# Essential Foundations of
# ECONOMICS

# Essential Foundations of
# ECONOMICS

Robin Bade

Michael Parkin
*University of Western Ontario*

**SEVENTH EDITION**

Global Edition

**PEARSON**

Boston   Columbus   Indianapolis   New York   San Francisco   Upper Saddle River
Amsterdam   Cape Town   Dubai   London   Madrid   Milan   Munich   Paris   Montréal   Toronto
Delhi   Mexico City   São Paulo   Sydney   Hong Kong   Seoul   Singapore   Taipei   Tokyo

Editor in Chief: Donna Battista
Executive Acquisitions Editor: Adrienne D'Ambrosio
Editorial Project Manager: Sarah Dumouchelle
Editorial Assistant: Elissa Senra-Sargent
Executive Marketing Manager: Lori DeShazo
Managing Editor: Jeff Holcomb
Production Project Manager: Nancy Freihofer
Head of Learning Asset Acquisition, Global Editions:
    Laura Dent
Senior Acquisitions Editor, Global Editions:
    Steven Jackson
Associate Acquisitions Editor, Global Editions:
    Toril Cooper

Project Editor, Global Editions: Arundati Dandapani
Senior Manufacturing Controller, Global Editions:
    Trudy Kimber
Media Publisher: Denise Clinton
Content Product Manager: Noel Lotz
Senior Media Producer: Melissa Honig
Image Permission Manager: Rachel Youdelman
Photo Researcher: Joseph Songco
Text Designer: Jonathan Boylan
Cover Design: Lumina Datamatics, Inc.
Cover Image: © Ortodox/Shutterstock
Copyeditor: Catherine Baum
Technical Illustrator: Richard Parkin

Credits and acknowledgments borrowed from other sources and reproduced, with permission, in this textbook appear on the appropriate page within text and on pages C-1–C-2.

FRED® is a registered trademark and the FRED® logo and ST.LOUIS FED are trademarks of the Federal Reserve Bank of St. Louis, http://researchstlouisfed.org/fred2/

Pearson Education Limited
Edinburgh Gate
Harlow
Essex CM20 2JE
England

and Associated Companies throughout the world

Visit us on the World Wide Web at:
www.pearsonglobaleditions.com

© Pearson Education Limited 2015

The rights of Robin Bade and Michael Parkin to be identified as the authors of this work have been asserted by them in accordance with the Copyright, Designs and Patents Act 1988.

*Authorized adaptation from the United States edition, entitled Essential Foundations of Economics 7th edition, ISBN 978-0-13-346254-8, by Robin Bade and Michael Parkin, published by Pearson Education © 2015.*

ISBN 10: 1-292-06044-1
ISBN 13: 978-1-292-06044-6

British Library Cataloguing-in-Publication Data
A catalogue record for this book is available from the British Library

10 9 8 7 6 5 4 3 2 1
17 16 15 14

Typeset in 10/12, Palatino-Roman by Integra Software Services
Printed and bound in China at CTPSC/01

To Erin, Tessa, Jack, Abby, and Sophie

# About the Authors

***Robin Bade*** was an undergraduate at the University of Queensland, Australia, where she earned degrees in mathematics and economics. After a spell teaching high school math and physics, she enrolled in the Ph.D. program at the Australian National University, from which she graduated in 1970. She has held faculty appointments at the University of Edinburgh in Scotland, at Bond University in Australia, and at the Universities of Manitoba, Toronto, and Western Ontario in Canada. Her research on international capital flows appears in the *International Economic Review* and the *Economic Record.*

Robin first taught the principles of economics course in 1970 and has taught it (alongside intermediate macroeconomics and international trade and finance) most years since then. She developed many of the ideas found in this text while conducting tutorials with her students at the University of Western Ontario.

***Michael Parkin*** studied economics in England and began his university teaching career immediately after graduating with a B.A. from the University of Leicester. He learned the subject on the job at the University of Essex, England's most exciting new university of the 1960s, and at the age of 30 became one of the youngest full professors. He is a past president of the Canadian Economics Association and has served on the editorial boards of the *American Economic Review* and the *Journal of Monetary Economics.* His research on macroeconomics, monetary economics, and international economics has resulted in more than 160 publications in journals and edited volumes, including the *American Economic Review*, the *Journal of Political Economy*, the *Review of Economic Studies*, the *Journal of Monetary Economics*, and the *Journal of Money, Credit, and Banking.* He is author of the bestselling textbook, *Economics* (Addison-Wesley), now in its Eleventh Edition.

Robin and Michael are a wife-and-husband team. Their most notable joint research created the Bade-Parkin Index of central bank independence and spawned a vast amount of research on that topic. They don't claim credit for the independence of the new European Central Bank, but its constitution and the movement toward greater independence of central banks around the world were aided by their pioneering work. Their joint textbooks include *Macroeconomics* (Prentice-Hall), *Modern Macroeconomics* (Pearson Education Canada), and *Economics: Canada in the Global Environment*, the Canadian adaptation of Parkin, *Economics* (Addison-Wesley). They are dedicated to the challenge of explaining economics ever more clearly to a growing body of students.

Music, the theater, art, walking on the beach, and five grandchildren provides their relaxation and fun.

# ECONOMICS

# Brief Contents

# ECONOMICS

## Brief Contents

# Contents

# PART 2 A CLOSER LOOK AT MARKETS

## PART 3    PRICES, PROFITS, AND INDUSTRY PERFORMANCE

## PART 4    MONITORING THE MACROECONOMY

# PART 5   UNDERSTANDING THE MACROECONOMY

■ **EYE on the U.S. ECONOMY**

■ **EYE on the U.S. ECONOMY**

■ **EYE on FISCAL STIMULUS**

■ **EYE on the FED IN A CRISIS**

■ **EYE on YOUR LIFE**

# Preface

Students know that throughout their lives they will make economic decisions and be influenced by economic forces. They want to understand the economic principles that can help them navigate these forces and guide their decisions. *Essential Foundations of Economics* is our attempt to satisfy this want.

The response to our earlier editions from hundreds of colleagues across the United States and throughout the world tells us that most of you agree with our view that the principles course must do four things well. It must

- Motivate with compelling issues and questions
- Focus on core ideas
- Steer a path between an overload of detail and too much left unsaid
- Encourage and aid learning by doing

The Foundations icon with its four blocks (on the cover and throughout the book) symbolizes this four-point approach that has guided all our choices in writing this text and creating its comprehensive teaching and learning supplements.

# WHAT'S NEW IN THE SEVENTH EDITION

Two big stories dominate this Seventh Edition revision: A careful fine-tuning of the heavily revised and successful Sixth Edition content, and a massive investment in enhanced electronic features to bring the text to life and provide an exciting interactive experience for the student on all platforms and devices.

## ■ Fine-Tuning the Content

The content of this revision is driven by the drama of the extraordinary period of economic history in which we are living and its rich display of events and forces through which students can be motivated to discover the economic way of thinking. Persistent unemployment and slow growth; headwinds from Europe's unresolved debt crisis; ongoing tensions arising from offshore outsourcing; a slowing pace of China's expansion; enhanced concern about climate change; falling U.S. energy imports as fracking boosts domestic production; relentless pressure on the federal budget from the demands of an aging population and a sometimes dysfunctional Congress; the dilemma posed by slow recovery and rising government debt; the question of when and how fast to exit an era of extreme monetary stimulus; and a fluctuating dollar are just a few of these interest-arousing events. All of them feature at the appropriate points in our new edition.

Every chapter contains many small changes, all designed to enhance clarity and currency, and the text and examples are all thoroughly updated to reflect the most recently available data and events. We have also made a few carefully selected larger changes that we describe below.

## ■ Notable Content Changes

Because the previous edition revision was so extensive and well-received, we have limited our interventions and changes in this Seventh Edition to addressing the small number of issues raised by our reviewers and users, to ensuring that we are thoroughly up-to-date, and to focusing on the new electronic tools that we've just described. Nonetheless, some changes that we now summarize are worth noting.

We have reorganized the section in Chapter 1 on "The Economic Way of Thinking" to provide a clearer sequencing of the key ideas.

In Chapter 2, The U.S. and Global Economies, we use the new example of the complex production of the Dreamliner to motivate and illustrate what, how, and for whom in the U.S. and global economies. A new *Eye on the Past* looks at the dramatic changes in manufacturing in the U.S. economy through the example of the domestic production of shoes. Also a new photo essay highlights global differences in how goods and services are produced and the section on government has been compressed and simplified.

In Chapter 3, The Economic Problem, we illustrate economic growth and the expansion of production possibilities with the dramatic example of hydraulic fracturing—fracking—in the United States and its effects on the production and opportunity cost of energy.

Chapter 4, Demand and Supply, has a new motivating issue: "Why does tuition keep rising?" Not only is the question a deeply personal one for students but it is also a good example of how the demand-supply model enables us to isolate increasing demand as the source of a rising price. Events in the increasingly important market for solar panels provide a contrasting example of the effects of an increase in supply. We have revised the section on changes in both demand and supply to better explain the unambiguous and ambiguous cases and leave the student to pull all possible cases together.

In Chapter 10, Externalities: Pollution, Education, and Health Care we have reorganized our discussion of ideas for achieving efficiency in the face of external costs. We now explain these ideas in four categories: establish property rights, mandate clean technology, tax pollution, and cap-and-trade pollution permits. The discussion of mandates is new.

In Chapter 13, Monopolistic Competition and Oligopoly, we have updated our description of how the HHI is used to evaluate the effects of proposed mergers.

In Chapter 17, Potential GDP and Economic Growth, we have simplified the explanation of the contributions of capital accumulation and technological change to the fluctuating pace of productivity growth.

Topical policy issues pervade the macro chapters. These include the persistence of high unemployment in the United States, Eurozone's extreme unemployment problem, and the falling U.S. labor force participation rate in Chapter 15; the ever-widening Lucas wedge, now greater than $400,000 per person, and the persistence of U.S./E.U. productivity differences in Chapter 17; QE3 and the explosion of monetary base, the rise in bank reserves, and the collapse of the money multiplier in Chapter 18; the persistent recessionary gap in Chapter 19; the persistent federal budget deficit and rising debt to GDP ratio, the ongoing structural deficit, the ongoing near-zero federal funds rate, and an update of the contrast between monetary policy today and during the Great Depression, in Chapter 20.

## THE FOUNDATIONS VISION

### ■ Focus on Core Concepts

Each chapter of *Foundations* concentrates on a manageable number of main ideas (most commonly three or four) and reinforces each idea several times throughout the chapter. This patient, confidence-building approach guides students through unfamiliar terrain and helps them to focus their efforts on the most important tools and concepts of our discipline.

### ■ Many Learning Tools for Many Learning Styles

*Foundations'* integrated print and electronic package builds on the basic fact that students have a variety of learning styles. Students have powerful tools at their fingertips: With links from eText, they can get an immediate sense of the content of a chapter by playing the Big Picture video; learn the key ideas by playing the Snapshot videos, and get a quick walkthrough of the Checkpoint Practice Problems and In the News exercises with the Solutions videos.

### ■ Diagrams That Tell the Whole Story

We developed the style of our diagrams with extensive feedback from faculty focus-group participants and student reviewers. All of our figures make consistent use of color to show the direction of shifts and contain detailed, numbered captions designed to direct students' attention step-by-step through the action.

Because beginning students of economics are often apprehensive about working with graphs, we have made a special effort to present material in as many as three ways—with graphs, words, and tables—in the same figure. In an innovation that seems necessary, but is to our knowledge unmatched, nearly all of the information supporting a figure appears on the same page as the figure itself. No more flipping pages back and forth!

### ■ Real-World Connections That Bring Theory to Life

Students learn best when they can see the purpose of what they are studying, apply it to illuminate the world around them, and use it in their lives.

*Eye on* boxes offer fresh new examples to help students see that economics is everywhere. Current and recent events appear in *Eye on the U.S. Economy* boxes; we place current U.S. economic events in global and historical perspectives in our *Eye on the Global Economy* and *Eye on the Past* boxes; and we show how students can use economics in day-to-day decisions in *Eye on Your Life* boxes.

The *Eye On* boxes that build off of the chapter-opening question help students see the economics behind key issues facing our world and highlight a major aspect of the chapter's story.

## ORGANIZATION

We have organized the sequence of material and chapters in what we think is the most natural order in which to cover the material. But we recognize that there are alternative views on the best order. We have kept this fact and the need for flexibility firmly in mind throughout the text. Many alternative sequences work, and the Flexibility Chart on p. 31 explains the alternative pathways through the chapters. In using the flexibility information, keep in mind that the best sequence is the one in which we present the material. And even chapters that the flexibility chart identifies as strictly optional are better covered than omitted.

# SUPPORT MATERIALS FOR INSTRUCTORS AND STUDENTS

*Essential Foundations of Economics* is accompanied by the most comprehensive set of teaching and learning tools ever assembled. Each component of our package is organized by Checkpoint topic for a tight, seamless integration with both the textbook and the other components. In addition to authoring the PowerPoint content, we have helped in the reviewing and revising of the Study Guide, Solutions Manual, Instructor's Manual, and Test Item Files to ensure that every element of the package achieves the consistency that students and teachers need.

## ■ PowerPoint Resources

We have created the PowerPoint resources based on our 20 years of experience using this tool in our own classrooms. We have created four sets of PowerPoint presentations for instructors.
They are:

- Lecture notes with full-color, animated figures, and tables from the textbook
- Figures and tables from the textbook, animated with step-by-step walk-through for instructors to use in their own personal slides
- *Eye On* features
- Checkpoint Practice Problems and solutions

## ■ Instructor's Manual

The Instructor's Manual, written by Luke Armstrong and reviewed by Mark Rush, contains chapter outlines and road maps, additional exercises with solutions, a comprehensive Chapter Lecture resource, and a virtual encyclopedia of suggestions on how to enrich class presentation and use class time efficiently. Both the micro and macro portions have been updated to reflect changes in the main text as well as infused with a fresh and intuitive approach to teaching this course. The Instructor's Manual is available for download in Word and PDF formats.

## ■ Solutions Manual

The Solutions Manual, written by Mark Rush and checked for accuracy by Jeannie Gillmore, contains the solutions to all Checkpoint Practice Problems, In the News exercises, and Chapter Checkpoint Problems and Applications. The Solutions Manual is available for download in Word and PDF formats.

## ■ Three Test Item Files and TestGen

More than 6,000 multiple-choice, numerical, fill-in-the-blank, short answer, essay, and integrative questions make up the three Test Item Files that support *Essential Foundations of Economics*. Mark Rush reviewed and edited questions from six dedicated principles instructors to form one of the most comprehensive testing systems on the market. Our microeconomics authors are Gregory E. Givens (University of Alabama); Lee Hoke (University of Tampa); Homer Guevara, Jr. (Northwest Vista College); and Carol Dole (Jacksonville University). Our macroeconomics questions were written by Gregory Givens, Buffie Schmidt (Augusta State University), and Rolando Sanchez (Northwest Vista College). The entire set of questions is available for download in Word, PDF, and TestGen formats.

All three Test Item Files are available in test generator software (TestGen with QuizMaster). TestGen's graphical interface enables instructors to view, edit, and add questions; transfer questions to tests; and print different forms of tests. Instructors also have the option to reformat tests with varying fonts and styles, margins, and headers and footers, as in any word-processing document. Search and sort features let the instructor quickly locate questions and arrange them in a preferred order. QuizMaster, working with your school's computer network, automatically grades the exams, stores the results on disk, and allows the instructor to view and print a variety of reports.

## ■ Study Guide for Students

Mark Rush of the University of Florida has prepared the Study Guide. It provides an expanded Chapter Checklist that enables the student to break the learning tasks down into smaller, bite-sized pieces; self-test materials; and additional practice problems. The Study Guide has been carefully coordinated with the text and the Test Item Files.

## ACKNOWLEDGMENTS

Working on a project such as this one generates many debts that can never be repaid. But they can be acknowledged, and it is a special pleasure to be able to do so here and to express our heartfelt thanks to each and every one of the following long list, without whose contributions we could not have produced *Foundations*.

Mark Rush again coordinated, managed, and contributed to our Study Guide, Solutions Manual, Instructor's Manual, and Test Item Files. He assembled, polished, wrote, and rewrote these materials to ensure their close consistency with the text. He and we were in constant contact as all the elements of our text and package came together. Mark also made many valuable suggestions for improving the text and the Checkpoint Problems. His contribution went well beyond that of a reviewer, and his effervescent sense of humor kept us all in good spirits along the way.

Working closely with Mark, Luke Armstrong wrote content for the Instructor's Manual. Carol Dole, Buffie Schmidt, Lee Hoke, Greg Givens, Rolando Sanchez, and Homer Guevara, Jr. authored new questions for the Test Item Files.

Michelle Sheran (University of North Carolina, Greensboro) and Carol Dole recorded the narrations that accompany the Big Picture, Snapshot, and Solutions videos in the eText. The engaging style and clarity of these outstanding teachers makes these videos a powerful learning tool. Fred Bounds (Georgia Perimeter College), Carol Dole, Trevor Collier (University of Dayton), and Paul Lande (Loyola University Maryland) provided outstanding reviews of the Study Plan and Assessment problems and helped us to make these exercises and their feedback messages as effective as possible.

The ideas from which *Foundations* grew began to form over dinner at the Andover Inn in Andover, Massachusetts, with Denise Clinton and Sylvia Mallory. We gratefully acknowledge Sylvia's role not only at the birth of this project but also in managing its initial development team. Denise has been an ongoing inspiration for 15 years, and we are privileged to have the benefit of her enormous experience.

The success of *Foundations* owes much to its outstanding Executive Acquisitions Editor, Adrienne D'Ambrosio. Adrienne's acute intelligence and sensitive understanding of the market have helped sharpen our vision of this text and package. Her value-added on this project is huge. It has been, and we hope it will for many future editions remain, a joy to work with her.

Sarah Dumouchelle, Editorial Project Manager, ensured that we were provided with outstanding and timely reviews and managed the photo research and our supplements. Elissa Senra-Sargent, Editorial Assistant, helped us in many ways, particularly in envisioning the new cover design.

Jonathan Boylan created the new impressive cover design and converted the raw ideas of our brainstorms into an outstandingly designed text.

Susan Schoenberg, Media Director, Denise Clinton, Media Publisher, Melissa Honig, Senior Media Producer, and Noel Lotz, Content Product Manager have set a new standard for online learning and teaching resources. Building on the pioneering work of Michelle Neil, Susan worked creatively to improve our technology systems. Noel managed reviews of the content. They have all been sources of high energy, good sense, and level-headed advice and quickly found creative solutions to all our technology problems.

Nancy Freihofer, our outstanding, ever calm, Senior Production Project Manager, worked with a talented team at Integra, Project Editor, Heather Johnson, and designer, art coordinator, and typesetter. Our copy editor, Catherine Baum, gave our work a thorough review and helpful polish, and our proofreader ensured the most error-free text we have yet produced.

Our Executive Marketing Manager, Lori DeShazo, has been a constant source of good judgment and sound advice on content and design issues, ranging over the entire package from text to print and electronic supplements.

Richard Parkin, our technical illustrator, created the figures in the text, the dynamic figures in the eText, the animated figures in the PowerPoint presentations, created the animations for and assembled the enhanced eText videos, and contributed many ideas to improving the clarity of our illustrations in all media.

Jeannie Gillmore, our long-standing personal assistant, worked closely with us to create exercises and guided solutions.

Don Davison of Galvaston College found an embarrassing error that has been present in the previous editions and that we are pleased to have been able to correct.

Sharmistha Nag, our new personal assistant, worked with us to create the Key Terms Quizzes for easy assignment.

Finally, our reviewers, whose names appear on the following pages, have made an enormous contribution to this text and its resources. Once again we find ourselves using superlatives, but they are called for. In the many texts that we've written, we've not seen reviewing of the quality that we enjoyed on this revision. It has been a pleasure (if at times a challenge) to respond constructively to their many excellent suggestions.

Robin Bade
Michael Parkin
London, Ontario, Canada
robin@econ100.com
michael.parkin@uwo.ca

Pearson gratefully acknowledges and thanks the following people for their work on the Global Edition:

*Contributors*
Charles Kwong Che Leung, The Open University of Hong Kong
Tajul Ariffin Masron,  Universiti Sains Malaysia
Yuka Chan Ka Yu, The Open University of Hong Kong

*Reviewers*
Eddie Cheung Chi Leung, The Open University of Hong Kong
Erkan Ilgün, International Burch University, Sarajevo
Michael Cope, London School of Business & Finance
Sami Hartikainen, HAAGA-HELIA University of Applied Sciences

## ESSENTIAL FOUNDATIONS OF ECONOMICS: FLEXIBILITY CHART

### Flexibility

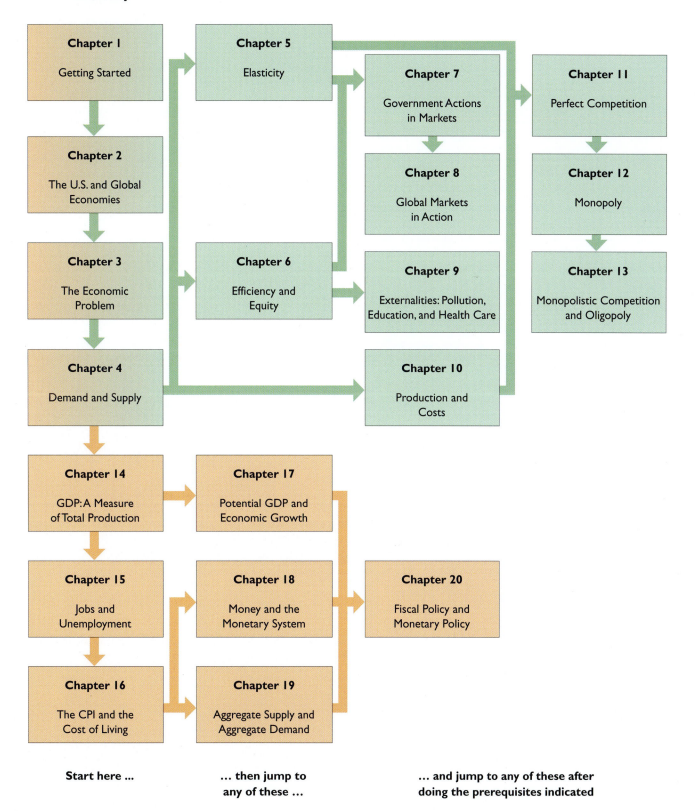

**Start here ...**                    **... then jump to
any of these ...**                         **... and jump to any of these after
doing the prerequisites indicated**

# Reviewers

Alfredo A. Romero Aguirre, North Carolina A&T State University

Seemi Ahmad, Dutchess Community College

William Aldridge, Shelton State Community College

Rashid B. Al-Hmoud, Texas Tech University

Neil Alper, Northeastern University

Nejat Anbarci, Deakin University

J.J. Arias, Georgia College & State University

Luke A. Armstrong, Lee College

Leland Ash, Skagit Valley College

Ali Ataiifar, Delaware County Community College

John Baffoe-Bonnie, Pennsylvania State University, Delaware County Campus

A. Paul Ballantyne, University of Colorado

Tyra D. Barrett, Pellissippi State Community College

Sue Bartlett, University of South Florida

Gerald Baumgardner, Penn College

Klaus Becker, Texas Tech University

Clive Belfield, Queen's College, City University of New York

William K. Bellinger, Dickinson College

John Bethune, Barton College

Prasun Bhattacharjee, East Tennessee State University

Gautam Bhattacharya, University of Kansas

Gerald W. Bialka, University of North Florida

David Bivin, Indiana University–Purdue University at Indianapolis

Geoffrey Black, Boise State University

Carey Anne Borkoski, Arundel Community College

Jurgen Brauer, Augusta State University

Greg Brock, Georgia Southern University

Barbara Brogan, Northern Virginia Community College

Bruce C. Brown, California State Polytechnic University, Pomona

Christopher Brown, Arkansas State University

James O. Brown, Delta State University

Brian Buckley, Clemson University

Donald Bumpass, Sam Houston State University

Seewoonundun Bunjun, East Stroudsburg University

Nancy Burnett, University of Wisconsin at Oshkosh

James L. Butkiewicz, University of Delaware

Barbara Caldwell, Saint Leo University

Bruce Caldwell, University of North Carolina, Greensboro

Joseph Calhoun, Florida State University

Robert Carlsson, University of South Carolina

Shawn Carter, Jacksonville State University

Regina Cassady, Valencia Community College

Jack Chambless, Valencia Community College

Joni Charles, Southwest Texas State University

Anoshua Chaudhuri, San Francisco State University

Robert Cherry, Brooklyn College

Chi-Young Choi, University of New Hampshire

Paul Cichello, Xavier University

Quentin Ciolfi, Brevard Community College

Victor V. Claar, Henderson State University

Jane L. Cline, Forsyth Technical Community College

Jim Cobbe, Florida State University

John Cochran, University of Chicago

Mike Cohick, Collin County Community College

Ludovic Comeau, De Paul University

Carol Conrad, Cerro Coso Community College

Christopher Cornell, Vassar College

Richard Cornwall, University of California, Davis

Kevin Cotter, Wayne State University

Erik Craft, University of Richmond

Tom Creahan, Morehead State University

Elizabeth Crowell, University of Michigan at Dearborn

Susan Dadres, Southern Methodist University

David Davenport, McLennan Community College

Troy Davig, College of William and Mary

Jeffrey Davis, ITT Technical Institute (Utah)

Lewis Davis, Union College

Dennis Debrecht, Carroll College

Al DeCooke, Broward Community College

Jason J. Delaney, Georgia Gwinnett College

Vince DiMartino, University of Texas at San Antonio

Vernon J. Dobis, Minnesota State University–Moorhead

Carol Dole, Jacksonville University

Kathleen Dorsainvil, American University

John Dorsey, University of Maryland, College Park

Amrik Singh Dua, Mt. San Antonio College

Marie Duggan, Keene State College

Allen Dupont, North Carolina State University

David Eaton, Murray State University

Kevin J. Egan, University of Toledo

Harold W. Elder, University of Alabama

Harry Ellis, University of North Texas

Stephen Ellis, North Central Texas College

Carl Enomoto, New Mexico State University

Chuen-mei Fan, Colorado State University

Chris Fant, Spartanburg Community College

Elena Ermolenko Fein, Oakton Community College

Gary Ferrier, University of Arkansas

Rudy Fichtenbaum, Wright State University

Donna K. Fisher, Georgia Southern University

Kaya Ford, Northern Virginia Community College

Robert Francis, Shoreline Community College

Roger Frantz, San Diego State University

Amanda S. Freeman, Kansas State University

Marc Fusaro, East Carolina University

Arthur Friedberg, Mohawk Valley Community College

Julie Gallaway, Southwest Missouri State University

Byron Gangnes, University of Hawaii

Gay GareschÈ, Glendale Community College

Neil Garston, California State University, Los Angeles

Lisa Geib-Gunderson, University of Maryland

Lisa M. George, City University of New York

Linda Ghent, Eastern Illinois University

Soma Ghosh, Bridgewater State College

Kirk Gifford, Ricks College

Scott Gilbert, Southern Illinois University

Maria Giuili, Diablo Valley Community College

Mark Gius, Quinnipiac College

Gregory E. Givens, University of Alabama

Randall Glover, Brevard Community College

Stephan Gohmann, University of Louisville

Richard Gosselin, Houston Community College

John Graham, Rutgers University

Patricia E. Graham, University of Northern Colorado

Warren Graham, Tulsa Community College

Homer Guevara, Jr., Northwest Vista College

Osman Gulseven, North Carolina State University

Jang-Ting Guo, University of California, Riverside

Dennis Hammett, University of Texas at El Paso

Leo Hardwick, Macomb Community College

Mehdi Haririan, Bloomsburg University

Paul Harris, Camden County Community College

Mark Healy, William Rainey Harper College

Rey Hernandez-Julian, Metropolitan State College of Denver

Gus Herring, Brookhaven College

Michael Heslop, Northern Virginia Community College

Steven Hickerson, Mankato State University

Frederick Steb Hipple, East Tennessee State University

Lee Hoke, University of Tampa

Andy Howard, Rio Hondo College

Yu Hsing, Southeastern Louisiana University

Greg Hunter, California State Polytechnic University, Pomona

Matthew Hyle, Winona State University

Todd Idson, Boston University

Harvey James, University of Hartford

Russell Janis, University of Massachusetts at Amherst

Ricot Jean, Valencia College

Jay A. Johnson, Southeastern Louisiana University

Ted Joyce, City University of New York, Baruch College

Ahmad A. Kader, University of Nevada, Las Vegas

Jonathan D. Kaplan, California State University, Sacramento

Arthur Kartman, San Diego State University

Chris Kauffman, University of Tennessee

Diane Keenan, Cerritos College

Brian Kench, University of Tampa

John Keith, Utah State University

Kristen Keith, University of Toledo

Joe Kerkvliet, Oregon State University

Randall Kesselring, Arkansas State University

Gary Kikuchi, University of Hawaii at Manoa

Douglas Kinnear, Colorado State University

Morris Knapp, Miami Dade Community College

Steven Koch, Georgia Southern University

Kate Krause, University of New Mexico

Stephan Kroll, California State University, Sacramento

Joyce Lapping, University of Southern Maine

Tom Larson, California State University, Los Angeles

Robert Lemke, Florida International University

J. Mark Leonard, University of Nebraska at Omaha

Tony Lima, California State University, Hayward

Joshua Long, Ivy Tech Community College

Kenneth Long, New River Community College

Noel Lotz, Middle Tennessee State University

Marty Ludlum, Oklahoma City Community College

Brian Lynch, Lake Land College

Michael Machiorlatti, Oklahoma City Community College

Roger Mack, De Anza College

Michael Magura, University of Toledo

Mark Maier, Glendale College

Svitlana Maksymenko, University of Pittsburgh

Paula Manns, Atlantic Cape Community College

Dan Marburger, Arkansas State University

Kathryn Marshall, Ohio State University

John V. Martin, Boise State University

Drew E. Mattson, Anoka-Ramsey Community College

Stephen McCafferty, Ohio State University

Thomas S. McCaleb, Florida State University

Katherine S. McCann, University of Delaware

William McLean, Oklahoma State University

Diego Mendez-Carbajo, Illinois Wesleyan University

Evelina Mengova, California State University, Fullerton

Thomas Meyer, Patrick Henry Community College

Meghan Millea, Mississippi State University

Michael Milligan, Front Range Community College

Jenny Minier, University of Miami

David Mitchell, Valdosta State University

Dr. Carl B. Montano, Lamar University

Christine Moser, Western Michigan University

William Mosher, Clark University

Mike Munoz, Northwest Vista College

John R. Mundy, St. Johns River State College

Kevin Murphy, Oakland University

Ronald Nate, Brigham Young University, Idaho

Nasrin Nazemzadeh, Rowan Cabarrus Community College

Michael Nelson, Texas A&M University

Rebecca Neumann, University of Wisconsin—Milwaukee

Charles Newton, Houston Community College Southwest

Melinda Nish, Salt Lake Community College

Lee Nordgren, Indiana University at Bloomington

Norman P. Obst, Michigan State University

Inge O'Connor, Syracuse University

William C. O'Connor, Western Montana College–University of Montana

Fola Odebunmi, Cypress College

Victor I. Oguledo, Florida A&M University

Charles Okeke, College of Southern Nevada

Lydia M. Ortega, St. Philip's College

P. Marcelo Oviedo, Iowa State University

Jennifer Pate, Ph.D., Loyola Marymount University

Sanjay Paul, Elizabethtown College

Ken Peterson, Furman University

Tim Petry, North Dakota State University

Charles Pflanz, Scottsdale Community College

Jonathon Phillips, North Carolina State University

Basharat Pitafi, Southern Illinois University

Anthony Plunkett, Harrison College

Paul Poast, Ohio State University

Greg Pratt, Mesa Community College

Fernando Quijano, Dickinson State University

Andy Radler, Butte Community College

Ratha Ramoo, Diablo Valley College

Karen Reid, University of Wisconsin, Parkside

Mary Rigdon, University of Texas, Austin

Helen Roberts, University of Illinois at Chicago

Greg Rose, Sacramento City College

Barbara Ross, Kapi'olani Community College

Elham Rouhani, Gwinnett Technical College

Jeffrey Rous, University of North Texas

June Roux, Salem Community College

Udayan Roy, Long Island University

Nancy C. Rumore, University of Louisiana–Lafayette

Mark Rush, University of Florida

Rolando Sanchez, Northwest Vista College

Joseph Santos, South Dakota State University

Roland Santos, Lakeland Community College

Mark Scanlan, Stephen F. Austin State University

Ted Scheinman, Mount Hood Community College

Buffie Schmidt, Augusta State University

Jerry Schwartz, Broward Community College

Gautam Sethi, Bard College

Margaret Anne Shannon, Georgia Southern University

Mushtaq Sheikh, Union County College

Michelle Sheran-Andrews, University of North Carolina at Greensboro

Virginia Shingleton, Valparaiso University

Steven S. Shwiff, Texas A & M University—Commerce

Charles Sicotte, Rock Valley College

Issoufou Soumaila, Texas Tech University

Martin Spechler, Indiana University

Leticia Starkov, Elgin Community College

Stela Stefanova, University of Delaware

John Stiver, University of Connecticut

Richard W. Stratton, The University of Akron

Abdulhamid Sukar, Cameron University

Terry Sutton, Southeast Missouri State University

Janet M. Thomas, Bentley College

Donna Thompson, Brookdale Community College

Deborah Thorsen, Palm Beach State College

James Thorson, Southern Connecticut State University

Marc Tomljanovich, Colgate University

Cynthia Royal Tori, Valdosta State University

Ngoc-Bich Tran, San Jacinto College South

Nora Underwood, University of California, Davis

Jogindar S. Uppal, State University of New York

Va Nee L. Van Vleck, California State University, Fresno

Victoria Vernon, Empire State College / SUNY

Christian Weber, Seattle University

Ethel Weeks, Nassau Community College

Jack Wegman, Santa Rosa Junior College

Jason White, Northwest Missouri State University

Benjamin Widner, Colorado State University

Barbara Wiens-Tuers, Pennsylvania State University, Altoona

Katherine Wolfe, University of Pittsburgh

Kristen Wolfe, St. Johns River State College

You're in school!
Did you make the right decision?

# Getting Started

**1**

**When you have completed your study of this chapter, you will be able to**

1 Define economics and explain the kinds of questions that economists try to answer.

2 Explain the ideas that define the economic way of thinking.

## 1.1    DEFINITION AND QUESTIONS

We want more than we can get. We want good health and long lives. We want spacious and comfortable homes. We want sports shoes and jet skis. We want the time to enjoy our favorite sports, video games, novels, music, and movies; to travel to exotic places; and just to hang out with friends. Wants exceed the resources available to satisfy them, and this fundamental fact is the source of all economic questions and problems.

### ■ Scarcity

**Scarcity**

The condition that arises because wants exceed the ability of resources to satisfy them.

Our inability to satisfy all our wants is called **scarcity**. The ability of each of us to satisfy our wants is limited by the time we have, the incomes we earn, and the prices we pay for the things we buy. These limits mean that everyone has unsatisfied wants. The ability of all of us as a society to satisfy our wants is limited by the productive resources that exist. These resources include the gifts of nature, our labor and ingenuity, and the tools and equipment that we have made.

Everyone, poor and rich alike, faces scarcity. A student wants Beyonce's latest album and a paperback but has only $10.00 in his pocket. He faces scarcity. Brad Pitt wants to spend a week in New Orleans discussing plans for his new eco-friendly housing and he also wants to spend the week promoting his new movie. He faces scarcity. The U.S. government wants to increase spending on homeland security and cut taxes. It faces scarcity. An entire society wants improved health care, an Internet connection in every classroom, clean lakes and rivers, and so on. Society faces scarcity. Scarcity is everywhere: Even parrots face scarcity!

Faced with scarcity, we must make choices. We must choose among the available alternatives. The student must choose the album or the paperback. Brad Pitt must choose New Orleans or promoting his new movie. The government must choose greater security or tax cuts. And society must choose among health care, computers, the environment, and so on.

Not only do I want a cracker—we all want a cracker!

### ■ Economics Defined

**Economics**

The social science that studies the choices that individuals, businesses, governments, and entire societies make as they cope with *scarcity*, the influences on those choices, and the arrangements that coordinate them.

**Economics** is the social science that studies the choices that individuals, businesses, governments, and entire societies make as they cope with *scarcity*, the influences on those choices, and the arrangements that coordinate them.

The subject has two broad parts:

- Microeconomics, and
- Macroeconomics

#### Microeconomics

**Microeconomics**

The study of the choices that individuals and businesses make and the way these choices interact and are influenced by governments.

**Microeconomics** is the study of the choices that individuals and businesses make and the way these choices interact and are influenced by governments. Some examples of microeconomic questions are: Will you buy a 3-D TV or a standard one? Will Nintendo sell more units of Wii if it cuts the price? Will a cut in the income tax rate encourage people to work longer hours? Will a hike in the gas tax encourage more people to drive hybrid or smaller automobiles? Are song downloads killing CDs?

## Macroeconomics

**Macroeconomics** is the study of the aggregate (or total) effects on the national economy and the global economy of the choices that individuals, businesses, and governments make. Some examples of macroeconomic questions are: Why did production and jobs expand slowly in the United States during 2012 and 2013? Why are incomes growing much faster in China and India than in the United States? Why is unemployment in Europe so high? Why are Americans borrowing more than $1 billion a day from the rest of the world?

> **Macroeconomics**
> The study of the aggregate (or total) effects on the national economy and the global economy of the choices that individuals, businesses, and governments make.

Two big questions define the scope of economics:

- How do choices end up determining *what, how,* and *for whom* goods and services get produced?
- When do choices made in the pursuit of *self-interest* also promote the *social interest*?

## ■ What, How, and For Whom?

**Goods and services** are the objects and actions that people value and produce to satisfy human wants. Goods are *objects* that satisfy wants. Sports shoes and ketchup are examples. Services are *actions* that satisfy wants. Haircuts and rock concerts are examples. We produce a dazzling array of goods and services that range from necessities such as food, houses, and health care to leisure items such as Blu-ray players and roller coaster rides.

> **Goods and services**
> The objects (goods) and the actions (services) that people value and produce to satisfy human wants.

### What?

*What* determines the quantities of corn we grow, homes we build, and health-care services we produce? Sixty years ago, farm output was 5 percent of total U.S. production. Today, it is 1 percent. Over the same period, the output of mines, construction, and utilities slipped from 9 percent to 7 percent of total production and manufacturing fell from 28 percent to 12 percent. These decreases in output are matched by increases in the production of a wide range of services, up from 58 percent of total production 60 years ago to 80 percent today. How will these quantities change in the future as ongoing changes in technology make an ever-wider array of goods and services available to us?

### How?

*How* are goods and services produced? In a vineyard in France, a hundred basket-carrying workers pick the annual grape crop by hand. In a vineyard in California, a huge machine and a few workers do the same job. Look around and you will see many examples of this phenomenon—the same job being done in different ways. In some stores, checkout clerks key in prices. In others, they use a laser scanner. One farmer keeps track of his livestock feeding schedules and inventories by using paper-and-pencil records, while another uses a computer. In some plants, GM hires workers to weld auto bodies and in others it uses robots to do the job.

Why do we use machines in some cases and people in others? Do mechanization and technological change destroy more jobs than they create? Do they make us better off or worse off?

*In a California vineyard a machine and a few workers do the same job as a hundred grape pickers in France.*

*A doctor gets more of the goods and services produced than a nurse or a medical assistant gets.*

**Self-interest**
The choices that are best for the individual who makes them.

**Social interest**
The choices that are best for society as a whole.

### For Whom?

*For whom* are goods and services produced? The answer to this question depends on the incomes that people earn and the prices they pay for the goods and services they buy. At given prices, a person who has a high income is able to buy more goods and services than a person who has a low income. Doctors earn much higher incomes than do nurses and medical assistants, so doctors get more of the goods and services produced than nurses and medical assistants get.

You probably know about many other persistent differences in incomes. Men, on average, earn more than women. Whites, on average, earn more than minorities. College graduates, on average, earn more than high school graduates. Americans, on average, earn more than Europeans, who in turn earn more, on average, than Asians and Africans. But there are some significant exceptions. The people of Japan and Hong Kong now earn an average income similar to that of Americans. And there is a lot of income inequality throughout the world.

What determines the incomes we earn? Why do doctors earn larger incomes than nurses? Why do men earn more, on average, than women? Why do college graduates earn more, on average, than high school graduates? Why do Americans earn more, on average, than Africans?

Economics explains how the choices that individuals, businesses, and governments make and the interactions of those choices end up determining *what, how,* and *for whom* goods and services are produced. In answering these questions, we have a deeper agenda in mind. We're not interested in just knowing how many Blu-ray players are produced, how they are produced, and who gets to enjoy them. We ultimately want to know the answer to the second big economic question that we'll now explore.

### ■ Can the Pursuit of Self-Interest Be in the Social Interest?

Every day, you and 316 million other Americans, along with 7.1 billion people in the rest of the world, make economic choices that result in *"what," "how,"* and *"for whom"* goods and services are produced.

Are the goods and services produced, and the quantities in which they are produced, the right ones? Do the scarce resources get used in the best possible way? Do the goods and services that we produce go to the people who benefit most from them?

### Self-Interest and the Social Interest

Choices that are the best for the individual who makes them are choices made in the pursuit of **self-interest**. Choices that are the best for society as a whole are said to be in the **social interest**. The social interest has two dimensions: *efficiency* and *equity.* We'll explore these concepts in later chapters. For now, think of efficiency as being achieved by baking the biggest possible pie, and think of equity as being achieved by sharing the pie in the fairest possible way.

You know that your own choices are the best ones for you—or at least you *think* they're the best at the time that you make them. You use your time and other resources in the way that you think is best. You might consider how your choices affect other people, but you order a home delivery pizza because you're hungry and want to eat, not because you're concerned that the delivery person or the cook needs an income. You make choices that are in your self-interest— choices that you think are best for you.

When you act on your economic decisions, you come into contact with thousands of other people who produce and deliver the goods and services that you decide to buy or who buy the things that you sell. These people have made their own decisions—what to produce and how to produce it, whom to hire or whom to work for, and so on. Like you, all these people make choices that they think are best for them. When the pizza delivery person shows up at your home, he's not doing you a favor. He's earning his income and hoping for a good tip.

Can it be possible that when each one of us makes choices that are in our own best interest—in our self-interest—it turns out that these choices are also the best choices for society as a whole—in the social interest?

Adam Smith, regarded as the founder of economic science, (see *Eye on the Past* on p. 51) said the answer is *yes*. He believed that when we pursue our self-interest, we are led by an *invisible hand* to promote the social interest.

Is Adam Smith correct? Can it really be possible that the pursuit of self-interest promotes the social interest? Much of the rest of this book helps you to learn what economists know about this question and its answer. To help you start thinking about the question, we're going to illustrate it with four topics that generate heated discussion in today's world. You're already at least a little bit familiar with each one of them. They are

- Globalization
- The "Information Age"
- Climate change
- Government budget deficit and debt

## Globalization

Globalization—the expansion of international trade and the production of components and services by firms in other countries—has been going on for centuries. But in recent years, its pace has accelerated. Microchips, satellites, and fiber-optic cables have lowered the cost of communication and globalized production decisions. When Nike produces more sports shoes, people in Malaysia get more work. When Steven Spielberg makes a new movie, programmers in New Zealand write the code that makes magical animations. And when China Airlines wants a new airplane, Americans who work for Boeing build it.

Globalization is bringing rapid income growth, especially in Asia. But globalization is leaving some people behind. Jobs in manufacturing and routine services are shrinking in the United States, and some nations of Africa and South America are not sharing in the prosperity enjoyed in other parts of the world.

*Workers in Asia make our shoes.*

The owners of multinational firms benefit from lower production costs and consumers benefit from low-cost imported goods. But don't displaced American workers lose? And doesn't even the worker in Malaysia, who sews your new shoes for a few cents an hour, also lose? Is globalization in the social interest, or does globalization benefit just some at the expense of others?

## The "Information Age"

We are living at a time of extraordinary economic change that has been called the *Information Revolution*. This name suggests a parallel with the *Industrial Revolution* that occurred around 1800 and the *Agricultural Revolution* of 12,000 years ago.

The changes that occurred during the last 30 years were based on one major technology: the microprocessor or computer chip. The spin-offs from faster and

*The computer chip has transformed our lives.*

cheaper computing have been widespread in telecommunications, music, and movie recording, and the automation of millions of routine tasks that previously required human decision and action. You encounter these automated tasks every day when you check out at the grocery store, use an ATM, or call a government department or large business. All the new products and processes and the low-cost computing power that made them possible resulted from people pursuing their self-interest. They did not result from any grand design or government plan.

When Gordon Moore set up Intel and started making chips, and Bill Gates quit Harvard to set up Microsoft, they weren't thinking how much easier it would be for you to turn in your essay on time if you had a better computer. Moore and Gates and thousands of other entrepreneurs were in hot pursuit of the big payoffs that many of them achieved. Yet their actions made many other people better off. They advanced the social interest.

But were resources used in the best possible way? Or did Intel and Microsoft set their prices too high and put their products out of reach for too many people? And did they really need to be rewarded with billions of dollars?

## Climate Change

The Earth is getting hotter and the ice at the two poles is melting. Since the late nineteenth century, the Earth's surface temperature has increased about 1 degree Fahrenheit, and close to a half of that increase occurred over the past 25 years.

Most climate scientists believe that the current warming has come at least in part from human economic activity—from self-interested choices—and that, if left unchecked, the warming will bring large future economic costs.

Are the choices that each of us makes to use energy damaging the social interest? What needs to be done to make our choices serve the social interest? Would the United States joining with other nations to limit carbon emissions serve the social interest? What other measures might be introduced?

*Human activity is raising the Earth's temperature.*

*A government budget time bomb is ticking as spending grows faster than tax revenues.*

## Government Budget Deficit and Debt

Every year since 2001, the U.S. government has run a budget deficit. On average, the government has spent $1.6 billion a day more than it has received in taxes. The government's debt has increased each day by that amount. Over the 12 year period from 2002 to 2013, government debt increased by $6.85 trillion. Your personal share of this debt is $22,000.

This large deficit and debt is just the beginning of an even bigger problem. From about 2020 onwards, the retirement and health-care benefits to which older Americans are entitled are going to cost increasingly more than current taxes can cover. With no changes in tax or benefit rates, the budget deficit will increase and the debt will swell ever higher.

Deficits and the debts they create cannot persist indefinitely, and debts must somehow be repaid. They will most likely be repaid by you, not by your parents. When we make our voter choices, we pursue our self-interest. Do our choices serve the social interest? Do the choices made by politicians and bureaucrats in Washington and the state capitals promote the social interest, or do they only serve their self-interests?

The four issues we've just reviewed raise questions that are hard to answer. We'll return to each of them at various points throughout this text and explain when the social interest is served and when there remain problems to be solved.

**CHECKPOINT 1.1**

**Define economics and explain the kinds of questions that economists try to answer.**

## Practice Problems

1. Economics studies choices that arise from one fact. What is that fact?

2. Provide three examples of wants in the United States today that are especially pressing but not satisfied.

3. In the following three news items, find examples of the *what*, *how*, and *for whom* questions: "With more research, we will cure cancer"; "A good education is the right of every child"; "Congress raises taxes to curb the deficit."

4. How does a new Starbucks in Beijing, China, influence self-interest and the social interest?

5. How does Facebook influence self-interest and the social interest?

## In the News

1. According to the Bureau of Labor Statistics (BLS), high-paying jobs in health care and jobs in leisure, hospitality, and education will expand quickly over the next five years. How does the BLS expect *what* and *for whom* goods and services are produced to change in the next five years?

2. In May 2011, businesses cut hiring because the higher price of gas pushed up costs and higher food prices forced consumers to cut spending.

    Source: CNNMoney, June 4, 2011

    Did businesses and consumers act in their self-interest or the social interest?

## Solutions to Practice Problems

1. The fact is scarcity—human wants exceed the resources available.

2. Examples would include security from terrorism, cleaner air in our cities, better public schools, and better public infrastructure. (Think of others.)

3. More research is a *how* question, and a cure for cancer is a *what* question. Good education is a *what* question, and every child is a *for whom* question. Raising taxes is a *for whom* question.

4. Decisions made by Starbucks are in Starbucks' self-interest but they also serve the self-interest of its customers and so contribute to the social interest.

5. Facebook serves the self-interest of its investors, users, and advertisers. It also serves the social interest by enabling people to share information.

## Solutions to In the News

1. The BLS expects the quantities of goods and services produced by workers in health care, leisure, hospitality, and education to increase. For whom they are produced depends on how people's incomes and the prices of goods and services will change in the next five years. The BLS expects workers in these high-paying jobs and expanding industries will get more of them.

2. Businesses made their decisions on the basis of their costs, so they acted in their self-interest. Consumers' decisions to cut spending were made on the basis of the prices they face, so they acted in their self-interest.

## 1.2    THE ECONOMIC WAY OF THINKING

The definition of economics and the kinds of questions that economists try to answer give you a flavor of the scope of economics. But they don't tell you how economists *think* about these questions and how they go about seeking answers to them. You're now going to see how economists approach their work.

We'll break this task into two parts. First, we'll explain the ideas that economists use to frame their view of the world. These ideas will soon have you thinking like an economist. Second, we'll look at economics both as a social science and as a policy tool that governments, businesses, and *you* can use.

### ■ Economic Ideas

Six ideas define the *economic way of thinking*:

- A choice is a *tradeoff*
- *Cost* is what you *must give up* to get something.
- *Benefit* is what you gain from something.
- People make *rational choices* by comparing benefits and costs.
- Most choices are "*how much*" choices made at the *margin*.
- Choices respond to *incentives*.

### ■ A Choice Is a Tradeoff

**Tradeoff**
An exchange—giving up one thing to get something else.

A **tradeoff** is an exchange—giving up one thing to get something else. Because we face scarcity, we must make choices. And when we make a choice, we select from the available alternatives. You can think about choices as tradeoffs. When you choose one thing, you give up something else that you could have chosen.

Think about what you will do on Saturday night. You can spend the night studying for your next economics test or having fun with your friends, but you can't do both of these activities at the same time. You must choose how much time to devote to each. Whatever choice you make, you could have chosen something else. When you choose how to spend your Saturday night, you face a tradeoff between studying and hanging out with your friends. To get more study time, you must give up some time with your friends.

### ■ Cost: What You *Must* Give Up

**Opportunity cost**
The opportunity cost of something is the best thing you must give up to get it.

*The opportunity cost of being in school: things you can't buy and do.*

The **opportunity cost** of something is the best thing you must give up to get it. You most likely think about the cost of something as the money you must spend to get it. But dig a bit deeper. If you spend $10 on a movie ticket, you can't spend it on a sandwich. The movie ticket really costs a sandwich. The *cost* of something is what must be given up to get it, not the money spent on it. Economists use the term *opportunity cost* to emphasize this view of cost.

The biggest opportunity cost you face is that of being in school. This opportunity cost has two components: things you can't afford to buy and things you can't do with your time.

Start with the things you can't afford to buy. You've spent all your income on tuition, residence fees, books, and a laptop. If you weren't in school, you would have spent this money on tickets to ball games and movies and all the other things that you enjoy. But that's only the start of the things you can't afford to buy because you're in school. You've also given up the opportunity to get a job and buy the things that you could afford with your higher income. Suppose that the best job you could get if you weren't in school is working at Citibank as a teller earning $24,000 a year. Another part of your opportunity cost of being in school is all the things that you would buy with that extra $24,000.

Now think about the time that being a student eats up. You spend many hours each week in class, doing homework assignments, preparing for tests, and so on. To do all these school activities, you must give up what would otherwise be leisure time spent with your friends.

The opportunity cost of being in school is the best alternative things that you can't afford and that you don't have the time to enjoy. You might put a dollar value on this cost but the cost is the things you give up, not dollars.

*The opportunity cost of being in school includes forgone earnings.*

## ■ Benefit: What You Gain

The **benefit** from something is the gain or pleasure that it brings, measured by what you are *willing to give up* to get it. Benefit is determined by personal *preferences*—by what a person likes and dislikes and the intensity of those feelings. If you get a huge kick out of *Madden Football* that video game brings you a large benefit. And if you have little interest in listening to Yo Yo Ma playing a Vivaldi cello concerto, that activity brings you a small benefit.

Some benefits are large and easy to identify, such as the benefit that you get from being in school. A big piece of that benefit is the goods and services that you will be able to enjoy with the boost to your earning power when you graduate. Some benefits are small, such as the benefit you receive from a slice of pizza.

Economists measure benefit as the most that a person is *willing to give up* to get something. You are willing to give up a lot for something that brings a large benefit. For example, because being in school brings a large benefit, you're *willing to give up* a lot of time and goods and services to get that benefit. But you're willing to give up very little for something that brings a small benefit. For example, you might be willing to give up one iTunes download to get a slice of pizza.

**Benefit**
The benefit from something is the gain or pleasure that it brings, measured by what you are *willing to give up* to get it.

## ■ Rational Choice

A basic idea of economics is that in making choices, people act rationally. A **rational choice** is one that uses the available resources to best achieve the objective of the person making the choice.

But how do people choose rationally? The answer is by comparing the *benefits* and *costs* of the alternative choices and choosing the alternative that makes *net benefit*—benefit minus cost—as large as possible.

You have chosen to be a student. If that choice is rational, as economists assume, your benefit from being in school exceeds the cost, so your net benefit is maximized by being in school. For an outstanding baseball player, a high earning potential makes the opportunity cost of school higher than the benefit from school, so for that person, net benefit is maxmized by choosing full-time sport. (*Eye on the Benefit and Cost of School* on p. 53 explores these examples more closely.)

The preferences of the person making a choice determine its benefit, so two people can make different rational choices even if they face the same cost. For example, you might like chocolate ice cream more than vanilla ice cream, but your friend prefers vanilla. So it is rational for you to choose chocolate and for your friend to choose vanilla.

**Rational choice**
A choice that uses the available resources to best achieve the objective of the person making the choice.

A rational choice might turn out not to have been the best choice after the event. For example, a farmer might decide to plant wheat rather than soybeans. Then, when the crop comes to market, the price of soybeans might be much higher than the price of wheat. The farmer's choice was rational when it was made, but subsequent events made it less profitable than the alternative choice.

All the rational choices we've just considered (school or not, chocolate or vanilla ice cream, soybeans or wheat) involve choosing between two things. One or the other is chosen. We call such choices *all-or-nothing* choices. Many choices are of this type, but most choices involve *how much* of an activity to do.

### ■ How Much? Choosing at the Margin

You can allocate the next hour between studying and instant messaging your friends, but the choice is not all or nothing. You must decide how many minutes to allocate to each activity. To make this decision, you compare the benefit of a little bit more study time with its cost—you make your choice *at the margin*.

Other words for "margin" are "border" or "edge." You can think of a choice at the margin as one that adjusts the border or edge of a plan to determine the best course of action. Making a choice at the **margin** means comparing the relevant alternatives systematically and incrementally.

### Marginal Cost

**Margin**

A choice on the margin is a choice that is made by comparing *all* the relevant alternatives systematically and incrementally.

The opportunity cost of a one-unit increase in an activity is called **marginal cost**. The marginal cost of something is what you *must* give up to get *one additional* unit of it. Think about your marginal cost of going to the movies for a third time in a week. Your marginal cost of seeing the movie is what you must give up to see that one additional movie. It is *not* what you give up to see all three movies. The reason is that you've already given up something for two movies, so you don't count that cost as resulting from the decision to see the third movie.

**Marginal cost**

The opportunity cost that arises from a one-unit increase in an activity. The marginal cost of something is what you *must* give up to get *one additional* unit of it.

The marginal cost of any activity increases as you do more of it. You know that going to the movies decreases your study time and lowers your grade. Suppose that seeing a second movie in a week lowers your grade by five percentage points. Seeing a third movie will lower your grade by more than five percentage points. Your marginal cost of moviegoing is increasing as you see more movies.

### Marginal Benefit

**Marginal benefit**

The benefit that arises from a one-unit increase in an activity. The marginal benefit of something is *measured* by what you *are willing* to give up to get *one additional* unit of it.

The benefit of a one-unit increase in an activity is called **marginal benefit**. Marginal benefit is what you gain from having *one more* unit of something. But the marginal benefit from something is *measured* by what you *are willing* to give up to get that *one additional* unit of it.

A fundamental feature of marginal benefit is that it diminishes. Think about your marginal benefit from movies. If you've been studying hard and haven't seen a movie this week, your marginal benefit from seeing your next movie is large. But if you've been on a movie binge this week, you now want a break and your marginal benefit from seeing your next movie is small.

Because the marginal benefit from a movie decreases as you see more movies, you are willing to give up less to see one additional movie. For example, you know that going to the movies decreases your study time and lowers your grade. You pay for seeing a movie with a lower grade. You might be willing to give up ten percentage points to see your first movie in a week, but you won't be willing to take such a big hit on your grade to see a second movie in a week. Your willingness to pay to see a movie decreases as the number of movies increases.

## Making a Rational Choice

So, will you go to the movies for that third time in a week? The answer is found by comparing marginal benefit and marginal cost.

If the marginal cost of the movie is less than the marginal benefit from it, seeing the third movie adds more to benefit than to cost. Your net benefit increases, so your rational choice is to see the third movie.

If the marginal cost of the movie exceeds the marginal benefit from it, seeing the third movie adds more to cost than to benefit. Your net benefit decreases, so your rational choice is to spend the evening studying.

When the marginal benefit from something equals its marginal cost, the choice is rational and it is not possible to make a better choice. Scarce resources are being used in the best possible way.

## ■ Choices Respond to Incentives

The choices we make depend on the incentives we face. An **incentive** is a reward or a penalty—a "carrot" or a "stick"—that encourages or discourages an action. We respond positively to "carrots" and negatively to "sticks." The carrots are marginal benefits; the sticks are marginal costs. A change in marginal benefit or a change in marginal cost changes the incentives that we face and leads us to change our actions.

Most students believe that the payoff from studying just before a test is greater than the payoff from studying a month before a test. In other words, as a test date approaches, the marginal benefit from studying increases and the incentive to study becomes stronger. For this reason, we observe an increase in study time and a decrease in leisure pursuits during the last few days before a test. And the more important the test, the greater is this effect.

A change in marginal cost also changes incentives. For example, suppose that last week, you found your course work easy and you scored 100 percent on your practice quizzes. You figured that the marginal cost of taking an evening off to enjoy a movie was low and that your grade on the next test would not suffer, so you had a movie feast. But this week the going has gotten tough. You're just not getting it, and your practice test scores are low. If you take off even one evening this week, your grade on the next test will suffer. The marginal cost of seeing a movie is now high, so you decide to give the movies a miss.

A central idea of economics is that by observing *changes in incentives*, we can predict how *choices change*.

**Incentive**
A reward or a penalty—a "carrot" or a "stick"—that encourages or discourages an action.

*Changes in marginal benefit and marginal cost change the incentive to study or to enjoy a movie.*

## ■ Economics as Social Science

Economists try to understand and predict the effects of economic forces by using the *scientific method* first developed by physicists. The scientific method is a commonsense way of systematically checking what works and what doesn't work.

A scientist begins with a question or a puzzle about cause and effect arising from some observed facts. An economist might wonder why computers are getting cheaper and more computers are being used. Are computers getting cheaper because more people are buying them? Or are more people buying computers because they are getting cheaper? Or is some third factor causing both the price of a computer to fall and the quantity of computers bought to increase?

### Economic Models

**Economic model**
A description of the economy or a part of the economy that includes only those features assumed necessary to explain the observed facts.

A scientist's second step is to build a model that provides a possible answer to the question of interest. All sciences use models. An **economic model** is a description of the economy or a part of the economy that includes only those features assumed necessary to explain the observed facts.

A model is analogous to a map. If you want to know about valleys and mountains, you use a physical map; if you're studying nations, you use a political map; if you want to drive from *A* to *B* in an unfamiliar city, you use a street map; and if you're a telephone engineer who is wanting to fix a broken connection, you use a map of the cables and conduit under the streets.

Sometimes, in the natural sciences, models are physical objects such as a plastic model of an atom or DNA. But models are also mathematical and often can be visualized in graphs. You can imagine a Lego model of an economy, but you can also see that such a model wouldn't be very revealing. So in economics we use mathematical and graph-based models.

The questions we posed about the price and quantity of computers bought are answered by an economic model called the "demand and supply model" that you will study in Chapter 4.

### Check Models Against Facts

A scientist's third step is to check the proposed model against the facts. Physicists can check whether their models correspond to the facts by doing experiments. For example, with a particle accelerator, a physicist can test a model of the structure of an atom.

Economists have a harder time than physicists, but they still approach the task in a scientific manner. To check an economic model against the facts, economists use natural experiments, statistical investigations, and laboratory experiments.

A natural experiment is a situation that arises in the ordinary course of economic life in which the one factor of interest is different and other things are equal (or similar). For example, Canada has higher unemployment benefits than the United States, but the people in the two nations are similar. So to study the effect of unemployment benefits on the unemployment rate, economists might compare the United States with Canada.

A statistical investigation looks for a *correlation*—a tendency for the values of two variables to move together (either in the same direction or in opposite directions) in a predictable and related way. For example, cigarette smoking and lung cancer are correlated. Sometimes a correlation shows a causal influence of one variable on the other. Smoking does cause lung cancer. But sometimes the direction of causation is hard to determine.

# EYE on the PAST
## Adam Smith and the Birth of Economics as a Social Science

Many people had written about economics before Adam Smith did, but he made economics a social science.

Born in 1723 in Kirkcaldy, a small fishing town near Edinburgh, Scotland, Smith was the only child of the town's customs officer. Lured from his professorship (he was a full professor at 28) by a wealthy Scottish duke who gave him a pension of £300 a year—ten times the average income at that time—Smith devoted ten years to writing his masterpiece, *An Inquiry into the Nature and Causes of the Wealth of Nations,* published in 1776.

Why, Adam Smith asked in that book, are some nations wealthy while others are poor? He was pondering these questions at the height of the Industrial Revolution. During these years, new technologies were applied to the manufacture of textiles, iron, transportation, and agriculture.

Adam Smith answered his questions by emphasizing the role of the division of labor and free markets. To illustrate his argument, he used the example of a pin factory. He guessed that one person, using the hand tools available in the 1770s, might make 20 pins a day. Yet, he observed, by using those same hand tools but breaking the process into a number of individually small operations in which people specialize—by the division of labor—ten people could make a staggering 48,000 pins a day.

But a large market is needed to support the division of labor: One factory employing ten workers would need to sell more than 15 million pins a year to stay in business!

Smith saw free competitive markets as another source of wealth. The self-interested pursuit of profit, led by an invisible hand, resulted in resources being used in ways that created the greatest possible value and wealth.

A laboratory experiment puts people in a decision-making situation and varies the influence of one factor at a time to discover how they respond.

## Disagreement: Normative versus Positive

Economists sometimes disagree about assumptions and models. They also sometimes disagree about what policy should be followed. Some disagreements can be settled by appealing to further facts, but others cannot.

Disagreements that can't be settled by facts are *normative statements*—statements about what *ought to be.* These statements depend on values and cannot be tested. The statement "We *ought to* cut back on our use of coal" is a normative statement. You may agree or disagree with it, but you can't test it. It doesn't assert a fact that can be checked. Economists as social scientists try to steer clear of normative statements.

Disagreements that *can* be settled by facts are *positive statements*—statements about *what is.* A positive statement might be right or wrong and we can discover which by careful observation of facts. "Our planet is warming because of the quantity of coal that we're burning" is a positive statement. It could be right or wrong, and it can be tested.

# ■ Economics as Policy Tool

Economics is useful, and you don't have to be an economist to think like one and to use the insights of economics as a policy tool. The subject provides a way of approaching problems in all aspects of our lives:

- Personal
- Business
- Government

## Personal Economic Policy

Should you take out a student loan? Should you get a weekend job? Should you buy a used car or a new one? Should you rent an apartment or take out a loan and buy a condominium? Should you pay off your credit card balance or make just the minimum payment? How should you allocate your time between study, working for a wage, caring for family members, and having fun? How should you allocate your time between studying economics and your other subjects? Should you leave school after getting a bachelor's degree or should you go for a master's or a professional qualification?

All these questions involve a marginal benefit and a marginal cost. Although some of the numbers might be hard to pin down, you will make more solid decisions if you approach these questions with the tools of economics.

## Business Economic Policy

Should Sony make only flat panel televisions and stop making conventional ones? Should Texaco get more oil and gas from the Gulf of Mexico or from Alaska? Should Palm outsource its online customer services to India or run the operation from California? Should Marvel Studios produce *Spider-Man 4*, a sequel to *Spider-Man 3*? Can Microsoft compete with Google in the search engine business? Can eBay compete with the surge of new Internet auction services? Is Alex Rodriguez really worth $32,000,000 to the New York Yankees?

Like personal economic questions, these business questions involve the evaluation of a marginal benefit and a marginal cost. Some of the questions require a broader investigation of the interactions of individuals and businesses. But again, by approaching these questions with the tools of economics and by hiring economists as advisers, businesses can make better decisions.

## Government Economic Policy

How can California balance its budget? Should the federal government cut taxes or raise them? How can the tax system be simplified? Should people be permitted to invest their Social Security money in stocks that they pick themselves? Should Medicaid and Medicare be extended to the entire population? Should there be a special tax to penalize corporations that send jobs overseas? Should cheap foreign imports of furniture and textiles be limited? Should the farms that grow tomatoes and sugar beets receive a subsidy? Should water be transported from Washington and Oregon to California?

These government policy questions call for decisions that involve the evaluation of a marginal benefit and a marginal cost and an investigation of the interactions of individuals and businesses. Yet again, by approaching these questions with the tools of economics, governments can make better decisions.

Notice that all the policy questions we've just posed involve a blend of the positive and the normative. Economics can't help with the normative part—the objective. But for a given objective, economics provides a method of evaluating alternative solutions. That method is to evaluate the marginal benefits and marginal costs and to find the solution that brings the greatest available gain.

# EYE on the BENEFIT AND COST OF SCHOOL
## Did You Make the Right Decision?

Did you make the right decision when you chose school over looking for a full-time job? Or, if you have a full-time job and you're studying in what would be your leisure time, did you make the right choice? Does school provide a big enough benefit to justify its cost?

### The Benefits of School

Being in school has many benefits for which people are willing to pay. They fall into two broad categories: present enjoyment and a higher future income.

You can easily make a list of all the fun things you do with your friends in school that would be harder to do if you didn't have these friends and opportunities for social interaction that school provides.

Putting a dollar value on the items in your list would be hard but it is possible to put a dollar value, or rather an expected dollar value, on the other benefit—a higher future income.

On average, a high-school graduate earns $40,000 a year. A graduate with a bachelor's degree earns, on average, $76,000 a year.

So by being in school, you can expect (on average) to increase your annual earnings by $36,000 a year.

This number is likely to grow as the economy becomes more productive and prices and earnings rise.

### The Costs of School

The opportunity cost of being in school for a full-time student includes:

- Tuition
- Books
- Other study costs
- Forgone earnings

For a student attending a state university in her or his home state, tuition is around $10,000 per year.

Books and other study aids cost around $1,000 per year.

Forgone earnings are the wage of a high-school graduate in a starter job, which is around $24,000 a year.

So the total annual cost is about $35,000 or $105,000 for a 3-year degree and $140,000 for a 4-year degree.

### Net Benefit

The benefit of extra earnings alone brings in $36,000 a year or $360,000 in 10 years and $1,440,000 in a working life of 40 years.

The costs are incurred in the present and the benefits accrue in the future, so we need to lower the benefits to be able to compare them properly with the costs. You'll learn how to do that later in your economics course. But even allowing for the fact that the costs are now and the benefits in the future, net benefit is big!

### Is School Always Best?

At the age of 18, Clayton Kershaw was considered the top high-schooler available entering the 2006 MLB Draft. He signed with the Los Angeles Dodgers with a bonus said to be $2.3 million, and turned down a baseball scholarship at Texas A & M.

As the Dodgers starting pitcher, Clayton's value to the team is high and earned him a salary of $11 million in 2013.

Clayton Kershaw's opportunity cost of a college education vastly exceeded the benefit he could expect to get from it. So Clayton, like you, maximized his net benefit and made the right decision.

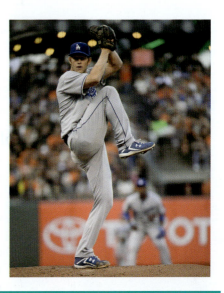

## CHECKPOINT 1.2

**Explain the ideas that define the economic way of thinking.**

## Practice Problems

Every week, Kate plays tennis for two hours, and her grade on each math test is 70 percent. Last week, after playing for two hours, Kate considered playing for another hour. She decided to play for another hour and cut her study time by one hour. But last week, her math grade fell to 60 percent. Use this information to work Problems **1** to **4**.

1. What was Kate's opportunity cost of the third hour of tennis?
2. Given that Kate played the third hour, what can you conclude about her marginal benefit and marginal cost of the second hour of tennis?
3. Was Kate's decision to play the third hour of tennis rational?
4. Did Kate make her decision on the margin?

## In the News

The *New York Times* reports that cruise lines have been slashing prices and cruise sales are up. It says this surge of interest tells us that despite the uncertain economic climate, people clearly need more fun in their lives and view their vacations as a valuable and necessary part of it.

1. In deciding whether to take a cruise, would you face a tradeoff?
2. How would you make a rational choice about taking a cruise?
3. What would be the marginal benefit from a cruise? What would be the marginal cost of a cruise?
4. Why would you expect a lower price to increase the number of people who decide to take a cruise?

## Solutions to Practice Problems

1. Kate's opportunity cost of the third hour of tennis was the drop in her grade of ten percentage points.
2. The marginal benefit from the second hour of tennis must have exceeded the marginal cost of the second hour because Kate chose to play the third hour.
3. If marginal benefit exceeded marginal cost, Kate's decision was rational.
4. Kate made her decision on the margin because she compared the benefit and cost of one more hour (marginal benefit and marginal cost).

## Solutions to In the News

1. You would face a tradeoff because you would have to forgo something else that you might otherwise do with your resources (time and budget).
2. You would make a rational choice by comparing the marginal benefit from a cruise and the marginal cost of taking one.
3. The marginal benefit from a cruise is the most you are willing to pay for one. The marginal cost is what you would have to pay to take a cruise.
4. With a lower price, more people will have a marginal benefit that exceeds the price and they will choose to take a cruise.

**CHAPTER SUMMARY**

## Key Points

**1.** **Define economics and explain the kinds of questions that economists try to answer.**

- Economics is the social science that studies the choices that we make as we cope with scarcity and the incentives that influence and reconcile our choices.
- Microeconomics is the study of individual choices and interactions, and macroeconomics is the study of the national economy and global economy.
- The first big question of economics is: How do the choices that people make end up determining *what, how,* and *for whom* goods and services are produced?
- The second big question is: When do choices made in the pursuit of *self-interest* also promote the *social interest*?

**2.** **Explain the ideas that define the economic way of thinking.**

- Six ideas define the economic way of thinking:
  1. A choice is a *tradeoff*.
  2. *Cost* is what you *must* give up to get something.
  3. *Benefit* is what you gain when you get something (measured by what you *are willing to* give up to get it).
  4. People make *rational* choices by comparing benefits and costs.
  5. A "how much" choice is made on the *margin* by comparing *marginal benefit* and *marginal cost*.
  6. Choices respond to *incentives*.
- Economists use the *scientific method* to try to understand how the economic world works. They create economic models and test them using natural experiments, statistical investigations, and laboratory experiments.
- Economics is a tool for personal, business, and government decisions.

## Key Terms

Benefit, 47
Economic model, 50
Economics, 40
Goods and services, 41
Incentive, 49
Macroeconomics, 41

Margin, 48
Marginal benefit, 48
Marginal cost, 48
Microeconomics, 40
Opportunity cost, 46
Rational choice, 47

Scarcity, 40
Self-interest, 42
Social interest, 42
Tradeoff, 46

# CHAPTER CHECKPOINT

## Study Plan Problems and Applications

**1.** Provide three examples of scarcity that illustrate why even the 1,210 billionaires in the world face scarcity.

**2.** Label each entry in List 1 as dealing with a microeconomic topic or a macroeconomic topic. Explain your answer.

Use the following information to work Problems **3** to **6**.

*The Social Network* had world-wide box office receipts of $225 million. The movie had a production budget of about $70 million and additional marketing costs of about $50 million. Creating a successful movie brings pleasure to millions, generates work for thousands, and makes a few people rich.

**3.** What contribution does a movie like *The Social Network* make to coping with scarcity? When you buy a movie ticket, are you buying a good or a service?

**4.** Who decides whether a movie is going to be a blockbuster? How do you think the creation of a blockbuster movie influences *what*, *how*, and *for whom* goods and services are produced?

**5.** What are some of the components of marginal cost and marginal benefit that the producer of a movie faces?

**6.** Suppose that Jesse Eisenberg had been offered a bigger and better part in another movie and that to hire him for *The Social Network*, the producer had to double Jesse's pay. What incentives would have changed? How might the changed incentives have changed the choices that people made?

**7.** What is the social interest? Distinguish it from self-interest. In your answer give an example of self-interest and an example of social interest.

**8.** Pam, Pru, and Pat are deciding how they will celebrate the New Year. Pam prefers to take a cruise, is happy to go to Hawaii, but does not want to go skiing. Pru prefers to go skiing, is happy to go to Hawaii, but does not want to take a cruise. Pat prefers to go to Hawaii or to take a cruise but does not want to go skiing. Their decision is to go to Hawaii. Is this decision rational? What is the opportunity cost of the trip to Hawaii for each of them? What is the benefit that each gets?

**9.** Label each of the entries in List 2 as a positive or a normative statement.

Use the following information to work Problems **10** to **12**.

**Hundreds line up for 5 p.m. Eminem ticket giveaway**

Eminem fans lined up all day to get a free ticket to his secret concert at which he will release his new album *Relapse* (his first in 5 years).

Source: *Detroit Free Press*, May 18, 2009

**10.** With tickets free and the show to be held in a 1,500-seat Detroit theater, what is free and what is scarce? Explain your answer.

**11.** What do you think Eminem's incentive is to give a free show? Was his decision made in self-interest or in the social interest? Explain your answer.

**12.** Is the marginal benefit from the concert zero? Explain your answer.

**13.** Read *Eye on the Benefit and Cost of School* on p. 53 and explain why both you and Alex Rodriguez made the right decision.

---

**LIST 1**

- Motor vehicles production in China is growing by 10 percent a year.
- Coffee prices rocket.
- Globalization has reduced African poverty.
- The government must cut its budget deficit.
- Apple sells 3 million iPhones a month.

---

**LIST 2**

- Low-income people pay too much for housing.
- The number of U.S. farms has decreased over the past 50 years.
- Toyota expands parts production in the United States.
- Imports from China are swamping U.S. department stores.
- The population of rural United States is declining.

## Instructor Assignable Problems and Applications

1. Which of the following are components of the opportunity cost of being a full-time student? The cost of
   - Tuition and books
   - Residence and a meal plan
   - A subscription to the *New Yorker* magazine
   - The income a student will earn after graduating

2. Think about the following news items and label each as involving a *what, how,* or *for whom* question:
   - Today, most stores use computers to keep their inventory records, whereas 20 years ago most stores used paper records.
   - Health-care professionals and drug companies recommend that Medicaid drug rebates be made available to everyone in need.
   - A doubling of the gas tax might lead to a better public transit system.

3. On May 3, 2013, the headlines in List 1 appeared in *The Wall Street Journal.* Classify each headline as a signal that the news article is about a microeconomic topic or a macroeconomic topic. Explain your answers.

4. Your school decides to increase the intake of new students next year. To make its decision, what economic concepts would it have considered? Would the school have used the "economic way of thinking" in reaching its decision? Would the school have made its decision on the margin?

5. Provide two examples of a monetary incentive and two examples of a non-monetary incentive, a carrot and a stick of each, that government policies use to influence behavior.

6. Think about each of the items in List 2 and explain how they affect incentives and might change the choices that people make.

7. Does the decision to make a blockbuster movie mean that some other more desirable activities get fewer resources than they deserve? Is your answer positive or normative? Explain your answer.

8. Provide two examples of economics being used as a tool by each of a student, a business, and a government. Classify your examples as dealing with microeconomic topics and macroeconomic topics.

Use the following news clip to work Problems **9** to **12**.

**Obama will drive up miles-per-gallon requirements**

Obama's revision of auto-emission and fuel-economy standards will require automakers to boost fuel economy to 35.5 miles per gallon by 2016, notching up 5% each year from 2012, to limit the amount of carbon dioxide cars can emit.

Source: *USA Today*, May 18, 2009

9. What are two benefits of the new miles-per-gallon requirements? Are these benefits in someone's self-interest or in the social interest?

10. What are two benefits of the new auto-emission standards?

11. What costs associated with the new miles-per-gallon requirements arise from decisions made in self-interest and in the social interest?

12. What costs associated with the new auto-emission standards arise from decisions made in self-interest and in the social interest?

---

**LIST 1**

- Job Gains Calm Slump Worries
- Washington Post's Profit Falls
- Overcapacity, Fuel Costs Hit Shipping
- Green Shoots in Greece?

---

**LIST 2**

- A hurricane hits Central Florida.
- The World Series begins tonight but a storm warning is in effect for the area around the stadium.
- The price of a personal computer falls to $50.
- Unrest in the Middle East sends the price of gas to $5 a gallon.

## Critical Thinking Discussion Questions

1. **Cardiff City FC gets more cash**

   Vincent Tan, the owner of Cardiff City FC, says a further £35m cash injection will be made, which will include £10m to pay off the historical debt and a substantial amount for signing new players.

   Source: *Wales Online*, June 14, 2012

   a. With a substantial cash injection, would Cardiff City FC still face a scarcity problem? Explain your answer.
   b. In whose self-interest is this cash injection: Vincent Tan, a Malaysian billionaire, or some other person? Is this cash injection in the social interest? Explain your answer.
   c. Did Mr. Tan make a rational decision? Explain your answer.

2. **From brewer to bio-tech entrepreneur**

   Kiran Mazumdar-Shaw trained as a master brewer and then used her skills to create a pharmaceuticals business. She employed uneducated workers and paid good wages. When the trade unions revolted, Kiran fired the workers, mechanized, and hired only highly skilled workers. She became a billionaire and opened a cancer treatment center to help thousands of poor patients.

   Source: *The New Yorker*, January 2, 2012

   a. Identify the economic decision-makers and the decisions made in self-interest.
   b. Did any decisions also serve the social interest?
   c. Did any decisions harm the social interest?

3. Amir is accepted to do a bachelor's degree at university but he can't afford the tuition fee, so he decides to take a full-time job. What economic concept did Amir use to make this decision?

4. **Tanaka: best Japanese pitcher ever?**

   Major League Baseball (MBL) teams in desperate need of an ace starting pitcher are lining up to make offers to Japanese superstar Masahiro Tanaka—and for good reason. His performance in Japan suggests he will be the best import ever.

   Source: *The Wall Street Journal*, January 3, 2014

   a. Is the above statement positive or normative? Explain your answer.
   b. Would a decision to sign Tanaka be made at the margin?
   c. What is the opportunity cost to Tanaka if he accepted an MBL offer?
   d. What is the opportunity cost to Tanaka if he rejected an MBL offer?

# APPENDIX: MAKING AND USING GRAPHS

## When you have completed your study of this appendix, you will be able to

**1** Interpret graphs that display data.

**2** Interpret the graphs used in economic models.

**3** Define and calculate slope.

**4** Graph relationships among more than two variables.

## Basic Idea

A graph represents a quantity as a distance and enables us to visualize the relationship between two variables. To make a graph, we set two lines called *axes* perpendicular to each other, like those in Figure A1.1. The vertical line is called the *y*-axis, and the horizontal line is called the *x*-axis. The common zero point is called the *origin*. In Figure A1.1, the *x*-axis measures temperature in degrees Fahrenheit. A movement to the right shows an increase in temperature, and a movement to the left shows a decrease in temperature. The *y*-axis represents ice cream consumption, measured in gallons per day.

To make a graph, we need a value of the variable on the *x*-axis and a corresponding value of the variable on the *y*-axis. For example, if the temperature is 40°F, ice cream consumption is 5 gallons a day at point *A* in Figure A1.1. If the temperature is 80°F, ice cream consumption is 20 gallons a day at point *B* in Figure A1.1. Graphs like that in Figure A1.1 can be used to show any type of quantitative data on two variables.

■ **FIGURE A1.1**

Making a Graph

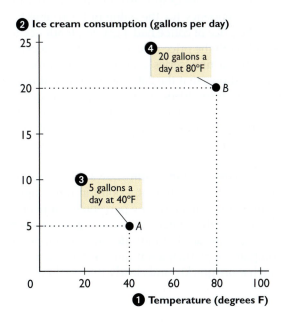

All graphs have axes that measure quantities as distances.

❶ The horizontal axis (*x*-axis) measures temperature in degrees Fahrenheit. A movement to the right shows an increase in temperature.

❷ The vertical axis (*y*-axis) measures ice cream consumption in gallons per day. A movement upward shows an increase in ice cream consumption.

❸ Point *A* shows that 5 gallons of ice cream are consumed on a day when the temperature is 40°F.

❹ Point *B* shows that 20 gallons of ice cream are consumed on a day when the temperature is 80°F.

## ■ Interpreting Data Graphs

**Scatter diagram**
A graph of the value of one variable against the value of another variable.

A **scatter diagram** is a graph of the value of one variable against the value of another variable. It is used to reveal whether a relationship exists between two variables and to describe the relationship. Figure A1.2 shows two examples.

Figure A1.2(a) shows the relationship between expenditure and income. Each point shows expenditure per person and income per person in the United States in a given year from 2000 to 2012. The points are "scattered" within the graph. The label on each point shows its year. The point marked 10 shows that in 2010, income per person was $32,335 and expenditure per person was $29,686. This scatter diagram reveals that as income increases, expenditure also increases.

Figure A1.2(b) shows the relationship during the 1990s between the percentage of Americans who own a cell phone and the average monthly cell-phone bill. This scatter diagram reveals that as the cost of using a cell phone falls, the number of cell-phone subscribers increases.

**Time-series graph**
A graph that measures time on the x-axis and the variable or variables in which we are interested on the y-axis.

A **time-series graph** measures time (for example, months or years) on the x-axis and the variable or variables in which we are interested on the y-axis. Figure A1.2(c) shows an example. In this graph, time (on the x-axis) is measured in years, which run from 1980 to 2012. The variable that we are interested in is the price of coffee, and it is measured on the y-axis.

A time-series graph conveys an enormous amount of information quickly and easily, as this example illustrates. It shows when the value is

1.  High or low. When the line is a long way from the x-axis, the price is high, as it was in 1986. When the line is close to the x-axis, the price is low, as it was in 2001.

2.  Rising or falling. When the line slopes upward, as in 1994, the price is rising. When the line slopes downward, as in 1996, the price is falling.

3.  Rising or falling quickly or slowly. If the line is steep, then the price is rising or falling quickly. If the line is not steep, the price is rising or falling slowly. For example, the price rose quickly in 1994 and slowly in 1995. The price fell quickly in 1996 and slowly in 2003.

**Trend**
A general tendency for the value of a variable to rise or fall over time.

A time-series graph also reveals whether the variable has a trend. A **trend** is a general tendency for the value of a variable to rise or fall over time. You can see that the price of coffee had a general tendency to fall from 1980 to late in 2000. That is, although the price rose and fell, it had a general tendency to fall.

With a time-series graph, we can compare different periods quickly. Figure A1.2(c) shows that the 2000s were different from the 1990s, which in turn were different from the 1980s. The price of coffee started the 1980s high and then fell for a number of years. During the 1990s, the price was on a roller coaster. And during the 2000s, the price rose steadily. This graph conveys a wealth of information about the price of coffee, and it does so in much less space than we have used to describe only some of its features.

**Cross-section graph**
A graph that shows the values of an economic variable for different groups in a population at a point in time.

A **cross-section graph** shows the values of an economic variable for different groups in a population at a point in time. Figure A1.2(d) is an example of a cross-section graph. It shows the percentage of people who participate in selected sports activities in the United States. This graph uses bars rather than dots and lines, and the length of each bar indicates the participation rate. Figure A1.2(d) enables you to compare the participation rates in these ten sporting activities. And you can do so much more quickly and clearly than by looking at a list of numbers.

### ■ FIGURE A1.2

## Data Graphs

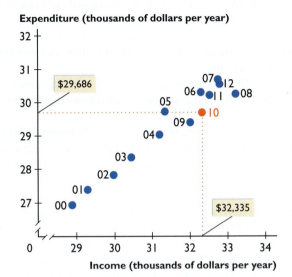

**(a) Scatter Diagram: Expenditure and income**

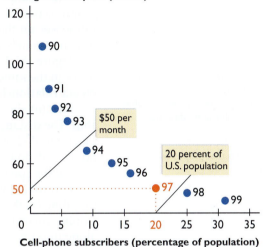

**(b) Scatter Diagram: Subscribers and cost**

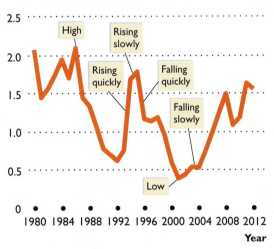

**(c) Time Series: The price of coffee**

**(d) Cross Section: Participation in selected sports activities**

A scatter diagram reveals the relationship between two variables. In part (a), as income increases, expenditure almost always increases. In part (b), as the monthly cell-phone bill falls, the percentage of people who own a cell phone increases.

A time-series graph plots the value of a variable on the *y*-axis against time on the *x*-axis. Part (c) plots the price of coffee each

year from 1980 to 2012. The graph shows when the price of coffee was high and low, when it increased and decreased, and when it changed quickly and changed slowly.

A cross-section graph shows the value of a variable across the members of a population. Part (d) shows the participation rate in the United States in each of ten sporting activities.

## ■ Interpreting Graphs Used in Economic Models

We use graphs to show the relationships among the variables in an economic model. An *economic model* is a simplified description of the economy or of a component of the economy such as a business or a household. It consists of statements about economic behavior that can be expressed as equations or as curves in a graph. Economists use models to explore the effects of different policies or other influences on the economy in ways similar to those used to test model airplanes in wind tunnels and models of the climate.

Figure A1.3 shows graphs of the relationships between two variables that move in the same direction. Such a relationship is called a **positive relationship** or **direct relationship**.

Part (a) shows a straight-line relationship, which is called a **linear relationship**. The distance traveled in 5 hours increases as the speed increases. For example, point *A* shows that 200 miles are traveled in 5 hours at a speed of 40 miles an hour. And point *B* shows that the distance traveled in 5 hours increases to 300 miles if the speed increases to 60 miles an hour.

Part (b) shows the relationship between distance sprinted and recovery time (the time it takes the heart rate to return to its normal resting rate). An upward-sloping curved line that starts out quite flat but then becomes steeper as we move along the curve away from the origin describes this relationship. The curve slopes upward and becomes steeper because the extra recovery time needed from sprinting another 100 yards increases. It takes 5 minutes to recover from sprinting 100 yards but 15 minutes to recover from sprinting 200 yards.

Part (c) shows the relationship between the number of problems worked by a student and the amount of study time. An upward-sloping curved line that starts out quite steep and becomes flatter as we move away from the origin shows this

**Positive relationship or direct relationship**
A relationship between two variables that move in the same direction.

**Linear relationship**
A relationship that graphs as a straight line.

■ **FIGURE A1.3**

Positive (Direct) Relationships

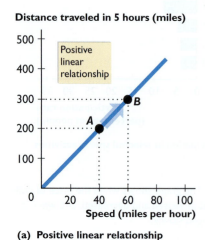

**(a)  Positive linear relationship**

Part (a) shows that as speed increases, the distance traveled in a given number of hours increases along a straight line.

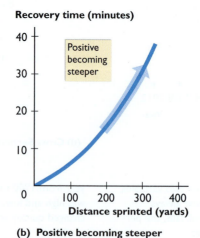

**(b)  Positive becoming steeper**

Part (b) shows that as the distance sprinted increases, recovery time increases along a curve that becomes steeper.

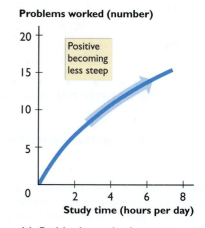

**(c)  Positive becoming less steep**

Part (c) shows that as study time increases, the number of problems worked increases along a curve that becomes less steep.

relationship. Study time becomes less effective as you increase the hours worked and become more tired.

Figure A1.4 shows relationships between two variables that move in opposite directions. Such a relationship is called a **negative relationship** or **inverse relationship**.

Part (a) shows the relationship between the number of hours spent playing squash and the number of hours spent playing tennis when the total number of hours available is five. One extra hour spent playing tennis means one hour less playing squash and vice versa. This relationship is negative and linear.

Part (b) shows the relationship between the cost per mile traveled and the length of a journey. The longer the journey, the lower is the cost per mile. But as the journey length increases, the fall in the cost per mile becomes smaller. This feature of the relationship is shown by the fact that the curve slopes downward, starting out steep at a short journey length and then becoming flatter as the journey length increases. This relationship arises because some of the costs, such as auto insurance, are fixed, and as the journey length increases, the fixed costs are spread over more miles.

Part (c) shows the relationship between the amount of leisure time and the number of problems worked by a student. Increasing leisure time produces an increasingly large reduction in the number of problems worked. This relationship is a negative one that starts out with a gentle slope at a small number of leisure hours and becomes steeper as the number of leisure hours increases. This relationship is a different view of the idea shown in Figure A1.3(c).

Many relationships in economic models have a maximum or a minimum. For example, firms try to make the largest possible profit and to produce at the lowest possible cost. Figure A1.5 shows relationships that have a maximum or a minimum.

**Negative relationship or inverse relationship**
A relationship between two variables that move in opposite directions.

■ **FIGURE A1.4**

Negative (Inverse) Relationships

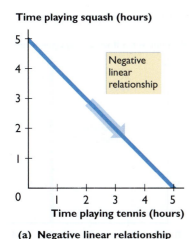

(a) **Negative linear relationship**

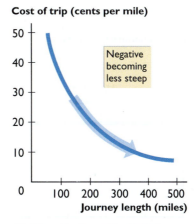

(b) **Negative becoming less steep**

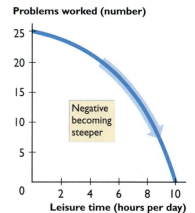

(c) **Negative becoming steeper**

Part (a) shows that as the time playing tennis increases, the time playing squash decreases along a straight line.

Part (b) shows that as the journey length increases, the cost of the trip falls along a curve that becomes less steep.

Part (c) shows that as leisure time increases, the number of problems worked decreases along a curve that becomes steeper.

■ **FIGURE A1.5**

## Maximum and Minimum Points

In part (a), as the rainfall increases, the curve ❶ slopes upward as the yield per acre rises, ❷ is flat at point *A*, the maximum yield, and then ❸ slopes downward as the yield per acre falls.

In part (b), as the speed increases, the curve ❶ slopes downward as the cost per mile falls, ❷ is flat at the minimum point *B*, and then ❸ slopes upward as the cost per mile rises.

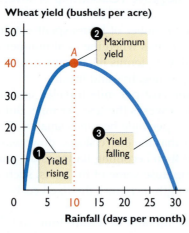

**(a)  Relationship with a maximum**

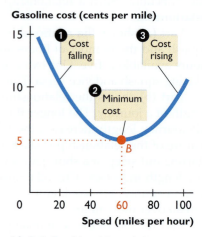

**(b)  Relationship with a minimum**

   Part (a) shows a relationship that starts out sloping upward, reaches a maximum, and then slopes downward. Part (b) shows a relationship that begins sloping downward, falls to a minimum, and then slopes upward.
   Finally, there are many situations in which, no matter what happens to the value of one variable, the other variable remains constant. Sometimes we want to show two variables that are unrelated in a graph. Figure A1.6 shows two graphs in which the variables are unrelated.

■ **FIGURE A1.6**

## Variables That Are Unrelated

In part (a), as the price of bananas increases, the student's grade in economics remains at 75 percent. These variables are unrelated, and the curve is horizontal.

In part (b), the vineyards of France produce 3 billion gallons of wine no matter what the rainfall is in California. These variables are unrelated, and the curve is vertical.

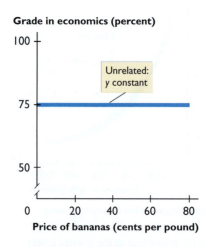

**(a)  Unrelated: y constant**

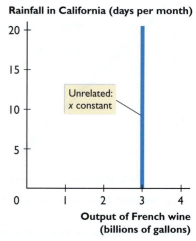

**(b)  Unrelated: x constant**

### ■ The Slope of a Relationship

We can measure the influence of one variable on another by the slope of the relationship. The **slope** of a relationship is the change in the value of the variable measured on the $y$-axis divided by the change in the value of the variable measured on the $x$-axis. We use the Greek letter $\Delta$ (delta) to represent "change in." So $\Delta y$ means the change in the value of $y$, and $\Delta x$ means the change in the value of $x$. The slope of the relationship is

$$\Delta y \div \Delta x.$$

If a large change in $y$ is associated with a small change in $x$, the slope is large and the curve is steep. If a small change in $y$ is associated with a large change in $x$, the slope is small and the curve is flat.

Figure A1.7 shows you how to calculate slope. The slope of a straight line is the same regardless of where on the line you calculate it—the slope is constant. In part (a), when $x$ increases from 2 to 6, $y$ increases from 3 to 6. The change in $x$ is 4—that is, $\Delta x$ is 4. The change in $y$ is 3—that is, $\Delta y$ is 3. The slope of that line is 3/4. In part (b), when $x$ increases from 2 to 6, $y$ *decreases* from 6 to 3. The change in $y$ is *minus* 3—that is, $\Delta y$ is $-3$ The change in $x$ is plus 4—that is, $\Delta x$ is 4. The slope of the curve is $-3/4$.

In part (c), we calculate the slope at a point on a curve. To do so, place a ruler on the graph so that it touches point $A$ and no other point on the curve, then draw a straight line along the edge of the ruler. The slope of this straight line is the slope of the curve at point $A$. This slope is 3/4.

**Slope**
The change in the value of the variable measured on the y-axis divided by the change in the value of the variable measured on the x-axis.

■ **FIGURE A1.7**

Calculating Slope

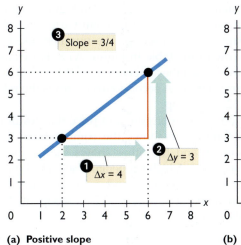

(a)  **Positive slope**

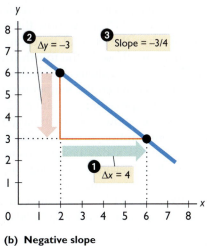

(b)  **Negative slope**

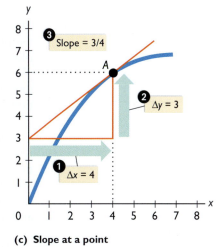

(c)  **Slope at a point**

In part (a), ❶ when $\Delta x$ is 4, ❷ $\Delta y$ is 3, so ❸ the slope ($\Delta y \div \Delta x$) is 3/4.

In part (b), ❶ when $\Delta x$ is 4, ❷ $\Delta y$ is $-3$, so ❸ the slope ($\Delta y \div \Delta x$) is $-3/4$.

In part (c), the slope of the curve at point $A$ equals the slope of the red line. ❶ When $\Delta x$ is 4, ❷ $\Delta y$ is 3, so ❸ the slope ($\Delta y \div \Delta x$) is 3/4.

## ■ Relationships Among More Than Two Variables

All the graphs that you have studied so far plot the relationship between two variables as a point formed by the $x$ and $y$ values. But most of the relationships in economics involve relationships among many variables, not just two. For example, the amount of ice cream consumed depends on the price of ice cream and the temperature. If ice cream is expensive and the temperature is low, people eat much less ice cream than when ice cream is inexpensive and the temperature is high. For any given price of ice cream, the quantity consumed varies with the temperature; and for any given temperature, the quantity of ice cream consumed varies with its price.

Figure A1.8 shows a relationship among three variables. The table shows the number of gallons of ice cream consumed per day at various temperatures and ice cream prices. How can we graph these numbers?

To graph a relationship that involves more than two variables, we use the *ceteris paribus* assumption.

### Ceteris Paribus

The Latin phrase *ceteris paribus* means "other things remaining the same." Every laboratory experiment is an attempt to create *ceteris paribus* and isolate the relationship of interest. We use the same method to make a graph.

Figure A1.8(a) shows an example. This graph shows what happens to the quantity of ice cream consumed when the price of ice cream varies while the temperature remains constant. The curve labeled 70°F shows the relationship between ice cream consumption and the price of ice cream if the temperature is 70°F. The numbers used to plot that curve are those in the first and fourth columns of the table in Figure A1.8. For example, if the temperature is 70°F, 10 gallons are consumed when the price is $2.75 a scoop and 18 gallons are consumed when the price is $2.25 a scoop. The curve labeled 90°F shows the relationship between consumption and the price when the temperature is 90°F.

We can also show the relationship between ice cream consumption and temperature while the price of ice cream remains constant, as shown in Figure A1.8(b). The curve labeled $2.75 shows how the consumption of ice cream varies with the temperature when the price of ice cream is $2.75 a scoop. The numbers used to plot that curve are those in the fourth row of the table in Figure A1.8. For example, at $2.75 a scoop, 10 gallons are consumed when the temperature is 70°F and 20 gallons are consumed when the temperature is 90°F. A second curve shows the relationship when the price of ice cream is $2.00 a scoop.

Figure A1.8(c) shows the combinations of temperature and price that result in a constant consumption of ice cream. One curve shows the combinations that result in 10 gallons a day being consumed, and the other shows the combinations that result in 7 gallons a day being consumed. A high temperature and a high price lead to the same consumption as a lower temperature and a lower price. For example, 10 gallons of ice cream are consumed at 90°F and $3.25 a scoop, at 70°F and $2.75 a scoop, and at 50°F and $2.50 a scoop.

With what you've learned about graphs in this Appendix, you can move forward with your study of economics. There are no graphs in this textbook that are more complicated than the ones you've studied here.

**FIGURE A1.8**

Graphing a Relationship Among Three Variables

| Price (dollars per scoop) | Ice cream consumption (gallons per day) | | | |
|---|---|---|---|---|
| | 30°F | 50°F | 70°F | 90°F |
| 2.00 | 12 | 18 | 25 | 50 |
| 2.25 | 10 | 12 | 18 | 37 |
| 2.50 | 7 | 10 | 13 | 27 |
| 2.75 | 5 | 7 | 10 | 20 |
| 3.00 | 3 | 5 | 7 | 14 |
| 3.25 | 2 | 3 | 5 | 10 |
| 3.50 | 1 | 2 | 3 | 6 |

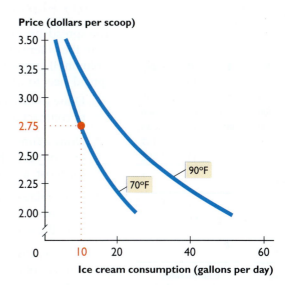

**(a) Price and consumption at a given temperature**

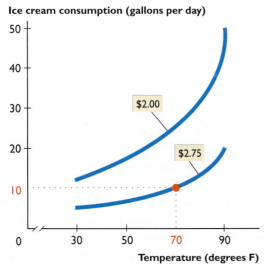

**(b) Temperature and consumption at a given price**

**(c) Temperature and price at a given consumption**

The table tells us how many gallons of ice cream are consumed at different prices and different temperatures. For example, if the price is $2.75 a scoop and the temperature is 70°F, 10 gallons of ice cream are consumed. This set of values is highlighted in the table and each part of the figure.

Part (a) shows the relationship between price and consumption when temperature is held constant. One curve holds temperature at 90°F, and the other at 70°F.

Part (b) shows the relationship between temperature and consumption when price is held constant. One curve holds the price at

$2.75 a scoop, and the other at $2.00 a scoop.

Part (c) shows the relationship between temperature and price when consumption is held constant. One curve holds consumption at 10 gallons a day, and the other at 7 gallons a day.

**APPENDIX CHECKPOINT**

## Study Plan Problems

The spreadsheet in Table 1 provides data on the U.S. economy: Column A is the year; the other columns are quantities sold in millions per year of compact discs (column B), music videos (column C), and singles downloads (column D). Use this spreadsheet to work Problems **1** and **2**.

**TABLE 1**

|   | A | B | C | D |
|---|---|---|---|---|
| **1** | 2002 | 803 | 15 | 51 |
| **2** | 2004 | 767 | 33 | 139 |
| **3** | 2006 | 620 | 23 | 586 |
| **4** | 2008 | 385 | 13 | 1,033 |
| **5** | 2010 | 226 | 9 | 1,162 |
| **6** | 2012 | 211 | 11 | 1,392 |

**TABLE 2**

| $x$ | 0 | 1 | 2 | 3 | 4 | 5 |
|---|---|---|---|---|---|---|
| $y$ | 32 | 31 | 28 | 23 | 16 | 7 |

**TABLE 3**

| Price (dollars per ride) | Balloon rides (number per day) | | |
|---|---|---|---|
| | 50°F | 70°F | 90°F |
| 5 | 32 | 50 | 40 |
| 10 | 27 | 40 | 32 |
| 15 | 18 | 32 | 27 |
| 20 | 10 | 27 | 18 |

**TABLE 4**

| $x$ | 0 | 1 | 2 | 3 | 4 | 5 |
|---|---|---|---|---|---|---|
| $y$ | 0 | 1 | 4 | 9 | 16 | 25 |

**TABLE 5**

| Price (dollars per cup) | Hot chocolate (number per week) | | |
|---|---|---|---|
| | 50°F | 70°F | 90°F |
| 2.00 | 40 | 30 | 20 |
| 2.50 | 30 | 20 | 10 |
| 3.00 | 20 | 10 | 0 |
| 3.50 | 10 | 0 | 0 |

1. Draw a scatter diagram to show the relationship between the quantities sold of compact discs and music videos. Describe the relationship.

2. Draw a time-series graph of the quantity of compact discs sold. Say in which year or years the quantity sold (a) was highest, (b) was lowest, (c) increased the most, and (d) decreased the most. If the data show a trend, describe it.

3. Is the relationship between $x$ and $y$ in Table 2 positive or negative? Calculate the slope of the relationship when $x$ equals 2 and when $x$ equals 4. How does the slope change as the value of $x$ increases?

4. Table 3 provides data on the price of a balloon ride, the temperature, and the number of rides a day. Draw graphs to show the relationship between
   • The price and the number of rides, when the temperature is 70°F.
   • The number of rides and the temperature, when the price is $15 a ride.

## Instructor Assignable Problems

Use the information in Table 1 to work Problems **1** and **2**.

1. Draw a scatter diagram to show the relationship between quantities sold of music videos and singles downloads. Describe the relationship.

2. Draw a time-series graph of the quantity of music videos sold. Say in which year or years the quantity sold (a) was highest, (b) was lowest, (c) decreased the most, and (d) decreased the least. If the data show a trend, describe it.

Use the information in Table 4 on the relationship between two variables $x$ and $y$ to work Problems **3** and **4**.

3. Is the relationship between $x$ and $y$ in Table 4 positive or negative? Explain.

4. Calculate the slope of the relationship when $x$ equals 2 and $x$ equals 4. How does the slope change as the value of $x$ increases?

5. Table 5 provides data on the price of hot chocolate, the temperature, and the number of cups a week. Draw graphs to show the relationship between
   • The price and the number of cups of hot chocolate, when the temperature is constant.
   • The temperature and the number of cups of hot chocolate, when the price is constant.

## Key Terms

Cross-section graph, 60
Direct relationship, 62
Inverse relationship, 63
Linear relationship, 62

Negative relationship, 63
Positive relationship, 62
Scatter diagram, 60
Slope, 65

Time-series graph, 60
Trend, 60

Who makes the Dreamliner?

# The U.S. and Global Economies

**When you have completed your study of this chapter, you will be able to**

**1** Describe what, how, and for whom goods and services are produced in the United States.

**2** Describe what, how, and for whom goods and services are produced in the global economy.

**3** Explain the circular flow model of the U.S. economy and of the global economy.

## 2.1  WHAT, HOW, AND FOR WHOM?

Walk around a shopping mall and pay close attention to the range of goods and services that are being offered for sale. Go inside some of the shops and look at the labels to see where various items are manufactured. The next time you travel on an interstate highway, look at the large trucks and pay attention to the names and products printed on their sides and the places in which the trucks are registered. Open the Yellow Pages and flip through a few sections. Notice the huge range of goods and services that businesses are offering.

You've just done a sampling of *what* goods and services are produced and consumed in the United States today.

### ■ What Do We Produce?

We place the goods and services produced into two large groups:

- Consumption goods and services
- Capital goods

### Consumption Goods and Services

**Consumption goods and services**
Goods and services that individuals and governments buy and use in the current period.

**Consumption goods and services** are items that individuals and governments buy and use up in the current period. Consumption goods and services bought by households include items such as housing, automobiles, bottled water, ramen noodles, chocolate bars, Po' Boy sandwiches, movies, downhill skiing lessons, and doctor and dental services. Consumption goods and services bought by governments include items such as police and fire services, garbage collection, and education.

### Capital Goods

**Capital goods**
Goods bought by businesses and governments to increase productive resources and to use over future periods to produce other goods and services.

**Capital goods** are goods that businesses and governments buy to increase productive resources to use over future periods to produce other goods and services. Capital goods bought by businesses include items such as auto assembly lines, shopping malls, airplanes, and oil tankers. Capital goods bought by governments include missiles and weapons systems for national security, public schools and universities, and interstate highways.

Consumption goods and services represent 85 percent of U.S. production by value and that percentage doesn't fluctuate much. *Eye on the U.S. Economy* opposite breaks the goods and services down into smaller categories.

Health services is the largest category, with 17.6 percent of the value of total production. Real estate services come next at 12.6 percent. The main components of this item are the services of rental and owner-occupied housing. Professional and business services, which include the services of accountants and lawyers, are 12.5 percent of total production. Other large components of services are education and retail and wholesale trades.

The manufacture of goods represents only 11.5 percent of total production and the largest category of goods produced, chemicals, accounts for less than 2 percent of total production.

Construction accounts for 3.5 percent of production, and utilities, mining, and agriculture together make up only 5 percent. The nation's farms produce only a bit more than 1 percent of total production.

# EYE on the U.S. ECONOMY
## What We Produce

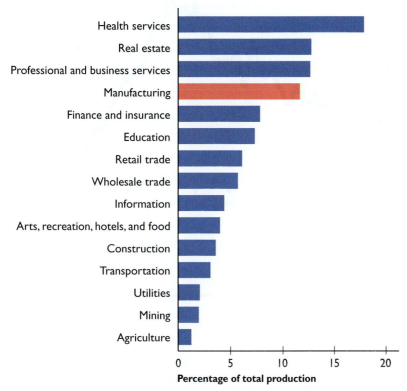

**(a) Goods and services produced in the U.S. economy**

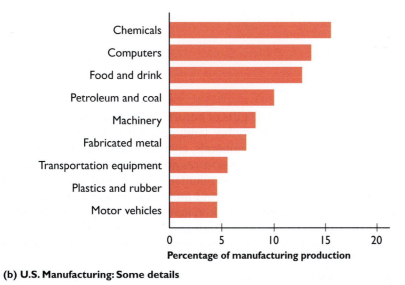

**(b) U.S. Manufacturing: Some details**

SOURCE OF DATA: Bureau of Economic Analysis.

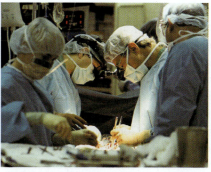

*Health-care services …*

*education services …*

*and retail trades are among the largest categories of services produced.*

*The largest category of goods produced is chemicals.*

# EYE on the PAST
## Changes in What We Produce

Freeport, Maine, became a shoemaking center in 1881 when the H.E. Davis Shoe Company opened its steam-powered factory in the town. Over the following years, many other shoe-makers set up in Freeport and produc-tion steadily expanded. The town's shoe production peaked in 1968 after which it shrank rapidly. When the Freeport Shoe Company closed its factory in 1972, it became the fifteenth shoe factory to close in Freeport in four years. Today, the Freeport econ-omy is based on shopping, not shoes.

Freeport's story of shoemaking was repeated across America and the graph tells this broader story. And as manu-facturing has shrunk, retail and other services have expanded.

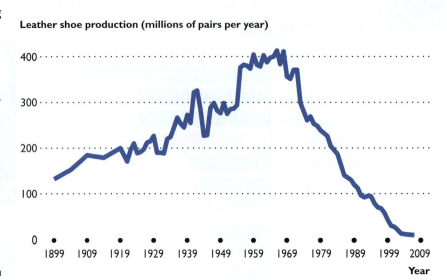

**Leather shoe production (millions of pairs per year)**

SOURCES OF DATA: *Historical Statistics of the United States Millennial Edition Online* and *Statistical Abstract of the United States,* 2012.

## ■ How Do We Produce?

**Factors of production**
The productive resources that are used to produce goods and services—land, labor, capital, and entrepreneurship.

Goods and services are produced by using productive resources. Economists call the productive resources **factors of production**. Factors of production are grouped into four categories:

- Land
- Labor
- Capital
- Entrepreneurship

### Land

**Land**
The "gifts of nature," or *natural resources,* that we use to produce goods and services.

In economics, **land** includes all the "gifts of nature" that we use to produce goods and services. Land is what, in everyday language, we call *natural resources.* It includes land in the everyday sense, minerals, energy, water, air, and wild plants, animals, birds, and fish. Some of these resources are renewable, and some are non-renewable. The U.S. Geological Survey maintains a national inventory of the quantity and quality of natural resources and monitors changes to that inventory.

The United States covers almost 2 billion acres. About 45 percent of the land is forest, lakes, and national parks. In 2009, almost 50 percent of the land was used for agriculture and 5 percent was urban, but urban land use is growing and agri-cultural land use is shrinking.

Our land surface and water resources are renewable, and some of our mineral resources can be recycled. But many mineral resources can be used only once. They are nonrenewable resources. Of these, the United States has vast known reserves of coal, oil, and natural gas.

## Labor

**Labor** is the work time and work effort that people devote to producing goods and services. Labor includes the physical and mental efforts of all the people who work on farms and construction sites and in factories, shops, and offices. The Census Bureau and Bureau of Labor Statistics measure the quantity of labor at work every month.

In the United States in April 2013, 155 million people had jobs or were available for work. Some worked full time, some worked part time, and some were unemployed but looking for an acceptable vacant job. The total amount of time worked during 2011 was about 275 billion hours.

The quantity of labor increases as the adult population increases. The quantity of labor also increases if a larger percentage of the population takes jobs. During the past 50 years, a larger proportion of women have taken paid work and this trend has increased the quantity of labor. At the same time, a slightly smaller proportion of men have taken paid work and this trend has decreased the quantity of labor.

The *quality* of labor depends on how skilled people are. A laborer who can push a hand cart but can't drive a truck is much less productive than one who can drive. An office worker who can use a computer is much more productive than one who can't. Economists use a special name for human skill: human capital. **Human capital** is the knowledge and skill that people obtain from education, on-the-job training, and work experience.

You are building your own human capital right now as you work on your economics course and other subjects. Your human capital will continue to grow when you get a full-time job and become better at it. Human capital improves the *quality* of labor and increases the quantity of goods and services that labor can produce.

**Labor**
The work time and work effort that people devote to producing goods and services.

**Human capital**
The knowledge and skill that people obtain from education, on-the-job training, and work experience.

## Capital

**Capital** consists of the tools, instruments, machines, buildings, and other items that have been produced in the past and that businesses now use to produce goods and services. Capital includes hammers and screwdrivers, computers, auto assembly lines, office towers and warehouses, dams and power plants, airplanes, shirt factories, and shopping malls.

Capital also includes inventories of unsold goods or of partly finished goods on a production line. And capital includes what is sometimes called *infrastructure capital*, such as highways and airports.

Capital, like human capital, makes labor more productive. A truck driver can produce vastly more transportation services than someone pushing a hand cart; the Interstate highway system enables us to produce vastly more transportation services than was possible on the old highway system that preceded it.

The Bureau of Economic Analysis in the U.S. Department of Commerce keeps track of the total value of capital in the United States and how it grows over time. Today, the value of capital in the U.S. economy is around $50 trillion.

**Capital**
Tools, instruments, machines, buildings, and other items that have been produced in the past and that businesses now use to produce goods and services.

### Financial Capital Is Not Capital

In everyday language, we talk about money, stocks, and bonds as being capital. These items are *financial capital*, and they are not productive resources. They enable people to provide businesses with financial resources, but they are *not* used to produce goods and services. They are not capital.

# EYE on the U.S. ECONOMY
## Changes in How We Produce in the Information Economy

The information economy consists of the jobs and businesses that produce and use computers and equipment powered by computer chips. This information economy is highly visible in your daily life.

The pairs of images here illustrate two examples. In each pair, a new technology enables capital to replace labor.

The top pair of pictures illustrate the replacement of bank tellers (labor) with ATMs (capital). Although the ATM was invented almost 40 years ago, when it made its first appearance, it was located only inside banks and was not able to update customers' accounts. It is only in the last decade that ATMs have spread to corner stores and enable us to get cash and check our bank balance from almost anywhere in the world.

The bottom pair of pictures illustrate a more recent replacement of labor with capital: self-check-in. Air passengers today issue their own boarding pass, often at their own computer before leaving home. For international

flights, some of these machines now even check passport details.

The number of bank teller and airport check-in clerk jobs is shrinking,

but these new technologies are creating a whole range of new jobs for people who make, program, install, and repair the vast number of machines.

## Entrepreneurship

**Entrepreneurship**
The human resource that organizes labor, land, and capital to produce goods and services.

**Entrepreneurship** is the human resource that organizes land, labor, and capital to produce goods and services. Entrepreneurs are creative and imaginative. They come up with new ideas about what and how to produce, make business decisions, and bear the risks that arise from these decisions. If their ideas work out, they earn a profit. If their ideas turn out to be wrong, they bear the loss.

The quantity of entrepreneurship is hard to describe or measure. During some periods, there appears to be a great deal of imaginative entrepreneurship around. People such as Sam Walton, who created Wal-Mart, one of the world's largest retailers; Bill Gates, who founded the Microsoft empire; and Mark Zuckerberg, who founded Facebook, are examples of extraordinary entrepreneurial talent. But these highly visible entrepreneurs are just the tip of an iceberg that consists of hundreds of thousands of people who run businesses, large and small.

# ■ For Whom Do We Produce?

Who gets the goods and services depends on the incomes that people earn. A large income enables a person to buy large quantities of goods and services. A small income leaves a person with a small quantity of goods and services.

People earn their incomes by selling the services of the factors of production they own. **Rent** is paid for the use of land, **wages** are paid for the services of labor, **interest** is paid for the use of capital, and entrepreneurs receive a **profit** (or incur a **loss**) for running their businesses. What are the shares of these four factor incomes in the United States? Which factor receives the largest share?

Figure 2.1(a) answers these questions. It shows that wages were 69 percent of total income in 2011 and rent, interest, and profit were 31 percent of total income. These percentages remain remarkably constant over time. We call the distribution of income among the factors of production the *functional distribution of income.*

Figure 2.1(b) shows the *personal distribution of income*—the distribution of income among households—in 2011. Some households, like that of Alex Rodriguez, earn many millions of dollars a year. These households are in the richest 20 percent who earn 50 percent of total income. Households at the other end of the scale, like those of fast-food servers, are in the poorest 20 percent who earn only 3 percent of total income. The distribution of income has been changing and becoming more unequal. The rich have become richer. But it isn't the case, on the whole, that the poor have become poorer. They just haven't become richer as fast as the rich have.

**Rent**
Income paid for the use of land.

**Wages**
Income paid for the services of labor.

**Interest**
Income paid for the use of capital.

**Profit (or loss)**
Income earned by an entrepreneur for running a business.

---

## ■ FIGURE 2.1

### *For Whom* in 2011

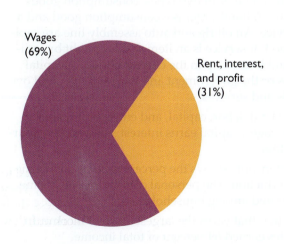

**(a) Functional distribution of income**

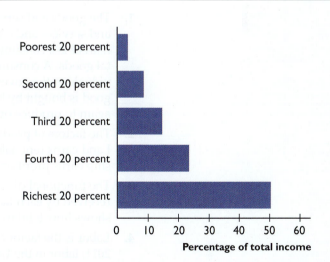

**(b) Personal distribution of income**

SOURCES OF DATA: Bureau of Economic Analysis, *National Income and Product Accounts*, Table 1.10 and U.S. Census Bureau, *Income, Poverty, and Health Insurance Coverage in the United States*: 2011, Current Population Reports P60-243, 2012.

In 2011, wages (the income from labor) were **69** percent of total income. Rent, interest, and profit (the income from the services of land, capital, and entrepreneurship) totaled the remaining 31 percent.

In 2011, the 20 percent of the population with the highest incomes received 50 percent of total income. The 20 percent with the lowest incomes received only 3 percent of total income.

## CHECKPOINT 2.1

**Describe what, how, and for whom goods and services are produced in the United States.**

## Practice Problems

1. What are the types of goods and services produced? Give an example of each (different from those in the chapter) and distinguish between them.
2. Name the four factors of production and the incomes they earn.
3. Distinguish between the functional distribution of income and the personal distribution of income.
4. In the United States, which factor of production earned the largest share of income in 2011 and what percentage did it earn?

## In the News

**What microloans miss**
The 2006 Nobel Peace Prize winner Muhammad Yunus has said that "all people are entrepreneurs" and that microloans will pull poor people out of poverty. Only 14 percent of Americans are entrepreneurs while almost 40 percent of Peruvians are.

Source: James Surowiecki, *The New Yorker*, March 17, 2008

With only 14 percent of Americans earning their income from entrepreneurship, from what factor of production do most Americans earn their income? What is that income called? Why might so many people in Peru be entrepreneurs?

## Solutions to Practice Problems

1. The goods and services produced fall into two types: consumption goods and services and capital goods. A hamburger is a consumption good and a haircut is a consumption service. An oil rig and auto assembly line are capital goods. A consumption good or service is an item that is bought by individuals or the government and is used up in the current period. A capital good is bought by businesses or the government and it is used over and over again to produce other goods and services.
2. The factors of production are land, labor, capital, and entrepreneurship. Land earns rent; labor earns wages; capital earns interest; and entrepreneurship earns profit or incurs a loss.
3. The functional distribution of income shows the percentage of total income received by each factor of production. The personal distribution of income shows how total income is shared among households.
4. Labor is the factor of production that earns the largest share of income. In 2011, labor in the United States earned 69 percent of total income.

## Solution to In the News

Most Americans earn their income from supplying labor services and the income they earn is called a wage. Peru is a poor country in which jobs are more limited than in the United States. So to earn an income, many Peruvians are self-employed and work as small entrepreneurs.

## 2.2    THE GLOBAL ECONOMY

We're now going to look at *what*, *how*, and *for whom* goods and services get produced in the global economy. We'll begin with a brief overview of the people and countries that form the global economy.

### ■ The People

Visit the Web site of the U.S. Census Bureau and go to the population clocks to find out how many people there are today in both the United States and the entire world. On the day these words were written, May 9, 2013, the U.S. clock recorded a population of 315,824,000. The world clock recorded a global population of 7,084,065,000. The U.S. clock ticks along showing a population increase of one person every 15 seconds. The world clock spins faster, adding 30 people in the same 15 seconds.

### ■ The Economies

The world's 7.1 billion (and rising) population lives in 176 economies, which the International Monetary Fund classifies into two broad groups:

- Advanced economies
- Emerging market and developing economies

#### Advanced Economies

Advanced economies are the richest 29 countries (or areas). The United States, Japan, Italy, Germany, France, the United Kingdom, and Canada belong to this group. So do four new industrial Asian economies: Hong Kong, South Korea, Singapore, and Taiwan. The other advanced economies include Australia, New Zealand, and most of the rest of Western Europe. Almost 1 billion people (15 percent of the world's population) live in the advanced economies.

#### Emerging Market and Developing Economies

*Emerging market economies* are 28 countries in Central and Eastern Europe and Asia. Almost 500 million people live in these countries—about half of the number in the advanced economies. These countries are important because they are emerging (hence the name) from a system of state-owned production, central economic planning, and heavily regulated markets moving toward a system of free enterprise and unregulated markets.

*Developing economies* are the 119 countries in Africa, Asia, the Middle East, Europe, and Central and South America. More than 5.5 billion people—almost four out of every five people—live in the developing economies.

Developing economies vary enormously in size, in the level of average income, and the rate of growth of production and incomes. But in all the developing economies, average incomes are much lower than those in the advanced economies, and in some cases, they are extremely low.

Five emerging market and developing economies, representing 3 billion people or 42 percent of the world's population and known as BRICS (Brazil, Russia, India, China, and South Africa), hold regular meetings to advance the interests of these nations and draw attention to their development problems.

## ■ *What* in the Global Economy?

First, let's look at the big picture. Imagine that each year the global economy produces an enormous pie. In 2013, the pie was worth about $87 trillion! To give this number some meaning, if the pie were shared equally among the world's 7.1 billion people, each of us would get a slice worth a bit more than $12,254.

### Where Is the Global Pie Baked?

Figure 2.2 shows us where in the world the pie is baked. The advanced economies produce 50 percent—19 percent in the United States, 14 percent in the Euro area, and 17 percent in the other advanced economies. This 50 percent of global output (by value) is produced by 15 percent of the world's population.

The BRICS economies, highlighted in the figure, together produce 28 percent of the world's output. China, with 15 percent of world production, dominates this group and South Africa, the group's smallest member, produces barely 1 percent of global output. This 28 percent of the global pie is baked by 42 percent of the world's population.

The remaining 22 percent of the global pie comes from other emerging market and developing economies and is baked by 43 percent of the world's people.

Unlike the slices of an apple pie, those of the global pie have different fillings. Some slices have more oil, some more food, some more clothing, some more housing services, some more autos, and so on. Let's look at some of these different fillings and at some similarities too.

---

### ■ FIGURE 2.2

*What* in the Global Economy in 2013

---

If we show the value of production in the world economy as a pie, the United States produces a slice that is 19 percent of the total. The Euro area produces 14 percent and other advanced economies 17 percent, so together, the advanced economies produce 50 percent of global output.

Another 28 percent of the global pie comes from the BRICS economies, and China, with 15 percent of world output, dominates this group.

The remaining 22 percent of world output comes from emerging market and developing economies in Africa, Asia, the Middle East, and the Western Hemisphere.

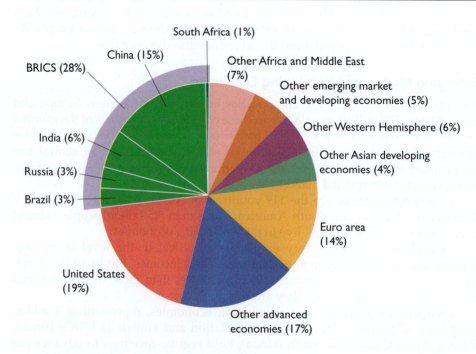

SOURCE OF DATA: International Monetary Fund, World Economic Outlook Database, April 2013.

# EYE on the DREAMLINER

## Who Makes the Dreamliner?

Boeing designed, assembles, and markets the Dreamliner, but the airplane is made by more than 400 firms on four continents that employ thousands of workers and millions of dollars' worth of specialized capital equipment. The graphic identifies some of the firms and the components they make.

Boeing and these firms make decisions and pay their workers, investors, and raw material suppliers to influence *what*, *how*, and *for whom* goods and services are produced. All these decisions are made in self-interest, and produce an airplane at the lowest possible cost.

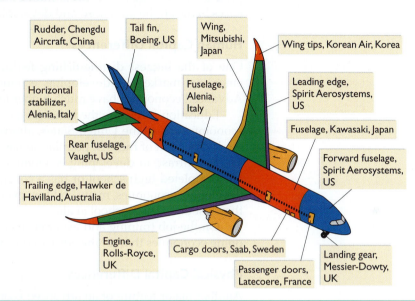

Rudder, Chengdu Aircraft, China
Tail fin, Boeing, US
Wing, Mitsubishi, Japan
Wing tips, Korean Air, Korea
Horizontal stabilizer, Alenia, Italy
Fuselage, Alenia, Italy
Leading edge, Spirit Aerosystems, US
Fuselage, Kawasaki, Japan
Rear fuselage, Vaught, US
Forward fuselage, Spirit Aerosystems, US
Trailing edge, Hawker de Havilland, Australia
Engine, Rolls-Royce, UK
Cargo doors, Saab, Sweden
Passenger doors, Latecoere, France
Landing gear, Messier-Dowty, UK

## Some Differences in What Is Produced

What is produced in the developing economies contrasts sharply with that of the advanced economies. Manufacturing is the big story. Developing economies have large and growing industries, which produce textiles, footwear, sports gear, toys, electronic goods, furniture, steel, and even automobiles and airplanes.

Food production is a small part of the U.S. and other advanced economies and a large part of the developing economies such as Brazil, China, and India. But the advanced economies produce about one third of the world's food. How come? *Total* production is much larger in the advanced economies than in the developing economies, but a small percentage of a big number can be *greater* than a large percentage of a small number!

## Some Similarities in What Is Produced

If you were to visit a shopping mall in Canada, England, Australia, Japan, or any of the other advanced economies, you would wonder whether you had left the United States. You would see Starbucks, Burger King, Pizza Hut, Domino's Pizza, KFC, Kmart, Wal-Mart, Target, Gap, Tommy Hilfiger, Lululemon, Banana Republic, the upscale Louis Vuitton and Burberry, and a host of other familiar names. And, of course, you would see McDonald's golden arches. You would see them in any of the 119 countries in which one or more of McDonald's 30,000 restaurants are located.

The similarities among the advanced economies go beyond the view from main street and the shopping mall. The structure of *what* is produced is similar in these economies. As percentages of the total economy, agriculture and manufacturing are small and shrinking whereas services are large and expanding.

*McDonald's in Shanghai.*

## ■ *How* in the Global Economy?

Goods and services are produced using land, labor, capital, and entrepreneurial resources, and the combinations of these resources used are chosen to produce at the lowest possible cost. Each country or region has its own blend of factors of production, but there are some interesting common patterns and crucial differences between the advanced and developing economies that we'll now examine.

### Human Capital Differences

One of the biggest distinguishing features of an advanced economy from an emerging market or developing economy is its quantity of *human capital*. Advanced economies have much higher levels of human capital.

Education levels are the handiest measure of human capital. In an advanced economy such as the United States, almost everyone has completed high school. And 30 percent of the U.S. population has completed 4 years or more of college.

In contrast, in developing economies, the proportion of the population who has completed high school or has a college degree is small. In the poorest of the developing economies, many children even miss out on basic primary education—they just don't go to school at all.

On-the-job training and experience are also much less extensive in the developing economies than in the advanced economies.

### Physical Capital Differences

Another major feature of an advanced economy that differentiates it from a developing economy is the amount of capital available for producing goods and services. The differences begin with the basic transportation system. In the advanced economies, a well-developed highway system connects all the major cities and points of production. You can see this difference vividly if you open a road atlas of North America: Contrast the U.S. interstate highway system with the sparse highways of Mexico. You would see a similar contrast if you flipped through a road atlas of Western Europe and Africa.

But it isn't the case that the developing economies have no highways and no modern trucks and cars. In fact, some of them have the newest and the best. But the new and best are usually inside and around the major cities—see *Eye on the Global Economy* opposite.

The contrasts in the transportation system are matched by those on farms and in factories. In general, the more advanced the economy, the greater are the amount and sophistication of the capital equipment used in production. But again, the contrast is not all or nothing. Some factories in India, China, and other parts of Asia use the very latest technologies. Furniture manufacturing is an example. To make furniture of a quality that Americans are willing to buy, firms in Asia use machines like those in the furniture factories of North Carolina.

The differences in human capital and physical capital between advanced and developing economies have a big effect on *who* gets the goods and services, which we'll now examine.

## ■ *For Whom* in the Global Economy?

Who gets the world's goods and services depends on the incomes that people earn. We're now going to see how incomes are distributed within economies and across the world.

# EYE on the GLOBAL ECONOMY
## Differences in How We Produce

Big differences exist in how goods and services are produced and the images here illustrate three examples.

Laundry services (top), transportation services (center), and highway systems (bottom) can use a large amount of capital and almost no labor (left) or use almost no capital and a large amount of labor (right).

Capital-intensive automatic laundry equipment, big trucks, and multi-lane paved freeways are common in advanced economies but rare in poorer developing economies.

Riverside clothes washing, human pedal power, and unsealed dirt tracks are seen only in developing economies.

But we also see huge differences even within a developing economy. The bottom pictures contrast Beijing's capital-intensive highway system with the unpaved and sometimes hazardous roads of rural China.

## Personal Distribution of Income

You saw earlier (on p. 75) that in the United States, the lowest-paid 20 percent of the population receives 3 percent of total income and the highest-paid 20 percent receives 50 percent of total income. The personal distribution of income in the world economy is much more unequal. According to World Bank data, the lowest-paid 20 percent of the world's population receives 2 percent of world income and the highest-paid 20 percent receives about 70 percent of world income.

## International Distribution

Much of the greater inequality at the global level arises from differences in average incomes among countries. Figure 2.3 shows some of these differences. It shows the dollar value of what people can afford each day on average. You can see that in the United States, that number is $137 a day—an average person in the United States can buy goods and services that cost $137. This amount is around five times the world average. The Euro area has an average income of around two thirds that of the United States at $93 per day. Income levels fall off quickly as we move farther down the graph, with Russia at $49 a day, China $25 a day, India $10 a day, and Africa only $7 a day.

As people have lost well-paid manufacturing jobs and found lower-paid service jobs, inequality has increased in the United States and in most other advanced economies. Inequality is also increasing in the developing economies. People with skills enjoy rapidly rising incomes but the incomes of the unskilled are falling.

### A Happy Paradox and a Huge Challenge

Despite the increase in inequality inside most countries, inequality across the entire world has decreased during the past 20 years. And most important, according to Xavier Sala-i-Martin, an economics professor at Columbia University, extreme poverty has declined. Professor Sala-i-Martin estimates that between 1976 and 1998, the number of people who earn $1 a day or less fell by 235 million and the number who earn $2 a day or less fell by 450 million. This positive situation arises because in China, the largest nation, incomes have increased rapidly and lifted millions from extreme poverty. Incomes are growing quickly in India too.

Lifting Africa from poverty is today's big challenge. In 1960, 11 percent of the world's poor lived in Africa, but in 1998, 66 percent did. Between 1976 and 1998, the number of people in Africa who earn $1 a day or less rose by 175 million, and the number who earn $2 a day or less rose by 227 million.

■ **FIGURE 2.3**

*For Whom* in the Global Economy in 2012

In 2012, the average income per person per day in the United States was $137. It was $93 in the Euro area and $49 in Russia. The number falls to $25 in China, $10 in India, and $7 in Africa.

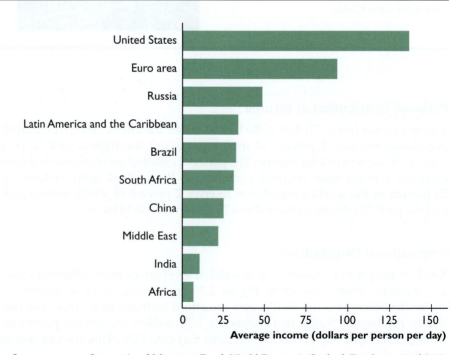

SOURCE OF DATA: International Monetary Fund, World Economic Outlook Database, April 2013.

# EYE on YOUR LIFE
## The U.S. and Global Economies in Your Life

You've encountered a lot of facts and trends about what, how, and for whom goods and services are produced in the U.S. economy and the global economy. How can you use this information? You can use it in two ways:

1. To inf orm your choice of career
2. To inform your stand on the politics of protecting U.S. jobs

### Career Choices

As you think about your future career, you are now better informed about some of the key trends. You know that manufacturing is shrinking. The U.S. economy is what is sometimes called a *post-industrial economy*. Industries that provided the backbone of the economy in previous generations have fallen to barely a fifth of the economy today, and the trend continues. It is possible that by the middle of the current century, manufacturing will be as small a source of jobs as agriculture is today.

So, a job in a manufacturing business is likely to lead to some tough situations and possibly the need for several job changes over a working life.

As manufacturing shrinks, so services expand, and this expansion will continue. The provision of health care, education, communication, wholesale and retail trades, and entertainment are all likely to expand in the future and be sources of increasing employment and rising wages. A job in a service-oriented business is more likely to lead to steady advances in income.

### Political Stand on Job Protection

As you think about the stand you will take on the political question of protecting U.S. jobs, you are better informed about the basic facts and trends.

When you hear that manufacturing jobs are disappearing to China, you will be able to place that news in historical perspective. You might reasonably be concerned, especially if you or a member of your family has lost a job. But you know that trying to reverse or even halt this process is flying in the face of stubborn historical trends.

In later chapters, you will learn that there are good economic reasons to be skeptical about any form of protection and placing limits on competition.

---

## CHECKPOINT 2.2

**Describe what, how, and for whom goods and services are produced in the global economy.**

### Practice Problems

1. Describe what, how, and for whom goods and services are produced in developing economies.
2. A Clinton Foundation success story is that it loaned $23,000 to Rwandan coffee growers to support improvements to coffee washing stations and provided technical support. What was the source of the success?

### Solutions to Practice Problems

1. In developing countries, agriculture is the largest percentage, manufacturing is an increasing percentage, and services are a small percentage of total production. Most production does not use modern capital-intensive technologies, but some industries do. People who work in factories have rising incomes while those who work in rural industries are left behind.
2. The technical support allowed Rwandan coffee growers to improve their knowledge of coffee farming, which increased their human capital. The improvements to washing stations was a change in physical capital that allowed farmers to increase the quan-tity of washed coffee.

## 2.3 THE CIRCULAR FLOWS

**Circular flow model**

A model of the economy that shows the circular flow of expenditures and incomes that result from decision makers' choices and the way those choices interact to determine what, how, and for whom goods and services are produced.

We can organize the data you've just studied using the **circular flow model**—a model of the economy that shows the circular flow of expenditures and incomes that result from decision makers' choices and the way those choices interact to determine what, how, and for whom goods and services are produced. Figure 2.4 shows the circular flow model.

### ■ Households and Firms

**Households** are individuals or groups of people living together. The 121 million households in the United States own the factors of production—land, labor, capital, and entrepreneurship—and choose the quantities of these resources to provide to firms. Households also choose the quantities of goods and services to buy.

**Firms** are the institutions that organize the production of goods and services. The 28 million firms in the United States choose the quantities of the factors of production to hire and the quantities of goods and services to produce.

**Households**

Individuals or groups of people living together.

**Firms**

The institutions that organize the production of goods and services.

### ■ Markets

Households choose the quantities of the factors of production to provide to firms, and firms choose the quantities of the services of the factors of production to hire. Firms choose the quantities of goods and services to produce, and households choose the quantities of goods and services to buy. How are these choices coordinated and made compatible? The answer is: by markets.

A **market** is any arrangement that brings buyers and sellers together and enables them to get information and do business with each other. An example is the market in which oil is bought and sold—the world oil market. The world oil market is not a place. It is the network of oil producers, oil users, wholesalers, and brokers who buy and sell oil. In the world oil market, decision makers do not meet physically. They make deals by telephone, fax, and the Internet.

Figure 2.4 identifies two types of markets: goods markets and factor markets. Goods and services are bought and sold in **goods markets;** and the services of factors of production are bought and sold in **factor markets.**

**Market**

Any arrangement that brings buyers and sellers together and enables them to get information and do business with each other.

**Goods markets**

Markets in which goods and services are bought and sold.

**Factor markets**

Markets in which the services of factors of production are bought and sold.

### ■ Real Flows and Money Flows

When households choose the quantities of services of land, labor, capital, and entrepreneurship to offer in factor markets, they respond to the incomes they receive—rent for land, wages for labor, interest for capital, and profit for entrepreneurship. When firms choose the quantities of factor services to hire, they respond to the rent, wages, interest, and profits they must pay to households.

Similarly, when firms choose the quantities of goods and services to produce and offer for sale in goods markets, they respond to the amounts that they receive from the expenditures that households make. And when households choose the quantities of goods and services to buy, they respond to the amounts they must pay to firms.

Figure 2.4 shows the flows that result from these choices made by households and firms. The flows shown in orange are *real flows:* the flows of the factors of production that go from households through factor markets to firms and of the goods and services that go from firms through goods markets to households. The flows in the opposite direction are *money flows:* the flows of payments made in exchange for the services of factors of production (shown in blue) and of expenditures on goods and services (shown in red).

Lying behind these real flows and money flows are millions of individual choices about what to consume and what and how to produce. These choices result in buying plans by households and selling plans by firms in goods markets. And the choices result in selling plans by households and buying plans by firms in factor markets that interact to determine the prices that people pay and the incomes they earn, and so determine for whom goods and services are produced. You'll learn in Chapter 4 how markets coordinate the buying plans and selling plans of households and firms and make them compatible.

Firms produce most of the goods and services that we consume, but governments provide some of the services that we enjoy. Governments also play a big role in modifying for whom goods and services are produced by changing the personal distribution of income. We're now going to look at the role of governments in the U.S. economy and add them to the circular flow model.

## ■ FIGURE 2.4

### The Circular Flow Model

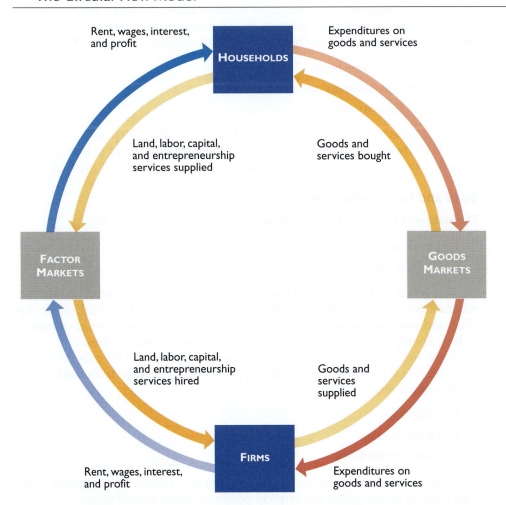

The orange flows are the services of factors of production that go from households through factor markets to firms and the goods and services that go from firms through goods markets to households. These flows are *real* flows.

The blue flow is the income earned by the factors of production, and the red flow is the expenditures on goods and services. These flows are *money* flows.

The choices that generate these real and money flows determine *what*, *how*, and *for whom* goods and services are produced.

# ■ Governments

More than 86,000 organizations operate as governments in the United States. Some are tiny like the Yuma, Arizona, school district and some are enormous like the U.S. federal government. We divide governments into two levels:

- Federal government
- State and local government

## Federal Government

The federal government's major expenditures provide

1. Goods and services
2. Social Security and welfare payments
3. Transfers to state and local governments

The goods and services provided by the federal government include the legal system, which protects property and enforces contracts, and national defense. Social Security and welfare benefits, which include income for retired people and programs such as Medicare and Medicaid, are transfers from the federal government to households. Federal government transfers to state and local governments are payments designed to provide more equality across the states and regions.

The federal government finances its expenditures by collecting a variety of taxes. The main taxes paid to the federal government are

1. Personal income taxes
2. Corporate (business) income taxes
3. Social Security taxes

In 2012, the federal government spent $3 trillion—about 19 percent of the total value of all the goods and services produced in the United States in that year. The taxes they raised were less than this amount—the government had a deficit.

## State and Local Government

The state and local governments' major expenditures are to provide

1. Goods and services
2. Welfare benefits

The goods and services provided by state and local governments include the state courts and police, schools, roads, garbage collection and disposal, water supplies, and sewage management. Welfare benefits provided by state governments include unemployment benefits and other aid to low-income families.

State and local governments finance these expenditures by collecting taxes and receiving transfers from the federal government. The main taxes paid to state and local governments are

1. Sales taxes
2. Property taxes
3. State income taxes

In 2012, state and local governments spent $2.2 trillion or 14 percent of the total value of all the goods and services produced in the United States.

# ■ Governments in the Circular Flow

Figure 2.5 adds governments to the circular flow model. As you study this figure, first notice that the outer circle is the same as in Figure 2.4. In addition to these flows, governments buy goods and services from firms. The red arrows that run from governments through the goods markets to firms show this expenditure.

Households and firms pay taxes to governments. The green arrows running directly from households and firms to governments show these flows. Also, governments make money payments to households and firms. The green arrows running directly from governments to households and firms show these flows. Taxes and transfers are direct transactions with governments and do not go through the goods markets and factor markets.

Not part of the circular flow and not visible in Figure 2.5, governments provide the legal framework within which all transactions occur. For example, governments operate the courts and legal system that enable contracts to be written and enforced.

■ **FIGURE 2.5**

Governments in the Circular Flow

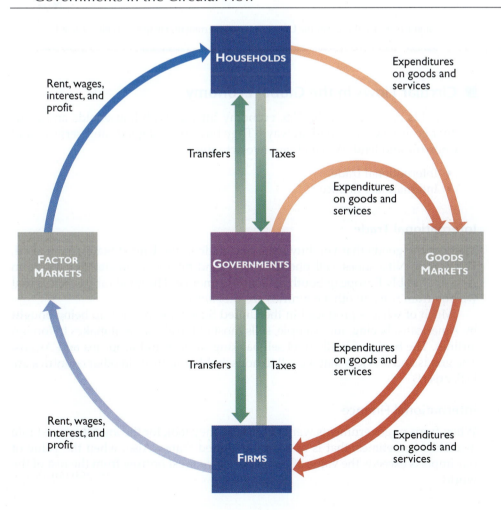

The green flows from households and firms to governments are taxes, and the green flows from governments to households and firms are money transfers.

The red flow from governments through the goods markets to firms is the expenditure on goods and services by governments.

# EYE on the PAST
## Growing Government

One hundred years ago, the federal government spent 2 cents out of each dollar earned. Today, the federal government spends 23 cents. Government grew during the two world wars and during the 1960s and 1970s as social programs expanded.

Only during the 1980s and 1990s did big government begin to shrink in a process begun by Ronald Reagan and continued by Bill Clinton. But 9-11 saw the start of a new era of growing government, and fiscal stimulus and bailouts to cope with the global financial crisis sent spending soaring.

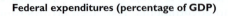

SOURCE OF DATA: Budget of the United States Government, Historical Tables, Table 1.1.

## ■ Circular Flows in the Global Economy

Households and firms in the U.S. economy interact with households and firms in other economies in two main ways: They buy and sell goods and services and they borrow and lend. We call these two activities:

- International trade
- International finance

### International Trade

Many of the goods that you buy were not made in the United States. Your iPod, Wii games, Nike shoes, cell phone, T-shirt, and bike were made somewhere in Asia or possibly Europe or South or Central America. The goods and services that we buy from firms in other countries are U.S. *imports.*

Much of what is produced in the United States doesn't end up being bought by Americans. Boeing, for example, sells most of the airplanes it makes to foreign airlines. The banks of Wall Street sell banking services to Europeans and Asians. The goods and services that we sell to households and firms in other countries are U.S. *exports.*

### International Finance

When firms or governments want to borrow, they look for the lowest interest rate available. Sometimes, that is outside the United States. Also, when the value of our imports exceeds the value of our exports, we must borrow from the rest of the world.

Firms and governments in the rest of the world behave in the same way. They look for the lowest interest rate at which to borrow and the highest at which to lend. They might borrow from or lend to Americans.

Figure 2.6 shows the flows through goods markets and financial markets in the global economy. Households and firms in the U.S. economy interact with those in the rest of the world (other economies) in goods markets and financial markets.

The red flow shows the expenditure by Americans on imports of goods and services, and the blue flow shows the expenditure by the rest of the world on U.S. exports (other countries' imports). The green flow shows U.S. lending to the rest of the world, and the orange flow shows U.S. borrowing from the rest of the world.

It is these international trade and international finance flows that tie nations together in the global economy and through which global booms and slumps are transmitted.

■ **FIGURE 2.6**

Circular Flows in the Global Economy

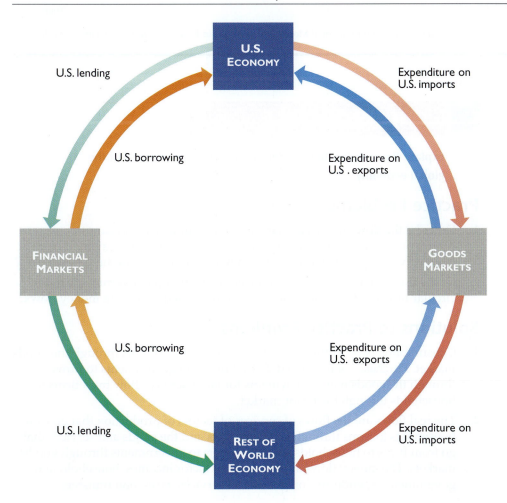

Households and firms in the U.S. economy interact with those in the rest of the world (other economies) in goods markets and financial markets.

The red flow shows the expenditure by Americans on imports of goods and services, and the blue flow shows the expenditure by the rest of the world on U.S. exports (other countries' imports).

The green flow shows U.S. lending to the rest of the world, and the orange flow shows U.S. borrowing from the rest of the world.

# EYE on the GLOBAL ECONOMY
## The Ups and Downs in International Trade

International trade expanded rapidly after China became a powerful player in the global economy.

At an average growth rate of close to 7 percent a year, world trade has doubled every decade and increased as a percentage of world production.

A mini-recession in 2001 slowed the growth in world trade to a crawl and the 2009 global economic slump reduced world trade.

After the slump of 2009, world trade bounced back to more than 30 percent of global production in 2011 and 2012.

**Global international trade (percentage of world GDP)**

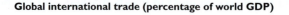

SOURCE OF DATA: International Monetary Fund, World Economic Outlook Database, April 2013.

# CHECKPOINT 2.3

**Explain the circular flow model of the U.S. economy and of the global economy.**

## Practice Problems

1. Describe the flows in the circular flow model in which consumption expenditure, purchases of new national defense equipment, and payments for labor services appear. Through which market does each of these flows pass?

2. Of the flows that run between households, firms, and governments in the circular flow model, which ones are real flows and which are money flows?

## Solutions to Practice Problems

1. Consumption expenditure flows from households to firms through the goods market. Purchases of national defense flow from governments to firms through the goods market. Payments for labor services flow from firms to households through the factor market.

2. The real flows are the flows of services of factors of production that go from households to firms through factor markets and the goods and services that go from firms to households and from firms to governments through goods markets. The money flows are the flows of factor incomes, household and government expenditures on goods and services, taxes, and transfers.

CHAPTER SUMMARY

## Key Points

**1.** **Describe what, how, and for whom goods and services are produced in the United States.**

- Consumption goods and services represent 85 percent of total production; capital goods represent 15 percent.
- Goods and services are produced by using the four factors of production: land, labor, capital, and entrepreneurship.
- The incomes people earn (rent for land, wages for labor, interest for capital, and profit for entrepreneurship) determine who gets the goods and services produced.

**2.** **Describe what, how, and for whom goods and services are produced in the global economy.**

- Sixty-one percent of the world's production (by value) comes from the advanced industrial countries and the emerging market economies.
- Production in the advanced economies uses more capital (both machines and human), but some developing economies use the latest capital and technologies.
- The global distribution of income is more unequal than the U.S. distribution. Poverty has fallen in Asia, but it has increased in Africa.

**3.** **Explain the circular flow model of the U.S. economy and of the global economy.**

- The circular flow model of the U.S. economy shows the real flows of factors of production and goods and the corresponding money flows of incomes and expenditures.
- Governments in the circular flow receive taxes, make transfers, and buy goods and services.
- The circular flow model of the global economy shows the flows of U.S. exports and imports and the international financial flows that result from lending to and borrowing from other countries.

## Key Terms

Capital, 73
Capital goods, 70
Circular flow model, 84
Consumption goods and services, 70
Entrepreneurship, 74
Factor markets, 84

Factors of production, 72
Firms, 84
Goods markets, 84
Households, 84
Human capital, 73
Interest, 75

Labor, 73
Land, 72
Market, 84
Profit (or loss), 75
Rent, 75
Wages, 75

# CHAPTER CHECKPOINT

## Study Plan Problems and Applications

**1.** Explain which of the following items are *not* consumption goods and services:
   - A chocolate bar
   - A ski lift
   - A golf ball

**2.** Explain which of the following items are *not* capital goods:
   - An auto assembly line
   - A shopping mall
   - A golf ball

**3.** Explain which of the following items are *not* factors of production:
   - Vans used by a baker to deliver bread
   - 1,000 shares of Amazon.com stock
   - Undiscovered oil in the Arctic Ocean

**4.** Which factor of production earns the highest percentage of total U.S. income? Define that factor of production. What is the income earned by this factor of production called?

**5.** With more job training and more scholarships to poor American students, which special factor of production is likely to grow faster than in the past?

**6.** Define the factor of production called capital. Give three examples of capital, different from those in the chapter. Distinguish between the factor of production capital and financial capital.

**7.** A Job Creation through Entrepreneurship Act, debated in the House of Representatives in 2009, would award grants to small business owners, some of which would be aimed at women, Native Americans, and veterans. The Act would provide $189 million in 2010 and $531 million between 2010 and 2014. Explain how you would expect this Act to influence *what*, *how*, and *for whom* goods and services are produced in the United States.

**8.** In the circular flow model, explain the real flow and/or the money flow in which each item in List 1 belongs. Show your answers on a graph.

**9. For-profit colleges may face aid cuts**

The Obama Administration proposes a new rule: Federal aid to for-profit colleges will be cut if students in vocational programs graduate without a degree. Millions of low-income students are borrowing heavily to attend colleges and too many of them are dropping out, and failing to get a job.

Source: *USA Today*, June 2, 2011

How do you think the personal distribution of income would change if all graduates could obtain a well-paying job that uses their knowledge gained in college?

**10.** Read *Eye on the Dreamliner* on p. 79 and then answer the following questions:
   - How many firms are involved in the production of the Dreamliner and how many are identified in the figure on p. 79?
   - Is the Dreamliner a capital good or a consumption good? Explain why.
   - State the factors of production that make the Dreamliner and provide an example of each.
   - Explain how the production of the Dreamliner influences *what*, *how*, and *for whom*, goods and services are produced.
   - Use a graph to show where in the circular flow model of the global economy the flows of the components listed on p. 79 appear and where the sales of Dreamliners appear.

---

**LIST 1**

- You buy a coffee at Starbucks.
- The government buys some Dell computers.
- A student works at Kinko.
- Donald Trump rents a building to Marriot hotels.
- You pay your income tax.

## Instructor Assignable Problems and Applications

**1.** Boeing's Dreamliner has had a rocky start.
  - Why doesn't Boeing manufacture all the components of the Dreamliner at its own factory in the United States?
  - Describe some of the changes in *what*, *how*, and *for whom*, that would occur if Boeing manufactured all the components of the Dreamliner at its own factories in the United States.
  - State some of the tradeoffs that Boeing faces in making the Dreamliner.
  - Why might Boeing's decisions in making the Dreamliner be in the social interest?

**2.** The global economy has three cell-phone users for every fixed line user. Two in every three cell-phone users live in a developing nation and the growth rate is fastest in Africa. In 2000, 1 African in 50 had a cell phone; in 2009, it was 14 in 50. Describe the changes in *what, how,* and *for whom* telecommunication services are produced in the global economy.

**3.** Which of the entries in List 1 are consumption goods and services? Explain your choice.

**4.** Which of the entries in List 1 are capital goods? Explain your choice.

**5.** Which of the entries in List 1 are factors of production? Explain your choice.

**6.** In the African nation of Senegal, to enroll in school a child needs a birth certificate that costs $25. This price is several weeks' income for many families. Explain how this requirement is likely to affect the growth of human capital in Senegal.

**7. China's prosperity brings income gap**

The Asian Development Bank [ADB] reports that China has the largest gap between the rich and the poor in Asia. Ifzal Ali, the ADB's chief economist, claims it is not that the rich are getting richer and the poor are getting poorer, but that the rich are getting richer faster than the poor.

Source: *Financial Times*, August 9, 2007

Explain how the distribution of personal income in China can be getting more unequal even though the poorest 20 percent are getting richer.

**8.** Compare the scale of agricultural production in the advanced and developing economies. In which is the percentage higher? In which is the total amount produced greater?

**9.** On a graph of the circular flow model, indicate in which real or money flow each entry in List 2 belongs.

Use the following information to work Problems **10** and **11**.

**Poor India makes millionaires at fastest pace**

India, with the world's largest population of poor people, also paradoxically created millionaires at the fastest pace in the world. Millionaires increased by 22.7 percent to 123,000. In contrast, the number of Indians living on less than a dollar a day is 350 million and those living on less than $2 a day is 700 million. In other words, there are 7,000 very poor Indians for every millionaire.

Source: *The Times of India*, June 25, 2008

**10.** How is the personal distribution of income in India changing?

**11.** Why might incomes of $1 a day and $2 a day underestimate the value of the goods and services that these households actually consume?

---

**LIST 1**

- An interstate highway
- A jet airplane
- A school teacher
- A stealth bomber
- A garbage truck
- A pack of bubble gum
- President of the United States
- A strawberry field
- A movie
- An ATM

---

**LIST 2**

- General Motors pays its workers wages.
- IBM pays a dividend to its stockholders.
- You buy your groceries.
- Chrysler buys robots.
- Southwest rents some aircraft.
- Nike pays Roger Federer for promoting its sports shoes.

# Critical Thinking Discussion Questions

1. **Mark Zuckerberg's big idea: The "next 5 billion"**

   Facebook founder Mark Zuckerberg wants to make it so that anyone, anywhere, can get online. To achieve this goal, he has created internet.org, "a global partnership between technology leaders, nonprofits, local communities, and experts who are working together to bring the Internet to the two-thirds of the world's population that doesn't have it."

   Sources: CNN Money, August 21, 2013 and internet.org

   a.  How does this news clip illustrate what, how, and for whom goods and services are produced?
   b.  Is Internet service a capital good or a consumer good or service?
   c.  What are the factors of production that produce Internet service?

2. The table provides data from the CIA World Fact Book about seven economies. If the economy in which you live isn't in the table, add the data from the CIA World Fact Book Web site.

   | Economy | Income per person (U.S. dollars per year) | Agriculture | Industry | Services |
   |---|---|---|---|---|
   | | | | (percent) | |
   | China | 9,800 | 10 | 44 | 46 |
   | India | 4,000 | 17 | 17 | 66 |
   | Korea | 33,200 | 3 | 39 | 58 |
   | Indonesia | 5,200 | 14 | 47 | 39 |
   | Malaysia | 17,500 | 11 | 41 | 48 |
   | Saudi Arabia | 31,300 | 2 | 63 | 35 |
   | South Africa | 11,500 | 3 | 29 | 68 |
   | Where you live | | | | |

   a.  What do these data tell us about differences in *what* is produced in the listed economies?
   b.  Compare and contrast what is produced in your own economy with what is produced in other economies.
   c.  Explore the correlation between income per person and agriculture production.
   d.  Draw a scatter diagram of income per person and agriculture production and think about reasons for the pattern you see.

3. Using the data in the table in Question 2, what can you say about *who* gets the goods and services produced? Compare and contrast the value of goods and services that people in your own economy can afford with what people in other economies can afford.

4. Using the data in the table in Question 2, what can you infer about *how* the goods and services are produced?
   Compare and contrast how goods and services are produced in your own economy with how they are produced in other economies. In which economies would you expect production to be capital intensive—using a large amount of capital per worker?

5. **China forecast to overtake U.S. by 2016**

   China is on track for a fourth consecutive decade of rapid growth and will overtake the U.S. as the world's biggest economy in 2016.

   Source: *Financial Times*, March 22, 2013

   What do the trends in economic growth imply about changes in the sizes of the Chinese and American slices in the global production pie in Figure 2.2 (p. 78)?

Is wind power free?

# The Economic Problem

**3**

When you have completed your study of this chapter, you will be able to

**1** Explain and illustrate the concepts of scarcity, production efficiency, and tradeoff using the production possibilities frontier.

**2** Calculate opportunity cost.

**3** Explain what makes production possibilities expand.

**4** Explain how people gain from specialization and trade.

## 3.1 PRODUCTION POSSIBILITIES

Every working day in mines, factories, shops, and offices and on farms and construction sites across the United States, we produce a vast array of goods and services. In the United States in 2011, 250 billion hours of labor equipped with $50 trillion worth of capital produced $15 trillion worth of goods and services.

Although our production capability is enormous, it is limited by our available resources and by technology. At any given time, we have fixed quantities of the factors of production and a fixed state of technology. Because our wants exceed our resources, we must make choices. We must rank our wants and decide which to satisfy and which to leave unsatisfied. In using our scarce resources, we make rational choices. And to make a rational choice, we must determine the costs and benefits of the alternatives.

Your first task in this chapter is to learn about an economic model of scarcity, choice, and opportunity cost—a model called the production possibilities frontier.

### ■ Production Possibilities Frontier

**Production possibilities frontier**
The boundary between the combinations of goods and services that can be produced and the combinations that cannot be produced, given the available factors of production and the state of technology.

The **production possibilities frontier** is the boundary between the combinations of goods and services that can be produced and the combinations that cannot be produced, given the available factors of production—land, labor, capital, and entrepreneurship—and the state of technology.

Although we produce millions of different goods and services, we can visualize the limits to production most easily if we imagine a simpler world that produces just two goods. Imagine an economy that produces only DVDs and cell phones. All the land, labor, capital, and entrepreneurship available gets used to produce these two goods.

Land can be used for movie studios and DVD factories or cell-phone factories. Labor can be trained to work as movie actors, camera and sound crews, movie producers, and DVD makers or as cell-phone makers. Capital can be used for making movies, making and coating disks, and transferring images to disks, or for the equipment that makes cell phones. Entrepreneurs can put their creative talents to managing movie studios and running electronics businesses that make DVDs or to running cell-phone businesses. In every case, the more resources that are used to produce DVDs, the fewer are left to produce cell phones.

Suppose that if no factors of production are allocated to producing cell phones, the maximum number of DVDs that can be produced is 15 million a year. So one production possibility is no cell phones and 15 million DVDs. Another possibility is to allocate sufficient resources to produce 1 million cell phones a year. But these resources must be taken from DVD factories. Suppose that the economy can now produce only 14 million DVDs a year. As resources are moved from producing DVDs to producing cell phones, the economy produces more cell phones but fewer DVDs.

The table in Figure 3.1 illustrates these two combinations of cell phones and DVDs as possibilities A and B. Suppose that C, D, E, and F are other combinations of the quantities of these two goods that the economy can produce. Possibility F uses all the resources to produce 5 million cell phones a year and allocates no resources to producing DVDs. These six possibilities are alternative combinations of the quantities of the two goods that the economy can produce by *using all of its resources, given the technology.*

The graph in Figure 3.1 illustrates the production possibilities frontier, *PPF*, for cell phones and DVDs. Each point on the graph labeled *A* through *F* represents the possibility in the table identified by the same letter. For example, point *B* represents the production of 1 million cell phones and 14 million DVDs. These quantities also appear in the table as possibility *B*.

The *PPF* shows the limits to production *with the available resources and technology*. If either resources or technology change, the *PPF* shifts. More resources or better technology shift it outward and a loss of resources shifts it inward.

The *PPF* is a valuable tool for illustrating the effects of scarcity and its consequences. The *PPF* puts three features of production possibilities in sharp focus. They are the distinctions between

- Attainable and unattainable combinations
- Efficient and inefficient production
- Tradeoffs and free lunches

■ **FIGURE 3.1**

The Production Possibilities Frontier

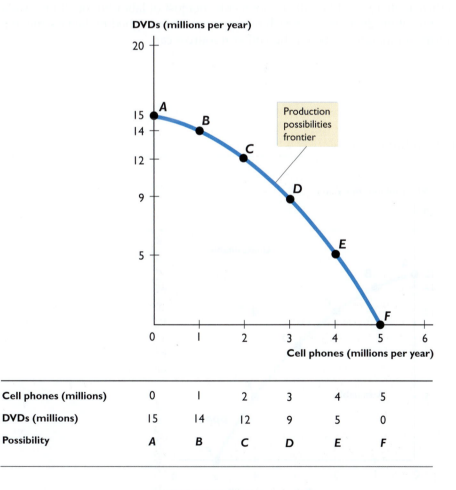

The table and the graph show the production possibilities frontier for cell phones and DVDs.

Point *A* tells us that if the economy produces no cell phones, the maximum quantity of DVDs it can produce is 15 million a year. Each point *A*, *B*, *C*, *D*, *E*, and *F* on the graph represents the possibility in the table identified by the same letter. The line passing through these points is the production possibilities frontier.

| Cell phones (millions) | 0 | 1 | 2 | 3 | 4 | 5 |
|---|---|---|---|---|---|---|
| DVDs (millions) | 15 | 14 | 12 | 9 | 5 | 0 |
| Possibility | *A* | *B* | *C* | *D* | *E* | *F* |

## Attainable and Unattainable Combinations

Because the *PPF* shows the *limits* to production, it separates attainable combinations from unattainable ones. The economy can produce combinations of cell phones and DVDs that are smaller than those on the *PPF*, and it can produce any of the combinations *on* the *PPF*. These combinations of cell phones and DVDs are attainable. But it is impossible to produce combinations that are larger than those on the *PPF*. These combinations are unattainable.

Figure 3.2 emphasizes the attainable and unattainable combinations. Only the points on the *PPF* and inside it (in the orange area) are attainable. The combinations of cell phones and DVDs beyond the *PPF* (in the white area), such as the combination at point *G*, are unattainable. These points illustrate combinations that cannot be produced with the current resources and technology. The *PPF* tells us that the economy can produce 4 million cell phones and 5 million DVDs at point *E or* 2 million cell phones and 12 million DVDs at point *C*. But the economy cannot produce 4 million cell phones and 12 million DVDs at point *G*.

## Efficient and Inefficient Production

**Production efficiency**
A situation in which the economy is getting all that it can from its resources and cannot produce more of one good or service without producing less of something else.

**Production efficiency** occurs when the economy is getting all that it can from its resources. When production is efficient it is not possible to produce more of one good or service without producing less of something else. For production to be efficient, there must be full employment—not just of labor but of all the available factors of production—and each resource must be assigned to the task that it performs comparatively better than other resources can.

■ **FIGURE 3.2**

Attainable and Unattainable Combinations

The production possibilities frontier, *PPF*, separates attainable combinations from unattainable ones. The economy can produce at any point *inside* the *PPF* (the orange area) or at any point *on* the frontier. Any point outside the production possibilities frontier, such as point *G*, is unattainable.

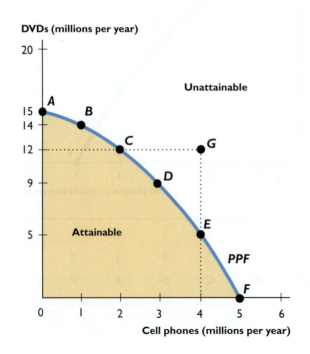

Cell phones (millions per year)

Figure 3.3 illustrates the distinction between efficient and inefficient production. With *inefficient* production, the economy might be producing 3 million cell phones and 5 million DVDs at point *H*. With an *efficient* use of the economy's resources, it is possible to produce at a point on the *PPF* such as point *D* or *E*. At point *D*, there are more DVDs and the same quantity of cell phones as at point *H*. And at point *E*, there are more cell phones and the same quantity of DVDs as at point *H*. At points *D* and *E*, production is efficient.

## Tradeoffs and Free Lunches

A **tradeoff** is an exchange—giving up one thing to get something else. You trade off income for a better grade when you decide to cut back on the hours you spend on your weekend job and allocate the time to extra study. The Ford Motor Company faces a tradeoff when it cuts the production of trucks and uses the resources saved to produce more hybrid SUVs. The federal government faces a tradeoff when it cuts NASA's space exploration program and allocates more resources to homeland security. As a society, we face a tradeoff when we decide to cut down a forest and destroy the habitat of the spotted owl.

The production possibilities frontier illustrates the idea of a tradeoff. The *PPF* in Figure 3.3 shows how. If the economy produces at point *E* and people want to produce more DVDs, they must forgo some cell phones. In the move from point *E* to point *D*, people trade off cell phones for DVDs.

Economists often express the central idea of economics—that choices involve tradeoff—with the saying "There is no such thing as a free lunch." A *free lunch* is a gift—getting something without giving up something else. What does the

**Tradeoff**
An exchange—giving up one thing to get something else.

## FIGURE 3.3

### Efficient and Inefficient Production, Tradeoffs, and Free Lunches

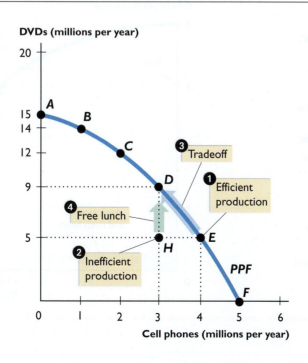

❶ When production occurs at a point on the *PPF*, such as point *E*, resources are used efficiently.

❷ When production occurs at a point inside the *PPF*, such as point *H*, resources are used inefficiently.

❸ When production is efficient— on the *PPF*—the economy faces a tradeoff. To move from point *E* to point *D* requires that some cell phones be given up for more DVDs.

❹ When production is inefficient— inside the *PPF*—there is a free lunch. To move from point *H* to point *D* does not involve a tradeoff.

famous saying mean? Suppose some resources are not being used or are not being used efficiently. Isn't it then possible to avoid a tradeoff and get a free lunch?

The answer is yes. You can see why in Figure 3.3. If production is taking place *inside* the *PPF* at point *H*, then it is possible to move to point *D* and increase the production of DVDs by using currently unused resources or by using resources in their most productive way. Nothing is forgone to increase production—there is a free lunch.

When production is efficient—at a point on the *PPF*—choosing to produce more of one good involves a tradeoff. But if production is inefficient—at a point inside the *PPF*—there is a free lunch. More of some goods and services can be produced without producing less of any others.

So "there is no such thing as a free lunch" means that when resources are used efficiently, every choice involves a tradeoff. Because economists view people as making rational choices, they expect that resources will be used efficiently. That is why they emphasize the tradeoff idea and deny the existence of free lunches. We might *sometimes* get a free lunch, but we *almost always* face a tradeoff.

# EYE on YOUR LIFE
## Your Production Possibilities Frontier

Two "goods" that concern you a great deal are your grade point average (GPA) and the amount of time you have available for leisure or earning an income. You face a tradeoff. To get a higher GPA you must give up leisure or income. Your forgone leisure or forgone income is the opportunity cost of a higher GPA. Similarly, to get more leisure or more income, you must accept a lower grade. A lower grade is the opportunity cost of increased leisure or increased income.

The figure illustrates a student's *PPF*. Any point on or beneath the *PPF* is attainable and any point above the *PPF* is unattainable. A student who wastes time or doesn't study efficiently ends up with a lower GPA than the highest attainable from the time spent studying. But a student who works efficiently achieves a point *on* the *PPF* and achieves production efficiency.

The student in the figure allocates the scarce 168 hours a week between studying (class and study hours) and other activities (work, leisure, and sleep hours). The student attends class

and studies for 48 hours each week and works or has fun (and sleeps) for the other 120 hours. With this allocation of time, and studying efficiently, the student's GPA is 3.

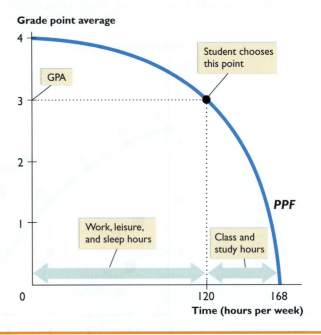

## CHECKPOINT 3.1

**Explain and illustrate the concepts of scarcity, production efficiency, and tradeoff using the production possibilities frontier.**

## Practice Problems

1. Table 1 sets out the production possibilities of a small Pacific island economy. Draw the economy's *PPF*.

Figure 1 shows an economy's *PPF* and identifies some production points. Use this figure to work Problems **2** to **4**.

2. Which points are attainable? Explain why.
3. Which points are efficient and which points are inefficient? Explain why.
4. Which points illustrate a tradeoff? Explain why.

## In the News

**Loss of honeybees is less but still a threat**
Honeybees are crucial for the pollination of almonds in California's Central Valley. During 2008, 30 percent of U.S. honeybees died.
Source: *USA Today*, May 20, 2009

Explain how this loss of honeybees affected the Central Valley's *PPF*.

## Solutions to Practice Problems

1. The *PPF* is the boundary between attainable and unattainable combinations of goods. Figure 2 shows the economy's *PPF*. The graph plots each row of the table as a point with the corresponding letter.
2. Attainable points: Any point on the *PPF* is attainable and any point below (inside) the *PPF* is attainable. Points outside the *PPF* (*F* and *G*) are unattainable. In Figure 1, the attainable points are *A*, *B*, *C*, *D*, and *E*.
3. Efficient points: Production is efficient when it is not possible to produce more of one good without producing less of another good. To be efficient, a point must be attainable, so points *F* and *G* can't be efficient. Points inside the *PPF* can't be efficient because more goods can be produced, so *D* and *E* are not efficient. The only efficient points are those *on* the *PPF*—*A*, *B*, and *C*.

   Inefficient points: Inefficiency occurs when resources are misallocated or unemployed. Such points are *inside* the *PPF*. These points are *D* and *E*.
4. Tradeoff: Begin by recalling that a tradeoff is an exchange—giving up something to get something else. A tradeoff occurs when moving along the *PPF* from one point to another point. So moving from any point *on* the *PPF*, point *A*, *B*, or *C*, to another point *on* the *PPF* illustrates a tradeoff.

## Solution to In the News

Honeybees are a resource used in the production of almonds. At the start of 2008, Central Valley farmers were at a point on their *PPF*. A 30 percent drop in honeybees reduced the quantity of almonds produced by about 30 percent. With no change in the quantity of other resources and technology, the quantity of other crops produced remained the same and the Central Valley *PPF* shifted inward.

**TABLE 1**

| Possibility | Fish (pounds) | | Berries (pounds) |
| --- | --- | --- | --- |
| A | 0 | and | 20 |
| B | 1 | and | 18 |
| C | 2 | and | 15 |
| D | 3 | and | 11 |
| E | 4 | and | 6 |
| F | 5 | and | 0 |

**FIGURE 1**
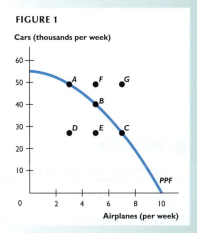

**FIGURE 2**
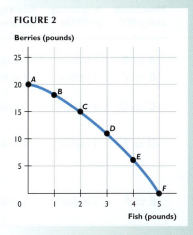

## 3.2   OPPORTUNITY COST

You've seen that moving from one point to another on the *PPF* involves a trade-off. But what are the terms of the tradeoff? *How much* of one item must be forgone to obtain an additional unit of another item—a large amount or a small amount? The answer is given by opportunity cost—the best thing you must give up to get something (see p. 46). We can use the *PPF* to calculate opportunity cost.

### ■ The Opportunity Cost of a Cell Phone

The opportunity cost of a cell phone is the number of DVDs forgone to get an additional cell phone. It is calculated as the number of DVDs forgone divided by the number of cell phones gained.

Figure 3.4 illustrates the calculation. At point *A*, the quantities produced are zero cell phones and 15 million DVDs; and at point *B*, the quantities produced are 1 million cell phones and 14 million DVDs. To gain 1 million cell phones by moving from point *A* to point *B*, 1 million DVDs are forgone, so the opportunity cost of 1 cell phone is 1 DVD.

At point *C*, the quantities produced are 2 million cell phones and 12 million DVDs. To gain 1 million cell phones by moving from point *B* to point *C*, 2 million DVDs are forgone. Now the opportunity cost of 1 cell phone is 2 DVDs.

If you repeat these calculations, moving from *C* to *D*, *D* to *E*, and *E* to *F*, you will obtain the opportunity costs shown in the table and the graph.

■ **FIGURE 3.4**

Calculating the Opportunity Cost of a Cell Phone

| Movement along *PPF* | Decrease in quantity of DVDs | Increase in quantity of cell phones | Decrease in DVDs divided by increase in cell phones |
|---|---|---|---|
| *A* to *B* | 1 million | 1 million | 1 DVD per phone |
| *B* to *C* | 2 million | 1 million | 2 DVDs per phone |
| *C* to *D* | 3 million | 1 million | 3 DVDs per phone |
| *D* to *E* | 4 million | 1 million | 4 DVDs per phone |
| *E* to *F* | 5 million | 1 million | 5 DVDs per phone |

Along the *PPF* from *A* to *F*, the opportunity cost of a cell phone increases as the quantity of cell phones produced increases.

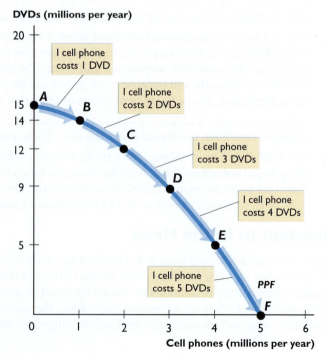

## ■ Opportunity Cost and the Slope of the *PPF*

Look at the numbers that we've just calculated for the opportunity cost of a cell phone and notice that they follow a striking pattern. The opportunity cost of a cell phone increases as the quantity of cell phones produced increases.

The magnitude of the *slope* of the *PPF* measures the opportunity cost. Because the *PPF* in Figure 3.4 is bowed outward, its slope changes and gets steeper as the quantity of cell phones produced increases.

When a small quantity of cell phones is produced—between points *A* and *B*—the *PPF* has a gentle slope and the opportunity cost of a cell phone is low. A given increase in the quantity of cell phones costs a small decrease in the quantity of DVDs. When a large quantity of cell phones is produced—between points *E* and *F*—the *PPF* is steep and the opportunity cost of a cell phone is high. A given increase in the quantity of cell phones costs a large decrease in the quantity of DVDs. Figure 3.5 shows the increasing opportunity cost of a cell phone.

## ■ Opportunity Cost Is a Ratio

The opportunity cost of a cell phone is the *ratio* of DVDs forgone to cell phones gained. Similarly, the opportunity cost of a DVD is the *ratio* of cell phones forgone to DVDs gained. So the opportunity cost of a DVD is equal to the inverse of the opportunity cost of a cell phone. For example, moving along the *PPF* in Figure 3.4 from *C* to *D* the opportunity cost of a cell phone is 3 DVDs. Moving along the *PPF* in the opposite direction, from *D* to *C*, the opportunity cost of a DVD is 1/3 of a cell phone.

■ **FIGURE 3.5**

The Opportunity Cost of a Cell Phone

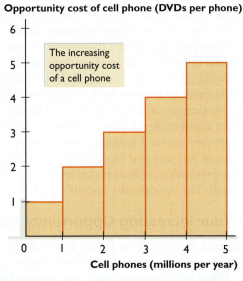

Because the *PPF* in Figure 3.4 is bowed outward, the opportunity cost of a cell phone increases as the quantity of cell phones produced increases.

| Cell phones (millions) | 0 to 1 | 1 to 2 | 2 to 3 | 3 to 4 | 4 to 5 |
|---|---|---|---|---|---|
| Opportunity cost (DVDs per phone) | 1 | 2 | 3 | 4 | 5 |

# EYE on the ENVIRONMENT

## Is Wind Power Free?

Wind power is not free. To use it, we must give up huge amounts of other goods and services to build wind turbines and transmission lines.

Wind turbines can produce electricity only when there is wind, which turns out, at best, to be 40 percent of the time and, on average, about 25 percent of the time. Also some of the best wind farm locations are a long way from major population centers, so transmission lines would be long and power transmission losses large.

If we produced 55 percent of our electricity using South Dakota wind power, we would be operating inside the *PPF* at a point such as *Z*.

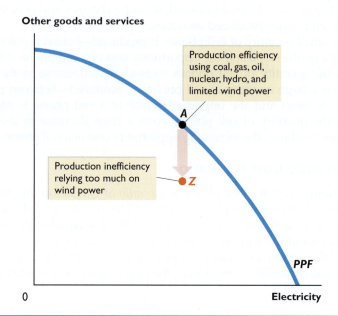

## ■ Increasing Opportunity Costs Are Everywhere

Just about every production activity that you can think of has increasing opportunity cost. We allocate the most skillful farmers and the most fertile land to producing food, and we allocate the best doctors and the least fertile land to producing health-care services. Some resources are equally productive in both activities. If we shift these equally productive resources away from farming to hospitals, we get an increase in health care at a low opportunity cost. But if we keep increasing health-care services, we must eventually build hospitals on the most fertile land and get the best farmers to become hospital porters. The production of food drops drastically and the increase in the production of health-care services is small. The opportunity cost of a unit of health-care services rises. Similarly, if we shift resources away from health care toward farming, we must eventually use more skilled doctors and nurses as farmers and more hospitals as hydroponic tomato factories. The decrease in the production of health-care services is large, but the increase in food production is small. The opportunity cost of a unit of food rises.

## ■ Your Increasing Opportunity Cost

Flip back to the *PPF* in *Eye on Your Life* on page 100 and think about its implications for your opportunity cost of a higher grade.

What is the opportunity cost of spending time with your friends in terms of the grade you might receive on your exam? What is the opportunity cost of a higher grade in terms of the activities you give up to study? Do you face increasing opportunity costs in these activities?

# CHECKPOINT 3.2

Calculate opportunity cost.

## Practice Problems

Table 1 shows Robinson Crusoe's production possibilities.

1. What is his opportunity cost of a pound of berries when Crusoe increases the quantity of berries from 21 pounds to 26 pounds and production is efficient? Does this opportunity cost increase as he produces more berries?

2. If Crusoe is producing 10 pounds of fish and 21 pounds of berries, what is his opportunity cost of an extra pound of berries? And what is his opportunity cost of an extra pound of fish? Explain your answers.

## In the News

### Obama drives up miles-per-gallon requirements

Emissions from all new vehicles must be cut from 354 grams to 250 grams. To meet this new standard, the price of a new vehicle will rise by $1,300.

Source: *USA Today*, May 20, 2009

Calculate the opportunity cost of reducing the emission level by 1 gram.

**TABLE 1**

| Possibility | Fish (pounds) | | Berries (pounds) |
|---|---|---|---|
| A | 0 | and | 36 |
| B | 4.0 | and | 35 |
| C | 7.5 | and | 33 |
| D | 10.5 | and | 30 |
| E | 13.0 | and | 26 |
| F | 15.0 | and | 21 |
| G | 16.5 | and | 15 |
| H | 17.5 | and | 8 |
| I | 18.0 | and | 0 |

## Solutions to Practice Problems

1. If Crusoe's production is efficient, he is producing at a point *on* his *PPF*. His opportunity cost of an extra pound of berries is the quantity of fish he must give up to get the berries. It is calculated as the decrease in the quantity of fish divided by the increase in the quantity of berries as he moves along his *PPF*.

   To increase the quantity of berries from 21 pounds to 26 pounds (from row *F* to row *E* of Table 1), production of fish decreases from 15 pounds to 13 pounds. To gain 5 pounds of berries, Crusoe must forgo 2 pounds of fish. The opportunity cost of 1 pound of berries is the 2 pounds of fish forgone divided by 5 pounds of berries gained—2/5 of a pound of fish.

   Crusoe's opportunity cost of berries increases as he produces more berries. To see why, move Crusoe from row *E* to row *D* in Table 1. His production of berries increases by 4 pounds and his production of fish falls by 2.5 pounds. His opportunity cost of 1 pound of berries increases to 5/8 of a pound of fish.

2. Figure 1 graphs the data in Table 1 and shows Crusoe's *PPF*. If Crusoe is producing 10 pounds of fish and 21 pounds of berries, he is producing at point *Z*. Point *Z* is a point *inside* Crusoe's *PPF*. When Crusoe produces 21 pounds of berries, he has enough time available to produce 15 pounds of fish at point *F* on his *PPF*. To produce more fish, Crusoe can move from *Z* toward *F* on his *PPF* and forgo no berries. His opportunity cost of a pound of fish is zero. Similarly, his opportunity cost of a pound of berries is zero.

**FIGURE 1**

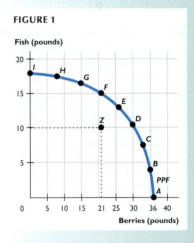

## Solution to In the News

By spending $1,300 extra on a new car, you forgo $1,300 of other goods. With a new car, your emissions fall from 354 grams to 250 grams, a reduction of 104 grams. The opportunity cost of a 1-gram reduction in emissions is $1,300 of other goods divided by 104 grams, or $12.50 of other goods.

## 3.3 ECONOMIC GROWTH

**Economic growth**
The sustained expansion of production possibilities.

**Economic growth** is the sustained expansion of production possibilities. Our economy grows when we develop better technologies for producing goods and services; improve the quality of labor by education, on-the-job training, and work experience; and acquire more machines to help us produce.

To study economic growth, we must change the two goods and look at the production possibilities for a consumption good and a capital good. A cell phone is a consumption good and a cell-phone factory is a capital good. By using today's resources to produce cell-phone factories, the economy can expand its future production possibilities. The greater the production of new capital—the number of new cell-phone factories—the faster is the expansion of production possibilities.

Figure 3.6 shows how the *PPF* can expand. If no new factories are produced (at point *L*), production possibilities do not expand and the *PPF* stays at its original position. By producing fewer cell phones and using resources to produce 2 new cell-phone factories (at point *K*), production possibilities expand and the *PPF* rotates outward to the new *PPF*.

But economic growth is *not* free. To make it happen, consumption must decrease. The move from *L* to *K* in Figure 3.6 means forgoing 2 million cell phones now. The opportunity cost of producing more cell-phone factories is producing fewer cell phones today.

Also, economic growth is no magic formula for abolishing scarcity. Economic growth shifts the *PPF* outward, but on the new *PPF* we continue to face opportunity costs. To keep producing capital, current consumption must be less than its maximum possible level.

■ **FIGURE 3.6**

Expanding Production Possibilities

❶ If firms allocate no resources to producing cell-phone factories and produce 5 million cell phones a year at point *L*, the *PPF* doesn't change.

❷ If firms decrease cell-phone production to 3 million a year and produce 2 cell-phone factories, at point *K*, production possibilities will expand. After a year, the *PPF* shifts outward to the new *PPF* and production can move to point *K'*.

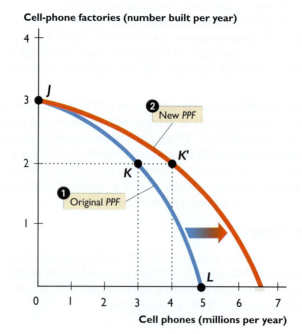

# EYE on the U.S. ECONOMY
## Expanding Our Production Possibilities

Horizontal drilling and hydraulic fracturing—fracking—combined with recent advances in remote sensing technology have made it possible to extract a large quantity of gas trapped in shale at low cost. The United States has an estimated 750 trillion cubic feet of this gas, enough for more than 90 years at today's extraction rate. The map below shows the locations of these gas deposits.

Figure 1 shows two recent years of shale gas production, which in January 2012 was double its rate just two years earlier.

Was this increase in gas production achieved by sliding along the *PPF* and producing less of other goods and servces? No! It was the result of advances in technology and opening up additional gas wells.

Figure 2 illustrates how these changes shifted the *PPF* from $PPF_{10}$ in 2010 to $PPF_{12}$ in 2012. Point *J* is the same on both curves because if we produced at that point (only other goods and services and no gas), we would not get the benefits of the technological advances in gas production. In 2010 we produced at point *K*, and in 2012 at point *K'*. Along $PPF_{12}$ the opportunity cost of gas is lower than along $PPF_{10}$.

**Shale gas production (trillions of cubic feet per year)**

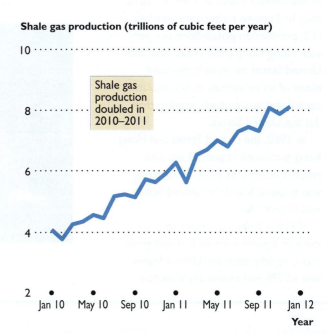

Shale gas production doubled in 2010–2011

**Figure 1 Shale Gas Production**

**Other goods and services (units)**

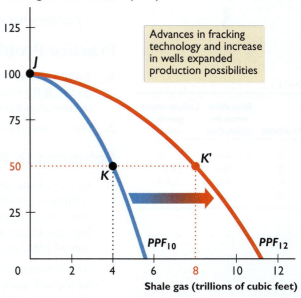

Advances in fracking technology and increase in wells expanded production possibilities

**Figure 2 Shale Gas Versus Other Goods and Services**

**Natural Gas Shale Basins in the United States**

Source of data: Energy Information Administration.

# EYE on the GLOBAL ECONOMY
## Hong Kong's Rapid Economic Growth

Hong Kong's production possibilities per person were 25 percent of those of the United States in 1960. By 2012, they had grown to become equal to U.S. production possibilities per person. Hong Kong grew faster than the United States because it allocated more of its resources to accumulating capital and less to consumption than did the United States.

In 1960, the United States and Hong Kong produced at point A on their respective PPFs. In 2012, Hong Kong was at point B and the United States was at point C.

If Hong Kong continues to produce at a point such as B, it will grow more rapidly than the United States and its PPF will eventually shift out

beyond the PPF of the United States. But if Hong Kong produces at a point such as D, the pace of expansion of its PPF will slow.

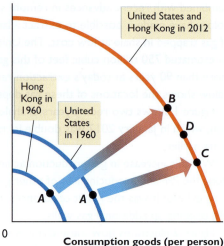

---

**Explain what makes production possibilities expand.**

## Practice Problems

1. Table 1 shows an economy that produces education services and consumption goods. If the economy currently produces 500 graduates a year and 2,000 units of consumption goods, what is the opportunity cost of one additional graduate?

2. How does an economy grow? Explain why economic growth is not free.

**TABLE 1**

| Possibility | Education services (graduates) | Consumption goods (units) |
|---|---|---|
| A | 1,000 | 0 |
| B | 750 | 1,000 |
| C | 500 | 2,000 |
| D | 0 | 3,000 |

## Solutions to Practice Problems

1. By increasing the number of graduates from 500 to 750, the quantity of consumption goods produced decreases from 2,000 to 1,000 units. The opportunity cost of a graduate is the decrease in consumption goods divided by the increase in the number of graduates. That is, the opportunity cost of a graduate is 1,000 units divided by 250, or 4 units of consumption goods.

2. An economy grows if it expands its production possibilities—if it develops better technologies; improves the quality of labor by education, on-the-job training, and work experience; and acquires more machines to use in production. Economic growth occurs when resources are used today to produce better technologies, better quality labor, or more machines. Those resources cannot be used to produce goods and services today, so the cost of economic growth is the goods and services forgone today. Economic growth is not free.

## 3.4    SPECIALIZATION AND TRADE

The next time you visit your favorite fast-food restaurant, watch what the workers are doing. You might see one person re-stocking the bread, salad materials, meat, sauces, boxes, and wrappers; another working the grill and another the fry maker; another assembling meals; and yet another taking orders and payments. Imagine how long you would wait for your burger if each worker performed all the tasks needed to fill each customer's not-so-fast-food order.

Specialization makes people more productive in two ways: It brings absolute advantage and comparative advantage.

### ■ Absolute Advantage and Comparative Advantage

A person has an **absolute advantage** if that person is more productive than another. Being more productive means using fewer inputs or taking less time to produce a good or perform a production task. Being more productive also means being able to produce more with given inputs in a given amount of time.

The specialized workers at McDonald's have an *absolute advantage* over the same number of workers each performing all the tasks needed to make a burger.

A person has a **comparative advantage** in an activity if that person can perform the activity at a lower opportunity cost than anyone else. Recall that the opportunity cost of something is what you must give up to get it.

Notice the contrast between *absolute advantage* and *comparative advantage*. Absolute advantage is about *productivity*—how long does it take to produce a unit of a good. Comparative advantage is about *opportunity cost*—how much of some other good must be forgone to produce a unit of a good.

*Specialization boosts productivity in a fast-food kitchen*

**Absolute advantage**
When one person (or nation) is more productive than another—needs fewer inputs or takes less time to produce a good or perform a production task.

**Comparative advantage**
The ability of a person to perform an activity or produce a good or service at a lower opportunity cost than anyone else.

# EYE on the U.S. ECONOMY
## No One Knows How to Make a Pencil

Not many products in today's world are as simple as a pencil. Yet the story of how the pencil in your hand got there illustrates the astonishing power of specialization and trade.

When you hold a pencil, you're holding cedar grown in Oregon, graphite mined in Sri Lanka, clay from Mississippi, wax from Mexico, rapeseed oil grown in the Dutch East Indies, pumice from Italy, copper from Arizona, and zinc from Alaska.

These materials were harvested and mined by thousands of workers equipped with hundreds of specialized tools, all of which were manufactured by thousands of other workers using hundreds more specialized tools. These tools were in turn made of steel, itself made from iron ore, and from other minerals and materials.

Rail, road, and ocean transportation systems moved all these things to custom-built factories that made graphite "leads," erasers, brass to hold the erasers, paint, and glue.

Finally, all these components were bought by a pencil factory, which, with its millions of dollars' worth of custom machinery, put them all together.

Millions of people contributed to making that pencil, many of whom don't even know what a pencil is and *not one of whom knows how to make a pencil*. No one directed all these people. Each worker and business went about its self-interested specialized task trading with each other in markets.

Adapted from *I Pencil*, by Leonard Read, Foundation for Economic Education, 1958.

## ■ Comparative Advantage: An Example

We're going to explore the idea of comparative advantage and make it concrete by looking at production in two smoothie bars: one operated by Liz and the other operated by Joe. You will see how we identify comparative advantage and how it creates an opportunity for Liz and Joe to gain from specialization and trade.

### Liz's Smoothie Bar

**TABLE 3.1    LIZ'S PRODUCTION POSSIBILITIES**

| Item | Minutes to produce 1 | Quantity per hour |
|------|----------------------|-------------------|
| Smoothies | 2 | 30 |
| Salads | 2 | 30 |

Liz produces smoothies and salads in a high-tech bar. She can turn out *either* a smoothie *or* a salad every 2 minutes. If she spends all her time making smoothies, she produces 30 an hour. If she spends all her time making salads, she also produces 30 an hour. If she splits her time equally between the two, she can produce 15 smoothies *and* 15 salads an hour. For each additional smoothie Liz produces, she must decrease her production of salads by one, and for each additional salad Liz produces, she must decrease her production of smoothies by one. So

> **Liz's opportunity cost of producing 1 smoothie is 1 salad,**

and

> **Liz's opportunity cost of producing 1 salad is 1 smoothie.**

Liz's customers buy smoothies and salads in equal quantities, so Liz splits her time equally between the items and produces 15 smoothies and 15 salads an hour.

### Joe's Smoothie Bar

**TABLE 3.2    JOE'S PRODUCTION POSSIBILITIES**

| Item | Minutes to produce 1 | Quantity per hour |
|------|----------------------|-------------------|
| Smoothies | 10 | 6 |
| Salads | 2 | 30 |

Joe also produces both smoothies and salads. Joe's bar is smaller than Liz's, and he has only one blender—a slow, old machine. Even if Joe uses all his resources to produce smoothies, he can produce only 6 an hour. But Joe is pretty good in the salad department, so if he uses all his resources to make salads, he can produce 30 an hour. Joe's ability to make smoothies and salads is the same regardless of how he splits an hour between the two tasks. He can make a salad in 2 minutes or a smoothie in 10 minutes. For each additional smoothie Joe produces, he must decrease his production of salads by 5. And for each additional salad Joe produces, he must decrease his production of smoothies by 1/5 of a smoothie. So

> **Joe's opportunity cost of producing 1 smoothie is 5 salads,**

and

> **Joe's opportunity cost of producing 1 salad is 1/5 of a smoothie.**

Joe's customers, like Liz's, buy smoothies and salads in equal quantities. Joe spends 50 minutes of each hour making smoothies and 10 minutes of each hour making salads. With this division of his time, Joe produces 5 smoothies and 5 salads an hour.

### Liz's and Joe's *PPFs*

The *PPFs* in Figure 3.7 illustrate the situation we've just described. In part (a), Liz faces a *PPF* that enables her to produce 15 smoothies and 15 salads. In part (b), Joe faces a *PPF* that enables him to produce 5 smoothies and 5 salads. On Liz's *PPF*, one smoothie costs one salad. On Joe's *PPF*, one smoothie costs 5 salads.

The *PPFs* in Figure 3.7 contrast with the outward-bowed *PPFs* that you've seen earlier in this chapter, which capture the general rule that the opportunity cost of a good increases as we increase its rate of production. It is easier to identify comparative advantage and see the gains from trade when individuals have

### ■ FIGURE 3.7

## Production Possibilities Frontiers

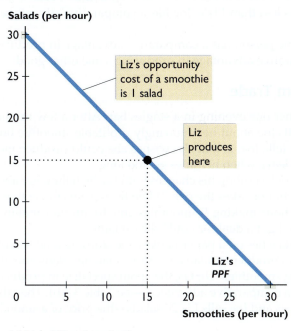

**(a) Liz's PPF and production**

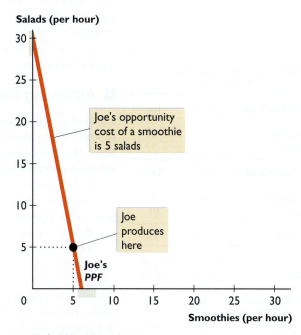

**(b) Joe's PPF and production**

Liz can produce 30 smoothies per hour or 30 salads per hour or any other combination along her *PPF* in part (a). Liz chooses to produce 15 smoothies and 15 salads per hour.

Joe can produce 6 smoothies per hour or 30 salads per hour or any other combination along his *PPF* in part (b). Joe chooses to produce 5 smoothies and 5 salads per hour.

constant opportunity cost. And as you will soon see, the social *PPF* is outward-bowed even when individuals have constant opportunity cost and linear *PPFs*.

## Liz's Greater Productivity

You can see from the production numbers that Liz is three times as productive as Joe—her 15 smoothies and 15 salads an hour are three times Joe's 5 smoothies and 5 salads. Liz is more productive than Joe in producing both smoothies and salads, but Liz has a comparative advantage in only one of the activities.

## Liz's Comparative Advantage

In which of the two activities does Liz have a *comparative* advantage? Recall that comparative advantage is a situation in which one person's opportunity cost of producing a good is lower than another person's opportunity cost of producing that same good.

You've seen that Liz's opportunity cost of a smoothie is 1 salad, whereas Joe's opportunity cost of a smoothie is 5 salads. To produce 1 smoothie, Liz must forgo 1 salad while Joe must forgo 5 salads. So, because Liz forgoes fewer salads to make a smoothie, she has a comparative advantage in producing smoothies.

What about Joe? Doesn't he have a comparative advantage at anything? He does as you're about to see.

### Joe's Comparative Advantage

Look at the opportunity costs of producing salads. For Liz, that opportunity cost is 1 smoothie. But for Joe, a salad costs only 1/5 of a smoothie. Because Joe's opportunity cost of a salad is less than Liz's, Joe has a comparative advantage in producing salads.

It is always true that if one person has a comparative advantage in producing a good, others have a comparative advantage in producing some other good.

## ■ Achieving Gains from Trade

Liz and Joe run into each other one evening in a singles bar. After a few minutes of getting acquainted, Liz tells Joe about her amazingly profitable smoothie business. Her only problem, she tells Joe, is that she wishes she could produce more because potential customers leave when her lines get too long.

Joe isn't sure whether to risk spoiling his chances with Liz by telling her about his own struggling business, but he takes the risk. When he explains to Liz that he spends 50 minutes of every hour making 5 smoothies and 10 minutes making 5 salads, Liz's eyes pop. "Have I got a deal for you!" she exclaims.

Here's the deal that Liz sketches on a paper napkin. Joe stops making smoothies and allocates all his time to producing salads. Liz stops making salads and allocates all her time to producing smoothies. That is, they both specialize in producing the good in which they have a comparative advantage—see Table 3.3(b). They then trade: Liz sells Joe 10 smoothies and Joe sells Liz 20 salads—the price of a smoothie is 2 salads—see Table 3.3(c).

After the trade, Joe has 10 salads (the 30 he produces minus the 20 he sells to Liz) and the 10 smoothies that he buys from Liz. So Joe doubles the quantities of smoothies and salads he can sell. Liz has 20 smoothies (the 30 she produces minus the 10 she sells to Joe) and the 20 salads she buys from Joe. See Table 3.3(d). From specialization and trade, each gains 5 smoothies and 5 salads—see Table 3.3(e).

**TABLE 3.3   LIZ AND JOE GAIN FROM TRADE**

| (a) Before Trade | Liz | Joe |
|---|---|---|
| Smoothies | 15 | 5 |
| Salads | 15 | 5 |

| (b) Specialization | Liz | Joe |
|---|---|---|
| Smoothies | 30 | 0 |
| Salads | 0 | 30 |

| (c) Trade | Liz | Joe |
|---|---|---|
| Smoothies | sell 10 | buy 10 |
| Salads | buy 20 | sell 20 |

| (d) After Trade | Liz | Joe |
|---|---|---|
| Smoothies | 20 | 10 |
| Salads | 20 | 10 |

| (e) Gains from Trade | Liz | Joe |
|---|---|---|
| Smoothies | +5 | +5 |
| Salads | +5 | +5 |

# EYE on YOUR LIFE
## Your Comparative Advantage

What you have learned in this chapter has huge implications for the way you organize your life. It also has implications for the position that you take on the controversial issue of offshore outsourcing.

Just as an economy expands its production possibilities by accumulating capital, so also will you expand your production possibilities by accumulating human capital. That is what you're doing right now in school.

By discovering your comparative advantage, you will be able to focus on producing the items that make you as well off as possible. Think hard about what you enjoy doing, and that you do comparatively better than others. That, most likely, is where your comparative advantage lies.

In today's world, it is a good idea to try to remain flexible so that you can switch jobs if you discover that your comparative advantage has changed.

Looking beyond your own self-interest, are you going to be a voice that supports or opposes offshore outsourcing?

You've learned in this chapter that regardless of whether outsourcing remains inside the United States, as it does with Liz and Joe at their smoothie bars, or is global like the outsourcing of jobs by U. S. producers to India, both parties gain from trade.

Americans pay less for goods and services and Indians earn higher incomes. But some Americans lose, at least in the short run.

Liz draws a figure (Figure 3.8) to illustrate her idea. The blue *PPF* is Liz's and the red *PPF* is Joe's. They are each producing at the points marked *A*. Liz's proposal is that they each produce at the points marked *B*. They then trade smoothies and salads.

Liz suggests that they trade at a price of 2 salads per smoothie (1/2 a smoothie per salad). This price turns out to give each of them equal gains.

Liz gets salads for 1/2 a smoothie each, which is less than the 1 smoothie that it costs her to produce them. Joe gets smoothies for 2 salads each, which is less than the 5 salads it costs him to produce them. Each moves to the points marked *C* where Liz has 20 smoothies and 20 salads, 5 of each more than she has producing only for herself. And Joe has 10 smoothies and 10 salads, also 5 more of each than he has producing only for himself. Because of the gains from trade, total production increases by 10 smoothies and 10 salads.

Notice that the points *C* are *outside* Liz's and Joe's *PPFs*. This is the magic of the gains from trade. Everyone gains and everyone can enjoy quantities of goods and services that exceed their own ability to produce them.

Notice finally, that for the Liz-Joe society, despite the fact that they each have constant opportunity costs, the society's opportunity cost is increasing. The first 30 smoothies can be produced (by Liz) for 1 salad per smoothie, but the 31st smoothie produced (by Joe) costs 5 salads.

**FIGURE 3.8**

The Gains from Specialization and Trade

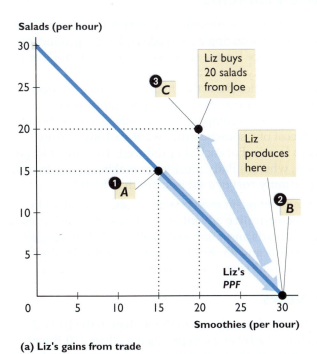

**(a) Liz's gains from trade**

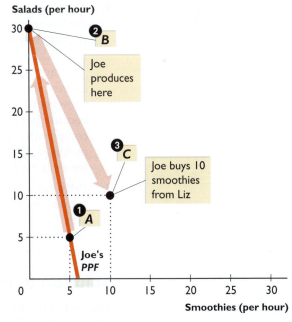

**(b) Joe's gains from trade**

❶ Liz and Joe each produce at point *A* on their respective *PPFs*. Liz has a comparative advantage in producing smoothies, and Joe has a comparative advantage in producing salads.

❷ Joe specializes in salads and Liz specializes in smoothies, so they each produce at point *B* on their respective *PPFs*.

❸ They exchange smoothies for salads at a price of 2 salads per smoothie. Each goes to point *C*—a point *outside* their individual *PPFs*. They each gain 5 salads and 5 smoothies—the quantities at point *C* minus the quantities at point *A*.

# CHECKPOINT 3.4

**Explain how people gain from specialization and trade.**

## Practice Problems

**TABLE 1   TONY'S PRODUCTION POSSIBILITIES**

| Snowboards (per week) | | Skis (per week) |
|---|---|---|
| 25 | and | 0 |
| 20 | and | 10 |
| 15 | and | 20 |
| 10 | and | 30 |
| 5 | and | 40 |
| 0 | and | 50 |

**TABLE 2   PATTY'S PRODUCTION POSSIBILITIES**

| Snowboards (per week) | | Skis (per week) |
|---|---|---|
| 20 | and | 0 |
| 10 | and | 5 |
| 0 | and | 10 |

Tony and Patty produce skis and snowboards. Tables 1 and 2 show their production possibilities. Each week, Tony produces 5 snowboards and 40 skis and Patty produces 10 snowboards and 5 skis.

1. Who has a comparative advantage in producing snowboards? Who has a comparative advantage in producing skis?

2. If Tony and Patty specialize and trade, what are the gains from trade?

## In the News

**With big boost from sugar cane, Brazil is satisfying its fuel needs**
Brazil is almost self-sufficient in ethanol. Brazilian ethanol is made from sugar and costs 83¢ per gallon whereas U.S. ethanol, made from corn, costs $1.14 per gallon. The United States does not import ethanol.

Source: *The New York Times*, April 12, 2006

Which country has a comparative advantage in producing ethanol? Explain why both the United States and Brazil can gain from specialization and trade.

## Solutions to Practice Problems

1. The person with a comparative advantage in snowboards is the one who has the lower opportunity cost of producing a snowboard. Tony's production possibilities show that to produce 5 more snowboards he must produce 10 fewer skis. So Tony's opportunity cost of a snowboard is 2 skis.

   Patty's production possibilities show that to produce 10 more snowboards, she must produce 5 fewer skis. So Patty's opportunity cost of a snowboard is 1/2 a ski. Patty has a comparative advantage in snowboards because her opportunity cost of a snowboard is less than Tony's. Tony's comparative advantage is in skis. For each ski produced, Tony must forgo making 1/2 a snowboard, whereas Patty must forgo making 2 snowboards for a ski. So Tony's opportunity cost of a ski is lower than Patty's.

2. Patty has a comparative advantage in snowboards, so she specializes in snowboards. Tony has a comparative advantage in skis, so he specializes in skis. Patty makes 20 snowboards and Tony makes 50 skis. Before specializing, they made 15 snowboards and 45 skis. By specializing, total output increases by 5 snowboards and 5 skis. They share this gain by trading.

## Solution to In the News

The cost of producing a gallon of ethanol is less in Brazil than in the United States, so Brazil has a comparative advantage in producing ethanol. If Brazil specializes in producing ethanol and the United States specializes in producing other goods (for example, movies or food) and the two countries engage in free trade, each country can gain because it will get to a point outside its own *PPF*.

# CHAPTER SUMMARY

## Key Points

1. **Explain and illustrate the concepts of scarcity, production efficiency, and tradeoff using the production possibilities frontier.**

   - The production possibilities frontier, *PPF*, describes the limits to what can be produced by using all the available resources efficiently.
   - Points inside and on the *PPF* are attainable. Points outside the *PPF* are unattainable.
   - Production at any point on the *PPF* achieves production efficiency. Production at a point inside the *PPF* is inefficient.
   - When production is efficient—on the *PPF*—people face a tradeoff. If production is at a point inside the *PPF*, there is a free lunch to be had.

2. **Calculate opportunity cost.**

   - Along the *PPF*, the opportunity cost of *X* (the item measured on the *x*-axis) is the decrease in *Y* (the item measured on the *y*-axis) divided by the increase in *X*.
   - The opportunity cost of *Y* is the inverse of the opportunity cost of *X*.
   - The opportunity cost of producing a good increases as the quantity of the good produced increases.

3. **Explain what makes production possibilities expand.**

   - Technological change and increases in capital and human capital expand production possibilities.
   - The opportunity cost of economic growth is the decrease in current consumption.

4. **Explain how people gain from specialization and trade.**

   - A person has a comparative advantage in an activity if he or she can perform that activity at a lower opportunity cost than someone else.
   - People gain by increasing the production of the item in which they have a comparative advantage and trading.

## Key Terms

Absolute advantage, 109
Comparative advantage, 109
Economic growth, 106

Production efficiency, 98
Production possibilities frontier, 96
Tradeoff, 99

# CHAPTER CHECKPOINT

## Study Plan Problems and Applications

**1.** Table 1 shows the quantities of corn and beef that a farm can produce in a year. Draw a graph of the farm's *PPF*. Mark on the graph:

- An inefficient combination of corn and beef—label this point *A*.
- An unattainable combination of corn and beef—label this point *B*.
- An efficient combination of corn and beef—label this point *C*.

Use the following information to work Problems **2** and **3**.

The people of Leisure Island have 50 hours of labor a day that can be used to produce entertainment and good food. Table 2 shows the maximum quantity of *either* entertainment *or* good food that Leisure Island can produce with different quantities of labor.

**2.** Is an output of 50 units of entertainment and 50 units of good food attainable and efficient? With a production of 50 units of entertainment and 50 units of good food, do the people of Leisure Island face a tradeoff?

**3.** What is the opportunity cost of producing an additional unit of entertainment? Explain how the opportunity cost of producing a unit of entertainment changes as more entertainment is produced.

Use the following information to work Problems **4** and **5**.

**Malaria can be controlled**

The World Health Organization's malaria chief says that it is too costly to try to fully eradicate the disease. He says that by using nets, medicine, and DDT it is possible to eliminate 90 percent of malaria cases. But to eliminate 100 percent of cases would be extremely costly.

Source: *The New York Times*, March 4, 2008

**4.** Make a graph of the production possibilities frontier with malaria control on the *x*-axis and other goods and services on the *y*-axis.

**5.** Describe how the opportunity cost of controlling malaria changes as more resources are used to reduce the number of malaria cases.

**6.** Explain how the following events influence U.S. production possibilities:

- Some retail workers are re-employed building dams and wind farms.
- More people take early retirement.
- Drought devastates California's economy.

Use the following information to work Problems **7** and **8**.

Figure 1 shows Tom's production possibilities and Figure 2 shows Abby's production possibilities. Tom uses all his resources and produces 2 rackets and 20 balls an hour. Abby uses all her resources and produces 2 rackets and 40 balls an hour.

**7.** What is Tom's opportunity cost of producing a racket? What is Abby's opportunity cost of a racket? Who has a comparative advantage in producing rackets? Who has a comparative advantage in producing balls?

**8.** If Tom and Abby specialize and trade 15 balls for 1 racket, what are the gains from trade?

**9.** Read *Eye on the Environment* on p. 104 and describe a tradeoff faced when deciding how to generate electricity and whether to use wind power.

**TABLE 1**

| Corn (bushels) | | Beef (pounds) |
|---|---|---|
| 250 | and | 0 |
| 200 | and | 300 |
| 100 | and | 500 |
| 0 | and | 600 |

**TABLE 2**

| Labor (hours) | Entertainment (units) | | Good food (units) |
|---|---|---|---|
| 0 | 0 | or | 0 |
| 10 | 20 | or | 30 |
| 20 | 40 | or | 50 |
| 30 | 60 | or | 60 |
| 40 | 80 | or | 65 |
| 50 | 100 | or | 67 |

**FIGURE 1**

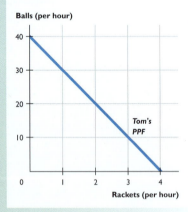

**FIGURE 2**

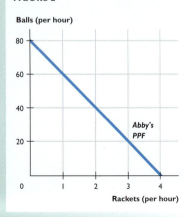

## Instructor Assignable Problems and Applications

Use the following information to work Problems **1** to **4**.

Representatives Waxman of California and Markey of Massachusetts proposed a law to limit greenhouse gas emissions from electricity generation and require electricity producers to generate a minimum percentage of power using renewable fuels, with some emission rights to be auctioned. The Congressional Budget Office estimated that the government would receive $846 billion from auctions and would spend $821 billion on incentive programs and compensation for higher energy prices. Electricity producers would spend $208 million a year to comply with the new rules. (Think of these dollar amounts as dollars' worth of other goods and services.)

1. Would the Waxman-Markey law achieve production efficiency?
2. Is the $846 billion that electricity producers would pay for the right to emit greenhouse gasses part of the opportunity cost of producing electricity?
3. Is the $821 billion that the government would spend on incentive programs and compensation for higher energy prices part of the opportunity cost of producing electricity?
4. Is the $208 million that electricity producers will spend to comply with the new rules part of the opportunity cost of producing electricity?
5. The people of Foodland have 40 hours of labor a day to bake pizza and bread. Table 1 shows the maximum quantity of *either* pizza *or* bread that Foodland can bake with different quantities of labor. Can Foodland produce 30 pizzas and 30 loaves of bread a day? If it can, is this output efficient, do the people of Foodland face a tradeoff, and what is the opportunity cost of producing an additional pizza?

Use Table 2, which shows a farm's production possibilities, to work Problems **6** and **7**.

6. If the farm uses its resources efficiently, what is the opportunity cost of an increase in chicken production from 300 pounds to 500 pounds a year? Explain your answer.
7. If the farm adopted a new technology, which allows it to use fewer resources to fatten chickens, explain how the farm's production possibilities will change. Explain how the opportunity cost of producing a bushel of soybean will be affected.
8. In an hour, Sue can produce 40 caps or 4 jackets and Tessa can produce 80 caps or 4 jackets. Who has a comparative advantage in producing caps? If Sue and Tessa specialize and trade, who will gain?

Use the following information to work Problems **9** to **11**.

**Cheap broadband's a winner**

Inexpensive broadband access has created a new generation of television producers and the Internet is their native medium.

Source: *The New York Times*, December 2, 2007

9. How has inexpensive broadband changed the production possibilities of video entertainment and other goods and services?
10. Sketch a *PPF* for video entertainment and other goods and services before broadband.
11. Explain how the arrival of inexpensive broadband has changed the *PPF*.

**TABLE 1**

| Labor (hours) | Pizzas | | Bread (loaves) |
|---|---|---|---|
| 0 | 0 | or | 0 |
| 10 | 30 | or | 10 |
| 20 | 50 | or | 20 |
| 30 | 60 | or | 30 |
| 40 | 65 | or | 40 |

**TABLE 2**

| Soybean (bushels per year) | | Chicken (pounds per year) |
|---|---|---|
| 500 | and | 0 |
| 400 | and | 300 |
| 200 | and | 500 |
| 0 | and | 600 |

## Critical Thinking Discussion Questions

**1. Google to open first Latin America data center in Chile**

The Chilean government's "Start-Up Chile" tech hub initiative is attracting information services entrepreneurs and firms from around the world. One of the firms attracted to Chile is Google, which has decided to base its first Latin American data center there.

Source: BBC, September 7, 2012

Think about the effects of the "Start-Up Chile" program and Google's decision:

How do Chile's production possibilities change?

How does Chile's opportunity cost of information services change?

How does Chile's opportunity cost of other goods and services change?

How does Chile's comparative advantage change?

**2. Men aren't pulling their weight at home**

In Italy, women work an average of 57 hours per week, 22 hours in a paid job and 35 hours in the home, doing unpaid housework. Italian men work a total of 46 hours per week, mainly for pay. In the United States, both men and women work an average of 51 hours a week. For women, 27 hours are worked in the home, and for men, 17 hours are in the home.

Source: CNN Money, November 5, 2013

Think about a household's production possibilities and tradeoffs:

What tradeoffs must the members of a household make?

Is it possible that Italian households are producing inside their production possibilities frontier?

Is it possible that American households are producing outside their production possibilities frontier?

If households are allocating their resources efficiently, who usually has a comparative advantage at working in the home, a man or a woman? How can you tell?

Can you think of an economic reason why Italian men work fewer total hours than Italian women, while American men and women work the same total hours?

What do the facts in this news clip tell us about the amount of human capital and physical capital in an Italian and American household?

# Demand and Supply

4

**When you have completed your study of this chapter, you will be able to**

**1** Distinguish between quantity demanded and demand, and explain what determines demand.

**2** Distinguish between quantity supplied and supply, and explain what determines supply.

**3** Explain how demand and supply determine price and quantity in a market, and explain the effects of changes in demand and supply.

119

# COMPETITIVE MARKETS

When you need a new pair of running shoes, want a bagel and a latte, or need to fly home for Thanksgiving, you must find a place where people sell those items or offer those services. The place where you find them is a *market*.

You learned in Chapter 2 that a market is any arrangement that brings buyers and sellers together. A market has two sides: demand (buyers) and supply (sellers). There are markets for *goods* such as apples and hiking boots, for *services* such as haircuts and tennis lessons, for *resources* such as computer programmers and tractors, and for other manufactured *inputs* such as memory chips and auto parts. There are also markets for money such as Japanese yen and for financial securities such as Yahoo! stock. Only imagination limits what can be traded in markets.

Some markets are physical places where buyers and sellers meet and where an auctioneer or a broker helps to determine the prices. Examples of this type of market are the New York Stock Exchange; wholesale fish, meat, and produce markets; and used car auctions.

Some markets are virtual spaces where buyers and sellers never meet face-to-face but connect over telephone lines or the Internet. Examples include currency markets, e-commerce Web sites such as Amazon.com and bananarepublic.com, and auction sites such as eBay.

But most markets are unorganized collections of buyers and sellers. You do most of your trading in this type of market. An example is the market for basketball shoes. The buyers in this $3-billion-a-year market are the 45 million Americans who play basketball (or who want to make a fashion statement) and are looking for a new pair of shoes. The sellers are the tens of thousands of retail sports equipment and footwear stores. Each buyer can visit several different stores, and each seller knows that the buyer has a choice of stores.

Markets vary in the intensity of competition that buyers and sellers face. In this chapter, we're going to study a *competitive market* that has so many buyers and so many sellers that no single buyer or seller can influence the price.

*Markets for running shoes …*

*coffee and a bagel …*

*and airline travel.*

## 4.1 DEMAND

First, we'll study the behavior of buyers in a competitive market. The **quantity demanded** of any good, service, or resource is the amount that people are willing and able to buy during a specified period at a specified price. For example, when spring water costs $1 a bottle, you decide to buy 2 bottles a day. The 2 bottles a day is your quantity demanded of spring water.

The quantity demanded is measured as an amount *per unit of time*. For example, your quantity demanded of water is 2 bottles *per day*. We could express this quantity as 14 bottles per week, or some other number per month or per year. A particular number of bottles without a time dimension has no meaning.

Many things influence buying plans, and one of them is price. We look first at the relationship between quantity demanded and price. To study this relationship, we keep all other influences on buying plans the same and we ask: How, other things remaining the same, does the quantity demanded of a good change as its price varies? The law of demand provides the answer.

**Quantity demanded**
The amount of any good, service, or resource that people are willing and able to buy during a specified period at a specified price.

### ■ The Law of Demand

The **law of demand** states

> Other things remaining the same, if the price of a good rises, the quantity demanded of that good decreases; and if the price of a good falls, the quantity demanded of that good increases.

So the law of demand states that when all other things remain the same, if the price of an iPhone falls, people will buy more iPhones; or if the price of a baseball ticket rises, people will buy fewer baseball tickets.

Why does the quantity demanded increase if the price falls, all other things remaining the same?

The answer is that, faced with a limited budget, people always have an incentive to find the best deals available. If the price of one item falls and the prices of all other items remain the same, the item with the lower price is a better deal than it was before, so some people buy more of this item. Suppose, for example, that the price of bottled water fell from $1 a bottle to 25 cents a bottle while the price of Gatorade remained at $1 a bottle. Wouldn't some people switch from Gatorade to water? By doing so, they save 75 cents a bottle, which they can spend on other things they previously couldn't afford.

Think about the things that you buy and ask yourself: Which of these items does *not* obey the law of demand? If the price of a new textbook were lower, other things remaining the same (including the price of a used textbook), would you buy more new textbooks? Then think about all the things that you do not buy but would if you could afford them. How cheap would a computer have to be for you to buy *both* a tablet and a laptop? There is a price that is low enough to entice you!

### ■ Demand Schedule and Demand Curve

**Demand** is the relationship between the quantity demanded and the price of a good when all other influences on buying plans remain the same. The quantity demanded is *one* quantity at *one* price. *Demand* is a *list of quantities at different prices* illustrated by a demand schedule and a demand curve.

**Demand**
The relationship between the quantity demanded and the price of a good when all other influences on buying plans remain the same.

**Demand schedule**

A list of the quantities demanded at each different price when all the other influences on buying plans remain the same.

**Demand curve**

A graph of the relationship between the quantity demanded of a good and its price when all the other influences on buying plans remain the same.

A **demand schedule** is a list of the quantities demanded at each different price when *all the other influences on buying plans remain the same.* The table in Figure 4.1 is one person's (Tina's) demand schedule for bottled water. It tells us that if the price of water is $2.00 a bottle, Tina buys no water. Her quantity demanded is 0 bottles a day. If the price of water is $1.50 a bottle, her quantity demanded is 1 bottle a day. Tina's quantity demanded increases to 2 bottles a day at a price of $1.00 a bottle and to 3 bottles a day at a price of 50 cents a bottle.

A **demand curve** is a graph of the relationship between the quantity demanded of a good and its price when all the other influences on buying plans remain the same. The points on the demand curve labeled *A* through *D* represent the rows *A* through *D* of the demand schedule. For example, point *B* on the graph represents row *B* of the demand schedule and shows that the quantity demanded is 1 bottle a day when the price is $1.50 a bottle. Point *C* on the demand curve represents row *C* of the demand schedule and shows that the quantity demanded is 2 bottles a day when the price is $1.00 a bottle.

The downward slope of the demand curve illustrates the law of demand. Along the demand curve, when the price of the good *falls*, the quantity demanded *increases.* For example, in Figure 4.1, when the price of a bottle of water falls from $1.00 to 50 cents, the quantity demanded increases from 2 bottles a day to 3 bottles a day. Conversely, when the price *rises*, the quantity demanded *decreases.* For example, when the price rises from $1.00 to $1.50 a bottle, the quantity demanded decreases from 2 bottles a day to 1 bottle a day.

■ **FIGURE 4.1**

Demand Schedule and Demand Curve

The table shows Tina's demand schedule that lists the quantity of water demanded at each price if all other influences on buying plans remain the same. At a price of $1.50 a bottle, the quantity demanded is 1 bottle a day.

The demand curve shows the relationship between the quantity demanded and price, other things remaining the same. The downward-sloping demand curve illustrates the law of demand. When the price falls, the quantity demanded increases; and when the price rises, the quantity demanded decreases.

|   | Price (dollars per bottle) | Quantity demanded (bottles per day) |
|---|---|---|
| A | 2.00 | 0 |
| B | 1.50 | 1 |
| C | 1.00 | 2 |
| D | 0.50 | 3 |

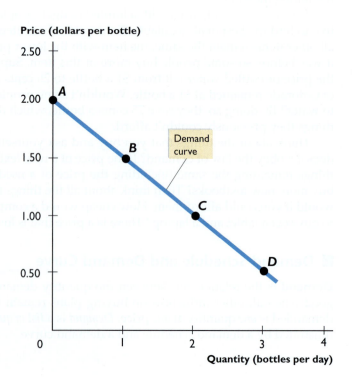

## Individual Demand and Market Demand

The demand schedule and the demand curve that you've just studied are for one person. To study a market, we must determine the market demand.

*Market demand* is the sum of the demands of all the buyers in a market. To find the market demand, imagine a market in which there are only two buyers: Tina and Tim. The table in Figure 4.2 shows three demand schedules: Tina's, Tim's, and the market demand schedule. Tina's demand schedule is the same as before. It shows the quantity of water demanded by Tina at each different price. Tim's demand schedule tells us the quantity of water demanded by Tim at each price. To find the quantity of water demanded in the market, we sum the quantities demanded by Tina and Tim. For example, at a price of $1.00 a bottle, the quantity demanded by Tina is 2 bottles a day, the quantity demanded by Tim is 1 bottle a day, and so the quantity demanded in the market is 3 bottles a day.

Tina's demand curve in part (a) and Tim's demand curve in part (b) are graphs of the two individual demand schedules. The market demand curve in part (c) is a graph of the market demand schedule. At a given price, the quantity demanded on the market demand curve equals the horizontal sum of the quantities demanded on the individual demand curves.

### FIGURE 4.2

#### Individual Demand and Market Demand

| Price (dollars per bottle) | Quantity demanded (bottles per day) | | |
|---|---|---|---|
| | Tina | Tim | Market |
| 2.00 | 0 | 0 | 0 |
| 1.50 | 1 | 0 | 1 |
| 1.00 | 2 + | 1 = | 3 |
| 0.50 | 3 | 2 | 5 |

The market demand schedule is the sum of the individual demand schedules, and the market demand curve is the horizontal sum of the individual demand curves.

At a price of $1 a bottle, the quantity demanded by Tina is 2 bottles a day and the quantity demanded by Tim is 1 bottle a day, so the total quantity demanded in the market is 3 bottles a day.

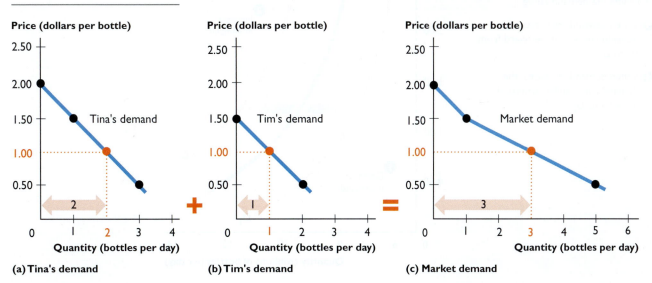

(a) Tina's demand

(b) Tim's demand

(c) Market demand

## ■ Changes in Demand

The demand curve shows how the quantity demanded changes when the price of the good changes but *all other influences on buying plans remain the same.* When any of these other influences on buying plans change, there is a **change in demand**, which means that there is a new demand schedule and new demand curve. *The demand curve shifts.*

Demand can either increase or decrease and Figure 4.3 illustrates the two cases. Initially, the demand curve is $D_0$. When demand decreases, the demand curve shifts leftward to $D_1$. On demand curve $D_1$, the quantity demanded at each price is smaller. When demand increases, the demand curve shifts rightward to $D_2$. On demand curve $D_2$, the quantity demanded at each price is greater.

The main influences on buying plans that change demand are

- Prices of related goods
- Expected future prices
- Income
- Expected future income and credit
- Number of buyers
- Preferences

### Prices of Related Goods

Goods have substitutes and complements. A **substitute** for a good is another good that can be consumed in its place. Chocolate cake is a substitute for cheesecake, and bottled water is a substitute for Gatorade. A **complement** of a good is another good that is consumed with it. Wrist guards are a complement of in-line skates, and bottled water is a complement of fitness center services.

**Change in demand**

A change in the quantity that people plan to buy when any influence on buying plans other than the price of the good changes.

**Substitute**

A good that can be consumed in place of another good.

**Complement**

A good that is consumed with another good.

---

■ **FIGURE 4.3**

Changes in Demand

A change in any influence on buying plans, other than a change in the price of the good itself, changes demand and shifts the demand curve.

❶ When demand decreases, the demand curve shifts leftward from $D_0$ to $D_1$.

❷ When demand increases, the demand curve shifts rightward from $D_0$ to $D_2$.

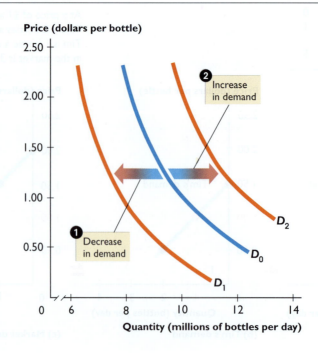

The demand for a good and the price of one of its substitutes move in the *same direction.* The demand for a good *increases* if the price of one of its substitutes *rises* and *decreases* if the price of one of its substitutes *falls.* For example, the demand for cheesecake increases when the price of chocolate cake rises.

The demand for a good and the price of one of its complements move in *opposite directions.* The demand for a good *decreases* if the price of one of its complements *rises* and *increases* if the price of one of its complements *falls.* For example, the demand for wrist guards decreases when the price of in-line skates rises.

## Expected Future Prices

A rise in the expected *future* price of a good increases the *current* demand for that good and a fall in the expected *future* price decreases *current* demand. If you expect the price of noodles to rise next week, you buy a big enough stockpile to get you through the next few weeks. Your demand for noodles today has increased. If you expect the price of noodles to fall next week, you buy none now and plan to buy next week. Your demand for noodles today has decreased.

## Income

A rise in income brings an increase in demand and a fall in income brings a decrease in demand for a **normal good**. A rise in income brings a *decrease* in demand and a fall in income brings an *increase* in demand for an **inferior good**. For example, if your income increases and you decide to buy more chicken and less pasta, for you, chicken is a normal good and pasta is an inferior good.

**Normal good**
A good for which demand increases when income increases and demand decreases when income decreases.

**Inferior good**
A good for which demand decreases when income increases and demand increases when income decreases.

## Expected Future Income and Credit

When income is expected to increase in the future, or when credit is easy to get and the cost of borrowing is low, the demand for some goods increases. And when income is expected to decrease in the future, or when credit is hard to get and the cost of borrowing is high, the demand for some goods decreases.

Changes in expected future income and the availability and cost of credit have the greatest effect on the demand for big ticket items such as homes and automobiles. Modest changes in expected future income or credit availability bring large swings in the demand for these items.

## Number of Buyers

The greater the number of buyers in a market, the larger is demand. For example, the demand for parking spaces, movies, bottled water, or just about anything is greater in New York City than it is in Boise, Idaho.

## Preferences

Tastes or *preferences,* as economists call them, influence demand. When preferences change, the demand for one item increases and the demand for another item (or items) decreases. For example, preferences have changed as people have become better informed about the health hazards of tobacco. This change in preferences has decreased the demand for cigarettes and has increased the demand for nicotine patches. Preferences also change when new goods become available. For example, the development of MP3 technology has decreased the demand for CDs and has increased the demand for Internet service and MP3 players.

## ■ Change in Quantity Demanded Versus Change in Demand

The influences on buyers' plans that you've just seen bring a *change in demand*. These are all the influences on buying plans *except for the price of the good*. To avoid confusion, when *the price of the good changes* and all other influences on buying plans remain the same, we say there has been a **change in the quantity demanded**.

**Change in the quantity demanded**
A change in the quantity of a good that people plan to buy that results from a change in the price of the good with all other influences on buying plans remaining the same.

The distinction between a change in demand and a change in the quantity demanded is crucial for working out how a market responds to the forces that hit it. Figure 4.4 illustrates and summarizes the distinction:

- If the price of bottled water *rises* when other things remain the same, the quantity demanded of bottled water *decreases* and there is a *movement up* along the demand curve $D_0$. If the price *falls* when other things remain the same, the quantity demanded *increases* and there is a *movement down* along the demand curve $D_0$.
- If some influence on buyers' plans other than the price of bottled water changes, there is a change in demand. When the demand for bottled water *decreases*, the demand curve *shifts leftward* to $D_1$. When the demand for bottled water *increases*, the demand curve *shifts rightward* to $D_2$.

When you are thinking about the influences on demand, try to get into the habit of asking: Does this influence change the quantity demanded or does it change demand? The test is: Did the price of the good change or did some other influence change? If the price changed, then quantity demanded changed. If some other influence changed and the price remained constant, then demand changed.

■ **FIGURE 4.4**

Change in Quantity Demanded Versus Change in Demand

❶ **A decrease in the quantity demanded**

The quantity demanded decreases and there is a movement up along the demand curve $D_0$ if the price of the good rises and other things remain the same.

❸ **A decrease in demand**

Demand decreases and the demand curve shifts leftward (from $D_0$ to $D_1$) if

- The price of a substitute falls or the price of a complement rises.
- The price of the good is expected to fall.
- Income decreases.*
- Expected future income or credit decreases.
- The number of buyers decreases.

*Bottled water is a normal good.

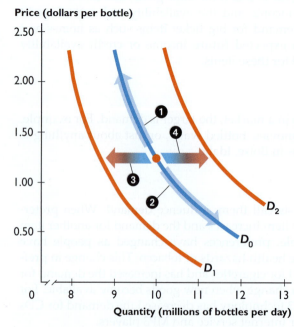

❷ **An increase in the quantity demanded**

The quantity demanded increases and there is a movement down along the demand curve $D_0$ if the price of the good falls and other things remain the same.

❹ **An increase in demand**

Demand increases and the demand curve shifts rightward (from $D_0$ to $D_2$) if

- The price of a substitute rises or the price of a complement falls.
- The price of the good is expected to rise.
- Income increases.
- Expected future income or credit increases.
- The number of buyers increases.

# CHECKPOINT 4.1

**Distinguish between quantity demanded and demand, and explain what determines demand.**

## Practice Problems

The following events occur one at a time in the market for cell phones:
- The price of a cell phone falls.
- Producers announce that cell-phone prices will fall next month.
- The price of a call made from a cell phone falls.
- The price of a call made from a land-line phone increases.
- The introduction of camera phones makes cell phones more popular.

1. Explain the effect of each event on the demand for cell phones.

2. Use a graph to illustrate the effect of each event.

3. Does any event (or events) illustrate the law of demand?

## In the News

**Airlines, now flush, fear a downturn**
So far this year, airlines have been able to raise fares but still fill their planes.
Source: *The New York Times*, June 10, 2011

Does this news clip imply that the law of demand doesn't work in the real world? Explain why or why not.

## Solutions to Practice Problems

1. A fall in the price of a cell phone increases the quantity of cell phones demanded but has no effect on the demand for cell phones.
   With the producers' announcement, the expected future price of a cell phone falls, which decreases the demand for cell phones today.
   A fall in the price of a call from a cell phone increases the demand for cell phones because a cell-phone call and a cell phone are complements.
   A rise in the price of a call from a land-line phone increases the demand for cell phones because a land-line phone and a cell phone are substitutes.
   With cell phones more popular, the demand for cell phones increases.

2. Figure 1 illustrates the effect of a fall in the price of a cell phone as a movement along the demand curve $D$.
   Figure 2 illustrates the effect of an increase in the demand for cell phones as the shift of the demand curve from $D_0$ to $D_1$ and a decrease in the demand for cell phones as the shift of the demand curve from $D_0$ to $D_2$.

3. A fall in the price of a cell phone (other things remaining the same) illustrates the law of demand. Figure 1 illustrates the law of demand. The other events change demand and do not illustrate the law of demand.

## Solution to In the News

The law of demand states: If the price of an airline ticket rises, other things remaining the same, the quantity demanded of airline tickets will decrease. The demand curve for airline tickets slopes downward. The law of demand does work in the real world. Airlines can still fill their planes because "other things" did not remain the same. Some event increased the demand for airline tickets.

**FIGURE 1**

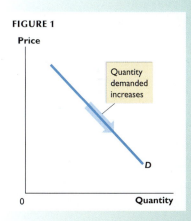

**FIGURE 2**

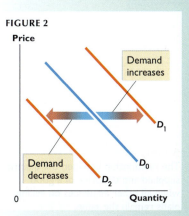

## 4.2 SUPPLY

A market has two sides. On one side are the buyers, or demanders, that we've just studied. On the other side of the market are the sellers, or suppliers. We now study the forces that determine suppliers' plans.

**Quantity supplied**
The amount of any good, service, or resource that people are willing and able to sell during a specified period at a specified price.

The **quantity supplied** of a good, service, or resource is the amount that people are willing and able to sell during a specified period at a specified price. For example, when the price of spring water is $1.50 a bottle, a spring owner decides to sell 2,000 bottles a day. The 2,000 bottles a day is the quantity supplied of spring water by this individual producer. (As in the case of demand, the quantity supplied is measured as an amount *per unit of time.*)

Many things influence selling plans, and one of them is the price. We look first at the relationship between quantity supplied of a good and its price. To study this relationship, we keep all other influences on selling plans the same, and we ask: Other things remaining the same, how does the quantity supplied of a good change as its price varies? The law of supply provides the answer.

### ■ The Law of Supply

The **law of supply** states

> **Other things remaining the same, if the price of a good rises, the quantity supplied of that good increases; and if the price of a good falls, the quantity supplied of that good decreases.**

So the law of supply states that when all other things remain the same, if the price of bottled water rises, spring owners will offer more water for sale; if the price of a flat panel TV falls, Sony Corp. will offer fewer flat panel TVs for sale.

Why, other things remaining the same, does the quantity supplied increase if the price rises and decrease if the price falls? Part of the answer lies in the principle of increasing opportunity cost (see p. 106). Because factors of production are not equally productive in all activities, as more of a good is produced, the opportunity cost of producing it increases. A higher price provides the incentive to bear the higher opportunity cost of increased production. Another part of the answer is that for a given cost, the higher price brings a larger profit, so sellers have greater incentive to increase production.

Think about the resources that you own and can offer for sale to others and ask yourself: Which of these items does *not* obey the law of supply? If the wage rate for summer jobs increased, would you have an incentive to work longer hours and bear the higher opportunity cost of forgone leisure? If the bank offered a higher interest rate on deposits, would you have an incentive to save more and bear the higher opportunity cost of forgone consumption? If the used book dealer offered a higher price for last year's textbooks, would you have an incentive to sell that handy math text and bear the higher opportunity cost of visiting the library (or finding a friend) whenever you needed the book?

### ■ Supply Schedule and Supply Curve

**Supply**
The relationship between the quantity supplied and the price of a good when all other influences on selling plans remain the same.

**Supply** is the relationship between the quantity supplied and the price of a good when all other influences on selling plans remain the same. The quantity supplied is *one* quantity at *one* price. *Supply* is a *list of quantities at different prices* illustrated by a supply schedule and a supply curve.

A **supply schedule** lists the quantities supplied at each different price when all the other influences on selling plans remain the same. The table in Figure 4.5 is one firm's (Agua's) supply schedule for bottled water. It tells us that if the price of water is 50 cents a bottle, Agua plans to sell no water. Its quantity supplied is 0 bottles a day. If the price of water is $1.00 a bottle, Agua's quantity supplied is 1,000 bottles a day. Agua's quantity supplied increases to 2,000 bottles a day at a price of $1.50 a bottle and to 3,000 bottles a day at a price of $2.00 a bottle.

A **supply curve** is a graph of the relationship between the quantity supplied of a good and its price when all the other influences on selling plans remain the same. The points on the supply curve labeled *A* through *D* represent the rows *A* through *D* of the supply schedule. For example, point *C* on the supply curve represents row *C* of the supply schedule and shows that the quantity supplied is 1,000 bottles a day when the price is $1.00 a bottle. Point *B* on the supply curve represents row *B* of the supply schedule and shows that the quantity supplied is 2,000 bottles a day when the price is $1.50 a bottle.

The upward slope of the supply curve illustrates the law of supply. Along the supply curve, when the price of the good *rises*, the quantity supplied *increases*. For example, in Figure 4.5, when the price of a bottle of water rises from $1.50 to $2.00, the quantity supplied increases from 2,000 bottles a day to 3,000 bottles a day. And when the price *falls*, the quantity supplied *decreases*. For example, when the price falls from $1.50 to $1.00 a bottle, the quantity supplied decreases from 2,000 bottles a day to 1,000 bottles a day.

**Supply schedule**
A list of the quantities supplied at each different price when all the other influences on selling plans remain the same.

**Supply curve**
A graph of the relationship between the quantity supplied of a good and its price when all the other influences on selling plans remain the same.

**FIGURE 4.5**

Supply Schedule and Supply Curve

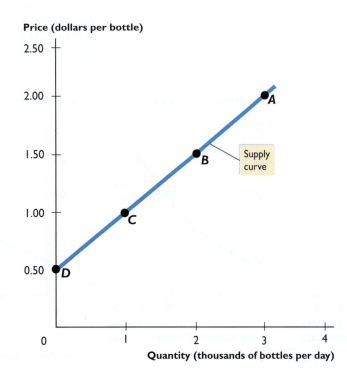

| | Price (dollars per bottle) | Quantity supplied (thousands of bottles per day) |
|---|---|---|
| A | 2.00 | 3 |
| B | 1.50 | 2 |
| C | 1.00 | 1 |
| D | 0.50 | 0 |

The table shows a supply schedule that lists the quantity of water supplied at each price if all other influences on selling plans remain the same. At a price of $1.50 a bottle, the quantity supplied is 2,000 bottles a day.

The supply curve shows the relationship between the quantity supplied and price, other things remaining the same. The upward-sloping supply curve illustrates the law of supply. When the price rises, the quantity supplied increases; and when the price falls, the quantity supplied decreases.

### ◼ Individual Supply and Market Supply

The supply schedule and the supply curve that you've just studied are for one seller. To study a market, we must determine the market supply.

*Market supply* is the sum of the supplies of all the sellers in the market. To find the market supply of water, imagine a market in which there are only two sellers: Agua and Prima. The table in Figure 4.6 shows three supply schedules: Agua's, Prima's, and the market supply schedule. Agua's supply schedule is the same as before. Prima's supply schedule tells us the quantity of water that Prima plans to sell at each price. To find the quantity of water supplied in the market, we sum the quantities supplied by Agua and Prima. For example, at a price of $1.00 a bottle, the quantity supplied by Agua is 1,000 bottles a day, the quantity supplied by Prima is 2,000 bottles a day, and the quantity supplied in the market is 3,000 bottles a day.

Agua's supply curve in part (a) and Prima's supply curve in part (b) are graphs of the two individual supply schedules. The market supply curve in part (c) is a graph of the market supply schedule. At a given price, the quantity supplied on the market supply curve equals the horizontal sum of the quantities supplied on the individual supply curves.

◼ **FIGURE 4.6**

Individual Supply and Market Supply

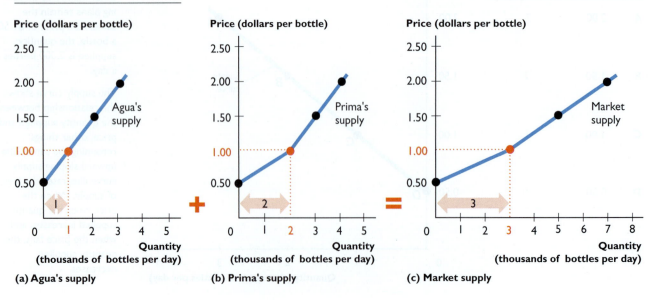

| Price (dollars per bottle) | Quantity supplied (thousands of bottles per day) | | |
|---|---|---|---|
| | Agua | Prima | Market |
| 2.00 | 3 | 4 | 7 |
| 1.50 | 2 | 3 | 5 |
| 1.00 | 1 + | 2 = | 3 |
| 0.50 | 0 | 0 | 0 |

The market supply schedule is the sum of the individual supply schedules, and the market supply curve is the horizontal sum of the individual supply curves.

At a price of $1 a bottle, the quantity supplied by Agua is 1,000 bottles a day and the quantity supplied by Prima is 2,000 bottles a day, so the total quantity supplied in the market is 3,000 bottles a day.

**(a) Agua's supply**

**(b) Prima's supply**

**(c) Market supply**

# ■ Changes in Supply

The supply curve shows how the quantity supplied changes when the price of the good changes but *all other influences on selling plans remain the same*. When any of these other influences on selling plans change, there is a **change in supply**, which means that there is a new supply schedule and new supply curve. *The supply curve shifts.*

Supply can either increase or decrease, and Figure 4.7 illustrates the two cases. Initially, the supply curve is $S_0$. When supply decreases, the supply curve shifts leftward to $S_1$. On supply curve $S_1$, the quantity supplied at each price is smaller. When supply increases, the supply curve shifts rightward to $S_2$. On supply curve $S_2$, the quantity supplied at each price is greater.

The main influences on selling plans that change supply are

- Prices of related goods
- Prices of resources and other inputs
- Expected future prices
- Number of sellers
- Productivity

**Change in supply**
A change in the quantity that suppliers plan to sell when any influence on selling plans other than the price of the good changes.

## Prices of Related Goods

Related goods are either substitutes *in production* or complements *in production*. A **substitute in production** for a good is another good that can be produced in its place. Skinny jeans are substitutes in production for boot cut jeans in a clothing factory.

A **complement in production** of a good is another good that is produced along with it. Cream is a complement in production of skim milk in a dairy.

**Substitute in production**
A good that can be produced in place of another good.

**Complement in production**
A good that is produced along with another good.

---

■ **FIGURE 4.7**

Changes in Supply

---

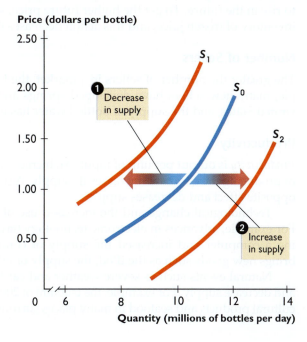

A change in any influence on selling plans other than a change in the price of the good itself changes supply and shifts the supply curve.

❶ When supply decreases, the supply curve shifts leftward from $S_0$ to $S_1$.

❷ When supply increases, the supply curve shifts rightward from $S_0$ to $S_2$.

*A Change in the Price of a Substitute in Production* The supply of a good *decreases* if the price of one of its substitutes in production *rises;* and the supply of a good *increases* if the price of one of its substitutes in production *falls.* That is, the supply of a good and the price of one of its substitutes in production move in *opposite directions.* For example, a clothing factory can produce chinos or button-fly jeans, so these goods are substitutes in production. When the price of button-fly jeans rises, the clothing factory switches production from chinos to button-fly jeans, so the supply of chinos decreases.

*A Change in the Price of a Complement in Production* The supply of a good *increases* if the price of one of its complements in production *rises;* and the supply of a good *decreases* if the price of one of its complements in production *falls.* That is, the supply of a good and the price of one of its complements in production move in the *same direction.* For example, when a dairy produces skim milk, it also produces cream, so these goods are complements in production. When the price of skim milk rises, the dairy produces more skim milk, so the supply of cream increases.

### Prices of Resources and Other Inputs

Supply changes when the price of a resource or other input used to produce the good changes. The reason is that resource and input prices influence the cost of production. The more it costs to produce a good, the smaller is the quantity supplied of that good at each price (other things remaining the same). For example, if the wage rate of bottling-plant workers rises, it costs more to produce a bottle of water, so the supply of bottled water decreases.

### Expected Future Prices

Expectations about future prices influence supply. For example, a severe frost that wipes out Florida's citrus crop doesn't change the production of orange juice today, but it does decrease production later in the year when the current crop would normally have been harvested. Sellers of orange juice will expect the price to rise in the future. To get the higher future price, some sellers will increase their inventory of frozen juice, and this action decreases the supply of juice today.

### Number of Sellers

The greater the number of sellers in a market, the larger is the supply. For example, many new sellers have developed springs and water-bottling plants in the United States, and the supply of bottled water has increased.

### Productivity

*Productivity* is output per unit of input. An increase in productivity lowers the cost of producing the good and increases its supply. A decrease in productivity has the opposite effect and decreases supply.

Technological change and the increased use of capital increase productivity. For example, advances in electronic technology have lowered the cost of producing a computer and increased the supply of computers. Technological change brings new goods such as the iPod, the supply of which was previously zero.

Natural events such as severe weather and earthquakes decrease productivity and decrease supply. For example, the tsunami of 2004 decreased the supply of agricultural products and seafood in many places surrounding the Indian Ocean.

## ■ Change in Quantity Supplied Versus Change in Supply

The influences on sellers' plans that you've just considered bring a *change in supply*. These are all the influences on sellers' plans *except the price of the good*. To avoid confusion, when the *price of the good changes* and all other influences on selling plans remain the same, we say there has been a **change in the quantity supplied**.

The distinction between a change in supply and a change in the quantity supplied is crucial for figuring out how a market responds to the forces that hit it. Figure 4.8 illustrates and summarizes the distinction:

- If the price of bottled water *falls* when other things remain the same, the quantity supplied of bottled water *decreases* and there is a *movement down* along the supply curve $S_0$. If the price *rises* when other things remain the same, the quantity supplied *increases* and there is a *movement up* along the supply curve $S_0$.
- If any influence on water bottlers' plans other than the price of bottled water changes, there is a change in the supply of bottled water. When the supply of bottled water *decreases*, the supply curve *shifts leftward* to $S_1$. When the supply of bottled water *increases*, the supply curve *shifts rightward* to $S_2$.

When you are thinking about the influences on supply, get into the habit of asking: Does this influence change the quantity supplied or does it change supply? The test is: Did the price change or did some other influence change? If the price of the good changed, then quantity supplied changed. If some other influence changed and the price of the good remained constant, then supply changed.

**Change in the quantity supplied**
A change in the quantity of a good that suppliers plan to sell that results from a change in the price of the good.

### FIGURE 4.8

Change in Quantity Supplied Versus Change in Supply

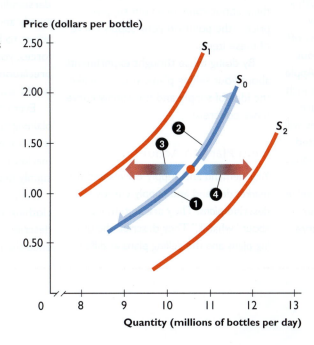

**❶ A decrease in the quantity supplied**

The quantity supplied decreases and there is a movement down along the supply curve $S_0$ if the price of the good falls and other things remain the same.

**❸ A decrease in supply**

Supply decreases and the supply curve shifts leftward (from $S_0$ to $S_1$) if

■ The price of a substitute in production rises.
■ The price of a complement in production falls.
■ A resource price or other input price rises.
■ The price of the good is expected to rise.
■ The number of sellers decreases.
■ Productivity decreases.

**❷ An increase in the quantity supplied**

The quantity supplied increases and there is a movement up along the supply curve $S_0$ if the price of the good rises and other things remain the same.

**❹ An increase in supply**

Supply increases and the supply curve shifts rightward (from $S_0$ to $S_2$) if

■ The price of a substitute in production falls.
■ The price of a complement in production rises.
■ A resource price or other input price falls.
■ The price of the good is expected to fall.
■ The number of sellers increases.
■ Productivity increases.

# EYE on YOUR LIFE
## Understanding and Using Demand and Supply

To truly understand the demand and supply model, it is a good idea to go beyond just memorizing the key terms and definitions and lists of factors that change demand or change supply. Take ownership of the model by seeing how it explains your buying plans and your selling plans.

### Your Buying Plans

Think about the things you buy: the quantities you buy and the prices you pay. These quantities and prices are points on your demand curves.

Now think about how some price changes would change your buying plans. How would your buying plans change if prices at the campus coffee shop increased? For which items would you change your quantity demanded? And for which items would you change your demand?

How would your buying plans change if you started a new job with a higher wage? What would you buy more of? What would you buy less of?

Suppose that you were just about to buy a new smart phone when Apple and Samsung announce plans to launch new phones next month. You figure that the prices of the older models will fall. How will this fall in the expected future price of a smart phone influence your buying plans?

For each thought experiment we've just described, think about whether you are sliding along a demand curve or shifting a demand curve.

### Your Selling Plans

Most likely, you don't sell much stuff, but you own one precious resource that you might sell: your time.

If you have a job, think about the number of hours you work and the wage rate you earn. Are you working as many hours as you want to? If you are, you're at a point on the supply curve of your labor services.

How would you respond to a rise in the wage rate? Would you plan to work more hours or fewer hours?

Another thing you own is a pile of textbooks. Think about your selling plan for when your courses are over at the end of the semester. What is the lowest price at which you will sell this textbook? That price is a point on your supply curve of this book to the used book market.

You might also have a few old things that you'd like to sell on eBay. Again, think about your minimum supply-price—the point on your supply curve of these items.

By doing these thought experiments about your selling plans, you can make the idea of supply and the supply curve more concrete.

### From Plans to Actions

*Your* demand and supply curves and the *market* demand and supply curves describe *plans*. They are statements about "what-if." They describe the buying plans and the selling plans at differ-ent possible prices. But when you act on your plan and buy something, someone else must have a plan to sell that item. Your buying plan must match someone else's selling plan.

Neither demand nor supply on its own tells us what actually happens in a market. To find buying plans and selling plans that match, we must look at demand and supply together. That's what you will do in the final section of this chapter. You will see how prices adjust to balance the opposing forces of demand and supply.

### The Rest of Your Life

The demand and supply model is going to be a big part of the rest of your life! You will use it again and again during your economics course, so having a firm grasp of it will bring an immediate payoff.

But much more important, by understanding the laws of demand and supply and being aware of how prices adjust to balance these two opposing forces, you will have a much better appreciation of how your economic world works.

Every time you hear someone complaining about a price hike and blaming it on someone's greed, think about the market forces and how demand and supply determine that price.

As you shop for your favorite clothing, music, and food items, try to describe how supply and demand influence the prices of these goods.

## CHECKPOINT 4.2

**Distinguish between quantity supplied and supply, and explain what determines supply.**

# Practice Problems

Lumber companies make timber beams from logs. In the process of making beams, the mill produces sawdust, which is made into pressed wood. In the market for timber beams, the following events occur one at a time:

- The wage rate of sawmill workers rises.
- The price of sawdust rises.
- The price of a timber beam rises.
- Next year's expected price of a timber beam rises.
- A new law reduces the amount of forest that can be cut for timber.
- A new technology lowers the cost of producing timber beams.

1. Explain the effect of each event on the supply of timber beams.

2. Use a graph to illustrate the effect of each event.

3. Does any event (or events) illustrate the law of supply?

# In the News

**Rising wages pose dilemma for China**

Chinese private-sector wages rose 14 percent in 2012. This trend in rapidly rising wage rates might hurt its manufacturing dominance.

Source: *The Wall Street Journal*, May 17, 2013

Explain the effect of the rising wage rates on the supply of manufactured goods.

# Solutions to Practice Problems

1. A rise in workers' wage rates increases the cost of producing a timber beam and decreases the supply of timber beams. A rise in the price of sawdust increases the supply of timber beams because sawdust and timber beams are complements in production. A rise in the price of a timber beam increases the quantity of timber beams supplied but has no effect on the supply of timber beams. A rise in the expected price of a timber beam decreases the supply of timber beams today as producers hold back and wait for the higher price. The new law decreases the supply of timber beams. The new technology increases the supply of timber beams.

2. In Figure 1, an increase in the supply shifts the supply curve from $S_0$ to $S_1$, and a decrease in the supply shifts the supply curve from $S_0$ to $S_2$. In Figure 2, the rise in the price of a beam creates a movement along the supply curve.

3. A rise in the price of a beam, other things remaining the same, is the only event that illustrates the law of supply—see Figure 2.

# Solution to In the News

Rising wage rates increase the cost of production and with no change in productivity China's supply of manufactured goods will decrease.

**FIGURE 1**

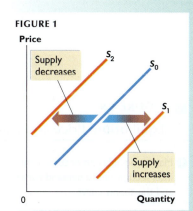

**FIGURE 2**

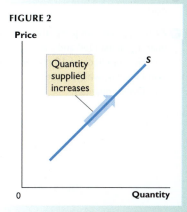

## 4.3 MARKET EQUILIBRIUM

**Market equilibrium**
When the quantity demanded equals the quantity supplied—buyers' and sellers' plans are in balance.

**Equilibrium price**
The price at which the quantity demanded equals the quantity supplied.

**Equilibrium quantity**
The quantity bought and sold at the equilibrium price.

In everyday language, "equilibrium" means "opposing forces are in balance." In a market, demand and supply are the opposing forces. **Market equilibrium** occurs when the quantity demanded equals the quantity supplied—when buyers' and sellers' plans are in balance. At the **equilibrium price**, the quantity demanded equals the quantity supplied. The **equilibrium quantity** is the quantity bought and sold at the equilibrium price.

In the market for bottled water in Figure 4.9, equilibrium occurs where the demand curve and the supply curve intersect. The equilibrium price is $1.00 a bottle, and the equilibrium quantity is 10 million bottles a day.

### ■ Price: A Market's Automatic Regulator

When equilibrium is disturbed, market forces restore it. The **law of market forces** states

> **When there is a surplus, the price falls; and when there is a shortage, the price rises.**

A *surplus* is the amount by which the quantity supplied exceeds the quantity demanded. If there is a surplus, suppliers must cut the price to sell more. Buyers are pleased to take the lower price, so the price falls. Because a surplus arises when the price is above the equilibrium price, a falling price is exactly what the market needs to restore equilibrium.

A *shortage* is the amount by which the quantity demanded exceeds the quantity supplied. If there is a shortage, buyers must pay a higher price to get more. Sellers are pleased to take the higher price, so the price rises. Because a shortage arises when the price is below the equilibrium price, a rising price is exactly what is needed to restore equilibrium.

■ **FIGURE 4.9**

Equilibrium Price and Equilibrium Quantity

❶ Market equilibrium occurs at the intersection of the demand curve and the supply curve.

❷ The equilibrium price is $1.00 a bottle.

❸ At the equilibrium price, the quantity demanded and the quantity supplied are 10 million bottles a day, which is the equilibrium quantity.

### ■ FIGURE 4.10

The Forces That Achieve Equilibrium

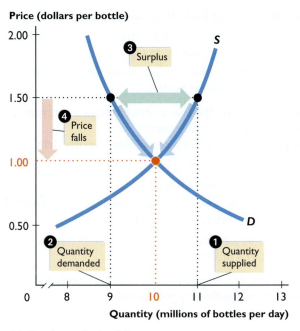

(a) Surplus and price falls

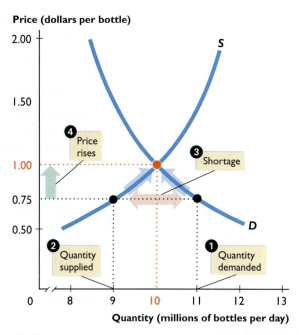

(b) Shortage and price rises

At $1.50 a bottle, ❶ the quantity supplied is 11 million bottles of water, ❷ the quantity demanded is 9 million bottles, ❸ the surplus is 2 million bottles, and ❹ the price falls.

At 75 cents a bottle, ❶ the quantity demanded is 11 million bottles of water, ❷ the quantity supplied is 9 million bottles, ❸ the shortage is 2 million bottles, and ❹ the price rises.

In Figure 4.10(a), at $1.50 a bottle, there is a surplus: The price falls, the quantity demanded increases, the quantity supplied decreases, and the surplus is eliminated at $1.00 a bottle.

In Figure 4.10(b), at 75 cents a bottle, there is a shortage of water: The price rises, the quantity demanded decreases, the quantity supplied increases, and the shortage is eliminated at $1.00 a bottle.

### ■ Predicting Price Changes: Three Questions

Because price adjustments eliminate shortages and surpluses, markets are normally in equilibrium. When an event disturbs an equilibrium, a new equilibrium soon emerges. To explain and predict changes in prices and quantities, we need to consider only changes in the *equilibrium* price and the *equilibrium* quantity. We can work out the effects of an event on a market by answering three questions:

1. Does the event influence demand or supply?

2. Does the event *increase* or *decrease* demand or supply—shift the demand curve or the supply curve *rightward* or *leftward*?

3. What are the new *equilibrium* price and *equilibrium* quantity and how have they changed?

## ■ Effects of Changes in Demand

Let's practice answering the three questions by working out the effects of an event in the market for bottled water: A new study says that tap water is unsafe.

1. With tap water unsafe, the demand for bottled water changes.
2. The demand for bottled water *increases*, and the demand curve *shifts rightward*. Figure 4.11(a) shows the shift from $D_0$ to $D_1$.
3. There is now a *shortage* at $1.00 a bottle. The *price rises* to $1.50 a bottle, and the quantity increases to 11 million bottles.

Note that there is *no change in supply*; the rise in price brings an *increase in the quantity supplied*—a movement along the supply curve.

Let's work out what happens if the price of a zero-calorie sports drink falls.

1. The sports drink is a substitute for bottled water, so when its price changes, the demand for bottled water changes.
2. The demand for bottled water *decreases*, and the demand curve *shifts leftward*. Figure 4.11(b) shows the shift from $D_0$ to $D_2$.
3. There is now a *surplus* at $1.00 a bottle. The price *falls* to 75 cents a bottle, and the quantity decreases to 9 million bottles.

Note again that there is *no change in supply*; the fall in price brings a *decrease in the quantity supplied*—a movement along the supply curve.

■ **FIGURE 4.11**

The Effects of a Change in Demand

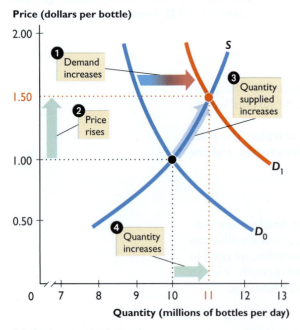

**(a)  An increase in demand**

❶ An increase in demand shifts the demand curve rightward to $D_1$ and creates a shortage of water. ❷ The price rises, ❸ the quantity supplied increases, and ❹ the equilibrium quantity increases.

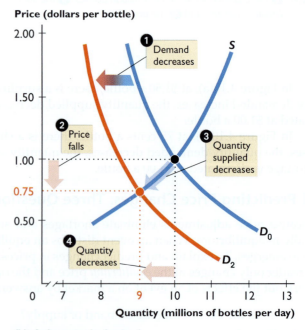

**(b)  A decrease in demand**

❶ A decrease in demand shifts the demand curve leftward to $D_2$ and creates a surplus of water. ❷ The price falls, ❸ the quantity supplied decreases, and ❹ the equilibrium quantity decreases.

# EYE on TUITION
## Why Does Tuition Keep Rising?

Tuition has increased every year since 1980 and at the same time, enrollment has steadily climbed. Figure 1 shows these facts. The points tell us the levels of enrollment (*x*-axis) and tuition (*y*-axis, measured in 2010 dollars) in 1981, 1991, and each year from 2001 to 2010. We can interpret the data using the demand and supply model

More than 4,500 public and private, 2-year and 4-year schools supply college education services and more than 20 million people demand these services.

The law of demand says: Other things remaining the same, if tuition rises, the quantity of college places demanded decreases. The law of supply says: Other things remaining the same, if tuition rises, the quantity of college places supplied increases. Tuition is determined at the level that makes the quantity of college places demanded equal the quantity supplied.

In a given year, other things remain the same, but from one year to the next, some things change. The population has grown, incomes have increased, jobs that require more than a high-school diploma have expanded while jobs for high-school graduates have shrunk, and government subsidized student loans programs have expanded. These changes increase the demand for college education.

Figure 2 illustrates the market for college education that we've just described. In 2001, demand was $D_{01}$ and supply was $S$. The market was in equilibrium with 16 million students enrolled paying an average tuition of $15,000. By 2010, demand had increased to $D_{10}$. At the tuition of 2001, there would be a severe shortage of college places, so tuition rises. In 2010, the market was in equilibrium at a tuition of $21,000 with 21 million students enrolled.

Demand for college places will keep increasing and tuition will keep rising.

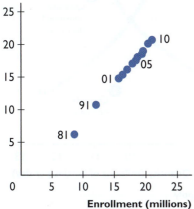

**Figure 1 The Data: A Scatter Diagram**

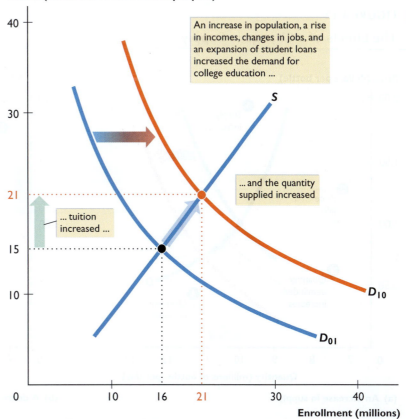

**Figure 2 The Market for College Education**

## ■ Effects of Changes in Supply

You can get more practice working out the effects of another event in the market for bottled water: European water bottlers buy springs and open new plants in the United States.

1. With more suppliers of bottled water, the supply changes.

2. The supply of bottled water *increases,* and the supply curve *shifts rightward.* Figure 4.12(a) shows the shift from $S_0$ to $S_1$.

3. There is now a *surplus* at $1.00 a bottle. The *price falls* to 75 cents a bottle, and the quantity increases to 11 million bottles.

Note that there is *no change in demand*; the fall in price brings an *increase in the quantity demanded*—a movement along the demand curve.

What happens if a drought dries up some springs?

1. The drought is a change in productivity, so the supply of water changes.

2. With fewer springs, the supply of bottled water *decreases,* and the supply curve *shifts leftward.* Figure 4.12(b) shows the shift from to $S_0$ to $S_2$.

3. There is now a *shortage* at $1.00 a bottle. The *price rises* to $1.50 a bottle, and the quantity decreases to 9 million bottles.

Again, there is *no change in demand*; the rise in price brings a *decrease in the quantity demanded*—a movement along the demand curve.

■ **FIGURE 4.12**

## The Effects of a Change in Supply

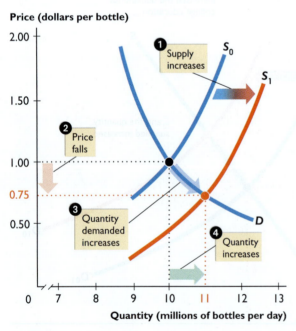

**(a) An increase in supply**

❶ An increase in supply shifts the supply curve rightward to $S_1$ and creates a surplus of water. ❷ The price falls, ❸ the quantity demanded increases, and ❹ the equilibrium quantity increases.

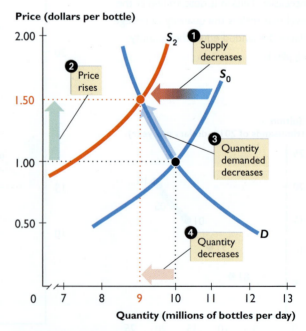

**(b) A decrease in supply**

❶ A decrease in supply shifts the supply curve leftward to $S_2$ and creates a shortage of water. ❷ The price rises, ❸ the quantity demanded decreases, and ❹ the equilibrium quantity decreases.

# EYE on the GLOBAL ECONOMY
## The Market for Solar Panels

Solar panels are produced in the United States, China, Japan, Korea, and Norway and used all over the world. The market for solar panels is a global market.

Figure 1 shows that the price of a solar panel has fallen and the quantity installed each year has increased. We can interpret these facts by using the demand and supply model of the market for solar panels.

The law of demand says: Other things remaining the same, if the price of a solar panel falls, the quantity of

solar panels demanded increases. The law of supply says: Other things remaining the same, if the price of a solar panel falls, the quantity of solar panels supplied decreases. The price of a solar panel is determined at the level that makes the quantity demanded equal the quantity supplied.

In Figure 2, the demand for solar panels is $D$ and in 2009, supply was $S_{09}$. The market was in equilibrium with 11 gigawatts (GW) of units installed at a price of $2 per unit.

Two things are changing in the market for solar panels: The price of silicon from which the panels are made is falling and solar panel technology is getting better. These changes lower the cost of producing solar panels and increase the supply. But they have no effect on the demand.

In Figure 2, supply increased to $S_{11}$ in 2011 and to $S_{13}$ in 2013. The price fell and the quantity of solar panels demanded has increased. The price will keep falling as technology advances.

*Installing solar panels on a home in California*

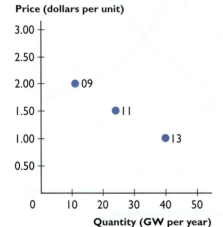

**Figure 1 The Data: A Scatter Diagram**

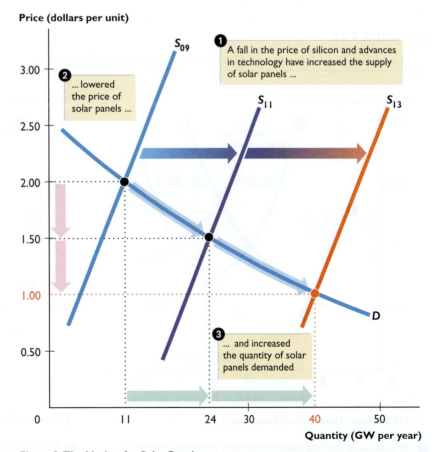

**Figure 2 The Market for Solar Panels**

### ■ Effects of Changes in Both Demand and Supply

When events occur that change *both* demand and supply, you can find the resulting change in the equilibrium price and equilibrium quantity by combining the cases you've just studied.

#### Both Demand and Supply Change in the Same Direction

When demand and supply change in the same direction, the equilibrium quantity changes in that same direction, but we need to know the magnitudes of the changes in demand and supply to predict whether the price rises or falls. If demand increases by more than supply increases, the price rises. But if supply increases by more than demand increases, the price falls.

Figure 4.13(a) shows the case when both demand and supply increase and by the same amount. The equilibrium quantity increases. But because the increase in demand equals the increase in supply, neither a shortage nor a surplus arises so the price doesn't change. A bigger increase in demand would have created a shortage and a rise in the price; a bigger increase in supply would have created a surplus and a fall in the price.

Figure 4.13(b) shows the case when both demand and supply decrease by the same amount. Here the equilibrium quantity decreases and again the price might either rise or fall.

### ■ FIGURE 4.13

The Effects of Change in *Both* Demand and Supply in the *Same Direction*

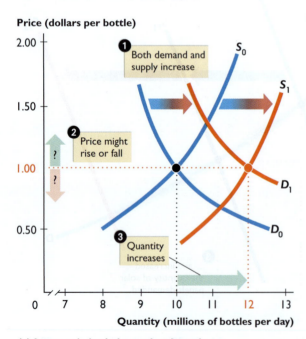

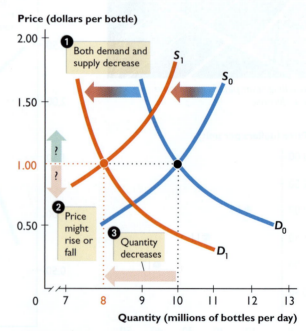

(a) Increase in both demand and supply

(b) Decrease in both demand and supply

❶ An increase in demand shifts the demand curve rightward to $D_1$ and an increase in supply shifts the supply curve rightward to $S_1$.
❷ The price might rise or fall, but ❸ the quantity increases.

❶ A decrease in demand shifts the demand curve leftward to $D_1$ and a decrease in supply shifts the supply curve leftward to $S_1$.
❷ The price might rise or fall, but ❸ the quantity decreases.

## Both Demand and Supply Change in Opposite Directions

When demand and supply change in opposite directions, we can predict how the price changes, but we need to know the magnitudes of the changes in demand and supply to say whether the equilibrium quantity increases or decreases. If demand changes by more than supply, the equilibrium quantity changes in the same direction as the change in demand. But if supply changes by more than demand, the equilibrium quantity changes in the same direction as the change in supply.

Figure 4.14(a) illustrates what happens when demand decreases and supply increases by the same amount. At the initial price, there is a surplus, so the price falls. A decrease in demand decreases the quantity and an increase in supply increases the quantity, so when these changes occur together, we can't say what happens to the quantity unless we know the magnitudes of the changes.

Figure 4.14(b) illustrates what happens when demand increases and supply decreases by the same amount. In this case, at the initial price, there is a shortage, so the price rises. An increase in demand increases the quantity and a decrease in supply decreases the quantity, so again, when these changes occur together, we can't say what happens to the quantity unless we know the magnitudes of the changes in demand and supply.

For all the cases in Figures 4.13 and 4.14 where you "can't say" what happens to price or quantity, draw some examples that go in each direction.

---

■ **FIGURE 4.14**

The Effects of Change in *Both* Demand and Supply in *Opposite Directions*

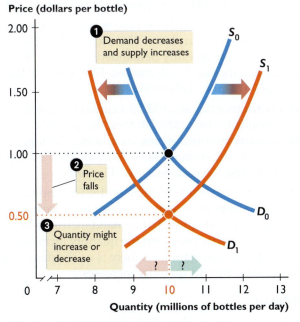

**(a) Decrease in demand and increase in supply**

❶ A decrease in demand shifts the demand curve leftward to $D_1$ and an increase in supply shifts the supply curve rightward to $S_1$.
❷ The price falls, but ❸ the quantity might increase or decrease.

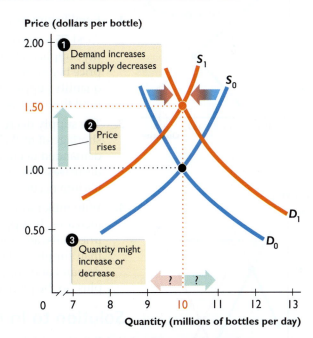

**(b) Increase in demand and decrease in supply**

❶ An increase in demand shifts the demand curve rightward to $D_1$ and a decrease in supply shifts the supply curve leftward to $S_1$.
❷ The price rises, but ❸ the quantity might increase or decrease.

Explain how demand and supply determine price and quantity in a market, and explain the effects of changes in demand and supply.

## Practice Problems

Table 1 sets out the demand and supply schedules for milk.

**TABLE 1**

| Price (dollars per carton) | Quantity demanded | Quantity supplied |
|---|---|---|
| | (cartons per day) | |
| 1.00 | 200 | 110 |
| 1.25 | 175 | 130 |
| 1.50 | 150 | 150 |
| 1.75 | 125 | 170 |
| 2.00 | 100 | 190 |

1. What is the equilibrium price and equilibrium quantity of milk?
2. Describe the situation in the milk market if the price were $1.75 a carton and explain how the market reaches equilibrium.
3. A drought decreases the quantity supplied by 45 cartons a day at each price. What is the new equilibrium and how does the market adjust to it?
4. If milk becomes more popular and better feeds increase milk production, describe how the equilibrium price and quantity of milk will change.

## In the News

**After wild weather, higher food prices on horizon**
After heavy rain this year, the corn harvest will be less than expected while the demand for corn will continue to increase. Food prices will continue to rise.
Source: npr, June 9, 2011

Using the demand and supply model, explain why food prices are expected to rise.

## Solutions to Practice Problems

1. Equilibrium price is $1.50 a carton; equilibrium quantity is 150 cartons a day.
2. At $1.75 a carton, the quantity demanded (125 cartons) is less than the quantity supplied (170 cartons), so there is a surplus of 45 cartons a day. The price begins to fall, and as it does, the quantity demanded increases, the quantity supplied decreases, and the surplus decreases. The price will fall until the surplus is eliminated. The price falls to $1.50 a carton.
3. The supply decreases by 45 cartons a day so at $1.50 a carton there is a shortage of milk. The price begins to rise, and as it does, the quantity demanded decreases, the quantity supplied increases, and the shortage decreases. The price will rise until the shortage is eliminated. The new equilibrium occurs at $1.75 a carton and 125 cartons a day (Figure 1).
4. With milk more popular, demand increases. With better feeds, supply increases. If supply increases by more than demand, a surplus arises. The price falls, and the quantity increases (Figure 2). If demand increases by more than supply, a shortage arises. The price rises, and the quantity increases. If demand and supply increase by the same amount, there is no shortage or surplus, so the price does not change, but the quantity increases.

## Solution to In the News

A fall in the corn harvest will decrease the supply of corn and shift the supply curve of corn leftward. The increase in the demand for corn will shift the demand curve rightward. The price of corn will rise. The higher price of corn will decrease the supply of food made from corn and raise the price of this food.

**FIGURE 1**

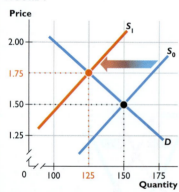

**FIGURE 2**

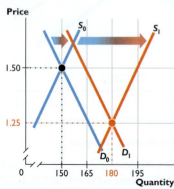

# CHAPTER SUMMARY

## Key Points

**1. Distinguish between quantity demanded and demand, and explain what determines demand.**

- Other things remaining the same, the quantity demanded increases as the price falls and decreases as the price rises—the law of demand.
- The demand for a good is influenced by the prices of related goods, expected future prices, income, expected future income and credit, the number of buyers, and preferences. A change in any of these influences changes the demand for the good.

**2. Distinguish between quantity supplied and supply, and explain what determines supply.**

- Other things remaining the same, the quantity supplied increases as the price rises and decreases as the price falls—the law of supply.
- The supply of a good is influenced by the prices of related goods, prices of resources and other inputs, expected future prices, the number of sellers, and productivity. A change in any of these influences changes the supply of the good.

**3. Explain how demand and supply determine price and quantity in a market, and explain the effects of changes in demand and supply.**

- The law of market forces brings market equilibrium—the equilibrium price and equilibrium quantity at which buyers and sellers trade.
- The price adjusts to maintain market equilibrium—to keep the quantity demanded equal to the quantity supplied. A surplus brings a fall in the price to restore market equilibrium; a shortage brings a rise in the price to restore market equilibrium.
- Market equilibrium responds to changes in demand and supply. An increase in demand increases both the price and the quantity; a decrease in demand decreases both the price and the quantity. An increase in supply increases the quantity but decreases the price; and a decrease in supply decreases the quantity but increases the price.

## Key Terms

Change in demand, 124
Change in the quantity demanded, 126
Change in the quantity supplied, 133
Change in supply, 131
Complement, 124
Complement in production, 131
Demand, 121
Demand curve, 122

Demand schedule, 122
Equilibrium price, 136
Equilibrium quantity, 136
Inferior good, 125
Law of demand, 121
Law of market forces, 136
Law of supply, 128
Market equilibrium, 136

Normal good, 125
Quantity demanded, 121
Quantity supplied, 128
Substitute, 124
Substitute in production, 131
Supply, 128
Supply curve, 129
Supply schedule, 129

# CHAPTER CHECKPOINT

## Study Plan Problems and Applications

1. Explain how each of the following events changes the demand for or supply of air travel.
   - Airfares tumble, while long-distance bus fares don't change.
   - The price of jet fuel rises.
   - Airlines reduce the number of flights each day.
   - People expect airfares to increase next summer.
   - The price of train travel falls.
   - The price of a pound of air cargo increases.

Use the laws of demand and supply to explain whether the statements in Problems **2** and **3** are true or false. In your explanation, distinguish between a change in demand and a change in the quantity demanded and between a change in supply and a change in the quantity supplied.

2. The United States does not allow oranges from Brazil (the world's largest producer of oranges) to enter the United States. If Brazilian oranges were sold in the United States, oranges and orange juice would be cheaper.

3. If the price of frozen yogurt falls, the quantity of ice cream consumed will decrease and the price of ice cream will rise.

4. Table 1 shows the demand and supply schedules for running shoes. What is the market equilibrium? If the price is $70 a pair, describe the situation in the market. Explain how market equilibrium is restored. If a rise in income increases the demand for running shoes by 100 pairs a day at each price, explain how the market adjusts to its new equilibrium.

5. "As more people buy fuel-efficient hybrid cars, the demand for gasoline will decrease and the price of gasoline will fall. The fall in the price of gasoline will decrease the supply of gasoline." Is this statement true? Explain.

6. **OPEC deadlocked on oil production hike**
   Oil prices exceeded the $100-a-barrel mark Wednesday after OPEC said it could not reach an agreement about raising crude production.
   Source: CNN Money, June 8, 2011

   Suppose that OPEC members had agreed to increase production. Use a graph of the oil market to show the effect of this decision on the market equilibrium.

Use the following information to work Problems **7** and **8**.

**Pricier bread and cereal. Coming soon?**
Wheat and corn prices surged last week and could hit the items in your grocery basket by mid-summer. It's a case of two extremes: drought in parts of the United States and in Europe have sparked fears of a supply crunch of wheat, while supplies of corn are being threatened by flooding and heavy rain in the Midwest.
Source: CNN Money, May 19, 2011

7. Explain why the drought will lead to a rise in the price of bread.

8. Use graphs to show why the price of corn has risen and show its effect on the price of cereals.

9. Read *Eye on Tuition* on p. 139 and explain how we know that tuition has risen because the demand for college places has increased and not because the supply has decreased?

**TABLE 1**

| Price (dollars per pair) | Quantity demanded | Quantity supplied |
|---|---|---|
| | (pairs per day) | |
| 60 | 1,000 | 400 |
| 70 | 900 | 500 |
| 80 | 800 | 600 |
| 90 | 700 | 700 |
| 100 | 600 | 800 |
| 110 | 500 | 900 |

## Instructor Assignable Problems and Applications

1. Why can we be confident that the market for college education is competitive and that an increase in demand rather than the greed of college administrators is the reason for the ongoing rise in tuition?

2. What is the effect on the equilibrium price and equilibrium quantity of orange juice if the price of apple juice decreases and the wage rate paid to orange grove workers increases?

3. What is the effect on the equilibrium in the orange juice market if orange juice becomes more popular and a cheaper robot is used to pick oranges?

4. **Rain falls on wheat parade**

   The price of wheat has fallen from $9 a bushel to $7 a bushel in the past seven months as rain and snow fell on the southern states.

   Source: *The Wall Street Journal*, February 12, 2013

   Explain the effect of the fall in the wheat price on the market for cereals.

Table 1 shows the demand and supply schedules for boxes of chocolates in an average week. Use this information to work Problems **5** and **6**.

5. If the price of chocolates is $17.00 a box, describe the situation in the market. Explain how market equilibrium is restored.

6. During Valentine's week, more people buy chocolates and chocolatiers offer their chocolates in special red boxes, which cost more to produce than the everyday box. Set out the three-step process of analysis and show on a graph the adjustment process to the new equilibrium. Describe the changes in the equilibrium price and the equilibrium quantity.

**TABLE 1**

| Price (dollars per box) | Quantity demanded | Quantity supplied |
|---|---|---|
| | (boxes per day) | |
| 13.00 | 1,200 | |
| 14.00 | 1,500 | 1,300 |
| 15.00 | 1,400 | 1,400 |
| 16.00 | 1,300 | 1,500 |
| 17.00 | 1,200 | 1,600 |
| 18.00 | 1,100 | 1,700 |

7. After a severe bout of foreclosures and defaults on home loans, banks made it harder for people to borrow. How does this change influence:
   - The demand for new homes?
   - The supply of new homes?
   - The price of new homes?

   Illustrate your answer with a graphical analysis.

8. **Alabama food prices jump in May**

   Alabama Farmers Federation announced that food prices in May will increase. In previous unprofitable years, farmers reduced their herds with the result that in 2009 meat production will fall. Bacon is expected to rise by 32 cents a pound to $4.18 and steaks by 57 cents to $8.41 a pound.

   Source: *The Birmingham News*, May 21, 2009

   Explain why the reduction of herds will lead to a rise in meat prices today. Draw a graph to illustrate.

9. "As more people buy cell phones, the demand for cell-phone service increases and the price of cell service falls, which decreases the supply of cell service." Is this statement true or false? Explain.

10. **Steel output set for historic drop**

    Steel producers expect to cut output by 10 percent in response to cancelled orders from construction companies and car and appliance producers.

    Source: *Financial Times*, December 28, 2008

    Explain how the cancellation of orders change the market for steel. What happens to the equilibrium price of steel?

# Critical Thinking Discussion Questions

1. **BMW at $213,000 is Singapore way to encourage train rides**

   The price of a BMW 328i sedan in Singapore is six times its price in the United States. The Singaporean government wants a larger percentage of the population to use the bus or train.

   Source: Bloomberg, January 9, 2014

   How does the high price of a car in Singapore encourage more people to travel by train?
   Answer by explaining the effects of the high price of a car on the demand for cars and train travel, on the quantity of cars and train travel demanded, and on the equilibrium quantities of cars and train travel.

2. **Rising onion prices bring India woes home**

   Indians normally consume more than 15 million tons of onions a year but severe drought has brought a sharp rise in the price of onions, leading shoppers to cut back.

   Source: CNN Money, September 12, 2013

   Why, when shoppers cut back on buying onions, does the demand for onions not change?

   Why does a drought lead to a rise in the price of onions?

   Provide a detailed step-by-step account of the process.

   How would you expect the rise in the price of onions to affect the demand for chicken and tomatoes?

   How would you expect the rise in the price of onions to affect the supply of chicken and tomatoes?

   How would you expect the rise in the price of onions to affect the prices and quantities of chicken and tomatoes?

3. **Selling your old iPhone? Do it now.**

   Old iPhones hold their price well, but the resale price of an old iPhone drops right before Apple announces a new version. Waiting until the actual announcement is too late. And the price keeps on dropping for weeks after the announcement.

   Source: CNN Money, August 22, 2013

   Does the anticipation of an announcement of a new iPhone change the demand for iPhones or the supply of iPhones, or both demand and supply, and in which direction?

   Why is waiting for the actual announcement leaving it to too late?

   Why does the price of an old iPhone keep falling after the announcement of a new model?

What do you do when the price of gasoline rises?

# Elasticities of Demand and Supply

5

**When you have completed your study of this chapter, you will be able to**

**1** Define and calculate the price elasticity of demand, and explain the factors that influence it.

**2** Define and calculate the price elasticity of supply, and explain the factors that influence it.

**3** Define the cross elasticity of demand and the income elasticity of demand, and explain the factors that influence them.

**Price elasticity of demand**
A measure of the responsiveness of the quantity demanded of a good to a change in its price when all other influences on buyers' plans remain the same.

## 5.1   THE PRICE ELASTICITY OF DEMAND

You know that if the supply of coffee decreases, the price of coffee rises and the equilibrium quantity of coffee decreases. But to predict by how much the price and quantity change, we need to know more about the demand for coffee than the fact that its curve slopes downward. We need to know how responsive the quantity demanded is to a price change. Elasticity provides this information.

The **price elasticity of demand** is a measure of the responsiveness of the quantity demanded of a good to a change in its price when all other influences on buyers' plans remain the same.

To determine the price elasticity of demand, we compare the percentage change in the quantity demanded with the percentage change in price.

### ■ Percentage Change in Price

If Starbucks changes its price of a latte by $2, the percentage change in price depends on whether the price has gone up or down.

#### A Rise in Price

Suppose that Starbucks raises the price of a latte from $3 to $5 a cup. The percentage change is calculated as the change in price divided by the initial price, all multiplied by 100. The formula for the percentage change is

$$\text{Percentage change in price} = \left( \frac{\text{New price} - \text{Initial price}}{\text{Initial price}} \right) \times 100.$$

In this example, the initial price is $3 and the new price is $5, so

$$\text{Percentage change in price} = \left( \frac{\$5 - \$3}{\$3} \right) \times 100 = \left( \frac{\$2}{\$3} \right) \times 100 = 66.67 \text{ percent}.$$

#### A Fall in Price

Now suppose that Starbucks cuts the price of a latte from $5 to $3 a cup. The initial price is now $5 and the new price is $3, so the percentage change in price is

$$\text{Percentage change in price} = \left( \frac{\$3 - \$5}{\$5} \right) \times 100 = \left( \frac{-\$2}{\$5} \right) \times 100 = -40 \text{ percent}.$$

The same price change, $2 a cup, over the same interval, between $3 and $5 a cup, is a different absolute percentage change—66.67 percent if the price rises and 40 percent if the price falls.

Because elasticity compares the percentage change in the quantity demanded with the percentage change in price, we need a measure of percentage change that does not depend on the direction of the price change. The measure that economists use is called the *midpoint method.*

#### The Midpoint Method

To calculate the percentage change in price using the midpoint method, we divide the change in the price by the *average price*—the *average* of the new price and the initial price—and then multiply by 100. The average price is at the midpoint between the initial and the new price, hence the name *midpoint method.*

The formula for the percentage change using the midpoint method is

$$\text{Percentage change in price} = \left( \frac{\text{New price} - \text{Initial price}}{(\text{New price} + \text{Initial price}) \div 2} \right) \times 100.$$

In this formula, the numerator, (New price − Initial Price) is the same as before. The denominator, (New price + Initial price) ÷ 2, is the average of the new price and the initial price.

To calculate the percentage change in the price of a Starbucks latte using the midpoint method, put $5 for new price and $3 for initial price in the formula:

$$\begin{aligned} \text{Percentage} \atop \text{change in price} &= \left( \frac{\$5 - \$3}{(\$5 + \$3) \div 2} \right) \times 100 = \left( \frac{\$2}{\$8 \div 2} \right) \times 100 \\[2mm] &= \left( \frac{\$2}{\$4} \right) \times 100 = 50 \text{ percent.} \end{aligned}$$

Because the average price is the same regardless of whether the price rises or falls, the percentage change in price calculated by the midpoint method is the same (magnitude) for a price rise and a price fall. In this example, it is 50 percent.

## ■ Percentage Change in Quantity Demanded

Suppose that when the price of a latte rises from $3 to $5 a cup, the quantity demanded decreases from 15 cups to 5 cups an hour. The percentage change in the quantity demanded using the midpoint method is

$$\begin{aligned} \text{Percentage change} \atop \text{in quantity} &= \left( \frac{\text{New quantity} - \text{Initial quantity}}{(\text{New quantity} + \text{Initial quantity}) \div 2} \right) \times 100 \\[2mm] &= \left( \frac{5 - 15}{(5 + 15) \div 2} \right) \times 100 = \left( \frac{-10}{20 \div 2} \right) \times 100 \\[2mm] &= \left( \frac{-10}{10} \right) \times 100 = -100 \text{ percent.} \end{aligned}$$

When the price of a good *rises*, the quantity demanded of it *decreases*—a *positive* change in price brings a *negative* change in the quantity demanded. Similarly, when the price of a good *falls*, the quantity demanded of it *increases*—this time a *negative* change in price brings a *positive* change in the quantity demanded.

To compare the percentage changes in price and quantity demanded, we use the magnitudes of the percentage changes and we ignore the minus sign.

## ■ Comparing the Percentage Changes in Price and Quantity

To determine the responsiveness of the quantity of Starbucks lattes demanded to its price, we compare the two percentage changes we've just calculated. The percentage change in quantity demanded is 100 and the percentage change in price is 50. So the percentage change in the quantity of Starbucks lattes demanded is greater than the percentage change in its price. But it might have been equal or less. Let's see how we classify degrees of responsiveness.

### ■ Elastic and Inelastic Demand

If we collected data on the prices and quantities of Starbucks lattes and a number of other goods and services and we were careful to check that other things had remained the same, we could calculate lots of percentage changes in prices and quantities demanded. We could then classify the demands by their degree of responsiveness of quantity demanded to price.

Our calculations would fall into three groups: The percentage change in the quantity demanded might exceed the percentage change in price (as in the example of Starbucks lattes), be equal to the percentage change in price, or be less than the percentage change in price. Each of these three possibilities defines three ranges for the price elasticity of demand:

**Elastic demand**
When the percentage change in the quantity demanded exceeds the percentage change in price.

**Unit elastic demand**
When the percentage change in the quantity demanded equals the percentage change in price.

**Inelastic demand**
When the percentage change in the quantity demanded is less than the percentage change in price.

**Perfectly elastic demand**
When the quantity demanded changes by a very large percentage in response to an almost zero percentage change in price.

**Perfectly inelastic demand**
When the percentage change in the quantity demanded is zero for any percentage change in the price.

- When the percentage change in the quantity demanded exceeds the percentage change in price, demand is **elastic.**
- When the percentage change in the quantity demanded equals the percentage change in price, demand is **unit elastic.**
- When the percentage change in the quantity demanded is less than the percentage change in price, demand is **inelastic.**

Figure 5.1 shows the different types of demand curves that illustrate the range of possible price elasticities of demand. Part (a) shows an extreme case of an elastic demand called a **perfectly elastic demand**—an almost zero percentage change in the price brings a very large percentage change in the quantity demanded. Consumers are willing to buy any quantity of the good at a given price but none at a higher price. Part (b) shows an elastic demand—the percentage change in the quantity demanded exceeds the percentage change in price. Part (c) shows a unit elastic demand—the percentage change in the quantity demanded equals the percentage change in price. Part (d) shows an inelastic demand—the percentage change in the quantity demanded is less than the percentage change in price. Finally, part (e) shows an extreme case of an inelastic demand called a **perfectly inelastic demand**—the percentage change in the quantity demanded is zero for any percentage change in price.

### ■ Influences on the Price Elasticity of Demand

What makes the demand for some things elastic and the demand for others inelastic? The influences on the price elasticity of demand fall into two groups:

- Availability of substitutes
- Proportion of income spent

#### Availability of Substitutes

The demand for a good is elastic if a substitute for it is easy to find. Soft drink containers can be made of either aluminum or plastic and it doesn't matter which, so the demand for aluminum is elastic.

The demand for a good is inelastic if a substitute for it is hard to find. Oil has poor substitutes (imagine a coal-fueled car), so the demand for oil is inelastic.

Three main factors influence the ability to find a substitute for a good: whether the good is a luxury or a necessity, how narrowly the good is defined, and the amount of time available to find a substitute for it.

## FIGURE 5.1

### The Range of Price Elasticities of Demand

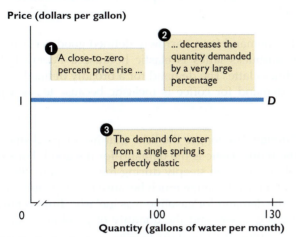

**(a) Perfectly elastic demand**

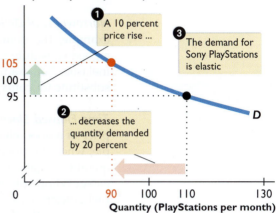

**(b) Elastic demand**

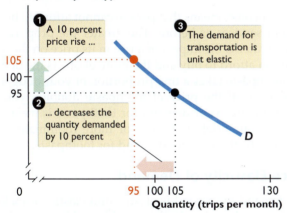

**(c) Unit elastic demand**

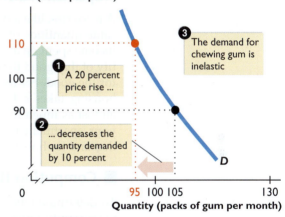

**(d) Inelastic demand**

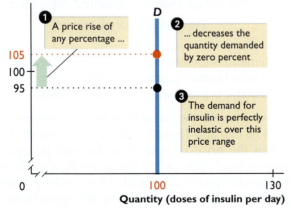

**(e) Perfectly inelastic demand**

❶A price rise brings ❷ a decrease in the quantity demanded. The relationship between the percentage change in the quantity demanded and the percentage change in price determines ❸ the price elasticity of demand, which ranges from perfectly elastic (part a) to perfectly inelastic (part e).

*Luxury Versus Necessity* We call goods such as food and housing *necessities* and goods such as exotic vacations *luxuries.* A necessity has poor substitutes—you must eat—so the demand for a necessity is inelastic. A luxury has many substitutes—you don't absolutely have to go to the Galapagos Islands this summer—so the demand for a luxury is elastic.

*Narrowness of Definition* The demand for a narrowly defined good is elastic. For example, the demand for Starbucks lattes is elastic because a Panera latte is a good substitute for a Starbucks latte. The demand for a broadly defined good is inelastic. For example, the demand for coffee is inelastic because tea is a poor substitute for coffee.

*Time Elapsed Since Price Change* The longer the time that has elapsed since the price of a good changed, the more elastic is the demand for the good. For example, when the price of gasoline increased steeply during the 1970s and 1980s, the quantity of gasoline demanded didn't change much because many people owned gas-guzzling automobiles—the demand for gasoline was inelastic. But eventually, fuel-efficient cars replaced gas guzzlers and the quantity of gasoline demanded decreased—the demand for gasoline became more elastic.

### Proportion of Income Spent

A price rise, like a decrease in income, means that people cannot afford to buy the same quantities of goods and services as before. The greater the proportion of income spent on a good, the greater is the impact of a rise in its price on the quantity of that good that people can afford to buy and the more elastic is the demand for the good. For example, toothpaste takes a tiny proportion of your budget and housing takes a large proportion. If the price of toothpaste doubles, you buy almost as much toothpaste as before. Your demand for toothpaste is inelastic. If your apartment rent doubles, you shriek and look for more roommates. Your demand for housing is more elastic than is your demand for toothpaste.

### ■ Computing the Price Elasticity of Demand

To determine whether the demand for a good is elastic, unit elastic, or inelastic, we compute a numerical value for the price elasticity of demand by using the following formula:

$$\text{Price elasticity of demand} = \frac{\text{Percentage change in quantity demanded}}{\text{Percentage change in price}}.$$

- If the price elasticity of demand is greater than 1, demand is elastic.
- If the price elasticity of demand equals 1, demand is unit elastic.
- If the price elasticity of demand is less than 1, demand is inelastic.

Figure 5.2 illustrates and summarizes the calculation for the Starbucks latte example. Initially, the price is $3 a cup and 15 cups an hour are demanded—the initial point in the figure. Then the price rises to $5 a cup and the quantity demanded decreases to 5 cups an hour—the new point in the figure. The price rises by $2 a cup and the average (midpoint) price is $4 a cup, so the percentage change in price is 50. The quantity demanded decreases by 10 cups an hour and the average (midpoint) quantity is 10 cups an hour, so the percentage change in quantity demanded is 100.

**FIGURE 5.2**

Price Elasticity of Demand Calculation

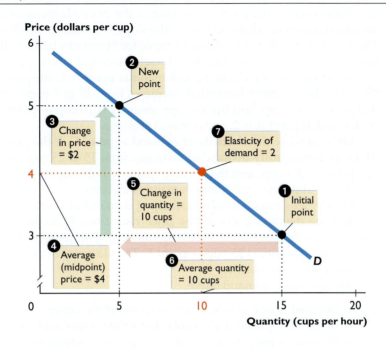

**1** At the initial point, the price is $3 a cup and the quantity demanded is 15 cups an hour.

**2** At the new point, the price is $5 a cup and the quantity demanded is 5 cups an hour.

**3** The change in price is $2 and **4** the average price is $4, so the percentage change in price equals ($2 ÷ $4) × 100, which is 50 percent.

**5** The change in the quantity demanded is 10 cups and **6** the average quantity demanded is 10 cups, so the percentage change in quantity demanded equals (10 cups ÷ 10 cups) × 100, which is 100 percent.

**7** The price elasticity of demand equals 100 percent ÷ 50 percent, which is 2.

Using the above formula, you can see that the price elasticity of demand for Starbucks lattes is

$$\text{Price elasticity of demand} = \frac{100 \text{ percent}}{50 \text{ percent}} = 2.$$

The price elasticity of demand is 2 at the midpoint between the initial price and the new price on the demand curve. Over this price range, the demand for Starbucks lattes is elastic.

## ■ Interpreting the Price Elasticity of Demand Number

The number we've just calculated for Starbucks lattes is only an example. We don't have real data on the price and quantity. But suppose we did have real data and we discovered that the price elasticity of demand for Starbucks lattes is 2. What does this number tell us?

It tells us three main things:

1.  The demand for Starbucks lattes is elastic. Being elastic, the good has plenty of convenient substitutes (such as other brands of latte) and takes only a small proportion of buyers' incomes.

2.  Starbucks must be careful not to charge too high a price for its latte. Pushing the price up brings in more revenue per cup but wipes out a lot of potential business.

3.  The flip side of the second point: Even a slightly lower price could create a lot of potential business and end up bringing in more revenue.

## ■ Elasticity Along a Linear Demand Curve

Slope measures responsiveness. But elasticity is *not* the same as *slope*. You can see the distinction most clearly by looking at the price elasticity of demand along a linear (straight-line) demand curve. The slope is constant, but the elasticity varies. Figure 5.3 shows the same demand curve for Starbucks lattes as that in Figure 5.2 but with the axes extended to show lower prices and larger quantities demanded.

Let's calculate the elasticity of demand at point *A*. If the price rises from $3 to $5 a cup, the quantity demanded decreases from 15 to 5 cups an hour. The average price is $4 a cup, and the average quantity is 10 cups—point *A*. The elasticity of demand at point *A* is 2, and demand is elastic.

Let's calculate the elasticity of demand at point *C*. If the price falls from $3 to $1 a cup, the quantity demanded increases from 15 to 25 cups an hour. The average price is $2 a cup, and the average quantity is 20 cups—point *C*. The elasticity of demand at point *C* is 0.5, and demand is inelastic.

Finally, let's calculate the elasticity of demand at point *B*, which is the midpoint of the demand curve. If the price rises from $2 to $4 a cup, the quantity demanded decreases from 20 to 10 cups an hour. The average price is $3 a cup, and the average quantity is 15 cups—point *B*. The elasticity of demand at point *B* is 1, and demand is unit elastic.

Along a linear demand curve,

- Demand is unit elastic at the midpoint of the curve.
- Demand is elastic at all points above the midpoint of the curve.
- Demand is inelastic at all points below the midpoint of the curve.

■ **FIGURE 5.3**

Elasticity Along a Linear Demand Curve

On a linear demand curve, the slope is constant but the elasticity decreases as the price falls and the quantity demanded increases.

❶ At point A, demand is elastic.

❷ At point B, which is the midpoint of the demand curve, demand is unit elastic.

❸ At point C, demand is inelastic.

Demand is elastic at all points above the midpoint of the demand curve and inelastic at all points below the midpoint of the demand curve.

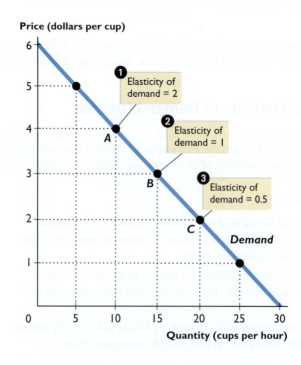

# EYE on the GLOBAL ECONOMY
## Price Elasticities of Demand

A rich American student is casual about her food. It costs only a few dollars a day, and she's going to have her burger, even at double the price. But a poor Tanzanian boy takes his food with deadly seriousness. He has a tough time getting, preparing, and even defending his food. A rise in the price of food means that he must cut back and eat even less.

The figure shows the percentage of income spent on food and the price elasticity of demand for food in ten countries. The larger the proportion of income spent on food, the larger is the price elasticity of demand for food.

As the low-income countries become richer, the proportion of income they spend on food will decrease and their demand for food will become more inelastic. Consequently, the world's demand for food will become more inelastic.

Harvests fluctuate and bring fluctuations in the price of food. As the world demand for food becomes

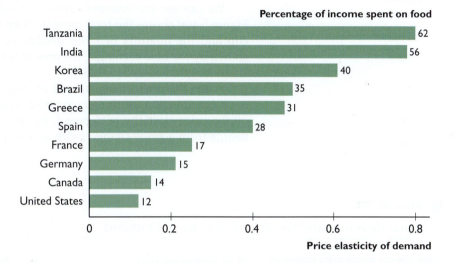

**Percentage of income spent on food**

| Country | Price elasticity of demand |
|---|---|
| Tanzania | 62 |
| India | 56 |
| Korea | 40 |
| Brazil | 35 |
| Greece | 31 |
| Spain | 28 |
| France | 17 |
| Germany | 15 |
| Canada | 14 |
| United States | 12 |

**Price elasticity of demand**

more and more inelastic, the fluctuations in the prices of food items will become larger.

The table shows a few real-world price elasticities of demand. The numbers in the table range from 1.52 for metals to 0.12 for food. Metals have good substitutes, such as plastics, while food has virtually no substitutes. As we move down the list of items, they have

fewer good substitutes and are more likely to be regarded as necessities.

## Some Price Elasticities of Demand

| Good or Service | Elasticity |
|---|---|
| **Elastic Demand** | |
| Metals | 1.52 |
| Electrical engineering products | 1.39 |
| Mechanical engineering products | 1.30 |
| Furniture | 1.26 |
| Motor vehicles | 1.14 |
| Instrument engineering products | 1.10 |
| Professional services | 1.09 |
| Transportation services | 1.03 |
| **Inelastic Demand** | |
| Gas, electricity, and water | 0.92 |
| Oil | 0.91 |
| Chemicals | 0.89 |
| Beverages (all types) | 0.78 |
| Clothing | 0.64 |
| Tobacco | 0.61 |
| Banking and insurance services | 0.56 |
| Housing services | 0.55 |
| Agricultural and fish products | 0.42 |
| Books, magazines, and newspapers | 0.34 |
| Food | 0.12 |

SOURCES OF DATA: See page C1.

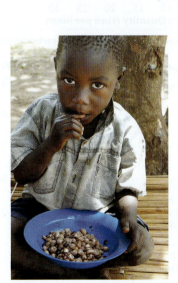

## ■ Total Revenue and the Price Elasticity of Demand

**Total revenue**
The amount spent on a good and received by its seller and equals the price of the good multiplied by the quantity sold.

**Total revenue** is the amount spent on a good and received by its sellers and equals the price of the good multiplied by the quantity of the good sold. For example, suppose that the price of a Starbucks latte is $3 and that 15 cups an hour are sold. Then total revenue is $3 a cup multiplied by 15 cups an hour, which equals $45 an hour.

We can use the demand curve for Starbucks lattes to illustrate total revenue. Figure 5.4(a) shows the total revenue from the sale of lattes when the price is $3 a cup and the quantity of lattes demanded is 15 cups an hour. Total revenue is shown by the blue rectangle, the area of which equals $3, its height, multiplied by 15, its length, which equals $45.

When the price changes, total revenue can change in the same direction, the opposite direction, or remain constant. Which of these outcomes occurs depends on the price elasticity of demand. By observing the change in total revenue that results from a price change (with all other influences on the quantity remaining

## ■ FIGURE 5.4

### Total Revenue and the Price Elasticity of Demand

Total revenue equals price multiplied by quantity. In part (a), when the price is $3 a cup, the quantity demanded is 15 cups an hour and total revenue equals $45 an hour. When the price rises to $5 a cup, the quantity demanded decreases to 5 cups an hour and total revenue decreases to $25 an hour. Demand for Starbucks lattes is elastic.

In part (b), when the price is $50 a book, the quantity demanded is 5 million books a year and total revenue equals $250 million a year. When the price rises to $75 a book, the quantity demanded decreases to 4 million books a year and total revenue increases to $300 million a year. Demand for textbooks is inelastic.

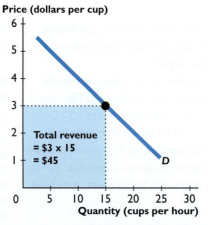
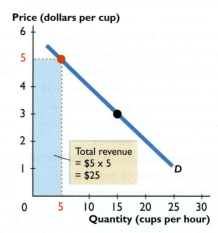

**(a) Total revenue and elastic demand: Starbucks lattes**

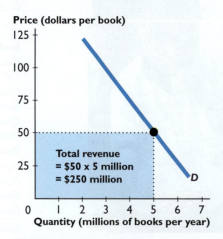
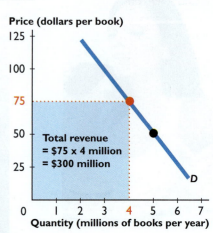

**(b) Total revenue and inelastic demand: textbooks**

unchanged), we can estimate the price elasticity of demand. This method of estimating the price elasticity of demand is called the **total revenue test.**

If demand is elastic, a given percentage rise in price brings a larger percentage decrease in the quantity demanded, so total revenue—price multiplied by quantity—decreases. Figure 5.4(a) shows this outcome. When the price of a latte is $3, the quantity demanded is 15 cups an hour and total revenue is $45 ($3 × 15). If the price of a latte rises to $5, the quantity demanded decreases to 5 cups an hour and total revenue *decreases* to $25 ($5 × 5).

If demand is inelastic, a given percentage rise in price brings a smaller percentage decrease in the quantity demanded, so total revenue increases. Figure 5.4(b) shows this outcome. When the price of a textbook is $50, the quantity demanded is 5 million textbooks a year and total revenue is $250 million ($50 × 5 million). If the price of a textbook rises to $75, the quantity demanded decreases to 4 million textbooks a year and total revenue *increases* to $300 million ($75 × 4 million).

The relationship between the price elasticity of demand and total revenue is

- If price and total revenue change in opposite directions, demand is elastic.
- If a price change leaves total revenue unchanged, demand is unit elastic.
- If price and total revenue change in the same direction, demand is inelastic.

**Total revenue test**

A method of estimating the price elasticity of demand by observing the change in total revenue that results from a price change (with all other influences on the quantity sold remaining unchanged).

# EYE on the PRICE OF GASOLINE

## What Do You Do When the Price of Gasoline Rises?

If you are like most people, you complain when the price of gasoline rises, but you don't cut back very much on the quantity you purchase.

University of London economists Phil Goodwin, Joyce Dargay, and Mark Hanly studied the effects of a hike in the price of gasoline on the quantity of gasoline demanded and on the volume of road traffic.

By using data for the United States and a large number of other countries, they estimated that a 10 percent rise in the price of gasoline decreases the quantity of gasoline used by 2.5 percent within one year and by 6 percent after five years.

### Price Elasticity of Demand

We can translate these numbers into price elasticities of demand for gasoline.

The short-run (up to one year) price elasticity of demand is 2.5 percent divided by 10 percent, which equals 0.25. The long-run (after five years) price elasticity of demand is 6 percent divided by 10 percent, which equals 0.6. Because these price elasticities are less than one, the demand for gasoline is inelastic.

When the price of gasoline rises, the quantity of gasoline demanded decreases but the amount spent on gasoline increases.

The effect of a rise in the price of gasoline on the volume of traffic is smaller than on the quantity of gasoline used.

A rise of 10 percent in the price of gasoline decreases the volume of traffic by only 1 percent within one year and by 3 percent after five years.

How can the volume of traffic fall by less than the quantity of gasoline used? The answer is by switching to smaller, more fuel-efficient vehicles.

The price elasticity of demand for gasoline is low—the demand for gasoline is inelastic—because gasoline has poor substitutes, but it does have one substitute—a smaller vehicle.

## ■ Applications of the Price Elasticity of Demand

Does a frost in Florida bring a massive or a modest rise in the price of oranges? And does a smaller orange crop mean bad news or good news for orange growers? Knowledge of the price elasticity of demand for oranges enables us to answer these questions.

### Orange Prices and Total Revenue

Economists have estimated the price elasticity of demand for agricultural products to be about 0.4—an inelastic demand. If this number applies to the demand for oranges, then

$$\text{Price elasticity of demand} = 0.4 = \frac{\text{Percentage change in quantity demanded}}{\text{Percentage change in price}}.$$

If supply changes and demand doesn't, the percentage change in the quantity demanded equals the percentage change in the equilibrium quantity. So if a frost in Florida decreases the orange harvest and decreases the equilibrium quantity of oranges by 1 percent, the price of oranges will rise by 2.5 percent. The percentage change in the quantity demanded (1 percent) divided by the percentage change in price (2.5 percent) equals the price elasticity of demand (0.4).

So the answer to the first question is that when the frost strikes, the price of oranges will rise by a larger percentage than the percentage decrease in the quantity of oranges. But what happens to the total revenue of the orange growers?

The answer is again provided by knowledge of the price elasticity of demand. Because the price rises by a larger percentage than the percentage decrease in quantity, total revenue increases. A frost is bad news for consumers and those growers who lose their crops, but good news for growers who escape the frost.

*A Florida frost is bad news for buyers of orange juice and for growers who lose their crops, but good news for growers who escape the frost.*

### Addiction and Elasticity

We can gain important insights that might help to design potentially effective policies for dealing with addiction to drugs, whether legal (such as tobacco and alcohol) or illegal (such as crack cocaine or heroin). Nonusers' demand for addictive substances is elastic. A moderately higher price leads to a substantially smaller number of people trying a drug and so exposing themselves to the possibility of becoming addicted to it. But the existing users' demand for addictive substances is inelastic. Even a substantial price rise brings only a modest decrease in the quantity demanded.

These facts about the price elasticity of demand mean that high taxes on cigarettes and alcohol limit the number of young people who become habitual users of these products, but high taxes have only a modest effect on the quantities consumed by established users.

Similarly, effective policing of imports of an illegal drug that limits its supply leads to a large price rise and a substantial decrease in the number of new users but only a small decrease in the quantity consumed by addicts. Expenditure on the drug by addicts increases. Further, because many drug addicts finance their purchases with crime, the amount of theft and burglary increases.

Because the price elasticity of demand for drugs is low for addicts, any successful policy to decrease drug use will be one that focuses on the demand for drugs and attempts to change preferences through rehabilitation programs.

*Cracking down on imports of illegal drugs limits supply, which leads to a large price increase. But it also increases the expenditure on drugs by addicts and increases the amount of crime that finances addiction.*

CHECKPOINT 5.1

**Define and calculate the price elasticity of demand, and explain the factors that influence it.**

## Practice Problems

When the price of a good increased by 10 percent, the quantity demanded of it decreased by 2 percent.

1.  Is the demand for this good elastic, unit elastic, or inelastic?
2.  Does this good have close substitutes or poor substitutes? Is this good more likely to be a necessity or a luxury and to be narrowly or broadly defined? Why?
3.  Calculate the price elasticity of demand for this good; explain how the total revenue from the sale of the good has changed; and explain which of the following goods this good is most likely to be: orange juice, bread, toothpaste, theater tickets, clothing, blue jeans, or Super Bowl tickets.

## In the News

**Music giant chops price to combat downloads**

In 2003, when music downloading first took off, Universal Music slashed the price of a CD from $21 to $15. The company said that it expected the price cut to boost the quantity of CDs sold by 30 percent, other things remaining the same.

Source: *Globe and Mail*, September 4, 2003

What was Universal Music's estimate of the price elasticity of demand for CDs? Was the demand estimated to be elastic or inelastic?

## Solutions to Practice Problems

1.  The demand for a good is *inelastic* if the percentage decrease in the quantity demanded is less than the percentage increase in its price. In this example, a 10 percent price rise brings a 2 percent decrease in the quantity demanded, so demand is inelastic.
2.  Because the good has an inelastic demand, it most likely has poor substitutes, is a necessity rather than a luxury, and is broadly defined.
3.  Price elasticity of demand = Percentage change in the quantity demanded ÷ Percentage change in price. In this example, the price elasticity of demand is 2 percent divided by 10 percent, or 0.2. An elasticity less than 1 means that demand is inelastic. When demand is inelastic, a price rise increases total revenue. This good is most likely a necessity (bread), or has poor substitutes (toothpaste), or is broadly defined (clothing).

## Solution to In the News

Price elasticity of demand = Percentage change in the quantity demanded ÷ Percentage change in price. The percentage change in the price equals [($21 − $15)/($18)] × 100, which is 33.3 percent. The percentage change in the quantity is 30 percent. So Universal Music's estimate of the price elasticity of demand for CDs was 30 percent ÷ 33.3 percent, or 0.9. Because the percentage change in the quantity is less than the percentage change in the price, demand is estimated to be inelastic, which is what an elasticity of 0.9 means.

## 5.2 THE PRICE ELASTICITY OF SUPPLY

You know that when demand increases, the equilibrium price rises and the equilibrium quantity increases. But does the price rise by a large amount and the quantity increase by a little? Or does the price barely rise and the quantity increase by a large amount? To answer this question, we need to know the price elasticity of supply.

The **price elasticity of supply** is a measure of the responsiveness of the quantity supplied of a good to a change in its price when all other influences on sellers' plans remain the same. We determine the price elasticity of supply by comparing the percentage change in the quantity supplied with the percentage change in price.

**Price elasticity of supply**
A measure of the responsiveness of the quantity supplied of a good to a change in its price when all other influences on sellers' plans remain the same.

### ■ Elastic and Inelastic Supply

The supply of a good might be

- Elastic
- Unit elastic
- Inelastic

Figure 5.5 illustrates the range of supply elasticities. Figure 5.5(a) shows the extreme case of a **perfectly elastic supply**—an almost zero percentage change in price brings a very large percentage change in the quantity supplied. Figure 5.5(b) shows an **elastic supply**—the percentage change in the quantity supplied exceeds the percentage change in price. Figure 5.5(c) shows a **unit elastic supply**—the percentage change in the quantity supplied equals the percentage change in price. Figure 5.5(d) shows an **inelastic supply**—the percentage change in the quantity supplied is less than the percentage change in price. And Figure 5.5(e) shows the extreme case of a **perfectly inelastic supply**—the percentage change in the quantity supplied is zero when the price changes.

**Perfectly elastic supply**
When the quantity supplied changes by a very large percentage in response to an almost zero percentage change in price.

**Elastic supply**
When the percentage change in the quantity supplied exceeds the percentage change in price.

**Unit elastic supply**
When the percentage change in the quantity supplied equals the percentage change in price.

### ■ Influences on the Price Elasticity of Supply

What makes the supply of some things elastic and the supply of others inelastic? The two main influences on the price elasticity of supply are

- Production possibilities
- Storage possibilities

**Inelastic supply**
When the percentage change in the quantity supplied is less than the percentage change in price.

**Perfectly inelastic supply**
When the percentage change in the quantity supplied is zero for any percentage change in the price.

### Production Possibilities

Some goods can be produced at a constant (or very gently rising) opportunity cost. These goods have an elastic supply. The silicon in your computer chips is an example of such a good. Silicon is extracted from sand at a tiny and almost constant opportunity cost, so the supply of silicon is perfectly elastic.

Some goods can be produced in only a fixed quantity. These goods have a perfectly inelastic supply. A beachfront home in Malibu can be built only on a unique beachfront lot, so the supply of these homes is perfectly inelastic.

Hotel rooms in New York City can't easily be used as office accommodation and office space cannot easily be converted into hotel rooms, so the supply of hotel rooms in New York City is inelastic. Paper and printing presses can be used to produce textbooks or magazines, and the supplies of these goods are elastic.

■ **FIGURE 5.5**

## The Range of Price Elasticities of Supply

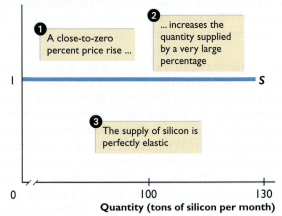

**(a)  Perfectly elastic supply**

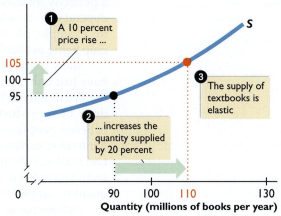

**(b)  Elastic supply**

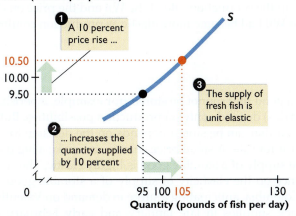

**(c)  Unit elastic supply**

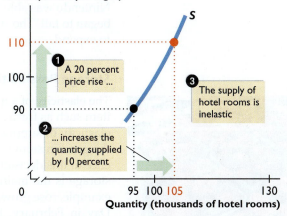

**(d)  Inelastic supply**

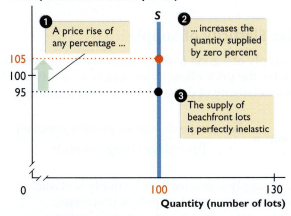

**(e)  Perfectly inelastic supply**

❶ A price rise brings ❷ an increase in the quantity supplied. The relationship between the percentage change in the quantity supplied and the percentage change in price determines ❸ the price elasticity of supply, which ranges from perfectly elastic (part a) to perfectly inelastic (part e).

***Time Elapsed Since Price Change*** As time passes after a price change, it becomes easier to change production plans and supply becomes more elastic. For some items—fruits and vegetables are examples—it is difficult or perhaps impossible to change the quantity supplied immediately after a price change. These goods have a perfectly inelastic supply on the day of a price change. The quantities supplied depend on crop-planting decisions that were made earlier. In the case of oranges, for example, planting decisions have to be made many years in advance of the crop being available.

Many manufactured goods also have an inelastic supply if production plans have had only a short period in which to change. For example, before it launched the Wii in November 2006, Nintendo made a forecast of demand, set a price, and drew up a production plan to supply the United States with the quantity that it believed people would be willing to buy. It turned out that demand outstripped Nintendo's earlier forecast. The price of the Wii increased on eBay, an Internet auction market, to bring market equilibrium. At the high price that emerged, Nintendo would have liked to ship more units of Wii, but it could do nothing to increase the quantity supplied in the near term. The supply of the Wii was inelastic.

As time passes, the elasticity of supply increases. After all the technologically possible ways of adjusting production have been exploited, supply is extremely elastic—perhaps perfectly elastic—for most manufactured items. In 2007, Nintendo was able to step up the production rate of the Wii and the price on eBay began to fall. The supply of Wii had become more elastic as production continued to expand.

### Storage Possibilities

The elasticity of supply of a good that cannot be stored (for example, a perishable item such as fresh strawberries) depends only on production possibilities. But the elasticity of supply of a good that can be stored depends on the decision to keep the good in storage or offer it for sale. A small price change can make a big difference to this decision, so the supply of a storable good is highly elastic. The cost of storage is the main influence on the elasticity of supply of a storable good. For example, rose growers in Colombia, anticipating a surge in demand on Valentine's Day in February, hold back supplies in late January and early February and increase their inventories of roses. They then release roses from inventory for Valentine's Day.

*Fresh strawberries must be sold before they deteriorate, so their supply is inelastic.*

### ■ Computing the Price Elasticity of Supply

To determine whether the supply of a good is elastic, unit elastic, or inelastic, we compute a numerical value for the price elasticity of supply in a way similar to that used to calculate the price elasticity of demand. We use the formula:

$$\text{Price elasticity of supply} = \frac{\text{Percentage change in quantity supplied}}{\text{Percentage change in price}}.$$

- If the price elasticity of supply is greater than 1, supply is elastic.
- If the price elasticity of supply equals 1, supply is unit elastic.
- If the price elasticity of supply is less than 1, supply is inelastic.

Let's calculate the price elasticity of supply of roses. Suppose that in a normal month, the price of roses is $40 a bouquet and 6 million bouquets are supplied. And suppose that in February, the price rises to $80 a bouquet and the quantity supplied increases to 24 million bouquets. Figure 5.6 illustrates the supply of roses and summarizes the calculation. The figure shows the initial point at $40 a bouquet and the new point at $80 a bouquet. The price increases by $40 a bouquet and the average, or midpoint, price is $60 a bouquet, so the percentage change in the price is 66.67 percent. The quantity supplied increases by 18 million bouquets and the average, or midpoint, quantity is 15 million bouquets, so the percentage change in the quantity supplied is 120 percent.

Using the above formula, you can see that the price elasticity of supply of roses is

$$\text{Price elasticity of supply} = \frac{120 \text{ percent}}{66.67 \text{ percent}} = 1.8.$$

The price elasticity of supply is 1.8 at the midpoint between the initial point and the new point on the supply curve. In this example, over this price range, the supply of roses is elastic.

**FIGURE 5.6**

Price Elasticity of Supply Calculation

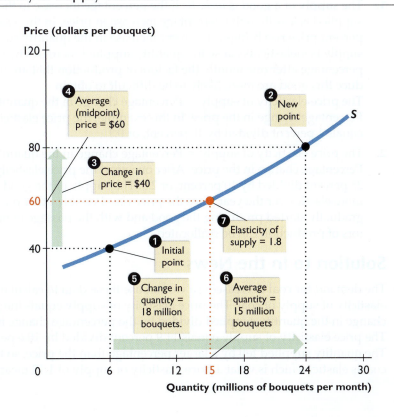

**1** At the initial point, the price is $40 a bouquet and the quantity supplied is 6 million bouquets a month.

**2** At the new point, the price is $80 a bouquet and the quantity supplied is 24 million bouquets a month.

**3** The change in price is $40, and **4** the average price is $60, so the percentage change in price equals ($40 ÷ $60) ×100, which is 66.67 percent.

**5** The change in the quantity supplied is 18 million bouquets and **6** the average quantity supplied is 15 million bouquets, so the percentage change in quantity supplied is (18 million ÷ 15 million) × 100, which is 120 percent.

**7** The price elasticity of supply equals 120 percent ÷ 66.67 percent, which is 1.8.

CHECKPOINT 5.2

**Define and calculate the price elasticity of supply, and explain the factors that influence it.**

## Practice Problems

A 10 percent increase in the price of a good increased the quantity supplied of the good by 1 percent after one month and by 25 percent after one year.

1. Is the supply of this good elastic, unit elastic, or inelastic? Is this good likely to be produced using factors of production that are easily obtained? What is the price elasticity of supply of this good?

2. What is the price elasticity of supply after one year? Has the supply of this good become more elastic or less elastic? Why?

## In the News

**Weak coal prices hit China's third-largest coal miner**

The chairman of Yanzhou Coal Mining, Wang Xin, reported that the demand for coal has fallen by 11.9 percent from a year earlier, despite the price falling by 10.6 percent.

Source: Dow Jones, April 27, 2009

Calculate the price elasticity of supply of coal. Is the supply of coal elastic or inelastic?

## Solutions to Practice Problems

1. The supply of a good is *inelastic* if the percentage increase in the quantity supplied is less than the percentage increase in price. In this example, a 10 percent price rise brings a 1 percent increase in the quantity supplied, so supply is inelastic. Because the quantity supplied increases by such a small percentage after one month, the factors of production that are used to produce this good are more likely to be difficult to obtain.
The price elasticity of supply = Percentage change in the quantity supplied ÷ Percentage change in the price. In this example, the price elasticity of supply equals 1 percent divided by 10 percent, or 0.1.

2. The price elasticity of supply = Percentage change in the quantity supplied ÷ Percentage change in the price. After one year, the price elasticity of supply is 25 percent divided by 10 percent, or 2.5. The supply of the good has become more elastic over the year since the price rise. Possibly other producers have gradually started producing the good and with the passage of time more factors of production can be reallocated.

## Solution to In the News

The demand for coal decreased, so we can use these data to calculate the price elasticity of supply of coal. The price elasticity of supply equals the percentage change in the quantity supplied divided by the percentage change in the price. The price elasticity of supply equals 11.9 percent divided by 10.6 percent, or 1.12. The quantity supplied fell by a larger percentage than the price, so the supply of coal is elastic, which is what a price elasticity of supply of 1.12 means.

## 5.3    CROSS ELASTICITY AND INCOME ELASTICITY

Domino's Pizza in Chula Vista has a problem. Burger King has just cut its prices. Domino's manager, Pat, knows that pizzas and burgers are substitutes. He also knows that when the price of a substitute for pizza falls, the demand for pizza decreases. But by how much will the quantity of pizza bought decrease if Pat maintains his current price?

Pat also knows that pizza and soda are complements. He knows that if the price of a complement of pizza falls, the demand for pizza increases. So he wonders whether he might keep his customers by cutting the price he charges for soda. But he wants to know by how much he must cut the price of soda to keep selling the same quantity of pizza with cheaper burgers all around him.

To answer these questions, Pat needs to calculate the cross elasticity of demand. Let's examine this elasticity measure.

### ■ Cross Elasticity of Demand

The **cross elasticity of demand** is a measure of the responsiveness of the demand for a good to a change in the price of a substitute or complement when other things remain the same. It is calculated by using the formula:

$$\text{Cross elasticity of demand} = \frac{\text{Percentage change in quantity demanded of a good}}{\text{Percentage change in price of one of its substitutes or complements}}.$$

**Cross elasticity of demand**
A measure of the responsiveness of the demand for a good to a change in the price of a substitute or complement when other things remain the same.

Suppose that when the price of a burger falls by 10 percent, the quantity of pizza demanded decreases by 5 percent.* The cross elasticity of demand for pizza with respect to the price of a burger is

$$\text{Cross elasticity of demand} = \frac{-5 \text{ percent}}{-10 \text{ percent}} = 0.5.$$

The cross elasticity of demand for a substitute is positive. A *fall* in the price of a substitute brings a *decrease* in the quantity demanded of the good. The quantity demanded of a good and the price of one of its substitutes change in the *same* direction.

Suppose that when the price of soda falls by 10 percent, the quantity of pizza demanded increases by 2 percent. The cross elasticity of demand for pizza with respect to the price of soda is

$$\text{Cross elasticity of demand} = \frac{+2 \text{ percent}}{-10 \text{ percent}} = -0.2.$$

The cross elasticity of demand for a complement is negative. A *fall* in the price of a complement brings an *increase* in the quantity demanded of the good. The quantity demanded of a good and the price of one of its complements change in *opposite* directions.

---

*As before, these percentage changes are calculated by using the midpoint method.

■ **FIGURE 5.7**

Cross Elasticity of Demand

❶ A burger is a *substitute* for pizza. When the price of a burger falls, the demand curve for pizza shifts leftward from $D_0$ to $D_1$. At the price of $10 a pizza, people plan to buy fewer pizzas. The cross elasticity of the demand for pizza with respect to the price of a burger is *positive*.

❷ Soda is a *complement* of pizza. When the price of soda falls, the demand for pizza increases and the demand curve for pizza shifts rightward from $D_0$ to $D_2$. At the price of $10 a pizza, people plan to buy more pizzas. The cross elasticity of the demand for pizza with respect to the price of soda is *negative*.

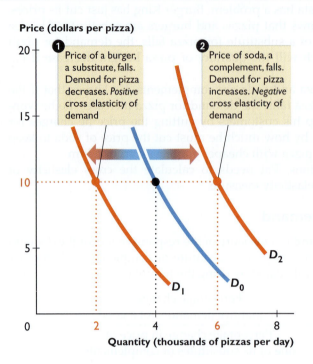

Figure 5.7 illustrates these two cross elasticities of demand for pizza. With the price of a pizza constant at $10, when the price of a burger falls, the demand for pizza decreases and the demand curve for pizza shifts leftward from $D_0$ to $D_1$. When the price of soda falls, the demand for pizza increases and the demand curve for pizza shifts rightward from $D_0$ to $D_2$. The magnitude of the cross elasticity determines how far the demand curve shifts.

## ■ Income Elasticity of Demand

The U.S. and global economies are expanding, and people are enjoying rising incomes. This increasing prosperity brings an increasing demand for most types of goods. But by how much will the demand for different items increase? Will the demand for some items increase so rapidly that we spend an increasing percentage of our incomes on them? And will the demand for some items decrease?

The answer depends on the income elasticity of demand. The **income elasticity of demand** is a measure of the responsiveness of the demand for a good to a change in income when other things remain the same. It is calculated by using the following formula:

$$\text{Income elasticity of demand} = \frac{\text{Percentage change in quantity demanded}}{\text{Percentage change in income}}.$$

The income elasticity of demand falls into three ranges:

- Greater than 1 (normal good, income elastic)
- Between zero and 1 (normal good, income inelastic)
- Less than zero (inferior good)

**Income elasticity of demand**
A measure of the responsiveness of the demand for a good to a change in income when other things remain the same.

As our incomes increase: items that have

- An income elastic demand take an increasing share of income
- An income inelastic demand take a decreasing share of income
- A negative income elasticity of demand take an absolutely smaller amount of income.

You can make some strong predictions about how the world will change over the coming years by knowing the income elasticities of demand of different goods and services. The table provides a sampling of numbers.

These estimated income elasticities of demand tell us that we can expect air travel—both domestic and international—to become hugely more important; an increasing share of our incomes will be spent on watching movies, eating out in restaurants, using public transportation, and getting haircuts. Two other prominent items not shown in the table, items for which demand is income elastic, are health care and education. As our incomes grow, we can expect education and health care to take increasing shares of our incomes.

As our incomes grow, we'll spend a decreasing percentage on clothing, phone calls, and food. The income elasticity of demand for food is less than one, even for the poorest people. So we can predict a continuation of the trends of the past— shrinking agriculture and manufacturing, and expanding services.

**Table 5.1**

### Some Income Elasticities of Demand

| Good or Service | Elasticity |
| --- | --- |
| **Income Elastic** | |
| Airline travel | 5.82 |
| Movies | 3.41 |
| Foreign travel | 3.08 |
| Electricity | 1.94 |
| Restaurant meals | 1.61 |
| Local buses and trains | 1.38 |
| Haircuts | 1.36 |
| **Income Inelastic** | |
| Tobacco | 0.86 |
| Alcoholic beverages | 0.62 |
| Clothing | 0.51 |
| Newspapers | 0.38 |
| Telephone | 0.32 |
| Food | 0.14 |

SOURCES OF DATA: See page C1.

# EYE on YOUR LIFE
## Your Price Elasticities of Demand

Pay close attention the next time the price of something that you buy rises. Did you spend more, the same, or less on this item?

Your expenditure on a good is equal to the price of the good multiplied by the quantity that you buy.

But recall that a seller's total revenue is equal to the price of the good multiplied by the quantity sold.

Because the buyer's expenditure on a good is equal to the seller's total revenue, the total revenue test that the seller uses to estimate the price elasticity of demand for the good sold can also be used by a buyer.

You can determine whether your demand for a good is elastic, unit elastic, or inelastic by noting what happens to your total expenditure on the good when its price changes.

When the price of a good rises, your demand for that good is

- *Elastic* if your expenditure on it decreases.
- *Unit elastic* if your expenditure on it remains constant.
- *Inelastic* if your expenditure on it increases.

Think about why your demand for a good might be elastic, unit elastic, or inelastic by checking back to the list of influences on the price elasticity of demand on p. 152.

Most likely, as we noted in the *Eye on the Price of Gasoline* on p. 159

when the price of gasoline rises, you use almost as much as you did at the lower price. Gasoline has poor substitutes and your demand for gasoline is inelastic.

What do you do if the price of cell-phone service falls? Do you spend less on cell-phone service, as you would if your demand for cell-phone service is inelastic? Or do you spend more on cell-phone service, which would indicate an elastic demand for cell-phone service?

What about your iPod and iTunes? Is your demand for these items elastic or inelastic? And is your demand for textbooks elastic or inelastic? You can estimate all these elasticities.

# CHECKPOINT 5.3

**Define the cross elasticity of demand and the income elasticity of demand, and explain the factors that influence them.**

## Practice Problems

1.  The quantity demanded of good *A* increases by 5 percent when the price of good *B* rises by 10 percent and other things remain the same. Are goods *A* and *B* complements or substitutes? Describe how the demand for good *A* changes and calculate the cross elasticity of demand.

2.  When income rises by 5 percent and other things remain the same, the quantity demanded of good *C* increases by 1 percent. Is good *C* a normal good or an inferior good? Describe how the demand for good *C* changes and calculate the income elasticity of demand for good *C*.

## In the News

### China will become the world's largest luxury goods market

With their fast-rising incomes, Chinese consumers will overtake those in today's rich economies to become the world's biggest spenders on luxury goods. They will rebalance their budgets in a gradual move from saving to consuming.

Source: ibtimes.com, February 2, 2011

Are luxury goods normal goods or just not necessities? Explain your answer.

## Solutions to Practice Problems

1.  Goods *A* and *B* are substitutes because when the price of good *B* rises, the quantity demanded of good *A* increases. People switch from good *B* to good *A*. The demand for good *A* increases (Figure 1).
    Cross elasticity of demand = Percentage change in the quantity demanded of good *A* ÷ Percentage increase in the price of good *B*.
    Cross elasticity of demand = 5 ÷ 10, or 0.5.

2.  Good *C* is a normal good; as income rises, the quantity demanded increases. The demand for good *C* increases (Figure 2).
    Income elasticity of demand = Percentage change in the quantity demanded of good *C* ÷ Percentage increase in income.
    Income elasticity of demand = 1 ÷ 5, or 0.2.

## Solution to In the News

To know whether a good is a normal good, we need to calculate the income elasticity of demand. A normal good is a good that has a positive income elasticity of demand. The source of the increase in the sales of luxury goods is rising incomes and people spending their past savings. As people spend more, the quantity of luxury goods bought increases, so the income elasticity of demand for luxury goods is positive. Luxury goods are normal goods.

**FIGURE 1**

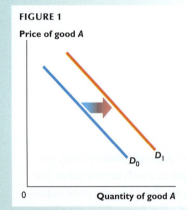

Price of good A

$D_0$  $D_1$

0    Quantity of good A

**FIGURE 2**

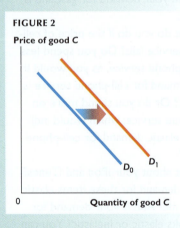

Price of good C

$D_0$  $D_1$

0    Quantity of good C

## CHAPTER SUMMARY

## Key Points

**1. Define and calculate the price elasticity of demand, and explain the factors that influence it.**

- The demand for a good is elastic if, when its price changes, the percentage change in the quantity demanded exceeds the percentage change in price.
- The demand for a good is inelastic if, when its price changes, the percentage change in the quantity demanded is less than the percentage change in price.
- The price elasticity of demand for a good depends on how easy it is to find substitutes for the good and on the proportion of income spent on it.
- Price elasticity of demand equals the percentage change in the quantity demanded divided by the percentage change in price.
- If demand is elastic, a rise in price leads to a decrease in total revenue. If demand is unit elastic, a rise in price leaves total revenue unchanged. And if demand is inelastic, a rise in price leads to an increase in total revenue.

**2. Define and calculate the price elasticity of supply, and explain the factors that influence it.**

- The supply of a good is elastic if, when its price changes, the percentage change in the quantity supplied exceeds the percentage change in price.
- The supply of a good is inelastic if, when its price changes, the percentage change in the quantity supplied is less than the percentage change in price.
- The main influences on the price elasticity of supply are the flexibility of production possibilities and storage possibilities.

**3. Define the cross elasticity of demand and the income elasticity of demand, and explain the factors that influence them.**

- Cross elasticity of demand shows how the demand for a good changes when the price of one of its substitutes or complements changes.
- Cross elasticity is positive for substitutes and negative for complements.
- Income elasticity of demand shows how the demand for a good changes when income changes. For a normal good, the income elasticity of demand is positive. For an inferior good, the income elasticity of demand is negative.

## Key Terms

Cross elasticity of demand, 167
Elastic demand, 152
Elastic supply, 162
Income elasticity of demand, 168
Inelastic demand, 152
Inelastic supply, 162

Perfectly elastic demand, 152
Perfectly elastic supply, 162
Perfectly inelastic demand, 152
Perfectly inelastic supply, 162
Price elasticity of demand, 150
Price elasticity of supply, 162

Total revenue, 158
Total revenue test, 159
Unit elastic demand, 152
Unit elastic supply, 162

CHAPTER CHECKPOINT

## Study Plan Problems and Applications

When the price of home heating oil increased by 20 percent, the quantity demanded decreased by 2 percent and the quantity of wool sweaters demanded increased by 10 percent. Use this information to work Problems **1** and **2**.

**1.** Use the total revenue test to determine whether the demand for home heating oil is elastic or inelastic.

**2.** If the price of a wool sweater did not change, calculate the cross elasticity of demand for wool sweaters with respect to the price of home heating oil. Are home heating oil and wool sweaters substitutes or complements? Why?

**3.** Figure 1 shows the demand for movie tickets. Is the demand for movie tickets elastic or inelastic over the price range $7 to $9 a ticket? If the price falls from $9 to $7 a ticket, explain how the total revenue from the sale of movie tickets will change. Calculate the price elasticity of demand for movie tickets when the price is $8 a ticket.

**4.** The price elasticity of demand for Pete's chocolate chip cookies is 1.5. Pete wants to increase his total revenue. Would you recommend that Pete raise or lower his price of cookies? Explain your answer.

Use the following information to work Problems **5** and **6**.

The price of a plane ride rises by 10 percent. The price elasticity of demand for plane rides is 0.5 and the price elasticity of demand for train rides is 0.2. The cross elasticity of demand for train rides with respect to the price of a plane ride is 0.4.

**5.** Calculate the percentage changes in the quantity demanded of plane rides and train rides.

**6.** Given the rise in the price of a plane ride, what percentage change in the price of a train ride will leave the quantity demanded of train rides unchanged?

**7.** A survey found that when incomes increased by 10 percent, the following changes in quantities demanded occurred: spring water up by 5 percent; sports drinks down by 2 percent; cruises up by 15 percent. Which demand is income elastic? Which is income inelastic? Which are normal goods?

Use the following information to work Problems **8** and **9**.

**Record U.S. corn crop, up 24%, is forecast**

The USDA reported that world corn production will be 9.9 percent greater than last year's, while U.S. corn production will be 24 percent larger. The price of corn is expected to be 46 percent higher than last year's price.

Source: *Bloomberg News*, August 11, 2007

**8.** Calculate the U.S. price elasticity of supply of corn. Is this supply elastic?

**9.** Calculate the world price elasticity of supply of corn.

 **10.** Read *Eye on the Price of Gasoline* on p. 159 and then explain why the demand for gasoline is more inelastic in the short run than in the long run. Which is likely to be more inelastic, the demand for premium gasoline or the demand for all grades of gasoline?

**FIGURE 1**

Price (dollars per ticket)

# Instructor Assignable Problems and Applications

 Use the following information to work Problems **1** and **2**.

**Why the tepid response to higher gasoline prices?**

Most studies report that when U.S. gasoline prices rise by 10 percent, the quantity purchased falls by 1 to 2 percent. In September 2005, the retail gasoline price was $2.90 a gallon, about $1.00 higher than in September 2004, but purchases of gasoline fell by only 3.5 percent.

Source: *The New York Times*, October 13, 2005

1. Calculate the price elasticity of demand for gasoline implied by what most studies have found.

2. Compare the elasticity implied by the data for the period from September 2004 to September 2005 with that implied by most studies. What might explain the difference?

3. When rain ruined the banana crop in Central America, the price of bananas rose from $1 to $2 a pound. Growers sold fewer bananas, but their total revenue was unchanged. By what percentage did the quantity demanded of bananas change? Is the demand for bananas elastic, unit elastic, or inelastic?

4. The income elasticity of demand for haircuts is 1.5, and the income elasticity of demand for food is 0.14. You take a weekend job, and the income you have to spend on food and haircuts doubles. If the prices of food and haircuts remain the same, will you double your expenditure on haircuts and double your expenditure on food? Explain why or why not.

5. Drought cuts the quantity of wheat grown by 2 percent. If the price elasticity of demand for wheat is 0.5, by how much will the price of wheat rise? If pasta makers estimate that this change in the price of wheat will increase the price of pasta by 25 percent and decrease the quantity demanded of pasta by 8 percent, what is the pasta makers' estimate of the price elasticity of demand for pasta? If pasta sauce makers estimate that, with the change in the price of pasta, the quantity of pasta sauce demanded will decrease by 5 percent, what is the pasta sauce makers' estimate of the cross elasticity of demand for pasta sauce with respect to the price of pasta?

6. "In a market in which demand is price inelastic, producers can gouge consumers and the government must set high standards of conduct for producers to ensure that consumers gets a fair deal." Do you agree or disagree with each part of this statement? Explain how you might go about testing the parts of the statement that are positive and lay bare the normative parts.

Use the following information to work Problems **7** and **8**.

**Almonds galore!**

The quantity of almonds harvested in 2008–2009 was expected to increase by 22 percent, while total receipts of growers was expected to increase by 17 percent.

Source: Almond Board of California

7. Was the price of almonds expected to rise or fall? Did a change in the supply of or demand for almonds bring about this expected change in the price?

8. If the price of almonds changed as a result of a change in the supply of almonds, is the demand for almonds elastic or inelastic? Explain your answer.

# Critical Thinking Discussion Questions

1. **The fluctuating market for nickel**

   World nickel consumption increased from 1.1 million tonnes in 2001 to 1.6 million tonnes in 2011. The increase was not smooth: in 2007, consumption fell to 1.3 million tonnes. From 2001 to 2003 the price of nickel remained below $10,000 per tonne but it increased through 2006 and peaked at $52,179 per tonne in May 2007. In 2011 the price was $26,015 per tonne.

   Source: INSG, December 17, 2013

   a. Why are the data reported in this news clip insufficient for us to be able to determine the price elasticity of demand for nickel?
   b. What additional information would you need to find the price elasticity of demand?
   c. Could the data be used to find the elasticity of supply of nickel? Explain your answer.

2. **Ryanair makes loss as low fares hit**

   Ryanair made a loss in the final three months of last year. Average fares were 9% lower and passenger numbers were 6% higher.

   Source: BBC News, February 3, 2014

   a. What must you assume to use the information in this news clip to determine the price elasticity of demand for Ryanair seats?
   b. Making the necessary assumption, what is Ryanair's price elasticity of demand?
   c. Is the demand for Ryanair flights elastic or inelastic?
   d. If the demand for Ryanair flights changed, what elasticities would we need to measure the change?
   e. Provide an example of a substitute for travel on Ryanair.

3. **Signed Beatles album Sgt. Pepper sells for $290,000**

   A signed copy of The Beatles' album Sgt. Pepper's Lonely Hearts Club Band has been bought at auction in the U.S. for $290,500.

   Source: BBC News, April 1, 2013

   a. What does the fact that the album went for a high price imply about the elasticity of supply of autographed Beatles' albums?
   b. What does the fact that the album went for a high price imply about the elasticity of demand for autographed Beatles' albums?
   c. What would you need to know to effectively determine the price elasticity of demand and the elasticity of supply in this market?

Should price gouging be illegal?

# Efficiency and Fairness of Markets

When you have completed your study of this chapter, you will be able to

**1** Describe the alternative methods of allocating scarce resources and define and explain the features of an efficient allocation.

**2** Distinguish between value and price and define consumer surplus.

**3** Distinguish between cost and price and define producer surplus.

**4** Evaluate the efficiency of the alternative methods of allocating resources.

**5** Explain the main ideas about fairness and evaluate the fairness of the alternative methods of allocating scarce resources.

## 6.1   ALLOCATION METHODS AND EFFICIENCY

Because resources are scarce, they must be allocated somehow among their competing uses. Doing nothing and leaving the allocation to chance is one method of allocation. The goal of this chapter is to evaluate the ability of markets to allocate resources efficiently and fairly—to allocate them in the social interest.

But trading in markets is only one of several methods of allocating resources. To know whether the market does a good job, we need to compare it with its alternatives. We also need to know what is meant by an efficient and fair allocation.

Economists have much more to say about efficiency than about fairness, so efficiency is the main focus of this chapter. We leave the difficult issue of fairness until the final section. We begin by describing the alternative ways in which resources might be allocated. Then we explain the characteristics of an efficient allocation.

### ■ Resource Allocation Methods

Resources might be allocated by using any one or some combination of the following methods:

- Market price
- Command
- Majority rule
- Contest
- First-come, first-served
- Sharing equally
- Lottery
- Personal characteristics
- Force

Let's see how each method works and look at an example of each.

### Market Price

*Market price allocates resources to those who are willing and able to pay.*

When a market price allocates a scarce resource, the people who get the resource are those who are willing and able to pay the market price. People who don't value the resource as highly as the market price leave it for others to buy and use.

Most of the scarce resources that you supply get allocated by market price. For example, you sell your labor services in a market, and you buy most of what you consume in markets.

Two kinds of people decide not to pay the market price: those who can afford to pay but choose not to buy and those who are too poor and simply can't afford to pay.

For many goods and services, distinguishing between those who choose not to buy and those who can't afford to pay doesn't matter. For a few items, that distinction does matter. For example, some poor people can't afford to pay school fees and doctor's fees. The inability of poor people to buy items that most people consider to be essential is not handled well by the market price method and is usually dealt with by one of the other allocation methods.

But for most goods and services, the market turns out to do a good job. We'll examine just how good a job it does later in this chapter.

## Command

A **command system** allocates resources by the order (command) of someone in authority. Many resources get allocated by command. In the U.S. economy, the command system is used extensively inside firms and government bureaus. For example, if you have a job, it is most likely that someone tells you what to do. Your labor time is allocated to specific tasks by a command.

Sometimes, a command system allocates the resources of an entire economy. The former Soviet Union is an example. North Korea and Cuba are the only remaining command economies.

A command system works well in organizations in which the lines of authority and responsibility are clear and it is easy to monitor the activities being performed. But a command system works badly when applied to an entire economy. The range of activities to be monitored is just too large, and it is easy for people to fool those in authority. The system works so badly in North Korea that it fails even to deliver an adequate supply of food.

## Majority Rule

Majority rule allocates resources in the way that a majority of voters choose. Societies use majority rule for some of their biggest decisions. For example, majority rule decides the tax rates that end up allocating scarce resources between private use and public use. And majority rule decides how tax dollars are allocated among competing uses such as national defense and health care for the aged.

Having 200 million people vote on every line in a nation's budget would be extremely costly, so instead of direct majority rule, the United States (and most other countries) use the system of representative government. Majority rule determines who will represent the people, and majority rule among the representatives decides the detailed allocation of scarce resources.

Majority rule works well when the decisions being made affect large numbers of people and self-interest must be suppressed to use resources most effectively.

## Contest

A contest allocates resources to a winner (or a group of winners). The most obvious contests are sporting events. Maria Sharapova and Sloane Stephens do battle on a tennis court, and the winner gets twice as much in prize money as the loser.

But contests are much more general than those in a sports arena, though we don't call them contests in ordinary speech. For example, Bill Gates won a big contest to provide the world's personal computer operating system, and Jennifer Lawrence won a type of contest to rise to the top of the movie-acting business.

Contests do a good job when the efforts of the "players" are hard to monitor and reward directly. By dangling the opportunity to win a big prize, people are motivated to work hard and try to be the "winner." Even though only a few people end up with a big prize, many people work harder in the process of trying to win and so total production is much greater than it would be without the contest.

## First-Come, First-Served

A first-come, first-served method allocates resources to those who are first in line. Most national parks allocate campsites in this way. Airlines use first-come, first-served to allocate standby seats at the departure gate. A freeway is an everyday example of first-come, first-served. This scarce transportation resource gets allocated

**Command system**
A system that allocates resources by the order of someone in authority.

*A command allocates resources by the order of someone in authority.*

*Voting allocates resources in the way that the majority wants.*

*A contest allocates resources to the winner, in sport and business.*

*First-come, first-served allocates resources to the first in line.*

to the first to arrive at the on-ramp. If too many vehicles enter the freeway, the speed slows and people, in effect, wait in line for a bit of the "freeway" to become free!

First-come, first-served works best when, as in the above examples, a scarce resource can serve just one user at a time in a sequence. By serving the user who arrives first, this method minimizes the time spent waiting in line for the resource to become free.

## Sharing Equally

When a resource is shared equally, everyone gets the same amount of it. You perhaps use this method to share dessert at a restaurant. People sometimes jointly own a vacation apartment and share its use equally.

To make equal shares work, people must agree on how to use the resource and must make an arrangement to implement the agreement. Sharing equally can work for small groups who share a set of common goals and ideals.

## Lottery

Lotteries allocate resources to those who pick the winning number, draw the lucky cards, or come up lucky on some other gaming system. State lotteries and casinos reallocate millions of dollars' worth of goods and services every year.

But lotteries are far more widespread than state jackpots and roulette wheels in casinos. They are used in a variety of situations to allocate scarce resources. For example, the Lawn Tennis Association operates ballots and draws to allocate Wimbledon tickets and some airports use them to allocate landing slots to airlines.

Lotteries work well when there is no effective way to distinguish among potential users of a scarce resource.

## Personal Characteristics

When resources are allocated on the basis of personal characteristics, people with the "right" characteristics get the resources. Some of the resources that matter most to you are allocated in this way. The people you like are the ones you spend the most time with. You try to avoid having to spend time with people you don't like. People choose marriage partners on the basis of personal characteristics. The use of personal characteristics to allocate resources is regarded as completely natural and acceptable.

But this method also gets used in unacceptable ways. Allocating the best jobs to white, Anglo-Saxon males and discriminating against minorities and women is an example.

## Force

Force plays a crucial role, for both good and ill, in allocating scarce resources. Let's start with the ill.

War, the use of military force by one nation against another, has played an enormous role historically in allocating resources. The economic supremacy of European settlers in the Americas and Australia owes much to the use of this method.

Theft, the taking of the property of others without their consent, also plays a large role. Both large-scale organized crime and small-scale petty crime collectively allocate billions of dollars' worth of resources annually. A large amount of

*Sharing allocates resources by mutual agreement.*

*A lottery allocates resources to the one who draws the winning number.*

*Personal characteristics allocate resources based on whom we like.*

*Force protects the rule of law and facilitates economic activity.*

theft today is conducted by using sophisticated electronic methods that move resources from banks and thousands of innocent people.

But force plays a crucial positive role in allocating resources. It provides an effective method for the state to transfer wealth from the rich to the poor and the legal framework in which voluntary exchange in markets takes place.

Most income and wealth redistribution in modern societies occurs through a taxation and benefits system that is enforced by the power of the state. We vote for taxes and benefits—a majority vote allocation—but we use the power of the state to ensure that everyone complies with the rules and pays their allotted share.

A legal system is the foundation on which our market economy functions. Without courts to enforce contracts, it would be difficult to do business. But the courts could not enforce contracts without the ability to apply force if necessary. The state provides the ultimate force that enables the courts to do their work.

More broadly, the force of the state is essential to uphold the principle of the *rule of law*. This principle is the bedrock of civilized economic (and social and political) life. With the rule of law upheld, people can go about their daily economic lives with the assurance that their property will be protected—that they can sue for violations of their property (and be sued if they violate the property of others).

Free from the burden of protecting their property and confident in the knowledge that those with whom they trade will honor their agreements, people can get on with focusing on the activity at which they have a comparative advantage and trading for mutual gain.

In the next sections of this chapter, we're going to see how a market achieves an efficient use of resources, examine obstacles to efficiency, and see how sometimes, an alternative method might improve on the market. But first we need to be clear about the meaning of efficiency. What are the characteristics of an efficient allocation of resources?

## ■ Using Resources Efficiently

In everyday language, *efficiency* means getting the most out of something. An efficient automobile is one that gets the best possible gas mileage; an efficient furnace is one that uses as little fuel as possible to deliver its heat. In economics, efficiency means getting the most out of the entire economy.

### Efficiency and the *PPF*

The **production possibilities frontier** (*PPF*) is the boundary between the combinations of goods and services that can be produced and those that cannot be produced given the available factors of production and state of technology (p. 96). Production is efficient when the economy is *on* its *PPF* (Chapter 3, pp. 98–99). Production at a point *inside* the *PPF* is *inefficient.*

**Allocative efficiency** is achieved when the quantities of goods and services produced are those that people *value most highly*. To put it another way, resources are allocated efficiently when we cannot produce more of one thing without giving up something else *that people value more highly*. If we can give up some units of one good to get more of something that is *valued more highly*, we haven't achieved the most valued point on the *PPF*.

The *PPF* tells us what it is *possible* to produce but it doesn't tell us about the *value* of what we produce. To find the *highest-valued* point on the *PPF*, we need some information about value. *Marginal benefit* provides that information.

**Production possibilities frontier**
The boundary between the combinations of goods and services that can be produced and the combinations that cannot be produced, given the available factors of production and the state of technology.

**Allocative efficiency**
A situation in which the quantities of goods and services produced are those that people *value most highly*—it is not possible to produce more of a good or service without giving up some of another good that people *value more highly*.

## Marginal Benefit

*Marginal benefit* is the benefit that people receive from consuming *one more unit* of a good or service. People's *preferences* determine marginal benefit and we can measure the marginal benefit from a good or service by what people *are willing to* give up to get *one more* unit of it.

The more we have of any good or service, the smaller is our marginal benefit from it—*the principle of decreasing marginal benefit*. Think about your own marginal benefit from pizza. You really enjoy the first slice. A second slice is fine, too, but not quite as satisfying as the first one. But eat three, four, five, six, and more slices, and each additional slice is less enjoyable than the previous one. You get diminishing marginal benefit from pizza. The more pizza you have, the less of some other good or service you are willing to give up to get one more slice.

Figure 6.1 illustrates the economy's marginal benefit schedule and marginal benefit curve for pizza. The schedule and curve show the same information. In the schedule and on the curve, the quantity of other goods that people *are willing to give up* to get one more pizza *decreases* as the quantity of pizza available *increases*.

## Marginal Cost

To achieve allocative efficiency, we must compare the marginal benefit from pizza with its marginal cost. *Marginal cost* is the opportunity cost of producing one more unit of a good or service (see p. 48) and is measured by the slope of the production possibilities frontier (see pp. 102–103). The marginal cost of a good increases as the quantity produced of that good increases.

■ **FIGURE 6.1**

Marginal Benefit from Pizza

The table and the graph show the marginal benefit from pizza.

Possibility A and point A tell us that if 2,000 pizzas a day are produced, people are willing to give up 15 units of other goods for a pizza. Each point A, B, and C in the graph represents the possibility in the table identified by the same letter.

The line passing through these points is the marginal benefit curve. The marginal benefit from pizza decreases as the quantity of pizza available increases.

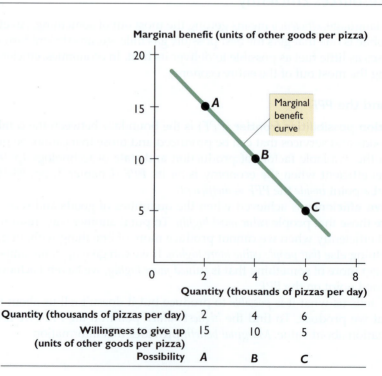

| Quantity (thousands of pizzas per day) | 2 | 4 | 6 |
|---|---|---|---|
| Willingness to give up (units of other goods per pizza) | 15 | 10 | 5 |
| Possibility | A | B | C |

Figure 6.2 illustrates the economy's marginal cost schedule and marginal cost curve. In the schedule and along the curve, which show the same information, the quantity of other goods that people *must give up* to get one more pizza *increases* as the quantity of pizza produced *increases*.

We can now use the concepts of marginal benefit and marginal cost to discover the efficient quantity of pizza to produce.

## Efficient Allocation

The efficient allocation is the highest-valued allocation. To find this allocation, we compare marginal benefit and marginal cost.

If the marginal benefit from pizza exceeds its marginal cost, we're producing too little pizza (and too many units of other goods). If we increase the quantity of pizza produced, we incur a cost but receive a larger benefit from the additional pizza. Our allocation of resources becomes more efficient.

If the marginal cost of pizza exceeds its marginal benefit, we're producing too much pizza (and too little of other goods). Now if we decrease the quantity of pizza produced, we receive a smaller benefit from pizza but save an even greater cost of pizza. Again, our allocation of resources becomes more efficient.

Only when the marginal benefit and marginal cost of pizza are equal are we allocating resources efficiently. Figure 6.3 on the next page illustrates this efficient allocation and provides a graphical summary of the above description of allocative efficiency.

### ■ FIGURE 6.2

## Marginal Cost of Pizza

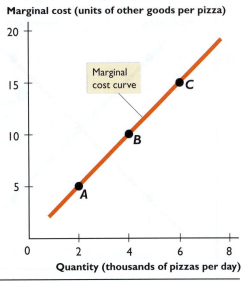

The table and the graph show the marginal cost of a pizza. Marginal cost is the opportunity cost of producing one more unit. It is derived from the *PPF* and is measured by the slope of the *PPF*.

Points *A*, *B*, and *C* in the graph represent the possibilities in the table. The marginal cost curve shows that the marginal cost of a pizza increases as the quantity of pizza produced increases.

| Quantity (thousands of pizzas per day) | 2 | 4 | 6 |
| --- | --- | --- | --- |
| Must give up (units of other goods per pizza) | 5 | 10 | 15 |
| Possibility | A | B | C |

### ■ FIGURE 6.3

## The Efficient Quantity of Pizza

*Production efficiency* occurs at all points on the *PPF*, but *allocative efficiency* occurs at only one point on the *PPF*.

**①** When 2,000 pizzas are produced in part (a), the marginal benefit from pizza exceeds its marginal cost in part (b). Too few pizzas are being produced. If more pizzas and less of other goods are produced, the value of production increases and resources are used more efficiently.

**②** When 6,000 pizzas are produced in part (a), the marginal cost of a pizza exceeds its marginal benefit in part (b). Too many pizzas are being produced. If fewer pizzas and more of other goods are produced, the value of production increases and resources are used more efficiently.

**③** When 4,000 pizzas a day are produced in part (a), the marginal cost of a pizza equals its marginal benefit in part (b). The efficient quantity of pizzas is being produced. It is not possible to get greater value from the economy's scarce resources. If one less pizza and more other goods are produced, the value of the lost pizza exceeds the value of the additional other goods, so total value falls. And if one more pizza and less other goods are produced, the value of the gained pizza is less than the value of the lost other goods, so again total value falls.

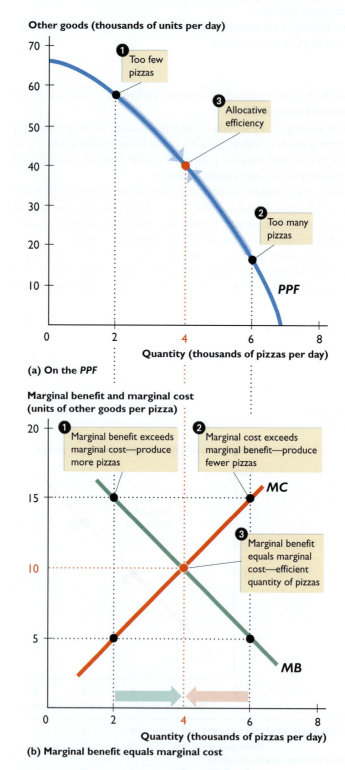

(a) On the *PPF*

(b) Marginal benefit equals marginal cost

# CHECKPOINT 6.1

**Describe the alternative methods of allocating scarce resources and define and explain the features of an efficient allocation.**

## Practice Problems

1. Which method is used to allocate the following scarce resources?
   * Campus parking space between student areas and faculty areas
   * A spot in a restricted student parking area
   * Textbooks
   * Host city for the Olympic Games

Use Figure 1, which shows a nation's *PPF*, and Table 1, which shows its marginal benefit and marginal cost schedules, to work Problems **2** and **3**.

2. What is the marginal benefit from bananas when 1 pound of bananas is grown? What is the marginal cost of growing 1 pound of bananas?

3. On Figure 1, mark two points: Point *A* at which production is efficient but too much coffee is produced for allocative efficiency; and point *B*, the point of allocative efficiency.

## In the News

### AC/DC's "Black Ice" tour breaks records down under
The 40,000 tickets for the March 6 gig sold out in seven minutes—a record. Many people who camped out overnight missed getting a ticket.

Source: *WAToday*, May 25, 2009

What method was used to allocate AC/DC concert tickets? Was it efficient?

## Solutions to Practice Problems

1. Campus parking is allocated by command. The spot in a restricted student parking area is allocated by first-come, first-served. Textbooks are allocated by market price. The Olympic Games' host city is allocated by contest.

2. The marginal benefit from 1 pound of bananas is 3 pounds of coffee. Marginal benefit is the amount of coffee that the nation is *willing to give up* to get *one additional* pound of bananas. The marginal cost of growing 1 pound of bananas is 1 pound of coffee. Marginal cost is the amount of coffee that the nation *must give up* to get *one additional* pound of bananas.

3. Point *A* on Figure 2 shows production efficiency (on the *PPF*) but not allocative efficiency because from Table 1 marginal benefit from bananas exceeds the marginal cost—too few bananas are produced. Point *B* is the point of allocative efficiency: It is on the *PPF* and marginal benefit equals marginal cost.

## Solution to In the News

The concert organizer used first-come, first-served to allocate tickets. The allocation was efficient if the concert-goer's willingness to pay (the ticket price plus the opportunity cost of time spent in the line), which is also the marginal benefit, equaled the organizer's marginal cost of providing one more seat.

**FIGURE 1**

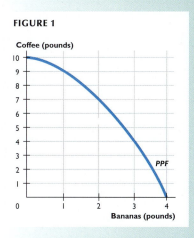

**TABLE 1    MARGINAL BENEFIT AND MARGINAL COST**

| | Willing to give up | Must give up |
|---|---|---|
| Bananas (pounds) | (pounds of coffee per pound of bananas) | |
| 1 | 3 | 1 |
| 2 | 2 | 2 |
| 3 | 1 | 3 |

**FIGURE 2**

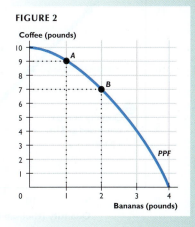

## 6.2  VALUE, PRICE, AND CONSUMER SURPLUS

To investigate whether a market is efficient, we need to understand the connection between demand and marginal benefit and between supply and marginal cost.

### ■ Demand and Marginal Benefit

In everyday life, when we talk about "getting value for money," we're distinguishing between *value* and *price*. Value is what we get, and price is what we pay. In economics, the everyday idea of value is *marginal benefit*, which we measure as the maximum price that people are willing to pay for another unit of the good or service. The demand curve tells us this price. In Figure 6.4(a), the demand curve shows the quantity demanded at a given price—when the price is $10 a pizza, the quantity demanded is 10,000 pizzas a day. In Figure 6.4(b), the demand curve shows the maximum price that people are willing to pay when there is a given quantity—when 10,000 pizzas a day are available, the most that people are willing to pay for the 10,000th pizza is $10. The marginal benefit from the 10,000th pizza is $10.

**A demand curve is a marginal benefit curve. The demand curve for pizza tells us the dollars' worth of other goods and services that people are willing to forgo to consume one more pizza.**

### ■ FIGURE 6.4

Demand, Willingness to Pay, and Marginal Benefit

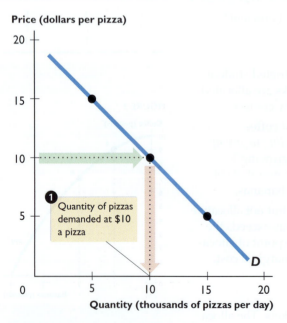

**(a) Price determines quantity demanded**

❶ The demand curve for pizza, *D*, shows the quantity of pizza demanded at each price, other things remaining the same. At $10 a pizza, the quantity demanded is 10,000 pizzas a day.

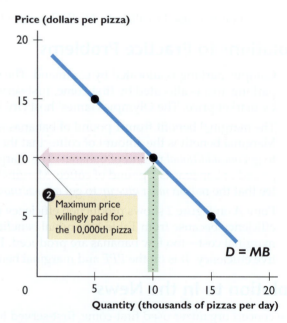

**(b) Quantity determines willingness to pay**

❷ The demand curve shows the maximum price willingly paid (marginal benefit) for a given quantity. If 10,000 pizzas are available, the maximum price willingly paid for the 10,000th pizza is $10. The demand curve is also the marginal benefit curve *MB*.

## ■ Consumer Surplus

We don't always have to pay as much as we're willing to pay. When people buy something for less than it is worth to them, they receive a consumer surplus. **Consumer surplus** is the excess of marginal benefit from a good over the price paid for it, summed over the quantity consumed.

Figure 6.5 illustrates consumer surplus. The demand curve for pizza tells us the quantity of pizza that people plan to buy at each price and the marginal benefit from pizza at each quantity. If the price of a pizza is $10, people buy 10,000 pizzas a day. Expenditure on pizza is $100,000, which is shown by the area of the blue rectangle.

To calculate consumer surplus, we must find the consumer surplus on each pizza and add these consumer surpluses together. For the 10,000th pizza, marginal benefit equals $10 and people pay $10, so the consumer surplus on this pizza is zero. For the 5,000th pizza (highlighted in the figure), marginal benefit is $15. So on this pizza, consumer surplus is $15 minus $10, which is $5. For the first pizza, marginal benefit is almost $20, so on this pizza, consumer surplus is almost $10.

Consumer surplus—the sum of the consumer surpluses on the 10,000 pizzas that people buy—is $50,000 a day, which is shown by the area of the green triangle. (The base of the triangle is 10,000 pizzas a day and its height is $10, so its area is (10,000 × $10) ÷ 2 = $50,000.)

The total benefit is the amount paid, $100,000 (blue rectangle), plus consumer surplus, $50,000 (green triangle), and is $150,000. Consumer surplus is the total benefit minus the amount paid, or net benefit to consumers.

**Consumer surplus**
The marginal benefit from a good or service in excess of the price paid for it, summed over the quantity consumed.

## FIGURE 6.5

### Demand and Consumer Surplus

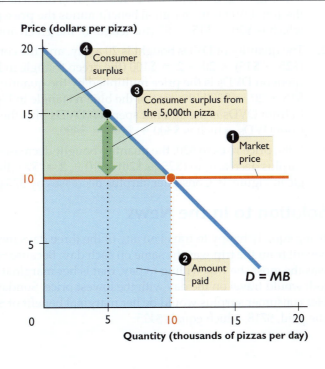

**Price (dollars per pizza)**

**④** Consumer surplus

**③** Consumer surplus from the 5,000th pizza

**①** Market price

**②** Amount paid

**D = MB**

**Quantity (thousands of pizzas per day)**

**①** The market price of a pizza is $10.

**②** At the market price, people buy 10,000 pizzas a day and spend $100,000 on pizza—the blue rectangle.

**③** The demand curve tells us that people are willing to pay $15 for the 5,000th pizza, so consumer surplus on the 5,000th pizza is $5.

**④** Consumer surplus from the 10,000 pizzas that people buy is $50,000—the area of the green triangle.

The total benefit from pizza is the $100,000 that people pay plus the $50,000 consumer surplus they receive, or $150,000.

# CHECKPOINT 6.2

**Distinguish between value and price and define consumer surplus.**

## Practice Problems

Figure 1 shows the demand curve for DVDs and the market price of a DVD.

1. What is the willingness to pay for the 20th DVD? Calculate the value of the 10th DVD and the consumer surplus on the 10th DVD.

2. What is the quantity of DVDs bought? Calculate the consumer surplus, the amount spent on DVDs, and the total benefit from the DVDs bought.

3. If the price of a DVD rises to $20, what is the change in consumer surplus?

## In the News

**Airfares stacked against consumers**
The airlines change prices from day to day. For example, the fare on one Delta flight from New York to Los Angeles jumped from $755 to $1,143 from a Friday to Saturday in April, then fell to $718 on Sunday.

Source: boston.com, June 22, 2011

Jodi planned a trip from New York to Los Angeles and was equally happy to travel on Friday, Saturday, or Sunday. The Saturday price was the most she was willing to pay. On which day do you predict she travelled and how much consumer surplus did she receive?

## Solutions to Practice Problems

1. The willingness to pay for the 20th DVD is the price on the demand curve at 20 DVDs, which is $15 (Figure 2). The value of the 10th DVD is its marginal benefit which is also the maximum price that someone is willing to pay for it. In Figure 2, the value of the 10th DVD is $20. The consumer surplus on the 10th DVD is its marginal benefit minus the price paid for the DVD, which is $20 − $15 = $5 (the length of the green arrow in Figure 2).

2. The quantity of DVDs bought is 20 a day, and the consumer surplus is ($25 − $15) × 20 ÷ 2 = $100 (the green triangle in Figure 2). The amount spent on DVDs is the price multiplied by the quantity bought, which is $15 × 20 = $300 (the area of the blue rectangle in Figure 2). The total benefit from DVDs is the amount spent on DVDs plus the consumer surplus from DVDs, which is $300 + $100 = $400.

3. If the price rises to $20, the quantity bought decreases to 10 a day. Consumer surplus decreases to ($25 − $20) × 10 ÷ 2 = $25 (the area of the green triangle in Figure 3). Consumer surplus decreases by $75 (from $100 to $25).

## Solution to In the News

Being equally happy to travel on any of the three days means that Jodi's marginal benefit from the trip was the same on each day. Because Saturday's price of $1,143 was the most she was willing to pay, that is her marginal benefit. Being rational, Jodi would travel on the day with the lowest price, Sunday, and pay a fare of $718. Her consumer surplus would be her marginal benefit of $1,143 minus the price she paid, $718, which equals $425.

---

**FIGURE 1**

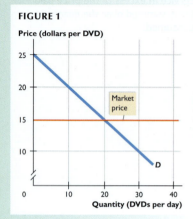

**FIGURE 2**

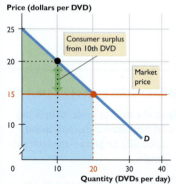

**FIGURE 3**

## 6.3  COST, PRICE, AND PRODUCER SURPLUS

You are now going to learn about cost, price, and producer surplus, which parallels what you've learned about value, price, and consumer surplus.

### ■ Supply and Marginal Cost

Just as buyers distinguish between *value* and *price,* so sellers distinguish between *cost* and *price.* Cost is what a seller must give up to produce the good, and price is what a seller receives when the good is sold. The cost of producing one more unit of a good or service is its *marginal cost.* It is just worth producing one more unit of a good or service if the price for which it can be sold equals marginal cost. The supply curve tells us this price. In Figure 6.6(a), the supply curve shows the quantity supplied at a given price—when the price of a pizza is $10, the quantity supplied is 10,000 pizzas a day. In Figure 6.6(b), the supply curve shows the minimum price that producers must receive to supply a given quantity—to supply 10,000 pizzas a day, producers must be able to get at least $10 for the 10,000th pizza. The marginal cost of the 10,000th pizza is $10. So:

> A supply curve is a marginal cost curve. The supply curve of pizza tells us the dollars' worth of other goods and services that people must forgo if firms produce one more pizza.

### ■ FIGURE 6.6

Supply, Minimum Supply Price, and Marginal Cost

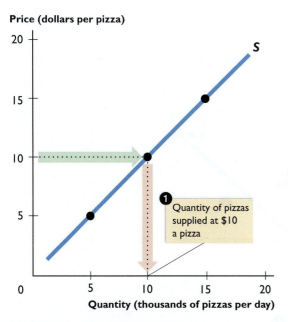

**(a) Price determines quantity supplied**

❶ The supply curve of pizza, S, shows the quantity of pizza supplied at each price, other things remaining the same. At $10 a pizza, the quantity supplied is 10,000 pizzas a day.

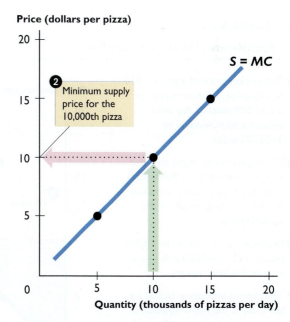

**(b) Quantity determines minimum supply price**

❷ The supply curve shows the minimum price that firms must be offered to supply a given quantity. The minimum supply price equals marginal cost, which for the 10,000th pizza is $10. The supply curve is also the marginal cost curve MC.

## ■ Producer Surplus

**Producer surplus**

The price of a good in excess of the marginal cost of producing it, summed over the quantity produced.

When the price exceeds marginal cost, the firm obtains a producer surplus. **Producer surplus** is the excess of the price of a good over the marginal cost of producing it, summed over the quantity produced.

Figure 6.7 illustrates the producer surplus for pizza producers. The supply curve of pizza tells us the quantity of pizza that producers plan to sell at each price. The supply curve also tells us the marginal cost of pizza at each quantity produced. If the price of a pizza is $10, producers plan to sell 10,000 pizzas a day. The total revenue from pizza is $100,000 per day.

To calculate producer surplus, we must find the producer surplus on each pizza and add these surpluses together. For the 10,000th pizza, marginal cost equals $10 and producers receive $10, so the producer surplus on this pizza is zero. For the 5,000th pizza (highlighted in the figure), marginal cost is $6. So on this pizza, producer surplus is $10 minus $6, which is $4. For the first pizza, marginal cost is $2, so on this pizza, producer surplus is $10 minus $2, which is $8.

Producer surplus—the sum of the producer surpluses on the 10,000 pizzas that firms produce—is $40,000 a day, which is shown by the area of the blue triangle. The base of the triangle is 10,000 pizzas a day and its height is $8, so its area is (10,000 × $8) ÷ 2 = $40,000.

The total cost of producing pizza is the amount received from selling it, $100,000, minus the producer surplus, $40,000 (blue triangle), and is $60,000 (the red area). Producer surplus is the total amount received minus the total cost, or net benefit to producers.

■ **FIGURE 6.7**

Supply and Producer Surplus

① The market price of a pizza is $10. At this price, producers plan to sell 10,000 pizzas a day and receive a total revenue of $100,000 a day.

② The supply curve shows that the marginal cost of the 5,000th pizza a day is $6, so producers receive a producer surplus of $4 on the 5,000th pizza.

③ Producer surplus from the 10,000 pizzas sold is $40,000 a day—the area of the blue triangle.

④ The cost of producing 10,000 pizzas a day is the red area beneath the marginal cost curve. It equals total revenue of $100,000 minus producer surplus of $40,000 and is $60,000 a day.

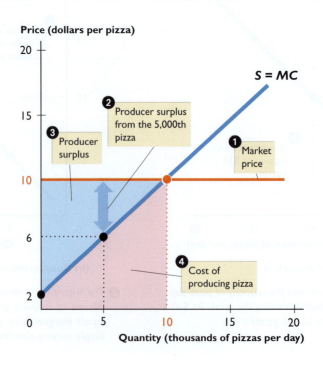

# CHECKPOINT 6.3

**Distinguish between cost and price and define producer surplus.**

## Practice Problems

Figure 1 shows the supply curve of DVDs and the market price of a DVD.

1. What is the minimum supply price of the 20th DVD? Calculate the marginal cost of the 10th DVD and the producer surplus on the 10th DVD.
2. What is the quantity of DVDs sold? Calculate the producer surplus, the total revenue from the DVDs sold, and the cost of producing the DVDs sold.
3. If the price of a DVD falls to $10, what is the change in producer surplus?

## In the News

**Is Australia's ski season headed for a wipeout?**
The Australian dollar has soared 26 percent against the U.S. dollar since last June, making those foreign lift tickets cheaper than those in Australia, and travel agents report a jump in interest in travel to North American ski destinations like Vail and Aspen.

Source: *The Wall Street Journal*, June 6, 2011

As Australians switch from skiing in Australia and flock to Vail and Aspen, how will the Australian ski operators' producer surplus change? How will the Vail and Aspen ski operators' producer surplus change?

## Solutions to Practice Problems

1. The minimum supply price of the 20th DVD is the marginal cost of the 20th DVD, which is $15 (Figure 2). The marginal cost of the 10th DVD is equal to the minimum supply price for the 10th DVD, which is $10. The producer surplus on the 10th DVD is its market price minus the marginal cost of producing it, which is $15 − $10 = $5 (the blue arrow in Figure 2).
2. The quantity sold is 20 a day. Producer surplus equals ($15 − $5) × 20 ÷ 2, which is $100 (the area of the blue triangle in Figure 2). The total revenue is price multiplied by quantity sold. Total revenue is $15 × 20 = $300. The cost of producing DVDs equals total revenue minus producer surplus, which is $300 − $100 = $200 (the red area in Figure 2).
3. The quantity sold decreases to 10 a day. The producer surplus decreases to ($10 − $5) × 10 ÷ 2 = $25 (the area of the blue triangle in Figure 3). The change in producer surplus is a decrease of $75 (from $100 down to $25).

## Solution to In the News

Producer surplus is the excess of the price of a good over the marginal cost of producing it, summed over the quantity produced.

In Australia, the demand for ski tickets decreases, the price and quantity of tickets sold decreases, and Australian ski operators' producer surplus decreases.

In Vail and Aspen, the demand for ski tickets increases, the price and quantity of tickets sold increases, and ski operators' producer surplus increases.

**FIGURE 1**

**FIGURE 2**

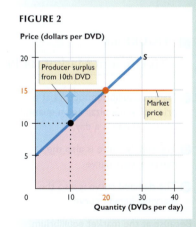

**FIGURE 3**

## 6.4 ARE MARKETS EFFICIENT?

Figure 6.8 shows the market for pizza. The demand curve is *D*, the supply curve is *S*, the equilibrium price is $10 a pizza, and the equilibrium quantity is 10,000 pizzas a day. The market forces that you studied in Chapter 4 (pp. 136–137) pull the pizza market to its equilibrium and coordinate the plans of buyers and sellers. But does this competitive equilibrium deliver the efficient quantity of pizza?

If the equilibrium is efficient, it does more than coordinate plans. It coordinates them in the best possible way. Resources are used to produce the quantity of pizza that people value most highly. It is not possible to produce more pizza without giving up some of another good or service that is valued more highly. And if a smaller quantity of pizza is produced, resources are used to produce some other good that is not valued as highly as the pizza that is forgone.

### ■ Marginal Benefit Equals Marginal Cost

To check whether the equilibrium in Figure 6.8 is efficient, recall the interpretation of the demand curve as a marginal benefit curve and the supply curve as a marginal cost curve. The demand curve tells us the marginal benefit from pizza. The supply curve tells us the marginal cost of pizza. Where the demand curve and the supply curve intersect, marginal benefit equals marginal cost.

### ■ FIGURE 6.8

#### An Efficient Market for Pizza

❶ Market equilibrium occurs at a price of $10 a pizza and a quantity of 10,000 pizzas a day.

❷ The supply curve is also the marginal cost curve.

❸ The demand curve is also the marginal benefit curve.

Because at the market equilibrium, marginal benefit equals marginal cost, the ❹ efficient quantity of pizza is produced. The sum of the ❺ consumer surplus and ❻ producer surplus is maximized.

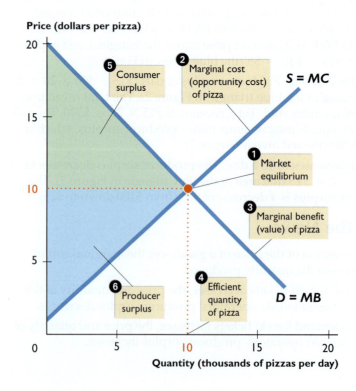

This condition—marginal benefit equals marginal cost—is the condition that delivers an efficient use of resources. Because a competitive equilibrium allocates resources to the activities that create the greatest possible value, it is efficient.

## ■ Total Surplus Is Maximized

Another way of checking that the equilibrium is efficient is to look at the total surplus that it generates. **Total surplus** is the sum of producer surplus and consumer surplus. A price above the equilibrium might increase producer surplus, but it would decrease consumer surplus by more. And a price below the equilibrium price might increase consumer surplus, but it would decrease producer surplus by more. The competitive equilibrium price maximizes total surplus.

**Total surplus**
The sum of producer surplus and consumer surplus.

In Figure 6.8, if production is less than 10,000 pizzas a day, someone is willing to buy a pizza for more than it costs to produce. Buyers and sellers will gain if production increases. If production exceeds 10,000 pizzas a day, it costs more to produce a pizza than anyone is willing to pay for it. Buyers and sellers will gain if production decreases. Only when 10,000 pizzas a day are produced is there no unexploited gain from changing the quantity of pizza produced, and total surplus is maximized.

Buyers and sellers each attempt to do the best they can for themselves—they pursue their self-interest. No one plans for an efficient outcome for society as a whole. No one worries about the social interest. Buyers seek the lowest possible price, and sellers seek the highest possible price. But as buyers and sellers pursue their self-interest, this astonishing outcome occurs: The social interest is served.

## ■ The Invisible Hand

Writing in his *Wealth of Nations* in 1776, Adam Smith was the first to suggest that competitive markets send resources to the uses in which they have the highest value. Smith believed that each participant in a competitive market is "led by an invisible hand to promote an end [the efficient use of resources] which was no part of his intention."

You can see the effects of the invisible hand at work every day. Your campus bookstore is stuffed with texts at the start of each term. It has the quantities that it predicts students will buy. The coffee shop has the variety and quantities of drinks and snacks that people plan to buy. Your local clothing store has the sweatpants and socks and other items that you plan to buy. Truckloads of textbooks, coffee and cookies, and sweatpants and socks roll along our highways and bring these items to where you and your friends want to buy them. Firms that don't know you anticipate your wants and work hard to help you satisfy them.

No government organizes all this production, and no government auditor monitors producers to ensure that they serve the social interest. The allocation of scarce resources is not planned. It happens because prices adjust to make buying plans and selling plans compatible, and it happens in a way that sends resources to the uses in which they have the highest value.

Adam Smith explained why all this amazing activity occurs. "It is not from the benevolence of the butcher, the brewer, or the baker that we expect our dinner," he wrote, "but from their regard to their own interest."

Publishing companies, coffee growers, garment manufacturers, and a host of other producers are led by their regard for *their* own interest to serve *your* interest.

# EYE on the U.S. ECONOMY
## The Invisible Hand and e-Commerce

You can see Adam Smith's invisible hand idea in the cartoon.

On a hot sunny day, a cold-drinks vendor approaches a man sitting in a park reading a newspaper (the top frame). The vendor has both cold drinks and shade and an opportunity cost and a minimum supply-price of each item. The park bench reader has a marginal benefit from a cold drink and from shade.

A transaction occurs and the invisible hand does its work (the middle frame). The park bench reader buys the vendor's sun shade. This transaction tells us that the reader's marginal benefit from shade exceeds the vendor's marginal cost of shade.

After the transaction (bottom frame), the vendor obtains a producer surplus from selling the shade for more than its opportunity cost, and the reader obtains a consumer surplus from buying the shade for less than its marginal benefit. Both the buyer of shade and the seller are better off.

The umbrella has moved to its highest-valued use and the resource is being used efficiently.

© The New Yorker Collection 1985
Mike Twohy from cartoonbank.com. All Rights Reserved.

The market economy performs activity similar to that illustrated in the cartoon to achieve an efficient allocation of resources. New technologies have cut the cost of using the Internet and during the past few years, hundreds of Web sites have been established that are dedicated to facilitating trade in all types of goods, services, and factors of production.

The electronic auction site eBay (http://www.ebay.com/), has brought a huge increase in consumer surplus and producer surplus, and helps to achieve ever-greater allocative efficiency.

## ■ Market Failure

**Market failure** occurs when a market delivers an inefficient outcome. Either too little of an item is produced—*underproduction*—or too much—*overproduction*.

**Market failure**
An inefficient market outcome.

### Underproduction and Overproduction

When underproduction occurs, marginal benefit exceeds marginal cost. Items *not* produced are worth more than they cost. When overproduction occurs, marginal cost exceeds marginal benefit. Items produced cost more than they are worth.

Figure 6.9(a) illustrates underproduction at 5,000 pizzas a day. Every pizza between 5,000 and 9,999 is worth more than it costs to make but it is not produced. Figure 6.9(b) illustrates overproduction at 15,000 a day. Every pizza produced between 10,001 and 15,000 costs more to make than it is worth.

### Deadweight Loss

A **deadweight loss** is the decrease in total surplus that results from inefficient underproduction or overproduction. The gray triangle in Figure 6.9(a) illustrates the deadweight loss from underproduction and in Figure 6.9(b) it shows the deadweight loss from overproduction. A deadweight loss is borne by the entire society. It is not a loss for producers and a gain for consumers. It is a *social* loss.

The deadweight loss from underproduction equals the area of the gray triangle in Figure 6.9(a). That area is $22,500 [($15 − $6) × 5,000 ÷ 2 = $22,500]. Can you calculate the deadweight loss from overproduction in Figure 6.9(b)?

**Deadweight loss**
The decrease in total surplus that results from an inefficient underproduction or overproduction.

### ■ FIGURE 6.9

Inefficient Outcomes

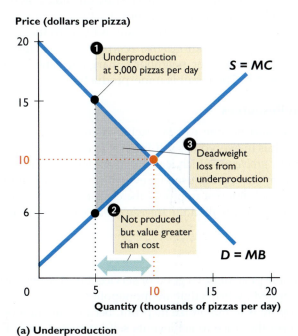

**(a) Underproduction**

❶ If production is 5,000 pizzas a day, ❷ pizzas not produced are worth more than they cost to make—there is inefficient underproduction. ❸ The gray triangle shows the deadweight loss that arises.

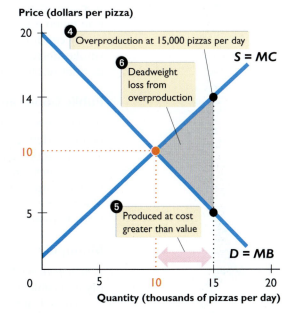

**(b) Overproduction**

❹ If production is 15,000 pizzas a day, ❺ pizzas produced cost more to make than they are worth—there is inefficient overproduction. ❻ The gray triangle shows the deadweight loss that arises.

## ■ Sources of Market Failure

Obstacles to efficiency that bring market failure and create deadweight losses are

- Price and quantity regulations
- Taxes and subsidies
- Externalities
- Public goods and common resources
- Monopoly
- High transactions costs

### Price and Quantity Regulations

*Price regulations* that put a cap on the rent a landlord is permitted to charge and laws that require employers to pay a minimum wage sometimes block the price adjustments that balance the quantity demanded and the quantity supplied and lead to underproduction. *Quantity regulations* that limit the amount that a farm is permitted to produce also lead to underproduction.

### Taxes and Subsidies

*Taxes* increase the prices paid by buyers and lower the prices received by sellers. So taxes decrease the quantity produced and lead to underproduction. *Subsidies,* which are payments by the government to producers, decrease the prices paid by buyers and increase the prices received by sellers. So subsidies increase the quantity produced and lead to overproduction.

### Externalities

An *externality* is a cost or a benefit that affects someone other than the seller and the buyer of a good. An electric utility creates an *external cost* by burning coal that brings acid rain and crop damage. The utility doesn't consider the cost of pollution when it decides how much power to produce. The result is overproduction.

A condominium owner would provide an *external benefit* if she installed a smoke detector. But she doesn't consider her neighbor's marginal benefit and decides not to install a smoke detector. The result is underproduction.

### Public Goods and Common Resources

A *public good* benefits everyone and no one can be excluded from its benefits. National defense is an example. It is in everyone's self-interest to avoid paying for a public good (called the *free-rider problem*), which leads to its underproduction.

A *common resource* is owned by no one but used by everyone. Atlantic salmon is an example. It is in everyone's self-interest to ignore the costs of their own use of a common resource that fall on others (called the *tragedy of the commons*), which leads to overproduction.

### Monopoly

A *monopoly* is a firm that is the sole provider of a good or service. Local water supply and cable television are supplied by firms that are monopolies.

The self-interest of a monopoly is to maximize its profit. Because the monopoly has no competitors, it can set the price to achieve its self-interested goal. To achieve its goal, a monopoly produces too little and charges too high a price, which leads to underproduction.

## High Transactions Costs

Stroll around a shopping mall and observe the retail markets in which you participate. You'll see that these markets employ enormous quantities of scarce labor and capital resources. It is costly to operate any market. Economists call the opportunity costs of making trades in a market **transactions costs**.

To use market prices as the allocators of scarce resources, it must be worth bearing the opportunity cost of establishing a market. Some markets are just too costly to operate. For example, when you want to play tennis on your local "free" court, you don't pay a market price for your slot on the court. You hang around until the court becomes vacant, and you "pay" with your waiting time.

When transactions costs are high, the market might underproduce.

**Transactions costs**
The opportunity costs of making trades in a market.

## ■ Alternatives to the Market

When a market is inefficient, can one of the alternative non-market methods that we described at the beginning of this chapter do a better job? Sometimes it can.

Table 6.1 summarizes the sources of market failure and the possible remedies. Often, majority rule might be used, but majority rule has its own shortcomings. A group that pursues the self-interest of its members can become the majority. For example, price and quantity regulations that create deadweight loss are almost always the result of a self-interested group becoming the majority and imposing costs on the minority. Also, with majority rule, votes must be translated into actions by bureaucrats who have their own agendas.

Managers in firms issue commands and avoid the transactions costs that they would incur if they went to a market every time they needed a job done. First-come, first-served saves a lot of hassle in waiting lines. These lines could have markets in which people trade their place in the line—but someone would have to enforce the agreements. Can you imagine the hassle at a busy Starbucks if you had to buy your spot at the head of the line?

There is no one mechanism for allocating resources efficiently. But markets bypassed by command systems inside firms and supplemented by majority rule and first-come, first-served do an amazingly good job.

### ■ Table 6.1

Market Failure and Some Possible Remedies

| Reason for market failure | Possible remedy |
| --- | --- |
| 1. Price and quantity regulations | Remove regulation by majority rule |
| 2. Taxes and subsidies | Minimize deadweight loss by majority rule |
| 3. Externalities | Minimize deadweight loss by majority rule |
| 4. Public goods | Allocate by majority rule |
| 5. Common resources | Allocate by majority rule |
| 6. Monopoly | Regulate by majority rule |
| 7. High transactions costs | Command or first-come, first-served |

# CHECKPOINT 6.4

**Evaluate the efficiency of the alternative methods of allocating resources.**

## Practice Problems

Figure 1 shows the market for paper.

1. At the market equilibrium, what are consumer surplus, producer surplus, and total surplus? Is the market for paper efficient? Why or why not?

2. Lobbyists for a group of news magazines persuade the government to pass a law that requires producers to sell 50 tons of paper a day. Is the market for paper efficient? Why or why not? Shade the deadweight loss on the figure.

3. An environmental lobbying group persuades the government to pass a law that limits the quantity of paper that producers sell to 20 tons a day. Is the market for paper efficient? If not, what is the deadweight loss?

## In the News

**Senate votes to end ethanol subsidies**
The Senate has voted to end the $6 billion a year in subsidies paid to the ethanol industry for the past three decades. Refiners would lose the 45-cent-a-gallon subsidy, and the tax on imported ethanol would be eliminated.

Source: *USA Today*, June 16, 2011

Describe the efficiency of the market for ethanol with the $6 billion subsidies in place. If the subsidies and taxes are eliminated, explain how the efficiency of the market for ethanol would change.

## Solutions to Practice Problems

1. Market equilibrium is 40 tons a day at a price of $3 a ton (Figure 2). Consumer surplus = ($9 − $3) × 40 ÷ 2 = $120 (the area of the green triangle in Figure 2). Producer surplus is ($3 − $1) × 40 ÷ 2, which equals $40 (the area of the blue triangle in Figure 2). Total surplus is the sum of consumer surplus and producer surplus, which is $160.
   The market is efficient because marginal benefit (on the demand curve) equals marginal cost (on the supply curve) and total surplus (consumer surplus plus producer surplus) is maximized.

2. The market is inefficient because marginal cost exceeds marginal benefit. Deadweight loss equals the area of the gray triangle 1 in Figure 3.

3. This market is now inefficient because marginal benefit exceeds marginal cost. The deadweight loss equals the area of the gray triangle 2 in Figure 3.

## Solution to In the News

Subsidies to producers increase the supply of the good, which decreases the market price. The price received by producers equals the market price plus the subsidy per gallon, which results in overproduction and inefficiency. A deadweight loss arises. By eliminating the subsidies and taxes, overproduction will decrease. The market for ethanol will be more efficient, and the deadweight loss will decrease.

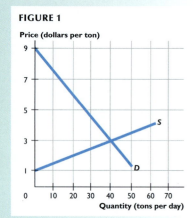

**FIGURE 1**

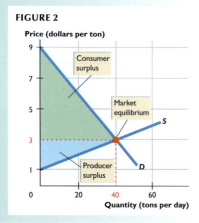

**FIGURE 2**

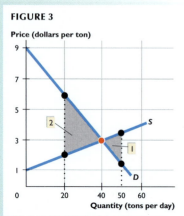

**FIGURE 3**

## 6.5    ARE MARKETS FAIR?

Following a severe winter storm or hurricane, the prices of many essential items jump. Is it fair that disaster victims should be hit with higher prices? Many low-skilled people work for a wage that is below what most would regard as a living wage. Is that fair? How do we decide whether something is fair or unfair?

Economists have a clear definition of efficiency but they do not have a similarly clear definition of fairness. Also, ideas about fairness are not exclusively economic ideas. They involve the study of ethics.

To study ideas about fairness, think of economic life as a game—a serious game—that has *rules* and a *result*. Two broad and generally conflicting approaches to fairness are

- It's not fair if the *rules* aren't fair.
- It's not fair if the *result* isn't fair.

### ■ It's Not Fair If the *Rules* Aren't Fair

Harvard philosopher Robert Nozick argued for the fair-rules view in a book entitled *Anarchy, State, and Utopia*, published in 1974. Nozick argued that fairness requires two rules:

- The state must establish and protect private property rights.
- Goods and services and the services of factors of production may be transferred from one person to another only by voluntary exchange with everyone free to engage in such exchange.

The first rule says that everything that is valuable—all scarce resources and goods—must be owned by individuals and that the state must protect private property rights. The second rule says that the only way a person can acquire something is to buy it in voluntary trade.

If these rules are followed, says Nozick, the outcome is fair. It doesn't matter how unequally the economic pie is shared provided that the people who bake it supply their services voluntarily in exchange for the share of the pie offered in compensation. Opportunity is equal but the result might be unequal. This fair-rules approach is consistent with allocative efficiency.

### ■ It's Not Fair If the *Result* Isn't Fair

Most people think that the fair-rules approach leads to too much inequality—to an unfair result: For example, it is unfair for a bank president to earn millions of dollars a year while a bank teller earns only thousands of dollars a year.

But what is "too unequal"? Is it fair for some people to receive twice as much as others but not ten times as much or a hundred times as much? Or is all that matters that the poorest people shouldn't be "too poor"?

There is no easy answer to these questions. Generally, greater equality is regarded as good but there is no measure of the most desirable shares.

The fair-result approach conflicts with allocative efficiency and leads to what is called the **big tradeoff**—a tradeoff between efficiency and fairness that recognizes the cost of making income transfers.

The big tradeoff is based on the fact that income can be transferred to people with low incomes only by taxing people with high incomes. But taxing people's

**Big tradeoff**
A tradeoff between efficiency and fairness that recognizes the cost of making income transfers.

# EYE on PRICE GOUGING
## Should Price Gouging Be Illegal?

*Price gouging* is the practice of selling an essential item for a much higher price than normal, and usually occurs following a natural disaster. In Florida and Texas, where hurricanes happen all too often, price gouging is illegal.

Whether price gouging *should* be illegal depends on the view of fairness employed and on the facts about whether the buyers or the sellers are the poorer group.

The standard view of economists is that price gouging should *not* be illegal and that it is the expected and *efficient* response to a change in demand.

After a hurricane, the demand for items such as generators, pumps, lamps, gasoline, and camp stoves increases and the prices of these items rise in a natural response to the change in demand.

The figure illustrates the market for camp stoves. The supply of stoves is the curve $S$, and in normal times, the demand for stoves is $D_0$. The price is $20 per stove and the equilibrium quantity is 5 stoves per day.

Following a hurricane that results in a lengthy power failure, the demand for camp stoves increases to $D_1$. Provided there is no price-gouging law, the equilibrium price of a stove jumps to $40 and the equilibrium quantity increases to 7 stoves per day.

This outcome is efficient because the marginal cost of a stove (on the supply curve) equals the marginal benefit from a stove (on the demand curve).

If a strict price-gouging law requires the price after the hurricane to be the *same* as the price before the hurricane, the price of a stove is stuck at $20.

At this price, the quantity of stoves supplied remains at 5 per day and a deadweight loss shown by the gray triangle arises. The price-gouging law is inefficient, and the price rise is efficient.

Whether a doubling of the price is *fair* depends on the idea of fairness used. On the *fair-rules* view, the price rise is fair. Trade is voluntary and both the buyer and the seller are better off. On the *fair-result* view, the price rise might be considered unfair if the buyers are poor and the sellers are rich. But if the buyers are rich and the sellers are poor, the price rise would be considered fair even on the fair-result view.

After Hurricane Katrina, John Shepperson bought 19 generators, loaded them into a rented U-Haul vehicle, and drove the 600 miles from his home in Kentucky to a place in Mississippi that had no power. He offered his generators to eager buyers for twice the price he had paid for them. But before he could complete a sale, the Mississippi police swooped in on him. They confiscated his generators and put him in jail for four days. His crime: price gouging.

Was it efficient to stop Mr. Shepperson from selling his generators? Was it fair either to him or his deprived customers?

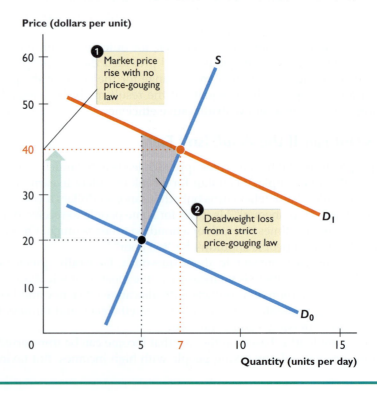

# EYE on YOUR LIFE
## Allocation Methods, Efficiency, and Fairness

You live in the national economy, your state economy, your regional economy, and your own household economy. The many decisions you must make affect efficiency and fairness at all these levels. Think about your household economy.

Make a spreadsheet and on it identify all the factors of production that your household owns. Count all the person-hours available and any capital.

Show how these resources are allocated.

By what methods are your household's scarce resources allocated? Identify those allocated by market price; by command; by first-come, first-served; and by equal shares. Are any resources allocated by majority vote?

Now the tough part: Are these resources allocated efficiently—is the value of your household's resources maximized? Think about how you can check whether marginal benefit equals marginal cost for each of your household's activities.

And now an even tougher question: Are your household's resources allocated fairly? Think about the two ideas of fairness and how they apply in your household.

---

income from employment discourages work. It results in the quantity of labor being less than the efficient quantity. Taxing people's income from capital discourages saving. It results in the quantity of capital being less than the efficient quantity. With smaller quantities of both labor and capital, the quantity of goods and services produced is less than the efficient quantity. The economic pie shrinks.

Income redistribution creates a tradeoff between the size of the economic pie and the equality with which it is shared. The greater the scale of income redistribution through income taxes, the greater is the inefficiency—the smaller is the pie.

There is a second source of inefficiency: A dollar taken from a rich person does not end up as a dollar in the hands of a poorer person. Some of the dollar is spent on administration of the tax and transfer system, which includes the cost of accountants, auditors, and lawyers. These activities use skilled labor and capital resources that could otherwise be used to produce other goods and services that people value.

You can see that when all these costs are taken into account, transferring a dollar from a rich person does not give a dollar to a poor person. It is even possible that those with low incomes end up being worse off. For example, if a highly taxed entrepreneur decides to work less hard and shut down a business, low-income workers get fired and must seek other, perhaps even lower-paid, work.

## ■ Compromise

Most people, and probably most economists, have sympathy with the Nozick view but think it too extreme. They see a role for taxes and government income support schemes to transfer some income from the rich to the poor. Such transfers could be considered voluntary in the sense that they are decided by majority voting, and even those who vote against such transfers voluntarily participate in the political process.

Once we agree that using the tax system to make transfers from the rich to the poor is fair, we need to determine just what we mean by a fair tax. We'll look at this big question when we study the tax system in Chapter 8.

**CHECKPOINT 6.5**

Explain the main ideas about fairness and evaluate the fairness of the alternative methods of allocating scarce resources.

## Practice Problems

A winter storm cuts the power supply and isolates a small town in the mountains. The people rush to buy candles from the town store, which is the only source of candles. The store owner decides to ration the candles to one per family but to keep the price of a candle unchanged.

1. Who gets to use the candles? Who receives the consumer surplus and who receives the producer surplus on candles?

2. Is the allocation efficient? Is the allocation fair?

## In the News

**Water use rising faster than world population**
Water use has been growing at more than twice the rate of population increase in the last century. Earth has lots of water, but 97.5 percent of it is salty. The problem is that over a billion people have no clean fresh drinking water.

Source: Reuters, October 25, 2011

Would a free world market in fresh water achieve a fair use of the world's water resources? Explain why or why not and be clear about the concept of fairness that you are using.

## Solutions to Practice Problems

1. The people who buy candles from the town store are not necessarily the people who use the candles. A buyer from the town store can sell a candle and will do so if he or she can get a price that exceeds his or her marginal benefit. The people who value the candles most—who are willing to pay the most—will use the candles.
   Only the people who are willing to pay the most for candles receive the consumer surplus on candles, and the store owner receives the same producer surplus as normal. People who sell the candles they buy from the store receive additional producer surplus.

2. The allocation is efficient because the people who value the candles most use them. Two views of fairness: The fair-rules view is that if the rule of one candle per family is followed and exchange is voluntary, then the outcome is fair. But the fair-result view is that if the candles are allocated unequally, then the allocation is unfair.

## Solution to In the News

In a free world market in fresh water, the market price would allocate the water. This allocation of water would be fair on the fair-rules view because the exchange of water would be voluntary, but it would not be fair on the fair-result view because poor people who own no water and those living in drought-stricken areas would not be able to afford water.

**CHAPTER SUMMARY**

## Key Points

**1. Describe the alternative methods of allocating scarce resources and define and explain the features of an efficient allocation.**

- The methods of allocating scarce resources are market price; command; majority rule; contest; first-come, first-served; sharing equally; lottery; personal characteristics; and force.
- Allocative efficiency occurs when resources are used to create the greatest value, which means that marginal benefit equals marginal cost.

**2. Distinguish between value and price and define consumer surplus.**

- Marginal benefit is measured by the maximum price that consumers are willing to pay for another unit of a good or service.
- A demand curve is a marginal benefit curve.
- Value is what people are *willing to* pay; price is what they *must* pay.
- Consumer surplus equals the excess of marginal benefit over price, summed over the quantity consumed.

**3. Distinguish between cost and price and define producer surplus.**

- Marginal cost is measured by the minimum price producers must be offered to increase production by one unit.
- A supply curve is a marginal cost curve.
- Opportunity cost is what producers *must* pay; price is what they *receive*.
- Producer surplus equals the excess of price over marginal cost, summed over the quantity produced.

**4. Evaluate the efficiency of the alternative methods of allocating resources.**

- In a competitive equilibrium, marginal benefit equals marginal cost and resource allocation is efficient.
- Price and quantity regulations, taxes, subsidies, externalities, public goods, common resources, monopoly, and high transactions costs lead to market failure and create deadweight loss.

**5. Explain the main ideas about fairness and evaluate the fairness of the alternative methods of allocating scarce resources.**

- Ideas about fairness divide into two groups: fair *rules* and a fair *result*.
- Fair rules require private property rights and voluntary exchange, and a fair result requires income transfers from the rich to the poor.

## Key Terms

Allocative efficiency, 179
Big tradeoff, 197
Command system, 177
Consumer surplus, 185

Deadweight loss, 193
Market failure, 193
Producer surplus, 188

Production possibilities frontier, 179
Total surplus, 191
Transactions costs, 195

# CHAPTER CHECKPOINT

## Study Plan Problems and Applications

At McDonald's, no reservations are accepted; at Panorama Restaurant at the St. Louis Art Museum, reservations are accepted; at Niche, reservations are essential. Use this information to answer Problems **1** to **3**.

**1.** Describe the method of allocating table resources in these three restaurants.

**2.** Why do you think restaurants have different reservation policies, and why might each restaurant be using an efficient allocation method?

**3.** Why don't all restaurants use the market price to allocate their tables?

Table 1 shows the demand and supply schedules for sandwiches. Use Table 1 to work Problems **4** to **7**.

**4.** Calculate the equilibrium price of a sandwich, the consumer surplus, and the producer surplus. What is the efficient quantity of sandwiches?

**5.** If the quantity demanded decreases by 100 sandwiches an hour at each price, what is the equilibrium price and what is the change in total surplus?

**6.** If the quantity supplied decreases by 100 sandwiches an hour at each price, what is the equilibrium price and what is the change in total surplus?

**7.** If Sandwiches To Go, Inc., buys all the sandwich producers and cuts production to 100 sandwiches an hour, what is the deadweight loss that is created? If Sandwiches To Go, Inc., rations sandwiches to two per person, by what view of fairness would the allocation be unfair?

Use the following information to work Problems **8** and **9**.

Table 2 shows the demand and supply schedules for sandbags before and during a major flood. During the flood, suppose that the government gave all families an equal quantity of sandbags. Resale of sandbags is not permitted.

**8.** How would total surplus and the price of a sandbag change?

**9.** Would the outcome be more efficient than if the government took no action? Explain.

**10.** The winner of the men's or women's tennis singles at the U.S. Open is paid twice as much as the runner-up, but it takes two players to have a singles final. Is this compensation arrangement efficient? Is it fair? Explain why it might illustrate the big tradeoff.

Use the following information to work Problems **11** and **12**.

### eBay saves billions for bidders

On eBay, the bidder who places the highest bid wins the auction and pays only what the second highest bidder offered. Researchers Wolfgang Jank and Galit Shmueli reported that purchasers on eBay in 2003 paid $7 billion less than their winning bids. Because each bid shows the buyer's willingness to pay, the winner receives an estimated consumer surplus of $4 or more.

Source: *InformationWeek*, January 28, 2008

**11.** What method is used to allocate goods on eBay? How does an eBay auction influence consumer surplus from the good?

**12.** Read *Eye on Price Gouging* on p. 198 and explain why it was inefficient to stop Mr. Shepperson from selling his generators.

**TABLE 1**

| Price (dollars per sandwich) | Quantity demanded | Quantity supplied |
|---|---|---|
| | (sandwiches per hour) | |
| 0 | 400 | 0 |
| 1 | 350 | 50 |
| 2 | 300 | 100 |
| 3 | 250 | 150 |
| 4 | 200 | 200 |
| 5 | 150 | 250 |
| 6 | 100 | 300 |
| 7 | 50 | 350 |
| 8 | 0 | 400 |

**TABLE 2**

| Price (dollars per bag) | Quantity demanded before flood | Quantity demanded during flood | Quantity supplied |
|---|---|---|---|
| | (thousands of bags) | | |
| 0 | 40 | 70 | 0 |
| 1 | 35 | 65 | 5 |
| 2 | 30 | 60 | 10 |
| 3 | 25 | 55 | 15 |
| 4 | 20 | 50 | 20 |
| 5 | 15 | 45 | 25 |
| 6 | 10 | 40 | 30 |
| 7 | 5 | 35 | 35 |
| 8 | 0 | 30 | 40 |

# Instructor Assignable Problems and Applications

 **1. Panic in paradise: Are high fares the new reality for Hawaii?**

On March 31, 2008, Hawaii lost 15 percent of its air service as Aloha Airlines and the cheap-flight airline ATA suddenly shut down. Stranded travelers were offered flights to West Coast cities at $1,000 one way. Within a month, the fare to West Coast cities dropped to about $200 a round trip. Stranded travelers complained of price gouging.

Source: *USA Today*, April 23, 2008

Under what conditions would the $1,000 fare be considered "price gouging"? Under what conditions would the $1,000 fare be an example of the market price method of allocating scarce airline seats?

Table 1 shows the demand schedule for haircuts and the supply schedule of haircuts. Use Table 1 to work Problems **2** and **3**.

**2.** What is the quantity of haircuts bought, the value of a haircut, and the total surplus from haircuts?

**3.** Suppose that all salons agree to charge $40 a haircut. How do consumer surplus and producer surplus change? What is the deadweight loss created?

In California, farmers pay a lower price for water than do city residents. Use this information to work Problems **4** to **6**.

**4.** What is this method of allocation of water resources? Is this allocation of water efficient? Is this use of scarce water fair? Why or why not?

**5.** If farmers were charged the same price as city residents pay, how would the price of agricultural produce, the quantity of produce grown, consumer surplus, and producer surplus change?

**6.** If all water in California is sold for the market equilibrium price, would the allocation of water be more efficient? Why or why not?

Use the following information to work Problems **7** and **8**.

**The world's largest tulip and flower market**

Every day over 19 million tulips and flowers are auctioned at the Dutch market called "The Bloemenveiling." These Dutch auctions match buyers and sellers.

Source: Tulip-Bulbs.com

In a Dutch auction, the auctioneer announces the highest price. If no one offers to buy the flowers, the auctioneer lowers the price until a buyer is found.

**7.** What method is used to allocate flowers at the Bloemenveiling?

**8.** How does a Dutch flower auction influence consumer surplus and producer surplus? Are the flower auctions at the Bloemenveiling efficient?

**9. New Zealand's private forests**

In the early 1990s, the government auctioned half the national forests, converting these forests from public ownership to private ownership. The government's decision was an incentive to get the owners to operate like farmers—that is, take care of the resource and to use it to make a profit.

Source: *Reuters*, September 7, 2007

Was the timber industry efficient before the auction and did logging companies operate in the social interest or self-interest? What effect has private ownership had on efficiency of the timber industry?

**TABLE 1**

| Price (dollars per haircut) | Quantity demanded | supplied |
|---|---|---|
| | (haircuts per day) | |
| 0 | 100 | 0 |
| 10 | 80 | 0 |
| 20 | 60 | 20 |
| 30 | 40 | 40 |
| 40 | 20 | 60 |
| 50 | 0 | 80 |

## Critical Thinking Discussion Questions

**1.** **OPEC would cover for any Ukraine-related oil shortage**

Saudi Arabia, which has played the leading role in cushioning against supply disruptions from Libya, Nigeria, Iraq, and South Sudan, will increase production if the Ukraine crisis creates an oil shortage.

Source: Reuters, May 12, 2014

   a.  Do Saudi Arabia's actions make the global oil market more efficient?
   b.  What would happen to consumer surplus as a consequence of Saudi Arabia's actions?
   c.  What would happen to producer surplus as a consequence of Saudi Arabia's actions?
   d.  Would Saudi Arabia's actions lead to underproduction, overproduction, or neither?

**2.** The English Premier League's club players are paid very highly compared to Division 1 players. Describe the method of allocating scarce resources amongst EPL members. Is it efficient?

**3.** To encourage energy saving, the government of Malaysia will set the price to zero for households whose electricity consumption is below RM20 a month, and hike the prices for those whose electricity consumption exceeds a limit.

   a.  Which method is the government of Malaysia using to allocate electricity?
   b.  Is the policy likely to be efficient? Explain your answer.
   c.  How does the policy influence consumer surplus for low-use and high-use households?
   d.  How does the policy influence producer surplus?
   e.  Is the policy fair? Evaluate on alternative criteria of fairness.

**4.** **Golden Apples: iPhone fetches $10,000 on eBay**

Someone paid $10,100 for a limited gold iPhone in an online bid. A high volume of sales came after China joined the list of launch countries.

Source: *Sydney Morning Herald*, September 24, 2013

   a.  Did the person who paid $10,100 for a gold iPhone on eBay receive a consumer surplus?
   b.  Did Apple's including China in its list of launch countries make the launch more efficient?
   c.  Do you think Apple deliberately created a shortage of iPhones for this launch? If yes, how does Apple gain producer surplus from this action?

Can the President repeal the laws of supply and demand?

# Government Actions in Markets

**7**

When you have completed your study of this chapter, you will be able to

1 Explain how taxes change prices and quantities, are shared by buyers and sellers, and create inefficiency.

2 Explain how a price ceiling works and show how a rent ceiling creates a housing shortage, inefficiency, and unfairness.

3 Explain how a price floor works and show how the minimum wage creates unemployment, inefficiency, and unfairness.

4 Explain how a price support in the market for an agricultural product creates a surplus, inefficiency, and unfairness.

## 7.1   TAXES ON BUYERS AND SELLERS

Almost every time you buy something—a late-night order of chow mein, a plane ticket, a tank of gasoline—you pay a tax. On some items, you pay a sales tax that is added to the advertised price. On other items, you pay an excise tax—often at a high rate like the tax on gasoline—that is included in the advertised price.

But do you really pay these taxes? When a tax is added to the advertised price, isn't it obvious that *you* pay the tax? Isn't the price higher than it otherwise would be by an amount equal to the tax?

What about a tax that is buried in the price, such as that on gasoline? Who pays that tax? Does the seller just pass on the full amount of the tax to you, the buyer? Or does the seller pay the tax by taking a lower price and leaving the price you pay unchanged?

To answer these questions, let's suppose that TIFS, the Tax Illegal File Sharing lobby, has persuaded the government to collect a $10 tax on every new MP3 player and to use the tax revenue to compensate artists. But an argument is raging between those who claim that the buyer benefits from using the MP3 player and should pay the tax and those who claim that the seller profits and should pay the tax.

*Does "No Sales Tax" mean that the seller pays the tax?*

### ■ Tax Incidence

**Tax incidence**

The division of the burden of a tax between the buyer and the seller.

**Tax incidence** is the division of the burden of a tax between the buyer and the seller. We're going to find the incidence of a $10 tax on MP3 players with two different taxes: a tax on the buyer and a tax on the seller.

Figure 7.1 shows the market for MP3 players. With no tax, the equilibrium price is $100 and the equilibrium quantity is 5,000 players a week.

When a good is taxed, it has two prices: a price that excludes the tax and a price that includes the tax. Buyers respond only to the price that includes the tax, because that is the price they pay. Sellers respond only to the price that excludes the tax, because that is the price they receive. The tax is like a wedge between these two prices.

Figure 7.1(a) shows what happens if the government taxes the buyer. The tax doesn't change the buyer's willingness and ability to pay. The demand curve, *D*, tells us the *total* amount that buyers are willing and able to pay. Because buyers must pay $10 to the government on each item bought, the red curve *D* − *tax* tells us what the buyers are willing to pay to the sellers. The red curve, *D* − *tax*, lies $10 *below* the blue demand curve.

Market equilibrium occurs where the red *D* − *tax* curve intersects the supply curve, *S*. The buyer pays the equilibrium net-of-tax price $95 plus the $10 tax: $105. The seller receives the net-of-tax price $95. The government collects a tax revenue of $10 a player on 2,000 players, or $20,000 (shown by the purple rectangle).

Figure 7.1(b) shows what happens if the government taxes the seller. The tax acts like an increase in the suppliers' cost, so supply decreases and the supply curve shifts to the red curve labeled *S* + *tax*. This curve tells us what sellers are willing to accept, given that they must pay the government $10 on each item sold. The red curve, *S* + *tax*, lies $10 *above* the blue supply curve.

Market equilibrium occurs where the red *S* + *tax* curve intersects the demand curve, *D*. The buyer pays the equilibrium price $105. The seller receives the net-of-tax price $95. The government collects a tax revenue of $20,000.

In both cases, the buyer and the seller split the $10 tax and pay $5 each.

**FIGURE 7.1**

A Tax on MP3 Players

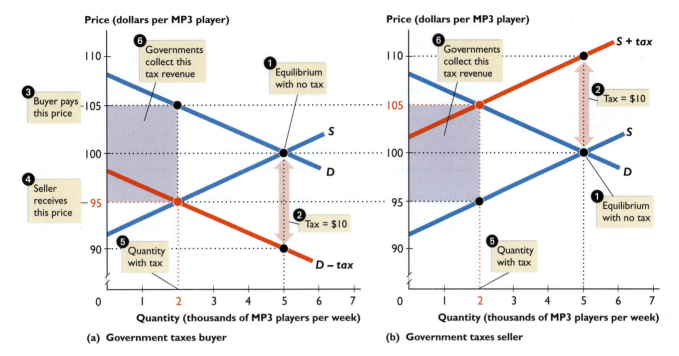

**(a) Government taxes buyer**

**(b) Government taxes seller**

❶ In both parts of the figure, with no tax, the price of an MP3 player is $100 and 5,000 players a week are bought.

❷ In part (a), a $10 tax on buyers of MP3 players shifts the demand curve down to $D - tax$ and in part (b), a $10 tax on sellers of MP3 players shifts the supply curve up to $S + tax$.

In both parts of the figure:

❸ The price paid by the buyer rises to $105—an increase of $5;

❹ The price received by the seller falls to $95—a decrease of $5;

❺ The quantity decreases to 2,000 players a week; and

❻ The government collects tax revenue of $20,000 a week—the purple rectangle.

In both cases, the burden of the tax is split equally between the buyer and the seller—each pays $5 per player.

You can now see that the argument about making the buyer pay or the seller pay is futile. The buyer pays the same price, the seller receives the same price, and the government receives the same tax revenue on the same quantity regardless of whether the government taxes the buyer or the seller.

In this example, the buyer and the seller share the burden of the tax equally. But in most cases, the burden will be shared unequally and might even fall entirely on one side of the market. We'll explore what determines the incidence of a tax, but first, let's see how a tax creates inefficiency.

## ■ Taxes and Efficiency

You've seen that resources are used efficiently when marginal benefit equals marginal cost. You've also seen that a tax places a wedge between the price the buyer pays and the price the seller receives. But the buyer's price equals marginal benefit and the seller's price equals marginal cost. So a tax puts a wedge between marginal benefit and marginal cost. The equilibrium quantity is less than the efficient quantity, and a deadweight loss arises.

Figure 7.2 shows the inefficiency of a tax. We'll assume that the government taxes the seller. In part (a), with no tax, marginal benefit equals marginal cost and the market is efficient. In part (b), with a tax, marginal benefit exceeds marginal cost. Consumer surplus and producer surplus shrink. Part of each surplus goes to the government as tax revenue—the purple area—and part of each surplus becomes a deadweight loss—the gray area.

Because a tax creates a deadweight loss, the burden of the tax exceeds the tax revenue. To remind us of this fact, we call the deadweight loss that arises from a tax the **excess burden** of the tax. But because the government uses the tax revenue to provide goods and services that people value, only the excess burden measures the inefficiency of the tax.

In this example, the excess burden is large. You can see how large by calculating the area of the deadweight loss triangle. This area is $15,000 ($10 × 3,000 ÷ 2). The tax revenue is $20,000, so the excess burden is 75 percent of the tax revenue.

**Excess burden**

The amount by which the burden of a tax exceeds the tax revenue received by the government—the deadweight loss from a tax.

### ■ Incidence, Inefficiency, and Elasticity

In the example of a $10 tax on MP3 players, the buyer and the seller split the tax equally and the excess burden is large. What determines how the tax is split and the size of its excess burden?

■ **FIGURE 7.2**

## Taxes and Efficiency

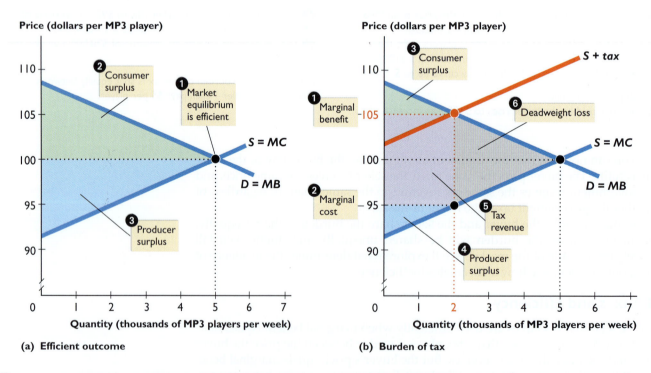

**(a) Efficient outcome**

**(b) Burden of tax**

❶ The market is efficient with marginal benefit equal to marginal cost. Total surplus—the sum of ❷ consumer surplus (green area) and ❸ producer surplus (blue area)—is at its maximum possible level.

A $10 tax drives a wedge between ❶ marginal benefit and ❷ marginal cost. ❸ Consumer surplus and ❹ producer surplus shrink by the amount of the ❺ tax revenue plus the ❻ deadweight loss. The deadweight loss is the excess burden of the tax.

The incidence of a tax and its excess burden depend on the elasticities of demand and supply in the following ways:

- For a given elasticity of supply, the more inelastic the demand for the good, the larger is the share of the tax paid by the buyer.
- For a given elasticity of demand, the more inelastic the supply of the good, the larger is the share of the tax paid by the seller.
- The excess burden is smaller, the more inelastic is demand *or* supply.

## ■ Incidence, Inefficiency, and the Elasticity of Demand

To see how the division of a tax between the buyer and the seller and the size of the excess burden depend on the elasticity of demand, we'll look at two extremes.

### Perfectly Inelastic Demand: Buyer Pays and Efficient

Figure 7.3(a) shows the market for insulin, a vital daily medication of diabetics. Demand is perfectly inelastic at 100,000 doses a week, as shown by the vertical demand curve. With no tax, the price is $2 a dose. A 20¢ a dose tax raises the price to $2.20, but the quantity does not change. The tax leaves the price received by the seller unchanged but raises the price paid by the buyer by the entire tax. The outcome is efficient (there is no deadweight loss) because marginal benefit equals marginal cost.

### Perfectly Elastic Demand: Seller Pays and Inefficient

Figure 7.3(b) shows the market for pink marker pens. Demand is perfectly elastic at $1 a pen, as shown by the horizontal demand curve. If pink pens are less expensive than other pens, everyone uses pink. If pink pens are more expensive than other pens, no one uses a pink pen. With no tax, the price of a pink pen is $1 and the quantity is 4,000 pens a week. A 10¢ a pen tax leaves the price at $1 a pen, but

## ■ FIGURE 7.3

Incidence, Inefficiency, and the Elasticity of Demand

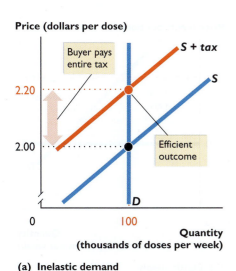

**(a) Inelastic demand**

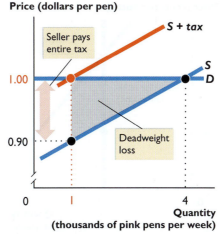

**(b) Elastic demand**

In part (a), the demand for insulin is perfectly inelastic. A tax of 20¢ a dose raises the price by 20¢, and the buyer pays all the tax. But marginal benefit still equals marginal cost, so the outcome is efficient.

In part (b), the demand for pink marker pens is perfectly elastic. A tax of 10¢ a pen lowers the price received by the seller by 10¢, and the seller pays all the tax. Marginal benefit exceeds marginal cost, so the outcome is inefficient. The deadweight loss is the excess burden of the tax and measures its inefficiency.

the quantity decreases to 1,000 a week. The price paid by the buyer is unchanged and the seller pays the entire tax. The outcome is inefficient because marginal benefit exceeds marginal cost and a deadweight loss arises.

## ■ Incidence, Inefficiency, and the Elasticity of Supply

To see how the division of a tax between the buyer and the seller depends on the elasticity of supply, we'll again look at two extremes.

### Perfectly Inelastic Supply: Seller Pays and Efficient

Figure 7.4(a) shows the market for spring water that flows at a constant rate that can't be controlled. Supply is perfectly inelastic at 100,000 bottles a week, as shown by the vertical supply curve. With no tax, the price is 50¢ a bottle and the 100,000 bottles that flow from the spring are bought. A tax of 5¢ a bottle leaves the quantity unchanged at 100,000 bottles a week. Buyers are willing to buy 100,000 bottles a week only if the price is 50¢ a bottle. The price remains at 50¢ a bottle, but the tax lowers the price received by the seller by 5¢ a bottle. The seller pays the entire tax.

Because marginal benefit equals marginal cost, there is no deadweight loss and the outcome is efficient.

### Perfectly Elastic Supply: Buyer Pays and Inefficient

Figure 7.4(b) shows the market for sand from which computer-chip makers extract silicon. Supply of this sand is perfectly elastic at a price of 10¢ a pound as shown by the horizontal supply curve. With no tax, the price is 10¢ a pound and 5,000 pounds a week are bought. A 1¢ a pound sand tax raises the price to 11¢, and the quantity decreases to 3,000 pounds a week. The buyer pays the entire tax.

Because marginal benefit exceeds marginal cost, a deadweight loss arises and the outcome is inefficient.

## ■ FIGURE 7.4

### Incidence, Inefficiency, and the Elasticity of Supply

In part (a), the supply of bottled spring water is perfectly inelastic. A tax of 5¢ a bottle lowers the price received by the seller by 5¢ a bottle, and the seller pays all the tax. Marginal benefit equals marginal cost, so the outcome is efficient.

In part (b), the supply of sand is perfectly elastic. A tax of 1¢ a pound increases the price by 1¢ a pound, and the buyer pays all the tax. Marginal benefit exceeds marginal cost, so the outcome is inefficient. The deadweight loss is the excess burden of the tax and measures its inefficiency.

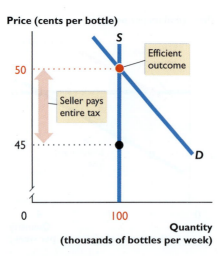

(a)  Inelastic supply

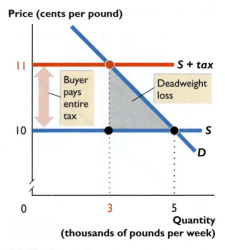

(b)  Elastic supply

# CHECKPOINT 7.1

**Explain how taxes change prices and quantities, are shared by buyers and sellers, and create inefficiency.**

## Practice Problems

Figure 1 shows the market for basketballs, when basketballs are not taxed.

1. If buyers of basketballs are taxed $6 a ball, what price does the buyer pay and how many do they buy? What is the tax revenue collected?

2. If sellers of basketballs are taxed $6 a ball, what price does the seller receive and how many do they sell? What is the tax revenue collected?

3. If basketballs are taxed at $6 a ball, what is the excess burden of the tax? Is the demand for basketballs or the supply of basketballs more inelastic? Explain your answer.

## In the News

**State gas taxes head higher**
Seventeen states are raising the gas tax. Wyoming increased its gas tax from 14 cents a gallon to 24 cents a gallon. Big trucks are switching to natural gas.

Source: *The Wall Street Journal*, April 4, 2013

Given the information in *Eye on the Price of Gasoline* on p. 159 and assuming the supply of gasoline is elastic, who will pay more of the increase in Wyoming's gas tax: the drivers or the gasoline companies? How will a big switch to natural gas change your answer?

## Solutions to Practice Problems

1. With a $6 tax on buyers, the demand curve shifts downward by $6 a ball as shown in Figure 2. The price that the buyer pays is $16 a basketball and 8 million basketballs a week are bought. The tax revenue is $6 × 8 million, which is $48 million a week (the purple rectangle in Figure 2).

2. With a $6 tax on sellers, the supply curve shifts upward by $6 a ball as shown in Figure 3. The price that the seller receives is $10 a basketball and 8 million basketballs a week are sold (Figure 3). The tax revenue is $6 × 8 million, which is $48 million a week (the purple rectangle in Figure 3).

3. The excess burden of the tax is $12 million. Excess burden equals the deadweight loss, the gray triangle, which is 4 million balls × $6 a ball ÷ 2. The $6 tax increases the price paid by buyers by $1 and lowers the price received by sellers by $5. Because the seller pays the larger share of the tax, the supply of basketballs is more inelastic than the demand for basketballs.

## Solution to In the News

The demand for gasoline is inelastic, so drivers will pay more of the increase in Wyoming's gas tax than the gasoline companies will pay. Although the demand for gasoline is inelastic, the widespread availablity of natural gas and big trucks switching to natural gas makes the demand for gasoline (and diesel) less inelastic, so the share of the tax paid by drivers will fall and the share paid by the gas companies will rise.

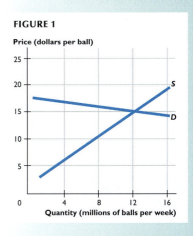

**FIGURE 1**

Price (dollars per ball)

Quantity (millions of balls per week)

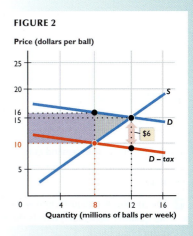

**FIGURE 2**

Price (dollars per ball)

Quantity (millions of balls per week)

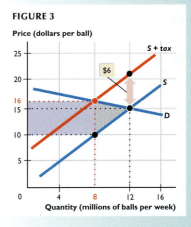

**FIGURE 3**

Price (dollars per ball)

Quantity (millions of balls per week)

## 7.2   PRICE CEILINGS

**Price ceiling** or **price cap**
A government regulation that places an *upper* limit on the price at which a particular good, service, or factor of production may be traded.

A **price ceiling** (also called a **price cap**) is a government regulation that places an *upper* limit on the price at which a particular good, service, or factor of production may be traded. Trading at a higher price is illegal.

A price ceiling has been used in several markets, but the one that looms largest in everyone's budget is the housing market. The price of housing is the rent that people pay for a house or apartment. Demand and supply in the housing market determine the rent and the quantity of housing available.

Figure 7.5 illustrates the apartment rental market in Biloxi, Mississippi. The rent is $550 a month, and 4,000 apartments are rented.

Suppose that Biloxi apartment rents have increased by $100 a month in the past two years and that a Citizens' Action Group asks the mayor to roll rents back.

### ■ A Rent Ceiling

**Rent ceiling**
A regulation that makes it illegal to charge more than a specified rent for housing.

Responding to the group's request, the mayor imposes a **rent ceiling**—a regulation that makes it illegal to charge more than a specified rent for housing.

The effect of a rent ceiling depends on whether it is imposed at a level above or below the equilibrium rent. In Figure 7.5, if the rent ceiling is set *above* $550 a month, nothing would change because people are already paying $550 a month.

But a rent ceiling that is set *below* the equilibrium rent has powerful effects on the market outcome. The reason is that the rent ceiling attempts to prevent the rent from rising high enough to regulate the quantities demanded and supplied. The law and the market are in conflict, and one (or both) of them must yield.

■ **FIGURE 7.5**

A Housing Market

The figure shows the demand curve, *D*, and the supply curve, *S*, for rental housing.

❶ The market is in equilibrium when the quantity demanded equals the quantity supplied.

❷ The equilibrium price (rent) is $550 a month.

❸ The equilibrium quantity is 4,000 units of housing.

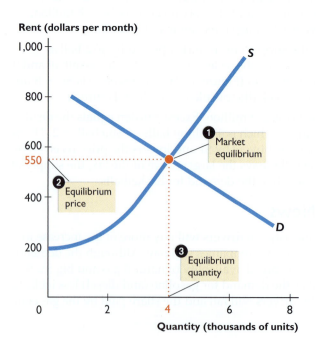

Figure 7.6 shows a rent ceiling that is set below the equilibrium rent at $400 a month. We've shaded the area *above* the rent ceiling because any rent in this region is illegal. The first effect of a rent ceiling is a housing shortage. At a rent of $400 a month, the quantity of housing supplied is 3,000 units and the quantity demanded is 6,000 units. So at $400 a month, there is a shortage of 3,000 units of housing.

But the story does not end here. The 3,000 units of housing that owners are willing to make available must somehow be allocated among people who are seeking 6,000 units. This allocation might be achieved in two ways:

- A black market
- Increased search activity

## A Black Market

A **black market** is an illegal market that operates alongside a government-regulated market. A rent ceiling sometimes creates a black market in housing as frustrated renters and landlords try to find ways of raising the rent above the legally imposed ceiling. Landlords want higher rents because they know that renters are willing to pay more for the existing quantity of housing. Renters are willing to pay more to jump to the front of the line.

Because raising the rent is illegal, landlords and renters use creative tricks to get around the law. One of these tricks is for a new tenant to pay a high price for worthless fittings—perhaps paying $2,000 for threadbare drapes. Another is for the tenant to pay a high price for new locks and keys—called "key money."

Figure 7.6 shows how high the black market rent might go in Biloxi. With strict enforcement of the rent ceiling, the quantity of housing available is 3,000

**Black market**
An illegal market that operates alongside a government-regulated market.

## FIGURE 7.6

### A Rent Ceiling Creates a Shortage

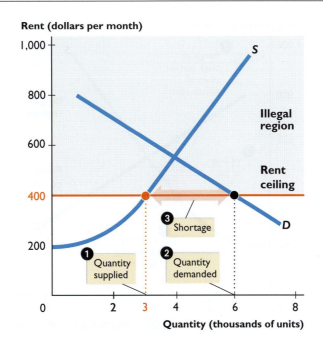

A rent ceiling is imposed below the equilibrium rent. In this example, the rent ceiling is $400 a month.

❶ The quantity of housing supplied decreases to 3,000 units.

❷ The quantity of housing demanded increases to 6,000 units.

❸ A shortage of 3,000 units arises.

units. But at this quantity, renters are willing to offer as much as $625 a month—the amount determined on the demand curve.

So a small number of landlords illegally offer housing for rents up to $625 a month. The black market rent might be at any level between the rent ceiling of $400 and the maximum that a renter is willing to pay of $625.

### Increased Search Activity

The time spent looking for someone with whom to do business is called **search activity.** We spend some time in search activity almost every time we buy something, and especially when we buy a big item such as a car or a home. When a price ceiling creates a shortage of housing, search activity *increases*. In a rent-controlled housing market, frustrated would-be renters scan the newspapers. Keen apartment seekers race to be first on the scene when news of a possible apartment breaks.

The *opportunity cost* of a good is equal to its price *plus* the value of the search time spent finding the good. So the opportunity cost of housing is equal to the rent plus the value of the search time spent looking for an apartment. Search activity is costly. It uses time and other resources, such as telephones, automobiles, and gasoline that could have been used in other productive ways. In Figure 7.7, to find accommodation at $400 a month, someone who is willing to pay a rent of $625 a month would be willing to spend on search activity an amount that is equivalent to adding $225 a month to the rent ceiling.

A rent ceiling controls the rent portion of the cost of housing but not the search cost. So when the search cost is added to the rent, some people end up paying a higher opportunity cost for housing than they would if there were no rent ceiling.

### FIGURE 7.7

#### A Rent Ceiling Creates a Black Market and Housing Search

With a rent ceiling of $400 a month,

**❶** 3,000 units of housing are available.

**❷** Someone is willing to pay $625 a month for the 3,000th unit of housing.

**❸** Black market rent might be as high as $625 a month or search activity might be equivalent to adding $225 a month to the rent ceiling.

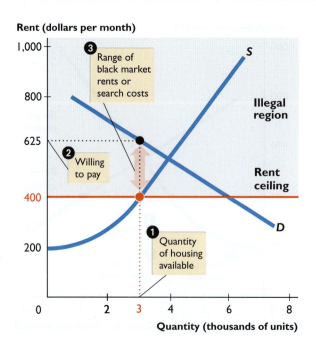

# ■ Are Rent Ceilings Efficient?

In a housing market with no rent ceiling, market forces determine the equilibrium rent. The quantity of housing demanded equals the quantity of housing supplied. In this situation, scarce housing resources are allocated efficiently because the marginal cost of housing equals the marginal benefit. Figure 7.8(a) shows this efficient outcome in the Biloxi apartment rental market. In this efficient market, total surplus—the sum of *consumer surplus* (the green area) and *producer surplus* (the blue area)—is maximized at the equilibrium rent and quantity of housing (see Chapter 6, p. 191).

Figure 7.8(b) shows that with a rent ceiling, the outcome is inefficient. Marginal benefit exceeds marginal cost. Producer surplus and consumer surplus shrink, and a deadweight loss (the gray area) arises. This loss is borne by the people who can't find housing and by landlords who can't offer housing at the lower rent ceiling.

But the total loss exceeds the deadweight loss. Resources get used in costly search activity or in evading the law in the black market. The value of these resources might be as large as the red rectangle. There is yet a further loss: the cost of enforcing the rent ceiling law. This loss, which is borne by taxpayers, is not visible in the figure.

■ **FIGURE 7.8**

The Inefficiency of a Rent Ceiling

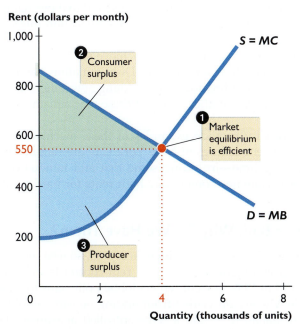

(a) Efficient housing market

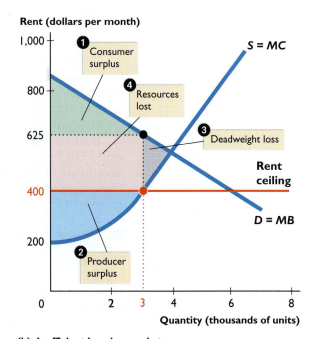

(b) Inefficient housing market

❶ The market equilibrium is efficient with marginal benefit equal to marginal cost. Total surplus, the sum of ❷ consumer surplus (green area) and ❸ producer surplus (blue area), is maximized.

A rent ceiling is inefficient. ❶ Consumer surplus and ❷ producer surplus shrink, a ❸ deadweight loss arises, and ❹ resources are lost in search activity and evading the rent ceiling law.

*With rent ceilings, landlords have no incentive to maintain buildings, and both the quality and quantity of housing supplied decrease.*

Although a rent ceiling creates inefficiency, not everyone loses. The people who pay the rent ceiling get an increase in consumer surplus, and landlords who charge a black market rent get an increase in producer surplus.

The costs of a rent ceiling that we've just considered are only the initial costs. With the rent below the market equilibrium rent, landlords have no incentive to maintain their buildings. So over time, both the quality and quantity of housing supplied *decrease* and the loss arising from a rent ceiling increases.

The size of the loss from a rent ceiling depends on the elasticities of supply and demand. If supply is inelastic, a rent ceiling brings a small decrease in the quantity of housing supplied. And if demand is inelastic, a rent ceiling brings a small increase in the quantity of housing demanded. So the more inelastic the supply or the demand, the smaller is the shortage of housing and the smaller is the deadweight loss.

### ■ Are Rent Ceilings Fair?

We've seen that rent ceilings prevent scarce resources from being allocated efficiently—resources do not flow to their highest-valued use. But don't they ensure that scarce housing resources are allocated more fairly?

You learned in Chapter 6 (pp. 197–199) that fairness is a complex idea about which there are two broad views: fair *rules* versus a fair *result.* Rent controls violate the fair-rules view of fairness because they block voluntary exchange. But do they deliver a fair result? Do rent ceilings ensure that scarce housing goes to the poor people whose need is greatest?

Blocking rent adjustments that bring the quantity of housing demanded into equality with the quantity supplied doesn't end scarcity. So when the law prevents the rent from adjusting and blocks the price mechanism from allocating scarce housing, some other allocation mechanism must be used. If that mechanism were one that provided the housing to the poorest, then the allocation might be regarded as fair.

But the mechanisms that get used do not usually achieve such an outcome. First-come, first-served is one allocation mechanism. Discrimination based on race, ethnicity, or sex is another. Discrimination against young newcomers and in favor of old established families is yet another. None of these mechanisms delivers a fair outcome.

Rent ceilings in New York City provide examples of these mechanisms at work. The main beneficiaries of rent ceilings in New York City are families that have lived in the city for a long time—including some rich and famous ones. These families enjoy low rents while newcomers pay high rents for hard-to-find apartments.

### ■ If Rent Ceilings Are So Bad, Why Do We Have Them?

The economic case against rent ceilings is now widely accepted, so *new* rent ceiling laws are rare. But when governments try to repeal rent control laws, as the New York City government did in 1999, current renters lobby politicians to maintain the ceilings. Also, people who are prevented from finding housing would be happy if they got lucky and managed to find a rent-controlled apartment. For these reasons, there is plenty of political support for rent ceilings.

Apartment owners who oppose rent ceilings are a minority, so their views are not a powerful influence on politicians. Because more people support rent ceilings than oppose them, politicians are sometimes willing to support them too.

# CHECKPOINT 7.2

**Explain how a price ceiling works and show how a rent ceiling creates a housing shortage, inefficiency, and unfairness.**

## Practice Problems

Figure 1 shows the rental market for apartments in Corsicana, Texas.

1. What is the rent and how many apartments are rented? If a rent ceiling of $900 a month is set, what is the rent and how many apartments are rented?

2. If the city government imposes a rent ceiling of $600 a month, what is the rent and how many apartments are rented? If a black market develops, how high could the black market rent be? Explain.

3. With a strictly enforced rent ceiling of $600 a month, is the housing market efficient? What is the deadweight loss? Is the housing market fair? Explain.

## In the News

**Beijing loosens fuel prices in boon to refiners**
China moved to raise the price ceiling on gasoline and diesel on Tuesday. Lin Boqiang of Xiamen University advised the government on pricing reform and said the "move is in the right direction, even if it's not a complete market price."

Source: *The Wall Street Journal*, March 26, 2013

Explain how raising the price ceiling on fuel will change consumer surplus, producer surplus, and deadweight loss.

## Solutions to Practice Problems

1. The equilibrium rent is $800 a month, and 3,000 apartments are rented. A rent ceiling of $900 a month is above the equilibrium rent, so the outcome is the market equilibrium rent of $800 a month with 3,000 apartments rented.

2. With the rent ceiling at $600 a month, the number of apartments rented is 1,000 and the rent is $600 a month (Figure 2). In a black market, some people are willing to rent an apartment for more than the rent ceiling. The highest rent that someone would offer is $1,200 a month. This rent equals someone's willingness to pay for the 1,000th apartment (Figure 2).

3. The housing market is not efficient. With 1,000 apartments rented, marginal benefit exceeds marginal cost and a deadweight loss arises (Figure 2). The deadweight loss is equal to the area of the gray triangle, which is $(1,200 - 600) \times (3,000 - 1,000) \div 2$. The deadweight loss is $600,000, The allocation of housing is less fair on both views of fairness: It blocks voluntary transactions and does not provide more housing to those most in need.

## Solution to In the News

By raising the price ceiling, the price received by producers will rise to the new price ceiling and the quantity produced will increase, but a shortage will remain. Buyers' willingness to pay falls as more fuel is available. Consumer surplus will increase. Producer surplus will increase as refiners produce more fuel and receive the higher price. A shortage of fuel will remain because the price is not a market-determined price. The marginal benefit from fuel exceeds the marginal cost of producing fuel, so a deadweight loss remains, but it is smaller.

**FIGURE 1**
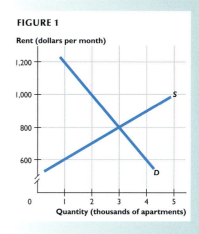

**FIGURE 2**
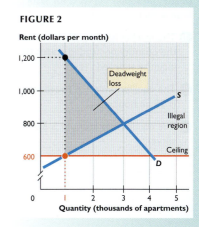

## 7.3 PRICE FLOORS

**Price floor**
A government regulation that places a *lower* limit on the price at which a particular good, service, or factor of production may be traded.

A **price floor** is a government regulation that places a *lower* limit on the price at which a particular good, service, or factor of production may be traded. Trading at a lower price is illegal.

Price floors are used in many markets, but the one that looms largest is the labor market. The price of labor is the wage rate that people earn. Demand and supply in the labor market determine the wage rate and the quantity of labor employed.

Figure 7.9 illustrates the market for fast-food servers in Yuma, Arizona. In this market, the demand for labor curve is *D*. On this demand curve, at a wage rate of $10 an hour, the quantity of fast-food servers demanded is zero. If Subway, Burger King, Taco Bell, McDonald's, Wendy's, and the other fast-food places had to pay servers $10 an hour, they wouldn't hire any. They would replace servers with vending machines! But at wage rates below $10 an hour, they would hire servers. At a wage rate of $5 an hour, firms would hire 5,000 servers.

On the supply side of the market, no one is willing to work for $2 an hour. To attract servers, firms must pay more than $2 an hour.

Equilibrium in this market occurs at a wage rate of $5 an hour with 5,000 people employed as servers.

Suppose that the government thinks that no one should have to work for a wage rate as low as $5 an hour and decides that it wants to increase the wage rate. Can the government improve conditions for these workers by passing a minimum wage law? Let's find out.

■ **FIGURE 7.9**

A Market for Fast-Food Servers

The figure shows the demand curve, *D*, and the supply curve, *S*, for fast-food servers.

❶ The market is in equilibrium when the quantity demanded equals the quantity supplied.

❷ The equilibrium price (wage rate) is $5 an hour.

❸ The equilibrium quantity is 5,000 servers.

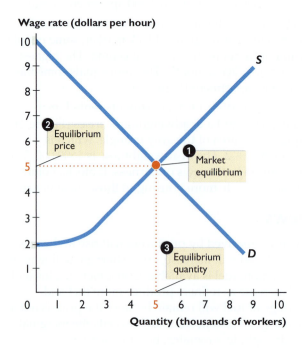

## ■ The Minimum Wage

A **minimum wage law** is a government regulation that makes hiring labor services for less than a specified wage illegal. Firms are free to pay a wage rate that exceeds the minimum wage but may not pay less than the minimum. A minimum wage is an example of a price floor.

The effect of a price floor depends on whether it is set below or above the equilibrium price. In Figure 7.9, the equilibrium wage rate is $5 an hour, and at this wage rate, firms hire 5,000 workers. If the government introduced a minimum wage below $5 an hour, nothing would change. The reason is that firms are already paying $5 an hour, and because this wage exceeds the minimum wage, the wage rate paid doesn't change. Firms continue to hire 5,000 workers.

But the aim of a minimum wage is to boost the incomes of low-wage earners. So in the markets for the lowest-paid workers, the minimum wage will exceed the equilibrium wage.

Suppose that the government introduces a minimum wage of $7 an hour. Figure 7.10 shows the effects of this law. Wage rates below $7 an hour are illegal, so we've shaded the illegal region *below* the minimum wage. Firms and workers are no longer permitted to operate at the equilibrium point in this market because it is in the illegal region. Market forces and political forces are in conflict.

The government can set a minimum wage, but it can't tell employers how many workers to hire. If firms must pay a wage rate of $7 an hour, they will hire only 3,000 workers. At the equilibrium wage rate of $5 an hour, firms hired 5,000 workers. So when the minimum wage is introduced, firms lay off 2,000 workers.

**Minimum wage law**

A government regulation that makes hiring labor services for less than a specified wage illegal.

### ■ FIGURE 7.10

A Minimum Wage Creates Unemployment

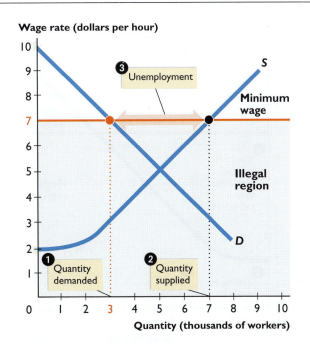

A minimum wage is introduced above the equilibrium wage rate. In this example, the minimum wage rate is $7 an hour.

❶ The quantity of labor demanded decreases to 3,000 workers.

❷ The quantity of labor supplied increases to 7,000 people.

❸ 4,000 people are unemployed.

But at a wage rate of $7 an hour, 2,000 people who didn't want to work for $5 an hour will now try to find work as servers. So at $7 an hour, the quantity supplied is 7,000 people. With 2,000 workers fired and another 2,000 looking for work at the higher wage rate, 4,000 people who would like to work as servers are unemployed.

The 3,000 jobs available must somehow be allocated among the 7,000 people who are willing to work as servers. How is this allocation achieved? The answer is by increased job-search activity and illegal hiring.

### Increased Job-Search Activity

Finding a good job takes a great deal of time and other resources. With a minimum wage, more people are looking for jobs than the number of jobs available. Frustrated unemployed people spend time and other resources searching for hard-to-find jobs. In Figure 7.11, to find a job at $7 an hour, someone who is willing to work for $3 an hour (on the supply curve) would be willing to spend $4 an hour (the minimum wage rate of $7 an hour minus $3 an hour) on job-search activity. For a job that might last a year or more, this amount is large.

### Illegal Hiring

With more people looking for work than the number of jobs available, some firms and workers might agree to do business at an illegal wage rate below the minimum wage in a black market. An illegal wage rate might be at any level between the minimum wage rate of $7 an hour and the lowest wage rate at which someone is willing to work, $3 an hour.

■ **FIGURE 7.11**

A Minimum Wage Creates Job Search and Illegal Hiring

The minimum wage rate is set at $7 an hour:

❶ 3,000 jobs are available.

❷ The lowest wage rate for which someone is willing to work is $3 an hour. In a black market, illegal wage rates might be as low as $3 an hour.

❸ The maximum that might be spent on job search is an amount equivalent to $4 an hour—the $7 they would receive if they found a job minus the $3 they are willing to work for.

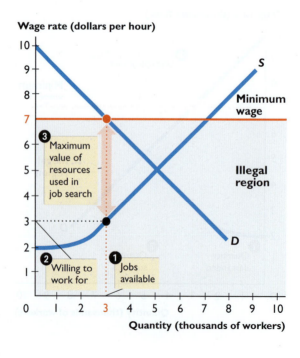

# EYE on the U.S. ECONOMY
## The Federal Minimum Wage

The *Fair Labor Standards Act* sets the federal minimum wage, but most states set their own minimum at a higher level than the federal minimum.

The figure shows the minimum wage since 1993 in terms of what it would buy at 2013 prices.

The minimum wage creates unemployment, but how much? Between 2007 and 2009, when the minimum wage increased by 38 percent (see figure), the employment of 16- to 19-year-olds fell by 28 percent. Part of that increase most likely was caused by the rise in the minimum wage.

Most economists believe that a 10 percent rise in the minimum wage decreases teenage employment by between 1 and 3 percent.

David Card of the University of California at Berkeley and Alan Krueger of Princeton University have challenged this consensus view. They say that a rise in the minimum wage in California, New Jersey, and Texas *increased* the employment rate of low-income workers. They suggest three reasons why a rise in the wage rate might increase employment:

(1) Workers become more conscientious and productive.

(2) Workers are less likely to quit, so costly labor turnover is reduced.

(3) Managers make a firm's operations more efficient.

Most economists are skeptical about these ideas and say that if higher wages make workers more productive and reduce labor turnover, firms will freely pay workers a higher wage. They also argue that there are other explanations for the employment increase that Card and Krueger found.

Daniel Hamermesh of the University of Texas at Austin says that Card and Krueger got the timing wrong. Firms anticipated the wage rise and so cut employment before it occurred. Looking at employment changes after the minimum wage increased missed its main effect. Finis Welch of Texas A&M University and Kevin Murphy of the University of Chicago say that the employment effects that Card and Krueger found are caused by regional differences in economic growth, not by changes in the minimum wage.

*Pizza delivery people gain from the minimum wage.*

Also, looking only at employment misses the supply-side effect of the minimum wage. It brings an increase in the number of people who drop out of high school to look for work.

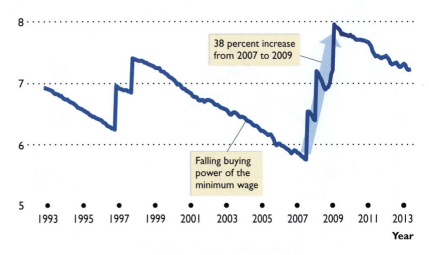

SOURCE OF DATA: Bureau of Labor Statistics.

### ■ Is the Minimum Wage Efficient?

The efficient allocation of a factor of production is similar to that of a good or service, which you studied in Chapter 6. The demand for labor tells us about the marginal benefit of labor to the firms that hire it. Firms benefit because the labor they hire produces the goods or services that they sell. Firms are willing to pay a wage rate equal to the benefit they receive from an additional hour of labor. In Figure 7.12(a), the demand curve for labor tells us the marginal benefit that the firms in Yuma receive from hiring fast-food servers. The marginal benefit minus the wage rate is a surplus for the firms.

The supply of labor tells us about the marginal cost of working. To work, people must forgo leisure or working in the home, activities that they value. The wage rate received minus the marginal cost of working is a surplus for workers.

An efficient allocation of labor occurs when the marginal benefit to firms equals the marginal cost borne by workers. Such an allocation occurs in the labor market in Figure 7.12(a). Firms enjoy a surplus (the blue area), and workers enjoy a surplus (the green area). The sum of these surpluses is maximized.

Figure 7.12(b) shows the loss from a minimum wage. With a minimum wage of $7 an hour, 3,000 workers are hired. Marginal benefit exceeds marginal cost. The firms' surplus and workers' surplus shrink, and a deadweight loss (the gray area) arises. This loss falls on the firms that cut back employment and the people who can't find jobs at the higher wage rate.

### ■ FIGURE 7.12

The Inefficiency of the Minimum Wage

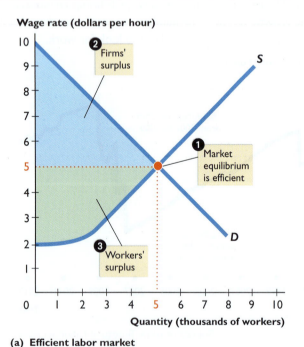

**(a) Efficient labor market**

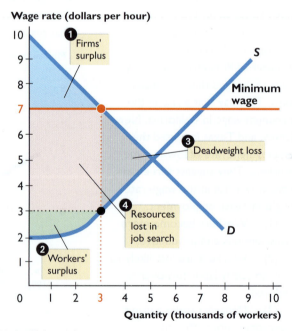

**(b) Inefficient labor market**

**❶** The market equilibrium is efficient with marginal benefit equal to marginal cost. The sum of **❷** the firms' surplus (blue area) and **❸** workers' surplus (green area) is maximized.

A minimum wage is inefficient. **❶** The firms' surplus and **❷** workers' surplus shrink, a **❸** deadweight loss arises, and **❹** resources are lost in job search.

But the total loss exceeds the deadweight loss. As each unemployed person keeps looking for a job, resources are used in costly job-search activity—writing letters, making phone calls, going to interviews, and so on. The value of these resources might be as large as the red rectangle.

### ■ Is the Minimum Wage Fair?

The minimum wage is unfair on both views of fairness: It delivers an unfair *result* and imposes unfair *rules*. The *result* is unfair because only those people who find jobs benefit. The unemployed end up worse off than they would be with no minimum wage. And those who get jobs were probably not the least well off. Personal characteristics, which means discrimination, allocates jobs and is another source of unfairness. The minimum wage imposes unfair *rules* because it blocks voluntary exchange. Firms are willing to hire more labor and people are willing to work more, but they are not permitted by the minimum wage law to do so.

### ■ If the Minimum Wage Is So Bad, Why Do We Have It?

Although the minimum wage is inefficient, not everyone loses from it. The people who find jobs at the minimum wage rate are better off. Other supporters of the minimum wage believe that the elasticities of demand and supply in the labor market are low, so not much unemployment results. Labor unions support the minimum wage because it puts upward pressure on all wage rates, including those of union workers. Nonunion labor is a substitute for union labor, so when the minimum wage rises, the demand for union labor increases.

## EYE on PRICE REGULATION
### Can the President Repeal the Laws of Supply and Demand?

The President has a powerful pen, but one that holds no magical powers. When the President signs a Bill or an Executive Order to bring in a new law or regulation, the outcome is not always exactly what was intended. A mismatch between intention and outcome is almost inevitable when a law or regulation seeks to block the laws of supply and demand.

You've seen the problems created by the federal minimum wage law, which leaves teenagers without jobs. There would also be problems at the other extreme of the labor market if the law tried to place a cap on executive pay.

In the spring of 2009, the "Cap Executive Officer Pay Act of 2009" was introduced in the Senate. The goal of the Act was to limit the compensation of executives and directors of firms receiving government handouts. The Act defined compensation broadly as all forms of cash receipts, property, and any perks. The cap envisaged was an annual compensation no greater than that of the President of the United States.

This Act never made it to the President's desk for his signature, but you can see some of the problems that would have risen if it had. Setting aside the difficult task of determining

the President's compensation (does it include the use of the White House and Air Force One?), placing a cap on executive pay would work like putting a ceiling on home rents that you've studied in this chapter. The quantity of executive services supplied would decrease and the most talented executives would seek jobs with the unregulated employers. The firms in the most difficulty—those receiving government funding—would face the added challenge of recruiting and keeping competent executives and directors. The deadweight loss from this action would be large. It is fortunate that the idea didn't have legs!

# CHECKPOINT 7.3

**Explain how a price floor works and show how the minimum wage creates unemployment, inefficiency, and unfairness.**

## Practice Problems

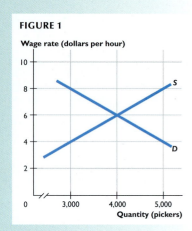

**FIGURE 1**

Figure 1 shows the market for tomato pickers in southern California.

1. What is the equilibrium wage rate and how many tomato pickers are employed? If California introduces a minimum wage of $4 an hour, how many tomato pickers are employed and how many are unemployed?

2. If California introduces a minimum wage of $8 an hour, how many tomato pickers are employed and how many are unemployed? What is the lowest wage that some workers might be able to earn if a black market develops?

3. Is the minimum wage of $8 an hour efficient? Who gains and who loses from the minimum wage of $8 an hour? Is it fair?

## In the News

**Hong Kong introduces a minimum wage**
Hong Kong's first minimum wage is set at $HK28 an hour—$HK5 less than labor unions wanted, but $HK5 more than the employers had offered. About 315,000 people will be affected by the new wage.

Source: *The Economist*, January 11, 2011

What will be the effects of the minimum wage if the employers' offer is equal to the equilibrium wage? What will be the effects of the minimum wage if the labor unions' demand is equal to the equilibrium wage?

## Solutions to Practice Problems

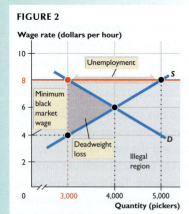

**FIGURE 2**

1. The equilibrium wage rate is $6 an hour, and 4,000 pickers are employed. The minimum wage of $4 an hour is below the equilibrium wage rate, so 4,000 tomato pickers are employed and no worker is unemployed.

2. The minimum wage of $8 an hour is above the equilibrium wage rate, so 3,000 pickers are employed (determined by the demand) and 5,000 people would like to work as pickers for $8 an hour (determined by the supply), so 2,000 are unemployed (Figure 2). If a black market developed, the lowest wage that someone might be able to earn would be $4 an hour (Figure 2).

3. The minimum wage of $8 an hour is not efficient because it creates a deadweight loss—the marginal benefit to growers exceeds the marginal cost to workers. Tomato pickers who find work at $8 an hour gain. Tomato growers and unemployed pickers lose. The minimum wage is unfair on both the fair-rules and fair-result views of fairness.

## Solution to In the News

If the employers' offer of $HK23 an hour is the equilibrium wage rate, then the minimum wage exceeds the equilibrium wage and some of the 315,000 workers will become unemployed. If the union's demand of $HK33 an hour is the equilibrium wage rate, then the minimum wage is below the equilibrium wage and the minimum wage has no effect on the quantity of labor employed.

## 7.4 PRICE SUPPORTS IN AGRICULTURE

"The nation has got to eat," declared President George W. Bush when he asked Congress to spend $170 billion to support U.S. farmers. The United States is not alone among the advanced economies in spending billions of dollars each year on farm support. Governments in all the advanced economies do it, and none more than those of the European Union and Japan.

### ■ How Governments Intervene in Markets for Farm Products

The methods that governments use to support farms vary, but they almost always involve three elements:

- Isolate the domestic market from global competition
- Introduce a price floor
- Pay farmers a subsidy

### Isolate the Domestic Market

A government can't regulate a market price without first isolating the domestic market from global competition. If the cost of production in the rest of the world is lower than that in the domestic economy and if foreign producers are free to sell in the domestic market, the forces of demand and supply drive the price down and swamp any efforts by the government to influence the price.

To isolate the domestic market, the government restricts imports from the rest of the world.

### Introduce a Price Floor

A price floor in an agricultural market is called a **price support,** because the floor is maintained by a government guarantee to buy any surplus output at that price. You saw that a price floor in the labor market—a minimum wage—creates a surplus of labor that shows up as unemployment. A price support in an agricultural market also generates a surplus. At the support price, the quantity supplied exceeds the quantity demanded. What happens to the surplus makes the effects of a price support different from those of a minimum wage. The government buys the surplus.

**Price support**
A price floor in an agricultural market maintained by a government guarantee to buy any surplus output at that price.

### Pay Farmers a Subsidy

A **subsidy** is a payment by the government to a producer to cover part of the cost of production. When the government buys the surplus produced by farmers, it provides them with a subsidy. Without the subsidy, farmers could not cover their costs because they would not be able to sell the surplus.

Let's see how a price support works.

**Subsidy**
A payment by the government to a producer to cover part of the cost of production.

### ■ Price Support: An Illustration

To see the effects of a price support, we'll look at the market for sugar beets. Both the United States and the European Union have price supports for sugar beets.

Figure 7.13 shows the market. This market is isolated from rest-of-world influences. The demand curve, $D$, tells us the quantities demanded at each price in the domestic economy only. And the supply curve, $S$, tells us the quantity supplied at each price by domestic farmers.

*With a price support program operated by the U.S. Department of Agriculture, farmers grew 26 million tons of sugar beets in 2011—a tenth of global production.*

## Free Market Reference Point

With no price support, the equilibrium price is $25 a ton and the equilibrium quantity is 25 million tons a year. The market is efficient only if the price in the rest of the world is also $25 a ton. If the price in the rest of the world is less than $25 a ton, it is efficient for the domestic farmers to produce less and for some sugar beets to be imported at the lower price (lower opportunity cost) available in the rest of the world. But if the price in the rest of the world exceeds $25 a ton, it is efficient for domestic farmers to increase production and export some sugar beets.

## Price Support and Subsidy

Suppose the government introduces a price support and sets the support price at $35 a ton. To make the price support work, the government agrees to pay farmers $35 for every ton of sugar beets they produce and can't sell in the market.

The farmers produce the quantity shown by the market supply curve. At a price of $35 a ton, the quantity supplied is 30 million tons a year, so production increases to this amount.

Domestic users of sugar beets cut back their purchases. At $35 a ton, the quantity demanded is 20 million tons a year, and purchases decrease to this amount.

Because farmers produce a greater quantity than domestic users are willing to buy, something must be done with the surplus. If the farmers just dumped the surplus on the market, you can see what would happen. The price would fall to that at which consumers are willing to pay for the quantity produced.

To make the price support work, the government buys the surplus. In this example, the government buys 10 million tons for $35 a ton and provides a subsidy to the farmers of $350 million.

## ■ FIGURE 7.13

### The Domestic Market for Sugar Beets

The market for sugar beets is isolated from global competition.

❶ With no intervention, the competitive equilibrium price is $25 a ton and the equilibrium quantity is 25 million tons a year.

❷ The government intervenes in this market and sets a support price at $35 a ton.

❸ The quantity produced increases to 30 million tons a year.

❹ The quantity bought by domestic users decreases to 20 million tons a year.

❺ The government buys the surplus of 10 million tons a year and pays farmers a subsidy of $350 million.

❻ A deadweight loss arises.

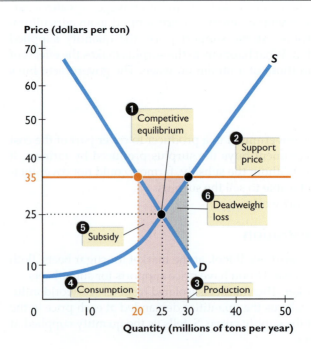

The price support increases farmers' total revenue. Without a subsidy, farmers would receive a total revenue of $625 million ($25 a ton multiplied by 25 million tons). With a subsidy, they receive a total revenue of $1,050 million ($35 a ton multiplied by 30 million tons).

The price support is inefficient because it creates a deadweight loss. Farmers gain but consumers, who are also the tax payers who end up paying the subsidy, lose. And consumers' losses exceed the farmers' gains by the amount of the deadweight loss.

## Effects on the Rest of the World

The rest of the world receives a double-whammy from price supports. First, import restrictions in advanced economies deny developing economies access to the food markets of the advanced economies. The result is lower prices and smaller farm production in the developing economies.

Second, the surplus produced in the advanced economies gets sold in the rest of the world. Both the price and the quantity produced in the rest of the world are depressed even further.

The subsidies received by U.S. farmers are paid not only by U.S. taxpayers and consumers but also by poor farmers in the developing economies.

We explore global markets in action in Chapter 8. There you will see other ways in which intervention in markets brings inefficiencies and redistributes the gains from trade.

# EYE on YOUR LIFE
## Price Ceilings and Price Floors

Price ceilings and price floors operate in many of the markets in which you trade, and they require you to take a stand as a citizen and voter.

Unless you live in New York City, you're not likely to live in a rent controlled house or apartment. Because economists have explained the unwanted effects of rent ceilings that you've learned about in this chapter, this type of market intervention is now rare.

But you run into a price ceiling almost every time you use a freeway.

The zero price for using a freeway is a type of price ceiling. The next time you're stuck in traffic and moving at a crawl, think about how a free market in road use would cut the congestion and allow you to zip along.

In Singapore, a transponder on your dashboard would be clocking up the dollars and cents as you drive around the city. The price varies with the time of day, the traffic density, and where in the city you are. As a result, you would never be stuck in slow-moving traffic.

You encounter a price floor in the labor market. Have you wanted a job and been willing and available to work, but unable to get hired? Would you have taken a job for a slightly lower wage if one had been available?

You also encounter price floors (price supports) in markets for food. You pay more for tomatoes, sugar, oranges, and many other food items than the minimum cost of producing them.

Develop your own policy position on price floors and price ceilings.

# CHECKPOINT 7.4

**Explain how a price support in the market for an agricultural product creates a surplus, inefficiency, and unfairness.**

## Practice Problems

Figure 1 shows the market for tomatoes.

1. What are the equilibrium price and quantity of tomatoes? Is the market for tomatoes efficient?

2. If the government introduces a price support and sets the support price at $8 per pound, what is the quantity of tomatoes produced, the quantity demanded, and the subsidy received by tomato farmers?

3. If the government introduces a price support and sets the support price at $8 per pound, is the market for tomatoes efficient? Who gains and who loses from the price support? What is the deadweight loss created? Could the price support be regarded as being fair?

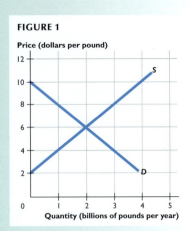

**FIGURE 1**

Price (dollars per pound)

Quantity (billions of pounds per year)

## In the News

**Big Sugar is set for a sweet bailout**
A bumper harvest of sugar beets and sugar cane has sent U.S. sugar prices tumbling to 21 cents a pound, below the USDA's support price of 25 cents a pound.

Source: *The Wall Street Journal*, March 12, 2013

How will the quantity of sugar produced and the quantity bought by consumers differ? Is there a surplus or shortage of sugar? Will the sugar market be efficient?

## Solutions to Practice Problems

1. The equilibrium price is $6 a pound; the equilibrium quantity is 2 billion pounds. The market is efficient—marginal benefit equals marginal cost.

2. At a support price of $8 a pound, 3 billion pounds are produced and 1 billion pounds are demanded, so there is a surplus of 2 billion pounds (Figure 2). The subsidy is $8 per pound on 2 billion pounds, which is $16 billion.

3. The market is not efficient because at the quantity produced, the marginal benefit (on the demand curve) is less than the marginal cost (on the supply curve). Farmers gain. They produce more and receive a higher price on what they sell in the market as well as the government subsidy. Consumers/taxpayers lose. They pay more for tomatoes and pay taxes to fund the subsidy. The deadweight loss is $2 billion (the area of the gray triangle). The outcome is unfair on both views of fairness unless farmers are poorer than consumers, in which case it might be fair to boost farmers' incomes.

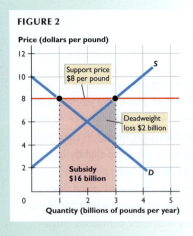

**FIGURE 2**

Price (dollars per pound)

Support price $8 per pound

Deadweight loss $2 billion

Subsidy $16 billion

Quantity (billions of pounds per year)

## Solution to In the News

The bumper harvest increases the supply of sugar. With no price support the quantity bought would equal the quantity produced and the market price would be 21 cents per pound. With a support price of 25 cents per pound, the quantity produced exceeds the quantity bought and a surplus arises. There is overproduction of sugar, which makes the sugar market inefficient.

# CHAPTER SUMMARY

## Key Points

1. **Explain how taxes change prices and quantities, are shared by buyers and sellers, and create inefficiency.**

   - A tax on buyers has the same effect as a tax on sellers. It increases the price paid by the buyer and lowers the price received by the seller.
   - A tax creates inefficiency by driving a wedge between marginal benefit and marginal cost and creating a deadweight loss.
   - The less elastic the demand or the more elastic the supply, the greater is the price increase and the larger is the share of the tax paid by the buyer.

2. **Explain how a price ceiling works and show how a rent ceiling creates a housing shortage, inefficiency, and unfairness.**

   - A price ceiling set above the equilibrium price has no effects.
   - A price ceiling set below the equilibrium price creates a shortage and increased search activity or a black market.
   - A price ceiling is inefficient and unfair.
   - A rent ceiling is an example of a price ceiling.

3. **Explain how a price floor works and show how the minimum wage creates unemployment, inefficiency, and unfairness.**

   - A price floor set below the equilibrium price has no effects.
   - A price floor set above the equilibrium price creates a surplus and increased search activity or illegal trading.
   - A price floor is inefficient and unfair.
   - A minimum wage is an example of a price floor.

4. **Explain how a price support in the market for an agricultural product creates a surplus, inefficiency, and unfairness.**

   - A price support increases the quantity produced, decreases the quantity consumed, and creates a surplus.
   - To maintain the support price, the government buys the surplus and subsidizes the producer.
   - A price support benefits the producer but costs the consumer/taxpayer more than the producer gains—it creates a deadweight loss.
   - A price support is inefficient and is usually unfair.

## Key Terms

Black market, 213
Excess burden, 208
Minimum wage law, 219
Price cap, 212

Price ceiling, 212
Price floor, 218
Price support, 225
Rent ceiling, 212

Search activity, 214
Subsidy, 225
Tax incidence, 206

# CHAPTER CHECKPOINT

## Study Plan Problems and Applications

**TABLE 1**

| Price (dollars per month) | Quantity demanded | Quantity supplied |
|---|---|---|
| | (units per month) | |
| 0 | 30 | 0 |
| 10 | 25 | 10 |
| 20 | 20 | 20 |
| 30 | 15 | 30 |
| 40 | 10 | 40 |

**FIGURE 1**

Price (dollars per month)

**TABLE 2**

| Wage rate (dollars per hour) | Quantity demanded | Quantity supplied |
|---|---|---|
| | (student workers) | |
| 10.00 | 600 | 300 |
| 10.50 | 500 | 350 |
| 11.00 | 400 | 400 |
| 11.50 | 300 | 450 |
| 12.00 | 200 | 500 |
| 12.50 | 100 | 550 |

**TABLE 3**

| Price (dollars per pound) | Quantity demanded | Quantity supplied |
|---|---|---|
| | (pounds per week) | |
| 1.00 | 5,000 | 2,000 |
| 2.00 | 4,500 | 2,500 |
| 3.00 | 4,000 | 3,000 |
| 4.00 | 3,500 | 3,500 |
| 5.00 | 3,000 | 4,000 |
| 6.00 | 2,500 | 4,500 |

**1.** In Florida, sunscreen and sunglasses are vital items. If the tax on sellers of these items is doubled from 5.5 percent to 11 percent, who will pay most of the tax increase: the buyer or the seller? Will the tax increase halve the quantity of sunscreen and sunglasses bought?

**2.** Suppose that the government imposes a $2 a cup tax on coffee. What determines by how much Starbucks will raise its price? How will the quantity of coffee bought in coffee shops change? Will this tax raise much revenue?

**3.** Table 1 illustrates the market for Internet service. What is the market price of Internet service? If the government taxes Internet service $15 a month, what is the price the buyer pays? What is the price the seller receives? Does the buyer or the seller pay more of the tax?

Use Figure 1, which shows the demand for on-campus housing, to work Problems **4** to **6**. The college has 200 rooms to rent.

**4.** If the college puts a rent ceiling on rooms of $650 a month, what is the rent, how many rooms are rented, and is the on-campus housing market efficient?

**5.** If the college puts a strictly enforced rent ceiling on rooms of $550 a month, what is the rent, how many rooms are rented, and is the on-campus housing market efficient? Explain why or why not.

**6.** Suppose that with a strictly enforced rent ceiling on rooms of $550 a month, a black market develops. How high could the black market rent be and would the on-campus housing market be fair? Explain your answer.

**7.** Table 2 shows the demand and supply schedules for student workers at on-campus venues. If the college introduces a strictly enforced minimum wage of $11.50 an hour, who gains and who loses from the minimum wage, and is the campus labor market efficient or fair?

**8.** Table 3 shows the demand and supply schedules for mushrooms. Suppose that the government introduces a support price for mushrooms of $6 per pound. Who gains and who loses? What are the quantity of mushrooms produced, the surplus of mushrooms, and the deadweight loss?

Use the following news clip to work Problems **9** and **10**.

**Coal shortage at China plants**
The government of China has set price controls on coal and gasoline in an attempt to shield families and farmers from rising world energy prices. Chinese power plants have run short of coal, sales of luxury, gas-guzzling cars have increased, and gasoline consumption has risen.

Source: CNN, May 20, 2008

**9.** Are China's price controls price floors or price ceilings? Draw a graph to illustrate the shortages of coal and gasoline created by the price controls.

**10.** Explain how China's price controls have changed consumer surplus, producer surplus, total surplus, and the deadweight loss in the markets for coal and gasoline. Draw a graph to illustrate your answer.

**11.** Read *Eye on Price Regulation* on p. 223 and explain why a mismatch between intention and outcome is inevitable if a price regulation seeks to block the laws of supply and demand.

# Instructor Assignable Problems and Applications

1. Suppose that Congress caps executive pay at a level below the equilibrium.
   - Explain how the quantity of executives demanded, the quantity supplied, and executive pay will change, and explain why the outcome is inefficient.
   - Draw a graph of the market for corporate executives. On your graph, show the market equilibrium, the pay cap, the quantity of executives supplied and the quantity demanded at the pay cap, and the deadweight loss created. Also show the highest pay that an executive might be offered in a black market.

Use the following information to work Problems **2** and **3**.

The supply of luxury boats is perfectly elastic, the demand for luxury boats is unit elastic, and with no tax on luxury boats, the price is $1 million and 240 luxury boats a week are bought. Now luxury boats are taxed at 20 percent.

2. What is the price that buyers pay? How is the tax split between the buyer and the seller? What is the government's tax revenue?

3. On a graph, show the excess burden of this tax. Is this tax efficient?

4. Figure 1 shows the demand for and supply of chocolate bars. Suppose that the government levies a $1.50 tax on a chocolate bar. What is the change in the quantity of chocolate bars bought, who pays most of the tax, and what is the deadweight loss?

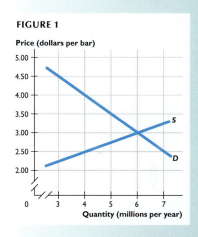

**FIGURE 1**

Price (dollars per bar)

Use the following information to work Problems **5** and **6**.

Concerned about the political fallout from rising gas prices, suppose that the U.S. government imposes a price ceiling of $3.00 a gallon on gasoline.

5. Explain how the market for gasoline would react to this price ceiling if the oil-producing nations increased production and drove the equilibrium price of gasoline to $2.50 a gallon. Would the U.S. gasoline market be efficient?

6. Explain how the market for gasoline would react to this price ceiling if a global shortage of oil sent the equilibrium price of gasoline to $3.50 a gallon. Would the U.S. gasoline market be efficient?

7. Suppose the government introduced a ceiling on lawyers' fees. How would the amount of work done by lawyers, the consumer surplus of people who hire lawyers, and the producer surplus of law firms change? Would this fee ceiling result in an efficient and fair use of resources? Why or why not?

Use the following information to work Problems **8** and **9**.

**Crop prices erode farm subsidy program**
High corn and soybean prices mean farmers are making the most money in their lives. At the same time, grain prices are far too high to trigger payouts under the U.S. primary farm-subsidy program's "price support" formula. The market has done what Congress couldn't do and that is "slash farm subsidies."

Source: *The Wall Street Journal*, July 25, 2011

8. Draw a graph to illustrate the soybean market when the soybean price was low. Show the quantity of soybeans produced, the subsidy farmers received, and the deadweight loss created.

9. In the market for corn with a price support, explain why the corn price has risen and ended up being too high to "trigger payouts."

## Critical Thinking Discussion Questions

1. **Venezuela's price controls**

   Since 2003, Venezuela's President Hugo Chavez had been setting prices on food, which have caused shortages and hoarding Venezuelan troops are cracking down on food smugglers and seizing their inventories.

   Sources: BBC News, January 26, 2006 and
   Associated Press, January 22, 2008

   a. Are the food prices price ceilings or price floors? Explain how you can tell.
   b. Why do Venezuelans attempt to sell smuggled foods?
   c. Do you think Venezuela's price controls are efficient? Explain and illustrate your answer.
   d. Do you think Venezuela's price controls are fair? Explain using alternative criteria of fairness.

2. **Living wage rise provides a boost for low-paid workers**

   More than 30,000 workers will receive a £400 a year pay rise in the voluntary "living wage" rate. The U.K. living wage rate is higher than the legal minimum wage of £6.31 an hour.

   Source: BBC News, November 4, 2013

   a. What is a living wage and how does it contrast with a legal minimum wage?
   b. Under what circumstances does a living wage result in unemployment?
   c. Draw a diagram to show the inefficiency of a living wage.
   d. Who benefits from a living wage? Who loses from a living wage?
   e. Is a living wage fair?

3. **Price ceiling for condoms**

   The Indian government has set a maximum price for a condom at 6.56 rupees. Manufacturers of more expensive "luxury" condom brands have criticized the move, saying it will have a negative impact on population-control measures. It is estimated that 1.8 billion luxury condoms are sold every year in India for up to 150 rupees. At the lower end of the price scale they are sold for about 25 rupees.

   Source: News India, December 20, 2013

   a. Explain why the manufacturers argued that setting the price ceiling for condoms would have a negative impact on population-control measures.
   b. Do you think that the price ceiling will increase the sales of condoms because more people can now afford to buy condoms?
   c. Do you agree with the new price ceiling? Why or why not?

Who wins and who loses from globalization?

# Global Markets in Action

When you have completed your study of this chapter, you will be able to

**1** Explain how markets work with international trade.

**2** Identify the gains from international trade and its winners and losers.

**3** Explain the effects of international trade barriers.

**4** Explain and evaluate arguments used to justify restricting international trade.

## 8.1 HOW GLOBAL MARKETS WORK

Because we trade with people in other countries, the goods and services that we buy and consume are not limited by what we produce. The goods and services that we buy from firms in other countries are our **imports;** the goods and services that we sell to people and firms in other countries are our **exports.**

**Imports**
The goods and services that people and firms in one country buy from firms in other countries.

**Exports**
The goods and services that firms in one country sell to people and firms in other countries.

### ■ International Trade Today

Global trade today is enormous. In 2012, global exports and imports (the two numbers are the same because what one country exports another imports) were about $23 trillion, which is 31 percent of the value of global production. The United States is the world's largest international trader and accounts for 10 percent of world exports and 12 percent of world imports. Germany and China, which rank 2 and 3 behind the United States, lag by a large margin.

In 2012, total U.S. exports were $2.2 trillion, which is about 14 percent of the value of U.S. production. Total U.S. imports were $2.8 trillion, which is about 17 percent of the value of total expenditure in the United States.

The United States trades both goods and services. In 2012, exports of services were $0.6 trillion (30 percent of total exports) and imports of services were $0.4 trillion (16 percent of total imports).

Our largest exports are services such as royalties, license fees, banking, business consulting, and other private services. Our largest exports of goods are industrial and service machinery. Our largest imports are crude oil and private services. *Eye on the U.S. Economy* (p. 235) provides a bit more detail on our ten largest exports and imports.

### ■ What Drives International Trade?

*Comparative advantage* is the fundamental force that drives international trade. We defined comparative advantage in Chapter 3 (p. 109) as the ability of a person to perform an activity or produce a good or service at a lower opportunity cost than anyone else. This same idea applies to nations. We can define *national comparative advantage* as the ability of a *nation* to perform an activity or produce a good or service at a lower opportunity cost than *any other nation*.

The opportunity cost of producing a T-shirt is lower in China than in the United States, so China has a comparative advantage in producing T-shirts. The opportunity cost of producing an airplane is lower in the United States than in China, so the United States has a comparative advantage in producing airplanes.

You saw in Chapter 3 how Liz and Joe reaped gains from trade by specializing in the production of the good at which they have a comparative advantage and then trading. Both were better off. This same principle applies to trade among nations.

China has a comparative advantage at producing T-shirts and the United States has a comparative advantage at producing airplanes, so the people of both countries can gain from specialization and trade. China can buy airplanes from the United States at a lower opportunity cost than that at which it can produce them. And Americans can buy T-shirts from China for a lower opportunity cost than that at which U.S. firms can produce them. Also, through international trade, Chinese producers can get higher prices for their T-shirts and Boeing can sell airplanes for a higher price. Both countries gain from international trade.

We're going to illustrate the gains from trade that we've just described by studying demand and supply in the global markets for T-shirts and airplanes.

# EYE on the U.S. ECONOMY
## U.S. Exports and Imports

The blue bars in part (a) of the figure show the ten largest U.S. exports and the red bars in part (b) show the ten largest U.S. imports. Some items appear in both parts (a) and (b) because the United States exports and imports items in many of the broad categories.

Three of the top ten U.S. exports are services—private services, which includes financial, business, professional, and technical services (such as the sale of advertising by Google to Adidas, a European sportswear maker), and education (foreign students in our colleges and universities), travel (such as the expenditure on a Florida vacation by a visitor from England), and royalties and license fees (such as fees received by Hollywood movie producers on films shown abroad).

Oil is the largest U.S. import. We also import large quantities of automobiles, clothing, furniture, TVs, DVD players, computers, and industrial machinery and equipment. Private services also feature in the ten largest imports.

Although we import a large quantity of computers, we export some too. We also export the semiconductors (computer chips) inside those imported computers. The Intel chip in a Lenovo laptop built in China and imported into the United States is an example. This chip is made in the United States and exported to China.

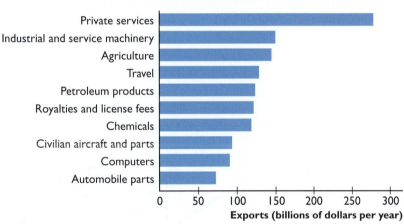

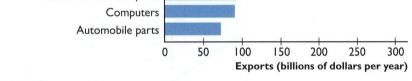

**(a) The 10 largest U.S. exports**

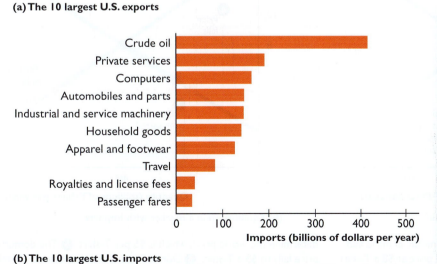

**(b) The 10 largest U.S. imports**

SOURCE OF DATA: Bureau of Economic Analysis.

*The United States exports airplanes …*

*and imports crude oil.*

## ■ Why the United States Imports T-Shirts

Figure 8.1 illustrates the effects of international trade in T-shirts. The demand curve $D_{US}$ and the supply curve $S_{US}$ show the demand and supply in the U.S. domestic market only. The demand curve tells us the quantity of T-shirts that Americans are willing to buy at various prices. The supply curve tells us the quantity of T-shirts that U.S. garment makers are willing to sell at various prices.

Figure 8.1(a) shows what the U.S. T-shirt market would be like with no international trade. The price of a T-shirt would be $8 and 40 million T-shirts a year would be produced by U.S. garment makers and bought by U.S. consumers.

Figure 8.1(b) shows the market for T-shirts *with* international trade. Now the price of a T-shirt is determined in the world market, not the U.S. domestic market. The world price is *less than* $8 a T-shirt, which means that the rest of the world has a comparative advantage in producing T-shirts. The world price line shows the world price as $5 a T-shirt.

The U.S. demand curve, $D_{US}$, tells us that at $5 a T-shirt, Americans buy 60 million T-shirts a year. The U.S. supply curve, $S_{US}$, tells us that at $5 a T-shirt, U.S. garment makers produce 20 million T-shirts. To buy 60 million T-shirts when only 20 million are produced in the United States, we must import T-shirts from the rest of the world. The quantity of T-shirts imported is 40 million a year.

■ **FIGURE 8.1**

A Market with Imports

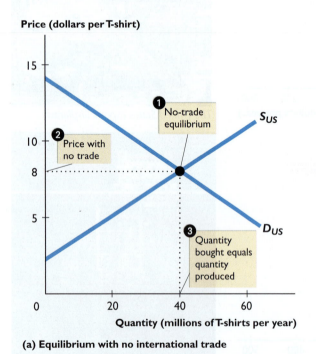

**(a) Equilibrium with no international trade**

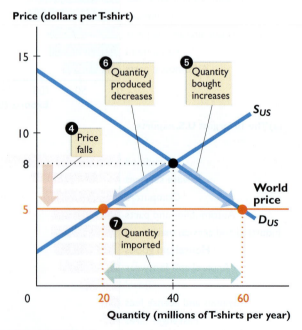

**(b) Equilibrium in a market with imports**

With no international trade, in part (a), ❶ domestic demand and domestic supply determine ❷ the equilibrium price at $8 a T-shirt and ❸ the quantity at 40 million T-shirts a year.
With international trade, in part (b), world demand and world supply determine the world price, which is $5 per T-shirt. ❹ The domestic price falls to $5 a T-shirt. ❺ Domestic purchases increase to 60 million T-shirts a year, and ❻ domestic production decreases to 20 million T-shirts a year. ❼ 40 million T-shirts a year are imported.

# ■ Why the United States Exports Airplanes

Figure 8.2 illustrates the effects of international trade in airplanes. The demand curve $D_{US}$ and the supply curve $S_{US}$ show the demand and supply in the U.S. domestic market only. The demand curve tells us the quantity of airplanes that U.S. airlines are willing to buy at various prices. The supply curve tells us the quantity of airplanes that U.S. aircraft makers are willing to sell at various prices.

Figure 8.2(a) shows what the U.S. airplane market would be like with no international trade. The price of an airplane would be $100 million and 400 airplanes a year would be produced by U.S. aircraft makers and bought by U.S. airlines.

Figure 8.2(b) shows the U.S. airplane market *with* international trade. Now the price of an airplane is determined in the world market, not the U.S. domestic market. The world price is *higher than* $100 million, which means that the United States has a comparative advantage in producing airplanes. The world price line shows the world price as $150 million.

The U.S. demand curve, $D_{US}$, tells us that at $150 million an airplane, U.S. airlines buy 200 airplanes a year. The U.S. supply curve, $S_{US}$, tells us that at $150 million an airplane, U.S. aircraft makers produce 700 airplanes a year. The quantity produced in the United States (700 a year) minus the quantity purchased by U.S. airlines (200 a year) is the quantity of U.S. exports, which is 500 airplanes a year.

■ **FIGURE 8.2**

A Market with Exports

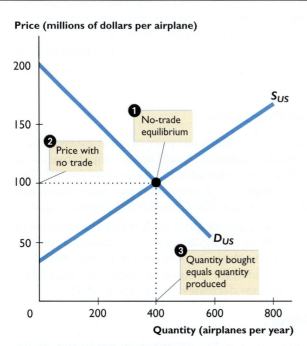

**(a) Equilibrium without international trade**

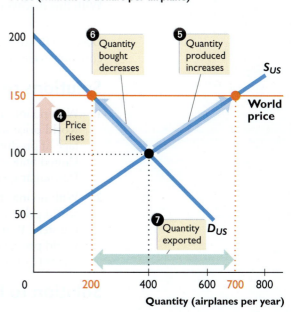

**(b) Equilibrium in a market with exports**

With no international trade, in part (a), ❶ domestic demand and domestic supply determine ❷ the equilibrium price at $100 million an airplane and ❸ the quantity at 400 airplanes a year. With international trade, in part (b), world demand and world supply determine the world price, which is $150 million an airplane.

❹ The domestic price rises. ❺ Domestic production increases to 700 airplanes a year, ❻ domestic purchases decrease to 200 airplanes a year, and ❼ 500 airplanes a year are exported.

# CHECKPOINT 8.1

**Explain how markets work with international trade.**

## Practice Problems

1. Suppose that the world price of sugar is 10 cents a pound, the United States does *not* trade internationally, and the U.S. equilibrium price of sugar is 20 cents a pound. The United States then begins to trade internationally.
   - How does the price of sugar in the United States change?
   - Do U.S. consumers buy more or less sugar?
   - Do U.S. sugar growers produce more or less sugar?
   - Does the United States export or import sugar?

2. Suppose that the world price of steel is $100 a ton, India does *not* trade internationally, and the equilibrium price of steel in India is $60 a ton. India then begins to trade internationally.
   - How does the price of steel in India change?
   - How does the quantity of steel produced in India change?
   - How does the quantity of steel bought by India change?
   - Does India export or import steel?

## In the News

**Underwater oil discovery to transform Brazil into a major exporter**

The discovery of a huge oil field could make Brazil a large exporter of gasoline. Until two years ago Brazil imported oil; then it became self-sufficient in oil. With this discovery, Brazil will become a major exporter of oil.

Source: *The New York Times*, January 11, 2008

Describe Brazil's comparative advantage in producing oil, and explain why its comparative advantage has changed.

## Solutions to Practice Problems

1. With no international trade, the U.S. domestic price of sugar exceeds the world price so we know that the rest of the world has a comparative advantage at producing sugar. With international trade, the price of sugar in the United States falls to the world price, U.S. consumers buy more sugar, and U.S. sugar growers produce less sugar. The United States imports sugar.

2. With no international trade, the domestic price of steel in India is below the world price so we know that India has a comparative advantage at producing steel. With international trade, the price of steel in India rises to the world price, steel mills in India increase the quantity they produce, and the quantity of steel bought by Indians decreases. India exports steel.

## Solution to In the News

Before 2008, Brazil did not have a comparative advantage in producing oil. Its cost of producing a barrel of oil was higher than the world market price, so Brazil imported oil. With the discovery of the new oil field, the cost of producing a barrel of oil in Brazil is below the world price. Now Brazil has a comparative advantage in the production of oil. With this new comparative advantage, Brazil had become an exporter of oil.

## 8.2    WINNERS, LOSERS, AND NET GAINS FROM TRADE

You've seen how international trade lowers the price of an imported good and raises the price of an exported good. Buyers of imported goods benefit from lower prices, and sellers of exported goods benefit from higher prices. But some people complain about international competition: Not everyone gains. We're now going to see who wins and who loses from free international trade. You will then be able to understand who complains about international competition and why.

We'll also see why we never hear the consumers of imported goods complaining and why we never hear exporters complaining, except when they want greater access to foreign markets. And we'll see why we *do* hear complaints from producers about cheap foreign imports.

# EYE on GLOBALIZATION

## Who Wins and Who Loses from Globalization?

Economists generally agree that the gains from globalization vastly outweigh the losses, but there are both winners and losers.

The U.S. consumer is a big winner. Globalization has brought iPads, Wii games, Nike shoes, and a wide range of other products to our shops at ever lower prices.

The Indian (and Chinese and other Asian) worker is another big winner. Globalization has brought a wider range of more interesting jobs and higher wages.

The U.S. (and European) textile workers and furniture makers are big losers. Their jobs have disappeared and many of them have struggled to find new jobs, even when they've been willing to take a pay cut.

But one of the biggest losers is the African farmer. Blocked from global agricultural markets by trade restrictions and subsidies in the United States and Europe, globalization is leaving much of Africa on the sidelines.

*The U.S. consumer …*

*and Indian workers gain from globalization.*

*But some U.S. workers and …*

*African farmers lose.*

## ■ Gains and Losses from Imports

We measure the gains and losses from imports by examining their effect on consumer surplus, producer surplus, and total surplus. The winners are those whose surplus increases and the losers are those whose surplus decreases.

Figure 8.3(a) shows what consumer surplus and producer surplus would be with no international trade. Domestic demand, $D_{US}$, and domestic supply, $S_{US}$, determine the price and quantity. The green area shows consumer surplus and the blue area shows producer surplus. Total surplus is the sum of consumer surplus and producer surplus.

Figure 8.3(b) shows how these surpluses change when the market opens to imports. The price falls to the world price. The quantity purchased increases to the quantity demanded at the world price, and consumer surplus expands to the larger green area $A + B + D$. The quantity produced decreases to the quantity supplied at the world price, and producer surplus shrinks to the smaller blue area $C$.

Part of the gain in consumer surplus, the area $B$, is a loss of producer surplus— a redistribution of total surplus. But the other part of the increase in consumer surplus, the area $D$, is a net gain. This increase in total surplus is the gain from imports and results from the lower price and increased purchases.

■ **FIGURE 8.3**

### Gains and Losses in a Market with Imports

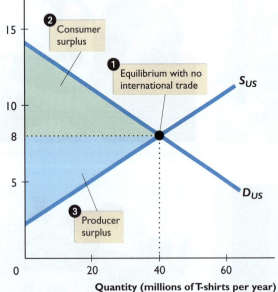

**(a) Consumer surplus and producer surplus with no international trade**

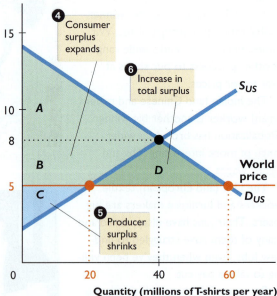

**(b) Gains and losses from imports**

With no international trade, ❶ equilibrium at the intersection of the domestic demand and domestic supply curves determines the price and quantity. ❷ The green area shows the consumer surplus and ❸ the blue area shows the producer surplus.

With international trade, the domestic price falls to the world price. ❹ Consumer surplus expands to the area $A + B + D$. Area $B$ is a transfer of surplus from producers to consumers, and ❺ producer surplus shrinks to area $C$. ❻ Area $D$ is an increase in total surplus.

# Gains and Losses from Exports

We measure the gains and losses from exports just like we measured those from imports, by examining their effect on consumer surplus, producer surplus, and total surplus.

Figure 8.4(a) shows what the consumer surplus and producer surplus would be with no international trade. Domestic demand, $D_{US}$, and domestic supply, $S_{US}$, determine the price and quantity. The green area shows consumer surplus and the blue area shows producer surplus. The two surpluses sum to total surplus.

Figure 8.4(b) shows how the consumer surplus and producer surplus change when the good is exported. The price rises to the world price. The quantity bought decreases to the quantity demanded at the world price, and the consumer surplus shrinks to the green area $A$. The quantity produced increases to the quantity supplied at the world price, and the producer surplus expands from the blue area $C$ to the larger blue area $B + C + D$.

Part of the gain in producer surplus, the area $B$, is a loss in consumer surplus—a redistribution of the total surplus. But the other part of the increase in producer surplus, the area $D$, is a net gain. This increase in total surplus is the gain from exports and results from the higher price and increased production.

## FIGURE 8.4

Gains and Losses in a Market with Exports

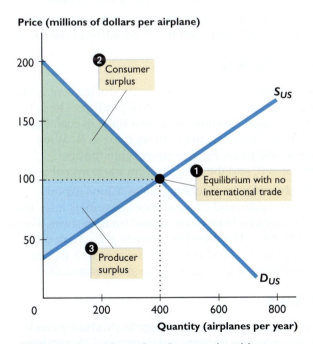

**(a) Consumer surplus and producer surplus with no international trade**

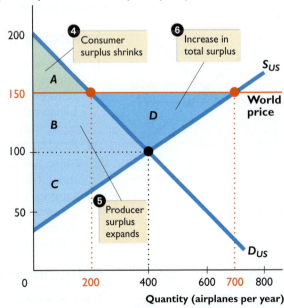

**(b) Gains and losses from exports**

With no international trade, ❶ equilibrium at the intersection of the domestic demand and domestic supply curves determines the price and quantity. ❷ The green area shows the consumer surplus and ❸ the blue area shows the producer surplus.

With international trade, the domestic price rises to the world price. ❹ Consumer surplus shrinks to the area $A$. ❺ Producer surplus expands to the area $B + C + D$. Area $B$ is transferred from consumers to producers. ❻ Area $D$ is an increase in total surplus.

# CHECKPOINT 8.2

**Identify the gains from international trade and its winners and losers.**

## Practice Problems

Before the 1980s, China did not trade internationally: It was self-sufficient. Then China began to trade internationally in, among other items, coal and shoes. The world price of coal was less than China's domestic price and the world price of shoes was higher than its domestic price.

1. Does China import or export coal? Who, in China, gains and who loses from international trade in coal? Does China gain from this trade in coal? On a graph of the market for coal in China show the gains, losses, and net gain or loss from international trade in coal.

2. Does China import or export shoes? Who, in China, gains and who loses from international trade in shoes? Does China gain from this trade in shoes? On a graph of the market for shoes in China, show the gains, losses, and net gain or loss from international trade in shoes.

## In the News

**Commodities post big drop**
World commodity prices have fallen in the past six weeks. Crude oil prices dropped 7%, beef prices fell 5%, and corn prices fell 4%.
Source: *Global Commodity Watch,* June 15, 2011

The United States imports crude oil and exports beef. How do these price falls change the U.S. gains from trade in each good and the distribution of the gains?

## Solutions to Practice Problems

1. The rest of the world has a comparative advantage in producing coal. China imports coal, Chinese coal users gain, and Chinese coal producers lose. The gains exceed the losses: China gains from international trade in coal. Figure 1 shows the market for coal in China. The price before trade is $P_0$. With trade, the price falls to the world price, $P_1$. Consumers gain the area $B + D$, producers lose the area $B$, and the net gain from trade in coal is $D$.

2. China has a comparative advantage in producing shoes. China exports shoes, Chinese shoe producers gain, and Chinese shoe consumers lose. The gains exceed the losses: China gains from international trade in shoes. Figure 2 shows the shoe market in China. The price before trade is $P_0$. With trade, the price rises to the world price, $P_1$. Producers gain the area $B + D$, consumers lose the area $B$, and the net gain from trade in shoes is area $D$.

## Solution to In the News

The United States does not have a comparative advantage in producing crude oil, so the fall in the world price increases imports and decreases U.S. production. Consumer surplus increases, producer surplus decreases, but consumers gain more than producers lose. The United States has a comparative advantage in producing beef, so the fall in the world price decreases U.S. production. Producer surplus decreases, consumer surplus increases, but producers lose more than consumers gain.

**FIGURE 1**

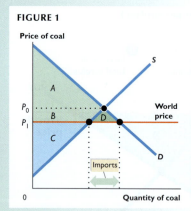

**FIGURE 2**

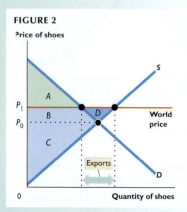

## 8.3  INTERNATIONAL TRADE RESTRICTIONS

Governments use four sets of tools to influence international trade and protect domestic industries from foreign competition. They are

- Tariffs
- Import quotas
- Other import barriers
- Export subsidies

### ■ Tariffs

A **tariff** is a tax that is imposed on a good when it is imported. For example, the government of India imposes a 100 percent tariff on wine imported from California. When an Indian firm imports a $10 bottle of Californian wine, it pays the Indian government a $10 import duty.

**Tariff**
A tax imposed on a good when it is imported.

The incentive for governments to impose tariffs is strong. First, they provide revenue to the government. Second, they enable the government to satisfy the self-interest of people who earn their incomes in import-competing industries. As you will see, tariffs and other restrictions on free international trade decrease the gains from trade and are not in the social interest. Let's see how.

# EYE on the PAST
## The History of U.S. Tariffs

The figure shows the average tariff rate on U.S. imports since 1930. Tariffs peaked during the 1930s when Congress passed the Smoot-Hawley Act. With other nations, the United States signed the General Agreement on Tariffs and Trade (GATT) in 1947. In a series of rounds of negotiations, GATT achieved widespread tariff cuts for the United States and many other nations. Today, the World Trade Organization (WTO) continues the work of GATT and seeks to promote unrestricted trade among all nations.

The United States is a party to many trade agreements with individual countries or regions. These include the North American Free Trade Agreement (NAFTA) and the Central American Free Trade Agreement (CAFTA). These agreements have eliminated tariffs on most goods traded between the United States and the countries of North and Central America.

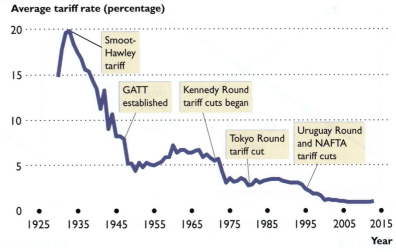

SOURCES OF DATA: The Budget for Fiscal Year 2013, Historical Tables, Table 2.5 and Bureau of Economic Analysis.

## The Effects of a Tariff

To see the effects of a tariff, let's return to the example in which, with free international trade, the United States imports T-shirts. The T-shirts are imported and sold at the world price. Then, under pressure from U.S. garment makers, the U.S. government imposes a tariff on imported T-shirts. Buyers of T-shirts must now pay the world price plus the tariff. Several consequences follow in the market for T-shirts. Figure 8.5 illustrates these consequences.

Figure 8.5(a) is the same as Figure 8.1(b) and shows the situation with free international trade. The United States produces 20 million T-shirts and imports 40 million T-shirts a year at the world price of $5 a T-shirt.

Figure 8.5(b) shows what happens with a tariff, which is set at $2 per T-shirt. The following changes occur in the U.S. market for T-shirts:

- The price of a T-shirt in the United States rises by $2.
- The quantity of T-shirts bought in the United States decreases.
- The quantity of T-shirts produced in the United States increases.
- The quantity of T-shirts imported into the United States decreases.
- The U.S. government collects a tariff revenue.

### FIGURE 8.5

The Effects of a Tariff

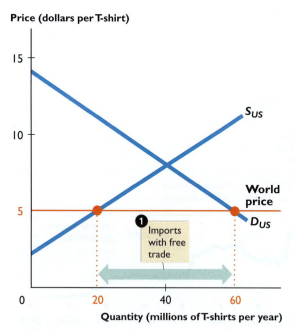

**(a) Free trade**

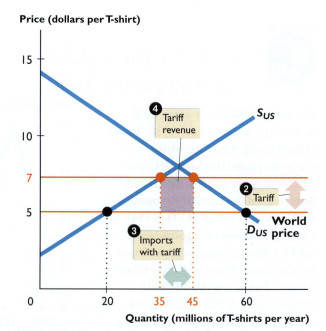

**(b) Market with tariff**

The world price of a T-shirt is $5. With free trade, in part (a), Americans buy 60 million T-shirts. The United States produces 20 million T-shirts and ❶ imports 40 million T-shirts.

❷ With a tariff of $2 per T-shirt in part (b), the domestic price rises to $7 a T-shirt (the world price plus the tariff). Domestic production increases, purchases decrease, and ❸ the quantity imported decreases. ❹ The U.S. government collects tariff revenue of $2 on each T-shirt imported, which is shown by the purple rectangle.

***Rise in Price of a T-Shirt***  To buy a T-shirt, Americans must pay the world price plus the tariff, so the price of a T-shirt rises by $2 to $7. Figure 8.5(b) shows the new domestic price line, which lies $2 above the world price line.

***Decrease in Purchases***  The higher price of a T-shirt brings a decrease in the quantity demanded, which Figure 8.5(b) shows as a movement along the demand curve from 60 million T-shirts at $5 a T-shirt to 45 million T-shirts at $7 a T-shirt.

***Increase in Domestic Production***  The higher price of a T-shirt stimulates domestic production, which Figure 8.5(b) shows as a movement along the supply curve from 20 million T-shirts at $5 a T-shirt to 35 million T-shirts at $7 a T-shirt.

***Decrease in Imports***  T-shirt imports decrease by 30 million from 40 million to 10 million a year. Both the decrease in purchases and the increase in domestic production contribute to this decrease in imports.

***Tariff Revenue***  The government's tariff revenue is $20 million—$2 per T-shirt on 10 million imported T-shirts—shown by the purple rectangle.

## Winners, Losers, and the Social Loss from a Tariff

A tariff on an imported good creates winners and losers. When the U.S. government imposes a tariff on an imported good,

- U.S. producers of the good gain.
- U.S. consumers of the good lose.
- U.S. consumers lose more than U.S. producers gain.

***U.S. Producers of the Good Gain***  Because the price of an imported T-shirt rises by the tariff, U.S. T-shirt producers are now able to sell their T-shirts for a higher price—the world price plus the tariff. As the price of a T-shirt rises, U.S. producers increase the quantity supplied. Because the marginal cost of producing a T-shirt in the United States is less than the higher price of all the T-shirts sold except for the marginal T-shirt, producer surplus increases. This increase in producer surplus is the gain to U.S. producers.

***U.S. Consumers of the Good Lose***  Because the price of a T-shirt in the United States rises, the quantity of T-shirts demanded decreases. The combination of a higher price and smaller quantity bought decreases consumer surplus.This loss of consumer surplus represents the loss to U.S. consumers that arises from a tariff.

***U.S. Consumers Lose More Than U.S. Producers Gain***  You've just seen that consumer surplus decreases and producer surplus increases, but which changes by more? Do consumers lose more than producers gain, or do producers gain more than consumers lose? Or is there just a straight transfer from consumers to producers? To answer these questions, we need to return to the demand and supply analysis of the market for T-shirts and compare the changes in consumer surplus and producer surplus.

Figure 8.6(a) is the same as Figure 8.3(b) and shows the consumer surplus and producer surplus with free international trade in T-shirts. The dark green area is the increase in total surplus that comes from free international trade. By comparing

■ **FIGURE 8.6**

The Winners and Losers from a Tariff

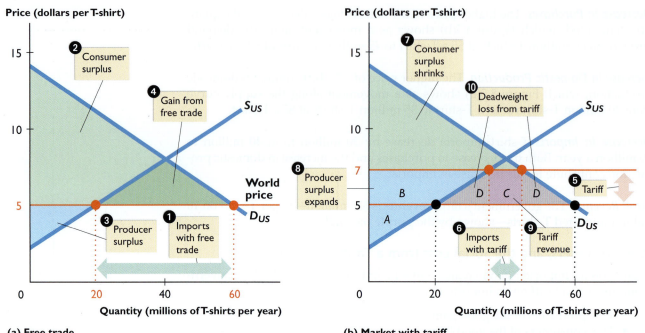

**(a) Free trade**

**(b) Market with tariff**

The world price of a T-shirt is $5. With free trade, ❶ the United States imports 40 million T-shirts. ❷ Consumer surplus, ❸ producer surplus, and ❹ the gains from free international trade are as large as possible. ❺ A tariff of $2 per T-shirt raises the price of a

T-shirt to $7. ❻ The quantity imported decreases. ❼ Consumer surplus shrinks by the areas *B*, *C*, and *D*. ❽ Producer surplus expands by area *B*. ❾ The government's tariff revenue is area *C*, and ❿ the tariff creates a deadweight loss equal to the areas *D*.

Figure 8.6(b) with Figure 8.6(a), you can see how a $2 tariff on imported T-shirts changes the surpluses. Producer surplus—the blue area—increases by the area labeled *B*. The increase in producer surplus is the gain to U.S. producers of T-shirts from the tariff. Consumer surplus—the green area—shrinks.

The decrease in consumer surplus divides into three parts. First, some of the consumer surplus is transferred to producers. The blue area *B* represents this loss of consumer surplus (and gain of producer surplus). Second, part of the consumer surplus is transferred to the government. The purple area *C* represents this loss of consumer surplus (and gain of government revenue). When the tariff revenue is spent, both consumers and producers receive some benefit, but there is no expectation that the buyers of T-shirts will receive the benefits of the expenditure of this tariff revenue from T-shirts. The tariff revenue is a loss to buyers of T-shirts.

The third part of the loss of consumer surplus is a transfer to no one: it is a *deadweight loss*. Consumers buy a smaller quantity at a higher price. The two gray areas labeled *D* represent this loss of consumer surplus. Total surplus decreases by this amount, which is the social loss from the tariff.

Let's now look at the second tool for restricting trade: quotas.

## ■ Import Quotas

An **import quota** is a quantitative restriction on the import of a good that limits the maximum quantity of a good that may be imported in a given period. The United States imposes import quotas on many items, including sugar, bananas, and textiles.

Quotas enable the government to satisfy the self-interest of people who earn their incomes in import-competing industries. You will see that like a tariff, a quota on imports decreases the gains from trade and is not in the social interest.

### The Effects of an Import Quota

The effects of an import quota are similar to those of a tariff. The price rises, the quantity bought decreases, and the quantity produced in the United States increases. Figure 8.7 illustrates the effects.

Figure 8.7(a) shows the situation with free international trade. Figure 8.7(b) shows what happens with a quota that limits imports to 10 million T-shirts a year. The U.S. supply curve of T-shirts becomes the domestic supply curve, $S_{US}$, plus the quantity that the quota permits to be imported. So the U.S. supply curve becomes the curve labeled $S_{US} + quota$. The price of a T-shirt rises to $7, the

**Import quota**
A quantitative restriction on the import of a good that limits the maximum quantity of a good that may be imported in a given period.

### ■ FIGURE 8.7

#### The Effects of an Import Quota

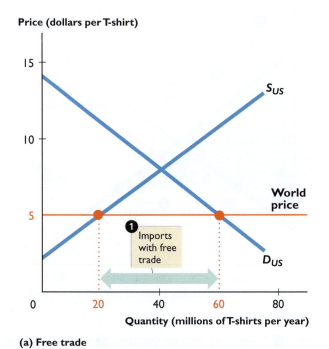

**(a) Free trade**

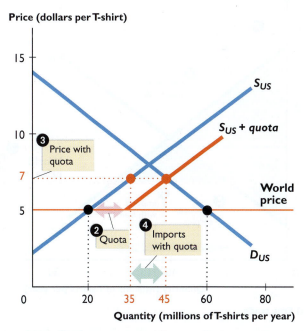

**(b) Market with quota**

With free trade, in part (a), Americans buy 60 million T-shirts at the world price. The United States produces 20 million T-shirts and ❶ imports 40 million T-shirts. ❷ With an import quota of 10 million

T-shirts, in part (b), the U.S. supply curve becomes $S_{US} + quota$. ❸ The price rises to $7 a T-shirt. Domestic production increases, purchases decrease, and ❹ the quantity imported decreases.

quantity of T-shirts bought in the United States decreases to 45 million a year, the quantity of T-shirts produced in the United States increases to 35 million a year, and the quantity of T-shirts imported into the United States decreases to the quota quantity of 10 million a year. All these effects of a quota are identical to the effects of a $2 per T-shirt tariff, as you can check in Figure 8.6(b).

### Winners, Losers, and the Social Loss from an Import Quota

An import quota creates winners and losers that are similar to those of a tariff but with an interesting difference. When the government imposes an import quota,

* U.S. producers of the good gain.
* U.S. consumers of the good lose.
* Importers of the good gain.
* U.S. consumers lose more than U.S. producers and importers gain.

Figure 8.8 compares the gains from trade under free trade with those under a quota. Figure 8.8(a) shows the consumer surplus and producer surplus with free international trade in T-shirts. By comparing Figure 8.8(b) with Figure 8.8(a), you can see how an import quota of 10 million T-shirts changes the surpluses. Producer surplus—the blue area—increases by the area labeled *B*. The increase in

### FIGURE 8.8

The Winners and Losers from an Import Quota

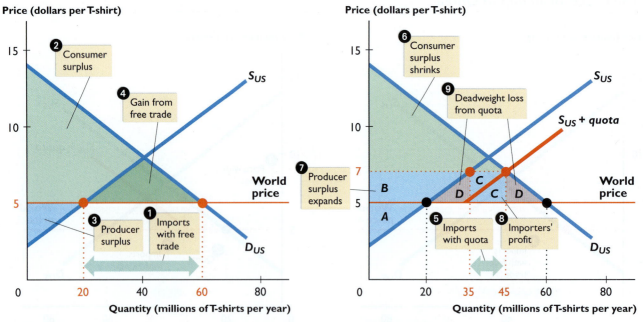

**(a) Free trade**

The world price of a T-shirt is $5. With free trade, ❶ the United States imports 40 million T-shirts. ❷ Consumer surplus, ❸ producer surplus, and ❹ the gains from free trade are as large as possible. In part (b), an import quota raises the domestic price to $7 a

**(b) Market with quota**

T-shirt. ❺ The quantity imported decreases. ❻ Consumer surplus shrinks by the areas *B*, *C*, and *D*. ❼ Producer surplus expands by area *B*. ❽ Importers' profit is the areas *C*, and ❾ the quota creates a deadweight loss equal to the areas *D*.

producer surplus is the gain by U.S. producers from the import quota. Consumer surplus—the green area—shrinks. This decrease is the loss to consumers from the import quota.

The decrease in consumer surplus divides into three parts. First, some of the consumer surplus is transferred to producers. The blue area *B* represents this loss of consumer surplus (and gain of producer surplus). Second, part of the consumer surplus is transferred to importers who buy T-shirts for $5 (the world price) and sell them for $7 (the domestic price). The blue areas *C* represent this loss of consumer surplus and profit for importers.

The third part of the loss of consumer surplus is a transfer to no one: it is a *deadweight loss*. Consumers buy a smaller quantity at a higher price. The two gray areas labeled *D* represent this loss of consumer surplus. Total surplus decreases by this amount, which is the social loss from the import quota.

You can now see the one difference between an import quota and a tariff. A tariff brings in revenue for the government while an import quota brings a profit for the importer. All the other effects are the same, provided the quota is set at the same level of imports that results from the tariff.

## ■ Other Import Barriers

Two sets of policies that influence imports are

- Health, safety, and regulation barriers
- Voluntary export restraints

### Health, Safety, and Regulation Barriers

Thousands of detailed health, safety, and other regulations restrict international trade. For example, U.S. food imports are examined by the Food and Drug Administration to determine whether the food is "pure, wholesome, safe to eat, and produced under sanitary conditions." The discovery of BSE (mad cow disease) in just one U.S. cow in 2003 was enough to close down international trade in U.S. beef. The European Union bans imports of most genetically modified foods, such as U.S.-produced soybeans. Although regulations of the type we've just described are not designed to limit international trade, they have that effect.

### Voluntary Export Restraints

A *voluntary export restraint* is like a quota allocated to a foreign exporter of the good. A voluntary export restraint decreases imports just like an import quota does, but the foreign exporter gets the profit from the gap between the domestic price and the world price.

## ■ Export Subsidies

An **export subsidy** is a payment by the government to the producer to cover part of the cost of production that is exported. The U.S. and European Union governments subsidize farm products. These subsidies stimulate the production and export of farm products, but they make it harder for producers in other countries, notably in Africa and Central and South America, to compete in global markets. Export subsidies bring gains to domestic producers, but they result in overproduction in the domestic economy and underproduction in the rest of the world and so create a deadweight loss (see Chapter 6, p. 193).

**Export subsidy**
A payment by the government to a producer to cover part of the cost of production that is exported.

# CHECKPOINT 8.3

**Explain the effects of international trade barriers.**

## Practice Problems

Before 1995, the United States imposed tariffs on goods imported from Mexico and Mexico imposed tariffs on goods imported from the United States. In 1995, Mexico joined NAFTA. U.S. tariffs on imports from Mexico and Mexican tariffs on imports from the United States are gradually being removed.

1.  Explain how the price that U.S. consumers pay for goods imported from Mexico and the quantity of U.S. imports from Mexico have changed. Who, in the United States, are the winners and losers from this free trade?

2.  Explain how the quantity of U.S. exports to Mexico and the U.S. government's tariff revenue from trade with Mexico have changed.

3.  Suppose that this year, tomato growers in Florida lobby the U.S. government to impose an import quota on Mexican tomatoes. Explain who, in the United States, would gain and who would lose from such a quota.

## In the News

**Indonesians bemoan Hollywood blockbuster blackout**
Four months ago Indonesia imposed an import tariff on Hollywood movies. The tariff was meant "to protect local film makers." The major Hollywood studios responded by withdrawing their films from Indonesia.

Source: *The Jakarta Post*, July 6, 2011

Explain how this tariff influences the price of seeing a movie in Indonesia, the quantity of movies produced in Indonesia, and Indonesia's gains from trade with the United States. Who, in Indonesia, gains from the tariff and who loses?

## Solutions to Practice Problems

1.  The price that U.S. consumers pay for goods imported from Mexico has fallen and the quantity of U.S. imports from Mexico has increased. The winners are U.S. consumers of goods imported from Mexico and the losers are U.S. producers of goods imported from Mexico.

2.  The quantity of U.S. exports to Mexico has increased and the U.S. government's tariff revenue from trade with Mexico has fallen.

3.  With an import quota, the price of tomatoes in the United States would rise and the quantity bought would decrease. Consumer surplus would decrease. Growers would receive a higher price, produce a larger quantity, and producer surplus would increase. The U.S. total surplus in the tomato market would be redistributed from consumers to producers, but it would decrease.

## Solution to In the News

The tariff raises the price of seeing a movie in Indonesia. The production of movies in Indonesia increases, and imports of Hollywood movies fall to zero. Indonesia's gains from trade with the United States decrease. With the higher price, consumer surplus decreases—consumers lose. Producer surplus increases—producers gain. The government collected zero tariff revenue.

## 8.4    THE CASE AGAINST PROTECTION

For as long as nations and international trade have existed, people have debated whether free international trade or protection from foreign competition is better for a country. The debate continues, but most economists believe that free trade promotes prosperity for all countries while protection reduces the potential gains from trade. We've seen the most powerful case for free trade: All countries benefit from their comparative advantage. But there is a broader range of issues in the free trade versus protection debate. Let's review these issues.

### ■ Three Traditional Arguments for Protection

Three traditional arguments for protection and restricting international trade are

- The national security argument
- The infant-industry argument
- The dumping argument

Let's look at each in turn.

### The National Security Argument

The national security argument is that a country must protect industries that produce defense equipment and armaments and those on which the defense industries rely for their raw materials and other intermediate inputs. This argument for protection can be taken too far.

First, it is an argument for international isolation, for in a time of war, there is no industry that does not contribute to national defense. Second, if the case is made for boosting the output of a strategic industry—say aerospace—it is more efficient to achieve this outcome with a subsidy financed out of taxes than with a tariff or import quota. A subsidy would keep the industry operating at the scale that is judged appropriate, and free international trade would keep the prices faced by consumers at their world market levels.

*Should producers of national security equipment be protected from international competition?*

### The Infant-Industry Argument

The **infant-industry argument** is that it is necessary to protect a new industry to enable it to grow into a mature industry that can compete in world markets. The argument is based on an idea called *learning-by-doing*. By working repeatedly at a task, workers become better at that task and can increase the amount they produce in a given period.

There is nothing wrong with the idea of learning-by-doing. It is a powerful engine of human capital accumulation and economic growth. Learning-by-doing can change comparative advantage. If on-the-job experience lowers the opportunity cost of producing a good, a country might develop a comparative advantage in producing that good.

But learning-by-doing does not justify protection. It is in the self-interest of firms and workers who benefit from learning-by-doing to produce the efficient quantities. If the government protected these firms to boost their production, there would be an inefficient overproduction (just like the overproduction in Chapter 6, p. 194).

The historical evidence is against the protection of infant industries. Countries in East Asia that have not given such protection have performed well. Countries that have protected infant industries, as India once did, have performed poorly.

**Infant-industry argument**
The argument that it is necessary to protect a new industry to enable it to grow into a mature industry that can compete in world markets.

*India's protection of manufacturing industries from international competition is generally regarded as a failure.*

## The Dumping Argument

**Dumping**
When a foreign firm sells its exports at a lower price than its cost of production.

**Dumping** occurs when a foreign firm sells its exports at a lower price than its cost of production. You might be wondering why a firm would ever want to sell any of its output at a price below the cost of production. Wouldn't such a firm be better off either selling nothing, or, if it could do so, raising its price to at least cover its costs? Two possible reasons why a firm might sell at a price below cost and therefore engage in dumping are

- Predatory pricing
- Subsidy

*China, a major producer of solar panels, is accused of dumping them on the U.S. and European markets.*

*Predatory Pricing* A firm that engages in *predatory pricing* sets its price below cost in the hope that it can drive its competitors out of the market. If a firm in one country tries to drive out competitors in another country, it will be *dumping* its product in the foreign market. The foreign firm sells its output at a price below its cost to drive domestic firms out of business. When the domestic firms have gone, the foreign firm takes advantage of its monopoly position and charges a higher price for its product. The higher price will attract new competitors, which makes it unlikely that this strategy will be profitable. For this reason, economists are skeptical that this type of dumping occurs.

*Subsidy* A *subsidy* is a payment by the government to a producer. A firm that receives a subsidy is able to sell profitably for a price below cost. Subsidies are very common in almost all countries. The United States and the European Union subsidize the production of many agricultural products and dump their surpluses on the world market. This action lowers the prices that farmers in developing nations receive and weakens the incentive to expand farming in poor countries. India and Europe have been suspected of dumping steel in the United States.

Whatever its source, dumping is illegal under the rules of the WTO, NAFTA, and CAFTA and is regarded as a justification for temporary tariffs. Consequently, anti-dumping tariffs have become important in today's world.

But there are powerful reasons to resist the dumping argument for protection. First, it is virtually impossible to detect dumping because it is hard to determine a firm's costs. As a result, the test for dumping is whether a firm's export price is below its domestic price. This test is a weak one because it can be rational for a firm to charge a lower price in markets in which the quantity demanded is highly sensitive to price and a higher price in a market in which demand is less price-sensitive.

Second, it is hard to think of a good that is produced by a single firm. Even if all the domestic firms were driven out of business in some industry, it would always be possible to find several and usually many alternative foreign sources of supply and to buy at prices determined in competitive markets.

Third, if a good or service were a truly global natural monopoly, the best way to deal with it would be by regulation—just as in the case of domestic monopolies. Such regulation would require international cooperation.

The three arguments for protection that we've just examined have an element of credibility. The counterarguments are in general stronger, so these arguments do not make the case for protection. They are not the only arguments that you might encounter. There are many others, four of which we'll now examine.

## ■ Four Newer Arguments for Protection

Four newer and commonly made arguments for restricting international trade are that protection

- Saves jobs
- Allows us to compete with cheap foreign labor
- Brings diversity and stability
- Penalizes lax environmental standards

### Saves Jobs

When Americans buy imported goods such as shoes from Brazil, U.S. workers who produce shoes lose their jobs. With no earnings and poor prospects, these workers become a drain on welfare and spend less, which creates a ripple effect of further job losses. The proposed solution is to protect U.S. jobs by banning imports of cheap foreign goods. The proposal is flawed for the following reasons.

First, free trade does cost some jobs, but it also creates other jobs. It brings about a global rationalization of labor and allocates labor resources to their highest-valued activities. Because of international trade in textiles, tens of thousands of workers in the United States have lost jobs because shoe factories and textile mills have closed. Tens of thousands of workers in other countries now have jobs because shoe factories and textile mills have opened there. And tens of thousands of U.S. workers now have better-paying jobs than as shoe makers or textile workers because other export industries have expanded and created more jobs than have been destroyed.

Second, imports create jobs. They create jobs for retailers that sell imported goods and for firms that service those goods. They also create jobs by creating incomes in the rest of the world, some of which are spent on imports of U.S.-made goods and services.

Protection saves some particular jobs, but it does so at a high cost. For example, until 2005, textile jobs in the United States were protected by import quotas imposed under an international agreement called the Multifiber Arrangement (or MFA). The U.S. International Trade Commission (ITC) estimated that because of import quotas, 72,000 jobs existed in textiles that would otherwise disappear and annual clothing expenditure in the United States was $15.9 billion ($160 per family) higher than it would be with free trade. An implication of the ITC estimate is that each textile job saved cost consumers $221,000 a year. The end of the MFA led to the destruction of a large number of textile jobs in the United States and Europe in 2005.

*Few shoe factories remain in the United States and manufacturing jobs have been lost …*

*… but well-paid professional and service jobs have been created to replace the lost manufacturing jobs.*

### Allows Us to Compete with Cheap Foreign Labor

With the removal of protective tariffs in U.S. trade with Mexico, some people said that jobs would be sucked into Mexico and that the United States would not be able to compete with its southern neighbor. Let's see what's wrong with this view.

Labor costs depend on the wage rate and the quantity a worker produces. For example, if a U.S. auto worker earns $30 an hour and produces 15 units of output an hour, the average labor cost of a unit of output is $2. If a Mexican auto worker earns $3 an hour and produces 1 unit of output an hour, the average labor cost of a unit of output is $3. Other things remaining the same, the greater the output a worker produces, the higher is the worker's wage rate. High-wage workers produce a large output. Low-wage workers produce a small output.

Although high-wage U.S. workers are more productive, on the average, than lower-wage Mexican workers, there are differences across industries. U.S. labor is relatively more productive in some activities than in others. For example, the productivity of U.S. workers in producing movies, financial services, and customized computer chips is relatively higher than their productivity in the production of metals and some standardized machine parts. The activities in which U.S. workers are relatively more productive than their Mexican counterparts are those in which the United States has a comparative advantage. By engaging in free trade, increasing our production and exports of the goods and services in which we have a comparative advantage, and decreasing our production and increasing our imports of the goods and services in which our trading partners have a comparative advantage, we can make ourselves and the citizens of other countries better off.

### Brings Diversity and Stability

A diversified investment portfolio is less risky than one that has all of its eggs in one basket. The same is true for an economy's production. A diversified economy fluctuates less than an economy that produces only one or two goods.

Most economies, whether the rich, advanced United States, Japan, and Europe or the developing China and Brazil, have diversified production and do not have this type of stability problem. A few economies, such as Saudi Arabia, have a comparative advantage that leads to the specialized production of only one good. But even these economies can stabilize their income and consumption by investing in a wide range of production activities in other countries.

### Penalizes Lax Environmental Standards

A new argument for protection is that many poorer countries, such as Mexico, do not have the same environmental standards that we have, and because they are willing to pollute and we are not, we cannot compete with them without tariffs. If these countries want free trade with the richer and "greener" countries, then they must raise their environmental standards.

This argument for trade restrictions is not entirely convincing. A poor country is less able than a rich one to devote resources to achieving high environmental standards. If free trade helps a poor country to become richer, then it will also help that country to develop the means to improve its environment. But there probably is a case for using the negotiation of free trade agreements such as NAFTA and CAFTA to hold member countries to higher environmental standards. There is an especially large payoff from using such bargaining to try to avoid irreversible damage to resources such as tropical rainforests.

So the four common arguments that we've just considered do not provide overwhelming support for protection. They all have flaws and leave the case for free international trade a strong one.

### ■ Why Is International Trade Restricted?

Why, despite all the arguments against protection, is international trade restricted? One reason that applies to developing nations is that the tariff is a convenient source of government revenue, but this reason does not apply to the United States where the government has access to income taxes and sales taxes.

Political support for international trade restrictions in the United States and most other developed countries arises from rent seeking. **Rent seeking** is lobbying and other political activity that seeks to capture the gains from trade. You've seen that free trade benefits consumers but shrinks the producer surplus of firms that compete in markets with imports.

The winners from free trade are the millions of consumers of low-cost imports, but the benefit per individual consumer is small. The losers from free trade are the producers of import-competing items. Compared to the millions of consumers, there are only a few thousand producers.

Now think about imposing a tariff on clothing. Millions of consumers will bear the cost in the form of a smaller consumer surplus and a few thousand garment makers and their employees will share the gain in producer surplus.

Because the gain from a tariff is large, producers have a strong incentive to incur the expense of lobbying *for* a tariff and *against* free trade. On the other hand, because each consumer's loss is small, consumers have little incentive to organize and incur the expense of lobbying *for* free trade. The gain from free trade for any one person is too small for that person to spend much time or money on a political organization to lobby for free trade. The loss from free trade will be seen as being so great by those bearing that loss that they will find it profitable to join a political organization to prevent free trade. Each group weighs benefits against costs and chooses the best action for themselves, but the anti-free-trade group will undertake more political lobbying than will the pro-free-trade group.

**Rent seeking**

Lobbying and other political activity that aims to capture the gains from trade.

# EYE on YOUR LIFE
## International Trade

International trade plays an extraordinarily large role in your life in three broad ways. It affects you as a

- Consumer
- Producer
- Voter

As a *consumer*, you benefit from the availability of a wide range of low-cost, high-quality goods and services that are produced in other countries.

Look closely at the labels on the items you buy. Where was your computer made? Where were your shirt and your shoes made? Where are the fruits and vegetables that you buy, especially in winter, grown?

The answers to all these questions are most likely Asia, Mexico, or South America. A few items were produced in Europe, Canada, and the United States.

As a *producer* (or as a potential producer if you don't yet have a job), you benefit from huge global markets for U.S. products. Your job prospects would be much dimmer if the firm for which you work didn't have global markets in which to sell its products.

People who work in the aircraft industry, for example, benefit from the huge global market for large passenger jets. Airlines from Canada to China are buying Boeing 777 aircraft as fast as they can be pushed out of the production line.

Even if you were to become a college professor, you would benefit from international trade in education services when your school admits foreign students.

As a *voter*, you have a big stake in the politics of free trade versus protection. As a buyer, your self-interest is hurt by tariffs and quotas on imported goods. Each time you buy a $20 sweater, you contribute $5 to the government in tariff revenue. But as a worker, your self-interest might be hurt by offshoring and by freer access to U.S. markets for foreign producers.

So as you decide how to vote, you must figure out what trade policy serves your self-interest and what best serves the social interest.

# CHECKPOINT 8.4

**Explain and evaluate arguments used to justify restricting international trade.**

## Practice Problems

1.  Japan sets an import quota on rice. California rice growers would like to export more rice to Japan. What are Japan's arguments for restricting imports of Californian rice? Are these arguments correct? Who loses from this restriction in trade?

2.  The United States has, from time to time, limited imports of steel from Europe. What argument has the United States used to justify this quota? Who wins from this restriction? Who loses?

3.  The United States maintains an import quota on sugar. What is the argument for this import quota? Is this argument flawed? If so, explain why.

## In the News

**Indonesians bemoan Hollywood blockbuster blackout**
The Indonesian import tariff on Hollywood movies was meant "to protect local film makers," but major Hollywood studios withdrew their films.
Source: *The Jakarta Post*, July 6, 2011

What argument is Indonesia using against free trade with the United States? What is wrong with Indonesia's argument?

## Solutions to Practice Problems

1.  The main arguments are that Japanese rice is a better quality rice and that the quota limits competition faced by Japanese farmers. The arguments are not correct. If Japanese consumers do not like the quality of Californian rice, they will not buy it. The quota does limit competition and the quota allows Japanese farmers to use their land less efficiently. The big losers are the Japanese consumers who pay about three times the U.S. price for rice.

2.  The U.S. argument is that European producers dump steel on the U.S. market. With an import quota, U.S. steel producers will face less competition and U.S. jobs will be saved. Workers in the steel industry and owners of steel companies will win at the expense of U.S. buyers of steel.

3.  The argument is that the import quota protects the jobs of U.S. workers. The argument is flawed because the United States does not have a comparative advantage in producing sugar and so an import quota allows the U.S. sugar industry to be inefficient. With free international trade in sugar, the U.S. sugar industry would exist but it would be much smaller and more efficient.

## Solution to In the News

Indonesia is using the infant-industry argument: Protection is needed to allow its movie industry to mature and, through learning-by-doing, Indonesia will develop a comparative advantage in movie production. What's wrong with this argument is that protected industries generally perform poorly and the country does not develop the comparative advantage.

# CHAPTER SUMMARY

## Key Points

**1. Explain how markets work with international trade.**

- Comparative advantage drives international trade.
- When the world price of a good is lower than the price that balances domestic demand and supply, a country gains by decreasing production and importing the good.
- When the world price of a good is higher than the price that balances domestic demand and supply, a country gains by increasing production and exporting the good.

**2. Identify the gains from international trade and its winners and losers.**

- Compared to a no-trade situation, in a market with imports, consumer surplus is larger, producer surplus is smaller, and total surplus is larger with free international trade.
- Compared to a no-trade situation, in a market with exports, consumer surplus is smaller, producer surplus is larger, and total surplus is larger with free international trade.

**3. Explain the effects of international trade barriers.**

- Countries restrict international trade by imposing tariffs, import quotas, other import barriers, and export subsidies.
- Trade restrictions raise the domestic price of imported goods, lower the quantity imported, decrease consumer surplus, increase producer surplus, and create a deadweight loss.

**4. Explain and evaluate arguments used to justify restricting international trade.**

- The arguments that protection is necessary for national security, for infant industries, and to prevent dumping are weak.
- Arguments that protection saves jobs, allows us to compete with cheap foreign labor, makes the economy diversified and stable, and is needed to penalize lax environmental standards are flawed.
- Trade is restricted because protection brings small losses to a large number of people and large gains to a small number of people.

## Key Terms

Dumping, 252  
Export subsidy, 249  
Exports, 234  

Import quota, 247  
Imports, 234  
Infant-industry argument, 251  

Rent seeking, 255  
Tariff, 243

# CHAPTER CHECKPOINT

## Study Plan Problems and Applications

Use Figures 1 and 2 to work Problems **1** to **4**. Figure 1 and Figure 2 show the markets for shoes if there is no trade between the United States and Brazil.

**1.** Which country has a comparative advantage in producing shoes? With international trade, explain which country would export shoes and how the price of shoes in the importing country and the quantity produced by the importing country would change. Explain which country gains from this trade.

**2.** The world price of a pair of shoes is $20. Explain how consumer surplus and producer surplus in the United States change as a result of international trade. On the graph, show the change in U.S. consumer surplus (label it *A*) and the change in U.S. producer surplus (label it *B*).

**3.** The world price of a pair of shoes is $20. Explain how consumer surplus and producer surplus in Brazil change as a result of international trade. Show the change in Brazil's consumer surplus (label it *C*) and the change in Brazil's producer surplus (label it *D*).

**4.** Who in the United States loses from free trade in shoes with Brazil? Explain.

Use the following information to work Problems **5** to **7**.

**5.** The supply of roses in the United States is made up of U.S.-grown roses and imported roses. Draw a graph to illustrate the U.S. rose market with free international trade. On your graph, mark the price of roses and the quantities of roses bought, produced, and imported into the United States.

**6.** Who in the United States loses from this trade in roses and would lobby for a restriction on the quantity of imported roses? If the U.S. government put a tariff on rose imports, show on your graph the U.S. consumer surplus that is redistributed to U.S. producers and also the government's tariff revenue.

**7.** Suppose that the U.S. government puts an import quota on roses. Show on your graph the consumer surplus that is redistributed to producers and importers and also the deadweight loss created by the import quota.

Use the following information to work Problems **8** to **10**.

### U.S. expands China paper anti-dumping tariff
The United States raised the tariff on glossy paper imports from China to 99.65 percent, as a result of complaints by NewPage Corp. of Dayton, Ohio. Imports from China increased 166 percent from 2005 to 2006. This glossy paper is used in art books, high-end magazines, and textbooks.

Source: *Reuters*, May 30, 2007

**8.** Explain who, in the United States, gains and who loses from this tariff on paper. How do you expect the prices of magazines and textbooks to change?

**9.** What is dumping? Who in the United States loses from China's dumping of glossy paper?

**10.** Explain what an anti-dumping tariff is. What argument might NewPage Corp. have used to get the government to raise the tariff to 99.65 percent?

 **11.** Read *Eye on Globalization* on p. 239 and draw two graphs to show how U.S. consumers gain from iPads manufactured in China and why Chinese workers also gain.

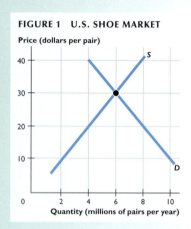

**FIGURE 1   U.S. SHOE MARKET**

Price (dollars per pair)

Quantity (millions of pairs per year)

**FIGURE 2   BRAZIL'S SHOE MARKET**

Price (dollars per pair)

Quantity (millions of pairs per year)

## Instructor Assignable Problems and Applications

Use the following information to work Problems **1** and **2**.

**The future of U.S.–India relations**

In May 2009, Secretary of State Hillary Clinton gave a major speech covering all the issues in U.S.–India relations. On economic and trade relations she noted that India maintains significant barriers to U.S. trade. The United States also maintains barriers against Indian imports such as textiles. Mrs. Clinton, President Obama, and Anand Sharma, the Indian Minister of Commerce and Industry, say they want to dismantle these trade barriers.

Source: www.state.gov

1. Explain who in the United States would gain and who might lose from dismantling trade barriers between the United States and India.

2. Draw a graph of the U.S. market for textiles and show how removing a tariff would change producer surplus, consumer surplus, and the deadweight loss from the tariff.

3. The United States exports wheat. Draw a graph to illustrate the U.S. wheat market if there is free international trade in wheat. On your graph, mark the price of wheat and the quantities bought, produced, and exported by the United States.

4. Suppose that the world price of sugar is 20 cents a pound, Brazil does not trade internationally, and the equilibrium price of sugar in Brazil is 10 cents a pound. Brazil then begins to trade internationally.
   • How does the price of sugar in Brazil change? Do Brazilians buy more or less sugar? Do Brazilian sugar growers produce more or less sugar?
   • Does Brazil export or import sugar and why?

5. The United States exports services and imports coffee. Why does the United States gain from exporting services and importing coffee? How do economists measure the net gain from this international trade?

Use Figure 1 and the following information to work Problems **6** to **8**.

Figure 1 shows the car market in Mexico when Mexico places no restriction on the quantity of cars imported. The world price of a car is $10,000.

6. If the government of Mexico introduces a $2,000 tariff on car imports, what will be the price of a car in Mexico, the quantity of cars produced in Mexico, the quantity imported into Mexico, and the government's tariff revenue?

7. If the government of Mexico introduces an import quota of 4 million cars a year, what will be the price of a car in Mexico, the quantity of cars produced in Mexico, and the quantity imported?

8. What argument might be used to encourage the government of Mexico to introduce a $2,000 tariff on car imports from the United States? Who will gain and who will lose as a result of Mexico's tariff?

9. In the 1950s, Ford and General Motors established a small car-producing industry in Australia and argued for a high tariff on car imports. The tariff has remained through the years. Until 2000, the tariff was 22.5 percent. What might have been Ford's and General Motors' argument for the high tariff? Is the tariff the best way to achieve the goals of the argument?

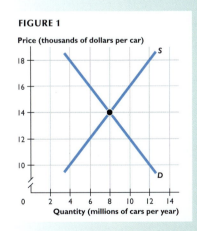

**FIGURE 1**

Price (thousands of dollars per car)

# Critical Thinking Discussion Questions

1. **Indonesia bans mineral ore exports**

   Indonesia's ban on mineral ore exports is part of a wider policy to boost state revenue by turning Indonesia from an exporter of raw commodities into a manufacturer of higher-value products. The ban will cut nickel available on the world market.

   Source: *Bloomberg News*, January 13, 2014

   a. What will happen to the world price of nickel ore, assuming that Indonesia is the largest supplier in the world?
   b. If Indonesia was producing only 1% of the world's nickel ore, would the world price of ore change?
   c. Who is the winner with this ban? Explain your answer.
   d. Who is the loser with this ban? Will current miners in Indonesia have to shut down their operations due to losses incurred? Explain your answer.
   e. Is there any deadweight loss created by this ban? Explain your answer.

2. The creation of the ASEAN Free Trade Area (AFTA) is proceeding smoothly. In Malaysia, a car maker wants to delay the lowering of the tariff on cars. What could be the argument(s) offered by the car maker in persuading the Malaysian government to postpone the date of tariff removal?

3. Japanese companies relocate their operations abroad to lower the costs of production. Yet, goods continue to be produced in Japan. Why? Why doesn't Japan just import all those products it does not have a comparative advantage in producing?

4. **Australian wine sales hit hard by Chinese austerity drive**

   Australian winemakers might have to wait until 2015 to see a return to growth in China. Until 2012, Chinese drinkers had been devouring Australian wine, but Beijing's anti-corruption drive, along with a broader austerity program, has smashed the demand for luxury goods, from wine to Ferraris.

   Source: *Sydney Morning Herald*, March 31, 2014

   a. Who gains and who loses when Australia decreases its wine exports to China?
   b. What other methods could the Chinese government use to decrease wine imports into China?
   c. Draw a diagram to illustrate your answer to part a.

5. **PM seeks to fast-track China free-trade deal**

   Prime Minister Tony Abbott has set down an ambitious deadline of just 12 months to conclude deadlocked free-trade talks with China.

   Source: *Sydney Morning Herald*, October 8, 2013

   Explain why it is in the self-interest of China and Australia to conclude a free-trade deal.

How can we limit climate change?

# Externalities: Pollution, Education, and Health Care

**9**

**When you have completed your study of this chapter, you will be able to**

**1** Explain why negative externalities lead to inefficient over-production and how property rights, pollution charges, and taxes can achieve a more efficient outcome.

**2** Explain why positive externalities lead to inefficient underproduction and how public provision, subsidies, and vouchers can achieve a more efficient outcome.

## EXTERNALITIES IN OUR DAILY LIVES

**Externality**
A cost or a benefit that arises from production and that falls on someone other than the producer; or a cost or benefit that arises from consumption and that falls on someone other than the consumer.

**Negative externality**
A production or consumption activity that creates an external cost.

**Positive externality**
A production or consumption activity that creates an external benefit.

An **externality** is a cost or a benefit that arises from production and that falls on someone other than the producer; or a cost or a benefit that arises from consumption and that falls on someone other than the consumer. Before we embark on the two main tasks of this chapter, we're going to review the range of externalities, classify them, and give some everyday examples.

First, an externality can arise from either a production activity or a consumption activity. Second, it can be either a **negative externality,** which imposes an external cost, or a **positive externality,** which provides an external benefit. So there are four types of externalities:

- Negative production externalities
- Positive production externalities
- Negative consumption externalities
- Positive consumption externalities

### ■ Negative Production Externalities

Burning coal to generate electricity emits carbon dioxide that warms the planet and other chemicals that pollute the atmosphere. Logging and the clearing of forests destroy the habitat of wildlife and also influence the amount of carbon dioxide in the atmosphere. These activities are major examples of production that brings negative externalities. The costs of these production activities are borne by everyone, and even by future generations.

Noise is another negative production externality. When the U.S. Open tennis tournament is being played at Flushing Meadows, players, spectators, and television viewers around the world share a cost that many New Yorkers experience every day: the noise of airplanes taking off from LaGuardia Airport. Aircraft noise imposes a large cost on millions of people who live under the flight paths to airports in every major city.

### ■ Positive Production Externalities

To produce orange blossom honey, Honey Run Honey of Chico, California, locates beehives next to an orange orchard. The honeybees collect pollen and nectar from the orange blossoms to make the honey. At the same time, they transfer pollen

*Negative production externality.*

*Positive production externality.*

between the blossoms, which helps to fertilize the blossoms. Two positive production externalities are present in this example. Honey Run Honey gets a positive production externality from the owner of the orange orchard; and the orange grower gets a positive production externality from Honey Run.

### ■ Negative Consumption Externalities

Negative consumption externalities are a source of irritation for most of us. Smoking tobacco in a confined space creates fumes that many people find unpleasant and that pose a health risk. So smoking in restaurants and on airplanes generates a negative externality. To avoid this negative externality, many restaurants and all airlines ban smoking. But while a smoking ban avoids a negative consumption externality for most people, it imposes a negative external cost on smokers who would prefer to enjoy the consumption of tobacco while dining or taking a plane trip.

Noisy parties and outdoor rock concerts are other examples of negative consumption externalities. They are also examples of the fact that a simple ban on an activity is not a solution. Banning noisy parties avoids the external cost on sleep-seeking neighbors, but it results in the sleepers imposing an external cost on the fun-seeking partygoers.

Permitting dandelions to grow in lawns, not picking up leaves in the fall, allowing a dog to bark loudly or to foul a neighbor's lawn, and letting a cell phone ring in class are other examples of negative consumption externalities.

### ■ Positive Consumption Externalities

When you get a flu vaccination, you lower your risk of being infected. If you avoid the flu, your neighbor, who didn't get vaccinated, has a better chance of remaining healthy. Flu vaccinations generate positive consumption externalities.

When the owner of a historic building restores it, everyone who sees the building gets pleasure from it. Similarly, when someone erects a spectacular home—such as those built by Frank Lloyd Wright during the 1920s and 1930s—or other exciting building—such as the Chrysler and Empire State Buildings in New York or the Walt Disney Concert Hall in Los Angeles—an external consumption benefit flows to everyone who has an opportunity to view it.

Education, which we examine in more detail in this chapter, is a major example of this type of externality.

*Negative consumption externality.*

*Positive consumption externality.*

## 9.1 NEGATIVE EXTERNALITIES: POLLUTION

Pollution is an example of a *negative externality*. Both production and consumption activities create pollution. Here, we'll focus on pollution as a negative production externality. When a paint factory dumps waste into a river, the people who live by the river and use it for fishing and boating bear the cost of the pollution. The paint factory does not consider the cost of pollution when it decides the quantity of paint to produce. The factory's supply curve is based on its own costs, not on the costs that it inflicts on others. You're going to see that when external costs are present, we produce more output than the efficient quantity and we get more pollution than the efficient quantity.

Pollution and other environmental problems are not new. Preindustrial towns and cities in Europe had severe sewage disposal problems that created cholera epidemics and plagues that killed millions. Nor is the desire to find solutions to environmental problems new. The development in the fourteenth century of a pure water supply and the hygienic disposal of garbage and sewage are examples of early efforts to improve the quality of the environment.

Popular discussions about pollution focus on physical aspects of the environment, not on costs and benefits. A common assumption is that activities that damage the environment are wrong and must cease. An economic study of the environment emphasizes costs and benefits and economists talk about the efficient amount of pollution or environmental damage. This emphasis on costs and benefits does not mean that economists, as citizens, don't have the same goals as others and value a healthy environment. Nor does it mean that economists have the right answers and everyone else has the wrong ones. Rather, economics provides a set of tools and principles that help to clarify the issues.

The starting point for an economic analysis of the environment is the distinction between private costs and social costs.

### ■ Private Costs and Social Costs

**Marginal private cost**
The cost of producing an additional unit of a good or service that is borne by the producer of that good or service.

**Marginal external cost**
The cost of producing an additional unit of a good or service that falls on people other than the producer.

**Marginal social cost**
The marginal cost incurred by the entire society—by the producer and by everyone else on whom the cost falls. It is the sum of marginal private cost and marginal external cost.

A *private cost* of production is a cost that is borne by the producer of a good or service. *Marginal cost* is the cost of producing an *additional unit* of a good or service. So **marginal private cost** (*MC*) is the cost of producing an additional unit of a good or service that is borne by the producer of that good or service.

You've seen that an *external cost* is a cost of producing a good or service that is *not* borne by the producer but borne by other people. A **marginal external cost** is the cost of producing an additional unit of a good or service that falls on people other than the producer.

**Marginal social cost** (*MSC*) is the marginal cost incurred by the entire society—by the producer and by everyone else on whom the cost falls—and is the sum of marginal private cost and marginal external cost. That is,

$$MSC = MC + \text{Marginal external cost.}$$

We express costs in dollars, but we must always remember that a cost is an opportunity cost—the best thing we give up to get something. A marginal external cost is what someone other than the producer of a good or service must give up when the producer makes one more unit of the item. Something real that people value, such as a clean river or clean air, is given up.

## Valuing an External Cost

Economists use market prices to put a dollar value on the cost of pollution. For example, suppose that there are two similar rivers, one polluted and the other clean, with identical homes along the side of each river. The homes on the clean river rent for $1,000 a month more than those on the polluted river. If pollution is the only detectable difference between the two locations, the $1,000 a month rent difference is the social cost per home of the pollution. The $1,000 multiplied by the number of homes on the polluted river is the total external cost of this pollution.

## External Cost and Output

Figure 9.1 shows an example of the relationship between output and cost in a polluting paint industry. The marginal cost curve, *MC*, describes the private marginal cost borne by the firms that produce the paint. Marginal cost increases as the quantity of the paint produced increases. If the firms dump waste into a river, they impose an external cost that increases with the amount of the paint produced. The marginal social cost curve, *MSC*, is the sum of marginal private cost and marginal external cost. For example, when firms produce 4 million gallons of paint a month, marginal private cost is $1.00 a gallon, marginal external cost is $1.25 a gallon, and marginal social cost is $2.25 a gallon.

In Figure 9.1, as the quantity of the paint produced increases, the amount of pollution increases and the external cost of pollution increases. The quantity of the paint produced and the pollution created depend on how the market for the paint operates. First, we'll see what happens when the industry is free to pollute.

■ **FIGURE 9.1**

### An External Cost

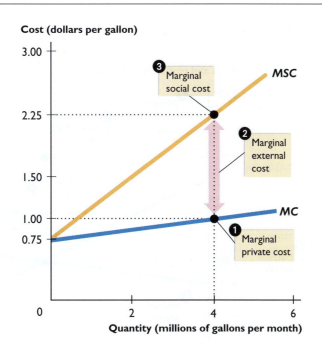

Cost (dollars per gallon)

The *MC* curve shows the marginal private cost borne by the factories that produce a paint. The *MSC* curve shows the sum of marginal private cost and marginal external cost.

When the quantity of paint produced is 4 million gallons a month, ❶ marginal private cost is $1.00 a gallon, ❷ marginal external cost is $1.25 a gallon, and ❸ marginal social cost is $2.25 a gallon.

## ■ Production and Pollution: How Much?

When a polluting industry is unregulated, the market outcome is one of inefficient *overproduction*. In the pursuit of their self-interest, firms produce too much, and they pollute too much. Figure 9.2, which illustrates a market for paint in which the producers pollute, explains why.

The demand curve and marginal benefit curve for paint is $D = MB$ (see Chapter 6, p. 184). The supply curve and marginal private cost curve of producers of the paint is $S = MC$ (see Chapter 6, p. 187). The supply curve is the marginal *private* cost curve because when firms make their supply decisions, they pursue their self-interest and consider only the costs that they will bear. The market *equilibrium* occurs where marginal benefit equals marginal *private* cost. The price is $1.00 a gallon and the quantity is 4 million gallons of paint a month. This outcome is inefficient because marginal *social* cost exceeds marginal benefit.

The efficient outcome is when marginal benefit *equals* marginal *social* cost. In Figure 9.2, the efficient quantity of the paint is 2 million gallons a month, where marginal social cost and marginal benefit each equal $1.50 per gallon.

The equilibrium outcome is one of inefficient *overproduction* and the gray triangle shows the deadweight loss that arises in this situation.

If some method can be found to get paint factories to create less pollution and eliminate the deadweight loss, everyone—the owners of the factories and the residents of the riverside homes—can gain. So what can be done to fix the inefficiency? Three methods are available and we'll examine each of them. They are

- Establish property rights
- Mandate clean technology
- Tax or price pollution

■ **FIGURE 9.2**

Inefficiency with an External Cost

The market supply curve is the marginal private cost curve, $S = MC$. The demand curve is the marginal benefit curve, $D = MB$. The marginal social cost curve is *MSC*.

❶ Market equilibrium at a price of $1.00 a gallon and 4 million gallons of paint a month is inefficient because ❷ marginal social cost exceeds ❸ marginal benefit.

❹ The efficient quantity of paint is 2 million gallons a month where marginal benefit equals marginal social cost.

❺ The gray triangle shows the deadweight loss created by the pollution externality.

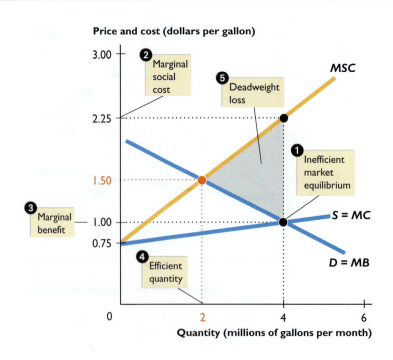

# ■ Establish Property Rights

**Property rights** are legally established titles to the ownership, use, and disposal of factors of production and goods and services that are enforceable in the courts. Establishing property rights where they do not currently exist can confront producers with the costs of their actions and provide them with an incentive to allocate resources efficiently.

To see how property rights work, suppose that the paint producers have property rights on a river and the homes alongside it—they own the river and the homes. The rental income that the paint producers earn on the homes depends on the amount of pollution they create. If people are willing to pay $1,000 a month more to live alongside a pollution-free river, the paint producers can earn that amount for each of the homes they own by not polluting the river.

The forgone rental income from homes alongside a polluted river is an opportunity cost of producing paint. It is part of the paint producers' marginal *private* cost and the paint producers must now decide how to respond to this cost. There are two things they might do:

- Use an abatement technology
- Produce less and pollute less

## Use an Abatement Technology

An **abatement technology** is a production technology that reduces or prevents pollution. The catalytic converter in every U.S. car is an example of an abatement technology. Its widespread adoption, along with lead-free gasoline, has dramatically reduced pollution from highway vehicles and helped to achieve the trends in U.S. air quality shown on p. 271.

Abatement technologies are available to reduce carbon emissions from electricity generation and pollution from industrial processes and paint manufacture.

## Produce Less and Pollute Less

An alternative to incurring the cost of using an abatement technology is to use the polluting technology but cut production, reduce pollution, and get a higher income from renting homes by the river. Firms will choose the least-cost alternative method of lowering pollution.

## The Coase Theorem

Does it matter whether the polluter or the victim of the pollution owns the resource that might be polluted? The Coase theorem (named for British economist Ronald Coase who was the first to have this remarkable insight) says it doesn't matter.

The **Coase theorem** is the proposition that if property rights exist and the costs of enforcing them are low, then the market outcome is efficient and it doesn't matter who has the property rights.

## Application of the Coase Theorem

Suppose that the residents own their homes and the river. Now the factories must pay a fee to the homeowners for the right to dump waste into the river. The greater the quantity of waste dumped, the more the factories must pay. So again, the factories face the opportunity cost of the pollution they create as part of their marginal *private* cost. The quantity of paint produced and the amount of waste

**Property rights**
Legally established titles to the ownership, use, and disposal of factors of production and goods and services that are enforceable in the courts.

**Abatement technology**
A technology that reduces or prevents pollution.

**Coase theorem**
The proposition that if property rights exist and the costs of enforcing them are low, then the market outcome is efficient and it doesn't matter who has the property rights.

dumped are the same whoever owns the homes and the river. If the factories own them, they bear the cost of pollution because they receive a lower income from home rents. If the residents own the homes and the river, the factories bear the cost of pollution because they must pay a fee to the homeowners. In both cases, the factories bear the cost of their pollution and dump the efficient amount of waste into the river.

### Efficient Market Equilibrium With Property Rights

Figure 9.3 illustrates the efficient market outcome with property rights in place. The paint producers face the pollution costs or the abatement costs, whichever is lower. The *MSC* curve includes the cost of producing paint plus either the cost of abatement or the cost of pollution (forgone rent), whichever is lower. This curve, labeled $S = MC = MSC$, is now the market supply curve.

Market equilibrium occurs at a price of $1.50 per gallon and 2 million gallons of paint per month. This outcome is efficient.

If the forgone rent is less than the abatement cost, the factories will still create some pollution, but it will be the efficient quantity. If the abatement cost is lower than the forgone rent, the factories will stop polluting, but they will produce less paint because marginal cost includes the abatement cost.

The Coase property rights solution works only when the cost of reaching an agreement between property owners is low. In many situations, these negotiation costs are high, so this solution is not available and government action is needed. One such action is to mandate the use of a clean abatement technology.

### FIGURE 9.3

Property Rights Achieve an Efficient Outcome

❶ With property rights, the marginal cost curve that excludes the cost of pollution shows only part of the producers' marginal cost.

The marginal private cost curve includes ❷ the cost of pollution, so the supply curve of paint is $S = MC = MSC$.

❸ Market equilibrium is at a price of $1.50 a gallon and a quantity of 2 million gallons of paint a month. This outcome is efficient because ❹ marginal social cost equals marginal benefit.

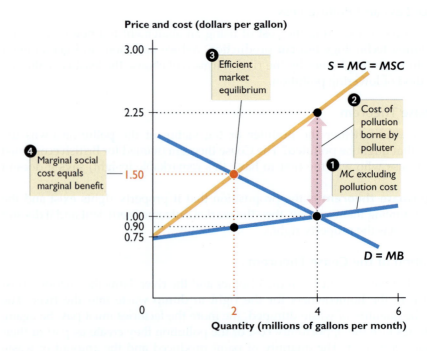

## ■ Mandate Clean Technology

The governments of most countries regulate what may be dumped in rivers and lakes and emitted into the atmosphere. Environmental resources of the United States are heavily regulated by the federal and state governments.

The most comprehensive environmental regulation is performed under the provisions of the Clean Air Act of 1970 and its later amendments, which gives the Environmental Protection Agency (EPA) the authority to issue regulations that limit emissions and achieve defined air quality standards.

The EPA has issued thousands of regulations that require chemical plants, utilities, and steel mills to adopt best-practice pollution abatement technologies and limit their emissions of specified air pollutants. Other regulations have been issued that govern road vehicle emission limits, which must be met by vehicle manufacturers.

But a major source of greenhouse gas emissions in the United States is electric power utilities that use coal and a deep controversy surrounds the question of whether the Clean Air Act extends to regulating these utilities. The legal battle turns on the question of whether carbon dioxide is a pollutant. The Supreme Court ruled in 2007 that carbon emissions *are* a pollutant, a ruling that requires the EPA to regulate these utilities, but because this issue is so deeply devisive, the EPA has stood on the sidelines.

*A Supreme Court decision says greenhouse gas emissions are pollution—the EPA must regulate them.*

Although direct regulation can and has reduced emissions and improved air quality, economists are generally skeptical about this approach. Abatement is not always the least-cost solution. Also, government agencies are not well placed to find the cost-minimizing solution to a pollution problem. Individual firms seeking to minimize cost and maximize profit and responding to price signals are more likely to achieve an efficient outcome. We'll now examine these other approaches to pollution.

## ■ Tax or Cap and Price Pollution

Governments use two main methods of confronting polluters with the costs of their decisions:

- Taxes
- Cap-and-trade

### Taxes

Governments can use taxes as an incentive for producers to reduce the pollution they create. Taxes used in this way are called Pigovian taxes (named for Arthur Cecil Pigou, the British economist who first worked out this method of dealing with external costs during the 1920s).

By setting the tax equal to the marginal external cost (or marginal abatement cost if it is lower), firms can be made to behave in the same way as they would if they bore the cost of the externality directly.

To see how government actions can change the outcome in a market with external costs, let's return to the example of paint factories and the river. Assume that the government has assessed the marginal external cost of pollution accurately and imposes a tax on the factories that exactly equals this cost. The producers are now confronted with the social cost of their actions. The market equilibrium is one in which price equals marginal social cost—an efficient outcome.

Figure 9.4 illustrates the effects of a Pigovian tax on pollution from paint factories. The curve $D = MB$ is the market demand for paint and the marginal benefit curve. The curve $MC$ is the marginal private cost of producing paint. The tax equals the marginal external cost of the pollution. We add this tax to the marginal private cost to find the market supply curve, the curve labeled $S = MC + tax$. This curve is the market supply curve because it tells us the quantity of paint supplied at each price, given the factories' marginal cost and the tax they must pay. This curve is also the marginal social cost curve $MSC$ because the pollution tax has been set equal to the marginal external cost at the quantity produced.

Demand and supply now determine the market equilibrium price at $1.50 per gallon and a quantity of 2 million gallons of paint a month. At this quantity of paint produced, the marginal social cost is $1.50 and the marginal benefit is $1.50, so the market outcome is efficient. The factories incur a marginal private cost of 90¢ per gallon and pay a pollution tax of 60¢ per gallon. The government collects tax revenue of $1.2 million per month.

## Cap-and-Trade

Cap-and-trade places a cap or ceiling on emissions and assigns or sells emission rights to individual producers who are then free to trade permits with each other. It is a tool that seeks to combine the power of government to limit total emissions with the power of the market to minimize cost and maximize benefit.

A government that uses this method must first estimate the efficient quantity of pollution and set the overall emissions cap to achieve the efficient outcome. Then the government must somehow allocate shares of the cap to individual

---

### FIGURE 9.4

A Pollution Charge or Pollution Tax

❶ A pollution charge or tax is imposed that is equal to the marginal external cost of pollution.

Because the pollution charge or tax equals the marginal external cost, the supply curve is the marginal social cost curve: $S = MC + tax = MSC$.

❷ Market equilibrium is efficient because ❸ marginal social cost equals marginal benefit.

❹ The government collects tax revenue equal to the area of the purple rectangle.

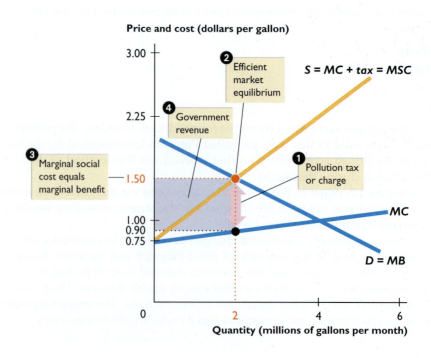

firms (and possibly even households). In an efficient allocation of emissions quotas to firms, each firm has the same marginal social cost of production and emissions abatement. So to allocate the cap efficiently across firms, the government would need to know a lot about each firm's production and abatement costs.

A Pigovian tax achieves an efficient allocation of pollution across firms because each firm chooses how much to produce and pollute taking the tax into account, and then produces the quantity at which marginal social cost equals price. Because all firms face the same market price, they also incur the same marginal social cost.

The government solves the allocation problem by making an initial distribution of the cap across firms and then allowing them to trade in a market for emission permits. Firms that have a low marginal abatement cost sell permits and make big cuts in pollution. Firms that have a high marginal abatement cost buy permits and make smaller cuts or perhaps even no cuts in pollution.

The market in permits determines the equilibrium price of emissions and each firm, confronted with that price, maximizes profit by setting its marginal pollution cost or marginal abatement cost, whichever is lower, equal to the market price of a permit. By confronting polluters with a price of pollution, trade in pollution permits can achieve the same efficient outcome as a Pigovian tax.

# EYE on the U.S. ECONOMY
## U.S. Air Pollution Trends

Air quality in the United States has improved. The figure shows the trends since 1980 for the atmospheric concentrations of five main air pollutants monitored by the Environmental Protection Agency (EPA) and a sixth pollutant (suspended particulates) monitored since 1990.

By using a mix of regulation, pollution limits, economic incentives, and permit trading, the EPA has almost eliminated lead and has substantially decreased sulfur dioxide, carbon monoxide, nitrogen dioxide, and suspended particulates.

Ozone is harder to eliminate, but it has nonetheless fallen to 70 percent of its 1980 level.

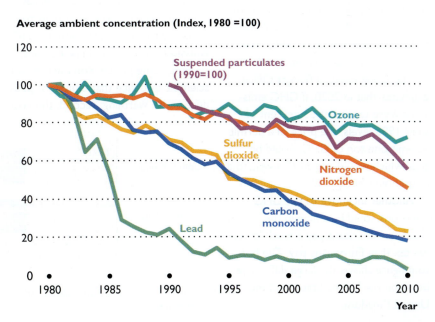

SOURCE OF DATA: Environmental Protection Agency, http://www.epa.gov/airtrends.

# EYE on CLIMATE CHANGE

## How Can We Limit Climate Change?

The average temperature of the Earth is rising and so is the atmospheric concentration of carbon dioxide, $CO_2$. The top figure shows these upward trends.

Scientists debate the contribution of human economic activity to the trends, but most believe it to be the source. Economists debate the costs and benefits of alternative ways of slowing $CO_2$ and other greenhouse gas (GHG) emissions, but most favor action.

Economists agree that lowering GHG emissions requires *incentives* to change.

One idea is to cap emissions and issue tradeable emissions permits, a system called *cap-and-trade*. Carbon emission permits are already priced on a global carbon trading market.

The idea has backers and opponents in Congress and although cap-and-trade has been used successfully by the EPA to cut local air pollutants, its use to limit carbon and other GHG emissions is not on the current agenda.

The Congressional Budget Office estimates that in 2020, if GHG emissions were capped at 83 percent of their 1995 levels, the price of a permit to emit one ton of GHG would be $28, which would add $175 a year to a household's energy bill.

Another incentive to cut GHG emissions could be a hike in the tax on gasoline. Americans pay a much lower gas tax than Europeans pay. The bottom figure shows the large difference between the United States and the United Kingdom.

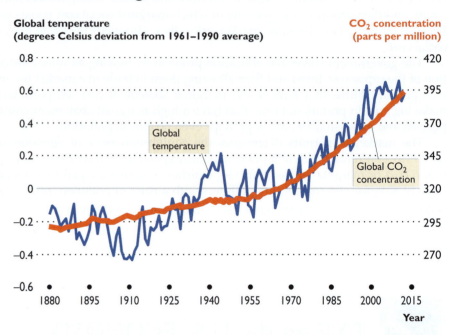

SOURCES OF DATA: Met Office Hadley Centre and Scripps Institution of Oceanography.

Why don't we have more aggressive caps and stronger incentives to encourage a larger reduction in GHG emissions? There are three reasons.

First, some people don't accept the scientific evidence that emissions produce global warming; second, the costs are certain and would be borne now, while the benefits would come many years in the future; and third, if current trends persist, by 2050, three quarters of carbon emissions will come not from the United States but from the developing economies.

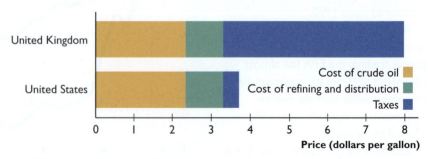

SOURCES OF DATA: Energy Information Administration, Automobile Association, and authors' assumptions.

## CHECKPOINT 9.1

**Explain why negative externalities lead to inefficient overproduction and how property rights, pollution charges, and taxes can achieve a more efficient outcome.**

## Practice Problems

Figure 1 illustrates the unregulated market for a pesticide. When factories produce pesticide, they also create waste, which they dump into a lake on the edge of the town. The marginal external cost of the dumped waste is equal to the marginal private cost of producing the pesticide (that is, the marginal social cost of producing the pesticide is double the marginal private cost).

1. What is the quantity of pesticide produced if no one owns the lake and what is the efficient quantity of pesticide? What is the deadweight loss?

2. If the town owns the lake, what is the quantity of pesticide produced and how much does the town charge the factories to dump waste?

3. If the pesticide factories own the lake, how much pesticide is produced?

4. If no one owns the lake and the government levies a pollution tax, what is the tax per ton of pesticide that achieves the efficient outcome?

## In the News

**New power-plant rule aids Northeast**
A new Obama air pollution rule requires coal-fired power plants to reduce both smog and acid-rain causing pollutants. The coal industry says this rule is among the most expensive ever imposed by the EPA.

Source: *The Wall Street Journal*, July 7, 2011

Explain how a pollution limit will change the quantity of electricity produced. For whom would the pollution limit be expensive?

## Solutions to Practice Problems

1. In Figure 2, production is 30 tons a week, the efficient quantity is 20 tons a week, and the deadweight loss is the area of the gray triangle.

2. The quantity of pesticide produced is the efficient quantity, 20 tons a week, and the town charges the factories $50 a ton of pesticide, which is the marginal external cost of the pollution produced by that quantity.

3. The factories produce the efficient quantity: 20 tons a week.

4. A pollution tax of $50 a ton paid by the factories achieves the efficient quantity of pesticide because the pollution tax equals the external cost.

## Solution to In the News

To reduce the amount of pollution, power plants must produce less. The quantity of electricity decreases and the price that consumers pay for electricity rises. The outcome is efficient if the quantity of electricity produced is that at which the marginal social cost of electricity equals its marginal benefit.

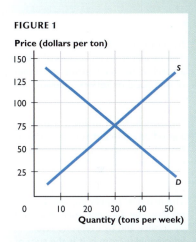

**FIGURE 1**

Price (dollars per ton)

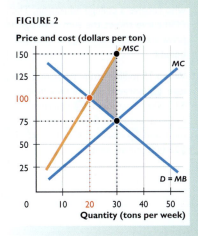

**FIGURE 2**

Price and cost (dollars per ton)

## 9.2   POSITIVE EXTERNALITIES: EDUCATION AND HEALTH CARE

Education and health care create positive externalities: Those who receive either service benefit, and so do the many other people with whom they interact. We'll use college education as the main example, and then apply the ideas to heath care To begin we must distinguish between its private benefits and its social benefits.

### ■ Private Benefits and Social Benefits

A *private benefit* is a benefit that the consumer of a good or service receives. The **marginal private benefit** (*MB*) is the benefit from an additional unit of a good or service that the consumer of that good or service receives.

An *external benefit* is a benefit from a good or service that someone other than the consumer receives. A **marginal external benefit** is the benefit from an additional unit of a good or service that people other than the consumer enjoy.

**Marginal social benefit** (*MSB*) is the marginal benefit enjoyed by society—by the consumers of a good or service (marginal private benefit) and by everyone else who benefits from it (the marginal external benefit). That is,

$$MSB = MB + \text{Marginal external benefit.}$$

Figure 9.5 illustrates these benefit concepts using as an example college education. (The same principles apply to all levels of education.) The marginal benefit curve, *MB*, describes the marginal private benefit—such as expanded job opportunities and higher incomes—enjoyed by college graduates. Marginal private benefit decreases as the quantity of education increases.

**Marginal private benefit**
The benefit from an additional unit of a good or service that the consumer of that good or service receives.

**Marginal external benefit**
The benefit from an additional unit of a good or service that people other than the consumer of that good or service enjoy.

**Marginal social benefit**
The marginal benefit enjoyed by society—by the consumer of a good or service and by everyone else who benefits from it. It is the sum of marginal private benefit and marginal external benefit.

■ **FIGURE 9.5**

### An External Benefit

The *MB* curve shows the marginal private benefit enjoyed by the people who receive a college education. The *MSB* curve shows the sum of marginal private benefit and marginal external benefit.

When 15 million students attend college, ❶ marginal private benefit is $10,000 per student, ❷ marginal external benefit is $15,000 per student, and ❸ marginal social benefit is $25,000 per student.

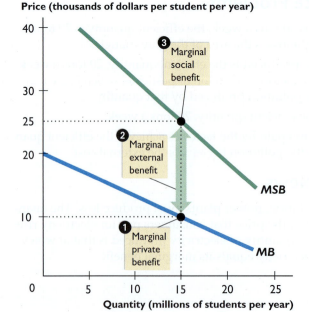

But college graduates generate external benefits. On the average, college graduates communicate more effectively with others and tend to be better citizens. Their crime rates are lower, and they are more tolerant of the views of others. A society with a large number of college graduates can support activities such as high-quality music, theater, and other organized social activities.

In the example in Figure 9.5, the marginal external benefit is $15,000 per student per year when 15 million students enroll in college. Marginal social benefit is the sum of marginal private benefit and marginal external benefit. For example, when 15 million students a year enroll in college, the marginal private benefit is $10,000 per student and the marginal external benefit is $15,000 per student, so the marginal social benefit is $25,000 per student.

The marginal social benefit curve, *MSB*, is the sum of marginal private benefit and marginal external benefit. It is steeper than the *MB* curve because marginal external benefit diminishes for the same reasons that *MB* diminishes.

When people make decisions about how much schooling to undertake, they consider only its private benefits and if education were provided by private schools that charged full-cost tuition, there would be too few college graduates.

Figure 9.6 shows the underproduction that would occur if all college education were left to the private market. The supply curve is the marginal cost curve of the private schools, $S = MC$. The demand curve is the marginal private benefit curve, $D = MB$. Market equilibrium is at a tuition of $15,000 per student per year and 7.5 million students per year. At this equilibrium, marginal social benefit is $38,000 per student, which exceeds marginal cost by $23,000. Too few students enroll in college. The efficient number is 15 million, where marginal social benefit equals marginal cost. The gray triangle shows the deadweight loss created by the underproduction.

### FIGURE 9.6

### Underproduction with an External Benefit

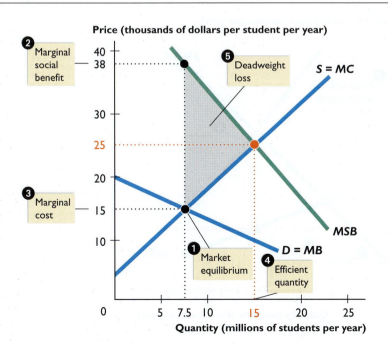

The market demand curve is the marginal private benefit curve, $D = MB$. The supply curve is the marginal cost curve, $S = MC$.

1 Market equilibrium is at a tuition of $15,000 a year and 7.5 million students and is inefficient because 2 marginal social benefit exceeds 3 marginal cost.

4 The marginal social benefit curve is *MSB*, so the efficient number of students is 15 million a year.

5 The gray triangle shows the dead-weight loss created because too few students enroll in college.

## ■ Government Actions in the Face of External Benefits

To get closer to producing the efficient quantity of a good or service that generates an external benefit, we make public choices through governments and modify the market outcome. To achieve a more efficient allocation of resources in the presence of external benefits, such as those that arise from education, governments can use three devices:

- Public provision
- Private subsidies
- Vouchers

### Public Provision

**Public provision**

The production of a good or service by a public authority that receives most of its revenue from the government.

**Public provision** is the production of a good or service by a public authority that receives most of its revenue from the government. Education services produced by the public universities, colleges, and schools are examples of public provision.

Figure 9.7 shows how public provision might overcome the underproduction that arises in Figure 9.6. Public provision cannot lower the cost of production, so marginal cost is the same as before. Marginal private benefit, marginal external benefit, and marginal social benefit are also the same as before.

The efficient quantity occurs where marginal social benefit equals marginal cost. In Figure 9.7, this quantity is 15 million students per year. Tuition is set to ensure that the efficient number of students enroll. That is, tuition is set at the level that equals the marginal private benefit at the efficient quantity. In Figure 9.7, tuition is $10,000 a year. The rest of the cost of the public university is borne by the taxpayers and, in this example, is $15,000 per student per year.

■ **FIGURE 9.7**

Public Provision to Achieve an Efficient Outcome

❶ Marginal social benefit equals marginal cost with 15 million students enrolled in college, the ❷ efficient quantity.

❸ Tuition is set at $10,000 per year, and ❹ the taxpayers cover the remaining $15,000 of marginal cost per student.

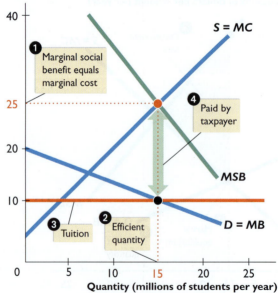

## Private Subsidies

A **subsidy** is a payment by the government to a producer to cover part of the costs of production. By giving producers a subsidy, the government can induce private decision makers to consider external benefits when they make their choices.

Figure 9.8 shows how a subsidy to private colleges works. In the absence of a subsidy, the marginal cost curve is the market supply curve of private college education, $S = MC$. The marginal benefit is the demand curve, $D = MB$. In this example, the government provides a subsidy to colleges of $15,000 per student per year. We must subtract the subsidy from the marginal cost of education to find the colleges' supply curve. That curve is $S = MC - subsidy$ in the figure. The equilibrium tuition (market price) is $10,000 a year, and the equilibrium quantity is 15 million students. To educate 15 million students, colleges incur a marginal cost of $25,000 a year. The marginal social benefit is also $25,000 a year. So with marginal cost equal to marginal social benefit, the subsidy has achieved an efficient outcome. The tuition and the subsidy just cover the colleges' marginal cost.

***Public Provision Versus Private Subsidy*** In the two methods we've just studied, the same number of students enroll and tuition is the same. So are these two methods of providing education services equally good? This question is difficult to resolve. The bureaucrats that operate public schools don't have as strong an incentive to minimize costs and maximize *quality* as those who run private schools. But for elementary and secondary education, *charter schools* (see p. 279) might be an efficient compromise between traditional public schools and subsidized private schools.

> **Subsidy**
> A payment by the government to a producer to cover part of the costs of production.

### FIGURE 9.8

Private Subsidy to Achieve an Efficient Outcome

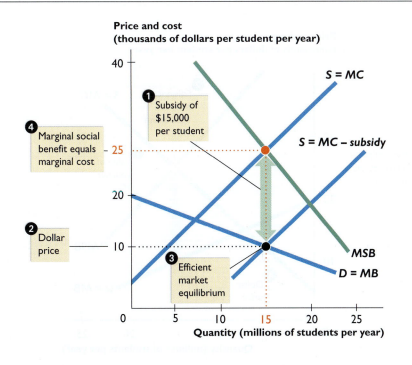

**Price and cost**
**(thousands of dollars per student per year)**

With a ❶ subsidy of $15,000 per student, the supply curve is $S = MC - subsidy$.

❷ The equilibrium price is $10,000.

❸ The market equilibrium is efficient with 15 million students enrolled in college because ❹ marginal social benefit equals marginal cost.

**Voucher**

A token that the government provides to households, which they can use to buy specified goods or services.

## Vouchers

A **voucher** is a token that the government provides to households, which they can use to buy specified goods or services. Food stamps that the U.S. Department of Agriculture provides under a federal Food Stamp Program are examples of vouchers. Vouchers for college education could be provided to students. Let's see how they would work.

The government would provide each student with a voucher. Students would choose the school to attend and pay the tuition with dollars plus a voucher. Schools would exchange the vouchers they receive for dollars from the government. If the government set the value of a voucher equal to the marginal external benefit of a year of college at the efficient quantity, the outcome would be efficient.

Figure 9.9 illustrates an efficient voucher scheme in action. The government issues vouchers worth $15,000 per student per year. Each student pays $10,000 tuition and the government pays $15,000 per voucher, so the school collects $25,000 per student. The voucher scheme results in 15 million students attending college, the marginal cost of a student equals the marginal social benefit, and the outcome is efficient.

***Do Vouchers Beat Public Provision and Subsidy?*** Vouchers provide public financial resources to the consumer rather than the producer. Economists generally believe that vouchers offer a more efficient outcome than public provision and subsidies because they combine the benefits of competition among private schools with the injection of the public funds needed to achieve an efficient level of output. Also, students and their parents can monitor school performance more effectively than the government can (see *Eye on the U.S. Economy* opposite.)

■ **FIGURE 9.9**

## Vouchers Achieve an Efficient Outcome

With vouchers, buyers are willing to pay *MB* plus the value of the voucher.

❶ The government issues vouchers to each student valued at $15,000.

❷ The market equilibrium is efficient. With 15 million students enrolled in college, ❸ marginal social benefit equals marginal cost.

❹ Each student pays tuition of $10,000 (the dollar price) and the school collects $15,000 (the value of the voucher) from the government.

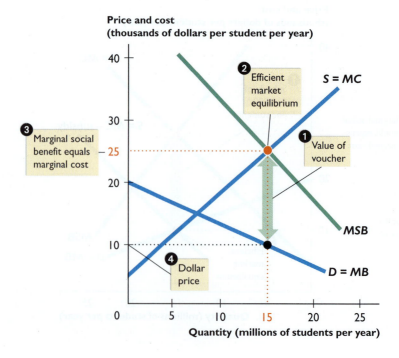

# EYE on the U.S. ECONOMY
## Education Quality: Charter Schools and Vouchers

The three methods of achieving efficient education have similar effects on the *quantity* of education but different effects on its *quality*, and quality has become a big issue: International league tables show U.S. students performing worse on standardized math and science tests than those in more than 20 other countries. Here, we look at two ways of trying to improve the quality of U.S. education: charter schools and school vouchers.

### Charter Schools

A *charter school* is a *public* school but one that is free to make its own education policy. Around 4,000 charter schools in 40 states are operating today and they teach more than 1 million students. When the demand for places in a charter school exceeds the supply, students are chosen by lottery.

How efficient are the charter schools?

School efficiency has two dimensions: cost per student and educational standard attained.

Charter schools perform well on both criteria. They cost less than public schools and they achieve more. Cost per student in New York charter schools is 18 percent less than regular public schools. And charter school students perform higher in math and reading than equivalent students who apply to but (randomly) don't get into a charter school.

### Vouchers

School vouchers are much less used than charter schools and more controversial. But an increasing number of states, among them Wisconsin, Louisiana, Ohio, the District of Columbia, and New York, operate a

*Stanford University professor Caroline Hoxby says: "Tell me your goals and I'll design you a voucher to achieve them."*

school voucher program.

Studies of the effects of vouchers have generated more controversies than firm conclusions, but some economists are convinced that they offer the best solution.

# EYE on YOUR LIFE
## Externalities in Your Life

Think about the externalities, both negative and positive, that play a huge part in *your* life; and think about the incentives that attempt to align your self-interest with the social interest.

You respond to the gasoline tax by buying a little bit less gas than you otherwise would. As you saw in *Eye on Climate Change* (p. 272), this incentive is small compared to that in some other countries. With a bigger gas tax, such

as that in the United Kingdom for example, you would find ways of getting by with a smaller quantity of gasoline and your actions and those of millions of others would make the traffic on our highways much lighter.

You are responding to the huge incentive of subsidized tuition by being in school. Without subsidized college education, fewer people would attend college and university and with fewer

college graduates, the benefits we all receive from living in a well-educated society would be smaller.

Think about your attitude as a citizen–voter to these two externalities. Should the gas tax be higher to discourage the use of the automobile? Should tuition be even lower to encourage even more people to enroll in school? Or have we got these incentives just right in the social interest?

280 Part 2 • A CLOSER LOOK AT MARKETS

## ■ Economic Problems in Health-Care Markets

Health care is two distinct products: health insurance—insurance that pays health-care bills—and health-care services—the services of physicians, specialists, nurses, other health-care professionals, and hospitals.

We're going to look at the health-care markets of the United States from an economic perspective. What are the economic problems these markets face? How do our health-care arrangements deal with these problems? How do other countries deal with the same problems? Does U.S. health care need reform?

The econonomic problem faced by health-care markets is that left to competitive market forces, both health insurance and health-care services would be underprovided. Underprovision would result from

- Asymmetric information
- Missing insurance market
- Public-health externalities

### Asymmetric Information

*Asymmetric information* is present in a market if either the buyer or the seller has *private information* relevant to a transaction. In the health-insurance market, buyers have private information about their behavior and in the health-care market, sellers have private information about the range and effectiveness of alternative treatments.

Asymmetric information brings adverse selection and moral hazard. **Adverse selection** occurs when a seller is better informed than a buyer or a buyer is better informed than a seller, and the deal that gets made benefits the one who is better informed. **Moral hazard** arises after a deal is done when the actions of the person with private information impose costs on the uninformed party.

***Adverse Selection and Moral Hazard in Health Insurance*** Some people exercise, eat healthy diets, watch their weight, and rarely get sick. Others are people who don't exercise, eat high-fat and high-sugar diets, are overweight, and not only get sick more often but also are at long-term risk for diabetes and heart disease.

Information about whether a person has a healthy or an unhealthy lifestyle is private information, which is not available to insurance companies.

*Adverse selection* arises because some of the healthiest people choose to be uninsured, at least during their younger years. *Moral hazard* arises because once insured, a person has less incentive to adopt a healthy lifestyle and some will yield to the temptation to drift into unhealthy habits.

Faced with a lack of information about individual lifestyle choices, health-insurance providers offer lower premiums with high deductibles so that buyers can reveal information about their lifestyle. The fittest and healthiest choose a high deductible and low premium, and the least fit and unhealthiest choose a low deductible and high premium.

***Adverse Selection and Moral Hazard in Health-Care Services*** High-quality providers of health-care services diagnose and prescribe treatments reliably and at the lowest possible cost. Low-quality providers make diagnosis errors and over-prescribe expensive drugs and other treatments. But the information about

**Adverse selection**
When a seller is better informed than a buyer or a buyer is better informed than a seller, and the deal that gets made benefits the one who is better informed.

**Moral hazard**
A situation that arises after a deal is done when the actions of the person with private information impose costs on the uninformed party.

the quality and reliability of the health-care provider is private. The buyers (patients and insurance companies) don't know the quality of the providers.

*Adverse selection* arises because buyers are unable to assess quality reliably enough, so too few high-quality providers would enter the market.

*Moral hazard* arises because health-care service providers have an incentive to play safe and overtreat a patient. Neither the patient nor the insurance company has information with which to prevent this inefficiency.

Arrangements exist to avoid the worst consequences of adverse selection and moral hazard. Licensing doctors ensures a high minimum standard of service quality and lessens the adverse selection problem. And Health Maintenance Organizations partly address the moral hazard problem. By working with a limited number of service providers, an insurance company can monitor the quality of the service and control costs. But service providers have more information than the insurer, so the problem is lessened but not completely overcome.

## Missing Insurance Market

Many people can't get private health insurance because they are too old or too sick or too disabled. Others with pre-existing conditions can get insurance but only with exclusions of the very health problems they are most likely to encounter. These are the people who have the greatest wants for health care but the least ability to get it without some alternative to the free market.

The missing insurance market is one that is blind to a person's known health risks. This market can be provided only with government intervention.

The U.S. health-care system deals with this problem by government provision of health insurance. Medicare pays the hospital costs and subsidizes the treatment costs of the aged (over 65) and some of the long-term disabled. Medicaid pays the health-care costs of those living in poverty and with long-term health-care needs.

These government programs provide health insurance for 93 million people but miss an estimated 48 million (see *Eye on the U.S. Economy* on p. 282). The total expenditure on these programs is driven by patient demand, not by decisions of Congress. As the population gets older and advances in medical technology keep people alive longer with expensive treatments, the cost of these programs grows.

## Public-Health Externalities

Infectious diseases have negative externalities. Marginal social cost exceeds the marginal private cost, so public sanitation systems, which general public health relies upon, are provided by governments to overcome a deadweight loss that would be generated by these externalities.

Vaccination against an infectious disease is a good that has a positive externality. People who get a flu shot protect not only themselves but everyone with whom they come into contact. The marginal social benefit of flu shots exceeds the marginal private benefit. The efficient quantity of flu shots exceeds the quantity that an unregulated market would provide. This feature of health care is a further reason why it is efficient to subsidize the care of the aged and those in poverty.

You've seen three economic reasons why health care isn't an ordinary good that we can expect the unregulated market to provide efficiently. You've also seen that U.S. health care is provided by a mixture of private and public insurance. How do the U.S. health-care markets compare with those in other countries?

# EYE on the U.S. ECONOMY
## Health Care in the United States: A Snapshot

Expenditure on health care takes 17.8 percent of U.S. incomes. Fifty-one percent of this expenditure is private—spending on health-care insurance and out-of-pocket payments for health-care services. The rest is financed by taxes—spending by federal and state governments on Medicare, Medicaid, and other public programs.

Figure 1 shows the distribution of the health-care dollar across these types of expenditure.

Of the 328 million people in the United States, 166 million have private health insurance.

More than one half of all employed people—about 70 million—buy health insurance through their employer.

Tax breaks are available on health insurance payments, the largest being for the self-employed who can deduct the entire payment.

About 75 million people limit their health-care cost by using a Health Maintenance Organization (HMO).

The federal and state Medicare and Medicaid programs cover 93 million people.

An estimated 48 million have no health-care insurance, and a further 25 million are reckoned to be underinsured—have some insurance but not enough for a big emergency.

Some of the uninsured are healthy and *choose* not to insure. Others can't afford insurance and don't qualify for Medicare or Medicaid.

Per person covered, government programs are more costly than private insurance because they serve the aged, the disabled, and the chronically sick.

Figure 2 shows expenditure per person. With 93 million people covered by Medicare and Medicaid at a total cost of $966 billion, governments spend $10,387 per person per year on public programs.

The cost of private insurance per person covered is 46 percent of the cost of the government programs at $4,826 per person per year.

Out-of-pocket expenditure, which includes spending by the uninsured, is $2,342 per person per year.

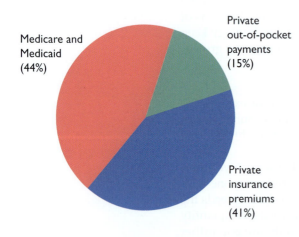

**Figure 1  Private and Public Expenditures on Health Care**

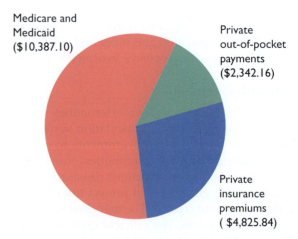

**Figure 2  Private and Public Expenditures per Person**

SOURCE OF DATA: U.S. Bureau of the Census, *Statistical Abstract of the United States: 2011*, Tables 135 and 1222.

## ■ Health-Care Systems in Other Countries

Every major country except the United States has a comprehensive national health-care system. Every person is insured under a government-funded national insurance program. Health-care services are provided by private clinics, hospitals, physicians, and specialists, but they are paid for by governments.

Government expenditure on health care is financed by specific health-insurance taxes and by general income taxes.

Resources in the public health-care system are allocated by physicians, specialists, and hospitals and are based on urgency of need, which results in patients often being placed on lengthy waiting lists.

No one is permitted to opt out of the national health service, but in most countries, everyone *is* permitted to buy private insurance and private health care. In these countries, what is called a "two-tier" system sometimes emerges in which the rich buy private insurance and get higher-quality care and the poor get their health care from a lower-quality state system.

In a few countries, there is no private option. It is illegal to open a private clinic and sell private insurance that covers the basic care provided by the state system. The idea of this restriction is to avoid the "two-tier" outcome.

The comprehensive national health systems limit choice and impose long waiting times. But they do contain costs and they do so without, apparently, compromising the overall quality of health outcomes.

## ■ A Reform Idea

The Medicare and Medicaid programs are in effect an open-ended commitment of public funds to the health care of the aged and those too poor to buy private health care. Health care in the United States faces two problems: Too many people are uninsured and health care costs too much. These problems are going to get worse if nothing major is done to reverse the trend.

The Patient Protection and Affordable Care Act (known as Obamacare) addresses the first of these problems by requiring everyone to be insured and by creating a new Pre-Existing Condition Insurance Plan, financed partly by the government. But the Act does little to address the problem of overexpenditure, and this problem is extremely serious. It is so serious that without massive change, the present open-ended health-care programs will bankrupt the United States.

A solution to both the problem of coverage and access and the problem of overexpenditure has been suggested by Laurence Kotlikoff, an economics professor at Boston University. His idea is to use health-care vouchers to ensure universal coverage and to cap total public expenditure on health care.

Professor Kotlikoff's proposal would scrap the entire existing Medicare and Medicaid programs and the Obamacare program and replace them with a new national health-care program based on a voucher system. Everyone would get a health-care voucher and those with higher expected health-care costs would get a bigger voucher.

Health-care vouchers would work like the education vouchers that we explain on p. 278. People would use a combination of their own money and vouchers to buy health insurance. This health-care system would provide the cost discipline of the European and Canadian systems with the choice that is so important to and valued by Americans.

*Professor Laurence J. Kotlikoff of Boston University; author of* The Healthcare Fix *and creator of* Medicare Part C for All.

# CHECKPOINT 9.2

**Explain why positive externalities lead to inefficient underproduction and how public provision, subsidies, and vouchers can achieve a more efficient outcome.**

## Practice Problems

Figure 1 shows the marginal private benefit from college education. The marginal cost of a college education is a constant $6,000 a year. The marginal external benefit from a college education is a constant $4,000 per student per year.

1. What is the efficient number of students? If colleges are private (no government involvement), how many people enroll, what is the tuition, and what is the deadweight loss?

2. If the government provides public colleges, what is the tuition that will achieve the efficient number of students? How much must taxpayers pay?

3. If the government subsidizes private colleges, what subsidy will achieve the efficient number of college students?

4. If the government offers each student a voucher, what value of the voucher will achieve the efficient number of students?

## In the News

**Tuition hikes should frighten students**

Despite the hard times, families will not be deprived of access to federal student loans. The real danger is a hike in tuition. Often in past recessions, states have cut funding for colleges and tuition has skyrocketed. The Cato Institute says a better policy would be for the states to maintain the subsidies to colleges.

Source: Michael Dannenberg, *USA Today*, October 22, 2008

If government cuts the subsidy to colleges, why will tuition rise and the number of students enrolled decrease? Why does the Cato Institute say that it's a better policy for government to maintain the subsidy?

## Solutions to Practice Problems

1. In Figure 2, the efficient number of students is 50,000 a year. With no government involvement, enrollment is 30,000 students a year and tuition is $6,000 a year. The gray triangle shows the deadweight loss.

2. To enroll the efficient 50,000 students, public colleges would charge $2,000 per student and taxpayers would pay $4,000 per student (Figure 2).

3. A subsidy of $4,000 per student (equal to marginal external benefit).

4. A voucher valued at $4,000 will achieve an efficient enrollment of 50,000. The private college tuition is $6,000. 50,000 students will enroll if the dollar cost is $2,000 per student. So the value of the voucher will have to be $4,000.

## Solution to In the News

A cut in the subsidy will increase the college's marginal cost. Tuition will rise and the number of students will decrease—a movement up along the demand curve. The Cato Institute says maintaining the subsidy is a better policy because it avoids the deadweight loss of a cut in the number of students.

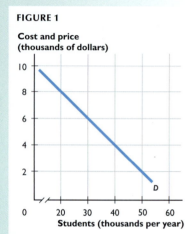

**FIGURE 1**

Cost and price
(thousands of dollars)

Students (thousands per year)

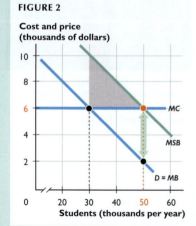

**FIGURE 2**

Cost and price
(thousands of dollars)

Students (thousands per year)

**CHAPTER SUMMARY**

## Key Points

**1.** **Explain why negative externalities lead to inefficient overproduction and how property rights, pollution charges, and taxes can achieve a more efficient outcome.**

- External costs are costs of production that fall on people other than the producer of a good or service. Marginal social cost equals marginal private cost plus marginal external cost.

- Producers take account only of marginal private cost and produce more than the efficient quantity when there is a marginal external cost.

- Sometimes it is possible to overcome a negative externality by assigning a property right.

- When property rights cannot be assigned, governments might overcome a negative externality by mandating clean technologies, imposing pollution taxes, or using a cap-and-trade program.

**2.** **Explain why positive externalities lead to inefficient underproduction and how public provision, subsidies, and vouchers can achieve a more efficient outcome.**

- External benefits are benefits that are received by people other than the consumer of a good or service. Marginal social benefit equals marginal private benefit plus marginal external benefit.

- External benefits from education arise because better-educated people are better citizens, commit fewer crimes, and support social activities.

- Vouchers or subsidies to private schools or the provision of public education below cost can achieve a more efficient provision of education.

- Vouchers can also achieve a more efficient provision of health care and at the same time contain health care costs.

## Key Terms

Abatement technology, 267
Adverse selection, 280
Coase theorem, 267
Externality, 262
Marginal external benefit, 274
Marginal external cost, 264
Marginal private benefit, 274
Marginal private cost, 264
Marginal social benefit, 274

Marginal social cost, 264
Moral hazard, 280
Negative externality, 262
Positive externality, 262
Property rights, 267
Public provision, 276
Subsidy, 277
Voucher, 278

# CHAPTER CHECKPOINT

## Study Plan Problems and Applications

Table 1 shows the demand schedule for electricity from a coal-burning utility. Table 2 shows the utility's cost of producing electricity and the external cost of the pollution created. Use this information to work Problems **1** to **3**.

**1.** With no pollution control, calculate the quantity of electricity produced, the price of electricity, and the marginal external cost of the pollution generated.

**2.** With no pollution control, calculate the quantity of electricity produced, the marginal social cost of the electricity generated, and the deadweight loss.

**3.** If the government levies a pollution tax such that the utility generates the efficient quantity of electricity, calculate the quantity of electricity generated, the price of electricity, the size of the pollution tax, and the tax revenue.

Use the following information to work Problems **4** and **5**.

Tom and Larry must spend a day working together. Tom likes to smoke cigars and the price of a cigar is $2. Larry likes a smoke-free environment.

**4.** If Tom's marginal benefit from a cigar a day is $20 and Larry's marginal benefit from a smoke-free environment is $25 a day, what is the outcome if they meet at Tom's home? What is the outcome if they meet at Larry's home?

**5.** If Tom's marginal benefit from a cigar a day is $25 and Larry's marginal benefit from a smoke-free environment is $20 a day, what is the outcome if they meet at Tom's home? What is the outcome if they meet at Larry's home?

Use Table 3 and the following information to work Problems **6** to **8**.

The marginal cost of educating a college student is $5,000 a year. Table 3 shows the marginal benefit schedule from a college education. The marginal external benefit from a college education is a constant $2,000 per student per year. There are no public colleges.

**6.** With no government involvement in college education, how many students enroll, what is the tuition, and what is the deadweight loss created?

**7.** If the government subsidizes colleges and sets the subsidy so that the efficient number of students enroll, what is the subsidy per student, how many students enroll, and what is the cost to taxpayers?

**8.** If the government offers vouchers to students, what is the value of the voucher that will encourage the efficient number of students to enroll?

**9. Global solutions for local gridlock**
Gridlock in Toronto already costs the region $6 billion a year, with average commute times of 80 minutes, among the highest in North America. By 2031, commute times will increase by 27 minutes. Civic leaders are looking at the options: road tolls, a regional gas tax, and parking levies.

Source: *Toronto Star*, June 24, 2011

With road tolls, a regional gas tax, and parking levies would Toronto roads become less congested? If the new charges cut commute times, would the Toronto road system be more efficient? Explain your answers.

**10.** Read *Eye on Climate Change* on p. 272 and then describe the government actions that could decrease carbon emissions and explain why the government is not using them more aggressively.

### TABLE 1   DEMAND FOR ELECTRICITY

| Price (cents per kilowatt) | Quantity demanded (kilowatts per day) |
|---|---|
| 4 | 500 |
| 8 | 400 |
| 12 | 300 |
| 16 | 200 |
| 20 | 100 |
| 24 | 0 |

### TABLE 2   PRIVATE AND EXTERNAL COSTS

| Quantity (kilowatts per day) | Marginal cost | Marginal external cost |
|---|---|---|
| | (cents per kilowatt) | |
| 0 | 0 | 0 |
| 100 | 2 | 2 |
| 200 | 4 | 4 |
| 300 | 6 | 6 |
| 400 | 8 | 8 |
| 500 | 10 | 10 |

### TABLE 3

| Students (millions per year) | Marginal private benefit (dollars per student per year) |
|---|---|
| 1 | 5,000 |
| 2 | 3,000 |
| 3 | 2,000 |
| 4 | 1,500 |
| 5 | 1,200 |
| 6 | 1,000 |
| 7 | 800 |
| 8 | 500 |

# Instructor Assignable Problems and Applications

1. The price of gasoline in Europe is about three times that in the United States, mainly because the European gas tax is higher than the U.S. gas tax. How would an increase in the gas tax in the United States to the European level change carbon emissions? Would this tax increase bring greater efficiency or would it increase deadweight loss?

2. **Polar ice cap shrinks further and thins**
   With global warming of the planet, the polar ice cap is shrinking. As the Arctic Sea expands, more underwater mineral resources will be accessible. Countries are staking out territorial claims to parts of the polar region.
   
   Source: *The Wall Street Journal*, April 7, 2009
   
   Explain how ownership of these mineral resources will influence the amount of damage done to the Arctic Sea and its wildlife.

Use the following information to work Problems **3** and **4**.

**Plans to curtail use of plastic bags, but not much action**
Last summer, Seattle approved a 20-cents charge on plastic shopping bags, which was intended to reduce pollution by encouraging reusable bags.

Source: *The New York Times*, February 23, 2009

3. Explain how Seattle's 20-cents charge will change the use of plastic bags and how the deadweight loss created by plastic bags will change.

4. Explain why a complete ban on plastic bags would be inefficient.

Use the following information to work Problems **5** to **7**.

The marginal cost of educating a college student online is $3,000 a year. Table 1 shows the marginal private benefit schedule from a college education. The marginal external benefit is 50 percent of the marginal private benefit.

5. With no government involvement in college education, how many students enroll and what is the tuition? Calculate the deadweight loss created.

6. If the government subsidizes colleges so that the efficient number of students will enroll, what is the cost to taxpayers?

7. If the government offers vouchers to students and values them so that the efficient number of students will enroll, what is the value of the voucher?

8. **U.S. environmentalists back EU emission plan**
   The European Union requires any airline operating to or from an EU airport to participate in the EU cap-and-trade system under which 15 percent of pollution credits for airlines will be auctioned off and the other 85 percent of credits are being given without charge.
   
   Source: *The Wall Street Journal*, June 30, 2011
   
   Explain the conditions under which a cap-and-trade system would reduce the amount of airline emissions to the efficient quantity.

9. **CBO report: the pros and cons of carbon tax**
   A carbon tax would raise the cost of producing goods and services that create large carbon emissions, but it would encourage Americans to use less carbon-intensive goods and services, which could slow global warming.
   
   Source: *The Wall Street Journal*, May 22, 2013
   
   Use a graph of the market for electricity produced from fossil fuel to show the "pro" and the "con" from a carbon tax.

**TABLE 1**

| Students (millions per year) | Marginal private benefit (dollars per student per year) |
|---|---|
| 1 | 6,000 |
| 2 | 5,000 |
| 3 | 4,000 |
| 4 | 3,000 |
| 5 | 2,000 |
| 6 | 1,000 |

# Critical Thinking Discussion Questions

**1. Virgin expands its green fuel options**

Virgin Australia has entered an agreement with another biofuel company to investigate the feasibility of producing aviation fuel using a proprietary Australian technology that turns biological waste into oil.

Source: *The Australian*, 14 December 2011

a. What are the marginal private costs of and marginal private benefits from using biofuel rather than fuel made from oil?

b. What are the marginal social costs of and marginal private benefits from using biofuel rather than fuel made from oil?

c. How does a carbon tax help to achieve an efficient quantity of air transport?

d. Why might a carbon tax end up generating almost no tax revenue?

**2. City traffic congestion a $20 billion problem**

Australia's big capital cities have been urged to introduce a London-style congestion tax payable on entry into the CBD traffic or make city parking even more expensive so car commuters stop taking everyone else for a ride. Parking levies have been introduced in Perth, Sydney, and Melbourne to raise money from private car parking operators and spend it on encouraging other forms of transport into the cities.

Source: *The Australian*, 6 October 2010

a. Will a charge on cars entering the city make city streets less congested?

b. Will a parking charge make city streets less congested?

c. Will a charge for entering the city be more effective than, less effective than, or equally effective as a parking charge? Explain.

d. If a new road-use pricing system cuts travel times, will the road system be more efficient? Explain.

**3. India makes polio vaccination mandatory for seven countries**

Having eradicated polio from within its borders, India has scaled up measures to prevent the polio virus from re-entering, making it mandatory for all travelers from certain countries, including Pakistan and Afghanistan, to take the polio vaccine.

Source: *DNA India*, March 3, 2014

a. Describe the private benefits and external benefits of vaccinations and explain why a private market for vaccinations would produce an inefficient outcome.

b. Draw a graph to illustrate a private market for vaccinations and show the deadweight loss.

c. Explain how government intervention could achieve an efficient quantity of vaccinations and draw a graph to illustrate this outcome.

Which store has the lower costs:
Wal-Mart or 7-Eleven?

# Production and Cost

**10**

**When you have completed your study of this chapter, you will be able to**

**1** Explain and distinguish between the economic and accounting measures of a firm's cost of production and profit.

**2** Explain the relationship between a firm's output and labor employed in the short run.

**3** Explain the relationship between a firm's output and costs in the short run.

**4** Derive and explain a firm's long-run average cost curve.

## 10.1 ECONOMIC COST AND PROFIT

The 20 million firms in the United States differ in size and in what they produce, but they all perform the same basic economic function: They hire factors of production and organize them to produce and sell goods and services. To understand the behavior of a firm, we need to know its goals.

### ■ The Firm's Goal

If you asked a group of entrepreneurs what they are trying to achieve, you would get many different answers. Some would talk about making a high-quality product, others about business growth, others about market share, and others about job satisfaction of the work force. All of these goals might be pursued, but they are not the fundamental goal. They are a means to a deeper goal.

The firm's goal is to *maximize profit*. A firm that does not seek to maximize profit is either eliminated or bought by firms that *do* seek to achieve that goal. To calculate a firm's profit, we must determine its total revenue and total cost. Economists have a special way of defining and measuring cost and profit, which we'll explain and illustrate by looking at Sam's Smoothies, a firm that is owned and operated by Samantha.

### ■ Accounting Cost and Profit

In 2011, Sam's Smoothies' total revenue from the sale of smoothies was $150,000. The firm paid $20,000 for fruit, yogurt, and honey; $22,000 in wages for the labor it hired; and $3,000 in interest to the bank. These expenses totaled $45,000.

Sam's accountant said that the depreciation of the firm's blenders, refrigerators, and shop during 2011 was $10,000. Depreciation is the fall in the value of the firm's capital, and accountants calculate it by using the Internal Revenue Service's rules, which are based on standards set by the Financial Accounting Standards Board. So the accountant reported Sam's Smoothies' total cost for 2011 as $55,000 and the firm's profit as $95,000—$150,000 of total revenue minus $55,000 of total costs.

Sam's accountant measures cost and profit to ensure that the firm pays the correct amount of income tax and to show the bank how Sam's has used its bank loan. Economists have a different purpose: to predict the decisions that a firm makes to maximize its profit. These decisions respond to *opportunity cost* and *economic profit*.

### ■ Opportunity Cost

To produce its output, a firm employs factors of production: land, labor, capital, and entrepreneurship. Another firm could have used these same resources to produce other goods or services. In Chapter 3 (pp. 102–103), resources can be used to produce either cell phones or DVDs, so the opportunity cost of producing a cell phone is the number of DVDs forgone. Pilots who fly passengers for Southwest Airlines can't at the same time fly freight for FedEx. Construction workers who are building an office high-rise can't simultaneously build apartments. A communications satellite operating at peak capacity can carry television signals or e-mail messages but not both at the same time. A journalist writing for the *New York Times* can't at the same time create Web news reports for CNN. And Samantha can't simultaneously run her smoothies business and a flower shop.

The highest-valued alternative forgone is the opportunity cost of a firm's production. From the viewpoint of the firm, this opportunity cost is the amount that the firm must pay the owners of the factors of production it employs to attract them from their best alternative use. So a firm's opportunity cost of production is the cost of the factors of production it employs.

To determine these costs, let's return to Sam's and look at the opportunity cost of producing smoothies.

## Explicit Costs and Implicit Costs

The amount that a firm pays to attract resources from their best alternative use is either an explicit cost or an implicit cost. A cost paid in money is an **explicit cost.** Because the amount spent could have been spent on something else, an explicit cost is an opportunity cost. The wages that Samantha pays labor, the interest she pays the bank, and her expenditure on fruit, yogurt, and honey are explicit costs.

A firm incurs an **implicit cost** when it uses a factor of production but does not make a direct money payment for its use. The two categories of implicit cost are economic depreciation and the cost of the resources of the firm's owner.

**Economic depreciation** is the opportunity cost of the firm using capital that it owns. It is measured as the change in the *market value* of capital—the market price of the capital at the beginning of the period minus its market price at the end of the period. Suppose that Samantha could have sold her blenders, refrigerators, and shop on December 31, 2010, for $250,000. If she can sell the same capital on December 31, 2011, for $246,000, her economic depreciation during 2011 is $4,000. This is the opportunity cost of using her capital during 2011, not the $10,000 depreciation calculated by Sam's accountant.

Interest is another cost of capital. When the firm's owner provides the funds used to buy capital, the opportunity cost of those funds is the interest income forgone by not using them in the best alternative way. If Sam loaned her firm funds that could have earned her $1,000 in interest, this amount is an implicit cost of producing smoothies.

When a firm's owner supplies labor, the opportunity cost of the owner's time spent working for the firm is the wage income forgone by not working in the best alternative job. For example, instead of working at her next best job that pays $34,000 a year, Sam supplies labor to her smoothies business. This implicit cost of $34,000 is part of the opportunity cost of producing smoothies.

Finally, a firm's owner often supplies entrepreneurship, the factor of production that organizes the business and bears the risk of running it. The return to entrepreneurship is **normal profit.** Normal profit is part of a firm's opportunity cost because it is the cost of a forgone alternative—running another firm. Instead of running Sam's Smoothies, Sam could earn $16,000 a year running a flower shop. This amount is an implicit cost of production at Sam's Smoothies.

## ■ Economic Profit

A firm's **economic profit** equals total revenue minus total cost. Total revenue is the amount received from the sale of the product. It is the price of the output multiplied by the quantity sold. Total cost is the sum of the explicit costs and implicit costs and is the opportunity cost of production.

**Explicit cost**
A cost paid in money.

**Implicit cost**
An opportunity cost incurred by a firm when it uses a factor of production for which it does not make a direct money payment.

**Economic depreciation**
An opportunity cost of a firm using capital that it owns—measured as the change in the *market value* of capital over a given period.

**Normal profit**
The return to entrepreneurship. Normal profit is part of a firm's opportunity cost because it is the cost of not running another firm.

**Economic profit**
A firm's total revenue minus total cost.

**TABLE 10.1**

## Economic Accounting

| Item | | |
|---|---|---|
| **Total Revenue** | | **$150,000** |
| *Explicit Costs* | | |
| Cost of fruit, yogurt, and honey | $20,000 | |
| Wages | $22,000 | |
| Interest | $3,000 | |
| *Implicit Costs* | | |
| Samantha's forgone wages | $34,000 | |
| Samantha's forgone interest | $1,000 | |
| Economic depreciation | $4,000 | |
| Normal profit | $16,000 | |
| **Opportunity Cost** | | **$100,000** |
| **Economic Profit** | | **$50,000** |

Because one of the firm's implicit costs is *normal profit*, the return to the entrepreneur equals normal profit plus economic profit. If a firm incurs an economic loss, the entrepreneur receives less than normal profit.

Table 10.1 summarizes the economic cost concepts, and Figure 10.1 compares the economic view and the accounting view of cost and profit. Sam's total revenue (price multiplied by quantity sold) is $150,000; the opportunity cost of the resources that Sam uses is $100,000; and Sam's economic profit is $50,000.

**FIGURE 10.1**

## Two Views of Cost and Profit

Both economists and accountants measure a firm's total revenue the same way. It equals the price multiplied by the quantity sold of each item. Economists measure economic profit as total revenue minus opportunity cost. Opportunity cost includes explicit costs and implicit costs. Normal profit is an implicit cost. Accountants measure profit as total revenue minus explicit costs—costs paid in money—and depreciation.

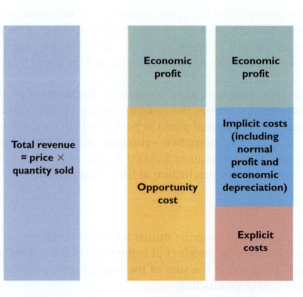

The economic view

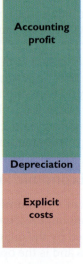

The accounting view

## CHECKPOINT 10.1

**Explain and distinguish between the economic and accounting measures of a firm's cost of production and profit.**

## Practice Problems

Lee, a programmer, earned $35,000 in 2010, but in 2011, he began to manufacture body boards. After one year, he submitted the following data to his accountant.

- He stopped renting out his cottage for $3,500 a year and used it as his factory. The market value of the cottage increased from $70,000 to $71,000.
- He spent $50,000 on materials, phone, utilities, etc.
- He leased machines for $10,000 a year.
- He paid $15,000 in wages.
- He used $10,000 from his savings account, which pays 5 percent a year interest.
- He borrowed $40,000 at 10 percent a year from the bank.
- He sold $160,000 worth of body boards.
- Normal profit is $25,000 a year.

1. Calculate Lee's explicit costs, implicit costs, and economic profit.
2. Lee's accountant recorded the depreciation on Lee's cottage during 2011 as $7,000. What did the accountant say Lee's profit or loss was?

## In the News

**What does it cost to make 100 pairs of running shoes?**
An Asian manufacturer of running shoes pays its workers $275 to make 100 pairs an hour. Workers use company-owned equipment that costs $300 an hour in forgone interest and economic depreciation. Materials cost $900.

Source: washpost.com

Which costs are explicit costs? Which are implicit costs? With total revenue from the sale of 100 pairs of shoes of $1,650, calculate economic profit.

## Solutions to Practice Problems

1. Lee's explicit costs are costs paid with money: $50,000 on materials, phone, utilities, etc; $10,000 on leased machines; $15,000 in wages; and $4,000 in bank interest. These items total $79,000. Lee's implicit costs are $35,000 in forgone wages; $3,500 in forgone rent; $1,000 increase in the value of his cottage is economic depreciation of –$1,000; $500 in forgone interest; and $25,000 in normal profit. These items total $63,000. Economic profit equals total revenue ($160,000) minus total cost ($79,000 + $63,000), which equals $142,000. So economic profit is $160,000 − $142,000, or $18,000.
2. The accountant measures Lee's profit as total revenue minus explicit costs minus depreciation: $160,000 − $79,000 − $7,000, or $74,000.

## Solution to In the News

Explicit costs are wages ($275) and materials ($900). Implicit costs are the forgone interest and economic depreciation ($300). Economic profit equals total revenue ($1,650) minus total cost ($1,475), which is $175.

# SHORT RUN AND LONG RUN

The main goal of this chapter is to explore the influences on a firm's costs. The key influence on cost is the quantity of output that the firm produces per period. The greater the output rate, the higher is the total cost of production. But the effect of a change in production on cost depends on how soon the firm wants to act. A firm that plans to change its output rate tomorrow has fewer options than a firm that plans ahead and intends to change its production six months from now.

To study the relationship between a firm's output decision and its costs, we distinguish between two decision time frames:

- The short run
- The long run

## The Short Run: Fixed Plant

**Short run**

The time frame in which the quantities of some resources are fixed. In the short run, a firm can usually change the quantity of labor it uses but not its technology and quantity of capital.

The **short run** is the time frame in which the quantities of some resources are fixed. For most firms, the fixed resources are the firm's technology and capital—its equipment and buildings. The management organization is also fixed in the short run. The fixed resources that a firm uses are its *fixed factors of production* and the resources that it can vary are its *variable factors of production*. The collection of fixed resources is the firm's *plant*. So in the short run, a firm's plant is fixed.

Sam's Smoothies' plant is its blenders, refrigerators, and shop. Sam's cannot change these inputs in the short run. An electric power utility can't change the number of generators it uses in the short run. An airport can't change the number of runways, terminal buildings, and traffic-control facilities in the short run.

To increase output in the short run, a firm must increase the quantity of variable factors it uses. Labor is usually the variable factor of production. To produce more smoothies, Sam must hire more labor. Similarly, to increase the production of electricity, a utility must hire more engineers and run its generators for longer hours. To increase the volume of traffic it handles, an airport must hire more check-in clerks, cargo handlers, and air-traffic controllers.

Short-run decisions are easily reversed. A firm can increase or decrease output in the short run by increasing or decreasing the number of labor hours it hires.

## The Long Run: Variable Plant

**Long run**

The time frame in which the quantities of *all* resources can be varied.

The **long run** is the time frame in which the quantities of *all* resources can be varied. That is, the long run is a period in which the firm can change its *plant*.

To increase output in the long run, a firm can increase the size of its plant. Sam's Smoothies can install more blenders and refrigerators and increase the size of its shop. An electric power utility can install more generators. And an airport can build more runways, terminals, and traffic-control facilities.

Long-run decisions are not easily reversed. Once a firm buys a new plant, its resale value is usually much less than the amount the firm paid for it. The fall in value is economic depreciation. It is called a *sunk cost* to emphasize that it is irrelevant to the firm's decisions. Only the short-run cost of changing its labor inputs and the long-run cost of changing its plant size are relevant to a firm's decisions.

We're going to study costs in the short run and the long run. We begin with the short run and describe the limits to the firm's production possibilities.

## 10.2  SHORT-RUN PRODUCTION

To increase the output of a fixed plant, a firm must increase the quantity of labor it employs. We describe the relationship between output and the quantity of labor employed by using three related concepts:

- Total product
- Marginal product
- Average product

### ■ Total Product

**Total product** (*TP*) is the total quantity of a good produced in a given period. Total product is an output *rate*—the number of units produced per unit of time (for example, per hour, day, or week). Total product changes as the quantity of labor employed increases and we illustrate this relationship as a total product schedule and total product curve like those in Figure 10.2. The total product schedule (the table below the graph) lists the maximum quantities of smoothies per hour that Sam can produce with her existing plant at each quantity of labor. Points *A* through *H* on the *TP* curve correspond to the columns in the table.

**Total product**
The total quantity of a good produced in a given period.

■ **FIGURE 10.2**

Total Product Schedule and Total Product Curve

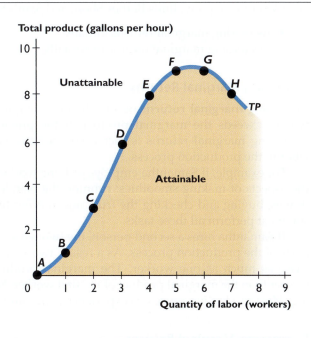

The total product schedule shows how the quantity of smoothies that Sam's can produce changes as the quantity of labor employed changes. In column *C*, Sam's employs 2 workers and can produce 3 gallons of smoothies an hour.

The total product curve, *TP*, graphs the data in the table. Points *A* through *H* on the curve correspond to the columns of the table. The total product curve separates attainable outputs from unattainable outputs. Points below the *TP* curve are inefficient. Points on the *TP* curve are efficient.

| Quantity of labor (workers) | 0 | 1 | 2 | 3 | 4 | 5 | 6 | 7 |
|---|---|---|---|---|---|---|---|---|
| Total product (gallons per hour) | 0 | 1 | 3 | 6 | 8 | 9 | 9 | 8 |
|  | *A* | *B* | *C* | *D* | *E* | *F* | *G* | *H* |

Like the *production possibilities frontier* (see Chapter 3, p. 98), the total product curve separates attainable outputs from unattainable outputs. All the points that lie above the curve are unattainable. Points that lie below the curve, in the orange area, are attainable, but they are inefficient: They use more labor than is necessary to produce a given output. Only the points *on* the total product curve are efficient.

## ■ Marginal Product

**Marginal product**

The change in total product that results from a one-unit increase in the quantity of labor employed.

**Marginal product** (*MP*) is the change in total product that results from a one-unit increase in the quantity of labor employed. It tells us the contribution to total product of adding one additional worker. When the quantity of labor increases by more than one worker, we calculate marginal product as

Marginal product = Change in total product ÷ Change in quanity of labor.

Figure 10.3 shows Sam's Smoothies' marginal product curve, *MP*, and its relationship with the total product curve. You can see that as the quantity of labor increases from 1 to 3 workers, marginal product increases. But as more than 3 workers are employed, marginal product decreases. When the seventh worker is employed, marginal product is negative.

Notice that the steeper the slope of the total product curve in part (a), the greater is marginal product in part (b). And when the total product curve turns downward in part (a), marginal product is negative in part (b).

The total product curve and marginal product curve in Figure 10.3 incorporate a feature that is shared by all production processes in firms as different as the Ford Motor Company, Jim's Barber Shop, and Sam's Smoothies:

- Increasing marginal returns initially
- Decreasing marginal returns eventually

### Increasing Marginal Returns

**Increasing marginal returns**

When the marginal product of an additional worker exceeds the marginal product of the previous worker.

**Increasing marginal returns** occur when the marginal product of an additional worker exceeds the marginal product of the previous worker. The source of increasing marginal returns is increased specialization and greater division of labor in the production process.

For example, if Samantha employs just one worker, that person must learn all the aspects of making smoothies: running the blender, cleaning it, fixing breakdowns, buying and checking the fruit, and serving the customers. That one person must perform all these tasks.

If Samantha hires a second person, the two workers can specialize in different parts of the production process. As a result, two workers can produce more than twice as much as one worker. The marginal product of the second worker is greater than the marginal product of the first worker. Marginal returns are increasing. Most production processes experience increasing marginal returns initially.

### Decreasing Marginal Returns

**Decreasing marginal returns**

When the marginal product of an additional worker is less than the marginal product of the previous worker.

All production processes eventually reach a point of *decreasing* marginal returns. **Decreasing marginal returns** occur when the marginal product of an additional worker is less than the marginal product of the previous worker. Decreasing marginal returns arise from the fact that more and more workers use the same equipment and work space. As more workers are employed, there is less and less that is productive for the additional worker to do. For example, if Samantha hires a

■ **FIGURE 10.3**

Total Product and Marginal Product

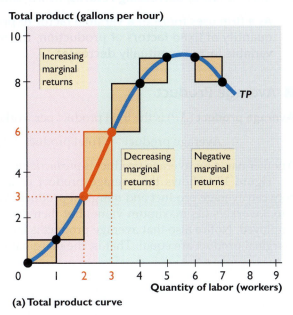

**(a) Total product curve**

The table calculates marginal product, and the orange bars illustrate it. When labor increases from 2 to 3 workers, total product increases from 3 gallons to 6 gallons of smoothies an hour. So marginal product is the orange bar whose height is 3 gallons (in both parts of the figure).

In part (b), marginal product is graphed midway between the labor inputs to emphasize that it is the result of *changing* inputs. Marginal product increases to a maximum (when 3 workers are employed in this example) and then declines— diminishing marginal product.

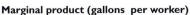

**(b) Marginal product curve**

| Quantity of labor (workers) | 0 | 1 | 2 | 3 | 4 | 5 | 6 | 7 |
|---|---|---|---|---|---|---|---|---|
| Total product (gallons per hour) | 0 | 1 | 3 | 6 | 8 | 9 | 9 | 8 |
| Marginal product (gallons per worker) | | 1 | 2 | 3 | 2 | 1 | 0 | –1 |

fourth worker, output increases but not by as much as it did when she hired the third worker. In this case, three workers exhaust all the possible gains from specialization and the division of labor. By hiring a fourth worker, Sam's produces more smoothies per hour, but the equipment is being operated closer to its limits. Sometimes the fourth worker has nothing to do because the machines are running without the need for further attention.

Hiring yet more workers continues to increase output but by successively smaller amounts until Samantha hires the sixth worker, at which point total product stops rising. Add a seventh worker, and the workplace is so congested that the workers get in each other's way and total product falls.

Decreasing marginal returns are so pervasive that they qualify for the status of a law: the **law of decreasing returns**, which states that

> **As a firm uses more of a variable factor of production, with a given quantity of fixed factors of production, the marginal product of the variable factor eventually decreases.**

### ■ Average Product

**Average product**

Total product divided by the quantity of a factor of production. The average product of labor is total product divided by the quantity of labor employed.

**Average product** (*AP*) is the total product per worker employed. It is calculated as

$$\text{Average product} = \text{Total product} \div \text{Quantity of labor.}$$

Another name for average product is *productivity*.

Figure 10.4 shows the average product of labor, *AP*, and the relationship between average product and marginal product. Average product increases from 1 to 3 workers (its maximum value) but then decreases as yet more workers are employed. Notice also that average product is largest when average product and marginal product are equal. That is, the marginal product curve cuts the average

---

■ **FIGURE 10.4**

Average Product and Marginal Product

The table calculates average product. For example, when the quantity of labor is 3 workers, total product is 6 gallons an hour, so average product is 6 gallons ÷ 3 workers = 2 gallons a worker.

The average product curve is *AP*. When marginal product exceeds average product, average product is increasing. When marginal product is less than average product, average product is decreasing.

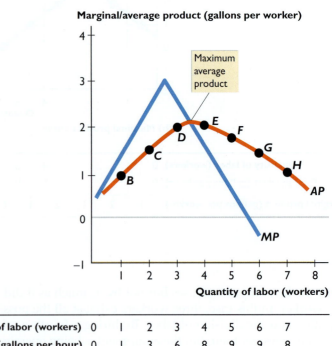

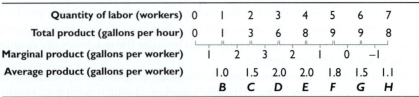

| Quantity of labor (workers) | 0 | 1 | 2 | 3 | 4 | 5 | 6 | 7 |
|---|---|---|---|---|---|---|---|---|
| Total product (gallons per hour) | 0 | 1 | 3 | 6 | 8 | 9 | 9 | 8 |
| Marginal product (gallons per worker) | | 1 | 2 | 3 | 2 | 1 | 0 | −1 |
| Average product (gallons per worker) | | 1.0 | 1.5 | 2.0 | 2.0 | 1.8 | 1.5 | 1.1 |
| | | *B* | *C* | *D* | *E* | *F* | *G* | *H* |

product curve at the point of maximum average product. For employment levels at which marginal product exceeds average product, the average product curve slopes upward and average product increases as more labor is employed. For employment levels at which marginal product is less than average product, the average product curve slopes downward and average product decreases as more labor is employed.

The relationship between average product and marginal product is a general feature of the relationship between the average value and the marginal value of any variable. *Eye on Your Life* looks at a familiar example.

# EYE on YOUR LIFE
## Your Average and Marginal Grades

Jen, a part-time student, takes one course each semester over five semesters. In the first semester, she takes calculus and her grade is a C (2). This grade is her marginal grade. It is also her average grade—her GPA.

In the next semester, Jen takes French and gets a B (3)—her new marginal grade. When the marginal value exceeds the average value, the average rises. Because Jen's marginal grade exceeds her average grade, the marginal grade pulls her average up. Her GPA rises to 2.5.

In the third semester, Jen takes economics and gets an A (4). Again her marginal grade exceeds her average, so the marginal grade pulls her average up. Jen's GPA is now 3—the average of 2, 3, and 4.

In the fourth semester, she takes history and gets a B (3). Now her marginal grade equals her average. When the marginal value equals the average value, the average doesn't change. So Jen's average remains at 3.

In the fifth semester, Jen takes English and gets a C (2). When the marginal value is below the average

value, the average falls. Because Jen's marginal grade, 2, is below her average of 3, the marginal grade pulls the average down. Her GPA falls.

This relationship between Jen's ❶ marginal grade and ❷ average grade is similar to the relationship between marginal product and average product.

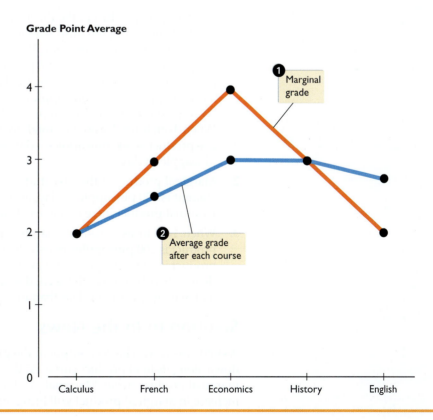

**CHECKPOINT 10.2**

**Explain the relationship between a firm's output and labor employed in the short run.**

## Practice Problems

**TABLE 1**

| Labor (students) | Total product (pineapples per day) |
|---|---|
| 0 | 0 |
| 1 | 100 |
| 2 | 220 |
| 3 | 300 |
| 4 | 360 |
| 5 | 400 |
| 6 | 420 |
| 7 | 430 |

Tom leases a farmer's field and grows pineapples. Tom hires students to pick and pack the pineapples. Table 1 sets out Tom's total product schedule.

1. Calculate the marginal product of the third student and the average product of three students.

2. Over what range of numbers of students does marginal product increase?

3. When marginal product increases, is average product greater than, less than, or equal to marginal product?

## In the News

**GM cuts jobs at its Australian manufacturing unit**

GM will cut 500 jobs, or about 12% of its workforce, at its Australian plant because of a sharp fall in demand for its locally-made "Cruze" small car.

Source: *The Wall Street Journal*, April 8, 2013

As GM cuts its workforce, how will the marginal product and average product of a worker change in the short run?

## Solutions to Practice Problems

1. The marginal product of the third student is the change in total product that results from hiring the third student. When Tom hires 2 students, total product is 220 pineapples a day. When Tom hires 3 students, total product is 300 pineapples a day. Marginal product of the third student is the total product of 3 students minus the total product of 2 students, which is 300 pineapples − 220 pineapples or 80 pineapples a day.
   Average product equals total product divided by the number of students. When Tom hires 3 students, total product is 300 pineapples a day, so average product is 300 pineapples a day ÷ 3 students, which equals 100 pineapples a day.

2. Marginal product of the first student is 100 pineapples a day, of the second student is 120 pineapples a day, and of the third is 80 pineapples a day. So marginal product increases when Tom hires the first and second students.

3. When Tom hires 1 student, marginal product is 100 pineapples and average product is 100 pineapples per student. When Tom hires 2 students, marginal product is 120 pineapples and average product is 110 pineapples per student. When Tom hires the second student, marginal product is increasing and average product is less than marginal product.

## Solution to In the News

As GM cuts its workforce, output at the plant will decrease as GM slides back down along its total product curve. At the same time, GM will slide up along its marginal product curve. Marginal product per worker will increase and the increase in marginal product will bring an increase in the average product.

## 10.3 SHORT-RUN COST

To produce more output (total product) in the short run, a firm must employ more labor, which means that it must increase its costs. We describe the relationship between output and cost using three cost concepts:

- Total cost
- Marginal cost
- Average cost

### ■ Total Cost

A firm's **total cost** (*TC*) is the cost of all the factors of production used by the firm. Total cost divides into two parts: total fixed cost and total variable cost. **Total fixed cost** (*TFC*) is the cost of a firm's fixed factors of production: land, capital, and entrepreneurship. In the short run, the quantities of these inputs don't change as output changes, so total fixed cost doesn't change as output changes. **Total variable cost** (*TVC*) is the cost of a firm's variable factor of production—labor. To change its output in the short run, a firm must change the quantity of labor it employs, so total variable cost changes as output changes.

Total cost is the sum of total fixed cost and total variable cost. That is,

$$TC = TFC + TVC.$$

Table 10.2 shows Sam's Smoothies' total costs. Sam's fixed costs are $10 an hour regardless of whether it operates or not—*TFC* is $10 an hour. To produce smoothies, Samantha hires labor, which costs $6 an hour. *TVC*, which increases as output increases, equals the number of workers per hour multiplied by $6. For example, to produce 6 gallons an hour, Samantha hires 3 workers, so *TVC* is $18 an hour. *TC* is the sum of *TFC* and *TVC*. So to produce 6 gallons an hour, *TC* is $28. Check the calculation in each row and note that to produce some quantities— 2 gallons an hour, for example—Sam hires a worker for only part of the hour.

**Total cost**
The cost of all the factors of production used by a firm.

**Total fixed cost**
The cost of the firm's fixed factors of production—the cost of land, capital, and entrepreneurship.

**Total variable cost**
The cost of the firm's variable factor of production—the cost of labor.

■ **TABLE 10.2**

Sam's Smoothies' Total Costs

| Labor (workers per hour) | Output (gallons per hour) | Total fixed cost | Total variable cost | Total cost |
|---|---|---|---|---|
| | | (dollars per hour) | | |
| 0 | 0 | 10 | 0 | 10.00 |
| 1.00 | 1 | 10 | 6.00 | 16.00 |
| 1.60 | 2 | 10 | 9.60 | 19.60 |
| 2.00 | 3 | 10 | 12.00 | 22.00 |
| 2.35 | 4 | 10 | 14.10 | 24.10 |
| 2.65 | 5 | 10 | 15.90 | 25.90 |
| 3.00 | 6 | 10 | 18.00 | 28.00 |
| 3.40 | 7 | 10 | 20.40 | 30.40 |
| 4.00 | 8 | 10 | 24.00 | 34.00 |
| 5.00 | 9 | 10 | 30.00 | 40.00 |

Sam's fixed factors of production are land, capital, and entrepreneurship. Total fixed cost is constant regardless of the quantity produced. Sam's variable factor of production is labor. Total variable cost is the cost of labor. Total cost is the sum of total fixed cost and total variable cost.

The highlighted row shows that to produce 6 gallons of smoothies, Sam's hires 3 workers. Total fixed cost is $10 an hour. Total variable cost is the cost of the 3 workers. At $6 an hour, 3 workers cost $18. Sam's total cost of producing 6 gallons an hour is $10 plus $18, which equals $28.

Figure 10.5 illustrates Sam's total cost curves. The green total fixed cost curve (*TFC*) is horizontal because total fixed cost does not change when output changes. It is a constant at $10 an hour. The purple total variable cost curve (*TVC*) and the blue total cost curve (*TC*) both slope upward because variable cost increases as output increases. The arrows highlight total fixed cost as the vertical distance between the *TVC* and *TC* curves.

Let's now look at Sam's Smoothies' marginal cost.

## ■ Marginal Cost

In Figure 10.5, total variable cost and total cost increase at a decreasing rate at small levels of output and then begin to increase at an increasing rate as output increases. To understand these patterns in the changes in total cost, we need to use the concept of *marginal cost*.

**Marginal cost**
The change in total cost that results from a one-unit increase in output.

A firm's **marginal cost** is the change in total cost that results from a one-unit increase in output. Table 10.3 calculates the marginal cost for Sam's Smoothies. When, for example, output increases from 5 gallons to 6 gallons an hour, total cost increases from $25.90 to $28. So the marginal cost of this gallon of smoothies is $2.10 ($28 − $25.90). Notice that marginal cost is located midway between the total costs to emphasize that it is the result of *changing* outputs

Marginal cost tells us how total cost changes as output changes. The final cost concept tells us what it costs, on average, to produce a unit of output. Let's now look at Sam's average costs.

**FIGURE 10.5**

Total Cost Curves at Sam's Smoothies

Total fixed cost (*TFC*) is constant—it graphs as a horizontal line—and total variable cost (*TVC*) increases as output increases. Total cost (*TC*) also increases as output increases. The vertical distance between the total cost curve and the total variable cost curve is total fixed cost, as illustrated by the two arrows.

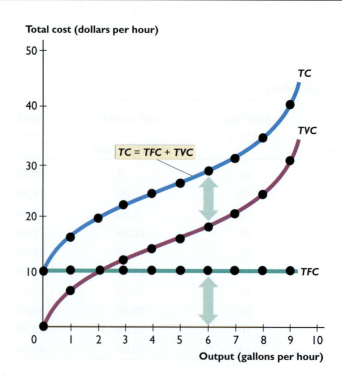

## ■ Average Cost

There are three average cost concepts:

- Average fixed cost
- Average variable cost
- Average total cost

**Average fixed cost** (*AFC*) is total fixed cost per unit of output. **Average variable cost** (*AVC*) is total variable cost per unit of output. **Average total cost** (*ATC*) is total cost per unit of output. The average cost concepts are calculated from the total cost concepts as follows:

$$TC = TFC + TVC.$$

Divide each total cost term by the quantity produced, *Q*, to give

$$\frac{TC}{Q} = \frac{TFC}{Q} + \frac{TVC}{Q}.$$

or

$$ATC = AFC + AVC.$$

Table 10.3 shows these average costs. For example, when output is 6 gallons an hour, *AFC* is ($10 ÷ 6), which equals $1.67; *AVC* is ($18 ÷ 6), which equals $3.00; and *ATC* is ($28 ÷ 6), which equals $4.67. Note that *ATC* ($4.67) equals *AFC* ($1.67) plus *AVC* ($3.00).

**Average fixed cost**
Total fixed cost per unit of output.

**Average variable cost**
Total variable cost per unit of output.

**Average total cost**
Total cost per unit of output, which equals average fixed cost plus average variable cost.

■ **TABLE 10.3**

### Sam's Smoothies' Marginal Cost and Average Cost

| Output (gallons per hour) | Total cost (dollars per hour) | Marginal cost (dollars per gallon) | Average fixed cost | Average variable cost | Average total cost |
|---|---|---|---|---|---|
| | | | | (dollars per gallon) | |
| 0 | 10.00 | | – | – | – |
| | | 6.00 | | | |
| 1 | 16.00 | | 10.00 | 6.00 | 16.00 |
| | | 3.60 | | | |
| 2 | 19.60 | | 5.00 | 4.80 | 9.80 |
| | | 2.40 | | | |
| 3 | 22.00 | | 3.33 | 4.00 | 7.33 |
| | | 2.10 | | | |
| 4 | 24.10 | | 2.50 | 3.53 | 6.03 |
| | | 1.80 | | | |
| 5 | 25.90 | | 2.00 | 3.18 | 5.18 |
| | | 2.10 | | | |
| 6 | 28.00 | | 1.67 | 3.00 | 4.67 |
| | | 2.40 | | | |
| 7 | 30.40 | | 1.43 | 2.91 | 4.34 |
| | | 3.60 | | | |
| 8 | 34.00 | | 1.25 | 3.00 | 4.25 |
| | | 6.00 | | | |
| 9 | 40.00 | | 1.11 | 3.33 | 4.44 |

To produce 6 gallons of smoothies an hour, Sam's total cost is $28. Table 10.2 shows that this total cost is the sum of total fixed cost ($10) and total variable cost ($18).

Marginal cost is the increase in total cost that results from a one-unit increase in output. When Sam's increases output from 5 gallons to 6 gallons an hour, total cost increases from $25.90 to $28.00, an increase of $2.10 a gallon. The marginal cost of the sixth gallon an hour is $2.10. Marginal cost is located midway between the total costs to emphasize that it is the result of *changing* output.

When Sam's produces 6 gallons an hour, average fixed cost ($10 ÷ 6 gallons) is $1.67 a gallon; average variable cost ($18 ÷ 6 gallons) is $3.00 a gallon; average total cost ($28 ÷ 6 gallons) is $4.67 a gallon.

Figure 10.6 graphs the marginal cost and average cost data in Table 10.3. The red marginal cost curve (*MC*) is U-shaped because of the way in which marginal product changes. Recall that when Samantha hires a second or a third worker, marginal product increases and output increases to 6 gallons an hour (Figure 10.3 on p. 297). Over this output range, marginal cost decreases as output increases. When Samantha hires a fourth or more workers, marginal product decreases but output increases up to 9 gallons an hour (Figure 10.3). Over this output range, marginal cost increases as output increases.

The green average fixed cost curve (*AFC*) slopes downward. As output increases, the same constant total fixed cost is spread over a larger output. The blue average total cost curve (*ATC*) and the purple average variable cost curve (*AVC*) are U-shaped. The vertical distance between the average total cost and average variable cost curves is equal to average fixed cost—as indicated by the two arrows. That distance shrinks as output increases because average fixed cost decreases with increasing output.

The marginal cost curve intersects the average variable cost curve and the average total cost curve at their minimum points. That is, when marginal cost is less than average cost, average cost is decreasing; and when marginal cost exceeds average cost, average cost is increasing. This relationship holds for both the *ATC* curve and the *AVC* curve and is another example of the relationship you saw in Figure 10.4 for average product and marginal product.

■ **FIGURE 10.6**

Average Cost Curves and Marginal Cost Curve at Sam's Smoothies

Average fixed cost decreases as output increases. The average fixed cost curve (*AFC*) slopes downward. The average total cost curve (*ATC*) and average variable cost curve (*AVC*) are U-shaped. The vertical distance between these two curves is equal to average fixed cost, as illustrated by the two arrows.

Marginal cost is the change in total cost when output increases by one unit. The marginal cost curve (*MC*) is U-shaped and intersects the average variable cost curve and the average total cost curve at their minimum points.

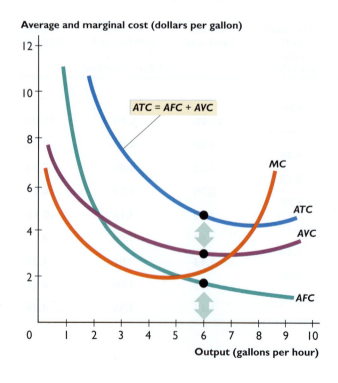

## ■ Why the Average Total Cost Curve Is U-Shaped

Average total cost, *ATC*, is the sum of average fixed cost, *AFC*, and average variable cost, *AVC*. So the shape of the *ATC* curve combines the shapes of the *AFC* and *AVC* curves. The U-shape of the average total cost curve arises from the influence of two opposing forces:

- Spreading total fixed cost over a larger output
- Decreasing marginal returns

When output increases, the firm spreads its total fixed costs over a larger output and its average fixed cost decreases—its average fixed cost curve slopes downward.

Decreasing marginal returns means that as output increases, ever larger amounts of labor are needed to produce an additional unit of output. So average variable cost eventually increases, and the *AVC* curve eventually slopes upward.

The shape of the average total cost curve combines these two effects. Initially, as output increases, both average fixed cost and average variable cost decrease, so average total cost decreases and the *ATC* curve slopes downward. But as output increases further and decreasing marginal returns set in, average variable cost begins to increase. Eventually, average variable cost increases more quickly than average fixed cost decreases, so average total cost increases and the *ATC* curve slopes upward.

All the short-run cost concepts that you've met are summarized in Table 10.4.

### ■ TABLE 10.4

### A Compact Glossary of Costs

| Term | Symbol | Definition | Equation |
|---|---|---|---|
| Fixed cost | | The cost of a fixed factor of production that is independent of the quantity produced | |
| Variable cost | | The cost of a variable factor of production that varies with the quantity produced | |
| Total fixed cost | *TFC* | Cost of the fixed factors of production | |
| Total variable cost | *TVC* | Cost of the variable factor of production | |
| Total cost | *TC* | Cost of all factors of production | $TC = TFC + TVC$ |
| Marginal cost | *MC* | Change in total cost resulting from a one-unit increase in output (*Q*) | $MC = \Delta TC \div \Delta Q*$ |
| Average fixed cost | *AFC* | Total fixed cost per unit of output | $AFC = TFC \div Q$ |
| Average variable cost | *AVC* | Total variable cost per unit of output | $AVC = TVC \div Q$ |
| Average total cost | *ATC* | Total cost per unit of output | $ATC = AFC + AVC$ |

*In this equation, the Greek letter delta (Δ) stands for "change in."

## ■ Cost Curves and Product Curves

A firm's cost curves and product curves are linked, and Figure 10.7 shows how. The upper graph shows the average product curve, *AP*, and the marginal product curve, *MP*. The lower graph shows the average variable cost curve, *AVC*, and the marginal cost curve, *MC*.

As labor increases up to 2.5 workers a day (upper graph), output increases to 4 units a day (lower graph). Marginal product and average product rise and marginal cost and average variable cost fall. At the point of maximum marginal product, marginal cost is at a minimum.

As labor increases to 3.5 workers a day (upper graph), output increases to 7 units a day (lower graph). Marginal product falls and marginal cost rises, but average product continues to rise and average variable cost continues to fall. At the point of maximum average product, average variable cost is at a minimum. As labor increases further, output increases. Average product diminishes and average variable cost increases.

## ■ Shifts in the Cost Curves

The position of a firm's short-run cost curves, in Figures 10.5 and 10.6, depends on two factors:

- Technology
- Prices of factors of production

### Technology

A technological change that increases productivity shifts the total product curve upward. It also shifts the marginal product curve and the average product curve upward. With a better technology that increases productivity, the same factors of production can produce more output, so an advance in technology lowers the average and marginal costs and shifts the short-run cost curves downward.

For example, advances in robotic technology have increased productivity in the automobile industry. As a result, the product curves of Chrysler, Ford, and GM have shifted upward, and their average and marginal cost curves have shifted downward. But the relationships between their product curves and cost curves have not changed. The curves are still linked, as in Figure 10.7.

Often a technological advance results in a firm using more capital, a fixed factor of production, and less labor, a variable factor of production. For example, today telephone companies use computers to connect long-distance calls instead of the human operators they used in the 1980s. When a telephone company makes this change, total variable cost decreases and total cost decreases, but total fixed cost increases. This change in the mix of fixed cost and variable cost means that at small output levels, average total cost might increase, but at large output levels, average total cost decreases.

### Prices of Factors of Production

An increase in the price of a factor of production increases costs and shifts the cost curves. But how the curves shift depends on which resource price changes. An increase in rent or some other component of *fixed* cost shifts the fixed cost curves (*TFC* and *AFC*) upward and shifts the total cost curve (*TC*) upward but leaves the variable cost curves (*AVC* and *TVC*) and the marginal cost curve (*MC*) unchanged.

## FIGURE 10.7

### Product Curves and Cost Curves

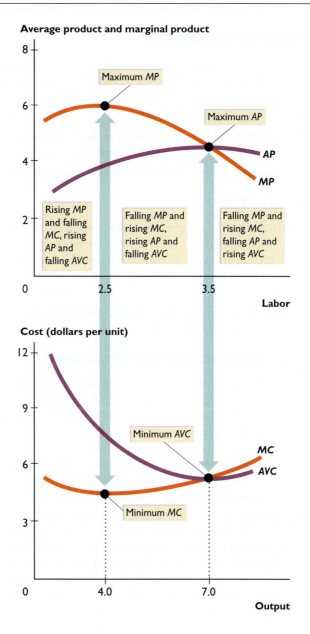

**Average product and marginal product**

Maximum MP

Maximum AP

AP

MP

Rising MP and falling MC, rising AP and falling AVC

Falling MP and rising MC, rising AP and falling AVC

Falling MP and rising MC, falling AP and rising AVC

0  2.5  3.5

Labor

**Cost (dollars per unit)**

Minimum AVC

MC

AVC

Minimum MC

0  4.0  7.0

Output

A firm's *MC* curve is linked to its *MP* curve. If, as the firm hires more labor up to 2.5 workers a day, the firm's marginal product rises, its marginal cost falls. If marginal product is at a maximum, marginal cost is at a minimum. If, as the firm hires more labor, its marginal product diminishes, its marginal cost rises.

A firm's *AVC* curve is linked to its *AP* curve. If, as the firm hires more labor up to 3.5 workers a day, its average product rises, its average variable cost falls. If average product is at a maximum, average variable cost is at a minimum. If as the firm hires more labor its average product diminishes, its average variable cost rises.

An increase in wage rates or some other component of *variable* cost shifts the variable cost curves (*TVC* and *AVC*) and the marginal cost curve (*MC*) upward but leaves the fixed cost curves (*AFC* and *TFC*) unchanged. So, for example, if the interest expense paid by a trucking company increases, the fixed cost of transportation services increases, but if the wage rate paid to truck drivers increases, the variable cost and marginal cost of transportation services increase.

# CHECKPOINT 10.3

**Explain the relationship between a firm's output and costs in the short run.**

## Practice Problems

Tom leases a farmer's field for $120 a day and grows pineapples. He pays students $100 a day each to pick pineapples and he leases capital at $80 a day. Table 1 shows Tom's daily output.

1. What is Tom's total cost and average total cost of 300 pineapples a day?

2. What is the marginal cost of picking a pineapple when the quantity increases from 360 to 400 pineapples a day?

3. At what output is Tom's average total cost a minimum?

## In the News

**Metropolitan Museum completes round of layoffs**
The museum cut 74 jobs and 95 other workers retired. The museum also laid off 127 other employees in its retail shops. The cut in labor costs is $10 million, but the museum expects no change in the number of visitors.
Source: *The New York Times*, June 22, 2009

Explain how the job cuts will change the museum's short-run average cost curves and marginal cost curve.

## Solutions to Practice Problems

1. Total cost is the sum of total fixed cost and total variable cost. Tom leases the field for $120 a day and capital for $80 a day, so Tom's total fixed cost is $200 a day. Total variable cost is the wages of the students. To produce 300 pineapples a day, Tom hires 3 students, so total variable cost is $300 a day and total cost is $500 a day. Table 2 shows the total cost (*TC*) schedule. Average total cost is the total cost divided by total product. The total cost of 300 pineapples a day is $500, so average total cost is $1.67 a pineapple. Table 2 shows the average total cost schedule.

2. Marginal cost is the increase in total cost that results from picking one additional pineapple a day. When the quantity picked increases from 360 to 400 pineapples a day, total cost (from Table 2) increases from $600 to $700. The increase in the number of pineapples is 40, and the increase in total cost is $100. Marginal cost is the increase in total cost ($100) divided by the increase in the number of pineapples (40), which is $2.50 per pineapple. So the marginal cost of a pineapple is $2.50.

3. At the minimum of average total cost, average total cost equals marginal cost. Minimum average total cost of a pineapple between 300 and 360 pineapples is $1.67. Table 2 shows that the marginal cost of increasing output from 300 to 360 pineapples a day is $1.67 a pineapple.

## Solution to In the News

A cut in labor but no change in output increases marginal product of labor and decreases marginal cost. The *MC*, *AVC*, and *ATC* curves shift downward.

**TABLE 1**

| Labor (students) | Output (pineapples per day) |
|---|---|
| 0 | 0 |
| 1 | 100 |
| 2 | 220 |
| 3 | 300 |
| 4 | 360 |
| 5 | 400 |
| 6 | 420 |
| 7 | 430 |

**TABLE 2**

| Labor | TP | TC | MC | ATC |
|---|---|---|---|---|
| 0 | 0 | 200 | | – |
| | | | 1.00 | |
| 1 | 100 | 300 | | 3.00 |
| | | | 0.83 | |
| 2 | 220 | 400 | | 1.82 |
| | | | 1.25 | |
| 3 | 300 | 500 | | 1.67 |
| | | | 1.67 | |
| 4 | 360 | 600 | | 1.67 |
| | | | 2.50 | |
| 5 | 400 | 700 | | 1.75 |
| | | | 5.00 | |
| 6 | 420 | 800 | | 1.90 |
| | | | 10.00 | |
| 7 | 430 | 900 | | 2.09 |

## 10.4 LONG-RUN COST

In the long run, a firm can vary both the quantity of labor and the quantity of capital. A small firm, such as Sam's Smoothies, can increase its plant size by moving into a larger building and installing more machines. A big firm such as General Motors can decrease its plant size by closing down some production lines.

We are now going to see how costs vary in the long run when a firm varies its plant—the quantity of capital it uses—along with the quantity of labor it uses.

The first thing that happens is that the distinction between fixed cost and variable cost disappears. All costs are variable in the long run.

### ■ Plant Size and Cost

When a firm changes its plant size, its cost of producing a given output changes. In Table 10.3 on p. 303 and Figure 10.6 on p. 304, the lowest average total cost that Samantha can achieve is $4.25 a gallon, which occurs when she produces 8 gallons of smoothies an hour. Samantha wonders what would happen to her average total cost if she increased the size of her plant by renting a bigger building and installing a larger number of blenders and refrigerators. Will the average total cost of producing a gallon of smoothies fall, rise, or remain the same?

Each of these three outcomes is possible, and they arise because when a firm changes the size of its plant, it might experience

- Economies of scale
- Diseconomies of scale
- Constant returns to scale

### Economies of Scale

**Economies of scale** are features of a firm's technology that make average total cost *fall* as output increases. The main source of economies of scale is greater specialization of both labor and capital.

*Specialization of Labor*  If Ford produced 100 cars a week, each production line worker would have to perform many different tasks. But if Ford produces 10,000 cars a week, each worker can specialize in a small number of tasks and become highly proficient at them. The result is that the average product of labor increases and the average total cost of producing a car falls.

Specialization also occurs off the production line. For example, a small firm usually does not have a specialist sales manager, personnel manager, and production manager. One person covers all these activities. But when a firm is large enough, specialists perform these activities. Average product increases, and the average total cost falls.

*Specialization of Capital*  At a small output rate, firms often must employ general-purpose machines and tools. For example, with an output of a few gallons an hour, Sam's Smoothies uses regular blenders like the one in your kitchen. But if Sam's produces hundreds of gallons an hour, it uses commercial blenders that fill, empty, and clean themselves. The result is that the output rate is larger and the average total cost of producing a gallon of smoothies is lower.

**Economies of scale**
Features of a firm's technology that make average total cost *fall* as output increases.

*Specialization of both labor and capital on an auto-assembly line.*

**Diseconomies of scale**
Features of a firm's technology that make average total cost *rise* as output increases.

**Constant returns to scale**
Features of a firm's technology that keep average total cost constant as output increases.

**Long-run average cost curve**
A curve that shows the lowest average total cost at which it is possible to produce each output when the firm has had sufficient time to change both its plant size and labor employed.

## Diseconomies of Scale

**Diseconomies of scale** are features of a firm's technology that make average total cost *rise* as output increases. Diseconomies of scale arise from the difficulty of coordinating and controlling a large enterprise. The larger the firm, the greater is the cost of communicating both up and down the management hierarchy and among managers. Eventually, management complexity brings rising average total cost. Diseconomies of scale occur in all production processes but in some perhaps only at a very large output rate.

## Constant Returns to Scale

**Constant returns to scale** are features of a firm's technology that keep average total cost *constant* as output increases. Constant returns to scale occur when a firm is able to replicate its existing production facility including its management system. For example, Ford might double its production of Fusion cars by doubling its production facility for those cars. It can build an identical production line and hire an identical number of workers. With the two identical production lines, Ford produces exactly twice as many cars. The average total cost of producing a Fusion is identical in the two plants. Ford's average total cost remains constant as it increases production.

## ■ The Long-Run Average Cost Curve

The **long-run average cost curve** shows the lowest average total cost at which it is possible to produce each output when the firm has had sufficient time to change both its plant size and its labor force.

Figure 10.8 shows Sam's Smoothies' long-run average cost curve *LRAC*. This long-run average cost curve is derived from the short-run average total cost curves for different possible plant sizes.

With its current small plant, Sam's Smoothies operates on the average total cost curve $ATC_1$ in Figure 10.8. The other three average total cost curves are for

■ **FIGURE 10.8**

## Long-Run Average Cost Curve

In the long run, Samantha can vary both the plant size and the quantity of labor she employs. The long-run average cost curve traces the lowest attainable average total cost of producing each output. The dark blue curve is the long-run average cost curve *LRAC*.

Sam's experiences economies of scale as output increases up to 14 gallons an hour, constant returns to scale for outputs between 14 gallons and 19 gallons an hour, and diseconomies of scale for outputs that exceed 19 gallons an hour.

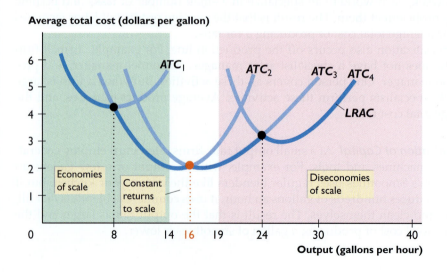

successively bigger plants. In this example, for outputs up to 8 gallons an hour, the existing plant with average total cost curve $ATC_1$ produces smoothies at the lowest attainable average cost. For outputs between 8 and 16 gallons an hour, average total cost is lowest on $ATC_2$. For outputs between 16 and 24 gallons an hour, average total cost is lowest on $ATC_3$. And for outputs in excess of 24 gallons an hour, average total cost is lowest on $ATC_4$.

The segment of each of the four average total cost curves for which that plant has the lowest average total cost is highlighted in dark blue in Figure 10.8. The scallop-shaped curve made up of these four segments is Sam's Smoothies' long-run average cost curve.

### Economies and Diseconomies of Scale

When economies of scale are present, the *LRAC* curve slopes downward. The *LRAC* curve in Figure 10.8 shows that Sam's Smoothies experiences economies of scale for output rates up to 14 gallons an hour. At output rates between 14 and 19 gallons an hour, the firm experiences constant returns to scale. And at output rates that exceed 19 gallons an hour, the firm experiences diseconomies of scale.

## EYE on RETAILERS' COSTS

### Which Store Has the Lower Costs: Wal-Mart or 7-Eleven?

Wal-Mart's "small" supercenters measure 99,000 square feet and serve an average of 30,000 customers a week. The average 7-Eleven store, most of which today are attached to gas stations, measures 2,000 square feet and serves 5,000 customers a week.

Which retailing technology has the lower operating cost? The answer depends on the scale of operation.

At a small number of customers per week, it costs less per customer to operate a store of 2,000 square feet than one of 99,000 square feet.

In the figure, the average total cost curve of operating a 7-Eleven store of 2,000 square feet is $ATC_{7\text{-}Eleven}$ and the average total cost curve of a store of 99,000 square feet is $ATC_{Wal\text{-}Mart}$. The dark blue curve is a retailer's long-run average cost curve *LRAC*.

If the number of customers is $Q$ a week, the average total cost per transaction is the same for both stores. For a store that serves more than $Q$ customers a week, the least-cost method

is the big store. For fewer than $Q$ customers a week, the least-cost method is the small store. The least-cost store is not always the biggest store.

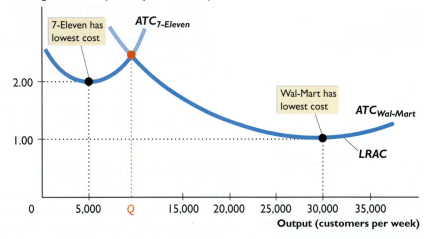

**CHECKPOINT 10.4**

Derive and explain a firm's long-run average cost curve.

## Practice Problems

To grow pineapples, Tom leases 1 field for $120 a day and capital for $80 a day and hires students at $100 a day each. Suppose that Tom now leases 2 fields for $240 a day and twice as much capital for $160 a day. Table 1 shows his outputs.

1. What is Tom's average total cost when he farms 2 fields and produces 220 pineapples a day?

2. Make a graph of Tom's average total cost curves using 1 field and 2 fields. Show on the graph Tom's long-run average cost curve. Over what output range will Tom use 1 field? 2 fields?

3. Does Tom experience constant returns to scale, economies of scale, or diseconomies of scale?

## In the News

**Ford to hire 2,000 and expand capacity**
Ford Motor Co. will hire 2,000 new workers and spend $1.1 billion to retool and refurbish its Kansas City plant.

Source: Automotive News, May 2, 2013

Explain the effects of the expansion plan on Ford's total fixed cost, total variable cost, short-run *ATC* curve, and *LRAC* curve at the Kansas City plant.

## Solutions to Practice Problems

1. Total cost equals fixed cost ($400 a day) plus $100 a day for each student. Tom can produce 220 pineapples with 2 fields and 1 student, so total cost is $500 a day. Average total cost is the total cost divided by output, which at 220 pineapples a day is $500 divided by 220, or $2.27. The "*ATC* (2 fields)" column of Table 2 shows Tom's average total cost schedule for 2 fields.

2. Figure 1 shows Tom's average total cost curve using 1 field as $ATC_1$. This curve graphs the data on *ATC* (1 field) and *TP* (1 field) in Table 2, which was calculated in Table 2 on p. 308. Using 2 fields, the average total cost curve is $ATC_2$. Tom's long-run average cost curve is the lower segments of the two *ATC* curves, highlighted in Figure 1. If Tom produces up to 300 pineapples a day, he will use 1 field. If he produces more than 300 pineapples a day, he will use 2 fields.

3. Tom experiences economies of scale up to an output of 740 pineapples a day because as he increases his plant and produces up to 740 pineapples a day, the average total cost of picking a pineapple decreases. (We don't have enough information to know what happens to Tom's average total cost if he uses three fields and three units of capital.)

## Solution to In the News

Retooling and refurbishing the Kansas City plant will raise Ford's total fixed cost; expanding production and increasing output will raise Ford's total variable cost. As Ford increases its output, it will move along its *ATC* curve. With a larger capacity, Ford will move rightward along its *LRAC* curve to the *ATC* curve associated with its larger scale.

**TABLE 1**

| Labor (students per day) | Output 1 field | Output 2 fields |
|---|---|---|
| | (pineapples per day) | |
| 0 | 0 | 0 |
| 1 | 100 | 220 |
| 2 | 220 | 460 |
| 3 | 300 | 620 |
| 4 | 360 | 740 |
| 5 | 400 | 820 |
| 6 | 420 | 860 |
| 7 | 430 | 880 |

**TABLE 2**

| TP (1 field) | ATC (1 field) | TP (2 fields) | ATC (2 fields) |
|---|---|---|---|
| 100 | 3.00 | 220 | 2.27 |
| 220 | 1.82 | 460 | 1.30 |
| 300 | 1.67 | 620 | 1.13 |
| 360 | 1.67 | 740 | 1.08 |
| 400 | 1.75 | 820 | 1.10 |
| 420 | 1.90 | 860 | 1.16 |
| 430 | 2.09 | 880 | 1.25 |

**FIGURE 1**

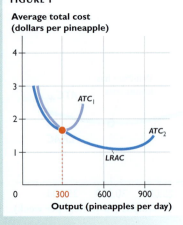

## CHAPTER SUMMARY

## Key Points

1. **Explain and distinguish between the economic and accounting measures of a firm's cost of production and profit.**

   - Firms seek to maximize economic profit, which is total revenue minus total cost.
   - Total cost equals opportunity cost—the sum of explicit costs and implicit costs, which include normal profit.

2. **Explain the relationship between a firm's output and labor employed in the short run.**

   - In the short run, the firm can change the output it produces by changing only the quantity of labor it employs.
   - A total product curve shows the limits to the output that the firm can produce with a given quantity of capital and different quantities of labor.
   - As the quantity of labor increases, the marginal product of labor increases initially but eventually decreases—the law of decreasing returns.

3. **Explain the relationship between a firm's output and costs in the short run.**

   - As total product increases, total fixed cost is constant, and total variable cost and total cost increase.
   - As total product increases, average fixed cost decreases; average variable cost, average total cost, and marginal cost decrease at small outputs and increase at large outputs so their curves are U-shaped.

4. **Derive and explain a firm's long-run average cost curve.**

   - In the long run, the firm can change the size of its plant.
   - Long-run cost is the cost of production when all inputs have been adjusted to produce at the lowest attainable cost.
   - The long-run average cost curve traces out the lowest attainable average total cost at each output when both the plant size and labor can be varied.
   - The long-run average cost curve slopes downward with economies of scale and upward with diseconomies of scale.

## Key Terms

# CHAPTER CHECKPOINT

## Study Plan Problems and Applications

1. Joe runs a shoe shine stand at the airport. Joe has no skills, no job experience, and no alternative job. Entrepreneurs in the shoe shine business earn $10,000 a year. Joe pays the rent of $2,000 a year, and his total revenue is $15,000 a year. He borrowed $1,000 at 20 percent a year to buy equipment. At the end of one year, Joe was offered $500 for his business and all its equipment. Calculate Joe's annual explicit costs, implicit costs, and economic profit.

2. Len's body board factory rents equipment for shaping boards and hires students. Table 1 sets out Len's total product schedule. Construct Len's marginal product and average product schedules. Over what range of workers do marginal returns increase?

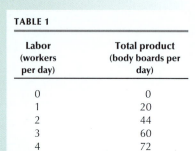

**TABLE 1**

| Labor (workers per day) | Total product (body boards per day) |
|---|---|
| 0 | 0 |
| 1 | 20 |
| 2 | 44 |
| 3 | 60 |
| 4 | 72 |

Use the following information to work Problems **3** to **6**.

Len's body board factory pays $60 a day for equipment and $200 a day to each student it hires. Table 1 sets out Len's total product schedule.

3. Construct Len's total variable cost and total cost schedules. What does the difference between total cost and total variable cost at each output equal?

4. Construct the average fixed cost, average variable cost, and average total cost schedules and the marginal cost schedule.

5. At what output is Len's average total cost at a minimum? At what output is Len's average variable cost at a minimum?

6. Explain why the output at which average variable cost is at a minimum is smaller than the output at which average total cost is at a minimum.

7. Table 2 shows the costs incurred at Pete's peanut farm. Complete the table.

**TABLE 2**

| Labor | TP | TVC | TC | AFC | AVC | ATC | MC |
|---|---|---|---|---|---|---|---|
| 0 | 0 | 0 | 100 | | | | |
| 1 | 10 | 35 | | | | | |
| 2 | 24 | 70 | | | | | |
| 3 | 38 | 105 | | | | | |
| 4 | 44 | 140 | | | | | |

8. **Gap will focus on smaller scale stores**
   Gap has too many 12,500 square feet stores. The target store size is 6,000 to 10,000 square feet, so Gap plans to combine previously separate stores. Some Gap Body, Gap Adult, and Gap Kids stores will be combined in one store.
   Source: CNN, June 10, 2008

   Thinking of a Gap store as a production plant, explain why Gap is reducing the size of its stores. Is Gap making a long-run decision or a short-run decision? Is Gap taking advantage of economies of scale?

9. Read *Eye on Retailers' Costs* on p. 311 and draw a graph to show how the retailers' cost curves would change if they introduced cost-saving self-checkouts.

# Instructor Assignable Problems and Applications

**1.** If the *ATC* curves of a Wal-Mart store and a 7-Eleven store are like those in *Eye on Retailers' Costs* on p. 308, and if each type of store operates at its minimum *ATC*, which store has the lower total cost? How can you be sure? Which has the lower marginal cost? How can you be sure? Sketch each firm's marginal cost curve.

**2.** Sonya used to earn $25,000 a year selling real estate, but she now sells greeting cards. The return to entrepreneurship in the greeting cards industry is $14,000 a year. Over the year, Sonya bought $10,000 worth of cards from manufacturers and sold them for $58,000. Sonya rents a shop for $5,000 a year and spends $1,000 on utilities and office expenses. Sonya owns a cash register, which she bought for $2,000 with funds from her savings account. Her bank pays 3 percent a year on savings accounts. At the end of the year, Sonya was offered $1,600 for her cash register. Calculate Sonya's explicit costs, implicit costs, and economic profit.

Use the following information to work Problems **3** to **5**.

Yolanda runs a bullfrog farm. When she employs 1 person, she produces 1,000 bullfrogs a week. When she hires a second worker, her total product doubles. Her total product doubles again when she hires a third worker. When she hires a fourth worker, her total product increases but by only 1,000 bullfrogs. Yolanda pays $1,000 a week for equipment and $500 a week to each worker she hires.

**3.** Construct Yolanda's marginal product and average product schedules. Over what range of workers does Yolanda's experience increasing marginal returns?

**4.** Construct Yolanda's total variable cost and total cost schedules. Calculate Yolanda's total fixed cost.

**5.** At what output is Yolanda's average total cost at a minimum?

**6.** Table 1 shows some of the costs incurred at Bill's Bakery. Calculate the values of *A*, *B*, *C*, *D*, and *E*. Show your work.

**TABLE 1**

| Labor | TP | TVC | TC | AFC | AVC | ATC | MC |
|---|---|---|---|---|---|---|---|
| 1 | 100 | 350 | 850 | *C* | 3.50 | *D* | |
| | | | | | | | 2.50 |
| 2 | 240 | 700 | *B* | 2.08 | 2.92 | 5.00 | |
| | | | | | | | *E* |
| 3 | 380 | *A* | 1,550 | 1.32 | 2.76 | 4.08 | |
| | | | | | | | 5.83 |
| 4 | 440 | 1,400 | 1,900 | 1.14 | 3.18 | 4.32 | |
| | | | | | | | 11.67 |
| 5 | 470 | 1,750 | 2,250 | 1.06 | 3.72 | 4.79 | |

**7. Grain prices go the way of the oil price**
Rising grain prices have started to impact the price of breakfast for millions of Americans—cereal prices are rising.

Source: *The Economist*, July 21, 2007

Explain how the rising price of grain affects the average total cost and marginal cost of producing breakfast cereals.

## Critical Thinking Discussion Questions

1. **Ford idles plant**

   Wixom, with Lincoln as its car model, was the most profitable plant in the industry during the 1980s. Due to Lincoln's falling sales, Ford announced on January 23, 2006, that the Wixom plant would be idled in 2007 as part of the way forward.

   Source: Wikipedia, Wixom Assembly Plant

   a. What costs does Ford avoid by idling its Wixom plant but not dismantling or selling it?
   b. What costs does Ford avoid by dismantling or selling its Wixom plant?
   c. Someone tells you that Ford should be able to maintain its Wixom plant operations indefinitely. Explain why that person is wrong.
   d. Draw a graph of the cost curves for the Wixom plant and use your graph to explain why a low output rate means a high average total cost.
   e. If Ford's research and development department developed a new machine that increased the productivity of the Wixom plant, how would the cost of production change?

2. **Airlines seek out new ways to save on fuel as costs soar**

   The financial pain of higher fuel prices is particularly acute for airlines because it is their single biggest expense. Airlines pump about 7,000 gallons into a Boeing 737 and about 60,000 gallons into the bigger 747 jet. Each generation of aircraft is more efficient: an Airbus A330 long-range jet uses 38% less fuel than the DC-10 it replaced, while the Airbus A319 medium range jet is 27% more efficient than the DC-9 it replaced.

   Source: *The New York Times*, 11 June 2008

   a. Is the price of fuel a fixed cost or a variable cost for an airline?
   b. Explain how an increase in the price of fuel changes an airline's total costs, average costs, and marginal cost.
   c. Draw a graph to show the effects of an increase in the price of fuel on an airline's *TFC, TVC, AFC, AVC,* and *MC* curves.
   d. Explain how a technological advance that makes an airplane engine more fuel-efficient changes an airline's total product, marginal product, and average product curves.
   e. Draw a graph to illustrate the effects of a more fuel-efficient aircraft on an airline's *TP, MP,* and *AP* curves.
   f. Explain how a technological advance that makes an airplane engine more fuel-efficient changes an airline's average variable cost, marginal cost, and average total cost.
   g. Draw a graph to illustrate how a technological advance that makes an airplane engine more fuel-efficient, changes an airline's *AVC, MC,* and *ATC* curves.

Where have all the record stores gone?

# Perfect Competition

**When you have completed your study of this chapter, you will be able to**

**1** Explain a perfectly competitive firm's profit-maximizing choices and derive its supply curve.

**2** Explain how output, price, and profit are determined in the short run.

**3** Explain how output, price, and profit are determined in the long run and explain why perfect competition is efficient.

# MARKET TYPES

The four market types are

- Perfect competition
- Monopoly
- Monopolistic competition
- Oligopoly

## ■ Perfect Competition

**Perfect competition**
A market in which there are many firms, each selling an identical product; many buyers; no barriers to the entry of new firms into the industry; no advantage to established firms; and buyers and sellers are well informed about prices.

**Perfect competition** exists when

- Many firms sell an identical product to many buyers.
- There are no barriers to entry into (or exit from) the market.
- Established firms have no advantage over new firms.
- Sellers and buyers are well informed about prices.

These conditions that define perfect competition arise when the market demand for the product is large relative to the output of a single producer. This situation arises when economies of scale are absent so the efficient scale of each firm is small. But a large market and the absence of economies of scale are not sufficient to create perfect competition. In addition, each firm must produce a good or service that has no characteristics that are unique to that firm so that consumers don't care from which firm they buy. Firms in perfect competition all look the same to the buyer.

Wheat farming, fishing, wood pulping and paper milling, the manufacture of paper cups and plastic shopping bags, lawn service, dry cleaning, and the provision of laundry services are all examples of highly competitive industries.

## ■ Other Market Types

**Monopoly**
A market in which one firm sells a good or service that has no close substitutes and a barrier blocks the entry of new firms.

**Monopoly** arises when one firm sells a good or service that has no close substitutes and a barrier blocks the entry of new firms. In some places, the phone, gas, electricity, and water suppliers are local monopolies—monopolies that are restricted to a given location. For many years, a global firm called DeBeers had a near international monopoly in diamonds. Microsoft has a near monopoly in producing the operating system for a personal computer.

**Monopolistic competition**
A market in which a large number of firms compete by making similar but slightly different products.

**Monopolistic competition** arises when a large number of firms compete by making similar but slightly different products. Each firm is the sole producer of the particular version of the good in question. For example, in the market for running shoes, Nike, Reebok, Fila, Asics, New Balance, and many others make their own versions of the perfect shoe. The term "monopolistic competition" reminds us that each firm has a monopoly on a particular brand of shoe but the firms compete with each other.

**Oligopoly**
A market in which a small number of interdependent firms compete.

**Oligopoly** arises when a small number of *interdependent* firms compete. Airplane manufacture is an example of oligopoly. Oligopolies might produce almost identical products, such as Duracell and Energizer batteries; or they might produce differentiated products, such as the colas produced by Coke and Pepsi.

We study perfect competition in this chapter, monopoly in Chapter 12, and monopolistic competition and oligopoly in Chapter 13.

## 11.1  A FIRM'S PROFIT-MAXIMIZING CHOICES

A firm's objective is to maximize *economic profit,* which is equal to *total revenue* minus the *total cost* of production. *Normal profit,* the return that the firm's entrepreneur can obtain on average, is part of the firm's cost.

In the short run, a firm achieves its objective by deciding the quantity to produce. This quantity influences the firm's total revenue, total cost, and economic profit. In the long run, a firm achieves its objective by deciding whether to enter or exit a market.

These are the key decisions that a firm in perfect competition makes. Such a firm does *not* choose the price at which to sell its output. The firm in perfect competition is a **price taker**—it cannot influence the price of its product.

**Price taker**
A firm that cannot influence the price of the good or service that it produces.

### ■ Price Taker

To see why a firm in perfect competition is a price taker, imagine that you are a wheat farmer in Kansas. You have a thousand acres under cultivation—which sounds like a lot. But then you go on a drive through Colorado, Oklahoma, Texas, and back up to Nebraska and the Dakotas. You find unbroken stretches of wheat covering millions of acres. And you know that there are similar vistas in Canada, Argentina, Australia, and Ukraine. Your thousand acres are a drop in the ocean. Nothing makes your wheat any better than any other farmer's, and all the buyers of wheat know the price they must pay. If the going price of wheat is $4 a bushel, you are stuck with that price. You can't get a higher price than $4, and you have no incentive to offer it for less than $4 because you can sell your entire output at that price.

The producers of most agricultural products are price takers. We'll illustrate perfect competition with another agriculture example: the market for maple syrup. The next time you pour syrup on your pancakes, think about the competitive market that gets this product from the sap of the maple tree to your table!

Dave's Maple Syrup is one of more than 11,000 similar firms in the maple syrup market of North America. Dave is a price taker. Like the Kansas wheat farmer, he can sell any quantity he chooses at the going price but none above that price. Dave faces a *perfectly elastic* demand. The demand for Dave's syrup is perfectly elastic because syrup from Don Harlow, Casper Sugar Shack, and all the other maple farms in North America are *perfect substitutes* for Dave's syrup.

*Wheat farmers and maple syrup farmers are price takers.*

We'll explore Dave's decisions and their implications for the way a competitive market works. We begin by defining some revenue concepts.

### ■ Revenue Concepts

In perfect competition, market demand and market supply determine the price. A firm's *total revenue* equals this given price multiplied by the quantity sold. A firm's **marginal revenue** is the change in total revenue that results from a one-unit increase in the quantity sold.

**Marginal revenue**
The change in total revenue that results from a one-unit increase in the quantity sold.

#### In perfect competition, marginal revenue equals price.

The reason is that the firm can sell any quantity it chooses at the going market price. So if the firm sells one more unit, it sells it for the market price and total revenue increases by that amount. This increase in total revenue is marginal revenue.

The table in Figure 11.1 illustrates the equality of marginal revenue and price. The price of syrup is $8 a can. Total revenue is equal to the price multiplied by the quantity sold. So if Dave sells 10 cans, his total revenue is 10 × $8 = $80. If the quantity sold increases from 10 cans to 11 cans, total revenue increases from $80 to $88, so marginal revenue is $8 a can, the same as the price.

Figure 11.1 illustrates price determination and revenue in the perfectly competitive market. Market demand and market supply in part (a) determine the market price. Dave is a price taker, so he sells his syrup for the market price. The demand curve for Dave's syrup is the horizontal line at the market price in part (b). Because price equals marginal revenue, the demand curve for Dave's syrup is Dave's marginal revenue curve (*MR*). The total revenue curve (*TR*), in part (c), shows the total revenue at each quantity sold. Because he sells each can for the market price, the total revenue curve is an upward-sloping straight line.

## ■ Profit-Maximizing Output

As output increases, total revenue increases, but total cost also increases. Because of *decreasing marginal returns* (see Chapter 10, pp. 296–298), total cost eventually increases faster than total revenue. There is one output level that maximizes economic profit, and a perfectly competitive firm chooses this output level.

## ■ FIGURE 11.1

### Demand, Price, and Revenue in Perfect Competition

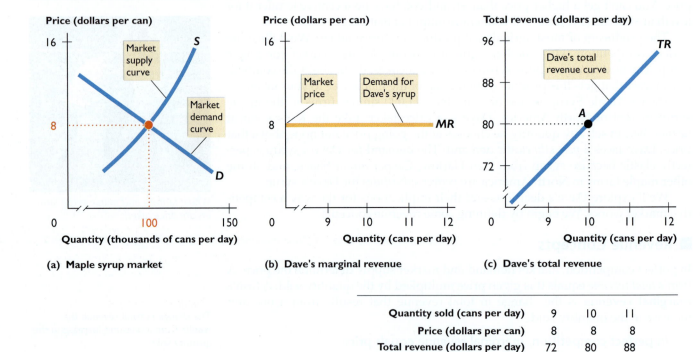

(a) Maple syrup market

(b) Dave's marginal revenue

(c) Dave's total revenue

| Quantity sold (cans per day) | 9 | 10 | 11 |
|---|---|---|---|
| Price (dollars per can) | 8 | 8 | 8 |
| Total revenue (dollars per day) | 72 | 80 | 88 |
| Marginal revenue (dollars per can) | | 8 | 8 |

Part (a) shows the market for maple syrup. The market price is $8 a can. The table calculates total revenue and marginal revenue.

Part (b) shows the demand curve for Dave's syrup, which is Dave's marginal revenue curve (*MR*).

Part (c) shows Dave's total revenue curve (*TR*). Point *A* corresponds to the second column of the table.

One way to find the profit-maximizing output is to use a firm's total revenue and total cost curves. Profit is maximized at the output level at which total revenue exceeds total cost by the largest amount. Figure 11.2 shows how to do this for Dave's Maple Syrup.

The table lists Dave's total revenue, total cost, and economic profit at different output levels. Figure 11.2(a) shows the total revenue and total cost curves. These curves are graphs of the numbers shown in the first three columns of the table. The total revenue curve (*TR*) is the same as that in Figure 11.1(c). The total cost curve (*TC*) is similar to the one that you met in Chapter 10 (p. 302). Figure 11.2(b) is an economic profit curve.

Dave makes an economic profit on outputs between 4 and 13 cans of syrup a day. At outputs of fewer than 4 cans a day and more than 13 cans a day, he incurs an economic loss. Outputs of 4 cans and 13 cans are *break-even points*—points at which total cost equals total revenue and economic profit is zero.

The profit curve is at its highest when the vertical distance between the *TR* and *TC* curves is greatest. In this example, profit maximization occurs at an output of 10 cans of syrup a day. At this output, Dave's economic profit is $29 a day.

## FIGURE 11.2

### Total Revenue, Total Cost, and Economic Profit

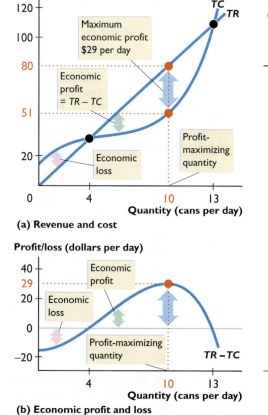

**(a) Revenue and cost**

**(b) Economic profit and loss**

| Quantity (Q) (cans per day) | Total revenue (TR) | Total cost (TC) | Economic profit (TR − TC) |
|---|---|---|---|
| | (dollars per day) | | |
| 0 | 0 | 15 | −15 |
| 1 | 8 | 22 | −14 |
| 2 | 16 | 27 | −11 |
| 3 | 24 | 30 | −6 |
| **4** | **32** | **32** | **0** |
| 5 | 40 | 33 | 7 |
| 6 | 48 | 34 | 14 |
| 7 | 56 | 36 | 20 |
| 8 | 64 | 40 | 24 |
| 9 | 72 | 44 | 28 |
| **10** | **80** | **51** | **29** |
| 11 | 88 | 60 | 28 |
| 12 | 96 | 76 | 20 |
| **13** | **104** | **104** | **0** |
| 14 | 112 | 144 | −32 |

The table calculates Dave's economic profit at each output of syrup.

In part (a), economic profit is the vertical distance between the total cost (*TC*) and total revenue (*TR*) curves.

In part (b), economic profit is the height of the profit curve.

If Dave produces less than 4 cans of syrup a day, he incurs an economic loss.

If Dave produces between 4 and 13 cans of syrup a day, he makes an economic profit. Dave's maximum economic profit is $29 a day when he produces 10 cans of syrup a day.

## ■ Marginal Analysis and the Supply Decision

Another way to find the profit-maximizing output is to use *marginal analysis,* which compares marginal revenue, *MR,* with marginal cost, *MC.* As output increases, marginal revenue is constant but marginal cost eventually increases.

If marginal revenue exceeds marginal cost ($MR > MC$), then the revenue from selling one more unit exceeds the cost of producing that unit and an *increase* in output increases economic profit. If marginal revenue is less than marginal cost ($MR < MC$), then the revenue from selling one more unit is less than the cost of producing that unit and a *decrease* in output increases economic profit. If marginal revenue equals marginal cost ($MR = MC$), then the revenue from selling one more unit equals the cost incurred to produce that unit. Economic profit is maximized and either an increase or a decrease in output *decreases* economic profit. The rule $MR = MC$ is a prime example of marginal analysis.

Figure 11.3 illustrates these propositions. If Dave increases output from 9 cans to 10 cans a day, marginal revenue ($8) exceeds marginal cost ($7), so by producing the 10th can economic profit increases. The last column of the table shows that economic profit increases from $28 to $29. The blue area in the figure shows the increase in economic profit when production increases from 9 to 10 cans per day.

If Dave increases production from 10 cans to 11 cans of syrup a day, marginal revenue ($8) is less than marginal cost ($9), so by producing the 11th can, economic profit decreases. The last column of the table shows that economic profit decreases from $29 to $28. The red area in the figure shows the economic loss that arises from increasing production from 10 to 11 cans per day.

■ **FIGURE 11.3**

Profit-Maximizing Output

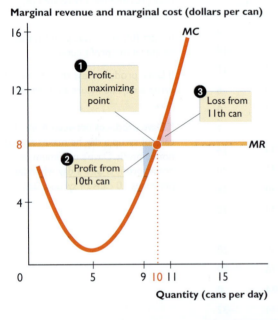

| Quantity (Q) (cans per day) | Total revenue (TR) (dollars per day) | Marginal revenue (MR) (dollars per can) | Total cost (TC) (dollars per day) | Marginal cost (MC) (dollars per can) | Economic profit (TR – TC) (dollars per day) |
|---|---|---|---|---|---|
| 8 | 64 | | 40 | | 24 |
| | | 8 | | 4 | |
| 9 | 72 | | 44 | | 28 |
| | | 8 | | 7 | |
| 10 | 80 | | 51 | | 29 |
| | | 8 | | 9 | |
| 11 | 88 | | 60 | | 28 |
| | | 8 | | 16 | |
| 12 | 96 | | 76 | | 20 |

❶ Profit is maximized when marginal revenue equals marginal cost at 10 cans of syrup a day. ❷ If output increases from 9 to 10 cans of syrup a day, marginal cost is $7, which is less than the marginal revenue of $8, and profit increases. ❸ If output increases from 10 to 11 cans of syrup a day, marginal cost is $9, which exceeds the marginal revenue of $8, and profit decreases.

Dave maximizes economic profit by producing 10 cans of syrup a day, the quantity at which marginal revenue equals marginal cost.

A firm's profit-maximizing output is its *quantity supplied*. Dave's *quantity supplied* at a price of $8 a can is 10 cans a day. If the price were higher than $8 a can, he would increase production. If the price were lower than $8 a can, he would decrease production. These profit-maximizing responses to different prices are the foundation of the law of supply:

**Other things remaining the same, the higher the price of a good, the greater is the quantity supplied of that good.**

## ■ Temporary Shutdown Decision

Sometimes, the price falls so low that a firm cannot cover its costs. What does the firm do in such a situation? The answer depends on whether the firm expects the low price to be permanent or temporary.

If a firm incurs an economic loss that it believes is permanent and sees no prospect of ending, the firm exits the market. We'll study this action later in this chapter when we look at the firm's decisions in the long run (pp. 332–335).

If a firm incurs an economic loss that it believes is temporary, it remains in the market, but it might temporarily shut down. To decide whether to produce or to shut down, the firm compares the loss it would incur in the two situations.

### Loss When Shut Down

If the firm shuts down temporarily, it receives no revenue and incurs no variable costs. The firm still incurs fixed costs. So, if a firm shuts down, it incurs an economic loss equal to total fixed cost. This loss is the largest that a firm need incur.

### Loss When Producing

A firm that produces an output receives revenue and incurs both fixed costs and variable costs. The firm incurs an economic loss equal to total fixed cost *plus* total variable cost *minus* total revenue. If total revenue exceeds total variable cost, the firm's economic loss is less than total fixed cost. But if total revenue is less than total variable cost, the firm's economic loss will exceed total fixed cost.

### The Shutdown Point

If total revenue is less than total variable cost, a firm shuts down temporarily and limits its loss to an amount equal to total fixed cost. If total revenue just equals total variable cost, a firm is indifferent between producing and shutting down. This situation arises when price equals minimum average variable cost and the firm produces the quantity at which average variable cost is a minimum—called the **shutdown point.**

Figure 11.4 illustrates the firm's shutdown decision and the shutdown point that we've just described for Dave's maple syrup farm. Dave's average variable cost curve is *AVC* and his marginal cost curve is *MC*. Average variable cost has a minimum of $3 a can when output is 7 cans a day. The *MC* curve intersects the *AVC* curve at its minimum. (We explained this relationship between the marginal and average values of a variable in Chapter 10; see pp. 298–299 and pp. 302–304.) The figure shows the marginal revenue curve *MR* when the price is $3 a can, a *price equal to minimum average variable cost*.

**Shutdown point**
The point at which price equals minimum average variable cost and the quantity produced is that at which average variable cost is at its minimum.

■ **FIGURE 11.4**

The Shutdown Decision

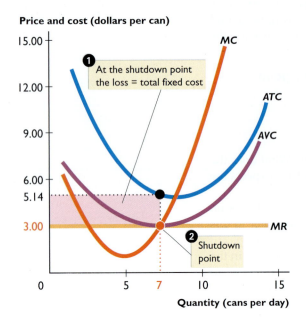

Price and cost (dollars per can)

| Quantity (Q) (cans per day) | Total revenue (TR) | Total variable cost (TVC) | Total fixed cost (TFC) | Total cost (TC) | Economic profit (TR – TC) |
|---|---|---|---|---|---|
| | | (dollars per day) | | | |
| 6 | 18 | 19 | 15 | 34 | –16 |
| 7 | 21 | 21 | 15 | 36 | –15 |
| 8 | 24 | 25 | 15 | 40 | –16 |

**1** The shutdown point is at minimum average variable cost. At a price below minimum average variable cost, the firm shuts down and produces no output. At a price equal to minimum average variable cost, the firm is indifferent between shutting down and producing no output or producing the output at minimum average variable cost. Either way, **2** the firm minimizes its economic loss and incurs a loss equal to total fixed cost.

If Dave produces at the shutdown point, he produces 7 cans a day and sells them for $3 a can. He incurs an economic loss equal to $2.14 a can and a total economic loss of $15 a day, which equals his total fixed cost. If Dave shuts down, he also incurs an economic loss equal to total fixed cost.

The table lists Dave's total revenue, total variable cost, total fixed cost, total cost, and economic profit at three output levels. The middle output, 7 cans a day, is that at which Dave's average variable cost is at its minimum—$3 a can. By examining the numbers in the table, you can see that when the price is $3 a can, Dave incurs a loss equal to total fixed cost by producing 7 cans a day.

### ■ The Firm's Short-Run Supply Curve

A perfectly competitive firm's short-run supply curve shows how the firm's profit-maximizing output varies as the price varies, other things remaining the same. This supply curve is based on the marginal analysis and shutdown decision that we've just explored.

Figure 11.5 derives Dave's supply curve. Part (a) shows the marginal cost and average variable cost curves, and part (b) shows the supply curve. There is a direct link between the marginal cost and average variable cost curves and the firm's supply curve. Let's see what that link is.

In Figure 11.5(a), if the price is above minimum average variable cost, Dave maximizes profit by producing the output at which marginal cost equals marginal revenue, which also equals price. We determine the quantity produced at each price from the marginal cost curve. At a price of $8 a can, the marginal revenue curve is $MR_1$ and Dave maximizes profit by producing 10 cans a day. If the price rises to $12 a can, the marginal revenue curve is $MR_2$ and Dave increases production to 11 cans a day.

If price equals minimum average variable cost, Dave maximizes profit (minimizes loss) by either producing the quantity at the shutdown point or shutting down and producing no output. But if the price is below minimum average variable cost, Dave shuts down and produces no output.

Figure 11.5(b) shows Dave's short-run supply curve. At prices that exceed minimum average variable cost, the supply curve is the same as the marginal cost curve. At prices below minimum average variable cost, Dave shuts down and produces nothing. His supply curve runs along the vertical axis. At a price of $3 a can, Dave is indifferent between shutting down and producing 7 cans a day at the shutdown point ($T$). Either way, he incurs a loss equal to total fixed cost.

So far, we have studied one firm in isolation. We have seen that the firm's profit-maximizing actions depend on the price, which the firm takes as given. In the next section, you'll learn how market supply is determined.

■ **FIGURE 11.5**

A Perfectly Competitive Firm's Supply Curve

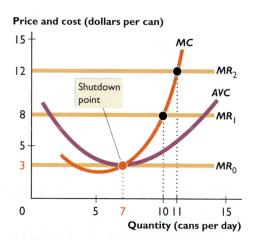

**(a) Marginal cost and average variable cost**

**(b) Firm's supply curve**

Part (a) shows that at $12 a can, Dave produces 11 cans a day; at $8 a can, he produces 10 cans a day; and at $3 a can, he produces either 7 cans a day or nothing. At any price below $3 a can, Dave produces nothing. The minimum average variable cost is the shutdown point.

Part (b) shows Dave's supply curve. At $3 a can, Dave is indifferent between producing the quantity at the shutdown point $T$ and not producing. At all prices above $3 a can, Dave's supply curve is made up of the marginal cost curve, in part (a), *above* minimum average variable cost. At all prices below $3 a can, Dave produces nothing and his supply curve runs along the vertical axis.

**CHECKPOINT 11.1**

**Explain a perfectly competitive firm's profit-maximizing choices and derive its supply curve.**

## Practice Problems

1. Sarah's Salmon Farm produced 1,000 fish last week. The marginal cost was $30 a fish, average variable cost was $20 a fish, and the market price was $25 a fish. Did Sarah maximize profit? If Sarah did not maximize profit and if nothing has changed will she increase or decrease the number of fish she produces to maximize her profit this week?

Use the following information to work Problems **2** to **4**.

Trout farming is a perfectly competitive industry and all trout farms have the same cost curves. When the market price is $25 a fish, farms maximize profit by producing 200 fish a week. At this output, average total cost is $20 a fish, and average variable cost is $15 a fish. Minimum average variable cost is $12 a fish.

2. If the price falls to $20 a fish, will a farm produce 200 fish a week?

3. If the price falls to $12 a fish, what will the trout farmer do?

4. What are two points on a trout farm's supply curve?

## In the News

**BHP Billiton to axe 6,000 jobs**
The price of coal has fallen to $125 a ton from $300 a ton. BHP Billiton will cut production, lay off 6,000 workers, and close some mines for six months.

Source: FT.com, January 21, 2009

As BHP responded to the fall in price, how did its marginal cost change? What is minimum average variable cost in the mines that closed?

## Solutions to Practice Problems

1. Profit is maximized when marginal cost equals marginal revenue. In perfect competition, marginal revenue equals the market price and is $25 a fish. Because marginal cost exceeded marginal revenue, Sarah did not maximize profit. To maximize profit, Sarah will decrease her output until marginal cost falls to $25 a fish (Figure 1).

2. The farm will produce fewer than 200 fish a week. The marginal cost curve slopes upward, so to lower marginal cost to $20, the farm cuts production.

3. If the price falls to $12 a fish, farms cut output until marginal cost equals $12. Because $12 a fish is also minimum average variable cost, farms are at the shutdown point—some farms produce the profit-maximizing output and others produce nothing.

4. One point on a farmer's supply curve is 200 fish at $25 a fish. Another point is the shutdown point (Solution **3**) or zero at a price below $12 a fish.

## Solution to In the News

Marginal cost decreased from $300 a ton to $125 a ton. The mines that closed temporarily were at the shutdown point. The price of $125 a ton is equal to or below the firm's minimum average variable cost.

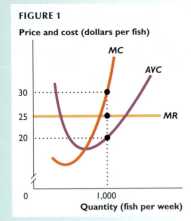

**FIGURE 1**

Price and cost (dollars per fish)

## 11.2  OUTPUT, PRICE, AND PROFIT IN THE SHORT RUN

Demand and supply determine the price and quantity in a perfectly competitive market. We first study short-run supply when the number of firms is fixed.

### ■ Market Supply in the Short Run

The market supply curve in the short run shows the quantity supplied at each price by a fixed number of firms. The quantity supplied at a given price is the sum of the quantities supplied by all firms at that price.

Figure 11.6 shows the supply curve for the competitive syrup market. In this example, the market consists of 10,000 firms exactly like Dave's Maple Syrup. The table shows how the market supply schedule is constructed. The shutdown point occurs at a price of $3 a can. At prices below $3 a can, every firm in the market shuts down; the quantity supplied is zero. At a price of $3 a can, each firm is indifferent between shutting down and producing nothing or operating and producing 7 cans a day. The quantity supplied by each firm is *either* 0 or 7 cans, and the quantity supplied in the market is *between* 0 (all firms shut down) and 70,000 (all firms produce 7 cans a day each). At prices above $3 a can, we sum the quantities supplied by the 10,000 firms, so the quantity supplied in the market is 10,000 times the quantity supplied by one firm.

At prices below $3 a can, the market supply curve runs along the price axis. Supply is perfectly inelastic. At $3 a can, the market supply curve is horizontal. Supply is perfectly elastic. Above $3 a can, the supply curve is upward sloping.

### ■ FIGURE 11.6

The Market Supply Curve

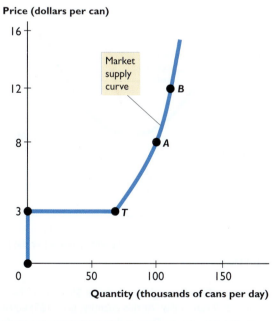

| | Price | Dave's quantity supplied | Market quantity supplied |
|---|---|---|---|
| | (dollars per can) | (cans per day) | |
| B | 12 | 11 | 110,000 |
| A | 8 | 10 | 100,000 |
| T | 3 | 0 or 7 | 0 to 70,000 |

A market with 10,000 identical firms has a supply schedule like that of an individual firm, but the quantity supplied is 10,000 times greater. Market supply is perfectly elastic at the price at which the shutdown point occurs.

### ■ Short-Run Equilibrium in Normal Times

Market demand and market supply determine the price and quantity bought and sold. Figure 11.7(a) shows a short-run equilibrium in the syrup market. The market supply curve $S$ is the same as that in Figure 11.6.

If the demand curve $D_1$ shows market demand, the equilibrium price is $5 a can. Although market demand and market supply determine this price, each firm takes the price as given and produces its profit-maximizing output, which is 9 cans a day. Because the market has 10,000 firms, market output is 90,000 cans a day.

Figure 11.7(b) shows the situation that Dave faces. The price is $5 a can, so Dave's marginal revenue is constant at $5 a can. Dave maximizes profit by producing 9 cans a day.

Figure 11.7(b) also shows Dave's average total cost curve ($ATC$). Recall that average total cost is the cost per unit produced. It equals total cost divided by the quantity of output produced.

Here, when Dave produces 9 cans a day, his average total cost is $5 a can, exactly the same as the market price. So Dave sells syrup for exactly the same price as his average cost of production and economic profit is zero.

Making zero economic profit means that Dave earns normal profit from running his business.

The short-run equilibrium in which a firm makes zero economic profit is just one of three possible situations. A competitive market might also deliver a positive economic profit or an economic loss. Let's look at these other two cases.

### ■ FIGURE 11.7

Zero Economic Profit in the Short Run

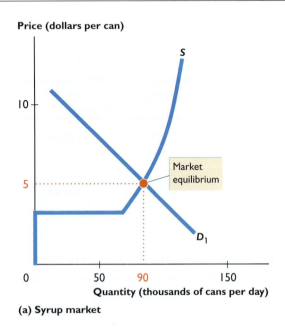

**(a) Syrup market**

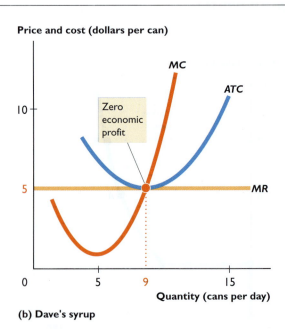

**(b) Dave's syrup**

In part (a), with the market demand curve $D_1$ and the market supply curve $S$, the equilibrium market price of syrup is $5 a can.

In part (b), Dave's marginal revenue is $5 a can, so he produces 9 cans a day. At this quantity, price ($5) equals average total cost, so Dave makes zero economic profit.

## ■ Short-Run Equilibrium in Good Times

Market demand might be greater or less than $D_1$ in Figure 11.7 and the price might be higher or lower than $5 a can. Figure 11.8(a) shows another short-run equilibrium in the syrup market. The supply curve $S$ is the same as that in Figure 11.6.

If the demand curve $D_2$ shows market demand, the equilibrium price is $8 a can. Although market demand and market supply determine this price, each firm takes the price as given and produces its profit-maximizing output, which is 10 cans a day. Because the market has 10,000 firms, market output is 100,000 cans a day.

Figure 11.8(b) shows the situation that Dave faces. The price is $8 a can, so Dave's marginal revenue is constant at $8 a can. Dave maximizes profit by producing 10 cans a day.

Figure 11.8(b) also shows Dave's average total cost curve ($ATC$). Recall that average total cost is the cost per unit produced. It equals total cost divided by the quantity of output produced. Here, when Dave produces 10 cans a day, his average total cost is $5.10 a can. So the price of $8 a can exceeds average total cost by $2.90 a can. This amount is Dave's economic profit per can.

If we multiply the economic profit per can of $2.90 by the number of cans, 10 a day, we arrive at Dave's economic profit, which is $29 a day.

The blue rectangle shows this economic profit. The height of that rectangle is the profit per can, $2.90, and the length is the quantity of cans, 10 a day, so the area of the rectangle (height × length) measures Dave's economic profit of $29 a day.

## ■ FIGURE 11.8

### Positive Economic Profit in the Short Run

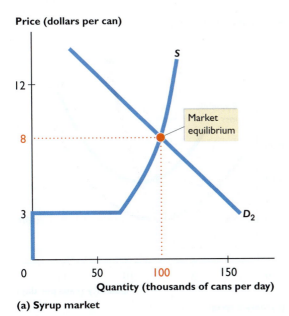

**(a) Syrup market**

In part (a), with the market demand curve $D_2$ and the market supply curve $S$, the equilibrium market price of syrup is $8 a can.

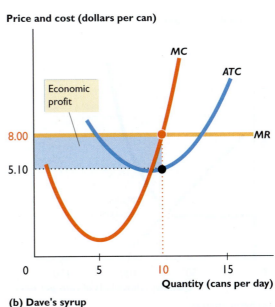

**(b) Dave's syrup**

In part (b), marginal revenue is $8 a can. Dave produces 10 cans a day. Because price ($8) exceeds average total cost ($5.10), Dave makes a positive economic profit.

### ■ Short-Run Equilibrium in Bad Times

Figure 11.9 shows the syrup market in a loss-incurring situation. The market demand curve is now $D_3$. The market still has 10,000 firms and their costs are the same as before, so the market supply curve, $S$, is also the same as before.

With the demand and supply curves shown in Figure 11.9(a), the equilibrium price of syrup is $3 a can and the equilibrium quantity is 70,000 cans a day.

Figure 11.9(b) shows the situation that Dave faces. The price is $3 a can, so Dave's marginal revenue is constant at $3 a can. Dave maximizes profit by producing 7 cans a day.

Figure 11.9(b) also shows Dave's average total cost curve (*ATC*), and you can see that when Dave produces 7 cans a day, his average total cost is $5.14 a can. Now the price of $3 a can is less than average total cost by $2.14 a can. This amount is Dave's economic loss per can. If we multiply the economic loss per can of $2.14 by the number of cans, 7 a day, we arrive at Dave's economic loss, which is shown by the red rectangle.

Figure 11.9(b) also shows Dave's average variable cost (*AVC*) curve. Notice that Dave is operating at the shutdown point. Dave might equally well produce no output. Either way, his economic loss would be equal to his total fixed cost. If the price were a bit higher than $3, Dave would still incur an economic loss, but a smaller one. And if the price were lower than $3, Dave would shut down and incur an economic loss equal to total fixed cost.

■ **FIGURE 11.9**

Economic Loss in the Short Run

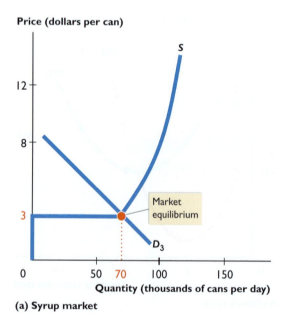

**(a) Syrup market**

In part (a), with the market demand curve $D_3$ and the market supply curve S, the equilibrium market price of syrup is $3 a can.

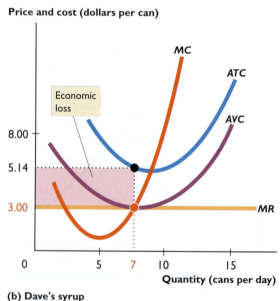

**(b) Dave's syrup**

In part (b), Dave's marginal revenue is $3 a can, so he produces 7 cans a day. At this quantity, price ($3) is less than average total cost ($5.14), so Dave incurs an economic loss shown by the red rectangle.

# CHECKPOINT 11.2

**Explain how output, price, and profit are determined in the short run.**

## Practice Problems

Tulip growing is perfectly competitive and all growers have the same costs. The market price is $25 a bunch, and each grower maximizes profit by producing 2,000 bunches a week. Average total cost is $20 a bunch, and average variable cost is $15 a bunch. Minimum average variable cost is $12 a bunch.

1.  What is the economic profit that each grower is making in the short run?

2.  What is the price at the grower's shutdown point?

3.  What is each grower's economic profit at the shutdown point?

## In the News

**Good news for wings restaurants**
With corn prices falling, the price of chicken wings is falling, and that's good news for wings restaurants.

Source: *The Wall Street Journal*, June 11, 2013

Explain how a fall in the price of corn (the main chicken feed) changes the marginal cost of producing wings and changes a farm's economic profit. What's the good news for restaurants?

## Solutions to Practice Problems

1.  The market price ($25) exceeds the average total cost ($20), so growers make an economic profit of $5 a bunch. Each grower produces 2,000 bunches a week, so a grower's economic profit is $10,000 a week. Figure 1 illustrates the situation. The grower's marginal revenue equals the market price ($25). The grower maximizes profit by producing 2,000 bunches, so at 2,000 bunches the marginal cost curve (*MC*) cuts the marginal revenue curve (*MR*). The average total cost of producing 2,000 bunches is $20, so the *ATC* curve passes through this point. Economic profit equals the area of the blue rectangle.

2.  The price at which a grower will shut down temporarily is equal to minimum average variable cost—$12 a bunch (Figure 1).

3.  At the shutdown point, the grower incurs an economic loss equal to total fixed cost. Figure 2 shows the data to calculate *TFC*. When 2,000 bunches a week are grown, *ATC* is $20 a bunch and *AVC* is $15 a bunch. *ATC* = *AFC* + *AVC*, so *AFC* is $5 a bunch. Total fixed cost equals $10,000 a week—*TFC* = *AFC* × *Q*, $5 a bunch × 2,000 bunches a week. At the shutdown point, the grower incurs an economic loss of $10,000 a week.

## Solution to In the News

A fall in the price of corn decreases the farm's marginal cost of producing chicken. The farm's marginal cost curve shifts downward and its economic profit increases. Marginal cost is now below marginal revenue, so to maximize profit the farm slides up its new *MC* curve, increasing its output. The good news for wings restaurants is: The supply of wings increases and the price falls.

**FIGURE 1**

Price and cost (dollars per bunch)

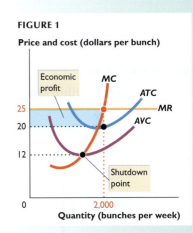

Quantity (bunches per week)

**FIGURE 2**

Price and cost (dollars per bunch)

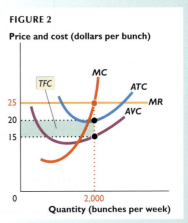

Quantity (bunches per week)

## 11.3 OUTPUT, PRICE, AND PROFIT IN THE LONG RUN

Competitive markets are in a constant state of change. Price, quantity, and economic profit fluctuate as demand and supply change. None of the three situations that we described on the previous pages—normal times, good times, or bad times—last forever in perfect competition. Market forces operate to compete away economic profits and eliminate economic losses to move the price toward the lowest possible price. That price equals minimum average total cost. In the long run, a firm in perfect competition produces at minimum average total cost and makes zero economic profit. (The firm's entrepreneur earns normal profit—part of the firm's total costs.)

Figure 11.10 illustrates a perfectly competitive market in long-run equilibrium and highlights the forces that bring the market to this situation. In Figure 11.10(a), the firm's average total cost curve is *ATC*, and the firm produces at the point of minimum average total cost—9 cans a day at an average total cost of $5 a can. If the price rises above or falls below $5 a can, market forces operate to move the price back toward $5 a can. The arrows pointing toward $5 represent these forces.

In Figure 11.10(b) the market demand curve is *D*. With this market demand, the price equals minimum average total cost only if the market supply curve is *S*. If supply is less than *S* (the supply curve is to the left of *S*), the price is above $5 a can; if supply exceeds *S* (the supply curve is to the right of *S*), the price is below $5 a can. Market forces operate to shift the supply curve back to *S*, and the arrows pointing toward *S* represent these forces.

■ **FIGURE 11.10**

Long-Run Equilibrium

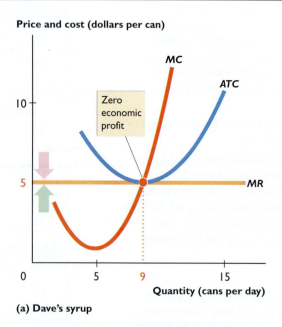

(a) Dave's syrup

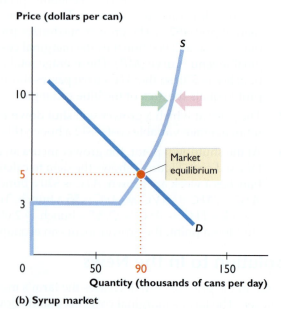

(b) Syrup market

In part (a), minimum average total cost is $5 a can. In long-run equilibrium, the price and marginal revenue are pulled to this level. The firm makes zero economic profit.

In part (b), if the price is above $5 a can, above minimum *ATC* in part (a), supply increases and the price falls. If the price is below $5, supply decreases and the price rises.

## ■ Entry and Exit

Entry and exit are the market forces that shift the supply curve and move the price to minimum average total cost in the long run. In the short run, firms might make a positive economic profit (as in Figure 11.8) or incur an economic loss (as in Figure 11.9). But in the long run, firms makes zero economic profit.

In the long run, firms respond to economic profit and economic loss by either entering or exiting a market. New firms enter a market in which the existing firms are making economic profits, and some existing firms exit a market in which firms are incurring economic losses. Temporary economic profit or temporary economic loss, like a win or loss at a casino, does not trigger entry and exit. But the prospect of persistent economic profit or economic loss does.

Entry and exit influence the market price, the quantity produced, and economic profit. The immediate effect of the decision to enter or exit a market is to shift the market supply curve. If more firms enter a market, supply increases and the market supply curve shifts rightward. If some firms exit a market, supply decreases and the market supply curve shifts leftward.

Let's see what happens when new firms enter a market.

### The Effects of Entry

Figure 11.11 shows the effects of entry. Initially, the market is in long-run equilibrium. Demand is $D_0$, supply is $S_0$, the price is $5 a can, and the quantity is 90,000 cans a day. A surge in the popularity of syrup increases demand, and the demand curve shifts to $D_1$. The price rises to $8 a can, and firms in the syrup market increase output to 100,000 cans a day and make an economic profit.

Times are good for syrup producers like Dave, so other potential syrup producers want some of the action. New firms begin to enter the market. As they do

*With the prospect of economic profit, a new business opens.*

### ■ FIGURE 11.11

### The Effects of Entry

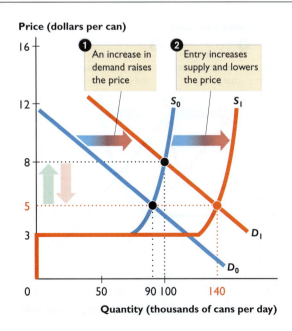

Starting in long-run equilibrium, ❶ demand increases and the market demand curve shifts from $D_0$ to $D_1$. The price rises from $5 to $8 a can.

Economic profit brings entry. ❷ As firms enter the market, the market supply curve shifts rightward, from $S_0$ to $S_1$. The equilibrium price falls from $8 to $5 a can, and the quantity produced increases from 100,000 to 140,000 cans a day.

so, supply increases and the market supply curve shifts rightward to $S_1$. With the greater market supply and unchanged market demand, the market price falls from $8 to $5 a can and the equilibrium quantity increases to 140,000 cans a day.

Market output increases, but because the price falls, Dave and the other producers decrease output. As the price falls, each firm's output gradually returns to its original level. Because the number of firms in the market increases, the market as a whole produces more.

As the price falls, each firm's economic profit decreases. When the price falls to $5 a can, economic profit disappears and each firm makes zero economic profit. The entry process stops, and the market is again in long-run equilibrium.

You have just discovered a key proposition:

**Economic profit is an incentive for new firms to enter a market, but as they do so, the price falls and the economic profit of each existing firm decreases.**

*Economic loss brings exit.*

## ■ The Effects of Exit

Figure 11.12 shows the effects of exit. Again we begin on demand curve $D_0$ and supply curve $S_0$ in long-run equilibrium. A new high-nutrition breakfast food decreases the demand for maple syrup. The demand curve shifts from $D_0$ to $D_2$. Firms' costs are the same as before, so the market supply curve is $S_0$.

With demand at $D_2$ and supply at $S_0$, the price falls to $3 a can and 70,000 cans a day are produced. The firms in the syrup market incur economic losses.

Times are tough for syrup producers, and Dave must seriously think about leaving his dream business and finding some other way of making a living. But other producers are in the same situation as Dave, and some start to exit the market while Dave is still thinking through his options.

## ■ FIGURE 11.12

The Effects of Exit

Starting in long-run equilibrium, ❶ demand decreases and the market demand curve shifts from $D_0$ to $D_2$. The price falls from $5 to $3 a can.

Economic loss brings exit. ❷ As firms exit the market, the market supply curve shifts leftward, from $S_0$ to $S_2$. The equilibrium price rises from $3 to $5 a can, and the quantity produced decreases from 70,000 to 50,000 cans a day.

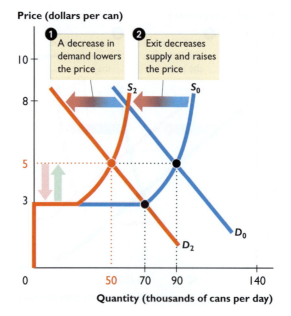

As firms exit, the market supply curve shifts leftward to $S_2$, output decreases from 70,000 to 50,000 cans and the market price rises from $3 to $5 a can.

As the price rises, Dave and each other firm that remains in the market move up along their supply curves and increase output. That is, for each firm that remains in the market, the profit-maximizing output *increases*. As the price rises and each firm sells more, economic loss decreases. When the price rises to $5 a can, each firm makes a zero economic profit. Dave earns normal profit (part of the firm's total cost) and he is happy that he can still make a living producing syrup.

You have just discovered a second key proposition:

**Economic loss is an incentive for firms to exit a market, but as they do so, the price rises and the economic loss of each remaining firm decreases.**

## ■ Change in Demand

Initially, a competitive market is in long-run equilibrium and the firms are making zero economic profit (and entrepreneurs are earning normal profit). Now market demand increases. The market price rises, firms increase production to keep marginal cost equal to price, and firms make an economic profit. The market is now in short-run equilibrium but not in long-run equilibrium.

Economic profit is an incentive for new firms to enter the market. As firms enter, market supply increases and the market price falls. With a lower price, firms decrease output to keep marginal cost equal to price.

Notice that as firms enter the market, market output increases, but each firm's output decreases. Eventually, enough firms enter to eliminate economic profit and the market returns to long-run equilibrium.

The key difference between the initial long-run equilibrium and the new long-run equilibrium is the number of firms. A permanent increase in demand increases the number of firms. Each firm produces the same output in the new long-run equilibrium as initially and makes zero economic profit. In the process of moving from the initial equilibrium to the new one, firms make economic profits.

The demand for airline travel in the world economy increased during the 1990s, and the deregulation of the airlines freed up firms to seek profit opportunities in this market. The result was a massive rate of entry of new airlines. The process of competition and change in the airline market were similar to what we have just studied.

A decrease in demand triggers a similar response, except in the opposite direction. The decrease in demand brings a lower price, economic loss, and exit. Exit decreases market supply, raises the price, and eliminates the economic loss.

## ■ Technological Change

New technologies lower cost, so as firms adopt a new technology, their cost curves shift downward. With lower costs, market supply increases and the price falls. Firms that use the new technology make an economic profit and firms that stick with the old technology incur economic losses. New-technology firms enter and old-technology firms exit. The price keeps falling until all the firms are using the new technology and economic profit is zero. The lower prices and better products that technological advances bring are permanent gains for consumers. *Eye on Record Stores* (on pp. 336–337) looks at the effects of technological change in the retail market for recorded music.

# EYE on RECORD STORES

## Where Have All the Record Stores Gone?

In 1995, more than 8,000 record stores traded in a very competitive market.

Figure 1 illustrates the average total cost curve, ATC, marginal cost curve, MC, and marginal revenue curve, $MR_0$, for one of these stores.

Competition was fierce in the record retail business and economic profit was hard to find. In Figure 1, the record store is earning zero economic profit and the market is in long-run equilibrium.

Although competition was fierce, it was about to notch up a gear. The dot-com boom had started.

The expansion of the Internet during the 1990s laid the foundation for many new ways of doing business. One of these was a new way of delivering recorded music.

Amazon was one of the first firms to take advantage of the technological advance made possible by the Internet when Amazon.com started trading in 1995.

At first, Amazon was an online bookstore. But entrepreneur Jeff Bezos quickly saw that the technologies being laid down for selling books could also be used to sell CDs (and just about anything).

*An Amazon server farm replaces hundreds of traditional record stores.*

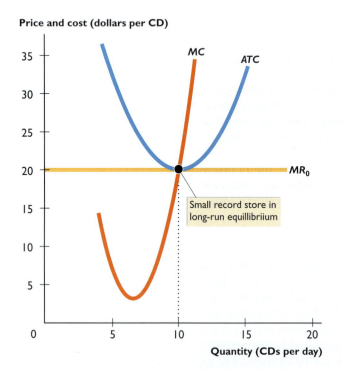

**Figure 1  Small Independent Record Store Before Internet**

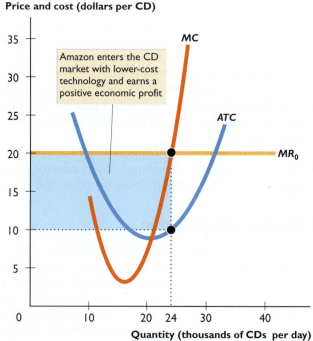

**Figure 2  Amazon Enters CD Retail Market**

This new technology also had much lower costs than traditional "bricks and mortar" retailing.

Figure 2 shows the average total cost curve and marginal cost curve using Amazon's lower-cost technology. The numbers are just examples, but first look carefully at the axes of Figures 1 and 2. Amazon can produce a larger output at a lower cost than the traditional record store can.

Online retailing wasn't profitable at first, but with its superior low-cost technology economic profit eventually rolled in. Figure 2 shows the economic profit available at the prices charged by traditional record stores but to a store using the new technology.

Positive economic profit attracts new entry. And that's what happened in the online music business. The

technology also kept advancing, with MP3 files replacing physical CDs. As Amazon, Apple's iTunes store, and others entered the market for MP3 downloads, the price of recorded music fell and profits were trimmed.

Figure 3 shows where perfect competition among online music download stores drives the price and quantity. Price falls to make marginal revenue $MR_1$, a level at which economic profit has vanished in a new long-run equilibrium.

This lower price means hard times for small independent record stores. The fall in price is too big for these small stores to cover even their average variable cost, $AVC$, and with no prospect of prices rising again, the independent stores avoid the economic losses by exiting.

Figure 4 illustrates the economic loss incurred by a traditional independent record store facing competition from online retailers when marginal revenue has fallen to $MR_1$.

Faced with this loss, the store exits. That's where the record stores have gone. They've exited to avoid the losses created by online competition.

*Sundance, in San Marcos, Texas, is one of 4,000 traditional record stores that exited.*

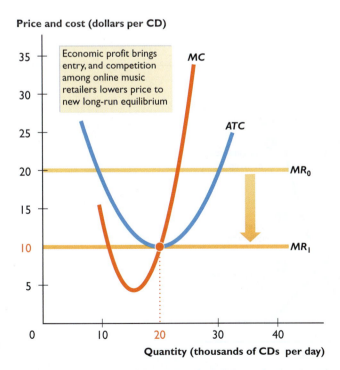

**Figure 3  More Large Online Music Stores Enter and Compete**

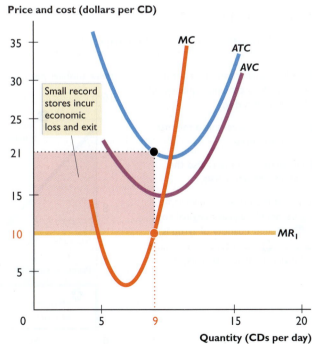

**Figure 4  Small Independent Record Store Exits**

## ■ Is Perfect Competition Efficient?

An efficient outcome is one in which scarce resources are allocated to their highest-value use. Perfect competition achieves such an outcome. It is efficient.

To see why, first recall the conditions for an efficient allocation of resources. Resources are used efficiently when it is not possible to get more of one good without giving up something that is valued more highly. When this outcome is achieved, marginal benefit equals marginal cost and total surplus (consumer surplus plus producer surplus) is maximized. That is the outcome achieved in perfect competition.

We derive a firm's supply curve in perfect competition from its marginal cost curve. The supply curve is the marginal cost curve at all points above the minimum of average variable cost (the shutdown price). Because the market supply curve is found by summing the quantities supplied by all the firms at each price, the market supply curve is the entire market's marginal cost curve.

The market demand curve is the marginal benefit curve. Because the market supply curve and market demand curve intersect at the equilibrium price, that price equals both marginal cost and marginal benefit.

Figure 11.13 illustrates the efficiency of perfect competition. We've labeled the market demand curve $D = MB$ and the market supply curve $S = MC$ to remind you that these curves are also the marginal benefit ($MB$) and marginal cost ($MC$) curves.

These demand and supply curves intersect at the equilibrium price and equilibrium quantity. The price equals marginal benefit and marginal cost, total surplus is maximized, and the equilibrium quantity is efficient. Any departure from this outcome is inferior to it and brings an avoidable deadweight loss.

■ **FIGURE 11.13**

The Efficiency of Perfect Competition

❶ Market equilibrium occurs at a price of $5 a can and a quantity of 90,000 cans a day.

❷ The supply curve is also the marginal cost curve.

❸ The demand curve is also the marginal benefit curve.

Because at the market equilibrium, marginal benefit equals marginal cost, the ❹ efficient quantity of syrup is produced. ❺ Total surplus (consumer surplus plus producer surplus) is maximized.

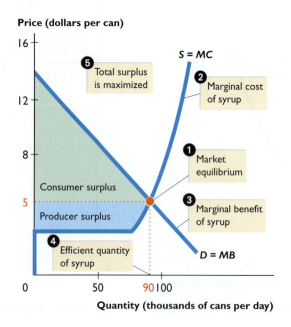

## ■ Is Perfect Competition Fair?

You've seen many situations in which perfect competition brings gains and losses. When the demand for an item decreases, most producers incur at least a temporary loss and some of them go out of business. When a technological change lowers costs, entrepreneurs who are quick to adopt the technology gain and others who respond slowly lose. Is it fair that some entrepreneurs gain and others lose?

When a natural disaster such as extreme weather or an earthquake strikes, the prices of essential items sold in competitive markets shoot upward, bringing gains for sellers and pain for buyers. Is that type of outcome fair?

You studied the fairness of markets in Chapter 6 (pp. 197–199) and saw two views of what is fair: fair rules and a fair result. According to the fair-rules view, an outcome is fair if property rights are enforced and people acquire resources, goods, and services through voluntary exchange. According to the fair-result view, an outcome is fair if the poorest aren't too poor and the richest aren't too rich. Are the competitive market outcomes we've just described fair on these two views of fairness?

The situations we've described appear to be fair on both views. Perfect competition places no restrictions on anyone's actions, all trade is voluntary, consumers pay the lowest possible prices, and entrepreneurs earn only normal profit. Price hikes arising from shortages following a natural disaster might be an exception. In such situations, large windfall gains for a few and high prices for essential items for many might be regarded as an unfair result. If it is considered unfair, it must be compared with the fairness of an alternative mechanism for allocating scarce resources.

## EYE on YOUR LIFE
### The Perfect Competition that You Encounter

Many of the markets that you encounter every day are highly competitive and almost perfectly competitive. And while you don't run into perfect competition on a daily basis, you do have dealings in some perfectly competitive markets. Two of those markets are the Internet auctions organized by eBay and one of its subsidiaries, StubHub.

If you have a ticket for a game between the Giants and the Braves but can't use it, you can sell it on StubHub for the going market price (minus a commission). And if you're desperate to see the game but missed out on getting a ticket, you can buy one for the going price (plus a commission) on the same Web site.

StubHub takes a commission and makes a profit. But competition between StubHub, Ticketmaster, and other ticket brokers ensure that profits are competed away in the long run, with entrepreneurs earning normal profit.

Just about every good or service that you buy and take for granted, no matter where you buy it, is available because of the forces of competition. Your home, your food, your clothing, your books, your DVDs, your MP3 files, your computer, your bike, your car, … ; the list is endless. No one organizes all the magic that enables

you to buy this vast array of products. Competitive markets and entrepreneurs striving to make the largest possible profit make it happen.

When either demand or technology changes and makes the current allocation of resources the wrong one, the market swiftly and silently acts. It sends signals to entrepreneurs that bring entry and exit and a new and efficient use of scarce resources.

It is no exaggeration or hype to say that your entire life is influenced by and benefits immeasurably from the forces of competition. Adam Smith's invisible hand might be hidden from view, but it is enormously powerful.

## CHECKPOINT 11.3

**Explain how output, price, and profit are determined in the long run and explain why perfect competition is efficient.**

## Practice Problems

Tulip growing is a perfectly competitive industry, and all tulip growers have the same cost curves. The market price of tulips is $15 a bunch, and each grower maximizes profit by producing 1,500 bunches a week. The average total cost of producing tulips is $21 a bunch. Minimum average variable cost is $12 a bunch, and the minimum average total cost is $18 a bunch.

1.  What is a tulip grower's economic profit in the short run and how does the number of tulip growers change in the long run?

2.  In the long run, what is the price and the tulip grower's economic profit?

## In the News

**Growers cut back on coffee**

New high-yield varieties have boosted Brazil's coffee production and coffee-bean prices have fallen 54 percent in the past two years. The drop has been so steep that some longtime Brazilian coffee farmers are considering other uses for their land, such as cattle pastures.

Source: *The Wall Street Journal*, June 13, 2013

Explain the effect of the fall in the price on the profit of growers in the short run. How will the market for coffee change in the long run?

## Solutions to Practice Problems

1.  The price is less than average total cost, so the tulip grower is incurring an economic loss in the short run. Because the price exceeds minimum average variable cost, the tulip grower continues to produce. The economic loss equals the loss per bunch ($21 minus $15) multiplied by the number of bunches (1,500), which equals $9,000 (Figure 1).
    Because tulip growers are incurring economic losses, some growers will exit in the long run. The number of tulip growers will decrease.

2.  In the long run, the price will be such that economic profit is zero. That is, as growers exit, the price will rise until it equals minimum average total cost. The long-run price will be $18 a bunch (Figure 2).
    A tulip grower's economic profit in the long run will be zero because average total cost equals price (Figure 2).

## Solution to In the News

An increase in the supply of coffee decreased the world price of coffee. As the price of coffee fell, coffee growers incurred economic losses. In the short run, growers continued to produce coffee, but in the long run as the price fell further some farmers allocated part of their land to other uses. As growers switch more and more of their land to other activities, the supply of coffee will fall, the price of coffee beans will rise, and growers' economic losses will decrease. Supply will continue to decrease until growers are making zero economic profit.

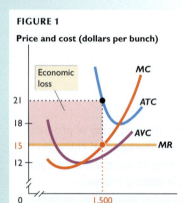

**FIGURE 1**

Price and cost (dollars per bunch)

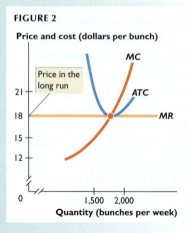

**FIGURE 2**

Price and cost (dollars per bunch)

## CHAPTER SUMMARY

### Key Points

**1. Explain a perfectly competitive firm's profit-maximizing choices and derive its supply curve.**

- A perfectly competitive firm is a price taker.
- Marginal revenue equals price.
- The firm produces the output at which price equals marginal cost.
- If price is less than minimum average variable cost, the firm temporarily shuts down.
- A firm's supply curve is the upward-sloping part of its marginal cost curve at all prices at or above minimum average variable cost (the shut-down point) and the vertical axis at all prices below minimum average variable cost.

**2. Explain how output, price, and profit are determined in the short run.**

- Market demand and market supply determine price.
- Firms choose the quantity to produce that maximizes profit, which is the quantity at which marginal cost equals price.
- In short-run equilibrium, a firm can make a positive economic profit, make zero economic profit, or incur an economic loss.

**3. Explain how output, price, and profit are determined in the long run and explain why perfect competition is efficient.**

- Economic profit induces entry, which increases market supply and lowers price and profit. Economic loss induces exit, which decreases market supply, raises price, and lowers the losses.
- In the long run, economic profit is zero and there is no entry or exit.
- An increase in demand increases the number of firms and increases the equilibrium quantity.
- An advance in technology that lowers the cost of producing a good increases market supply, lowers the price, and increases the quantity.
- Perfect competition is efficient because it makes marginal benefit equal marginal cost, and it is fair because trade is voluntary, consumers pay the lowest possible prices, and entrepreneurs earn normal profit.

### Key Terms

Marginal revenue, 319
Monopolistic competition, 318
Monopoly, 318
Oligopoly, 318

Perfect competition, 318
Price taker, 319
Shutdown point, 323

# CHAPTER CHECKPOINT

## Study Plan Problems and Applications

**LIST**

- Wheat
- Jeans
- Printer cartridges
- Toothpaste
- Gym membership in a town with one gym

1. Look at the list to the left. In what type of market is each good or service in the list sold? Explain your answers.

2. Explain why in a perfectly competitive market, the firm is a price taker. Why can't the firm choose the price at which it sells its good?

3. Table 1 shows the demand schedule for Lin's Fortune Cookies. Calculate Lin's marginal revenue for each quantity demanded. Compare Lin's marginal revenue and price. In what type of market does Lin's Fortune Cookies operate?

Table 1 shows the demand schedule for Lin's Fortune Cookies. Table 2 shows some cost data for Lin's. Use this information to work Problems **4** to **7**. (Hint: Make a sketch of Lin's short-run cost curves.)

4. At a market price of $50 a batch, what quantity does Lin's produce and what is the firm's economic profit in the short run?

5. At a market price of $35.20 a batch, what quantity does Lin's produce and what is the firm's economic profit in the short run?

6. Create Lin's short-run supply schedule and make a graph of Lin's short-run supply curve. Explain why only part of Lin's short-run supply curve is the same as its marginal cost curve.

7. At a market price of $83 a batch, what quantity does Lin's produce and what is the firm's economic profit in the short run? Do firms enter or exit the market and what is Lin's economic profit in the long run?

**TABLE 1**

| Price (dollars per batch) | Quantity demanded (batches per day) |
|---|---|
| 50 | 0 |
| 50 | 1 |
| 50 | 2 |
| 50 | 3 |
| 50 | 4 |
| 50 | 5 |
| 50 | 6 |

Use the following information to work Problems **8** to **10**.

**Maple-syrup makers strike gold**

Sugaring season in Vermont is going full blast. Vermont, the biggest U.S. syrup producer, produces about 500,000 gallons a year. In 2007, maple syrup cost an average of $35 a gallon; this year, the price is $45 a gallon. Canada is usually a huge producer, but with a poor season it has seen a 30 percent drop in production. As consumers turn to natural and organic products and buy locally made food, demand for maple syrup has rocketed.

Source: *USA Today*, March 30, 2009

8. Draw a graph to describe the maple syrup market and the cost and revenue of one firm in 2007, assuming that all firms are making zero economic profit.

9. Starting with the industry in long-run equilibrium, explain how the drop in the Canadian supply, other things remaining the same, affects the maple syrup market and an individual producer in the short run.

10. Starting with the industry in long-run equilibrium, explain how the increase in the demand for maple syrup, other things remaining the same, affects the maple syrup market and an individual producer in the short run.

11. Read *Eye on Record Stores* on 298–299 and explain how Internet retailing of recorded music changed the constraints faced by small traditional record stores. Why did many record stores exit rather than shut down temporarily?

**TABLE 2**

| Quantity (batches per day) | AFC | AVC | ATC | MC |
|---|---|---|---|---|
| | (dollars per batch) | | | |
| 1 | 84.0 | 51.0 | 135 | |
| | | | | 37 |
| 2 | 42.0 | 44.0 | 86 | |
| | | | | 29 |
| 3 | 28.0 | 39.0 | 67 | |
| | | | | 27 |
| 4 | 21.0 | 36.0 | 57 | |
| | | | | 32 |
| 5 | 16.8 | 35.2 | 52 | |
| | | | | 40 |
| 6 | 14.0 | 36.0 | 50 | |
| | | | | 57 |
| 7 | 12.0 | 39.0 | 51 | |
| | | | | 83 |
| 8 | 10.5 | 44.5 | 55 | |

# Instructor Assignable Problems and Applications

1. Why did Amazon enter the market for recorded music and why did independent record stores exit?

2. How does competition among online music retailers influence economic profit?

3. Look at the list to the right. In what type of market is each of the goods and services in the list sold? Explain your answers.

4. Suppose that the restaurant industry is perfectly competitive. Joe's Diner is always packed in the evening but rarely has a customer at lunchtime. Why doesn't Joe's Diner close—temporarily shut down—at lunchtime?

Use the following information to work Problems 5 to 7.

Figure 1 shows the short-run cost curves of a toy producer. The market has 1,000 identical producers and Table 1 shows the market demand schedule for toys.

5. At a market price of $21 a toy, what quantity does the firm produce in the short run and does the firm make a positive economic profit, a zero economic profit, or an economic loss?

6. At a market price of $12 a toy, how many toys does the firm produce and what is its economic profit in the short run? How will the number of firms in the market change in the long run?

7. At what market prices would the firm shut down temporarily? What is the market price of a toy in long-run equilibrium? How many firms will be in the toy market in the long run? Explain your answer.

Use the following information to work Problems 8 and 9.

California plans to crack down on the use of fumigants by growers of strawberries. The biggest burden will fall on Ventura County's growers, who produce about 90 percent of the nation's crop.

8. Draw graphs of the U.S. strawberry market in long-run equilibrium before the pollution crackdown: one of the U.S. market and one of a California grower. Now show the short-run effects of the pollution crackdown.

9. On the graph, show the long-run effects of the pollution crackdown.

Use the following information to work Problems 10 and 11.

**Big drops in prices for crops make it tough down on the farm**
Corn, soybean, and wheat prices have fallen roughly 50 percent from the historic highs of earlier this year. With better-than-expected crop yields, world grain production will rise nearly 5 percent this year. Grain prices have also become more closely tied to oil prices because of the growing corn-based ethanol industry.

Source: *USA Today*, October 23, 2008

10. Why did grain prices fall in 2008? Draw a graph to show the short-run effect on an individual farmer's economic profit.

11. Explain the effect of a fall in the oil price on the market for ethanol. If the price of oil remains low for some years, what will be the long-run effects on the market for ethanol and the number of ethanol producers?

**LIST**

- Breakfast cereals
- Cell phones
- The only restaurant in a small town
- Oranges
- Air travel in a town serviced by one airline

**FIGURE 1**

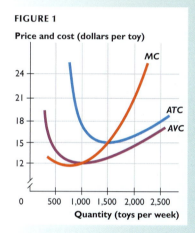

**TABLE 1**

| Price (dollars per toy) | Quantity demanded (thousands of toys per week) |
|---|---|
| 24 | 1,000 |
| 21 | 1,500 |
| 18 | 2,000 |
| 15 | 2,500 |
| 12 | 3,000 |

## Critical Thinking Discussion Questions

1. What features of the market for smart-phone apps make it competitive and what features of that market are impediments to competition?

2. **Singaporeans are big online shoppers**

   Online shopping in Singapore is booming. By 2015, e-shoppers will be snapping up clothes, shoes, books, and gadgets to the tune of S$4.4 billion, up from an estimated S$1.9 billion last year. PayPal's general manager for Southeast Asia and India says consumers are shifting their spending from physical stores to online stores because of lower prices, greater convenience, and a broader selection.

   Source: *The Straits Times*, August 18, 2013

   a. Does the Internet make markets more competitive or less competitive? Explain your answer.
   b. How do you think the cost of providing Internet retail services differs from the cost of providing bricks-and-mortar retail services? Which most likely has the higher fixed cost and which the higher variable cost?
   c. Which is likely to earn the higher economic profit, Internet retailing or bricks-and-mortar retailing (i) in the short run and (ii) in the long run? Explain your answer.
   d. Do you think the Internet makes markets more efficient? Explain your answer.

3. **Honda workers return after four-month shutdown**

   Honda shut down its U.K. Swindon car plant for four months in 2009, cutting annual production by 50 percent to 11,300 vehicles and shedding 1,300 workers through voluntary redundancies. Workers were paid 2 months' full pay and 2 months on 60 percent of pay during the shutdown.

   Source: *The Independent*, 17 February 2009

   a. Explain how Honda's shutdown decision would have affected the company's total cost, total variable cost, and total fixed cost.
   b. Under what conditions would this shutdown decision maximize Honda's economic profit (or minimize its economic loss)?
   c. Why would Honda start production again?

4. **Samsung Mobile sales fall as Chinese rivals win customers**

   Samsung, the largest smart-phone maker, faces fierce competition from Chinese producers in emerging markets with cheaper, feature-packed devices. Apple Inc. is boosting iPhone sales through China Mobile Ltd. Huawei Technologies Co. and Xiaomi Corp. are hence packing features into smart phones costing about $100 to target budget customers.

   Source: Bloomberg, April 29, 2014

   a. Explain why Samsung faces competition from new Chinese smartphone producers.
   b. Draw a graph to illustrate your answer in part (a).
   c. Explain the long-run effects of new producers entering the smartphone market.

Are Microsoft's prices too high?

# Monopoly

**When you have completed your study of this chapter, you will be able to**

**1** Explain how monopoly arises and distinguish between single-price monopoly and price-discriminating monopoly.

**2** Explain how a single-price monopoly determines its output and price.

**3** Compare the performance of a single-price monopoly with that of perfect competition.

**4** Explain how price discrimination increases profit.

**5** Explain why natural monopoly is regulated and the effects of regulation.

## 12.1 MONOPOLY AND HOW IT ARISES

**Monopoly**

A market in which one firm sells a good or service that has no close substitutes and a barrier blocks the entry of new firms.

*The market for raw uncut diamonds is close to being a monopoly.*

A **monopoly** is a market in which one firm sells a good or service that has no close substitutes and in which a barrier to entry prevents competition from new firms.

Markets for local telephone service, gas, electricity, and water are examples of local monopoly. GlaxoSmithKline has a monopoly on AZT, a drug that is used to treat AIDS. DeBeers, a South African firm, controls 80 percent of the world's production of raw diamonds—close to being a monopoly but not quite one.

### ■ How Monopoly Arises

Monopoly arises when there is

- No close substitute
- A barrier to entry

### No Close Substitute

If a good has a close substitute, even though only one firm produces it, that firm effectively faces competition from the producers of substitutes. Water supplied by a local public utility is an example of a good that does not have close substitutes. While it does have a close substitute for drinking—bottled spring water—it has no effective substitutes for doing the laundry, taking a shower, or washing a car.

The availability of close substitutes isn't static. Technological change can create substitutes and weaken a monopoly. For example, the creation of courier services such as UPS and the development of the fax machine and e-mail provide close substitutes for the mail-carrying services provided by the U.S. Postal Service and have weakened its monopoly. Broadband fiber-optic phone lines and satellite dishes have weakened the monopoly of cable television companies.

The arrival of a new product can also create a monopoly. For example, the technologies of the information age have provided opportunities for Google and Microsoft to become near monopolies in their markets.

### A Barrier to Entry

**Barrier to entry**

Any constraint that protects a firm from competitors.

Any constraint that protects a firm from the arrival of new competitors is a **barrier to entry.** There are three types of barrier to entry:

- Natural
- Ownership
- Legal

**Natural monopoly**

A monopoly that arises because one firm can meet the entire market demand at a lower average total cost than two or more firms could.

*Natural Barrier to Entry* A **natural monopoly** exists when the technology for producing a good or service enables one firm to meet the entire market demand at a lower average total cost than two or more firms could. One electric power distributor can meet the market demand for electricity at a lower cost than two or more firms could. Imagine two or more sets of wires running to your home so that you could choose your electric power supplier.

Figure 12.1 illustrates a natural monopoly in the distribution of electric power. Here, the demand curve for electric power is *D,* and the long-run average cost curve is *LRAC.* Economies of scale prevail over the entire length of this *LRAC* curve, indicated by the fact that the curve slopes downward. One firm can produce 4 million kilowatt-hours at 5¢ a kilowatt-hour. At this price, the quantity

### FIGURE 12.1

### Natural Monopoly

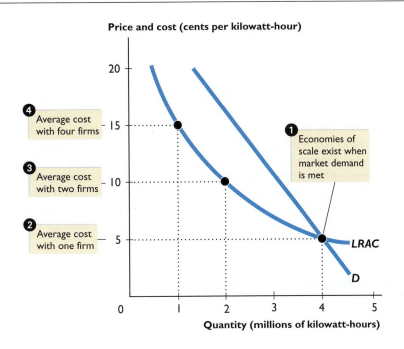

**Price and cost (cents per kilowatt-hour)**

**④** Average cost with four firms

**③** Average cost with two firms

**②** Average cost with one firm

**①** Economies of scale exist when market demand is met

**LRAC**

**D**

**Quantity (millions of kilowatt-hours)**

The demand curve for electric power is *D*, and the long-run average cost curve is *LRAC*.

**①** Economies of scale exist over the entire *LRAC* curve.

One firm can distribute 4 million kilowatt-hours at a **②** cost of 5¢ a kilowatt-hour.

Two firms can distribute this same total output at a **③** cost of 10¢ a kilowatt-hour.

Four firms can distribute this same total output at a **④** cost of 15¢ a kilowatt-hour.

One firm can meet the market demand at a lower cost than two or more firms can, and the market is a natural monopoly.

demanded is 4 million kilowatt-hours. So if the price was 5¢ a kilowatt-hour, one firm could supply the entire market. If two or more firms shared the market, average total cost would be higher.

To see why the situation shown in Figure 12.1 creates a barrier to entry, think about what would happen if a second firm tried to enter the market. Such a firm would find it impossible to make a profit. If it produced less than the original firm, it would have to charge a higher price and it would have no customers. If it produced the same quantity as the original firm, the price would fall below average total cost for both firms and one of them would be forced out of business. There is room for only one firm in this market.

*Ownership Barrier to Entry* A monopoly can arise in a market in which competition and entry are restricted by the concentration of ownership of a natural resource. If DeBeers controlled 100 percent of the world's production of raw diamonds, it would be an example of this type of monopoly. There is no natural barrier to entry in diamonds. Even though the diamond is a relatively rare mineral, its sources of supply could have many owners who compete in a global competitive auction market. Only by buying control over all the world's diamonds would DeBeers be able to prevent entry and competition.

*Legal Barrier to Entry* A legal barrier to entry creates a legal monopoly. A **legal monopoly** is a market in which competition and entry are restricted by the granting of a public franchise, government license, patent, or copyright.

A *public franchise* is an exclusive right granted to a firm to supply a good or service, an example of which is the U.S. Postal Service's exclusive right to deliver

**Legal monopoly**
A market in which competition and entry are restricted by the granting of a public franchise, government license, patent, or copyright.

first-class mail. A *government license* controls entry into particular occupations, professions, and industries. An example is Michael's Texaco in Charleston, Rhode Island, which is the only firm in the area licensed to test for vehicle emissions.

A *patent* is an exclusive right granted to the inventor of a product or service. A *copyright* is an exclusive right granted to the author or composer of a literary, musical, dramatic, or artistic work. Patents and copyrights are valid for a limited time period that varies from country to country. In the United States, a patent is valid for 20 years. Patents are designed to encourage the *invention* of new products and production methods. They also stimulate *innovation*—the use of new inventions—by encouraging inventors to publicize their discoveries and offer them for use under license. Patents have stimulated innovations in areas as diverse as soybean seeds, pharmaceuticals, memory chips, and video games.

Most monopolies are regulated by government agencies. To understand why governments regulate monopolies and what effects regulations have, we need to know how an unregulated monopoly behaves. So we'll first study an unregulated monopoly and then look at monopoly regulation at the end of this chapter.

A monopoly sets its own price, but in doing so, it faces a market constraint. Let's see how the market limits a monopoly's pricing choices.

## ■ Monopoly Price-Setting Strategies

A monopoly faces a tradeoff between price and the quantity sold. To sell a larger quantity, the monopoly must set a lower price. But there are two price-setting possibilities that create different tradeoffs:

- Single price
- Price discrimination

### Single Price

**Single-price monopoly**
A monopoly that must sell each unit of its output for the same price to all its customers.

A **single-price monopoly** is a firm that must sell each unit of its output for the same price to all its customers. DeBeers sells diamonds (of a given size and quality) for the same price to all its customers. DeBeers is a *single-price* monopoly because if it tried to sell at a higher price to some customers than to others, only the low-price customers would buy from DeBeers. The others would buy from DeBeers's low-price customers.

### Price Discrimination

**Price-discriminating monopoly**
A monopoly that sells different units of a good or service for different prices not related to cost differences.

A **price-discriminating monopoly** is a firm that sells different units for different prices not related to cost differences. Many firms price discriminate. Airlines offer a dizzying array of different prices for the same trip. Pizza producers charge one price for a single pizza and almost give away a second one. Different customers might pay different prices (like airfares), or one customer might pay different prices for different quantities bought (like the bargain price for a second pizza).

When a firm price discriminates, it appears to be doing its customers a favor. In fact, it is charging each group of customers the highest price it can get them to pay and is increasing its profit.

Not all monopolies can price discriminate. The main obstacle to the practice of price discrimination is resale by the customers who buy for a low price. Because of resale possibilities, price discrimination is limited to monopolies that sell goods and services that cannot be resold.

# CHECKPOINT 12.1

**Explain how monopoly arises and distinguish between single-price monopoly and price-discriminating monopoly.**

## Practice Problems

Use the information about the firms listed below to work Problems **1** and **2**.

    **a.** Coca-Cola cuts its price below that of Pepsi-Cola to increase profit.
    **b.** A single firm, protected by a barrier to entry, produces a personal service that has no close substitutes.
    **c.** A barrier to entry exists, but the good has some close substitutes.
    **d.** A museum offers discounts to students and seniors.
    **e.** A firm can sell any quantity it chooses at the going price.
    **f.** A firm experiences economies of scale even when it produces the quantity that meets the entire market demand.

**1.** Which of the six cases are monopolies or might give rise to monopoly?

**2.** Which are legal monopolies and which are natural monopolies? Can any of them price discriminate? If so, why?

## In the News

**Allegiant Air: The tardy, gas-guzzling, most profitable airline in America**

With 64 jets, Allegiant Air has achieved the lowest costs, fullest planes, and highest margins in the U.S. airline industry. It serves 75 small U.S. cities and faces competition on just 17 of its 203 routes. It offers a no-frills fare and charges for everything else, from carry-on luggage to water.

Source: *The Wall Street Journal*, June 4, 2013

What type of monopoly is Allegiant Air? What would be the barrier to entry?

## Solutions to Practice Problems

**1.** Monopoly arises when a single firm produces a good or service that has no close substitutes and a barrier to entry exists. Monopoly arises in **b** and **f**. In **a**, there is more than one firm. In **c**, the good has close substitutes. In **d**, a monopoly might be able to price discriminate, but other types of firms (for example, pizza producers) price discriminate and they are not monopolies. In **e**, the demand for the firm's output is perfectly elastic and there is no limit to what it can sell. This firm operates in a perfectly competitive market.

**2.** Natural monopoly exists when one firm can meet the entire market demand at a lower price than two or more firms could: **f** is a natural monopoly, but **b** could be. Legal monopoly exists when the granting of a right creates a barrier to entry: **b** might be a legal monopoly. Because a personal service cannot be resold, **b** could price discriminate.

## Solution to In the News

Allegiant Air is a natural monopoly on 186 routes. With lower costs than other airlines, it can meet the market demand and make a large profit. Its lower costs give it a natural barrier to entry. It does not have a legal barrier to entry as another airline can enter the market.

## 12.2   SINGLE-PRICE MONOPOLY

To understand how a single-price monopoly makes its output and price decisions, we must first study the link between price and marginal revenue.

### ■ Price and Marginal Revenue

Because in a monopoly there is only one firm, the demand for the firm's output is the market demand. Let's look at Bobbie's Barbershop, the sole supplier of haircuts in Cairo, Nebraska. The table in Figure 12.2 shows the demand schedule for Bobbie's haircuts. For example, at $12, consumers demand 4 haircuts an hour (row *E*).

*Total revenue* is the price multiplied by the quantity sold. For example, in row *D*, Bobbie sells 3 haircuts at $14 each, so total revenue is $42. *Marginal revenue* is the change in total revenue resulting from a one-unit increase in the quantity sold. For example, if the price falls from $16 (row *C*) to $14 (row *D*), the quantity sold increases from 2 to 3 haircuts. Total revenue rises from $32 to $42, so the change in total revenue is $10. Because the quantity sold increases by 1 haircut, marginal revenue equals the change in total revenue and is $10. Marginal revenue is placed between the two rows to emphasize that marginal revenue relates to the *change* in the quantity sold.

Figure 12.2 shows the market demand curve and Bobbie's marginal revenue curve (*MR*) and also illustrates the calculation that we've just made. At each output, marginal revenue is less than price—the marginal revenue curve lies below the demand curve because a lower price is received on *all* units sold, not just on the marginal unit. For example, at a price of $16, Bobbie sells 2 haircuts (point *C*). If she lowers the price to $14 a haircut, she sells 3 haircuts and has a revenue gain

■ **FIGURE 12.2**

Demand and Marginal Revenue

The table shows the market demand schedule and Bobbie's total revenue and marginal revenue schedules.

If the price falls from $16 to $14, the quantity sold increases from 2 to 3 haircuts.

❶ Total revenue lost on 2 haircuts is $4; ❷ total revenue gained on 1 haircut is $14; and ❸ marginal revenue is $10.

| | Price (dollars per haircut) | Quantity demanded (haircuts per hour) | Total revenue (dollars per hour) | Marginal revenue (dollars per haircut) |
|---|---|---|---|---|
| A | 20 | 0 | 0 | |
| | | | | 18 |
| B | 18 | 1 | 18 | |
| | | | | 14 |
| C | 16 | 2 | 32 | |
| | | | | 10 |
| D | 14 | 3 | 42 | |
| | | | | 6 |
| E | 12 | 4 | 48 | |
| | | | | 2 |
| F | 10 | 5 | 50 | |

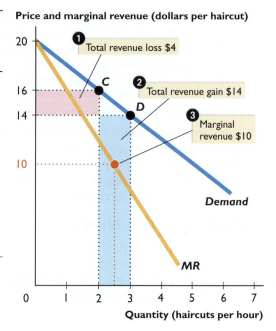

Price and marginal revenue (dollars per haircut)

of $14 on the third haircut. But she now receives only $14 a haircut on the first two—$2 a haircut less than before. So she loses $4 of revenue on the first 2 haircuts. To calculate marginal revenue, she must deduct this amount from the revenue gain of $14. So her marginal revenue is $10, which is less than the price.

Notice that the marginal revenue curve has *twice the slope* of the demand curve. When the price falls from $20 to $10, the quantity demanded increases from zero to 5 but the quantity on the *MR* curve increases from zero to 2.5.

## ■ Marginal Revenue and Elasticity

In Chapter 5 (pp. 158–159), you learned about the *total revenue test* for the price elasticity of demand. If a *fall* in price *increases* total revenue, demand is elastic; and if a *fall* in price *decreases* total revenue, demand is inelastic.

The total revenue test implies that when demand is elastic, marginal revenue is positive and when demand is inelastic, marginal revenue is negative. Figure 12.3 illustrates this relationship between elasticity and marginal revenue.

In part (a) as the price *falls* from $20 to $10, marginal revenue (shown by the blue bars) is *positive* and total revenue in part (b) *increases*, so demand is elastic. In part (a) as the price *falls* from $10 to zero, marginal revenue (the red bars) is *negative* and total revenue in part (b) *decreases*, so demand is *inelastic*. At a price of $10, total revenue is at a maximum, demand is unit elastic, and marginal revenue is zero.

■ **FIGURE 12.3**

Marginal Revenue and Elasticity

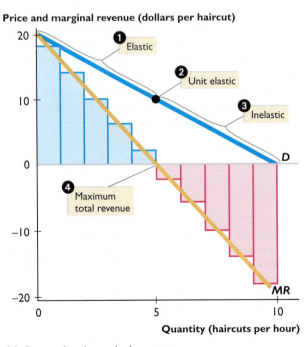

**(a) Demand and marginal revenue**

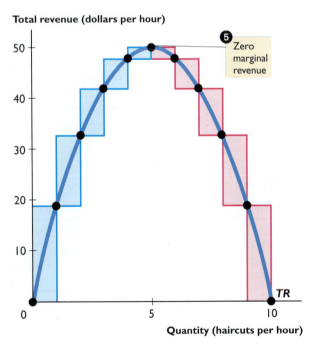

**(b) Total revenue**

As the price falls, if marginal revenue is positive (the blue bars), ❶ demand is elastic; if marginal revenue is zero, ❷ demand is unit elastic; if marginal revenue is negative (the red bars), ❸ demand is inelastic. At zero marginal revenue in part (a), ❹ total revenue is maximized. And at maximum total revenue in part (b), ❺ marginal revenue is zero.

The relationship between marginal revenue and elasticity implies that a monopoly never profitably produces along the inelastic range of its demand curve. If a monopoly did produce along the inelastic range of its demand curve, it could increase total revenue by raising its price and selling a smaller quantity. Also, by producing less, the firm's total cost would fall and the firm's profit would increase. Let's look at a monopoly's output and price decision.

## ■ Output and Price Decision

To determine the output level and price that maximize a monopoly's profit, we study the behavior of both revenue and costs as output varies.

Table 12.1 summarizes the information we need about Bobbie's revenue, costs, and economic profit. Economic profit, which equals total revenue minus total cost, is maximized at $12 an hour when Bobbie sells 3 haircuts an hour for $14 each. If she sold 2 haircuts for $16 each, her economic profit would be only $9. And if she sold 4 haircuts for $12 each, her economic profit would be only $8.

You can see why 3 haircuts is Bobbie's profit-maximizing output by looking at the marginal revenue and marginal cost. When Bobbie increases output from 2 to 3 haircuts, her marginal revenue is $10 and her marginal cost is $7. Profit increases by the difference, $3 an hour. If Bobbie increases output yet further, from 3 to 4 haircuts, her marginal revenue is $6 and her marginal cost is $10. In this case, marginal cost exceeds marginal revenue by $4, so profit decreases by $4 an hour.

Figure 12.4 illustrates the information contained in Table 12.1. Part (a) shows Bobbie's total revenue curve (TR) and her total cost curve (TC). It also shows Bobbie's economic profit as the vertical distance between the TR and TC curves. Bobbie maximizes her profit at 3 haircuts an hour and earns an economic profit of $12 an hour ($42 of total revenue minus $30 of total cost).

Figure 12.4(b) shows the market demand curve (D) and Bobbie's marginal revenue curve (MR) along with her marginal cost curve (MC) and average total cost curve (ATC). Bobbie maximizes profit by producing the output at which marginal cost equals marginal revenue—3 haircuts an hour. But what price does she charge for a haircut? To set the price, the monopoly uses the demand curve and finds the highest price at which it can sell the profit-maximizing output. In Bobbie's case, the highest price at which she can sell 3 haircuts an hour is $14 a haircut.

## ■ TABLE 12.1

A Monopoly's Output and Price Decision

| | Price (dollars per haircut) | Quantity demanded (haircuts per hour) | Total revenue (dollars per hour) | Marginal revenue (dollars per haircut) | Total cost (dollars per hour) | Marginal cost (dollars per haircut) | Profit (dollars per hour) |
|---|---|---|---|---|---|---|---|
| A | 20 | 0 | 0 | | 12 | | −12 |
| | | | | 18 | | 5 | |
| B | 18 | 1 | 18 | | 17 | | 1 |
| | | | | 14 | | 6 | |
| C | 16 | 2 | 32 | | 23 | | 9 |
| | | | | 10 | | 7 | |
| D | 14 | 3 | 42 | | 30 | | 12 |
| | | | | 6 | | 10 | |
| E | 12 | 4 | 48 | | 40 | | 8 |
| | | | | 2 | | 15 | |
| F | 10 | 5 | 50 | | 55 | | −5 |

When Bobbie produces 3 haircuts an hour, her average total cost is $10 (read from the *ATC* curve at the quantity 3 haircuts) and her price is $14 (read from the *D* curve). Her profit per haircut is $4 ($14 minus $10). Bobbie's economic profit is shown by the blue rectangle, which equals the profit per haircut ($4) multiplied by the number of haircuts (3 an hour), for a total of $12 an hour.

A positive economic profit is an incentive for firms to enter a market. But barriers to entry prevent that from happening in a monopoly. So in a monopoly, the firm can make a positive economic profit and continue to do so indefinitely.

A monopoly charges a price that exceeds marginal cost, but does it always make an economic profit? The answer is no. Bobbie makes a positive economic profit in Figure 12.4. But suppose that Bobbie's landlord increases the rent she pays for her barbershop. If Bobbie pays an additional $12 an hour in shop rent, her fixed cost increases by that amount. Her marginal cost and marginal revenue don't change, so her profit-maximizing output remains at 3 haircuts an hour. Her profit decreases by the additional rent of $12 an hour to zero. If Bobbie pays more than an additional $12 an hour for rent, she incurs an economic loss. If this situation were permanent, Bobbie would go out of business. But monopoly entrepreneurs are creative, and Bobbie might find another shop at a lower rent.

■ **FIGURE 12.4**

A Monopoly's Profit-Maximizing Output and Price

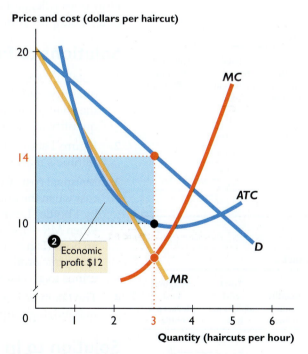

(a) Total revenue and total cost

(b) Demand, marginal revenue, and marginal cost

In part (a), economic profit is maximized when total revenue (*TR*) minus total cost (*TC*) is greatest. ❶ Economic profit, the vertical distance between *TR* and *TC*, is $12 an hour at 3 haircuts an hour.

In part (b), economic profit is maximized when marginal cost (*MC*) equals marginal revenue (*MR*). The price is determined by the demand curve (*D*) and is $14. ❷ Economic profit, the blue rectangle, is $12—the profit per haircut ($4) multiplied by 3 haircuts.

**CHECKPOINT 12.2**

**Explain how a single-price monopoly determines its output and price.**

## Practice Problems

**TABLE 1**

| Price (dollars per bottle) | Quantity (bottles per hour) | Total cost (dollars per hour) |
|---|---|---|
| 10 | 0 | 1 |
| 9 | 1 | 2 |
| 8 | 2 | 4 |
| 7 | 3 | 7 |
| 6 | 4 | 12 |
| 5 | 5 | 18 |

Minnie's Mineral Springs is a single-price monopoly. Table 1 shows the demand schedule for Minnie's spring water (columns 1 and 2) and the firm's total cost schedule (columns 2 and 3).

1. Calculate Minnie's total revenue and marginal revenue schedules.

2. Draw the demand curve and Minnie's marginal revenue curve.

3. Calculate Minnie's profit-maximizing output, price, and economic profit.

4. If Minnie's is hit with a conservation tax of $14 an hour, what are Minnie's new profit-maximizing output, price, and economic profit?

## In the News

**Allegiant Air: The most profitable airline in America**

Allegiant carries leisure travelers from 75 small U.S. cities to 14 warm-weather places. The airline faces no competition on 186 of its routes and has the lowest costs, the fullest planes, and the highest margins in the U.S. airline industry.

Source: *The Wall Street Journal*, June 4, 2013

How does Allegiant determine the fare and the number of seats to offer on each of its monopoly routes?

## Solutions to Practice Problems

**TABLE 2**

| Quantity (bottles per hour) | Total revenue (dollars per hour) | Marginal revenue (dollars per bottle) |
|---|---|---|
| 0 | 0 | |
| 1 | 9 | 9 |
| 2 | 16 | 7 |
| 3 | 21 | 5 |
| 4 | 24 | 3 |
| 5 | 25 | 1 |

**TABLE 3**

| Quantity (bottles per hour) | Total cost (dollars per hour) | Marginal cost (dollars per bottle) |
|---|---|---|
| 0 | 1 | |
| 1 | 2 | 1 |
| 2 | 4 | 2 |
| 3 | 7 | 3 |
| 4 | 12 | 5 |
| 5 | 18 | 6 |

1. Total revenue equals price multiplied by quantity sold. Marginal revenue equals the change in total revenue when the quantity increases by one unit (Table 2).

2. Figure 1 shows the demand curve and Minnie's marginal revenue curve, *MR*.

3. Marginal cost, *MC*, is the change in total cost when the quantity produced increases by 1 bottle (Table 3). Profit is maximized when *MR* = *MC* by producing 3 bottles an hour (Figure 1). The price is $7 a bottle. Economic profit equals total revenue ($21) minus total cost ($7), which is $14 an hour.

4. The tax increases Minnie's fixed cost but not its marginal cost, so the profit-maximizing output and price are unchanged. Economic profit is zero.

**FIGURE 1**

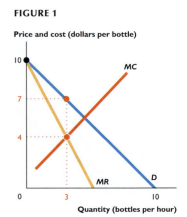

## Solution to In the News

Allegiant is a monopoly on many routes and it sets its fares to maximize economic profit. Allegiant knows its total costs, so it calculates the marginal cost of a passenger on each route. Allegiant uses its market experience to estimate the demand on each route and calculates marginal revenue. It offers the number of seats on each route that makes marginal revenue equal to marginal cost and it sets the highest fare that its customers are willing to pay for the profit-maximizing quantity.

## 12.3    MONOPOLY AND COMPETITION COMPARED

Imagine a market in which many small firms operate in perfect competition. Then suppose that a single firm buys out all these small firms and creates a monopoly. What happens in this market to the quantity produced, the price, and efficiency?

### ■ Output and Price

Figure 12.5 shows the market that we'll study. The market demand curve is $D$. Initially, with many small firms in the market, the market supply curve is $S$, which is the sum of the supply curves—and marginal cost curves—of the firms. The equilibrium price is $P_C$, which makes the quantity demanded equal the quantity supplied. The equilibrium quantity is $Q_C$. Each firm takes the price $P_C$ and maximizes its profit by producing the output at which its own marginal cost equals the price.

A single firm now buys all the firms in this market. Consumers don't change, so the demand curve doesn't change. But the monopoly recognizes this demand curve as a constraint on its sales and knows that its marginal revenue curve is $MR$.

The market supply curve in perfect competition is the sum of the marginal cost curves of the firms in the industry. So the monopoly's marginal cost curve is the market supply curve of perfect competition—labeled $S = MC$. The monopoly maximizes profit by producing the quantity at which marginal revenue equals marginal cost, which is $Q_M$. This output is smaller than the competitive output, $Q_C$. The monopoly charges the price $P_M$, which is higher than $P_C$.

**Compared to perfect competition, a single-price monopoly produces a smaller output and charges a higher price.**

### ■ FIGURE 12.5

Monopoly's Smaller Output and Higher Price

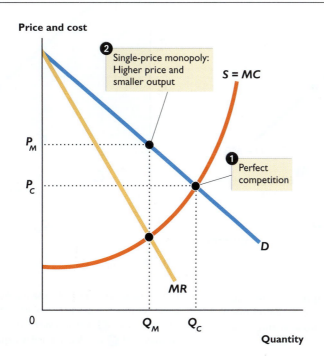

**①** A competitive industry produces the quantity $Q_C$ at price $P_C$.

**②** A single-price monopoly produces the quantity $Q_M$ at which marginal revenue equals marginal cost and sells that quantity for the price $P_M$. Compared to perfect competition, a single-price monopoly produces a smaller output and raises the price.

### ■ Is Monopoly Efficient?

You learned in Chapter 6 that resources are used efficiently when marginal benefit equals marginal cost. Figure 12.6(a) shows that perfect competition achieves this efficient use of resources. The demand curve ($D = MB$) shows the marginal benefit to consumers. The supply curve ($S = MC$) shows the marginal cost (opportunity cost) to producers. At the competitive equilibrium, the price is $P_C$ and the quantity is $Q_C$. Marginal benefit equals marginal cost, and resource use is efficient. Total surplus (Chapter 6, p. 191), the sum of *consumer surplus*, the green triangle, and *producer surplus*, the blue area, is maximized.

Figure 12.6(b) shows that monopoly is inefficient. Monopoly output is $Q_M$ and price is $P_M$. Price (marginal benefit) exceeds marginal cost and the underproduction creates a *deadweight loss* (Chapter 6, p. 193), which is shown by the gray area. Consumers lose partly by getting less of the good, shown by the gray triangle above $P_C$, and partly by paying more for the good. Consumer surplus shrinks to the smaller green triangle. Producers lose by selling less of the good, shown by the part of the gray area below $P_C$, but gain by selling their output for a higher price, shown by the dark blue rectangle. Producer surplus expands and is larger in monopoly than in perfect competition.

### ■ FIGURE 12.6

### The Inefficiency of Monopoly

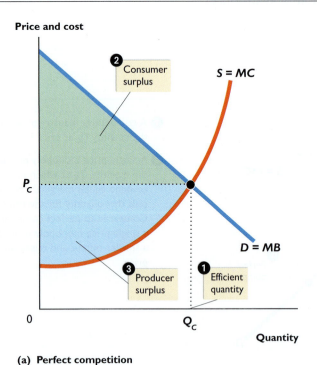

**(a) Perfect competition**

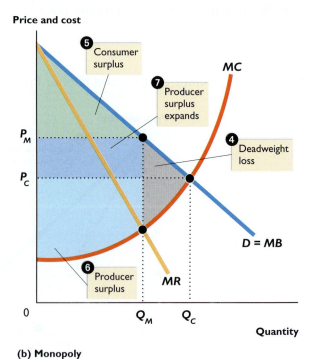

**(b) Monopoly**

In perfect competition, ❶ the equilibrium quantity is the efficient quantity, $Q_C$, because at that quantity the price, $P_C$, equals marginal benefit and marginal cost. The sum of ❷ consumer surplus and ❸ producer surplus is maximized.

In a single-price monopoly, the equilibrium quantity, $Q_M$, is inefficient because the price, $P_M$, which equals marginal benefit, exceeds marginal cost. ❹ A deadweight loss arises. ❺ Consumer surplus shrinks, and ❻ producer surplus expands by the area ❼.

## ■ Is Monopoly Fair?

Monopoly is inefficient because it creates a deadweight loss. But monopoly also *redistributes* consumer surplus. The producer gains, and the consumers lose.

Figure 12.6 shows this redistribution. The monopoly gets the difference between the higher price, $P_M$, and the competitive price, $P_C$, on the quantity sold, $Q_M$. So the dark blue rectangle shows the part of the consumer surplus taken by the monopoly. This portion of the loss of consumer surplus is not a loss to society. It is redistribution from consumers to the monopoly producer.

Are the gain for the monopoly and loss for consumers fair? You learned about two standards of fairness in Chapter 6: fair *rules* and a fair *result*. Redistribution from the rich to the poor is consistent with the fair-result view. So on this view of fairness, whether monopoly redistribution is fair or unfair depends on who is richer: the monopoly or the consumers of its product. It might be either. Whether the *rules* are fair depends on whether the monopoly has benefited from a protected position that is not available to anyone else. If everyone is free to acquire the monopoly, then the rules are fair. So monopoly is inefficient and it might be, but is not always, unfair.

The pursuit of monopoly profit leads to an additional costly activity that we'll now describe: rent seeking.

## ■ Rent Seeking

**Rent seeking** is the lobbying for special treatment from the government to create economic profit or to divert consumer surplus or producer surplus away from others. ("Rent" is a general term in economics that includes all forms of surplus such as consumer surplus, producer surplus, and economic profit.) Rent seeking does not always create a monopoly, but it always restricts competition and often creates a monopoly.

**Rent seeking**
The lobbying for special treatment from the government to create economic profit or to divert consumer surplus or producer surplus away from others.

Scarce resources can be used to produce the goods and services that people value or they can be used in rent seeking. Rent seeking is potentially profitable for the rent seeker but costly to society because it uses scarce resources purely to transfer wealth from one person or group to another person or group rather than to produce the things that people value.

To see why rent seeking occurs, think about the two ways in which a person might become the owner of a monopoly:

- Buy a monopoly.
- Create a monopoly.

### Buy a Monopoly

A person might try to make a monopoly profit by buying a firm (or a right) that is protected by a barrier to entry. Buying a taxicab medallion in New York City is an example. The number of medallions is restricted, so their owners are protected from unlimited entry into the industry. A person who wants to operate a taxi must buy a medallion from someone who already has one.

But anyone is free to enter the bidding for a medallion. So competition among buyers drives the price up to the point at which they make only zero economic profit. For example, competition for the right to operate a taxi in New York City has led to a price of $600,000 for a taxi medallion, which is sufficiently high to eliminate economic profit for taxi operators and leave entrepreneurs with only normal profit.

### Create a Monopoly

Because buying a monopoly means paying a price that soaks up the economic profit, creating a monopoly by rent seeking is an attractive alternative to buying one. Rent seeking is a political activity. It takes the form of lobbying and trying to influence the political process to get laws that create legal barriers to entry. Such influence might be sought by making campaign contributions in exchange for legislative support or by indirectly seeking to influence political outcomes through publicity in the media or by direct contact with politicians and bureaucrats. An example of a rent created in this way is the law that restricts the quantities of textiles that can be imported into the United States. Another is a law that limits the quantity of tomatoes that can be imported into the United States. These laws restrict competition, which decreases the quantity for sale and increases prices.

### Rent-Seeking Equilibrium

Rent seeking is a competitive activity. If an economic profit is available, a rent seeker will try to get some of it. Competition among rent seekers pushes up the cost of rent seeking until it leaves the monopoly earning only a zero economic profit after paying the rent-seeking costs.

Figure 12.7 shows a rent-seeking equilibrium. The cost of rent seeking is a fixed cost that must be added to a monopoly's other costs. The average total cost curve, which includes the fixed cost of rent seeking, shifts upward until it just touches the demand curve. Consumer surplus is unaffected. But the deadweight loss of monopoly now includes the original deadweight loss plus the economic profit consumed by rent seeking, which the enlarged gray area shows.

■ **FIGURE 12.7**

Rent-Seeking Equilibrium

❶ Rent-seeking costs exhaust economic profit. The firm's rent-seeking costs are fixed costs. They increase total fixed cost and average total cost. The *ATC* curve shifts upward until, at the profit-maximizing price, the firm breaks even.

❷ Monopoly profit-maximization shrinks consumer surplus relative to its maximum level in perfect competition, but rent-seeking doesn't shrink consumer surplus any further.

❸ The deadweight loss increases.

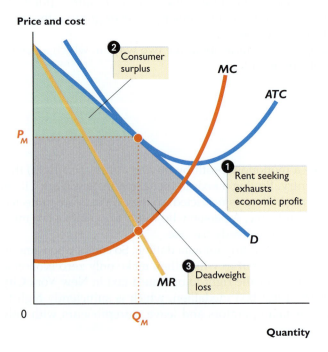

# CHECKPOINT 12.3

**Compare the performance of a single-price monopoly with that of perfect competition.**

## Practice Problems

Township is a small isolated community served by one newspaper that can meet the market demand at a lower cost than two or more newspapers could. The *Township Gazette* is the only source of news. Figure 1 shows the marginal cost of printing the *Township Gazette* and the market demand for it. The *Township Gazette* is a profit-maximizing, single-price monopoly.

1. How many copies of the *Township Gazette* are printed each day and what is the price of the *Township Gazette*?
2. What is the efficient number of copies of the *Township Gazette* and what is the price at which the efficient number of copies could be sold?
3. Is the number of copies printed the efficient quantity? Explain your answer.
4. On the graph, show the consumer surplus that is redistributed from consumers to the *Township Gazette* and the deadweight loss that arises because the *Township Gazette* is a monopoly.

## In the News

**Ticketmaster's near monopoly challenged as technology changes**
In the 1990s, to see Michael Jordan or Garth Brooks live you had to buy the ticket through Ticketmaster, or from a scalper. Today, Ticketmaster has merged with concert promoter Live Nation and now controls the sale of tickets to sports and music events. Competitors have entered the market, and events tickets are now sold through Internet auction markets.

How will the increased competition in the sale of tickets affect the service fee component of the price and the efficiency of the market? Will scalpers survive?

## Solutions to Practice Problems

1. The profit-maximizing quantity of the *Township Gazette* is 150 a day, where marginal revenue equals marginal cost. The price is 70¢ a copy (Figure 2).
2. The efficient quantity is 250 copies, where quantity demanded (marginal benefit) equals marginal cost and the price would be 50¢ a copy (Figure 2).
3. The number of copies printed is not efficient because the marginal benefit of the 150th copy (70¢) exceeds its marginal cost (40¢) (Figure 2).
4. In Figure 2, the blue rectangle ❶ shows the consumer surplus transferred from the consumers to the *Township Gazette* and the gray triangle ❷ shows the deadweight loss created.

## Solution to In the News

The price you pay for an event ticket is the sum of the price of the event plus a service fee. As a monopoly, Ticketmaster charges the profit-maximizing fee. The monopoly has weakened and competition has increased, but sellers still charge the profit-maximizing fee, although a lower fee. The ticket-selling market is more efficient, but scalpers now compete with resale auctions and appear to survive.

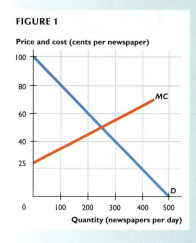

**FIGURE 2**

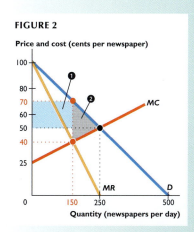

## 12.4 PRICE DISCRIMINATION

*Why does a hairdresser charge seniors, veterans, and kids $3 less than other customers?*

Price discrimination—selling a good or service at a number of different prices—is widespread. You encounter it when you travel, go to the movies, get your hair cut, buy pizza, or visit an art museum. At first sight, it appears that price discrimination contradicts the assumption of profit maximization. Why would a movie operator allow children to see movies at half price? Why would a hairdresser charge students and senior citizens less? Aren't these firms losing profit by being nice to their customers?

Deeper investigation shows that far from lowering profit, price discriminators make a bigger profit than they would otherwise. So a monopoly has an incentive to find ways of discriminating and charging each buyer the highest possible price. Some people pay less with price discrimination, but others pay more.

Most price discriminators are *not* monopolies, but monopolies do price discriminate when they can. To be able to price discriminate, a firm must

- Identify and separate different types of buyers.
- Sell a product that cannot be resold.

Price discrimination is charging different prices for a single good or service because the willingness to pay varies across buyers. Not all price *differences* are price *discrimination*. Some goods that are similar but not identical have different prices because they have different production costs. For example, the cost of producing electricity depends on time of day. If an electric power company charges a higher price for consumption between 7:00 and 9:00 in the morning and between 4:00 and 7:00 in the evening than it does at other times of the day, the company is not price discriminating.

### ■ Price Discrimination and Consumer Surplus

The key idea behind price discrimination is to convert consumer surplus into economic profit. To extract every dollar of consumer surplus from every buyer, the monopoly would have to offer each individual customer a separate price schedule based on that customer's own willingness to pay. Such price discrimination cannot be carried out in practice because a firm does not have enough information about each consumer's demand curve. But firms try to extract as much consumer surplus as possible, and to do so, they discriminate in two broad ways:

- Among groups of buyers
- Among units of a good

#### Discriminating Among Groups of Buyers

To price discriminate among groups of buyers, the firm offers different prices to different types of buyers, based on things such as age, employment status, or some other easily distinguished characteristic. This type of price discrimination works when each group has a different average willingness to pay for the good or service.

For example, a face-to-face sales meeting with a customer might bring a large and profitable order. For salespeople and other business travelers, the marginal benefit from an airplane trip is large and the price that such a traveler will pay for a trip is high. In contrast, for a vacation traveler, any of several different trips or even no vacation trip are options. So for vacation travelers, the marginal benefit of a trip is small and the price that such a traveler will pay for a trip is low. Because business travelers are willing to pay more than vacation travelers are, it is possible for an airline to profit by price discriminating between these two groups.

### Discriminating Among Units of a Good

To price discriminate among units of a good, the firm charges the same prices to all its customers but offers a lower price per unit for a larger number of units bought. When Pizza Hut charges $10 for one home-delivered pizza and $14 for two, it is using this type of price discrimination. In this example, the price of the second pizza is only $4.

Let's see how an airline exploits the differences in demand by business and vacation travelers and increases its profit by price discriminating.

### ■ Profiting by Price Discriminating

Global Air has a monopoly on an exotic route. Figure 12.8 shows the demand curve (*D*) for travel on this route and Global Air's marginal revenue curve (*MR*). It also shows Global Air's marginal cost (*MC*) and average total cost (*ATC*) curves.

Initially, Global is a single-price monopoly and maximizes its profit by producing 8,000 trips a year (the quantity at which *MR* equals *MC*). The price is $1,200 a trip. The average total cost of a trip is $600, so economic profit is $600 a trip. On 8,000 trips, Global's economic profit is $4.8 million a year, shown by the blue rectangle. Global's customers enjoy a consumer surplus shown by the green triangle.

### ■ FIGURE 12.8

A Single-Price Monopoly's Price and Economic Profit

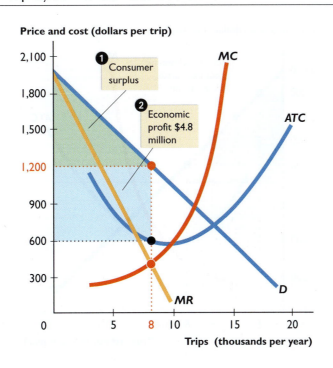

Global Air has a monopoly on an air route. The demand curve for travel on this route is *D*, and Global's marginal revenue curve is *MR*. Its marginal cost curve is *MC*, and its average total cost curve is *ATC*.

As a single-price monopoly, Global maximizes profit by selling 8,000 trips a year at $1,200 a trip.

❶ Global's customers enjoy a consumer surplus—the green triangle.

❷ Global's economic profit is $4.8 million a year—the blue rectangle.

Global is struck by the fact that many of its customers are business travelers, and Global suspects that they are willing to pay more than $1,200 a trip. So Global does some market research, which tells Global that some business travelers are willing to pay as much as $1,800 a trip. Also, these customers almost always make their travel plans at the last moment. Another group of business travelers is willing to pay $1,600. These customers know a week ahead when they will travel, and prefer a refundable ticket. Yet another group is willing to pay up to $1,400. These travelers know two weeks ahead when they will travel, and they are happy to buy a nonrefundable ticket.

So Global announces a new fare schedule: No restrictions, $1,800; 7-day advance purchase, refundable, $1,600; 14-day advance purchase, nonrefundable, $1,400; 14-day advance purchase, must stay at least 7 days, $1,200.

Figure 12.9 shows the outcome with this new fare structure and also shows why Global is pleased with its new fares. It sells 2,000 trips at each of its four prices. Global's economic profit increases by the area of the blue steps in the figure. Its economic profit is now its original $4.8 million a year plus an additional $2.4 million from its new higher fares. Consumer surplus has shrunk to the sum of the smaller green triangles.

## ■ Perfect Price Discrimination

**Perfect price discrimination**
Price discrimination that extracts the entire consumer surplus by charging the highest price that consumers are willing to pay for each unit.

But Global thinks that it can do even better. It plans to achieve **perfect price discrimination,** which extracts the entire consumer surplus by charging the highest price that consumers are willing to pay for each unit. To do so, Global must get creative and come up with a host of additional business fares ranging between $2,000 and $1,200, each one of which appeals to a small segment of the business market.

## ■ FIGURE 12.9

### Price Discrimination

Global revises its fare structure. It now offers no restrictions at $1,800; 7-day advance purchase, refundable at $1,600; 14-day advance purchase, nonrefundable at $1,400; and 14-day advance purchase, must stay at least 7 days, at $1,200.

Global sells 2,000 units at each of its four new fares. Its economic profit increases by $2.4 million a year to $7.2 million a year, which is shown by the original profit (light blue rectangle) plus the blue steps. Global's customers' consumer surplus shrinks to the sum of the green areas.

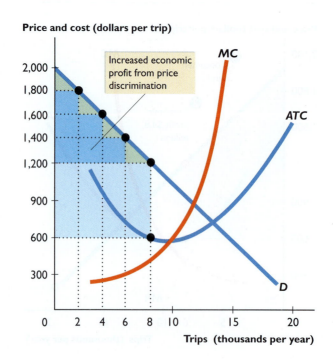

Once Global is discriminating finely between different customers and getting from each customer the maximum he or she is willing to pay, something special happens to marginal revenue. Recall that for the single-price monopoly, marginal revenue is less than price. The reason is that when the price is cut to sell a larger quantity, the price is lower on all units sold. But with perfect price discrimination, Global sells only the marginal seat at the lower price. All the other customers continue to buy for the highest price they are willing to pay. So for the perfect price discriminator, marginal revenue equals price and the demand curve becomes the marginal revenue curve.

With marginal revenue equal to price, Global can obtain yet greater profit by increasing output up to the point at which price (and marginal revenue) is equal to marginal cost.

So Global now seeks additional travelers who will not pay as much as $1,200 a trip but who will pay more than marginal cost. More creative pricing comes up with vacation specials and other fares that have combinations of advance reservation, minimum stay, and other restrictions that make these fares unattractive to Global's existing customers but attractive to a further group of travelers. With all these fares and specials, Global extracts the entire consumer surplus and maximizes economic profit.

Figure 12.10 shows the outcome with perfect price discrimination. The dozens of fares paid by the original travelers who are willing to pay between $1,200 and $2,000 have extracted the entire consumer surplus from this group and converted it into economic profit for Global. The new fares between $900 and $1,200 have attracted 3,000 additional travelers but have taken their entire consumer surplus also. Global is earning an economic profit of more than $9 million a year.

### FIGURE 12.10

Perfect Price Discrimination

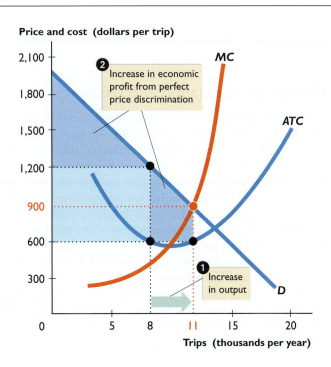

Price and cost (dollars per trip)

Trips (thousands per year)

With perfect price discrimination, the demand curve becomes Global's marginal revenue curve. Economic profit is maximized when the lowest price equals marginal cost.

❶ Output increases to 11,000 passengers a year, and ❷ Global's economic profit increases to $9.35 million a year.

# EYE on the U.S. ECONOMY
## Airline Price Discrimination

The normal coach fare from San Francisco to Washington, D.C., is $837; with a nonrefundable ticket, no change fee, one checked bag, and priority boarding is $506; and with a non-refundable ticket is $245. On a typical flight, passengers might be paying as many as 20 different fares.

The airlines sort their customers according to their willingness to pay by offering a variety of options that attract price-sensitive leisure travelers but don't get bought by business travelers.

Despite the sophistication of the airlines' pricing schemes, almost 20 percent of seats fly empty. The marginal cost of filling an empty seat is close to zero, so a ticket sold at a few dollars would be profitable.

Low fares are now feasible, thanks to priceline.com and dozens of other online travel agents. Shopping around the airlines with bids from travelers, these agents broker thousands of tickets a day and obtain the lowest possible fares for their customers.

Would it bother you to hear how little I paid for this flight?

Credit: William Hamilton

## ■ Price Discrimination and Efficiency

With perfect price discrimination, the monopoly increases output to the point at which price equals marginal cost. This output is identical to that of perfect competition. Perfect price discrimination pushes consumer surplus to zero but increases producer surplus to equal the sum of consumer surplus and producer surplus in perfect competition. Deadweight loss with perfect price discrimination is zero. So perfect price discrimination produces the efficient quantity.

But there are two differences between perfect competition and perfect price discrimination. First, the distribution of the total surplus is different. It is shared by consumers and producers in perfect competition while the producer gets it all with perfect price discrimination. Second, because the producer grabs all the total surplus, rent seeking becomes profitable.

Rent seekers use resources in pursuit of monopoly, and the bigger the rents, the greater is the incentive to use resources to pursue those rents. With free entry into rent seeking, the long-run equilibrium outcome is that rent seekers use up the entire producer surplus.

**CHECKPOINT 12.4**

Explain how price discrimination increases profit.

## Practice Problems

Village, a small isolated town, has one doctor. For a 30-minute consultation, the doctor charges a rich person twice as much as a poor person.

1. Does the doctor practice price discrimination? Is the doctor using resources efficiently? Does the doctor's pricing scheme redistribute consumer surplus? If so, explain how.

2. If the doctor decided to charge everyone the maximum price that he or she would be willing to pay, what would be the consumer surplus? Would the market for medical service in Village be efficient?

## In the News

**Feast on these great dining deals**

Entrées at Patina in Los Angeles start at $40, but the four-course fixed menu is $59. And pair that with the waived corkage fee on Tuesdays. At Michael Mina, San Francisco, enjoy a three-course, prix-fixe lunch for $49 or pay up to $65 when ordering the same items individually at dinner.

Source: *USA Today*, July 29, 2011

Are Patina and Michael Mina price discriminating? Explain your answer.

## Solutions to Practice Problems

1. The doctor practices price discrimination because rich people and poor people pay a different price for the same service: a 30-minute consultation. The doctor provides the profit-maximizing number of consultations and charges rich people more than poor people. As a monopoly, the total number of consultations is less than that at which marginal benefit equals the marginal cost of providing the medical service. Because marginal benefit does not equal marginal cost, the doctor is not using resources efficiently. With price discrimination, some consumer surplus is redistributed to the doctor as profit.

2. The doctor decides to practice perfect price discrimination. If successful, with perfect price discrimination, marginal revenue equals price. To maximize economic profit, the doctor increases the number of consultations to make the lowest price charged equal to the marginal cost of providing the service. The doctor takes the entire consumer surplus, so consumer surplus is zero.
   Marginal benefit equals price, so resources are being used efficiently.

## Solution to In the News

A restaurant meal cannot be resold, so price discrimination is possible. Offering a four-course fixed menu at a lower price than the sum of the prices of the individual items is price discrimination. Diners who want fewer than four courses and want to be more selective about what they eat pay more. Waiving the corkage fee on Tuesdays is not price discrimination. Demand is lower on Tuesdays, so the profit-maximizing price is lower. Waiving the corkage fee is a way of price cutting without reprinting the menu.

## 12.5   MONOPOLY REGULATION

Natural monopoly presents a dilemma. With economies of scale, a natural monopoly produces at the lowest possible cost. But with market power, the monopoly has an incentive to raise the price above the competitive price and produce too little—to operate in the self-interest of the monopoly and not in the social interest.

**Regulation**

Rules administered by a government agency to influence prices, quantities, entry, and other aspects of economic activity in a firm or industry.

**Regulation**—rules administered by a government agency to influence prices, quantities, entry, and other aspects of economic activity in a firm or industry—is a possible solution to this dilemma.

To implement regulation, the government establishes agencies to oversee and enforce the rules. For example, the Surface Transportation Board regulates prices on interstate railroads and some trucking and bus lines, and water and oil pipelines. By the 1970s, almost a quarter of the nation's output was produced by regulated industries (far more than just natural monopolies) and a process of deregulation began.

**Deregulation**

The process of removing regulation of prices, quantities, entry, and other aspects of economic activity in a firm or industry.

**Deregulation** is the process of removing regulation of prices, quantities, entry, and other aspects of economic activity in a firm or industry. During the past 30 years, deregulation has occurred in domestic air transportation, telephone service, interstate trucking, and banking and financial services. Cable TV was deregulated in 1984, re-regulated in 1992, and deregulated again in 1996.

Regulation is a *possible* solution to the dilemma presented by monopoly but not a sure-bet solution. There are two theories about how regulation actually works: the *social interest theory* and the *capture theory*.

**Social interest theory**

The theory that regulation achieves an efficient allocation of resources.

The **social interest theory** is that the political and regulatory process relentlessly seeks out inefficiency and introduces regulation that eliminates deadweight loss and allocates resources efficiently.

**Capture theory**

The theory that the regulation serves the self-interest of the producer and results in maximum profit, underproduction, and deadweight loss.

The **capture theory** is that the political and regulatory process gets captured by the regulated firm and ends up serving its self-interest, with maximum economic profit, underproduction, and deadweight loss. The regulator gets captured because the producer's gain is large and visible while each individual consumer's gain is small and invisible. No individual consumer has an incentive to oppose the regulation, but the producer has a big incentive to lobby for it.

Which theory of regulation best explains real-world regulations? Does regulation serve the social interest or the self-interest of monopoly producers?

### ■ Efficient Regulation of a Natural Monopoly

A cable TV company is a *natural monopoly* (pp. 346–347)—it can supply the entire market at a lower price than two or more competing firms can. Cox Communications, based in Atlanta, supplies cable TV to households in 16 states. It has invested heavily in satellite receiving dishes, cables, and control equipment and so has large fixed costs. These fixed costs are part of the company's average total cost. Its average total cost decreases as the number of households served increases because the fixed cost is spread over a larger number of households. Unregulated, Cox Communications serves the number of households that maximizes profit. Like all single-price monopolies, the profit-maximizing quantity is less than the efficient quantity and underproduction results in a deadweight loss (see Figure 12.6, p. 356).

**Marginal cost pricing rule**

A rule that sets price equal to marginal cost to achieve an efficient output.

How can Cox be regulated to produce the efficient quantity of cable TV service? The answer is by being regulated to set its price equal to marginal cost, known as the **marginal cost pricing rule.** The quantity demanded at a price equal to marginal cost is the efficient quantity—the quantity at which marginal benefit equals marginal cost.

Figure 12.11 illustrates the marginal cost pricing rule. The demand curve for cable TV is *D*. Cox's marginal cost curve is *MC*. That marginal cost curve is (assumed to be) horizontal at $10 per household per month—that is, the cost of providing each additional household with a month of cable programming is $10. The efficient outcome occurs if the price is regulated at $10 per household per month with 8 million households served.

But there is a problem: Because average total cost exceeds marginal cost, a firm that follows the marginal cost pricing rule incurs an economic loss. So a cable TV company that is required to use a marginal cost pricing rule will not stay in business for long. How can the firm cover its costs and, at the same time, obey a marginal cost pricing rule?

One possibility is price discrimination (see pp. 360–364). Another possibility is to use a two-part price (called a *two-part tariff*). For example, local telephone companies charge consumers a monthly fee for being connected to the telephone system and then charge a price equal to marginal cost (zero) for each local call. A cable TV operator can charge a one-time connection fee that covers its fixed cost and then charge a monthly fee equal to marginal cost.

## ■ Second-Best Regulation of a Natural Monopoly

Regulation of a natural monopoly cannot always achieve an efficient outcome. Two possible ways of enabling a regulated monopoly to avoid an economic loss are

- Average cost pricing
- Government subsidy

■ **FIGURE 12.11**

### Natural Monopoly: Marginal Cost Pricing

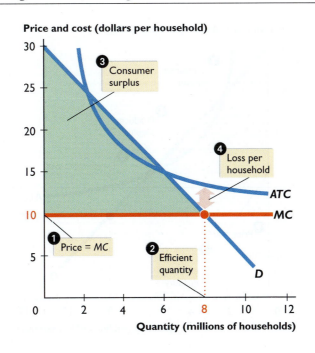

The market demand curve for cable TV is *D*. A cable TV operator's marginal cost *MC* is a constant $10 per household per month. Its fixed cost is large, and the average total cost curve, which includes average fixed cost, is *ATC*.

❶ Price is set equal to marginal cost at $10 a month.

❷ At this price, the efficient quantity (8 million households) is served.

❸ Consumer surplus is maximized as shown by the green triangle.

❹ The firm incurs a loss on each household served, shown by the red arrow.

## Average Cost Pricing

**Average cost pricing rule**
A rule that sets price equal to average total cost to enable a regulated firm to avoid economic loss.

The **average cost pricing rule** sets price equal to average total cost. With this rule the firm produces the quantity at which the average total cost curve cuts the demand curve. This rule results in the firm making zero economic profit—breaking even. But because for a natural monopoly average total cost exceeds marginal cost, the quantity produced is less than the efficient quantity and a deadweight loss arises. Figure 12.12 illustrates the average cost pricing rule. The price is $15 a month and 6 million households get cable TV. The gray triangle shows the deadweight loss.

## Government Subsidy

A government subsidy is a direct payment to the firm equal to its economic loss. But to pay a subsidy, the government must raise the revenue by taxing some other activity. You saw in Chapter 7 that taxes themselves generate deadweight loss.

## And the Second-Best Is...

Which is the better option, average cost pricing or marginal cost pricing with a government subsidy? The answer turns on the relative magnitudes of the two deadweight losses. Average cost pricing generates a deadweight loss in the market served by the natural monopoly. A subsidy generates deadweight losses in the markets for the items that are taxed to pay the subsidy. The smaller deadweight loss is the second-best solution to regulating a natural monopoly. Making this calculation in practice is too difficult and average cost pricing is generally preferred to a subsidy.

■ **FIGURE 12.12**

Natural Monopoly: Average Cost Pricing

❶ Price is set equal to average total cost at $15 a month.

At this price, ❷ the quantity served (6 million households) is less than the efficient quantity (8 million households).

❸ Consumer surplus shrinks to the smaller green triangle.

❹ A producer surplus enables the firm to pay its total fixed cost and break even.

❺ A deadweight loss, shown by the gray triangle, arises.

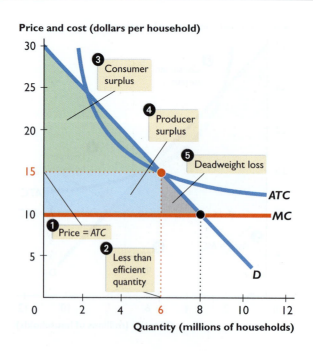

# EYE on MICROSOFT

## Are Microsoft's Prices Too High?

Microsoft's prices are too high in the sense that they exceed marginal cost and result in fewer copies sold of the Windows operating system and Office application than the efficient quantities.

### Profit Maximization

The figure illustrates how Microsoft prices its products to maximize profit. The demand for copies of the Windows Vista operating system is D. The marginal revenue curve is MR. The marginal cost of an additional copy of Vista is very small and we assume it to be zero, with marginal cost curve MC.

Profit is maximized by producing the quantity at which marginal revenue equals marginal cost. In the figure, that quantity is 4 million copies of Vista per month. The price is $300 per copy and Microsoft receives a producer surplus shown by the blue rectangle.

### Inefficiency

The efficient quantity is 8 million copies per month, where price and marginal benefit equal marginal cost. Because the actual quantity is smaller than the efficient quantity, a deadweight loss arises and the gray triangle shows its magnitude. The green triangle shows the consumer surplus.

### Fixed Cost

The marginal cost of a copy of Windows Vista might be close to zero but the fixed cost of developing the software is large. Microsoft must at least earn enough revenue to pay these fixed costs.

Earning enough to pay the firm's fixed costs does not inevitably lead to inefficiency. Some firms with zero marginal cost and the market power to charge a high price do choose to provide the efficient quantity of their services at a zero price.

### The Google Solution

Google is one such firm. The price of an Internet search on Google is zero. The quantity of searches is that at which the marginal benefit of a search equals the zero marginal cost, so the quantity of searches is the efficient quantity.

Google earns revenue, and a very large revenue, by selling advertising that more than pays its fixed operating costs.

### Efficiency

Advertising on Google is more effective than a TV or poster advertisement because it is targeted at potential buyers of products based on the topics of their searches.

The Google solution delivers the efficient quantity of zero-marginal-cost Internet search activity.

The Google solution might also deliver the efficient quantity of advertising. It will do so if Google is able to achieve perfect price discrimination in the market for advertising.

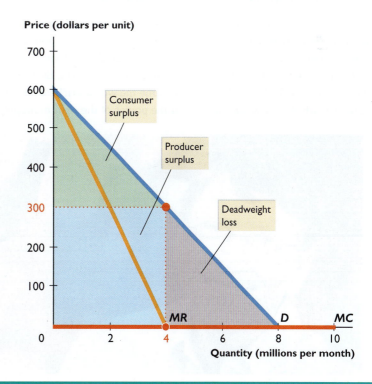

Implementing average cost pricing presents the regulator with a challenge because it is not possible to be sure of a firm's costs. So regulators use one of two practical rules:

- Rate of return regulation
- Price cap regulation

### Rate of Return Regulation

**Rate of return regulation**

A regulation that sets the price at a level that enables a firm to earn a specified target rate of return on its capital.

Under **rate of return regulation,** the price is set at a level that enables the firm to earn a specified target rate of return on its capital. This type of regulation can end up serving the self-interest of the firm rather than the social interest. The firm's managers have an incentive to inflate costs by spending on items such as private jets, free baseball tickets (disguised as public relations expenses), and lavish entertainment. Managers also have an incentive to use more capital than the efficient amount. The *rate* of return on capital is regulated but not the *total* return on capital, and the greater the amount of capital, the greater is the total return.

# EYE on YOUR LIFE
## Monopoly in Your Everyday Life

When Bill Gates decided to quit Harvard in 1975, he realized that PCs would need an operating system and applications programs to interact with the computer's hardware. He also knew that whoever owned the copyright on these programs would have a license to print money. And he wanted to be that person.

In less than 30 years, Bill Gates became the world's richest person. Such is the power of the right monopoly.

You, along with millions of other PC users, have willingly paid the monopoly price for Windows and Microsoft Office. Sure, the marginal cost of a copy of these programs is close to zero, so the quantity sold is way too few. There is a big deadweight loss.

Compared with the alternative of no Windows, you're better off. But are you better off than you would be if there were many alternatives to Windows competing for your attention? To answer this question, think about the applications—spreadsheets, word processing, and so on—that you need to make your computer useful. With lots of operating systems, what would happen to the cost of developing applications? Would you have more or less choice?

## Price Cap Regulation

For the reason that we've just examined, rate of return regulation is increasingly being replaced by price cap regulation. A **price cap regulation** is a price ceiling—a rule that specifies the highest price the firm is permitted to set. This type of regulation lowers the price and gives the firm an incentive to minimize its costs. But what happens to the quantity produced?

Recall that in a competitive market, a price ceiling set below the equilibrium price decreases output and creates a shortage (see Chapter 7, pp. 212–214). In contrast, in natural monopoly a price ceiling increases output. The reason is that at the regulated price, the firm can sell any quantity it chooses up to the quantity demanded. So each additional unit sold brings in the same additional revenue: marginal revenue equals price. The regulated price exceeds marginal cost, so the profit-maximizing quantity becomes the quantity demanded at the price ceiling.

Figure 12.13 illustrates this outcome. Unregulated, a cable TV operator maximizes profit by serving 4 million households at a price of $20 a month. With a price cap set at $15 a month, the firm is permitted to sell any quantity it chooses at that price or at a lower price. The profit-maximizing quantity now increases to 6 million households. Serving fewer than 6 million households, the firm incurs a loss—average total cost exceeds the price cap. Serving more than 6 million households is possible but only by lowering the price along the demand curve. Again, average total cost exceeds price and the firm incurs a loss.

In Figure 12.13, the price cap delivers average cost pricing. In practice, the regulator might set the cap too high. For this reason, price cap regulation is often combined with *earnings sharing regulation*—a regulation that requires firms to make refunds to customers when profits rise above a target level.

**Price cap regulation**
A rule that specifies the highest price that a firm is permitted to set—a price ceiling.

### FIGURE 12.13

Natural Monopoly: Price Cap Regulation

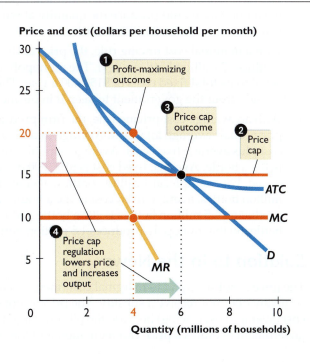

**❶** With no regulation, a cable TV operator serves 4 million households at a price of $20 a month.

**❷** A price cap regulation sets the maximum price at $15 a month.

**❸** Only when 6 million households are served can the firm break even. (When fewer than 6 million households are served or more than 6 million households are served, the firm incurs an economic loss.) The firm has an incentive to keep costs as low as possible and to produce the quantity demanded at the price cap.

**❹** The price cap regulation lowers the price and increases the quantity.

# CHECKPOINT 12.5

**Explain why natural monopoly is regulated and the effects of regulation.**

## Practice Problems

An unregulated natural monopoly bottles Elixir, a unique health product that has no substitutes. The monopoly's total fixed cost is $150,000, and its marginal cost is 10¢ a bottle. Figure 1 illustrates the demand for Elixir.

1. How many bottles of Elixir does the monopoly sell and what is the price of a bottle of Elixir? Is the monopoly's use of resources efficient?

2. Suppose that the government introduces a marginal cost pricing rule. What is the price of Elixir, the quantity sold, and the monopoly's economic profit?

3. Suppose that the government introduces an average cost pricing rule. What is the price of Elixir, the quantity sold, and the monopoly's economic profit?

## In the News

**Mexicans protest the plan to end the state oil monopoly**
Protesters fight the plan to open Mexico's state oil monopoly to private investment. In Mexico, the government sets the price and taxes the monopoly's profit. The price in Mexico is $2.48 a gallon and in the United States is $3.37 a gallon.
*Source: USA Today*, April 13, 2008

Describe how the Mexican government regulates the domestic oil market.

## Solutions to Practice Problems

1. The monopoly will produce 1 million bottles a year—the quantity at which marginal revenue equals marginal cost. The price is 30¢ a bottle—the highest price at which the monopoly can sell the 1 million bottles a year (Figure 2). The monopoly's use of resources is inefficient. If resource use were efficient, the monopoly would produce the quantity at which marginal benefit (price) equals marginal cost: 2 million bottles a year.

2. With a marginal cost pricing rule, the price is 10¢ a bottle and the monopoly produces 2 million bottles a year. The monopoly incurs an economic loss equal to its total fixed costs of $150,000 a year. The monopoly would need a subsidy from the government to keep it in business.

3. With an average cost pricing rule, the firm produces the quantity at which price equals average total cost. Average total cost equals average variable cost plus average fixed cost. Average variable cost equals marginal cost and is 10¢ a bottle. Average fixed cost is $150,000 divided by the quantity produced. For example, at 1 million bottles, average fixed cost is 15¢ and at 1.5 million bottles, average fixed cost is 10¢ a bottle. The average total cost of producing 1.5 million bottles is 20¢ a bottle and they can be sold for 20¢ a bottle. So the monopoly produces 1.5 million bottles a year and breaks even.

## Solution to In the News

The price is not set equal to marginal cost (marginal cost pricing) because the oil company does not receive a subsidy. The price is not set equal to average total cost (average cost pricing) because the oil company does not break even. The government operates a price cap regulation and the company pays a profit tax.

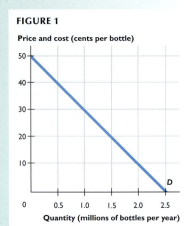

**FIGURE 1**

Price and cost (cents per bottle)

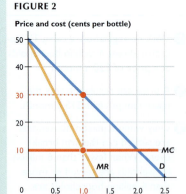

**FIGURE 2**

Price and cost (cents per bottle)

## CHAPTER SUMMARY

## Key Points

1. **Explain how monopoly arises and distinguish between single-price monopoly and price-discriminating monopoly.**

   - In monopoly, a single producer of a good or service that has no close substitutes operates behind natural, ownership, or legal barriers to entry.
   - A monopoly can price discriminate when there is no resale possibility.
   - Where resale is possible, a firm charges a single price.

2. **Explain how a single-price monopoly determines its output and price.**

   - The demand for a monopoly's output is the market demand, and a single-price monopoly's marginal revenue is less than price.
   - A monopoly maximizes profit by producing the quantity at which marginal revenue equals marginal cost and by charging the maximum price that consumers are willing to pay for that quantity.

3. **Compare the performance of a single-price monopoly with that of perfect competition.**

   - A single-price monopoly charges a higher price and produces a smaller quantity than does a perfectly competitive market and creates a deadweight loss.
   - Monopoly imposes a loss on society that equals its deadweight loss plus the cost of the resources devoted to rent seeking.

4. **Explain how price discrimination increases profit.**

   - Perfect price discrimination captures the entire consumer surplus. Prices are the highest that each consumer is willing to pay for each unit.
   - With perfect price discrimination, the monopoly is efficient but rent seeking uses some or all of the producer surplus.

5. **Explain why natural monopoly is regulated and the effects of regulation.**

   - Regulation might achieve an efficient use of resources or help the monopoly to maximize economic profit.
   - A natural monopoly is efficient if its price equals marginal cost, but a second-best outcome is for price to equal average total cost.
   - A price cap supported by earnings sharing regulation is the most effective practical method of regulating a natural monopoly.

## Key Terms

Average cost pricing rule, 368
Barrier to entry, 346
Capture theory, 366
Deregulation, 366
Legal monopoly, 347
Marginal cost pricing rule, 366

Monopoly, 346
Natural monopoly, 346
Perfect price discrimination, 362
Price cap regulation, 371
Price-discriminating monopoly, 348
Rate of return regulation, 370

Regulation, 366
Rent seeking, 357
Single-price monopoly, 348
Social interest theory, 366

# CHAPTER CHECKPOINT

## Study Plan Problems and Applications

Use the following information to work Problems **1** to **3**.

Elixir Spring produces a unique and highly prized mineral water. The firm's total fixed cost is $5,000 a day, and its marginal cost is zero. Table 1 shows the demand schedule for Elixir water.

**TABLE 1**

| Price (dollars per bottle) | Quantity (bottles per day) |
| --- | --- |
| 10 | 0 |
| 8 | 2,000 |
| 6 | 4,000 |
| 4 | 6,000 |
| 2 | 8,000 |
| 0 | 10,000 |

1. On a graph, show the demand curve for Elixir water and Elixir Spring's marginal revenue curve. What are Elixir's profit-maximizing price, output, and economic profit?

2. Compare Elixir's profit-maximizing price with the marginal cost of producing the profit-maximizing output. At the profit-maximizing price, is the demand for Elixir water inelastic or elastic?

3. Suppose that there are 1,000 springs, all able to produce this water at zero marginal cost and with zero fixed costs. Compare the equilibrium price and quantity produced with the price and quantity produced by Elixir water.

4. Blue Rose Inc. is the only flower grower to have cracked the secret of making a blue rose. Figure 1 shows the demand for blue roses and the marginal cost of producing a blue rose. What is Blue Rose's profit-maximizing output? What price does Blue Rose Inc. charge and is it efficient?

**FIGURE 1**

Hawaii Cable Television is a natural monopoly. Sketch a market demand curve and the firm's cost curves. Use your graph to work Problems **5** to **8**.

5. If Hawaii Cable is unregulated and maximizes profit, show in your graph the price, quantity, economic profit, consumer surplus, and deadweight loss.

6. If Hawaii Cable is unregulated and it gives householders a 50 percent discount for second and third connections, describe how its economic profit, consumer surplus, and deadweight loss would change.

7. If Hawaii Cable is regulated in the social interest, show in your graph the price, quantity, economic profit, consumer surplus, and deadweight loss.

8. If Hawaii Cable is subject to a price cap regulation that enables it to break even, show in your graph the price, quantity, economic profit, consumer surplus, and deadweight loss.

Use the following information to work Problems **9** and **10**.

**FCC planning rules to open cable market**
The Federal Communications Commission (FCC) will make it easier for independent programmers and rival video services to lease access to cable channels. The FCC will also limit the market share of a cable company to 30 percent.
Source: *The New York Times*, November 10, 2007

9. What barriers to entry exist in the cable television market? Are high cable prices evidence of monopoly power?

10. Draw a graph to illustrate the effects of the FCC's new regulations on the price, quantity, consumer surplus, producer surplus, and deadweight loss.

11. Read *Eye on Microsoft* on p. 369 and explain how Windows' price, quantity, consumer surplus, producer surplus, and deadweight loss would change if Microsoft were able to sell ads that appear every time a user opens a program. Illustrate your answer with a graph.

## Instructor Assignable Problems and Applications

Use the following information to work Problems **1** and **2**.

**Microsoft: We're not gouging Europe on Windows 7 pricing**
Regulators in the European Union have charged Microsoft with illegally tying Internet Explorer (IE) to Windows and mandated that a version of Windows be offered stripped of IE. A news report suggested that when Microsoft launches Windows 7, it will charge a higher price for the IE-stripped version than the price for a full version that includes IE. Microsoft denied this report but announced that it would offer the full version of Windows 7 at a lower upgrade price.

Source: computerworld.com

1. How does Microsoft set the price of Windows and would it be in the firm's self-interest to set a different price for a version stripped of IE?

2. Why might Microsoft offer the full version of Windows 7 to European customers at a lower upgrade price?

Use the following information to work Problems **3** and **4**.

Bobbie's Hair Care is a natural monopoly. Table 1 shows the demand schedule (the first two columns) and Bobbie's marginal cost schedule (the middle and third columns). Bobbie has done a survey and discovered that she has four types of customers each hour: one woman who is willing to pay $18, one senior who is willing to pay $16, one student who is willing to pay $14, and one boy who is willing to pay $12. Suppose that Bobbie's fixed costs are $20 an hour and Bobbie's price discriminates.

3. What is the price each type of customer is charged and how many haircuts an hour does Bobbie's sell? What is the increase in Bobbie's economic profit that results from price discrimination?

4. Who benefits from Bobbie's price discrimination? Is the quantity of haircuts efficient?

Use the following information to work Problems **5** to **10**.

Big Top is the only circus in the nation. Table 2 sets out the demand schedule for circus tickets and the cost schedule for producing the circus.

5. Calculate Big Top's profit-maximizing price, output, and economic profit if it charges a single price for all tickets.

6. When Big Top maximizes profit, what is the consumer surplus and producer surplus and is the circus efficient? Explain why or why not.

7. At the market equilibrium price, no children under 10 years old attend the circus. Big Top offers children under 10 a discount of 50 percent. How will this discount change the consumer surplus and producer surplus? Will Big Top be more efficient by offering the discount to children?

8. If Big Top is regulated to produce the efficient output, what is the quantity of tickets sold, what is the price of a ticket, and what would be the consumer surplus?

9. If Big Top is regulated to charge a price equal to average total cost, what is the quantity of tickets sold, the price of a ticket, and economic profit?

10. Draw a graph to illustrate the circus market if regulators set a price cap that enables Big Top to break even. Show the deadweight loss in your graph.

**TABLE 1**

| Price (dollars per haircut) | Quantity (haircuts per hour) | Marginal cost (dollars per hour) |
|---|---|---|
| 20 | 0 | — |
| 18 | 1 | 1 |
| 16 | 2 | 4 |
| 14 | 3 | 8 |
| 12 | 4 | 12 |
| 10 | 5 | 18 |

**TABLE 2**

| Price (dollars per ticket) | Quantity (tickets per show) | Total cost (dollars per show) |
|---|---|---|
| 20 | 0 | 1,000 |
| 18 | 100 | 1,600 |
| 16 | 200 | 2,200 |
| 14 | 300 | 2,800 |
| 12 | 400 | 3,400 |
| 10 | 500 | 4,000 |
| 8 | 600 | 4,600 |
| 6 | 700 | 5,200 |
| 4 | 800 | 5,800 |

## Critical Thinking Discussion Questions

**1. Mexicans protest the plan to end the state oil monopoly**

Protesters fight the plan to open Mexico's state oil monopoly to private investment. In Mexico, the government sets the price and taxes the monopoly's profit. The price in Mexico is $2.48 a gallon, and in the United States it is $3.37 a gallon.

Source: *USA Today*, April 13, 2008

a. Why do you think some people protest privatizing Mexico's state oil monopoly?

b. If the government decided to proceed with the privatization plan, what accompanying action might end the protest?

**2. Fiji TV**

Data shows that Fiji TV has made a profit since the 1997–98 financial year. Profits rose from $105,916 in 1997–98 to $213,857 in 1998–99. During the year 1999–2000, Fiji TV recorded a profit of $826,126.

Source: Asia-Pacific Network, November 6, 2002

a. In what type of market is Fiji TV operating? Explain your answer.

b. If the primary objective of Fiji TV channel is to educate the public, explain why the market might be inefficient?

c. Would Fijian economic welfare be improved if Fiji TV was privatized? Would a private TV company have lower costs, higher prices, and larger economic profit?

d. Would a private Fiji TV monopoly be able to price discriminate? Explain why and how or why not?

**3. Transportation monopoly in South Africa**

For a decade, South Africa's Transnet, enjoyed absolute monopoly of the country's transportation sector. It had control over virtually the entire transportation sector there. However, recently the company has been heading towards a deep financial crisis.

Source: Association of African Business School

a. Using only what you've learned in this chapter, what was the likely reason for Transnet's crisis?

b. Do you think that the transportation monopoly is a natural monopoly? Explain your answer.

c. How could the transportation market be regulated to be efficient?

**4. Sky high prices**

The U.K. competition regulator may force Sky TV to put a cap on its wholesale prices to rivals like BT Vision for showing sports and film channels. BT is ready to undercut Sky's prices for sports channels if prices are capped.

Source: BBC News, 30 March 2010

a. What is the effect of Sky's monopoly of U.K. satellite television provision on the prices charged to access the satellite network?

b. Explain why a price cap might be the most appropriate way to ensure fair and effective competition.

## Which cell phone?
## Is two too few?

# Monopolistic Competition and Oligopoly

**13**

**CHAPTER CHECKLIST**

**When you have completed your study of this chapter, you will be able to**

**1** Explain how a firm in monopolistic competition determines its price and quantity.

**2** Explain why advertising costs are high in monopolistic competition.

**3** Explain the dilemma faced by firms in oligopoly.

**4** Use game theory to explain how price and quantity are determined in oligopoly.

## 13.1   WHAT IS MONOPOLISTIC COMPETITION?

Most real-world markets lie between the extremes of perfect competition in Chapter 11 and monopoly in Chapter 12. Most firms possess some power to set their prices as monopolies do, and they face competition from the entry of new firms as the firms in perfect competition do. We call the markets in which such firms operate *monopolistic competition*. The other market that we study in this chapter, *oligopoly*, also lies between perfect competition and monopoly.

*Monopolistic competition* is a market structure in which

- A large number of firms compete.
- Each firm produces a differentiated product.
- Firms compete on price, product quality, and marketing.
- Firms are free to enter and exit.

### ■ Large Number of Firms

In monopolistic competition, as in perfect competition, the industry consists of a large number of firms. The presence of a large number of firms has three implications for the firms in the industry.

#### Small Market Share

Each firm supplies a small part of the market. Consequently, while each firm can influence the price of its own product, it has little power to influence the average market price.

#### No Market Dominance

Each firm must be sensitive to the average market price of the product, but it does not pay attention to any one individual competitor. Because all the firms are relatively small, no single firm can dictate market conditions, so no one firm's actions directly affect the actions of the other firms.

#### Collusion Impossible

Firms sometimes try to profit from illegal agreements—collusion—with other firms to fix prices and not undercut each other. Collusion is impossible when the market has a large number of firms, as it does in monopolistic competition.

### ■ Product Differentiation

**Product differentiation** is making a product that is slightly different from the products of competing firms. A differentiated product has close substitutes but it does not have perfect substitutes. Some people will pay more for one variety of the product, so when its price rises, the quantity demanded decreases but it does not (necessarily) decrease to zero. For example, Adidas, Asics, Diadora, Etonic, Fila, New Balance, Nike, Puma, and Reebok all make differentiated running shoes. Other things remaining the same, if the price of Adidas running shoes rises and the prices of the other shoes remain constant, Adidas sells fewer shoes.

### ■ Competing on Quality, Price, and Marketing

Product differentiation enables a firm to compete with other firms in three areas: quality, price, and marketing.

*About 20 firms, each with a small market share, produce a wide variety of treadmills.*

**Product differentiation**
Making a product that is slightly different from the products of competing firms.

## Quality

The quality of a product is the physical attributes that make it different from the products of other firms. Quality includes design, reliability, the service provided to the buyer, and the buyer's ease of access to the product. Quality lies on a spectrum that runs from high to low. Go to the J.D. Power Consumer Center at jdpower.com, and you'll see the many dimensions on which this rating agency describes the quality of autos, boats, financial services, travel and accommodation services, telecommunication services, and new homes—all examples of products that have a large range of quality variety.

## Price

Because of product differentiation, a firm in monopolistic competition faces a downward-sloping demand curve. So, like a monopoly, the firm can set both its price and its output. But there is a tradeoff between the product's quality and price. A firm that makes a high-quality product can charge a higher price than a firm that makes a low-quality product.

## Marketing

Because of product differentiation, a firm in monopolistic competition must market its product. Marketing takes two main forms: advertising and packaging. A firm that produces a high-quality product wants to sell it for a suitably high price. To be able to do so, it must advertise and package its product in a way that convinces buyers that they are getting the higher quality for which they are paying. For example, drug companies advertise and package their brand-name drugs to persuade buyers that these items are superior to the lower-priced generic alternatives. Similarly, a low-quality producer uses advertising and packaging to persuade buyers that although the quality is low, the low price more than compensates for this fact.

## ■ Entry and Exit

In monopolistic competition, there are no barriers to entry. Consequently, a firm cannot make an economic profit in the long run. When firms make economic profits, new firms enter the industry. This entry lowers prices and eventually eliminates economic profits. When economic losses are incurred, some firms leave the industry. This exit increases prices and profits of the remaining firms and eventually eliminates the economic losses. In long-run equilibrium, firms neither enter nor leave the industry and the firms in the industry make zero economic profit.

## ■ Identifying Monopolistic Competition

Several factors must be considered to identify monopolistic competition and distinguish it from perfect competition on the one side and oligopoly and monopoly on the other side. One of these factors is the extent to which a market is dominated by a small number of firms. To measure this feature of markets, economists use two indexes called measures of concentration. These indexes are

- The four-firm concentration ratio
- The Herfindahl-Hirschman Index

**Four-firm concentration ratio**
The percentage of the total revenue in an industry accounted for by the four largest firms in the industry.

**Herfindahl-Hirschman Index**
The square of the percentage market share of each firm summed over the 50 largest firms (or summed over all the firms if there are fewer than 50) in a market.

The **four-firm concentration ratio** is the percentage of the total revenue of the industry accounted for by the four largest firms in the industry. The range of the concentration ratio is from almost zero for perfect competition to 100 percent for monopoly The boundary between monopolistic competition and oligopoly is generally regarded as being around 40 percent. A ratio of less than 40 percent is regarded as an indication of a competitive market—monopolistic competition.

The **Herfindahl-Hirschman Index**—also called the HHI—is the square of the percentage market share of each firm summed over the 50 largest firms (or summed over all the firms if there are fewer than 50) in a market. For example, if there are four firms in a market and the market shares of the firms are 50 percent, 25 percent, 15 percent, and 10 percent, the Herfindahl-Hirschman Index is

$$HHI = 50^2 + 25^2 + 15^2 + 10^2 = 3,450.$$

In perfect competition, the HHI is small. For example, if each of the 50 largest firms in an industry has a market share of 0.1 percent, the HHI is $0.1^2 \times 50 = 0.5$. In a monopoly, the HHI is 10,000—the firm has 100 percent of the market: $100^2 = 10,000$.

The HHI is one of the measures of the degree of competition used by the U.S. Department of Justice to classify markets and guide decisions on mergers. A market in which the HHI is less than 1,500 is regarded as being competitive and an example of monopolistic competition. A market in which the HHI lies between 1,500 and 2,500 is regarded as being moderately competitive. It is also an example of monopolistic competition. But a market in which the HHI exceeds 2,500 is regarded as being uncompetitive.

A market with a high concentration ratio or HHI might nonetheless be competitive because the few firms in a market face competition from many firms that can easily enter the market and will do so if economic profits are available.

# EYE on the U.S. ECONOMY
## Examples of Monopolistic Competition

These ten industries operate in monopolistic competition. They have a large number of firms, shown in parentheses after the industry's name. The red bars show the percentage of industry total revenue received by the 4 largest firms. The green bars show the percentage of industry total revenue received by the next 4 largest firms. The entire red, green, and blue bars show the percentage of industry total revenue received by the 20 largest firms. The Herfindahl-Hirschman Index is shown on the right.

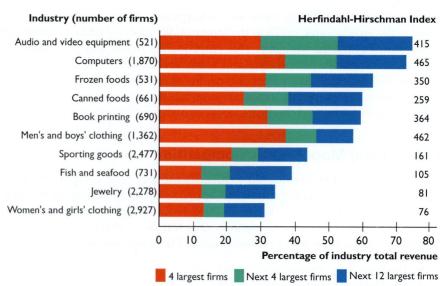

SOURCE OF DATA: U.S. Census Bureau.

## ■ Output and Price in Monopolistic Competition

Think about the decisions that Lucky Brand must make about the jeans it produces. First, Lucky Brand must decide on the design and quality of its jeans and on its marketing program. We'll suppose that the firm has already made these decisions so that we can concentrate on the firm's output and pricing decision. But we'll study quality and marketing decisions in the next section.

Because Lucky Brand has chosen the quality of its jeans and the amount of marketing activity, it faces given costs and market demand. How, with these costs and market demand for its jeans, does the firm decide the *quantity* of jeans to produce and the *price* at which to sell them?

## ■ The Firm's Profit-Maximizing Decision

A firm in monopolistic competition makes its output and price decision just as a monopoly firm does. Lucky Brand maximizes profit by producing the quantity at which marginal revenue equals marginal cost and by charging the highest price that buyers are willing to pay for this quantity.

Figure 13.1 illustrates this decision for Lucky jeans. The demand curve for Lucky jeans is *D*. The *MR* curve shows the marginal revenue curve associated with this demand curve and is derived just like the marginal revenue curve of a single-price monopoly in Chapter 12. The *ATC* curve shows the average total cost of producing Lucky jeans, and *MC* is the marginal cost curve. Profit is maximized by producing 125 pairs of jeans a day and selling them at a price of $100 a pair. When the firm produces 125 pairs of jeans a day, average total cost is $50 a pair and economic profit is $6,250 a day ($50 a pair multiplied by 125 pairs a day). The blue rectangle shows Lucky Brand's economic profit.

■ **FIGURE 13.1**

Output and Price in Monopolistic Competition

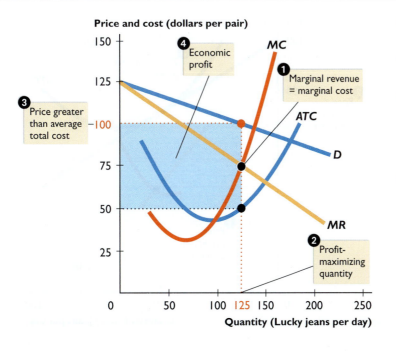

❶ Profit is maximized where marginal revenue equals marginal cost.

❷ The profit-maximizing quantity is 125 pairs of Lucky jeans a day.

❸ The profit-maximizing price is $100 a pair, which exceeds the average total cost of $50 a pair, so the firm makes an economic profit of $50 a pair.

❹ The blue rectangle illustrates economic profit and its area, which equals $6,250 a day ($50 a pair multiplied by 125 pairs) measures economic profit.

So far, the firm in monopolistic competition looks like a single-price monopoly. It produces the quantity at which marginal revenue equals marginal cost and charges the price that buyers are willing to pay for that quantity. The key difference between monopoly and monopolistic competition lies in what happens next.

## ■ Long Run: Zero Economic Profit

In monopolistic competition there is no restriction on entry, so if firms in an industry are making economic profits, other firms have an incentive to enter that industry and each firm's economic profit falls. So in the long run, firms will enter until all firms are making zero economic profit.

Lucky Brand is making an economic profit, which is an incentive for the Gap and Calvin Klein to start to make jeans similar to Lucky jeans. As they enter the jeans market, the demand for Lucky jeans decreases. At each point in time, the firm maximizes its profit by producing the quantity at which marginal revenue equals marginal cost and by charging the highest price that buyers are willing to pay for this quantity. But as demand decreases, marginal revenue decreases and the profit-maximizing quantity and price fall.

Figure 13.2 shows the long-run equilibrium. The demand curve for Lucky jeans and the marginal revenue curve have shifted leftward. The firm produces 75 pairs of jeans a day and sells them for $70 each. At this output level, average total cost is also $70 a pair. So Lucky Brand is making zero economic profit on its jeans. When all the firms in the industry are making zero economic profit, there is no incentive for new firms to enter.

If demand is so low relative to costs that firms incur economic losses, exit will occur. As firms leave an industry, the demand for the products of the remaining firms increases and their demand curves shift rightward. The exit process ends when all the firms in the industry are making zero economic profit.

## ■ FIGURE 13.2

### Output and Price in the Long Run

Economic profit encourages entry, which decreases the demand for each firm's product. Economic loss encourages exit, which increases the demand for each remaining firm's product.

When the demand curve touches the average total cost curve at the quantity at which marginal revenue equals marginal cost, the market is in long-run equilibrium.

❶ The output that maximizes profit is 75 pairs of Lucky jeans a day.

❷ The price, $70 a pair, equals average total cost.

❸ Economic profit is zero.

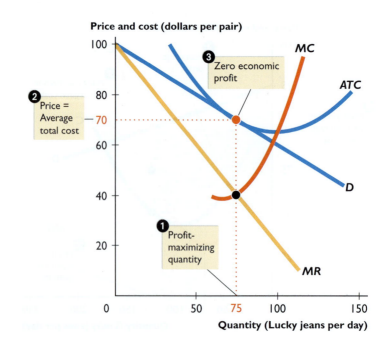

## Monopolistic Competition and Perfect Competition

Efficiency requires that the marginal benefit of the consumer equal the marginal cost of the producer. Price measures marginal benefit, so efficiency requires price to equal marginal cost. In monopolistic competition, price exceeds marginal revenue and marginal revenue equals marginal cost, so price exceeds marginal cost—a sign of inefficiency.

But this inefficiency arises from product differentiation—variety—that consumers value and for which they are willing to pay. So the loss that arises because marginal benefit exceeds marginal cost must be weighed against the gain that arises from greater product variety. It is almost inconceivable that consumers would be better off with no variety and price equal to marginal cost. So in a broader view of efficiency, monopolistic competition brings gains for consumers.

Another interesting feature of firms in monopolistic competition is that they always have excess capacity in long-run equilibrium.

### Excess Capacity

A firm's **efficient scale** is the quantity at which average total cost is a minimum—the quantity at the bottom of the U-shaped *ATC* curve. A firm's **excess capacity** is the amount by which its efficient scale exceeds the quantity that it produces. Figure 13.3 shows that in the long run Lucky Brand produces 75 pairs of jeans a day and has excess capacity of 25 pairs of jeans a day. That is, Lucky Brand produces a smaller output than that which minimizes average total cost. And because the demand curve slopes downward, the consumer pays a price that exceeds minimum average total cost. The demand curve slopes downward because of product differentiation. Product differentiation creates excess capacity.

**Efficient scale**
The quantity at which average total cost is a minimum.

**Excess capacity**
The amount by which the efficient scale exceeds the quantity that the firm produces.

## FIGURE 13.3

### Excess Capacity

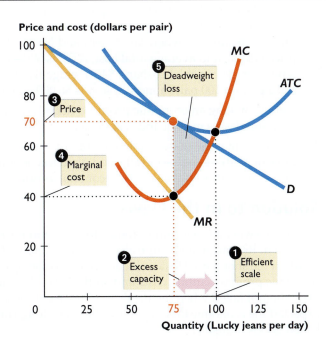

**1** The efficient scale (at minimum *ATC*) is 100 pairs a day.

In monopolistic competition in the long run, the firm produces 75 pairs of jeans a day and has **2** excess capacity of 25 pairs of jeans.

**3** The consumers pays a price that exceeds **4** marginal cost, and **5** a deadweight loss arises.

## CHECKPOINT 13.1

**Explain how a firm in monopolistic competition determines its price and quantity.**

## Practice Problems

Natti is a dot.com entrepreneur who has established a Web site at which people can design and buy awesome sunglasses. Natti pays $4,000 a month for her Web server and Internet connection. The sunglasses that her customers design are made to order by another firm, and Natti pays this firm $50 a pair. Natti has no other costs. Table 1 shows the demand schedule for Natti's sunglasses.

1. Calculate Natti's profit-maximizing output, price, and economic profit.
2. Do you expect other firms to enter the market and compete with Natti?
3. What happens to the demand for Natti's sunglasses in the long run? What happens to Natti's economic profit in the long run?

**TABLE 1**

| Price (dollars per pair) | Quantity (pairs per month) |
|---|---|
| 250 | 0 |
| 200 | 50 |
| 150 | 100 |
| 100 | 150 |
| 50 | 200 |
| 0 | 250 |

## In the News

### Hostess Brands closing for good

When its customers switched to healthier foods, Hostess incurred losses. To return to profit, the firm proposed a wage cut, but its workers went on strike. Hostess shut down its 33 bakeries, 565 distribution centers, and 570 outlet stores.

Source: CNN Money, November 16, 2012

Explain why the switch to healthier foods brought economic loss to Hostess in the short run. Why did Hostess exit in the long run?

## Solutions to Practice Problems

1. Marginal cost, *MC*, is $50 a pair—the price that Natti pays her supplier of sunglasses. To find marginal revenue, calculate the change in total revenue when the quantity increases by 1 pair of sunglasses. Figure 1 shows the demand curve, the marginal revenue curve, and the marginal cost curve. Profit is maximized when $MC = MR$ and Natti sells 100 pairs a month. The price is $150, and average total cost, *ATC*, is $90—the sum of $50 marginal (and average variable) cost and $40 average fixed cost. Economic profit is $60 a pair on 100 pairs a month, so it is $6,000 a month.

2. Natti is making an economic profit, so firms have an incentive to enter the Web sunglasses market and will do so.

3. As firms enter the market, the demand for Natti's sunglasses decreases, the price of Natti's sunglasses falls, and Natti's economic profit decreases. In the long run, Natti's will make zero economic profit.

**FIGURE 1**

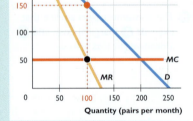

Price and cost (dollars per pair)

## Solution to In the News

As people switched to healthier foods, the demand for Hostess' baked goods decreased. Its marginal revenue also decreased and its *MR* curve shifted leftward. In the short run, Hostess incurred an economic loss and tried to return to economic profit by cutting costs and shifting its *ATC* and *MC* curves downward. That attempt failed when the firm's workers went on strike. So when Hostess expected the economic loss to persist, it made a long-run decision to exit the baked goods industry.

## 13.2    PRODUCT DEVELOPMENT AND MARKETING

When we studied a firm's output and price decisions, we supposed that it had already made its product quality and marketing decisions. We're now going to study these decisions and the impact they have on the firm's output, price, and economic profit.

### ■ Innovation and Product Development

To enjoy economic profits, firms in monopolistic competition must be continually developing new products. The reason is that wherever economic profits are earned, imitators emerge and set up business. So to maintain its economic profit, a firm must seek out new products that will provide it with a competitive edge, even if only temporarily. A firm that manages to introduce a new and differentiated product will temporarily have a less elastic demand for its product and will be able to increase its price temporarily. It will make an economic profit. Eventually, new firms that make close substitutes for the innovative product will enter and compete away the economic profit. So to restore economic profit, the firm must again innovate.

#### Cost Versus Benefit of Product Innovation

The decision to innovate is based on the same type of profit-maximizing calculation that you've already studied. Innovation and product development are costly activities, but they also bring in additional revenues. The firm must balance the cost and benefit at the margin. At a low level of product development, the marginal revenue from a better product exceeds the marginal cost. When the marginal dollar of product development expenditure (the marginal cost of product development) brings in a dollar of additional revenue (the marginal benefit from product development), the firm is spending the profit-maximizing amount on product development.

For example, when Electronic Arts releases its latest version of Madden NFL, it is probably not the best game that Electronic Arts could have created. But it was a game with features whose marginal benefit—and consumers' willingness to pay—equaled the marginal cost of those features.

*A profit-maximizing game has features that users value at least as highly as the marginal cost of programming the features.*

#### Efficiency and Product Innovation

Is product innovation an efficient activity? Does it benefit the consumer? There are two views about the answers to these questions. One view is that monopolistic competition brings to market many improved products that bring great benefits to the consumer. Clothing, kitchen and other household appliances, computers, computer programs, cars, and many other products keep getting better every year, and the consumer benefits from these improved products.

But many so-called improvements amount to little more than changing the appearance of a product or giving a different look to the packaging. In these cases, there is little objective benefit to the consumer.

But regardless of whether a product improvement is real or imagined, its value to the consumer is its marginal benefit, which equals the amount the consumer is willing to pay. In other words, the value of product improvements is the increase in price that the consumer is willing to pay. The marginal benefit to the producer is marginal revenue, which in equilibrium equals marginal cost. Because price exceeds marginal cost in monopolistic competition, product improvement is not pushed to its efficient level.

## ■ Marketing

Firms differentiate their products by designing and developing features that differ from those of their competitors' products. But firms also attempt to create a consumer perception of product differentiation even when actual differences are small. Advertising and packaging are the principal means firms use to achieve this end. An American Express card is a different product from a Visa card, but the actual differences are not the main ones that American Express emphasizes in its marketing. The deeper message is that if you use an American Express card, you can be like a celebrity or a high-profile successful person.

### Marketing Expenditures

Firms incur huge costs to ensure that buyers appreciate and value the differences between their own products and those of their competitors. So a large proportion of the price that we pay covers the cost of selling a good, and this proportion is increasing. Advertising in newspapers and magazines and on radio, television, and the Internet is one type of selling cost, but it is not the only one. Selling costs include the cost of shopping malls that look like movie sets; glossy catalogs and brochures; and the salaries, airfares, and hotel bills of salespeople.

The total scale of advertising costs is hard to estimate, but some components can be measured. A survey conducted by a commercial agency found that about 15 percent of the price of liquor, 12 percent of the prices of movies and medical doctors, and about 10 percent of the price of beer cover advertising expenditures.

# EYE on CELL PHONES

## Which Cell Phone?

There is a lot of product differentiation in cell phones: Samsung makes 38 varieties; HTC makes 35; Nokia makes 30; and Sony makes 25. In the three months from April through June 2013, dozens of new varieties of cell phones were introduced by the top 20 firms in this market. Why is there so much variety in cell phones?

The answer is that preferences are diverse and the cost of matching the diversity of preference is low.

Think about the ways in which cell phones differ: just a few of them are their dimensions, weight, navigation tools, talk time, standby time, screen, camera features, audio features, memory, connectivity, processor speed, storage, and network capability.

Each one of these features comes in dozens of varieties. If we combine only 10 of these features, each having 6 varieties, there are 1 million different possible cell-phone designs.

Firms produce variety only when the marginal cost of doing so is less than the marginal benefit. The marginal cost of some cell-phone variety is not large. Adding a feature to a camera, making the memory a bit bigger, and using a more economical battery are all relatively low-cost adjustments that phone designers can make.

But a technology exists for adding variety at almost zero cost that increases product differentiation to make each cell phone unique to the preferences of each individual. This technology is the app.

Apple has only six versions of the iPhone, but because of the large and growing number of program apps, each iPhone owner can load their phone with exactly the apps they want.

In long-run equilibrium, entry and innovation by each competitor will drive economic profit toward zero. Each cell-phone maker will offer a degree of product differentiation that equates the marginal cost of variety with its marginal revenue. But the pursuit of economic profit will spur ever more innovation and consumers will be confronted with ever wider choice.

In the U.S. economy as a whole, there are some 20,000 advertising agencies, which employ more than 200,000 people and have total revenue of $45 billion. But these numbers are only part of the total cost of advertising because many firms have their own internal advertising departments, the costs of which we can only guess.

Advertising expenditures and other selling costs affect firms' profits in two ways: They increase costs and they change demand. Let's look at these effects.

## Selling Costs and Total Costs

Selling costs such as advertising expenditures increase the costs of a monopolistically competitive firm above those of a perfectly competitive firm or a monopoly. Advertising costs and other selling costs are fixed costs. They do not vary as total output varies. So, just like fixed production costs, advertising costs per unit of output decrease as production increases.

Figure 13.4 shows how selling costs and advertising expenditures change a firm's average total cost. The blue curve shows the average total cost of production. The red curve shows the firm's average total cost of production plus advertising. The height of the shaded area between the two curves shows the average fixed cost of advertising. The *total* cost of advertising is fixed. But the *average* cost of advertising decreases as output increases.

Figure 13.4 shows that if advertising increases the quantity sold by a large enough amount, it can lower average total cost. For example, if the quantity sold increases from 25 pairs of jeans a day with no advertising to 100 pairs of jeans a day with advertising, average total cost falls from $60 a pair to $40 a pair. The reason is that although the *total* fixed cost has increased, the greater fixed cost is spread over a greater output, so average total cost falls.

■ **FIGURE 13.4**

Selling Costs and Total Costs

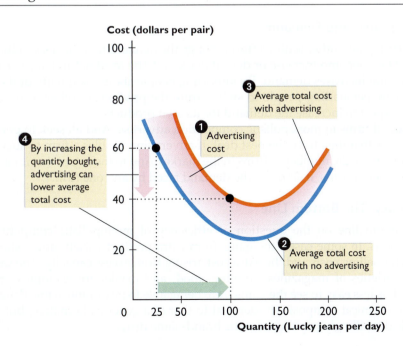

**Cost (dollars per pair)**

③ Average total cost with advertising

① Advertising cost

④ By increasing the quantity bought, advertising can lower average total cost

② Average total cost with no advertising

**Quantity (Lucky jeans per day)**

Selling costs such as the cost of advertising are fixed costs.

① When advertising costs are added to ② the average total cost of production, ③ average total cost increases by more at small outputs than at large outputs.

④ If advertising enables the quantity sold to increase from 25 pairs of jeans a day to 100 pairs a day, it *lowers* average total cost from $60 a pair to $40 a pair.

# EYE on YOUR LIFE
## Some Selling Costs You Pay

When you buy a new pair of running shoes, you're buying materials that cost $9, paying the producer in Asia and the shipping company for production and transportation costs of $8, paying the U.S. government an import duty of $3, and paying advertisers, retailers, and others who provide sales and distribution services $50.

The table provides a breakdown of the cost of a pair of shoes. Notice the huge gap between the retailer's cost and the price that you pay. The retail markup is about 100 percent.

Running shoes are not unusual. Almost everything that you buy includes a selling cost component that exceeds one half of the total cost. Your clothing, food, electronic items, DVDs, magazines, and even your textbooks cost more to sell than they cost to produce.

| Raw materials $9 | Production costs $8 | Import duty $3 | | | Selling costs $50 | |
|---|---|---|---|---|---|---|
| **Manufacturer (Asia)** | | **Nike (Beaverton, Oregon)** | | **Retailer (your town)** | | |
| Materials | $9.00 | | | | | |
| Cost of labor | $2.75 | Cost of shoe to Nike | $20.00 | Cost of shoe to retailer | | $35.50 |
| Cost of capital | $3.00 | Sales, distribution, and administration | $5.00 | Sales clerk's wages | | $9.50 |
| Profit | $1.75 | Advertising | $4.00 | Shop rent | | $9.00 |
| Shipping | $0.50 | Research & development | $0.25 | Retailer's other costs | | $7.00 |
| Import duty | $3.00 | Nike's profit | $6.25 | Retailer's profit | | $9.00 |
| **Nike's cost** | **$20.00** | **Retailer's cost** | **$35.50** | **Price paid by you** | | **$70.00** |

## Selling Costs and Demand

Advertising and other selling efforts change the demand for a firm's product. But how? Does demand increase or does it decrease? The most natural answer is that advertising increases demand. By informing people about the quality of its products or by persuading people to switch from the products of other firms, a firm might expect to increase the demand for its own products.

But all firms in monopolistic competition advertise. And all seek to persuade customers that they have the best deal. If advertising enables a firm to survive, it might increase the number of firms in the market. And to the extent that it increases the number of firms, it *decreases* the demand faced by any one firm.

## Efficiency: The Bottom Line

The bottom line on the question of efficiency of monopolistic competition is ambiguous. In some cases, the gains from extra product variety unquestionably offset the selling costs and the extra cost arising from excess capacity. The tremendous varieties of magazines, clothing, food, and drinks are examples of such gains. It is less easy to see the gains from being able to buy brand-name drugs that have a chemical composition identical to that of a generic alternative, but many people do willingly pay more for the brand-name drug.

# CHECKPOINT 13.2

**Explain why advertising costs are high in monopolistic competition.**

## Practice Problems

Bianca bakes delicious cookies. Her total fixed cost is $40 a day, and her average variable cost is $1 a bag. Few people know about Bianca's Cookies, and she maximizes her profit by selling 10 bags a day for $5 a bag. Bianca thinks that if she spends $50 a day on advertising, she will sell 25 bags a day for $5 a bag.

1. If Bianca's belief about the effect of advertising is correct, can she increase her economic profit by advertising?

2. If Bianca advertises, will her average total cost increase or decrease at the quantity produced?

3. If Bianca advertises, will she continue to sell her cookies for $5 a bag or will she raise her price or lower her price?

## In the News

**Is innovation killing the soap business?**
Americans like to pour their own laundry detergent and when concentrated detergent was introduced, Americans continued to pour the same amount and soap sales boomed. But when P&G introduced its laundry capsule, a 1-unit measure per wash, total detergent sales fell 5 percent from 3 years earlier.

Source: *The Wall Street Journal*, April 3, 2013

Why would P&G create a capsule when people are happy with powder and liquid detergent and laundry sales are booming?

## Solutions to Practice Problems

1. With no advertising, Bianca's total revenue is $50 (10 bags at $5 a bag) and her total cost is $50 ($40 total fixed cost plus $10 total variable cost). Bianca's economic profit is zero. With advertising expenditure of $50 a day, total revenue is $125 (25 bags at $5 a bag) and total cost is $115 ($90 total fixed cost plus $25 total variable cost). Bianca's economic profit with no price change is $10, so Bianca can increase her economic profit by advertising.

2. If Bianca advertises, her average total cost will decrease. With no advertising, her average total cost is $5 a bag ($50 ÷ 10). With advertising, her average total cost is $4.60 a bag ($115 ÷ 25).

3. We can't say if Bianca will sell her cookies for $5 a bag. Advertising changes the demand for her cookies. Although it increases fixed cost, marginal cost remains at $1 a bag. Bianca will sell the profit-maximizing quantity at the highest price she can charge for that quantity.

## Solution to In the News

In monopolistic competition, entry keeps driving economic profit to zero. Innovation— the development of a new differentiated product—is necessary to boost economic profit. P&G introduced a capsule, the marginal cost of which equals its marginal revenue, to maximize profit.

## 13.3 OLIGOPOLY

Another type of market that stands between the extremes of perfect competition and monopoly is oligopoly. *Oligopoly* is a market structure in which

- A small number of firms compete.
- Natural or legal barriers prevent the entry of new firms.

Oligopoly is a market with a small number of firms. Each firm has a large market share, the firms are interdependent, and they face the temptation to collude. In any market, the price depends on the total quantity supplied. In monopoly, one firm controls this quantity and so also controls the price. In perfect competition, no firm is big enough to influence the total quantity supplied, so no firm can influence the price. Oligopoly is unlike both of these cases. More than one firm controls the quantity supplied, so no *one* firm controls the price. But each firm is large, and the quantity produced by each firm influences the price.

Like monopoly, the firms in an oligopoly operate behind a barrier to entry. And also like monopoly, the barriers to entry can arise for either natural reasons or legal reasons. A natural oligopoly is a market in which economies of scale exist but the output of a few firms is required to meet the market demand at the lowest possible cost. One firm could not meet the market demand at as low a price as a few firms could, but economies of scale are sufficiently large that more than a few firms could not survive and earn a zero profit.

A legal oligopoly arises when a legal barrier to entry protects the small number of firms in a market. A city might license two taxi firms, or two bus companies, for example.

Firms in an oligopoly might produce identical or differentiated products.

The problem for a firm in oligopoly is that its own profit-maximizing actions might decrease the profits of its competitors. But if each firm's actions decrease the profits of the other firms, all the firms end up with a lower profit.

### ■ Collusion

**Cartel**
A group of firms acting together to limit output, raise price, and increase economic profit.

One possible way of avoiding a self-defeating outcome is for the firms in an oligopoly to form a cartel. A **cartel** is a group of firms acting together—in collusion—to limit output, raise price, and increase economic profit. Cartels are illegal in the United States (and in most other countries) and are undertaken in secret. Firms in an oligopoly would like to be able to agree with each other to fix the price at a level that maximizes their joint profit.

**Duopoly**
A market in which there are only two producers.

It turns out that collusion usually breaks down. To understand why, and to learn how price and output are determined in an oligopoly, we're going to study a special case called duopoly. **Duopoly** is a market in which there are only two producers. You can probably see some examples of duopoly where you live. Many cities have only two local newspapers, two taxi companies, two copy centers, or two college bookstores. In the global economy, there are only two major producers of commercial jet aircraft—Boeing in the United States and Airbus Industrie in Europe.

Although duopoly is common, the main reason for studying it is not its realism. We study it because it captures the essence of oligopoly and reveals the mutual interdependence of firms most effectively. Also, if collusion is difficult for a duopoly, it is even more difficult for an oligopoly with three or more firms.

## ■ Duopoly in Airplanes

Airbus and Boeing are the only makers of large commercial jet aircraft. Suppose that they have identical production costs. To keep things simple, we'll assume that the marginal cost of an airplane is $1 million and that total fixed cost is zero. Figure 13.5 shows the market for airplanes that Airbus and Boeing share.

### Competitive Outcome

If this industry was perfectly competitive, the marginal cost curve would be the industry supply curve. The equilibrium is where the industry supply curve intersects the demand curve—12 airplanes a week would be sold for $1 million each. Total cost would be $12 million and total revenue would also be $12 million, so economic profit would be zero—a long-run equilibrium in perfect competition.

### Monopoly Outcome

If this industry had only one firm, the firm would be a single-price monopoly because an airplane can be resold. The marginal revenue curve would be the one shown in Figure 13.5. The monopoly would produce 6 airplanes a week and sell them for $13 million each. Total cost would be $6 million and total revenue would be $78 million, so economic profit would be $72 million a week.

*Boeing and Airbus share the market for big passenger airplanes.*

### ■ FIGURE 13.5

#### A Market for Airplanes

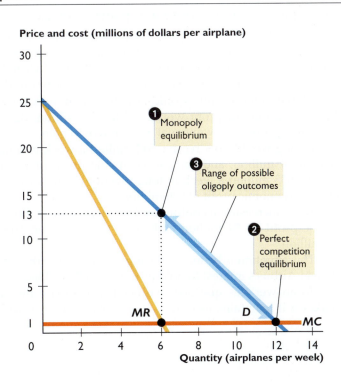

❶ With market demand curve, *D*, marginal revenue curve, *MR*, and marginal cost curve, *MC*, a monopoly airplane maker maximizes profit by producing 6 airplanes a week and selling them at a price of $13 million an airplane.

❷ With perfect competition among airplane makers, the market equilibrium quantity is 12 airplanes a week and the equilibrium price is $1 million an airplane.

❸ A cartel might achieve the monopoly equilibrium, break down and result in the perfect competition equilibrium, or operate somewhere between these two extreme outcomes.

### Range of Possible Oligopoly Outcomes

Because oligopoly is a market structure that lies between perfect competition and monopoly, these extremes that we've just found provide the maximum range within which the oligopoly outcome might lie. If Airbus and Boeing persistently cut their prices to increase their production and quantity sold, they might drive the price down all the way to the perfectly competitive price and end up with no economic profit. In contrast, if the two firms were able to collude and set the monopoly price, they could end up sharing the maximum available monopoly profit.

## ■ The Duopolists' Dilemma

You've just seen that if this industry had only one firm, 6 airplanes a week would be produced and the price of an airplane would be $13 million. Economic profit would be $72 million a week. If this same outcome could be achieved with two firms in the industry, Airbus and Boeing might each produce 3 airplanes a week and make an economic profit of $36 million each (see Table 13.1).

Because this outcome is the one that maximizes monopoly profit, we know that there is no better outcome for the two firms in total. That is, their joint profits cannot be any higher than the $72 million a week that a monopoly can achieve.

But can one firm make a larger profit than $36 million a week at the expense of the other firm? To answer this question, we need to see what happens if one of the firms increases output by 1 airplane a week. Because the two firms in this example are identical, we can explore this question with either Boeing or Airbus increasing production by 1 airplane a week and the other holding output at 3 a week. We'll suppose that Boeing increases output to 4 airplanes a week and Airbus at first continues to produce 3 airplanes a week.

### Boeing Increases Output to 4 Airplanes a Week

Table 13.2 shows what happens if Boeing produces 4 airplanes a week and Airbus produces 3 airplanes a week. To sell a total output of 7 airplanes a week, the price must fall. The market demand curve in Figure 13.5 tells us that the quantity demanded is 7 airplanes a week when the price is $11 million per airplane.

Market total revenue would now be $77 million, total cost would be $7 million, and economic profit would fall to $70 million. But the distribution of this economic profit is now unequal. Boeing would gain, and Airbus would lose.

Boeing would now receive $44 million a week in total revenue, have a total cost of $4 million, and earn an economic profit of $40 million. Airbus would receive $33 million a week in total revenue, incur a total cost of $3 million, and earn an economic profit of $30 million.

So by increasing its output by 1 airplane a week, Boeing can increase its economic profit by $4 million and cause the economic profit of Airbus to fall by $6 million.

This situation is better for Boeing, but would Airbus go along with it? Would it be in Airbus's interest to hold its output at 3 airplanes a week?

To answer this question, we need to compare the economic profit Airbus makes if it maintains its output at 3 airplanes a week with the profit it makes if

**TABLE 13.1   MONOPOLY OUTCOME**

|  | Boeing | Airbus | Market total |
|---|---|---|---|
| Quantity (airplanes a week) | 3 | 3 | 6 |
| Price ($ million per airplane) | 13 | 13 | 13 |
| Total revenue ($ million) | 39 | 39 | 78 |
| Total cost ($ million) | 3 | 3 | 6 |
| Economic profit ($ million) | 36 | 36 | 72 |

**TABLE 13.2   BOEING INCREASES OUTPUT TO 4 AIRPLANES A WEEK**

|  | Boeing | Airbus | Market total |
|---|---|---|---|
| Quantity (airplanes a week) | 4 | 3 | 7 |
| Price ($ million per airplane) | 11 | 11 | 11 |
| Total revenue ($ million) | 44 | 33 | 77 |
| Total cost ($ million) | 4 | 3 | 7 |
| Economic profit ($ million) | 40 | 30 | 70 |

it produces 4 airplanes a week. How much economic profit does Airbus make if it produces 4 airplanes a week with Boeing also producing 4 a week?

## Airbus Increases Output to 4 Airplanes a Week

With both firms producing 4 airplanes a week, total output is 8 airplanes a week. To sell 8 airplanes a week, the price must fall further. The market demand curve in Figure 13.5 tells us that the quantity demanded is 8 airplanes a week when the price is $9 million an airplane.

Table 13.3 keeps track of the data. Market total revenue would now be $72 million, total cost would be $8 million, and economic profit would fall to $64 million. With both firms producing the same output, the distribution of this economic profit is now equal.

Both firms would now receive $36 million a week in total revenue, have a total cost of $4 million, and earn an economic profit of $32 million. For Airbus, this outcome is an improvement on the previous one by $2 million a week. For Boeing, this outcome is worse than the previous one by $8 million a week.

This situation is better for Airbus, but would Boeing go along with it? You know that Boeing would be worse off if it decreased its output to 3 airplanes a week because it would get the outcome that Airbus has in Table 13.2—an economic profit of only $30 million a week. But would Boeing be better off if it increased output to 5 airplanes a week?

## Boeing Increases Output to 5 Airplanes a Week

To answer the question we've just posed, we need to calculate Boeing's economic profit if Airbus maintains its output at 4 airplanes a week and Boeing increases output to 5 a week.

Table 13.4 keeps track of the data. Total output is now 9 airplanes a week. To sell this quantity, the price must fall to $7 million per airplane. Market total revenue is $63 million and total cost is $9 million, so economic profit for the two firms is $54 million. The distribution of this economic profit is again unequal. But now both firms would lose.

Boeing would now receive $35 million a week in total revenue, have a total cost of $5 million, and earn an economic profit of $30 million—$2 million less than if it maintained its output at 4 airplanes a week (in Table 13.3). Airbus would receive $28 million a week in total revenue, incur a total cost of $4 million, and earn an economic profit of $24 million—$8 million less than before.

So neither firm can gain by increasing output beyond 4 airplanes a week. But there is a dilemma. If both firms stick to the monopoly output, they both produce 3 airplanes and make $36 million. If they both increase production to 4 airplanes a week, they both make $32 million. If only one of them increases production to 4 airplanes a week, that firm makes an economic profit of $40 million while the one that keeps production constant at 3 airplanes makes a lower economic profit of $30 million. So what will the firms do?

We can speculate about what they will do. But to work out the answer, we need to use some game theory. We'll leave the question that we've just asked dangling and return to it after we've learned the basic ideas about game theory.

**TABLE 13.3   AIRBUS INCREASES OUTPUT TO 4 AIRPLANES A WEEK**

| | Boeing | Airbus | Market total |
|---|---|---|---|
| Quantity (airplanes a week) | 4 | 4 | 8 |
| Price ($ million per airplane) | 9 | 9 | 9 |
| Total revenue ($ million) | 36 | 36 | 72 |
| Total cost ($ million) | 4 | 4 | 8 |
| Economic profit ($ million) | 32 | 32 | 64 |

**TABLE 13.4   BOEING INCREASES OUTPUT TO 5 AIRPLANES A WEEK**

| | Boeing | Airbus | Market total |
|---|---|---|---|
| Quantity (airplanes a week) | 5 | 4 | 9 |
| Price ($ million per airplane) | 7 | 7 | 7 |
| Total revenue ($ million) | 35 | 28 | 63 |
| Total cost ($ million) | 5 | 4 | 9 |
| Economic profit ($ million) | 30 | 24 | 54 |

CHECKPOINT 13.3

**Explain the dilemma faced by firms in oligopoly.**

## Practice Problems

Isolated Island has two natural gas wells, one owned by Tom and the other owned by Jerry. Each well has a valve that controls the flow of gas. The marginal cost of producing gas is zero. Table 1 gives the demand schedule for the gas.

1. If Tom and Jerry form a cartel and maximize their joint profit, what will be the price of gas and the quantity produced?

2. If Tom and Jerry are forced to sell at the perfectly competitive price, what will be the price of gas and the total quantity produced?

3. If Tom and Jerry compete as duopolists, what will be the price of gas?

## In the News

**Rice exporters eye cartel to boost prices**
Southeast Asia's rice-exporting nations are in talks to create a formal alliance aimed at boosting prices and increasing export revenues. But the previous attempt to form a cartel failed as countries failed to cooperate.

Source: *The Wall Street Journal*, August 23, 2012

Explain how an Asian profit-maximizing rice cartel would influence the global market for rice and the world price of rice. Why might a cartel not boost prices?

## Solutions to Practice Problems

1. If Tom and Jerry form a cartel and maximize their joint profit, they will charge the monopoly price. This price is the highest price the market will bear when together they produce the quantity at which marginal revenue equals marginal cost. Marginal cost is zero, so we need to find the price at which marginal revenue is zero. Marginal revenue is zero when total revenue is a maximum, which occurs when output is 6 units a day (Table 2) and price is $6 a unit (see the demand schedule in Table 1).

2. If Tom and Jerry are forced to sell at the perfectly competitive price, the price will equal marginal cost. Marginal cost is zero, so in this case, the price will be zero and the total quantity produced will be 12 units a day.

3. If Tom and Jerry compete as duopolists, they will increase production to more than the monopoly quantity. The price will fall, but they will not drive the price down to zero.

## Solution to In the News

A rice cartel would operate as a profit-maximizing monopoly and produce the quantity at which marginal revenue equals marginal cost. The profit-maximizing quantity that a monopoly produces is less than the quantity that competitive rice growers currently produce. The supply of rice on the world market will decrease and the world price will rise. For a cartel to be effective, each country would have to agree to a production quota. If countries cannot cooperate and maintain the agreed production quotas, then the cartel will fail and the price will not rise.

**TABLE 1**

| Price (dollars per unit) | Quantity demanded (units per day |
|---|---|
| 12 | 0 |
| 11 | 1 |
| 10 | 2 |
| 9 | 3 |
| 8 | 4 |
| 7 | 5 |
| 6 | 6 |
| 5 | 7 |
| 4 | 8 |
| 3 | 9 |
| 2 | 10 |
| 1 | 11 |
| 0 | 12 |

**TABLE 2**

| Quantity (units per day) | Total revenue (dollars per day) | Marginal revenue (dollars per unit) |
|---|---|---|
| 0 | 0 | |
| | | 11 |
| 1 | 11 | |
| | | 9 |
| 2 | 20 | |
| | | 7 |
| 3 | 27 | |
| | | 5 |
| 4 | 32 | |
| | | 3 |
| 5 | 35 | |
| | | 1 |
| 6 | 36 | |
| | | −1 |
| 7 | 35 | |
| | | −3 |
| 8 | 32 | |
| | | −5 |
| 9 | 27 | |
| | | −7 |
| 10 | 20 | |
| | | −9 |
| 11 | 11 | |
| | | −11 |
| 12 | 0 | |

## 13.4 GAME THEORY

**Game theory** is the tool that economists use to analyze *strategic behavior*—behavior that recognizes mutual interdependence and takes account of the expected behavior of others. John von Neumann invented game theory in 1937, and today it is a major research field in economics.

Game theory helps us to understand oligopoly and many other forms of economic, political, social, and even biological rivalries. We will begin our study of game theory and its application to the behavior of firms by thinking about familiar games that we play for fun.

### ■ What Is a Game?

What is a game? At first thought, the question seems silly. After all, there are many different games. There are ball games and parlor games, games of chance and games of skill. But what is it about all these different activities that make them games? What do all these games have in common? All games share three features:

- Rules
- Strategies
- Payoffs

Let's see how these common features of games apply to a game called "the prisoners' dilemma." The **prisoners' dilemma** is a game between two prisoners that shows why it is hard to cooperate even when it would be beneficial to both players to do so. This game captures the essential feature of the duopolists' dilemma that we've just been studying. The prisoners' dilemma also provides a good illustration of how game theory works and how it generates predictions.

### ■ The Prisoners' Dilemma

Art and Bob have been caught red-handed, stealing a car. During the district attorney's interviews with the prisoners, he begins to suspect that he has stumbled on the two people who committed a multimillion-dollar bank robbery some months earlier. But this is just a suspicion. The district attorney has no evidence on which he can convict them of the greater crime unless he can get them to confess. He makes the prisoners play a game with the following rules.

#### Rules

Each prisoner (player) is placed in a separate room and cannot communicate with the other player. Each is told that he is suspected of having carried out the bank robbery and that

- If both of them confess to the larger crime, each will receive a reduced sentence of 3 years for both crimes.
- If he alone confesses and his accomplice does not, he will receive an even shorter sentence of 1 year, while his accomplice will receive a 10-year sentence.
- If neither of them confesses to the larger crime, each will receive a 2-year sentence for car theft.

**Game theory**
The tool that economists use to analyze *strategic behavior*—behavior that recognizes mutual interdependence and takes account of the expected behavior of others.

**Prisoners' dilemma**
A game between two prisoners that shows why it is hard to cooperate even when it would be beneficial to both players to do so.

**Strategies**
All the possible actions of each player in a game.

**Payoff matrix**
A table that shows the payoffs for each player for every possible combination of actions by the players.

TABLE 13.5   PRISONERS' DILEMMA PAYOFF MATRIX

Each square shows the payoffs for the two players, Art and Bob, for each possible pair of actions. In each square, the red triangle shows Art's payoff and the blue triangle shows Bob's. For example, if both confess, the payoffs are in the top left square.

**Nash equilibrium**
An equilibrium in which each player takes the best possible action given the action of the other player.

## Strategies

In game theory, **strategies** are all the possible actions of each player. Art and Bob each have two possible strategies:

- Confess to the bank robbery.
- Deny having committed the bank robbery.

## Payoffs

Because there are two players, each with two strategies, there are four possible outcomes:

- Both confess.
- Both deny.
- Art confesses and Bob denies.
- Bob confesses and Art denies.

Each prisoner can work out exactly what happens to him—his *payoff*—in each of these four situations. We can tabulate the four possible payoffs for each of the prisoners in what is called a payoff matrix for the game. A **payoff matrix** is a table that shows the payoffs for every possible action by each player given every possible action by the other player.

Table 13.5 shows a payoff matrix for Art and Bob. The squares show the payoffs for the two prisoners—the red triangle in each square shows Art's, and the blue triangle shows Bob's. If both prisoners confess (top left), each gets a prison term of 3 years. If Bob confesses but Art denies (top right), Art gets a 10-year sentence and Bob gets a 1-year sentence. If Art confesses and Bob denies (bottom left), Art gets a 1-year sentence and Bob gets a 10-year sentence. Finally, if both of them deny (bottom right), neither can be convicted of the bank robbery charge but both are sentenced for the car theft—a 2-year sentence.

## Equilibrium

The equilibrium of a game occurs when each player takes the best possible action given the action of the other player. This equilibrium concept is called **Nash equilibrium**. It is so named because John Nash of Princeton University, who received the Nobel Prize for Economic Science in 1994, proposed it. (The same John Nash was portrayed by Russell Crowe in *A Beautiful Mind*.)

In the case of the prisoners' dilemma, equilibrium occurs when Art makes his best choice given Bob's choice and when Bob makes his best choice given Art's choice. Let's find the equilibrium.

First, look at the situation from Art's point of view. If Bob confesses, it pays Art to confess because in that case, he is sentenced to 3 years rather than 10 years. If Bob does not confess, it still pays Art to confess because in that case, he receives 1 year rather than 2 years. So no matter what Bob does, Art's best action is to confess.

Second, look at the situation from Bob's point of view. If Art confesses, it pays Bob to confess because in that case, he is sentenced to 3 years rather than 10 years. If Art does not confess, it still pays Bob to confess because in that case, he receives 1 year rather than 2 years. So no matter what Art does, Bob's best action is to confess.

Because each player's best action is to confess, each does confess, each gets a 3-year prison term, and the district attorney has solved the bank robbery. This is the equilibrium of the game.

### Not the Best Outcome

The equilibrium of the prisoners' dilemma game is not the best outcome for the prisoners. Isn't there some way in which they can cooperate and get the smaller 2-year prison term? There is not, because the players cannot communicate with each other. Each player can put himself in the other player's place and can figure out what the other will do. The prisoners are in a dilemma. Each knows that he can serve only 2 years if he can trust the other to deny. But each also knows that it is not in the best interest of the other to deny. So each prisoner knows that he must confess, thereby delivering a bad outcome for both.

Let's now see how we can use the ideas we've just developed to understand the behavior of firms in oligopoly. We'll start by returning to the duopolists' dilemma.

## ■ The Duopolists' Dilemma

The dilemma of Airbus and Boeing is similar to that of Art and Bob. Each firm has two strategies. It can produce airplanes at the rate of

- 3 a week
- 4 a week

Because each firm has two strategies, there are four possible combinations of actions for the two firms:

- Both firms produce 3 a week (monopoly outcome).
- Both firms produce 4 a week.
- Airbus produces 3 a week and Boeing produces 4 a week.
- Boeing produces 3 a week and Airbus produces 4 a week.

### The Payoff Matrix

Table 13.6 sets out the payoff matrix for this game. It is constructed in exactly the same way as the payoff matrix for the prisoners' dilemma in Table 13.5. The squares show the payoffs for Airbus and Boeing. In this case, the payoffs are economic profits. (In the case of the prisoners' dilemma, the payoffs were losses.)

The table shows that if both firms produce 4 a week (top left), each firm makes an economic profit of $32 million. If both firms produce 3 a week (bottom right), they make the monopoly profit, and each firm makes an economic profit of $36 million. The top right and bottom left squares show what happens if one firm produces 4 a week while the other produces 3 a week. The firm that increases production makes an economic profit of $40 million, and the one that keeps production at the monopoly quantity makes an economic profit of $30 million.

### Equilibrium of the Duopolists' Dilemma

What do the firms do? To answer this question, we must find the equilibrium of the duopoly game.

**TABLE 13.6   DUOPOLISTS' DILEMMA PAYOFF MATRIX**

Each square shows the payoffs from a pair of actions. For example, if both firms produce 3 airplanes a week, the payoffs are recorded in the bottom right square. The red triangle shows Airbus's payoff, and the blue triangle shows Boeing's.

**TABLE 13.7    THE NASH
EQUILIBRIUM**

The Nash equilibrium is for each firm to produce 4 airplanes a week.

Using the information in Table 13.7, look at things from Airbus's point of view. Airbus reasons as follows: Suppose that Boeing produces 4 airplanes a week. If I, Airbus, produce 3 a week, I will make an economic profit of $30 million. If I also produce 4 a week, I will make an economic profit of $32 million. So I'm better off producing 4 airplanes a week. Airbus continues to reason: Now suppose Boeing produces 3 a week. If I produce 4 a week, I will make an economic profit of $40 million, and if I produce 3 a week, I will make an economic profit of $36 million. An economic profit of $40 million is better than an economic profit of $36 million, so I'm better off if I produce 4 airplanes a week. So regardless of whether Boeing produces 3 a week or 4 a week, it pays Airbus to produce 4 airplanes a week.

Because the two firms face identical situations, Boeing comes to the same conclusion as Airbus, so both firms produce 4 a week. The equilibrium of the duopoly game is that both firms produce 4 airplanes a week.

### Collusion Is Profitable but Difficult to Achieve

In the duopolists' dilemma that you've just studied, Airbus and Boeing end up in a situation that is similar to that of the prisoners in the prisoners' dilemma game. They don't achieve the best joint outcome. Because each produces 4 airplanes a week, each makes an economic profit of $32 million a week.

If firms were able to collude, they would agree to limit their production to 3 airplanes a week each and they would each make the monopoly profit of $36 million a week.

The outcome of the duopolists' dilemma shows why it is difficult for firms to collude. Even if collusion were a legal activity, firms in duopoly would find it difficult to implement an agreement to restrict output. Like the players of the prisoners' dilemma game, the duopolists would reach a Nash equilibrium in which they produce more than the joint profit-maximizing quantity.

If two firms have difficulty maintaining a collusive agreement, oligopolies with more than two firms have an even harder time. The operation of the Organization of the Petroleum Exporting Countries (OPEC) illustrates this difficulty. To raise the price of oil, OPEC must limit global oil production. The members of this cartel meet from time to time and set a production limit for each member nation. Almost always, within a few months of a decision to restrict production, some (usually smaller) members of the cartel break their quotas, production increases, and the price sags below the cartel's desired target. The OPEC cartel plays an oligopoly dilemma game similar to the prisoners' dilemma. Only in 1973, 1979–1980, and 2005–2007 did OPEC manage to keep its members' production under control and raise the price of oil.

### ■ Advertising and Research Games in Oligopoly

Every month, Coke and Pepsi, Nike and Adidas, Procter & Gamble and Kimberly-Clark, Nokia and Motorola, and hundreds of other pairs of big firms locked in fierce competition spend millions of dollars on advertising campaigns and on research and development (R&D). They make decisions about whether to increase or cut the advertising budget or whether to undertake a large R&D effort aimed at lowering production costs or at making the product more reliable (usually, the more reliable a product, the more expensive it is to produce, but the more people are willing to pay for it). These choices can be analyzed as games. Let's look at some examples of these types of games.

## Advertising Game

A key to success in the soft drink industry is to run huge advertising campaigns. These campaigns affect market share but are costly to run. Table 13.8 shows some hypothetical numbers for the advertising game that Pepsi and Coke play. Each firm has two strategies: Advertise or don't advertise. If neither firm advertises, they each make $50 million (bottom right of the payoff matrix). If each firm advertises, each firm's profit is lower by the amount spent on advertising (top left square of the payoff matrix). If Pepsi advertises but Coke does not, Pepsi gains and Coke loses (top right square of the payoff matrix). Finally, if Coke advertises and Pepsi does not, Coke gains and Pepsi loses (bottom left square).

Pepsi reasons as follows: Regardless of whether Coke advertises, we're better off advertising. Coke reasons similarly: Regardless of whether Pepsi advertises, we're better off advertising. Because advertising is the best strategy for both players, it is the Nash equilibrium. The outcome of this game is that both firms advertise and make less profit than they would if they could collude to achieve the cooperative outcome of no advertising.

## Research and Development Game

A key to success in the disposable diaper industry is to design a product that people value highly relative to the cost of producing it. The firm that develops the most highly valued product and also develops the least-cost technology for producing it gains a competitive edge. It can undercut the rest of the market, increase its market share, and increase its economic profit. But it is costly to undertake the R&D that can ultimately result in an improved product and increased profit. So the cost of R&D must be deducted from the increased profit. If no firm does R&D, every firm can be better off, but if one firm initiates the R&D activity, all firms must follow.

Table 13.9 illustrates the dilemma (with hypothetical numbers) for the R&D game that Kimberly-Clark and Procter & Gamble play. Each firm has two strategies: Do R&D or do no R&D. If neither firm does R&D, Kimberly-Clark makes $30 million and Procter & Gamble makes $70 million (bottom right of the payoff matrix). If each firm does R&D, each firm's profit is lower by the amount spent on R&D (top left square of the payoff matrix). If Kimberly-Clark does R&D but Procter & Gamble does not, Kimberly-Clark gains and Procter & Gamble loses (top right square of the payoff matrix). Finally, if Procter & Gamble conducts R&D and Kimberly-Clark does not, Procter & Gamble gains and Kimberly-Clark loses (bottom left square).

Kimberly-Clark reasons as follows: Regardless of whether Procter & Gamble undertakes R&D, we're better off doing R&D. Procter & Gamble reasons similarly: Regardless of whether Kimberly-Clark does R&D, we're better off doing R&D.

Because R&D is the best strategy for both players, it is the Nash equilibrium. The outcome of this game is that both firms conduct R&D. They make less profit than they would if they could collude to achieve the cooperative outcome of no R&D.

The real-world situation has more players than Kimberly-Clark and Procter & Gamble. A large number of other firms strive to capture market share from Procter & Gamble and Kimberly-Clark. So the R&D effort by these two firms not only serves the purpose of maintaining shares in their own battle but also helps to keep barriers to entry high enough to preserve their joint market share.

TABLE 13.8   THE ADVERTISING GAME PAYOFF MATRIX

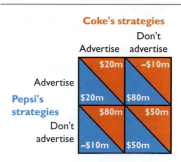

For each pair of strategies, the red triangle shows Coke's payoff, and the blue triangle shows Pepsi's. If both firms advertise, they make less than if neither firm advertises. But each firm is better off advertising if the other doesn't advertise. The Nash equilibrium for this prisoners' dilemma advertising game is for both firms to advertise.

TABLE 13.9   THE R&D GAME PAYOFF MATRIX

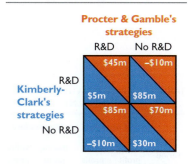

For each pair of strategies, the red triangle shows Procter & Gamble's payoff, and the blue triangle shows Kimberly-Clark's. If both firms do R&D, they make less than if neither firm undertakes R&D. But each firm is better off doing R&D if the other does no R&D. The Nash equilibrium for this prisoners' dilemma R&D game is for both firms to do R&D.

# EYE on YOUR LIFE
## A Game You Might Play

The payoff matrix here describes a game that might be familiar to you. But it isn't a prisoners' dilemma. It's a lovers' dilemma.

Jane and Jim have more fun if they do something together than if they do things alone.

But Jane likes the movies more than the ball game, and Jim likes the ball game more than the movies.

The payoff matrix describes how much they like the various outcomes (measured in units of utility).

What do they do?

By comparing the utility numbers for different strategies, you can figure out that Jim never goes to the movies alone and Jane never goes to the ball game alone.

You can also figure out that Jim doesn't go to the ball game alone and Jane doesn't go to the movies alone.

They always go out together. But do they go to the movies or the ball game?

The answer is that we can't tell. This game has no unique equilibrium. The payoffs tell you that Jane and Jim might go to either the game or the movies.

In a repeated game, they'll probably alternate between the two and might even toss a coin to decide which to go to on any given evening.

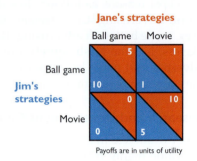

Payoffs are in units of utility

## ■ Repeated Games

The games that we've studied are played just once. In contrast, most real-world games get played repeatedly. This fact suggests that real-world duopolists might find some way of learning to cooperate so that they can enjoy a monopoly profit. If a game is played repeatedly, one player has the opportunity to penalize the other player for previous "bad" behavior. If Airbus produces 4 airplanes this week, perhaps Boeing will produce 4 next week. Before Airbus produces 4 this week, won't it take account of the possibility of Boeing producing 4 next week? What is the equilibrium of this more complicated dilemma game when it is repeated indefinitely?

The monopoly equilibrium might occur if each firm knows that the other will punish overproduction with overproduction, "tit for tat." Let's see why.

Table 13.10 keeps track of the numbers. Suppose that Boeing contemplates producing 4 airplanes in week 1. This move will bring it an economic profit of $40 million and will cut the economic profit of Airbus to $30 million. In week 2, Airbus will punish Boeing and produce 4 airplanes. But Boeing must go back to 3 airplanes to induce Airbus to cooperate again in week 3. So in week 2, Airbus makes an economic profit of $40 million, and Boeing makes an economic profit of $30 million. Adding up the profits over these two weeks of play, Boeing would have made $72 million by cooperating (2 × $36 million) compared with $70 million from producing 4 airplanes in week 1 and generating Airbus's tit-for-tat response.

What is true for Boeing is also true for Airbus. Because each firm makes a larger profit by sticking to the monopoly output, both firms do so and the monopoly price, quantity, and profit prevail.

In reality, whether a duopoly (or more generally an oligopoly) works like a one-play game or a repeated game depends primarily on the number of players and the ease of detecting and punishing overproduction. The larger the number of players, the harder it is to maintain the monopoly outcome.

**TABLE 13.10 PAYOFFS WITH PUNISHMENT**

| Period of play | Cooperate | | Overproduce | |
|---|---|---|---|---|
| | Boeing profit | Airbus profit | Boeing profit | Airbus profit |
| | (millions of dollars) | | | |
| 1 | 36 | 36 | 40 | 30 |
| 2 | 36 | 36 | 30 | 40 |

# EYE on the CELL-PHONE OLIGOPOLY

## Is Two Too Few?

A cell phone combines two products: hardware and the software that runs it. And two firms, Apple and Samsung, dominate the cell phone market. Apple powers the iPhone with its own operating system, iOS, and Samsung installs the Android operating system on its cell phones.

The pie charts show some worldwide market share data. In Figure 1, Android is by far the most popular operating system with a 75 percent market share. Figure 2 shows that although Samsung dominates the cellphone market, it competes with other Android smart-phone producers.

Is the cell-phone market efficient? Profit is one test of efficiency, and profits in the cell-phone market are large. One sign of the large profit is the battle among the big players, which frequently find themselves in court either making or defending a claim for royalties and compensation. In one

high-profile case, Microsoft claimed that Samsung's use of Android made indirect use of Microsoft's intellectual property. Samsung lost and now pays Microsoft a royalty of several dollars on each Android phone it sells.

The large profit suggests that this market is closer to monopoly than perfect competition. Producer surplus is maximized and consumer surplus is less than it would be in a competitive market. There is underproduction and a deadweight loss is created.

Some firms—Apple, Microsoft, Google (having bought Motorola)—seek maximum profit by controlling both the hardware and the software. Others—Samsung, LG, and many more—focus on hardware only. In either case, hardware is the key to profit, and economies of scale in its design and production mean that this market is likely to remain a highly contentrated oligopoly.

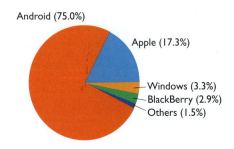

**Figure 1 Cell-Phone Operating System: Market Shares, 2013 Q1**

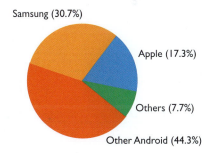

**Figure 2 Cell-Phone Makers: Market Shares, 2013 Q1**

SOURCE OF DATA: http://www.icharts.net.

## ■ Is Oligopoly Efficient?

The quantity produced of any good or service is the efficient quantity if the price (which measures marginal benefit) equals marginal cost. Does oligopoly produce efficient quantities of goods and services?

You've seen that if firms in oligopoly play a repeated prisoners' dilemma game, they can end up restricting output to the monopoly level and making the same economic profit as a monopoly would make. You've also seen that even when the firms don't cooperate, they don't necessarily drive the price down to marginal cost. So generally, oligopoly is not efficient. It suffers from the same source of inefficiency as monopoly.

Also, firms in oligopoly might end up operating at a higher average total cost than the lowest attainable cost because their advertising and research budgets are higher than the socially efficient level.

Because oligopoly creates inefficiency and firms in oligopoly have an incentive to try to behave like a monopoly, the United States has established antitrust laws that seek to reduce market power and move the oligopoly outcome closer to that of competition and efficiency.

CHECKPOINT 13.4

**Use game theory to explain how price and quantity are determined in oligopoly.**

## Practice Problems

Bud and Wise are the only two producers of a New Age beer, which is designed to displace root beer. Bud and Wise are trying to work out the quantity to produce. They know that if

- Both limit production to 10,000 gallons a day, they will make the maximum attainable joint profit of $200,000 a day—$100,000 a day each.
- One produces 20,000 gallons a day while the other produces 10,000 a day, the one that produces 20,000 gallons will make an economic profit of $150,000 and the one that sticks with 10,000 gallons will incur an economic loss of $50,000.
- Both produce 20,000 gallons a day, each will make zero economic profit.

1. Construct a payoff matrix for the game that Bud and Wise must play.
2. Find the Nash equilibrium of the game that Bud and Wise play.
3. What is the equilibrium of the game if Bud and Wise play it repeatedly?

## In the News

**Big soda fights decline: more products, for niche markets**
Soda sales are declining, but big drinks companies are fighting back with a more finely-tuned selection of product targeting smaller consumer niches. As the total market is expected to grow at 6 percent over the next seven years, Coke aims to take a larger share than its competitors.

Source: *The Wall Street Journal*, June 24, 2013

What is the game that Coke and its competitors will play over the next few years?

## Solutions to Practice Problems

1. Table 1 shows the payoff matrix for the game that Bud and Wise must play.
2. The Nash equilibrium is for both to produce 20,000 gallons a day. To see why, notice that regardless of the quantity that Bud produces, Wise makes more profit by producing 20,000 gallons a day. The same is true for Bud. So Bud and Wise each produce 20,000 gallons a day.
3. If Bud and Wise play this game repeatedly, each produces 10,000 gallons a day and makes maximum economic profit. They can achieve this outcome by playing a tit-for-tat strategy.

**TABLE 1**

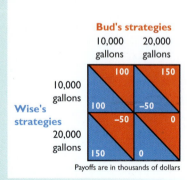

Payoffs are in thousands of dollars

## Solution to In the News

Coke and its competitors will play a product development and marketing game: introducing new products or marketing them to customers in niche (small) markets. The outcome will be that the mix of products offered in any niche market will be small and will satisfy local preferences rather than the national average. And as the preferences of the niche market change over time, so will the mix of drinks that the companies will supply to that market.

CHAPTER SUMMARY

## Key Points

**1. Explain how a firm in monopolistic competition determines its price and quantity.**

- The firm in monopolistic competition faces a downward-sloping demand curve and produces the quantity at which marginal revenue equals marginal cost.
- Entry and exit result in zero economic profit and excess capacity in long-run equilibrium.

**2. Explain why advertising costs are high in monopolistic competition.**

- Firms in monopolistic competition innovate and develop new products to maintain economic profit.
- Advertising expenditures increase total cost, but they might lower average total cost if the quantity sold increases by enough.
- Advertising expenditures might increase demand, but they might also increase competition and decrease the demand facing a firm.
- Whether monopolistic competition is inefficient depends on the value people place on product variety.

**3. Explain the dilemma faced by firms in oligopoly.**

- If firms in oligopoly act together to restrict output, they make the same economic profit as a monopoly, but each firm can make a larger profit by increasing production.
- The oligopoly dilemma is whether to restrict or expand output.

**4. Use game theory to explain how price and quantity are determined in oligopoly.**

- In the prisoners' dilemma game, two players acting in their own interests harm their joint interest. Oligopoly is a prisoners' dilemma game.
- If firms cooperated, they could earn the monopoly profit, but in a one-play game, they overproduce and can drive the price and economic profit to the levels of perfect competition.
- Advertising and research and development create a prisoners' dilemma for firms in oligopoly.
- In a repeated game, a punishment strategy can lead to monopoly output, price, and economic profit.
- Oligopoly is usually inefficient because the price (marginal benefit) exceeds marginal cost and cost might not be the lowest attainable.

## Key Terms

Cartel, 390
Duopoly, 390
Efficient scale, 383
Excess capacity, 383

Four-firm concentration ratio, 380
Game theory, 395
Herfindahl-Hirschman Index, 380
Nash equilibrium, 396

Payoff matrix, 396
Prisoners' dilemma, 395
Product differentiation, 378
Strategies, 396

# CHAPTER CHECKPOINT

## Study Plan Problems and Applications

**1.** Which of the items in List 1 are sold by firms in monopolistic competition? Explain your selections.

Use Figure 1, which shows the demand curve, marginal revenue curve, and cost curves of Lite and Kool, Inc., a producer of running shoes in monopolistic competition, to work Problems **2** to **4**.

**2.** In the short run, what quantity does Lite and Kool produce, what price does it charge, and does it make an economic profit?

**3.** In the short run, does Lite and Kool have excess capacity and what is its markup?

**4.** Do you expect firms to enter the running shoes market or exit from that market in the long run? Explain your answer.

Use the following information to work Problems **5** and **6**.

Isolated Island has two taxi companies, one owned by Ann and the other owned by Zack. Figure 2 shows the demand curve for taxi rides, *D*, and the cost curves of one of the firms. Suppose that Ann and Zack have two strategies: Collude, fix the monopoly price, and limit the number of rides, or break the collusion, cut the price, and produce more rides.

**5.** Create a payoff matrix for the game that Ann and Zack play, and find the Nash equilibrium for this game if it is played just once. Do the people of Isolated Island get the efficient quantity of taxi rides?

**6.** If Ann and Zack play the game repeatedly, what additional strategies become available to them and how might the outcome change?

Use the following information to work Problems **7** and **8**.

**Cola wars: What's your soft drink of choice?**
Soft drink sales have fallen for six straight years as consumers switched to healthier alternatives such as juices, and cut back on spending in the recession. The two rivals have moved into bottled water, fruit juices, energy drinks, and sports drinks to try to maintain market share. Both companies saw decreased sales, but Pepsi had the greater loss. Overall, Coke product sales were down 0.5 percent while Pepsi saw a 2.6 percent decline.

Source: CBC News, March 18, 2011

**7.** Describe the strategies in the game that Coca-Cola and PepsiCo play. With some assumed payoffs, create a payoff matrix for the game and find the equilibrium outcome.

**8.** Read *Eye on Cell Phones* on p. 386 and explain why cell-phone producers offer such a large variety of their products. Draw a graph of a firm's cost and revenue curves if all cell phones are identical. Use your graph to illustrate the effects of the firm introducing a new, differentiated cell phone.

**9.** Read *Eye on the Cell-Phone Oligopoly* on p. 401 and then explain the effects of economies of scale on the market for cell phones.

---

### LIST 1

- Cable TV service
- Wheat
- Athletic shoes
- Soda
- Toothbrushes
- Ready-mix concrete

---

**FIGURE 1**

Price and cost (dollars per pair)

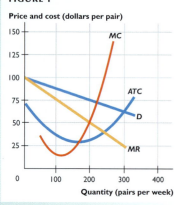

Quantity (pairs per week)

---

**FIGURE 2**

Price and cost (dollars per ride)

Quantity (taxi rides per day)

## Instructor Assignable Problems and Applications

**1.** Washtenaw Dairy in Ann Arbor, Michigan, sells 63 flavors of Strohs Mooney's ice cream, and Ben and Jerry's Web site also lists 63 different flavors of ice cream. These numbers are similar to the varieties of cell phones sold by Samsung, Nokia, and Motorola. Toyota makes only 16 varieties of vehicle and Boeing makes 16 varieties of airplane. Why is there more variety in cell phones and ice cream than in automobiles and airplanes?

**2.** Apple and Samsung have two pricing strategies: Set a high (monopoly) price or set a low (competitive) price. Suppose that if they both set a competitive price, economic profit for both is zero. If both set a monopoly price, Apple makes an economic profit of $100 million and Samsung of $200 million. If Apple sets a low price and Samsung sets a high price, Apple makes an economic profit of $200 million and Samsung incurs an economic loss of $100 million; if Apple sets a high price and Samsung sets a low price, Apple incurs an economic loss of $50 million and Samsung makes an economic profit of $250 million.
   - Create the payoff matrix for this game.
   - What is the equilibrium of this game?
   - Is the equilibrium efficient?
   - Is this game a prisoners' dilemma?

Use Figure 1, which shows the demand curve, marginal revenue curve, and cost curves of La Bella Pizza, a firm in monopolistic competition, to work Problems **3** and **4**.

**3.** In the short run, what is the quantity that La Bella Pizza produces, the price it charges, and its excess capacity?

**4.** In the long run, how will the number of pizza producers change? What are the excess capacity and the deadweight loss created? Explain your answer.

**5.** Which of the items in List 1 are sold by firms in monopolistic competition? Explain your selection.

**6. Sparks fly for Energizer**
   Energizer is gaining market share against competitor Duracell and its profit is rising despite the sharp rise in the price of zinc, a key battery ingredient.
   
   Source: www.businessweek.com, August 2007

   In what type of market are batteries sold? Explain your answer.

Use the following information to work Problems **7** and **8**.

The United States claims that Canada subsidizes its softwood lumber production and that imports of Canadian lumber damage the interests of U.S. producers. The United States has levied a tariff on Canadian imports to counter the subsidy. Canada is thinking of retaliating by refusing to export water to California. Table 1 shows a payoff matrix for the game that the United States and Canada play.

**7.** What is the United States' best strategy? What is Canada's best strategy? What is the outcome of this game? Explain.

**8.** Is this game like a prisoners' dilemma or different in some crucial way? Explain. Which country would benefit more from a free-trade agreement?

**FIGURE 1**

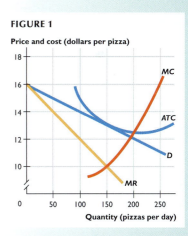

**LIST 1**
- Orange juice
- Canned soup
- PCs
- Chewing gum
- Breakfast cereals
- Corn

**TABLE 1**

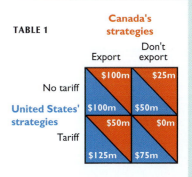

## Critical Thinking Discussion Questions

**1.** Suppose the four-firm concentration ratio for travel agencies in Turkey is 70% and the HHI is 2580.

   a. What do these numbers tell you about the market for travel agencies?
   b. Explain why these figures most likely underestimate the degree of competition in this market.

**2.** The shoe that won't quit

Amy finally decided to take the plunge and buy a pair of Uggs, but when she got around to shopping for her Uggs, the style that she wanted was sold out.

Source: *Fortune*, 5 June 2008

   a. Explain why it might be in Uggs' self-interest to restrict the quantity of Uggs available.
   b. Draw a graph to illustrate how the economic profit from Uggs is maximized.

**3.** Oil city

In the late 1990s, Reliance spent $6 billion to build a world-class oil refinery at Jamnagar, India. Now Reliance is more than doubling the size of the facility, which will make it the world's biggest producer of petrol—1.2 million gallons of petrol per day, or about 5% of global capacity. Reliance plans to sell the petrol in Europe and in the U.S., where it's too expensive and politically difficult to build new refineries. The bulked-up Jamnagar will be able to move the market and Singapore traders expect a drop in fuel prices as soon as it's going at full steam.

Source: *Fortune*, 28 April 2008

   a. Explain why the news clip implies that the global market for petrol has monopolistic as well as competitive elements.
   b. What barriers to entry might limit competition in this market and give a firm like Reliance the power to influence the market price?

**4.** Boeing vs. Airbus: Can't we all just get along?

Airbus beat out Boeing for a $24 billion contract to supply long-time Boeing customer Lion Air. Because Boeing has order backlogs, Lion Air is diversifying its fleet to avoid having a tough time procuring planes.

Source: *Fortune*, March 19, 2013

   a. In what type of market do Airbus and Boeing compete?
   b. What are some of the strategies used by Boeing and Airbus?
   c. Assume some strategies and payoffs, and set out a payoff matrix for the game between Boeing and Airbus that shows their economic profit from selling airplanes. Find the equilibrium of the game.
   d. How does repeating the game change the equilibrium?

How do we track the booms and busts in our economy?

# GDP: A Measure of Total Production and Income

**14**

When you have completed your study of this chapter, you will be able to

1 Define GDP and explain why the value of production, income, and expenditure are the same for an economy.

2 Describe how economic statisticians measure GDP and distinguish between nominal GDP and real GDP.

3 Describe the uses of real GDP and explain its limitations as a measure of the standard of living.

## 14.1  GDP, INCOME, AND EXPENDITURE

Where is the U.S. economy heading? Will it remain weak, begin to expand more rapidly, or sink into a deeper recession?

Everyone wants to know the answers to these questions. The people who make business decisions—homebuilders, auto producers, cell-phone service providers, airlines, oil producers, airplane makers, farmers, and retailers—want to know the answers so they can plan their production to align with demand. Governments want the answers because the amount of tax revenue that they collect depends on how much people earn and spend, which in turn depends on the state of the economy. Governments and the Federal Reserve want to know because they might be able to take actions that avoid excessive bust or boom. Ordinary citizens want the answers to plan their big decisions such as how long to remain in school, whether to rent or buy a new home, and how much to save toward retirement.

To assess the state of the economy we measure gross domestic product, or GDP. You're about to discover that GDP measures the value of total production, total income, and total expenditure.

### ◼ GDP Defined

**Gross domestic product (GDP)**

The market value of all the final goods and services produced within a country in a given time period.

We measure total production as **gross domestic product**, or **GDP,** which is the market value of all the final goods and services produced within a country in a given time period. This definition has four parts, which we'll examine in turn.

### Value Produced

To measure total production, we must add together the production of apples and oranges, bats and balls. Just counting the items doesn't get us very far. Which is the greater total production: 100 apples and 50 oranges or 50 apples and 100 oranges?

GDP answers this question by valuing items at their *market value*—at the prices at which the items are traded in markets. If the price of an apple is 10 cents and the price of an orange is 20 cents, the market value of 100 apples plus 50 oranges is $20 and the market value of 50 apples and 100 oranges is $25. By using market prices to value production, we can add the apples and oranges together.

### What Produced

**Final good or service**

A good or service that is produced for its final user and not as a component of another good or service.

**Intermediate good or service**

A good or service that is used as a component of a final good or service.

A **final good or service** is something that is produced for its final user and not as a component of another good or service. A final good or service contrasts with an **intermediate good or service,** which is used as a component of a final good or service. For example, a Ford car is a final good, but a Firestone tire that Ford buys and installs on the car is an intermediate good. In contrast, if you buy a replacement Firestone tire for your car, then that tire is a final good. The same good can be either final or intermediate depending on how it is used.

GDP does not count the value of everything that is produced. With one exception, it includes only those items that are traded in markets and does not include the value of goods and services that people produce for their own use. For example, if you buy a car wash, the value produced is included in GDP. But if you wash your own car, your production is not counted as part of GDP. The exception is the market value of homes that people own. GDP puts a rental value on these homes and pretends that the owners rent their homes to themselves.

## Where Produced

Only goods and services that are produced *within a country* count as part of that country's GDP. Nike Corporation, a U.S. firm, produces sneakers in Vietnam, and the market value of those shoes is part of Vietnam's GDP, not part of U.S. GDP. Toyota, a Japanese firm, produces automobiles in Georgetown, Kentucky, and the value of this production is part of U.S. GDP, not part of Japan's GDP.

## When Produced

GDP measures the value of production *during a given time period.* This time period is either a quarter of a year—called the quarterly GDP data—or a year—called the annual GDP data. The Federal Reserve and others use the quarterly GDP data to keep track of the short-term evolution of the economy, and economists use the annual GDP data to examine long-term trends.

GDP measures not only the value of total production but also total income and total expenditure. The circular flow model that you studied in Chapter 2 explains why.

## ■ Circular Flows in the U.S. Economy

Four groups buy the final goods and services produced: households, firms, governments, and the rest of the world. Four types of expenditure correspond to these groups:

- Consumption expenditure
- Investment
- Government expenditure on goods and services
- Net exports of goods and services

## Consumption Expenditure

**Consumption expenditure** is the expenditure by households on consumption goods and services. It includes expenditures on *nondurable goods* such as orange juice and pizza, *durable goods* such as televisions and DVD players, and *services* such as rock concerts and haircuts. Consumption expenditure also includes house and apartment rents, including the rental value of owner-occupied housing.

**Consumption expenditure**
The expenditure by households on consumption goods and services.

## Investment

**Investment** is the purchase of new *capital goods* (tools, instruments, machines, and buildings) and additions to inventories. Capital goods are *durable goods* produced by one firm and bought by another. Examples are PCs produced by Dell and bought by Ford Motor Company, and airplanes produced by Boeing and bought by United Airlines. Investment also includes the purchase of new homes by households.

**Investment**
The purchase of new *capital goods* (tools, instruments, machines, buildings) and additions to inventories.

At the end of a year, some of a firm's output might remain unsold. For example, if Ford produces 4 million cars and sells 3.9 million of them, the other 0.1 million (100,000) cars remain unsold. In this case, Ford's inventory of cars increases by 100,000. When a firm adds unsold output to inventory, we count those items as part of investment.

It is important to note that investment does *not* include the purchase of stocks and bonds. In macroeconomics, we reserve the term "investment" for the purchase of new capital goods and the additions to inventories.

**Government expenditure on goods and services**
The expenditure by all levels of government on goods and services.

## Government Expenditure on Goods and Services

**Government expenditure on goods and services** is expenditure by all levels of government on goods and services. For example, the U.S. Defense Department buys missiles and other weapons systems, the State Department buys travel services, the White House buys Internet services, and state and local governments buy cruisers for law enforcement officers.

## Net Exports of Goods and Services

**Net exports of goods and services**
The value of exports of goods and services minus the value of imports of goods and services.

**Exports of goods and services**
Items that firms in the United States produce and sell to the rest of the world.

**Imports of goods and services**
Items that households, firms, and governments in the United States buy from the rest of the world.

**Net exports of goods and services** is the value of exports of goods and services minus the value of imports of goods and services. **Exports of goods and services** are items that firms in the United States produce and sell to the rest of the world. **Imports of goods and services** are items that households, firms, and governments in the United States buy from the rest of the world. Imports are produced in other countries, so expenditure on imports is not included in expenditure on U.S.-produced goods and services. If exports exceed imports, net exports are positive and expenditure on U.S.-produced goods and services increases. If imports exceed exports, net exports are negative and expenditure on U.S.-produced goods and services decreases.

## Total Expenditure

Total expenditure on goods and services produced in the United States is the sum of the four items that you've just examined. We call consumption expenditure $C$, investment $I$, government expenditure on goods and services $G$, and net exports of goods and services $NX$. So total expenditure, which is also the total amount received by the producers of final goods and services, is

$$\text{Total expenditure} = C + I + G + NX.$$

## Income

Labor earns wages, capital earns interest, land earns rent, and entrepreneurship earns profits. Households receive these incomes. Some part of total income, called *undistributed profit*, is a combination of interest and profit that firms retain and do not pay to households. But from an economic viewpoint, undistributed profit is income paid to households and then loaned to firms.

## ■ Expenditure Equals Income

Figure 14.1 shows the circular flows of income and expenditure that we've just described. The figure is based on Figures 2.4 and 2.5 (on p. 85 and p. 87), but it includes some more details and additional flows.

We call total income $Y$ and show it by the blue flow from firms to households. When households receive their incomes, they pay some in taxes and save some. Some households receive benefits from governments. **Net taxes** equal taxes paid minus cash benefits received and are the green flow from households to governments labeled $NT$. **Saving** is the amount of income that is not paid in net taxes or spent on consumption goods and services. Saving flows from households to financial markets and is the green flow labeled $S$. These two green flows are not expenditures on goods and services. They are just flows of money. Because households allocate all their incomes after paying net taxes to consumption and saving,

**Net taxes**
Taxes paid minus cash benefits received from governments.

**Saving**
The amount of income that is not paid in net taxes or spent on consumption goods and services.

$$Y = C + S + NT.$$

The red flows show the four expenditure flows: consumption expenditure from households to firms, government expenditure from governments to firms, and net exports from the rest of the world to firms. Investment flows from the financial markets, where firms borrow, to the firms that produce capital goods.

Because firms pay out everything they receive as incomes to the factors of production, total expenditure equals total income. That is,

$$Y = C + I + G + NX.$$

From the viewpoint of firms, the value of production is the cost of production, which equals income. From the viewpoint of purchasers of goods and services, the value of production is the cost of buying it, which equals expenditure. So

**The value of production equals income equals expenditure.**

The circular flow and the equality of income and expenditure provide two approaches to measuring GDP that we'll study in the next section.

## FIGURE 14.1

The Circular Flow of Income and Expenditure

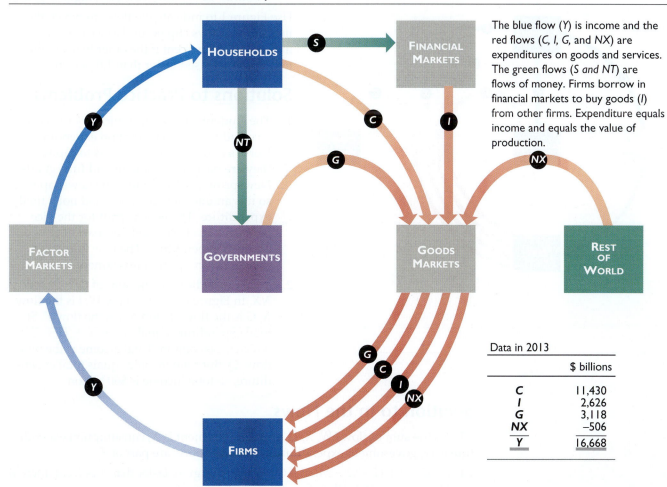

The blue flow (*Y*) is income and the red flows (*C, I, G,* and *NX*) are expenditures on goods and services. The green flows (*S and NT*) are flows of money. Firms borrow in financial markets to buy goods (*I*) from other firms. Expenditure equals income and equals the value of production.

Data in 2013

|  | $ billions |
|---|---|
| *C* | 11,430 |
| *I* | 2,626 |
| *G* | 3,118 |
| *NX* | −506 |
| *Y* | 16,668 |

# CHECKPOINT 14.1

**Define GDP and explain why the value of production, income, and expenditure are the same for an economy.**

## Practice Problems

**LIST 1**

- Banking services bought by a student
- New cars bought by Hertz, the car rental firm
- Newsprint bought by *USA Today* from International Paper
- The purchase of a new aircraft for the vice president
- New house bought by Beyoncé

1. Classify each of the items in List 1 as a final good or service or as an intermediate good or service and identify which is a component of consumption expenditure, investment, or government expenditure on goods and services.

2. Figure 1 shows the flows of expenditure and income on Lotus Island. In 2013, R was $10 billion; W was $30 billion; U was $12 billion; X was $15 billion; and Z was $3 billion. Calculate total expenditure and total income.

## In the News

**U.S. economy grew slower in spring than previously reported**
Real GDP increased at an annual rate of 1.0 percent in the second quarter of 2011. Investment, exports, consumption expenditure, and government expenditure increased faster than 1.0 percent.

Source: BEA News Release, August 26, 2011

Use Figure 1 to indicate the flows in which the items in the news clip occur. How can GDP increase by 1.0 percent if the other items in the news clip increased faster than 1.0 percent?

**FIGURE 1**

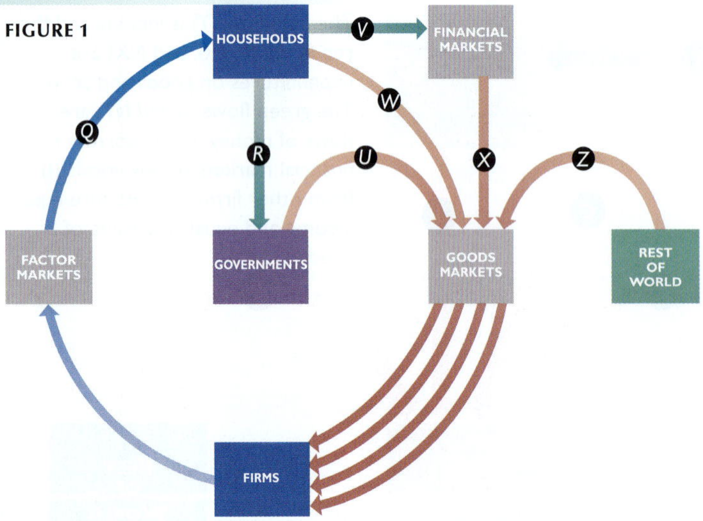

HOUSEHOLDS — V → FINANCIAL MARKETS

W

Q

R U X Z

FACTOR MARKETS   GOVERNMENTS   GOODS MARKETS   REST OF WORLD

FIRMS

## Solutions to Practice Problems

1. The student's banking service is a final service and part of consumption expenditure. Hertz's new cars are additions to capital, so they are part of investment and final goods. Newsprint is an input into the newspaper, so it is an intermediate good and not a final expenditure. The new aircraft for the vice president is a final good and part of government expenditure. The new house is a final good and part of investment.

2. Total expenditure is the sum of C, I, G, and NX. In Figure 1, C is the flow W; I is the flow X; G is the flow U; and NX is the flow Z. So total expenditure equals W + X + U + Z, which is $60 billion. Total income is the blue flow, Q. But total income equals total expenditure, so total income is $60 billion.

## Solution to In the News

GDP is the sum of flows W, X, U, and Z. Investment is X, consumption expenditure is W, government expenditure is U, and exports are part of Z.

GDP = C + I + G + X − M, so if C + I + G + X grew faster than 1 percent, then M must have grown faster than C + I + G + X.

## 14.2  MEASURING U.S. GDP

U.S. GDP is the market value of all the final goods and services produced within the United States during a year. In 2013, U.S. GDP was $16.7 trillion. The Bureau of Economic Analysis in the U.S. Department of Commerce measures GDP by using two approaches:

- Expenditure approach
- Income approach

### ■ The Expenditure Approach

The expenditure approach measures GDP by using data on consumption expenditure, investment, government expenditure on goods and services, and net exports. This approach is like attaching a meter to the circular flow diagram on all the flows running through the goods markets to firms and measuring the magnitudes of those flows. Table 14.1 shows this approach. The first column gives the terms used in the U.S. National Income and Product Accounts. The next column gives the symbols we used in the previous section.

Using the expenditure approach, GDP is the sum of consumption expenditure on goods and services ($C$), investment ($I$), government expenditure on goods and services ($G$), and net exports of goods and services ($NX$). The third column gives the expenditures in 2013. GDP measured by the expenditure approach was $16,668 billion (the data are for the second quarter of 2013).

Net exports were negative in 2013 because imports exceeded exports. Imports were $2,748 billion and exports were $2,242 billion, so net exports—exports minus imports—were −$506 billion as shown in the table.

The fourth column in Table 14.1 shows the relative magnitudes of the expenditures. Consumption expenditure is by far the largest component of total expenditure; government expenditure is the next largest. Investment and exports are a similar size; and net exports is the smallest component. In 2013, consumption expenditure was 68.6 percent, investment was 15.8 percent, government expenditure was 18.7 percent, and net exports were a negative 3.0 percent of GDP.

**TABLE 14.1**

### GDP: The Expenditure Approach

| Item | Symbol | Amount in 2013 (second quarter) (billions of dollars) | Percentage of GDP |
|------|--------|--------------------------------|-----------------|
| Consumption expenditure | $C$ | 11,430 | 68.6 |
| Investment | $I$ | 2,626 | 15.8 |
| Government expenditure | $G$ | 3,118 | 18.7 |
| Net exports | $NX$ | −506 | −3.0 |
| GDP | $Y$ | 16,668 | 100.0 |

The expenditure approach measures GDP by adding together consumption expenditure ($C$), investment ($I$), government expenditure ($G$), and net exports ($NX$).

In 2013, GDP measured by the expenditure approach was $16,668 billion.

SOURCE OF DATA: U.S. Department of Commerce, Bureau of Economic Analysis.

---

### Expenditures Not in GDP

Total expenditure (and GDP) does not include all the things that people and businesses buy. GDP is the value of *final goods and services,* so spending that is *not* on final goods and services is not part of GDP. Spending on intermediate goods and services is not part of GDP, although it is not always obvious whether an item is an intermediate good or a final good (see *Eye on the U.S. Economy* below). Also, we do not count as part of GDP spending on

- Used goods
- Financial assets

*Used Goods*   Expenditure on used goods is not part of GDP because these goods were part of GDP in the period in which they were produced and during which time they were new goods. For example, a 2010 automobile was part of GDP in 2010. If the car is traded on the used car market in 2014, the amount paid for the car is not part of GDP in 2014.

*Financial Assets*   When households buy financial assets such as bonds and stocks, they are making loans, not buying goods and services. The expenditure on newly produced capital goods is part of GDP, but the purchase of financial assets is not.

# EYE on the U.S. ECONOMY
## Is a Computer Program an Intermediate Good or a Final Good?

When American Airlines buys a new reservations software package, is that like General Motors buying tires? If it is, then software is an *intermediate good* and it is not counted as part of GDP. Airline ticket sales, like GM cars, are part of GDP, but the intermediate goods that are used to produce air transportation or cars are *not* part of GDP.

Or when American Airlines buys new software, is that like General Motors buying a new assembly-line robot? If it is, then the software is a capital good and its purchase is the purchase of a final good. In this case, the software purchase is an *investment* and it *is* counted as part of GDP.

Brent Moulton worked as a government economist in the Bureau of Economic Analysis (BEA). Moulton's job was to oversee periodic adjustments to the GDP estimates to incorporate new data and new ideas about the economy.

The biggest change made was in how the purchase of computer software by firms is classified. Before 1999, it was regarded as an *intermediate good.* But since 1999, it has been treated as an *investment.*

How big a deal is this? When the BEA recalculated the 1996 GDP, the change increased the estimate of the 1996 GDP by $115 billion. That is a lot of money. To put it in perspective: GDP

in 1996 was $7,662 billion. So the adjustment was 1.5 percent of GDP.

This change is a good example of the ongoing effort by the BEA to keep the GDP measure as accurate as possible.

## ■ The Income Approach

To measure GDP using the income approach, the Bureau of Economic Analysis uses income data collected by the Internal Revenue Service and other agencies. The BEA takes the incomes that firms pay households for the services of the factors of production they hire—wages for labor services, interest for the use of capital, rent for the use of land, and profits for entrepreneurship—and sums those incomes. This approach is like attaching a meter to the circular flow diagram on all the flows running through factor markets from firms to households and measuring the magnitudes of those flows. Let's see how the income approach works.

The U.S. National Income and Product Accounts divide incomes into two big categories:

- Wage income
- Interest, rent, and profit income

### Wage Income

Wage income, called *compensation of employees* in the national accounts, is the total payment for labor services. It includes net wages and salaries plus fringe benefits paid by employers such as health-care insurance, Social Security contributions, and pension fund contributions.

### Interest, Rent, and Profit Income

Interest, rent, and profit income, called *net operating surplus* in the national accounts, is the total income earned by capital, land, and entrepreneurship.

Interest income is the interest that households receive on capital. A household's capital is equal to its net worth—its assets minus its borrowing.

Rent includes payments for the use of land and other rented factors of production. It includes payments for rented housing and imputed rent for owner-occupied housing. (Imputed rent is an estimate of what homeowners would pay to rent the housing they own and use themselves. By including this item in the national accounts, we measure the total value of housing services, whether they are owned or rented.)

Profit includes the profits of corporations and the incomes of proprietors who run their own businesses. These incomes are a mixture of interest and profit.

Table 14.2 shows the relative magnitudes of these components of incomes.

### Net Domestic Product at Factor Cost

The sum of wages, interest, rent, and profit is *net domestic product at factor cost*. Net domestic product at factor cost is not GDP, and we must make two further adjustments to get to GDP: one from factor cost to market prices and another from net product to gross product.

### From Factor Cost to Market Price

The expenditure approach values goods and services at market prices, and the income approach values them at factor cost—the cost of the factors of production used to produce them. Indirect taxes (such as sales taxes) and subsidies (payments by government to firms) make these two values differ. Sales taxes make market prices exceed factor cost, and subsidies make factor cost exceed market prices. To convert the value at factor cost to the value at market prices, we must add indirect taxes and subtract subsidies.

## TABLE 14.2

### GDP: The Income Approach

The sum of all incomes equals net domestic product at factor cost. The income approach measure of GDP equals net domestic product at factor cost plus indirect taxes less subsidies plus depreciation (capital consumption).

In 2013, GDP measured by the income approach was $16,668 billion. This amount is $154 billion more than GDP measured by the expenditure approach—a statistical discrepancy of −$154 billion.

Wages are by far the largest part of total income.

| Item | Amount in 2013 (second quarter) (billions of dollars) | Percentage of GDP |
|---|---|---|
| Wages (compensation of employees) | 8,820 | 52.9 |
| Interest, rent, and profit (net operating surplus) | 4,290 | 25.7 |
| Net domestic product at factor cost | 13,110 | 78.7 |
| Indirect taxes less subsidies | 1,080 | 6.5 |
| Depreciation (capital consumption) | 2,632 | 15.8 |
| GDP (income approach) | 16,822 | 100.9 |
| Statistical discrepancy | −154 | −0.9 |
| GDP (expenditure approach) | 16,668 | 100.0 |

SOURCE OF DATA: U.S. Department of Commerce, Bureau of Economic Analysis.

**Depreciation**
The decrease in the value of capital that results from its use and from obsolescence.

### From Net Product to Gross Product

The income approach measures *net* product and the expenditure approach measures *gross* product. The difference is **depreciation,** which is the decrease in the value of capital that results from its use and from obsolescence. Firms' profits, which are included in the income approach, are net of depreciation, so the income approach gives a *net* measure. Investment, which is included in the expenditure approach, includes the purchase of capital to replace worn out or obsolete capital, so the expenditure approach gives a *gross* measure. To get *gross* domestic product from the income approach, we must *add* depreciation to total income.

### Statistical Discrepancy

The expenditure approach and income approach do not deliver exactly the same estimate of GDP. If a taxi driver doesn't report all his tips, they get missed in the income approach, but they get caught by the expenditure approach when he spends his income. So the sum of expenditures might exceed the sum of incomes. But most income gets reported to the Internal Revenue Service on tax returns while many items of expenditure are not recorded and must be estimated. So the sum of incomes might exceed the sum of estimated expenditures.

The discrepancy between the expenditure approach and the income approach estimates of GDP is called the *statistical discrepancy,* and it is calculated as the GDP expenditure total minus the GDP income total.

The two measures of GDP provide a check on the accuracy of the numbers. If the two are wildly different, we will want to know what mistakes we've made. Have we omitted some item? Have we counted something twice? The fact that the two estimates are close gives some confidence that they are reasonably accurate. But the expenditure total is regarded as the more reliable estimate of GDP, so the discrepancy is added to or subtracted from income to reconcile the two estimates.

Table 14.2 summarizes the calculation of GDP using the income approach and its reconciliation with GDP using the expenditure approach. The table also shows the relative magnitudes of the components of the income measure.

## ■ GDP and Related Measures of Production and Income

Although GDP is the main measure of total production, you will sometimes encounter another: gross *national* product or GNP.

### Gross National Product

A country's *gross national product*, or *GNP*, is the market value of all the final goods and services produced anywhere in the world in a given time period by the factors of production supplied by the residents of that country. For example, Nike's income from the capital that it supplies to its Vietnam shoe factory is part of U.S. GNP but not part of U.S. GDP. It is part of Vietnam's GDP. Similarly, Toyota's income on the capital it supplies to its Kentucky auto plant is part of U.S. GDP but not part of U.S. GNP. It is part of Japan's GNP.

GNP equals GDP plus net factor income received from or paid to other countries. The difference between U.S. GDP and GNP is small. But in an oil-rich Middle Eastern country such as Bahrain, where a large amount of capital is owned by foreigners, GNP is much smaller than GDP; and in a poor country such as Bangladesh, whose people work abroad and send income home, GNP is much larger than GDP.

### Disposable Personal Income

You've seen that consumption expenditure is the largest component of aggregate expenditure. The main influence on consumption expenditure is *disposable personal income*, which is the income received by households minus personal income taxes paid. Because disposable personal income plays an important role in influencing spending, the national accounts measure this item along with a number of intermediate totals that you can see in Figure 14.2. This figure shows how disposable personal income is calculated and how it relates to GDP and GNP.

■ **FIGURE 14.2**

GDP and Related Product and Income Measures

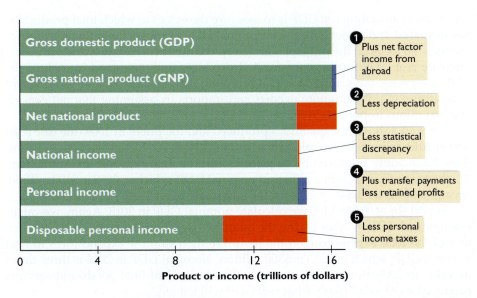

The bars show six related product and income measures and the relationship among them.

❶ Add net factor income from abroad to GDP to get GNP.

❷ Subtract depreciation from GNP to get net national product.

❸ Subtract the statistical discrepancy between the expenditure and income measures (almost invisible in the figure because it is tiny) to get national income.

❹ Add transfer payments by governments less profits retained by firms to get personal income.

❺ Finally, subtract personal income taxes to get disposable personal income.

Source of data: U.S. Department of Commerce, Bureau of Economic Analysis.

## ■ Real GDP and Nominal GDP

You've seen that GDP measures total expenditure on final goods and services in a given period. Suppose that we want to compare GDP in two periods, say 2009 and 2013. In 2009, GDP was $14,418 billion and by 2013, it was $16,668 billion—14 percent higher than in 2009. What does this 14 percent increase mean?

The answer is a combination of two things:

• We produced more goods and services.
• We paid higher prices for our goods and services.

Producing more goods and services contributes to an improvement in our standard of living. Paying higher prices means that our *cost of living* has increased but our standard of living has not. So it matters a great deal why GDP has increased. If the 14 percent increase is accounted for mainly by higher prices, our standard of living hasn't changed much. But if the 14 percent increase is accounted for mainly by the production of more goods and services, our standard of living might have increased a lot.

You're now going to see how economists at the Bureau of Economic Analysis isolate the effects on GDP of an increase in production. Their first step is to distinguish between two GDP concepts: real GDP and nominal GDP.

**Real GDP** is the value of the final goods and services produced in a given year expressed in terms of the prices in a *reference base year*. The *reference base year* is the year we choose against which to compare all other years. In the United States today, the *reference base year* is 2009.

Real GDP contrasts with **nominal GDP,** which is the value of the final goods and services produced in a given year expressed in terms of the prices of that same year. Nominal GDP is just a more precise name for GDP.

The method used to calculate real GDP has changed in recent years and is now a bit technical, but the essence of the calculation hasn't changed. Here, we describe the essence of the calculation. An appendix to this chapter describes the technical details of the method used by the Bureau of Economic Analysis.

**Real GDP**
The value of the final goods and services produced in a given year expressed in terms of the prices in a *base year.*

**Nominal GDP**
The value of the final goods and services produced in a given year expressed in terms of the prices of that same year.

## ■ Calculating Real GDP

The goal of calculating *real GDP* is to measure the extent to which total production has increased and remove from the nominal GDP numbers the influence of price changes. To focus on the principles and keep the numbers easy to work with, we'll calculate real GDP for an economy that produces only one good in each of the GDP categories: consumption expenditure (*C*), investment (*I*), and government expenditure (*G*). We'll ignore exports and imports by assuming that net exports (exports minus imports) is zero.

Table 14.3 shows the quantities produced and the prices in 2009 (the *base year*) and in 2013. In part (a), we calculate nominal GDP in 2009. For each item, we multiply the quantity produced by its price to find the total expenditure on the item. We then sum the expenditures to find nominal GDP, which in 2009 is $100 million. Because 2009 is the base year, real GDP and nominal GDP are equal in 2009.

In part (b) of Table 14.3, we calculate nominal GDP in 2013. Again, we calculate nominal GDP by multiplying the quantity of each item produced by its price to find the total expenditure on the item. We then sum the expenditures to find nominal GDP, which in 2013 is $300 million. Nominal GDP in 2013 is three times its value in 2009. But by how much has the quantity of final goods and services produced increased? That's what real GDP will tell us.

■ **TABLE 14.3**

Calculating Nominal GDP and Real GDP in 2009 and 2013

| Item | | Quantity (millions of units) | Price (dollars per unit) | Expenditure (millions of dollars) |
|---|---|---|---|---|
| **(a) In 2009** | | | | |
| C | T-shirts | 10 | 5 | 50 |
| I | Computer chips | 3 | 10 | 30 |
| G | Security services | 1 | 20 | 20 |
| Y | Real GDP and Nominal GDP in 2009 | | | 100 |
| **(b) In 2013** | | | | |
| C | T-shirts | 4 | 5 | 20 |
| I | Computer chips | 2 | 20 | 40 |
| G | Security services | 6 | 40 | 240 |
| Y | Nominal GDP in 2013 | | | 300 |
| **(c) Quantities of 2013 valued at prices of 2009** | | | | |
| C | T-shirts | 4 | 5 | 20 |
| I | Computer chips | 2 | 10 | 20 |
| G | Security services | 6 | 20 | 120 |
| Y | Real GDP in 2013 | | | 160 |

The base year is 2009, so real GDP and nominal GDP are equal in that year.

Between 2009 and 2013, the production of security services (G) increased, but the production of T-shirts (C) and computer chips (I) decreased. In the same period, the price of a T-shirt remained constant, but the other two prices doubled.

Nominal GDP increased from $100 million in 2009 in part (a) to $300 million in 2013 in part (b).

Real GDP in part (c), which is calculated by using the quantities of 2013 in part (b) and the prices of 2009 in part (a), increased from $100 million in 2009 to $160 million in 2013, a 60 percent increase.

In part (c) of Table 14.3, we calculate real GDP in 2013. You can see that the quantity of each good and service produced in part (c) is the same as that in part (b). They are the quantities of 2013. You can also see that the prices in part (c) are the same as those in part (a). They are the prices of the base year—2009.

For each item, we now multiply the quantity produced in 2013 by its price in 2009 to find what the total expenditure would have been in 2013 if prices had remained the same as they were in 2009. We then sum these expenditures to find real GDP in 2013, which is $160 million.

Nominal GDP in 2013 is three times its value in 2009, but real GDP in 2013 is only 1.6 times its 2009 value—a 60 percent increase in *real* GDP.

■ **Using the Real GDP Numbers**

In the example that we've just worked through, we found the value of real GDP in 2013 based on the prices of 2009. This number alone enables us to compare production in two years only. By repeating the calculation that we have done for 2013 using the data for each year between 2009 and 2013, we can calculate the *annual percentage change of real GDP*—the annual growth rate of real GDP. This is the most common use of the real GDP numbers. Also, by calculating real GDP every three months—known as *quarterly real GDP*—the Bureau of Economic Analysis is able to provide valuable information that is used to interpret the current state of the economy. This information is used to guide both government macroeconomic policy and business production and investment decisions.

# CHECKPOINT 14.2

**Describe how economic statisticians measure GDP and distinguish between nominal GDP and real GDP.**

## Practice Problems

Table 1 shows some of the items in the U.S. National Income and Product Accounts in 2010. Use Table 1 to work Problems **1** to **3**.

1. Use the expenditure approach to calculate U.S. GDP in 2010.
2. What was U.S. GDP as measured by the income approach in 2010? By how much did gross domestic product and net domestic product differ in 2010?
3. Calculate U.S. GNP and U.S. national income in 2010.
4. Table 2 shows some data for an economy. If the base year is 2013, calculate the economy's nominal GDP and real GDP in 2014.

### TABLE 1

| Item | Amount (trillions of dollars) |
| --- | --- |
| Consumption expenditure | 10.2 |
| Government expenditure | 3.1 |
| Indirect taxes less subsidies | 1.0 |
| Depreciation | 1.9 |
| Net factor income from abroad | 0.2 |
| Investment | 1.7 |
| Net exports | −0.5 |
| Statistical discrepancy | 0 |

### TABLE 2

**(a) In 2013:**

| Item | Quantity | Price |
| --- | --- | --- |
| Apples | 60 | $0.50 |
| Oranges | 80 | $0.25 |

**(b) In 2014:**

| Item | Quantity | Price |
| --- | --- | --- |
| Apples | 160 | $1.00 |
| Oranges | 220 | $2.00 |

## In the News

**Factory orders fell 4 percent in March**
The Commerce Department reported orders for manufactured goods decreased 4 percent, with nondurable goods falling 2.4 percent and durable goods falling 5.8 percent, while business inventories of durable goods increased 0.9 percent.

Source: *The Wall Street Journal*, May 3, 2013

Which component of GDP changes when sales of (i) nondurable goods fall and (ii) durable goods fall, and (iii) inventories of durable goods increase? Provide an example of each item of expenditure.

## Solutions to Practice Problems

1. GDP was $14.5 trillion. The expenditure approach sums the expenditure on final goods and services. That is, GDP $= C + I + G + NX$.
   In 2010, U.S. GDP $= (\$10.2 + \$1.7 + \$3.1 − \$0.5)$ trillion $= \$14.5$ trillion.
2. GDP as measured by the income approach was $14.5 trillion. With the statistical discrepancy zero, GDP (expenditure approach) = GDP (income approach). Gross domestic product minus net domestic product equals depreciation, which was $1.9 trillion.
3. GNP = GDP + Net factor income from abroad. In 2010, GNP was $14.7 trillion ($14.5 trillion + $0.2 trillion). National income = GNP − Depreciation, which equals $14.7 trillion − $1.9 trillion = $12.8 trillion.
4. Nominal GDP in 2014 equals (160 apples $\times$ $1) + (220 oranges $\times$ $2) = $600. Real GDP in 2014 at 2013 prices equals (160 apples $\times$ $0.50 per apple) + (220 oranges $\times$ $0.25 per orange) = $135.

## Solution to In the News

(i) Nondurable goods, such as gasoline and coffee bought by households, are part of consumption expenditure, *C*. (ii) Durable goods, such as iPhones bought by households, are part of consumption expenditure, *C*, and durable goods, such as aircraft bought by firms, are part of investment, *I*. (iii) An inventory of durable goods, such as the auto parts at a Ford plant, is part of investment, *I*.

## 14.3  THE USES AND LIMITATIONS OF REAL GDP

We use estimates of real GDP for three main purposes:

- To compare the standard of living over time
- To track the course of the business cycle
- To compare the standard of living among countries

### ■ The Standard of Living Over Time

A nation's *standard of living* is measured by the value of goods and services that its people enjoy, *on average*. Income per person determines what people can afford to buy and real GDP is a measure of real income. So *real GDP per person*—real GDP divided by the population—is a commonly used measure for comparing the standard of living over time.

Real GDP per person tells us the value of goods and services that the average person can enjoy. By using *real* GDP, we remove any influence that rising prices and a rising cost of living might have had on our comparison.

A handy way of comparing real GDP per person over time is to express it as a ratio of its value in some reference year. Table 14.4 provides the numbers for the United States that compare 2013 with 53 years earlier, 1960. In 1960, real GDP per person was $17,212 and in 2013 it was $49,636, or 2.9 times its 1960 level. To the extent that real GDP per person measures the standard of living, people were 2.9 times as well off in 2013 as their grandparents had been in 1960.

Figure 14.3 shows the entire 53 years of real GDP per person from 1960 to 2013 and displays two features of our changing standard of living:

1. The growth of potential GDP per person
2. Fluctuations of real GDP per person around potential GDP

**Potential GDP** is the level of real GDP when all the economy's factors of production—labor, capital, land, and entrepreneurial ability—are fully employed. When some factors of production are *unemployed*, real GDP is *below* potential GDP. And when some factors of production are *over-employed* and working harder and for longer hours than can be maintained in the long run, real GDP *exceeds* potential GDP.

You've seen that real GDP per person in 2013 was 2.9 times that of 1960. But in 2013, some labor and other factors of production were unemployed and the economy was producing less than potential GDP. To measure the trend in the standard of living, we must remove the influence of short-term fluctuations and focus on the path of potential GDP.

The growth rate of potential GDP fluctuates less than the growth rate of real GDP. During the 1960s, potential GDP per person grew at an average rate of 2.8 percent a year, but since 1970, its growth rate has slowed to 1.9 percent a year. This growth slowdown means that potential GDP is lower today (and lower by a large amount) than it would have been if the 1960s growth rate could have been maintained. If potential GDP had kept growing at the 1960s pace, potential GDP per person in 2013 would have been $30,000 more than it actually was. The cumulatively lost income from the growth slowdown of the 1970s is a staggering $406,000 per person. Understanding the reasons for the growth slowdown is one of the major tasks of macroeconomists.

**TABLE 14.4    REAL GDP PER PERSON IN 1960 AND 2013**

| Year | 1960 | 2013 |
| --- | --- | --- |
| Real GDP (billions) | $3,106 | $15,680 |
| Population (millions) | 180.4 | 315.9 |
| Real GDP per person | $17,212 | $49,636 |

**Potential GDP**
The value of real GDP when all the economy's factors of production—labor, capital, land, and entrepreneurial ability—are fully employed.

### FIGURE 14.3

## Real GDP and Potential GDP Per Person in the United States: 1960–2013

Real GDP grows and fluctuates around the growth path of potential GDP. Potential GDP per person grew at an annual rate of 2.8 percent during the 1960s and slowed to 1.9 percent after 1970.

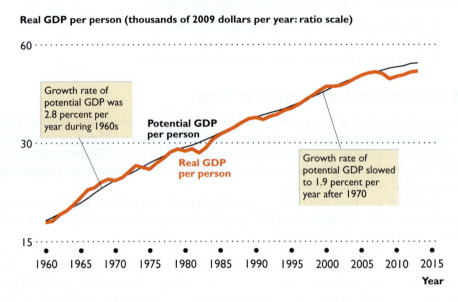

**Real GDP per person (thousands of 2009 dollars per year: ratio scale)**

Growth rate of potential GDP was 2.8 percent per year during 1960s

Potential GDP per person

Real GDP per person

Growth rate of potential GDP slowed to 1.9 percent per year after 1970

Sources of data: Bureau of Economic Analysis and the Congressional Budget Office.

**Business cycle**
A periodic but irregular up-and-down movement of total production and other measures of economic activity.

**Recession**
A period during which real GDP decreases for at least two successive quarters; or defined by the NBER as "a period of significant decline in total output, income, employment, and trade, usually lasting from six months to a year, and marked by contractions in many sectors of the economy."

### ■ Tracking the Course of the Business Cycle

We call the fluctuations in the pace of economic activity the business cycle. A **business cycle** is a periodic but irregular up-and-down movement of total production and other measures of economic activity such as employment and income. The business cycle isn't a regular, predictable, and repeating cycle like the phases of the moon. The timing and the intensity of the business cycle vary a lot, but every cycle has two phases:

1. Expansion
2. Recession

and two turning points:

1. Peak
2. Trough

Figure 14.4 shows these features of the most recent U.S. business cycle using real GDP as the measure of economic activity. An *expansion* is a period during which real GDP increases. In the early stage of an expansion, real GDP remains below potential GDP and as the expansion progresses, real GDP eventually exceeds potential GDP.

A common definition of **recession** is a period during which real GDP decreases—its growth rate is negative—for at least two successive quarters. The National Bureau of Economic Research (NBER), which dates the U.S. business cycle phases and turning points, defines a recession more broadly as "a significant decline in economic activity spread across the economy, lasting more than a few

■ **FIGURE 14.4**

The Most Recent U.S. Business Cycle

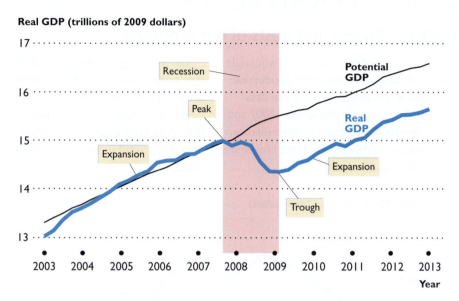

The most recent business cycle peak was in the fourth quarter of 2007 and the trough was in the second quarter of 2009 after which a new expansion began. Between the peak and the trough, the economy was in a recession. The recession was extremely deep and the expansion that followed was extremely weak—real GDP has remained a long way below potential GDP.

SOURCES OF DATA: Bureau of Economic Analysis, the Congressional Budget Office, and the National Bureau of Economic Research.

months, normally visible in real GDP, real income, employment, industrial production, and wholesale-retail sales." This definition means that sometimes the NBER declares a recession even though real GDP has not decreased for two successive quarters. A recession in 2001 was such a recession. An expansion ends and a recession begins at a business cycle peak. A peak is the highest level of real GDP that has been attained up to that time. A recession ends at a trough when real GDP reaches a low point and from which a new expansion begins.

The shaded bar in Figure 14.4 highlights the 2008–2009 recession. This recession was unusually severe. It lowered real GDP to its 2005 level. The end of a recession isn't the end of pain. When an expansion begins, real GDP is below potential GDP. And even after two years into the expansion that followed the 2008–2009 recession, real GDP had not returned to its previous peak level and the gap between real GDP and potential GDP was wide.

The period that began in 1991 following a severe recession and that ended with the global financial crisis of 2008 was so free from serious downturns in real GDP and other indicators of economic activity that it was called the *Great Moderation*, a name that contrasts it with the Great Depression. Some starry-eyed optimists even began to declare that the business cycle was dead. This long period of expansion also turned the attention of macroeconomists away from the business cycle and toward a focus on economic growth and the possibility of achieving faster growth.

But the 2008–2009 recession put the business cycle back on the agenda. Economists were criticized for not predicting it, and old divisions among economists that many thought were healed erupted in the pages of *The Economist* and *The New York Times* and online on a host of blogs.

We'll be examining the causes of recession and the alternative views among economists in greater detail as you progress through the rest of your study of macroeconomics.

# EYE on the BOOMS AND BUSTS

## How Do We Track the Booms and Busts of our Economy?

The National Bureau of Economic Research (NBER) Business Cycle Dating Committee determines the dates of U.S. business cycle turning points.

To identify the date of a business cycle peak, the NBER committee looks at data on industrial production, total employment, real GDP, and wholesale and retail sales.

Of these variables, real GDP is the most reliable measure of aggregate domestic production.

But when the NBER committee met in November 2008 to determine when the economy went into recession, the two measures of real GDP—the expenditure approach and the income approach—told conflicting stories.

For a few quarters in 2007 and 2008, because of the statistical discrepancy, the two estimates of real GDP did "not speak clearly about the date of a peak in activity."

So the NBER committee looked closely at the data on real personal income, real manufacturing, wholesale and retail sales, industrial production, and employment. All of these data peaked between November 2007 and June 2008. Weighing all the evidence, the committee decided that November 2007 was the peak.

But as the figure shows, real GDP didn't begin a sustained fall until the second quarter of 2008.

In contrast to the difficult task of dating the cycle peak, the trough was clear. It occured in the second quarter of 2009.

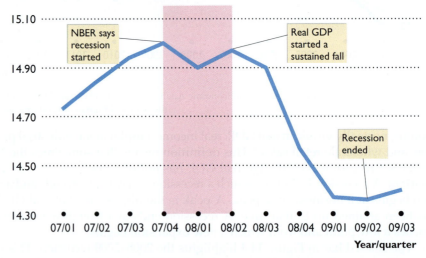

SOURCES OF DATA: Bureau of Economic Analysis and the National Bureau of Economic Research.

Let's now leave comparisons of the standard of living over time and business cycles and briefly see how we compare the standard of living among countries.

## ■ The Standard of Living Among Countries

To use real GDP per person to compare the standard of living among countries, we must convert the numbers for other countries into U.S. dollars. To calculate real GDP, we must also use a common set of prices—called *purchasing power parity prices*—for all countries. The International Monetary Fund performs these calculations and if you turn back to Figure 2.3 on p. 82 you can see some comparisons based on these data. They tell, for example, that an average American has a standard of living (income per person) almost 6 times that of an average person in China.

Real GDP provides an easy way of comparing living standards. But real GDP doesn't include *all* the goods and services produced. Also, real GDP has nothing to say about factors other than the goods and services that affect the standard of living. Let's explore these limitations of real GDP.

## ■ Goods and Services Omitted from GDP

GDP measures the value of goods and services that are bought in markets. GDP excludes

- Household production
- Underground production
- Leisure time
- Environment quality

### Household Production

*Household production* is the production of goods and services (mainly services) in the home. Examples of this production are preparing meals, changing a light bulb, cutting grass, washing a car, and helping a student with homework. Because we don't buy these services in markets, they are not counted as part of GDP. The result is that GDP *underestimates* the value of the production.

Many items that were traditionally produced at home are now bought in the market. For example, more families now eat in fast-food restaurants—one of the fastest-growing industries in the United States—and use day-care services. These trends mean that food preparation and child-care services that were once part of household production are now measured as part of GDP. So real GDP grows more rapidly than does real GDP plus home production.

### Underground Production

*Underground production* is the production of goods and services hidden from the view of government because people want to avoid taxes and regulations or their actions are illegal. Because underground production is unreported, it is omitted from GDP.

Examples of underground production are the distribution of illegal drugs, farm work that uses illegal workers who are paid less than the minimum wage, and jobs that are done for cash to avoid paying income taxes. This last category might be quite large and includes tips earned by cab drivers, hairdressers, and hotel and restaurant workers.

Edgar L. Feige, an economist at the University of Wisconsin, estimates that U.S. underground production was about 16 percent of GDP during the early 1990s. Underground production in many countries, especially in most developing countries, is estimated to be larger than that in the United States.

### Leisure Time

Leisure time is an economic good that is not valued as part of GDP. Yet the marginal hour of leisure time must be at least as valuable to us as the wage we earn for working. If it were not, we would work instead. Over the years, leisure time has steadily increased as the workweek gets shorter, more people take early retirement, and the number of vacation days increases. These improvements in our standard of living are not measured in real GDP.

### Environment Quality

Pollution is an economic *bad* (the opposite of a *good*). The more we pollute our environment, other things remaining the same, the lower is our standard of living. This lowering of our standard of living is not measured by real GDP.

### ■ Other Influences on the Standard of Living

The quantity of goods and services consumed is a major influence on the standard of living. But other influences are

- Health and life expectancy
- Political freedom and social justice

### Health and Life Expectancy

Good health and a long life—the hopes of everyone—do not show up directly in real GDP. A higher real GDP enables us to spend more on medical research, health care, a good diet, and exercise equipment. As real GDP has increased, our life expectancy has lengthened. But we face new health and life expectancy problems every year. Diseases, such as AIDS, and drug abuse are taking young lives at a rate that causes serious concern. When we take these negative influences into account, real GDP growth might overstate the improvements in the standard of living.

### Political Freedom and Social Justice

A country might have a very large real GDP per person but have limited political freedom and social justice. For example, a small elite might enjoy political liberty and extreme wealth while the majority of people have limited freedom and live in poverty. Such an economy would generally be regarded as having a lower standard of living than one that had the same amount of real GDP but in which everyone enjoyed political freedom.

## EYE on YOUR LIFE
### Making GDP Personal

As you read a newspaper or business magazine, watch a TV news show, or browse a news Web site, you often come across reports about GDP.

What do these reports mean for you? Where in the National Income and Product Accounts do *your* transactions appear? How can you use information about GDP in your life?

### Your Contribution to GDP

Your own economic transactions show up in the National Income and Product Accounts on both the expenditure side and the income side—as part of the expenditure approach and

part of the income approach to measuring GDP.

Most of your expenditure is part of Consumption Expenditure. If you were to buy a new home, that item would appear as part of Investment. Because much of what you buy is produced in another country, expenditure on these goods shows up as part of Imports.

If you have a job, your income appears in Compensation of Employees.

Because the GDP measure of the value of production includes only market transactions, some of your own production of goods and services is most likely not counted in GDP.

What are the nonmarket goods and services that you produce? How would you go about valuing them?

### Making Sense of the Numbers

To use the GDP numbers in a news report, you must first check whether the reporter is referring to *nominal* GDP or *real* GDP.

Using U.S. real GDP per person, check how your income compares with the average income in the United States. When you see GDP numbers for other countries, compare your income with that of a person in France, or Canada, or China.

# EYE on the GLOBAL ECONOMY
## Which Country Has the Highest Standard of Living?

You've seen that as a measure of the standard of living, GDP has limitations. To compare the standard of living across countries, we must consider other factors in addition to GDP.

GDP measures only the market value of all the final goods and services produced and bought in markets. GDP omits some goods and services (those produced in the home and in the hidden economy). It omits the value of leisure time, of good health and long life expectancy, as well as of political freedom and social justice. It also omits the damage (negative value) that pollution does to the environment.

These limitations of GDP as a measure of the standard of living apply in every country. So to make international comparisons of the standard of living, we must look at real GDP and other indicators. Nonetheless, real GDP per person is a major component of international comparisons.

Many alternatives to GDP have been proposed. One, called Green GDP, subtracts from GDP an estimate of the cost of greenhouse gas emissions and other negative influences on the environment. Another measure, called the Happy Planet Index, or HPI, goes further and subtracts from GDP an estimate of the cost of depleting nonrenewable resources.

Neither the Green GDP nor the HPI are reliable measures because they rely on guesses about the costs of pollution and resource depletion that are subjective and unreliable.

Taking an approach that focuses on the quality of life factors, the United Nations (UN) has constructed a Human Development Index (HDI), which combines real GDP, life expectancy and health, and education.

The figure shows the relationship between the HDI and GDP in 2012. (In the figure, each dot represents a country.) These two measures of the standard of living tell a similar but not identical story.

The United States has the third highest HDI in the figure, lower than Norway and Australia. Why does the United States not have a higher HDI?

The UN says that the people who live in the two countries with higher HDIs live longer, have access to universal health care, and have better schools than do people in the United States. The HDI emphasized equality of access to these services.

The HDI doesn't include political freedom and social justice. If it did, the United States would score highly on that component of the index.

The bottom line is that we don't know which country has the highest standard of living. But we do know that GDP per person alone does not provide the complete answer.

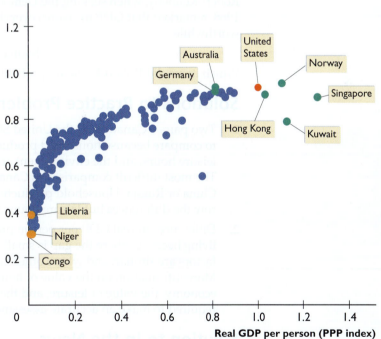

Source of data: *United Nations Human Development Report*, 2011, http://hdr.undp.org/.

# CHECKPOINT 14.3

**Describe the uses of real GDP and explain its limitations as a measure of the standard of living.**

## Practice Problems

The United Nations Human Development Report gives the data for 2011 in Table 1. Other information suggests that household production is similar in Canada and the United States and smaller than in China and Russia. The underground economy is larger in Russia and China and a similar proportion of each of these economies. Canadians and Americans enjoy more leisure hours than do the Chinese and Russians. Canada and the United States spend significantly more on the environment than do China and Russia. Use this information and ignore any other influences to work Problems **1** and **2**.

1. In which pair (or pairs) of countries is it easiest to compare the standard of living? And in which pair (or pairs) is it most difficult? Explain why.

2. Do the differences in real GDP per person correctly rank the standard of living in these four countries? What additional information would we need to be able to make an accurate assessment of the relative standard of living in these four countries?

**TABLE 1**

| Country | Real GDP per person |
| --- | --- |
| China | $4,833 |
| Russia | $13,543 |
| United States | $48,666 |
| Canada | $50,265 |

## In the News

**Economists look to expand GDP to include the quality of life**
Robert Kennedy, when seeking the Democratic presidential nomination in 1968, remarked that GDP measures everything except that which makes life worthwhile.

Source: *The New York Times*, September 1, 2008

Which items did Robert Kennedy probably think were missing?

## Solutions to Practice Problems

1. Two pairs—Canada and the United States, and China and Russia—are easy to compare because household production, the underground economy, leisure hours, and the environment are similar in the countries in each pair. The most difficult comparison is Canada and the United States with either China or Russia. Household production and the underground economy narrow the differences but leisure hours and the environment widen them.

2. Differences in real GDP per person probably correctly rank the standard of living because where the gap is small (Canada and the United States), other factors are similar, and where other factors differ, the gaps are huge. More information on the value of household production, the underground economy, the value of leisure, and the value of environmental differences is required to make an accurate assessment of relative living standards.

## Solution to In the News

GDP measures production that is traded in markets. GDP does not include household production, leisure time, health and life expectancy, political freedom, and social justice. These items are probably the ones that Kennedy believed were missing from GDP as a measure of the quality of life.

**CHAPTER SUMMARY**

## Key Points

1. **Define GDP and explain why the value of production, income, and expenditure are the same for an economy.**

   - GDP is the market value of all final goods and services produced within a country in a given time period.
   - We can value goods and services either by what they cost to produce (incomes) or by what people are willing to pay (expenditures).
   - The value of production equals income equals expenditure.

2. **Describe how economic statisticians measure GDP and distinguish between nominal GDP and real GDP.**

   - BEA measures GDP by summing expenditures and by summing incomes. With no errors of measurement the two totals are the same, but in practice, a small statistical discrepancy arises.
   - A country's GNP is similar to its GDP, but GNP is the value of production by factors of production supplied by the residents of a country.
   - Nominal GDP is the value of production using the prices of the current year and the quantities produced in the current year.
   - Real GDP is the value of production using the prices of a base year and the quantities produced in the current year.

3. **Describe the uses of real GDP and explain its limitations as a measure of the standard of living.**

   - We use real GDP per person to compare the standard of living over time.
   - We use real GDP to determine when the economy has reached a business cycle peak or trough.
   - We use real GDP per person expressed in purchasing power parity dollars to compare the standard of living among countries.
   - Real GDP omits some goods and services and ignores some factors that influence the standard of living.
   - The Human Development Index takes some other factors into account.

## Key Terms

Business cycle, 422
Consumption expenditure, 409
Depreciation, 416
Exports of goods and services, 410
Final good or service, 408
Government expenditure on goods
   and services, 410

Gross domestic product (GDP), 408
Imports of goods and services, 410
Intermediate good or service, 408
Investment, 409
Net exports of goods
   and services, 410
Net taxes, 410

Nominal GDP, 418
Potential GDP, 421
Real GDP, 418
Recession, 422
Saving, 410

## CHAPTER CHECKPOINT

### Study Plan Problems and Applications

**1.** Figure 1 shows the flows of income and expenditure in an economy. In 2013, *U* was $2 trillion, *V* was $1.5 trillion, *W* was $7 trillion, *X* was $1.5 trillion, and *Z* was zero. Calculate total income, net taxes, and GDP.

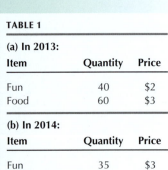

FIGURE 1

Use the following data to work Problems **2** and **3**.

The national accounts of Parchment Paradise are kept on (you guessed it) parchment. A fire in the statistics office destroys some accounts, leaving only the following data:

- GDP (income approach) $2,900
- Consumption expenditure $2,000
- Indirect taxes less subsidies $100
- Interest, rent, and profit $500
- Investment $800
- Government expenditure $400
- Wages $2,000
- Net factor income from abroad $50
- Net exports −$200

**2.** Calculate GDP (expenditure approach) and depreciation.

**3.** Calculate net domestic product at factor cost, the statistical discrepancy, and GNP.

Use the following information to work Problems **4** to **6**.

An economy produces only fun and food. Table 1 shows the prices and the quantities of fun and food produced in 2013 and 2014. The base year is 2013.

**4.** Calculate nominal GDP in 2013 and 2014.

**5.** Calculate the percentage increase in production in 2014.

**6.** If potential GDP was $270 in 2013 and it grew by 1 percent in 2014, in which phase of the business cycle is the economy? Explain.

TABLE 1

**(a) In 2013:**

| Item | Quantity | Price |
|------|----------|-------|
| Fun | 40 | $2 |
| Food | 60 | $3 |

**(b) In 2014:**

| Item | Quantity | Price |
|------|----------|-------|
| Fun | 35 | $3 |
| Food | 65 | $2 |

Use the following information to work Problems **7** to **9**.

**Expansion remains slow**

The Commerce Department reported that retail sales increased 1.3 percent in June. Net exports were up 0.8 percent in the first quarter and inventories held by businesses rose by 0.3 percent in June. Total sales by businesses rose 0.3 percent.

Source: Commerce Department, 2013

**7.** Which component of GDP changed because retail sales increased? Which component of GDP changed because inventories held by businesses fell?

**8.** Explain the effect of the rise in net exports on GDP.

**9.** Does the statement that total sales by businesses were up 0.3 percent mean that GDP increased by 0.3 percent? Explain your answer.

 **10.** Read *Eye on the Booms and Busts* on p. 424 and explain why the NBER reported that the 2008 recession began before real GDP had fallen for two successive quarters.

# Instructor Assignable Problems and Applications

**1.** In France, real GDP was the same in 2012 as it had been in 2011, but in the last quarter of 2012 and the first quarter of 2013, France's real GDP decreased. In the United States, real GDP increased in 2012, and in the first quarter of 2013, it was higher than in the last quarter of 2012.

Based on this information, which country was in a recession at the beginning of 2013? What features of the information provided led you to your conclusion?

**2.** Classify each of the items in List 1 as a final good or service or an intermediate good or service and identify it as a component of consumption expenditure, investment, or government expenditure on goods and services.

Use the following information to work Problems **3** and **4**.

Mitsubishi Heavy Industries makes the wings of the new Boeing 787 Dreamliner in Japan. Toyota assembles cars for the U.S. market in Kentucky.

**3.** Explain where these activities appear in the National Income and Product Accounts of the United States.

**4.** Explain where these activities appear in the National Income and Product Accounts of Japan.

Use the data on the economy of Iberia in Table 1 to work Problems **5** and **6**.

**5.** Calculate Iberia's GDP.

**6.** Calculate Iberia's imports of goods and services.

Use Table 2, which shows an economy's total production and the prices of the final goods it produced in 2013 and 2014, to work Problems **7** to **9**.

**7.** Calculate nominal GDP in 2013 and 2014.

**8.** The base year is 2013. Calculate real GDP in 2013 and 2014.

**9.** Calculate the percentage increase in production in 2014.

Use the following information to work Problems **10** and **11**.

**Cash-paying vultures pick bones of U.S. housing market as mortgages dry up**
New-home sales fell to an annual pace of 250,000 in February, an all-time low in records dating to 1963, the Commerce Department reported March 23. Existing-home sales dropped to a 4.88 million annualized pace in February, down 2.8 percent from a year earlier, the National Association of Realtors said, while the median price of existing homes fell to $156,100, the lowest since February 2002.

Source: Bloomberg, March 29, 2011

**10.** Where do new-home sales appear in the circular flow of expenditure and income? Explain how a fall in new home sales affects real GDP.

**11.** Where do sales of previously owned homes appear in the circular flow of expenditure and income? Explain how a fall in sales of previously owned homes affects real GDP.

**12.** **The road less traveled**
If we are right, this year is different and global growth will rise to an above-trend pace during the second half of 2013.

Source: J.P. Morgan Global Data Watch, May, 2013

Does this news mean that the 2008–2009 recession was expected to end in the second half of 2013? Does recession end only when real GDP growth rises above trend??

---

**LIST 1**

- Banking services bought by Target
- Security system bought by the White House
- Coffee beans bought by Starbucks
- New coffee machines bought by Starbucks
- Starbucks grande mocha frappuccino bought by a student
- New battle ship bought by the U.S. navy

---

**TABLE 1**

| Item | Amount |
| --- | --- |
| Net taxes | $18 billion |
| Government expenditure | $20 billion |
| Saving | $15 billion |
| Consumption expenditure | $67 billion |
| Investment | $21 billion |
| Exports | $30 billion. |

---

**TABLE 2**

**(a) In 2013:**

| Item | Quantity | Price |
| --- | --- | --- |
| Fish | 100 | $2 |
| Berries | 50 | $6 |

**(b) In 2014:**

| Item | Quantity | Price |
| --- | --- | --- |
| Fish | 75 | $5 |
| Berries | 65 | $10 |

## Critical Thinking Discussion Questions

**1. Japan wins bid to host 2020 Olympic Games**

Japan's Prime Minister, Shinzo Abe believes that Japan's infrastructure and tourism will grow as a result of Japan hosting the 2020 Olympic Games.

Source: *Mail Online*, 9 September 2013

Think about the effects of hosting the Olympic Games on Japan's economy:

What category of Japan's GDP records expenditure on Japan's infrastructure?

Is expenditure on infrastructure expenditure on a final good or on an intermediate good?

What category of Japan's GDP records expenditure by tourists?

Is expenditure by foreign tourists in Japan included in the GDP of their home country?

**2. German economy grows at a modest pace**

With recession in other parts of the European Union, the growth rate of Germany's real GDP slowed to 0.4 percent in 2013, down from a growth rate of 0.7 percent in 2012. Expenditure on machinery and other equipment by the government and firms decreased, but consumption expenditure increased by 0.9 percent.

Source: *New York Times*, 16 January 2014

Think about the growth of Germany's real GDP:

How does recession in other parts of the European Union affect Germany's real GDP?

Was the German economy in a recession in 2013?

What components of Germany's real GDP experienced negative growth in 2013?

If the growth rate of Germany's real GDP slows, does the growth rate of Germany's nominal real GDP also slow?

**3. Growth rate of nominal GDP**

Between 2002 and 2012, Finland's nominal GDP increased by 83 percent, while Indonesia's nominal GDP increased by 349 percent.

Source: The World Bank

Think about the standard of living in Finland and in Indonesia:

Did Finland's standard of living increase between 2002 and 2012?

Did Indonesia's standard of living increase between 2002 and 2012?

Did Indonesia's standard of living increase four times more than Finland's between 2002 and 2012?

**APPENDIX: MEASURING REAL GDP**

This appendix explains the method used by the Bureau of Economic Analysis (BEA) to calculate real GDP using a measure called **chained-dollar real GDP**. We begin by explaining the problem that arises from using the prices of the base year (the method on pp. 418–419) and how the problem can be overcome.

**Chained-dollar real GDP**
The measure of real GDP calculated by the Bureau of Economic Analysis.

## ■ The Problem With Base-Year Prices

When we calculated real GDP on pp. 418–419, we found that real GDP in 2013 was 60 percent greater than it was in 2009. But instead of using the prices of 2009 as the constant prices, we could have used the prices of 2013. In this case, we would have valued the quantities produced in 2009 at the prices of 2013. By comparing the values of real GDP in 2009 and 2013 at the constant prices of 2013, we get a different number for the percentage increase in production. If you use the numbers in Table 14.3 on p. 419 to value 2009 production at 2013 prices, you will get a real GDP in 2009 of $150 million (2013 dollars). Real GDP in 2013 at 2013 prices is $300 million. So by using the prices of 2013, production doubled—a 100 percent increase—from 2009 to 2013. Did production in fact increase by 60 percent or 100 percent?

The problem arises because to calculate real GDP, we weight the quantity of each item produced by its price. If all prices change by the same percentage, then the *relative* weight on each good or service doesn't change and the percentage change in real GDP from the first year to the second is the same regardless of which year's prices we use. But if prices change by different percentages, then the *relative* weight on each good or service *does* change and the percentage change in real GDP from the first year to the second depends on which prices we use. So which year's prices should we use: those of the first year or those of the second?

The answer given by the BEA method is to use the prices of both years. If we calculate the percentage change in real GDP twice, once using the prices of the first year and again using the prices of the second year, and then take the average of those two percentage changes, we get a unique measure of the change in real GDP and one that gives equal importance to the *relative* prices of both years.

To illustrate the calculation of the BEA measure of real GDP, we'll work through an example. The method has three steps:

- Value production in the prices of adjacent years.
- Find the average of two percentage changes.
- Link (chain) to the base year.

## ■ Value Production in the Prices of Adjacent Years

The first step is to value production in *adjacent* years at the prices of both years. We'll make these calculations for 2013, and its preceding year, 2012.

Table A14.1 shows the quantities produced and prices in the two years. Part (a) shows the nominal GDP calculation for 2012—the quantities produced in 2012 valued at the prices of 2012. Nominal GDP in 2012 is $145 million. Part (b) shows the nominal GDP calculation for 2013—the quantities produced in 2013 valued at the prices of 2013. Nominal GDP in 2013 is $172 million. Part (c) shows the value of the quantities produced in 2013 at the prices of 2012. This total is $160 million. Finally, part (d) shows the value of the quantities produced in 2012 at the prices of 2013. This total is $158 million.

■ **TABLE A14.1**

Real GDP Calculation Step 1: Value Production in Adjacent Years at Prices of Both Years

Step 1 is to value the production of adjacent years at the prices of both years.

Here, we value the production of 2012 and 2013 at the prices of both 2012 and 2013.

The value of 2012 production at 2012 prices, in part (a), is nominal GDP in 2012.

The value of 2013 production at 2013 prices, in part (b), is nominal GDP in 2013.

Part (c) calculates the value of 2013 production at 2012 prices, and part (d) calculates the value of 2012 production at 2013 prices.

We use these numbers in Step 2.

| Item | | Quantity (millions of units) | Price (dollars per unit) | Expenditure (millions of dollars) |
|---|---|---|---|---|
| **(a) In 2012** | | | | |
| C | T-shirts | 3 | 5 | 15 |
| I | Computer chips | 3 | 10 | 30 |
| G | Security services | 5 | 20 | 100 |
| Y | Nominal GDP in 2012 | | | 145 |
| **(b) In 2013** | | | | |
| C | T-shirts | 4 | 4 | 16 |
| I | Computer chips | 2 | 12 | 24 |
| G | Security services | 6 | 22 | 132 |
| Y | Nominal GDP in 2013 | | | 172 |
| **(c) Quantities of 2013 valued at prices of 2012** | | | | |
| C | T-shirts | 4 | 5 | 20 |
| I | Computer chips | 2 | 10 | 20 |
| G | Security services | 6 | 20 | 120 |
| Y | 2013 production at 2012 prices | | | 160 |
| **(d) Quantities of 2012 valued at prices of 2013** | | | | |
| C | T-shirts | 3 | 4 | 12 |
| I | Computer chips | 3 | 12 | 36 |
| G | Security services | 5 | 22 | 110 |
| Y | 2012 production at 2013 prices | | | 158 |

### Find the Average of Two Percentage Changes

The second step is to find the percentage change in the value of production based on the prices in the two adjacent years. Table A14.2 summarizes these calculations.

Valued at the prices of 2012, production increased from $145 million in 2012 to $160 million in 2013, an increase of 10.3 percent. Valued at the prices of 2013, production increased from $158 million in 2012 to $172 million in 2013, an increase of 8.9 percent. The average of these two percentage changes in the value of production is 9.6. That is, $(10.3 + 8.9) \div 2 = 9.6$.

We've now found the *growth rate* of real GDP in 2013. But we also want to calculate the *level* of real GDP. This level depends on the *reference base year*. The simplest example is when the previous year (2012 in this case) is the base year. In 2012, real GDP equals nominal GDP, which is $145 million. Real GDP in 2013, valued in 2012 dollars is 9.6 percent higher, which equals $159 million.

Although the real GDP of $159 million is expressed in 2012 dollars, the calculation uses the average of the *relative prices* of the final goods and services that make up GDP in 2012 and 2013.

When the base year is not the previous year, we need to link or chain the current year to the base year. Let's see how we do this linking.

■ **TABLE A14.2**

Real GDP Calculation Step 2: Find Average of Two Percentage Changes

| Value of Production in Adjacent Years | | Millions of dollars |
| --- | --- | --- |
| 2012 production at 2012 prices | | 145 |
| 2013 production at 2012 prices | | 160 |
| Percentage change in production at 2012 prices | 10.3 | |
| 2012 production at 2013 prices | | 158 |
| 2013 production at 2013 prices | | 172 |
| Percentage change in production at 2013 prices | 8.9 | |
| Average of two percentage changes in production | 9.6 | |

Using the numbers calculated in Step 1, we find the percentage change in production from 2012 to 2013 valued at 2012 prices, which is 10.3 percent.

We also find the percentage change in production from 2012 to 2013 valued at 2013 prices, which is 8.9 percent.

We then find the average of these two percentage changes, which is 9.6 percent.

## Link (Chain) to the Base Year

To link to the base year, we repeat the calculation that we've just described to obtain the real GDP growth rate each year. Real GDP equals nominal GDP in the base year, which currently is 2009. By applying the calculated growth rates to each successive year, we can obtain *chained-dollar real GDP* in 2009 dollars.

Figure A14.1 shows an example with real GDP equal to nominal GDP at $75 million in the base year, 2009, and assumed growth rates of real GDP for each year between 2006 and 2013. The 2013 growth rate is the 9.6 percent that we calculated in Table A14.2 above.

Starting with real GDP in the base year, we apply the calculated percentage change of 2.7 percent, so real GDP in 2010 was 2.7 percent higher than $75 million, which is $77 million. Repeating the calculation, real GDP in 2011 is 3.5 percent higher, which is $80 million, and in 2012, real GDP is 4.6 percent higher, which is $83 million. In 2013, real GDP is 9.6 percent higher than $83 million, which is $91 million.

The same method is used to chain-link the years before the base year. For example, real GDP in 2008 is 8.2 percent lower than in 2009 at $69 million.

■ **FIGURE A14.1**

Real GDP Calculation Step 3: Link (Chain) to the Base Year

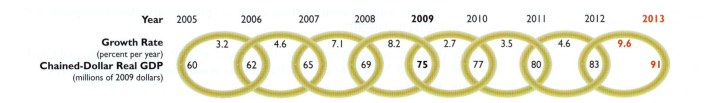

| Year | 2005 | 2006 | 2007 | 2008 | 2009 | 2010 | 2011 | 2012 | 2013 |
| --- | --- | --- | --- | --- | --- | --- | --- | --- | --- |
| Growth Rate (percent per year) | | 3.2 | 4.6 | 7.1 | 8.2 | 2.7 | 3.5 | 4.6 | 9.6 |
| Chained-Dollar Real GDP (millions of 2009 dollars) | 60 | 62 | 65 | 69 | 75 | 77 | 80 | 83 | 91 |

The growth rate of real GDP from one year to the next is calculated for every pair of years and then linked to the base year. Suppose that real GDP was $75 million in the base year, 2009. By applying the growth rate between each pair of years, we find the chained-dollar real GDP for each year, expressed in terms of the value of the dollar in the base year. Here, the percentages for 2007 through to 2013 are assumed. By 2013, the chained-dollar real GDP has increased to $91 million in 2009 dollars.

APPENDIX CHECKPOINT

## Study Plan Problems

**TABLE 1**

**(a) In 2012:**

| Item | Quantity | Price |
|---|---|---|
| Bananas | 100 | $10 |
| Coconuts | 50 | $12 |

**(b) In 2013:**

| Item | Quantity | Price |
|---|---|---|
| Bananas | 110 | $15 |
| Coconuts | 60 | $10 |

An island economy produces only bananas and coconuts. Table 1 gives the quantities produced and prices in 2012 and in 2013. The base year is 2012.

1. Calculate nominal GDP in 2012 and nominal GDP in 2013.

2. Calculate the value of 2013 production in 2012 prices and the percentage increase in production when valued at 2012 prices.

3. Calculate the value of 2012 production in 2013 prices and the percentage increase in production when valued at 2013 prices.

4. Use the chained-dollar method to calculate real GDP in 2012 and 2013. In terms of what dollars is each of these two real GDPs measured?

5. Using the chained-dollar method, compare the growth rates of nominal GDP and real GDP in 2013.

6. If the base year is 2013, use the chained-dollar method to calculate real GDP in 2012 and 2013. In terms of what dollars is each of these two real GDPs measured?

7. If the base year is 2013, compare the growth rates of nominal GDP and real GDP in 2013.

## Instructor Assignable Problems

**TABLE 2**

**(a) In 2012:**

| Item | Quantity | Price |
|---|---|---|
| Food | 100 | $2 |
| Fun | 50 | $6 |

**(b) In 2013:**

| Item | Quantity | Price |
|---|---|---|
| Food | 75 | $5 |
| Fun | 65 | $10 |

An economy produces only food and fun. Table 2 shows the quantities produced and prices in 2012 and 2013. The base year is 2013.

1. Calculate nominal GDP in 2012 and nominal GDP in 2013.

2. Calculate the value of 2013 production in 2012 prices and the percentage increase in production when valued at 2012 prices.

3. Calculate the value of 2012 production in 2013 prices and the percentage increase in production when valued at 2013 prices.

4. Using the chained-dollar method, calculate real GDP in 2012 and 2013. In terms of what dollars is each of these two real GDPs measured?

5. Using the chained-dollar method, compare the growth rates of nominal GDP and real GDP in 2013.

6. If the base year is 2012, use the chained-dollar method to calculate real GDP in 2012 and 2013. In terms of what dollars is each of these two real GDPs measured?

7. If the base year is 2012, compare the growth rates of nominal GDP and real GDP in 2013.

## Key Term

Chained-dollar real GDP, 433

How long does it take
to find a job?

# Jobs and Unemployment

## 15

**When you have completed your study of this chapter,
you will be able to**

**1** Define the unemployment rate and other labor market indicators.

**2** Describe the trends and fluctuations in the indicators of labor market performance in the United States.

**3** Describe the types of unemployment, define full employment, and explain the link between unemployment and real GDP.

Every month, 1,600 field interviewers and supervisors working on a joint project between the Bureau of Labor Statistics (or BLS) and the Bureau of the Census survey 60,000 households and ask a series of questions about the age and labor market status of their members. This survey is called the *Current Population Survey*. Let's look at the types of data collected by this survey.

### ■ Current Population Survey

Figure 15.1 shows the categories into which the BLS divides the population. It also shows the relationships among the categories. The first category divides the population into two groups: the working-age civilian population and others. The **working-age population** is the total number of people aged 16 years and over who are not in jail, hospital, or some other form of institutional care or in the U.S. Armed Forces. In May 2013, the estimated population of the United States was 316.1 million, the working-age population was 245.6 million, and 70.5 million people were under 16 years of age, in the military, or living in institutions.

The second category divides the working-age population into two groups: those in the labor force and those not in the labor force. The **labor force** is the number of people employed plus the number unemployed. In May 2013, the U.S. labor force was 155.7 million and 89.9 million people were not in the labor force. Most of those not in the labor force were in school full time or had retired from work.

The third category divides the labor force into two groups: the employed and the unemployed. In May 2013 in the United States, 143.9 million people were employed and 11.8 million people were unemployed.

### ■ Population Survey Criteria

The survey counts as *employed* all persons who, during the week before the survey, either

1. Worked at least 1 hour as paid employees or worked 15 hours or more as unpaid workers in their family business or
2. Were not working but had jobs or businesses from which they were temporarily absent.

The survey counts as *unemployed* all persons who, during the week before the survey,

1. Had no employment,
2. Were available for work,

and either

1. Had made specific efforts to find employment during the previous four weeks or
2. Were waiting to be recalled to a job from which they had been laid off.

People in the working-age population who by the above criteria are neither employed nor unemployed are classified as not in the labor force.

**Working-age population**
The total number of people aged 16 years and over who are not in jail, hospital, or some other form of institutional care or in the U.S. Armed Forces.

**Labor force**
The number of people employed plus the number unemployed.

*To be counted as unemployed, a person must not only want a job but also have tried to find one.*

■ **FIGURE 15.1**

Population Labor Force Categories

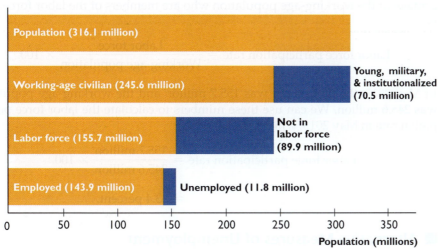

The U.S. population is divided into the working-age population and the young, military, and institutionalized. The working-age population is divided into the labor force and those not in the labor force. The labor force is divided into those employed and those unemployed. The figure shows the data for May 2013.

SOURCE OF DATA: Bureau of Labor Statistics.

## ■ Two Main Labor Market Indicators

Using the numbers from the Current Population Survey, the BLS calculates several indicators of the state of the labor market. The two main labor market indicators are

- The unemployment rate
- The labor force participation rate

### The Unemployment Rate

The amount of unemployment is an indicator of the extent to which people who want jobs can't find them. It tells us the amount of slack in the labor market. The **unemployment rate** is the percentage of the people in the labor force who are unemployed. That is,

$$\text{Unemployment rate} = \frac{\text{Number of people unemployed}}{\text{Labor force}} \times 100.$$

In May 2013, the number of people unemployed was 11.8 million and the labor force was 155.7 million. We can use these numbers to calculate the unemployment rate in May 2013, which is

$$\text{Unemployment rate} = \frac{11.8 \text{ million}}{155.7 \text{ million}} \times 100$$

$$= 7.6 \text{ percent.}$$

**Unemployment rate**
The percentage of the people in the labor force who are unemployed.

### The Labor Force Participation Rate

**Labor force participation rate**
The percentage of the working-age population who are members of the labor force.

The number of people in the labor force is an indicator of the willingness of people of working age to take jobs. The **labor force participation rate** is the percentage of the working-age population who are members of the labor force. That is,

$$\text{Labor force participation rate} = \frac{\text{Labor force}}{\text{Working-age population}} \times 100.$$

In May 2013, the labor force was 155.7 million and the working-age population was 245.6 million. We can use these numbers to calculate the labor force participation rate in May 2013, which is

$$\text{Labor force participation rate} = \frac{155.7 \text{ million}}{245.6 \text{ million}} \times 100.$$

$$= 63.4 \text{ percent.}$$

## ■ Alternative Measures of Unemployment

The unemployment rate based on the official definition of unemployment omits some types of underutilization of labor. The omissions are

- Marginally attached workers
- Part-time workers

### Marginally Attached Workers

**Marginally attached worker**
A person who does not have a job, is available and willing to work, has not made specific efforts to find a job within the previous four weeks, but has looked for work sometime in the recent past.

**Discouraged worker**
A marginally attached worker who has not made specific efforts to find a job within the past four weeks because previous unsuccessful attempts to find a job were discouraging.

Some people who think of themselves as being in the labor force and unemployed are not counted in the official labor force numbers. They are marginally attached workers. A **marginally attached worker** is a person who does not have a job, is available and willing to work, has not made specific efforts to find a job within the previous four weeks, but has looked for work sometime in the recent past. A **discouraged worker** is a marginally attached worker who has not made specific efforts to find a job within the previous four weeks because previous unsuccessful attempts were discouraging.

Other marginally attached workers differ from discouraged workers only in their reasons for not having looked for a job during the previous four weeks. For example, Martin doesn't have a job and is available for work, but he has not looked for work in the past four weeks because he was busy cleaning his home after a flood. He is a marginally attached worker but not a discouraged worker. Lena, Martin's wife, doesn't have a job and is available for work, but she hasn't looked for work in the past four weeks because she's been looking for six months and hasn't had a single job offer. She is a discouraged worker.

Neither the unemployment rate nor the labor force participation rate includes marginally attached workers. In May 2013, 753,000 people were discouraged workers. If we add them to both the number unemployed and the labor force, the unemployment rate becomes 8.0 percent—only slightly higher than the standard definition of the unemployment rate. Also in May 2013, 1,372,000 people were other marginally attached workers. If we add them and the discouraged workers to both the number unemployed and the labor force, the unemployment rate becomes 8.8 percent—1.2 percentage points higher than the standard definition.

# EYE on the U.S. ECONOMY
## The Current Population Survey

The Bureau of Labor Statistics and the Bureau of the Census go to great lengths to collect accurate labor force data. They constantly train and retrain around 1,600 field interviewers and supervisors. Each month, each field interviewer contacts 37 households and asks basic demographic questions about everyone living at the address and detailed labor force questions about those aged 16 or over.

Once a household has been selected for the survey, it is questioned for four consecutive months and then again for the same four months a year later. Each month, the addresses that have been in the panel eight times are removed and 6,250 new addresses are added. The rotation and overlap of households provide

very reliable information about month-to-month and year-to-year changes in the labor market.

The first time that a household is in the panel, an interviewer, armed with a hand-held computer, visits it. If the household has a telephone, most of the subsequent interviews are

conducted by phone, many of them from one of the three telephone interviewing centers in Hagerstown, Maryland; Jeffersonville, Indiana; and Tucson, Arizona.

For more information about the Current Population Survey, visit www.bls.gov/cps/cps_faq.htm.

## Part-Time Workers

The Current Population Survey measures the number of full-time workers and part-time workers. **Full-time workers** are those who usually work 35 hours or more a week. **Part-time workers** are those who usually work less than 35 hours a week. Part-time workers are divided into two groups: part time for economic reasons and part time for noneconomic reasons.

People who work **part time for economic reasons** (also called *involuntary part-time workers)* are people who work 1 to 34 hours but are looking for full-time work. These people are unable to find full-time work because of unfavorable business conditions or seasonal decreases in the availability of full-time work.

People who work part time for noneconomic reasons do not want full-time work and are not available for such work. This group includes people with health problems, family or personal responsibilities, or education commitments that limit their availability for work.

The Bureau of Labor Statistics uses the data on full-time and part-time status to measure the slack in the labor market that results from people being underemployed—employed but not able to find as much employment as they would like.

In May 2013, when employment was 143.9 million, full-time employment was 117.1 million and part-time employment was 26.8 million. An estimated 7.9 million people worked part time for economic reasons. When this number, along with marginally attached workers, is added to the number unemployed, the unemployment rate becomes 13.8 percent.

**Full-time workers**
People who usually work 35 hours or more a week.

**Part-time workers**
People who usually work less than 35 hours a week.

**Part time for economic reasons**
People who work 1 to 34 hours per week but are looking for full-time work and cannot find it because of unfavorable business conditions.

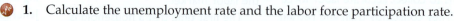
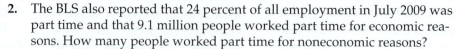

## CHECKPOINT 15.1

**Define the unemployment rate and other labor market indicators.**

## Practice Problems

The BLS reported that in July 2009, the labor force was 154.5 million, employment was 140.0 million, and the working-age population was 235.9 million.

 1.  Calculate the unemployment rate and the labor force participation rate.

2.  The BLS also reported that 24 percent of all employment in July 2009 was part time and that 9.1 million people worked part time for economic reasons. How many people worked part time for noneconomic reasons?

## In the News

**Summer 2012 youth labor market**
From April to July 2012, the number of employed youth 16- to 24-years old rose by 2.1 million to 19.5 million. Unemployment of youth increased from 3.2 million to 4.0 million. In July, the youth labor force grew by 2.9 million to a total of 23.5 million and the youth population was 38 million.

Source: BLS Press Release, August 12, 2012

How did the youth unemployment rate change from April to July? Calculate the youth labor force participation rate in July.

## Solutions to Practice Problems

1.  The unemployment rate is 9.4 percent. The labor force is the sum of the number employed plus the number unemployed. So the number unemployed equals the labor force minus the number employed, which equals 154.5 million minus 140.0 million, or 14.5 million. The unemployment rate is the number unemployed as a percentage of the labor force. The Unemployment rate = (14.5 million ÷ 154.5 million) × 100 or 9.4 percent. The labor force participation rate is 65.5 percent. The labor force participation rate is the percentage of the working-age population who are in the labor force. Labor force participation rate = (154.5 ÷ 235.9) × 100, or 65.5 percent.

2.  24.5 million people worked part time for noneconomic reasons. Employment was 140 million. Part-time employment was 24 percent of 140 million, which equals 33.6 million. Given that 9.1 million worked part time for economic reasons, 33.6 million minus 9.1 million, or 24.5 million worked part time for noneconomic reasons.

## Solution to In the News

The unemployment rate is the number unemployed as a percentage of the labor force. The April labor force equals the July labor force (23.5 million) minus the increase of 2.9 million from April to July. That is, the April labor force was 20.6 million. In April, 3.2 million youths were unemployed, so the April unemployment rate was (3.2 ÷ 20.6) × 100, or 15.5 percent. In July, 4.0 million youths were unemployed and the labor force was 23.5 million, so the unemployment rate was 17 percent. From April to July, the unemployment rate rose from 15.5 percent to 17 percent. The labor force participation rate equals the labor force (23.5 million) as a percentage of the population (38 million), which was 61.8 percent.

## 15.2 LABOR MARKET TRENDS AND FLUCTUATIONS

What do we learn about the U.S. labor market from changes in the unemployment rate, the labor force participation rate, and the alternative measures of unemployment? Let's explore the trends and fluctuations in these indicators.

### ■ Unemployment Rate

Figure 15.2 shows the U.S. unemployment rate over the 84 years from 1929 to 2013. Over these years, the average U.S. unemployment rate was 7.2 percent, but from 1948 to 2013, the long-term average was 5.8 percent. The unemployment rate was below this long-term average during the 1940s through the 1960s and during the late 1990s and early 2000s. It was above the long-term average during the 1970s to the mid-1990s and 2009–2013.

During the 1960s, the unemployment rate gradually fell to 3.5 percent. These years saw a rapid rate of job creation, partly from the demands placed on the economy by the growth of defense production during the Vietnam War and partly from an expansion of consumer spending encouraged by an expansion of social programs. Another burst of rapid job creation driven by the "new economy"—the high-technology sector driven by the expansion of the Internet—lowered the unemployment rate to below average from 1995 through the early 2000s.

The most striking event visible in Figure 15.2 is the **Great Depression,** a period of high unemployment, low incomes, and extreme economic hardship that lasted from 1929 to 1939. By 1933, the worst of the Great Depression years, real GDP had fallen by a huge 30 percent and as the figure shows, one in four of the people who wanted jobs couldn't find them. The horrors of the Great Depression led to the New Deal and shaped political attitudes that persist today.

**Great Depression**
A period of high unemployment, low incomes, and extreme economic hardship that lasted from 1929 to 1939.

■ **FIGURE 15.2**

The U.S. Unemployment Rate: 1929–2013

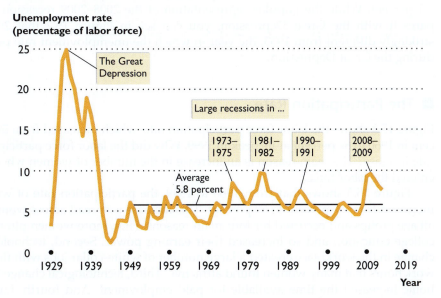

The average unemployment rate from 1948 to 2013 was 5.8 percent. The unemployment rate increases in recessions and decreases in expansions. Unemployment was at its lowest during World War II and the expansions of the 1950s, 1960s, and the 1990s and at its highest during the Great Depression and the recessions of 1981–1982 and 2008–2009.

SOURCE OF DATA: Bureau of Labor Statistics.

# EYE on the GLOBAL ECONOMY
## Unemployment Around the World

U.S. unemployment falls inside the range experienced by other countries. The highest unemployment rates have been in the United Kingdom, Canada, and the Eurozone; and the lowest have been in Japan and the newly industrializing Asian economies.

Differences in unemployment rates were large during the early 1980s, narrowed through the 1990s and early 2000s and widened after the 2008 recession.

The Eurozone, with a higher average unemployment rate than the United States, also has higher unemployment benefits and more regulated labor markets.

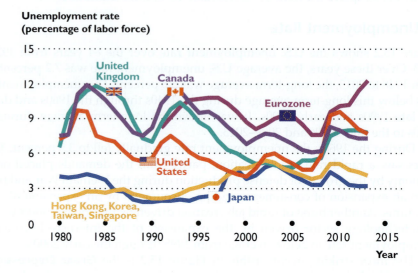

SOURCE OF DATA: International Monetary Fund, *World Economic Outlook,* April 2013.

During the recessions of 1973–1975, 1981–1982, 1990–1991, and 2008–2009, the unemployment rate increased. During the post-war years, the unemployment rate peaked in November–December 1982, when 10.8 percent of the labor force were unemployed. By mid-2011, although the economy had come out of recession and entered into a slow expansion, the unemployment rate stood at 9.1 percent. While the popular representation of the 2008–2009 recession compares it with the Great Depression, you can see in Figure 15.2 that 2010 is strikingly different from 1933, the year in which the unemployment rate peaked during the Great Depression.

## ■ The Participation Rate

Figure 15.3 shows the labor force participation rate, which increased from 59 percent in 1960 to 67 percent at its peak in 1999. Why did the labor force participation rate increase? The main reason is an increase in the number of women who have entered the labor force.

Figure 15.3 shows that from 1960 to 1999, the participation rate of women increased from 37 percent to 60 percent. This increase is spread across women of all age groups and occurred for four main reasons. First, more women pursued a college education and so increased their earning power. Second, technological change in the workplace created a large number of white-collar jobs with flexible work hours that many women found attractive. Third, technological change in the home increased the time available for paid employment. And fourth, families looked increasingly to a second income to balance tight budgets.

**■ FIGURE 15.3**

The Changing Face of the Labor Market: 1960–2013

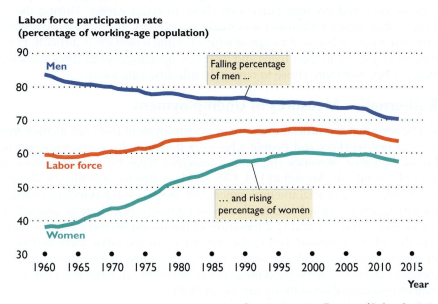

SOURCE OF DATA: Bureau of Labor Statistics.

The labor force participation rate increased from 1960 to 1999 but then decreased slightly.

The labor force participation rate of women has driven these trends, increasing strongly from 37 percent in 1960 to 60 percent in 1999.

The labor force participation rate of men has decreased steadily through the past 53 years.

# EYE on the GLOBAL ECONOMY
## Women in the Labor Force

The labor force participation rate of women has increased in most advanced nations. But the participation rate of women in the labor force varies a great deal around the world. The figure compares eight other countries with the United States.

The U.S. rank is surprisingly low and economists Francine D. Blau and Lawrence M. Kahn who have studied these data say that other countries have more "family-friendly" labor market policies. But they say these policies encourage part-time work and U.S. women are more likely than women in other countries to have good full-time jobs as managers or professionals.

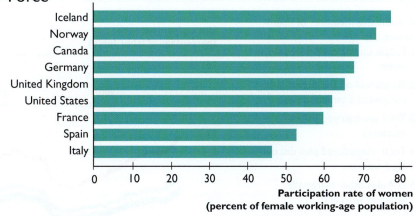

SOURCE OF DATA: OECD.

Cultural factors play a central role in influencing national differences in women's work choices. But education, and particularly the percentage of women with a college degree, is the dominant source of international differences in women's and men's job market prospects.

Figure 15.3 also shows another remarkable trend in the U.S. labor force: The participation rate of men *decreased* from 83 percent in 1960 to 70 percent in 2013. As in the case of women, this decrease is spread across all age groups. Some of the decrease occurred because older men chose to retire earlier. During the 1990s, some of this earlier retirement was made possible by an increase in wealth. But some arose from job loss at an age at which finding a new job is difficult. For other men, mainly those in their teens and twenties, decreased labor force participation occurred because more chose to remain in full-time education.

### ■ Alternative Measures of Unemployment

You've seen that the official measure of unemployment does not include marginally attached workers and people who work part time for economic reasons. The Bureau of Labor Statistics (BLS) now provides three broader measures of the unemployment rate, known as U-4, U-5, and U-6, that include these wider groups of the jobless. The official unemployment rate (based on the standard definition of unemployment) is called U-3 and as these names imply, there is also a U-1 and U-2 measure. The U-1 and U-2 measures of the unemployment rate are narrower than the official measure. U-1 is the percentage of the labor force that has been unemployed for 15 weeks or more and is a measure of long-term involuntary unemployment. U-2 is the percentage of the labor force that has been laid off and is another measure of involuntary unemployment.

Figure 15.4 shows the history of these six measures of unemployment since 1994 (the year in which the BLS started to measure them). The relative magnitudes of the six measures are explained by what they include—the broader the measure, the higher the average. The six measures follow similar but not identical tracks,

■ **FIGURE 15.4**

Alternative Measures of Unemployment: 1994–2013

The alternative measures of unemployment are:

U-1 People unemployed 15 weeks or longer

U-2 People laid off and others who completed a temporary job

U-3 Total unemployed (official measure)

U-4 Total unemployed plus discouraged workers

U-5 U-4 plus other marginally attached workers

U-6 U-5 plus employed part time for economic reasons

U-1, U-2, and U-3 are percentages of the labor force.

U-4, U-5, and U-6 are percentages of the labor force plus the unemployed in the added category.

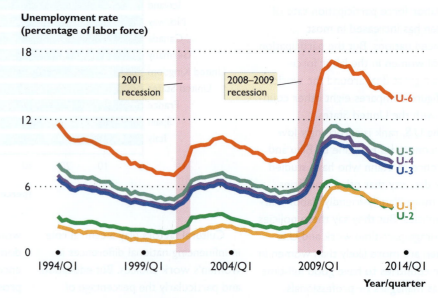

SOURCE OF DATA: Bureau of Labor Statistics.

rising during the recessions and falling in the expansions between the recessions. But during the 2001 recession, U-1 barely changed while during the 2008–2009 recession, it more than doubled in less than a year.

## ■ A Closer Look at Part-Time Employment

The broadest measure of the unemployment rate, U-6, includes people who work part time for economic reasons. Let's take a closer look at part-time employment.

A part-time job is attractive to many workers because it enables them to balance family and other commitments with work. Part-time jobs are attractive to employers because they don't have to pay benefits to part-time workers and are less constrained by government regulations. People who choose part-time jobs are part time for noneconomic reasons. People who take a part-time job because they can't find a full-time job are part time for economic reasons. The BLS measures these two groups and Figure 15.5 shows the data since 1980 (but with a change in the definitions in 1994).

The number of people who work part time for noneconomic reasons is double the number who work part time for economic reasons. Also, the percentage of the labor force who are part time for noneconomic reasons is remarkably steady at an average of 13 percent (old definition) and 14 percent (new definition) of the labor force, and that percentage barely fluctuates with the business cycle.

The percentage of the labor force who work part-time for economic reasons experiences large swings. In the 1981–1982 recession, it climbed to 6.2 percent and in the 2008–2009 recession, it climbed to 6.4 percent.

■ **FIGURE 15.5**

Part-Time Workers: 1980–2013

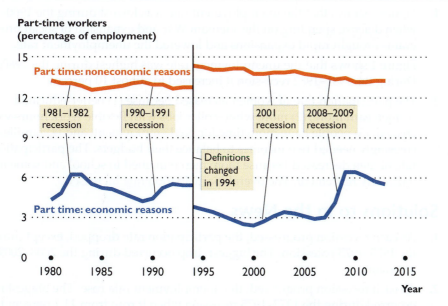

The annual average percentage of all employed workers who are part time for noneconomic reasons is a steady 13 percent (old definition) and 14 percent (new definition) and this percentage barely fluctuates with the business cycle.

But the percentage of all employed workers who are part time for economic reasons fluctuates with the business cycle. It increases in a recession and decreases in an expansion.

SOURCE OF DATA: Bureau of Labor Statistics.

# CHECKPOINT 15.2

Describe the trends and fluctuations in the indicators of labor market performance in the United States.

## Practice Problems

**FIGURE 1**

Unemployment rate
(percentage of labor force)

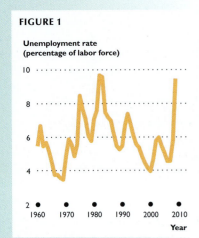

**TABLE 1**

| Recession years | Participation rate | Unemployment rate |
|---|---|---|
| | (percent in July) | |
| 1973 | 71.9 | 11.1 |
| 1974 | 73.2 | 12.4 |
| 1975 | 73.0 | 16.3 |
| 1981 | 75.3 | 16.2 |
| 1982 | 74.7 | 18.6 |
| 1990 | 75.1 | 10.9 |
| 1991 | 73.6 | 13.7 |
| 2008 | 65.1 | 14.0 |
| 2009 | 63.0 | 18.5 |

1.  Figure 1 shows the unemployment rate in the United States from 1960 to 2010. In which decade—the 1960s, 1970s, 1980s, 1990s, or 2000s—was the average unemployment rate the lowest and what brought low unemployment in that decade? In which decade was the average unemployment rate the highest and what brought high unemployment in that decade?

2.  Describe the trends in the participation rates of men and women and of all workers.

## In the News

**For young people, a jobless summer**
In July 2009, the youth unemployment rate hit 18.5 percent—the highest level since the BLS started recording youth labor statistics. The proportion of young people working was 51.4 percent, another historic low for the month of July.

Source: *The Wall Street Journal*, August 27, 2009

In addition, Table 1 sets out data for the youth labor force participation rate and unemployment rate during four major recent U.S. recessions.

1.  Compare the changes in the labor force participation rate during the recessions in Table 1. During which recession did the labor force participation rate drop the most?

2.  Compare the changes in the unemployment rate during the recessions in Table 1. During which recession did the unemployment rate rise the most?

## Solutions to Practice Problems

1.  Figure 1 shows that the unemployment rate was lowest during the 1960s when defense spending on the Vietnam War and expansion of social programs brought rapid expansions and lowered the unemployment rate.

    Figure 1 shows that the unemployment rate was highest during the 1980s. During the 1981–1982 recession it increased to almost 10 percent.

2.  The participation rate of women increased because (1) better-educated women earn more, (2) more white-collar jobs with flexible work hours were created, (3) people have more time for paid employment, and (4) families increasingly needed two incomes to balance their budgets. The participation rate of men decreased because more men remained in school and some men took early retirement. The overall participation rate increased.

## Solutions to In the News

1.  As each recession progressed, the participation rate dropped, except during the 1973–1975 recession. The biggest drop occurred during the 2008–2009 recession.

2.  As each recession progressed, the unemployment rate rose. The biggest rise occurred during the 1973–1975 recession when it rose from 11.1 percent to 16.3 percent—a 5.2 percentage point rise.

## 15.3 UNEMPLOYMENT AND FULL EMPLOYMENT

There is always someone without a job who is searching for one, so there is always some unemployment. The key reason is that the labor market is constantly churning. New jobs are created and old jobs die; and some people move into the labor force and some move out of it. This churning creates unemployment.

We distinguish among three types of unemployment:

- Frictional unemployment
- Structural unemployment
- Cyclical unemployment

### ■ Frictional Unemployment

**Frictional unemployment** is the unemployment that arises from people entering and leaving the labor force, from quitting jobs to find better ones, and from the ongoing creation and destruction of jobs—from normal labor turnover. Frictional unemployment is a permanent and healthy phenomenon in a dynamic, growing economy.

There is an unending flow of people into and out of the labor force as people move through the stages of life—from being in school to finding a job, to working, perhaps to becoming unhappy with a job and looking for a new one, and finally, to retiring from full-time work.

There is also an unending process of job creation and job destruction as new firms are born, firms expand or contract, and some firms fail and go out of business.

The flows into and out of the labor force and the processes of job creation and job destruction create the need for people to search for jobs and for businesses to search for workers. Businesses don't usually hire the first person who applies for a job, and unemployed people don't usually take the first job that comes their way. Instead, both firms and workers spend time searching for what they believe will be the best available match. By this process of search, people can match their own skills and interests with the available jobs and find a satisfying job and a good income.

**Frictional unemployment**
The unemployment that arises from people entering and leaving the labor force, from quitting jobs to find better ones, and from the ongoing creation and destruction of jobs—from normal labor turnover.

*A new graduate interviews for a job.*

### ■ Structural Unemployment

**Structural unemployment** is the unemployment that arises when changes in technology or international competition change the skills needed to perform jobs or change the locations of jobs. Structural unemployment usually lasts longer than frictional unemployment because workers must retrain and possibly relocate to find a job. For example, when banks introduced the automatic teller machine in the 1970s, many bank-teller jobs were destroyed. Meanwhile, new jobs for life-insurance salespeople and retail clerks were created. The former bank tellers remained unemployed for several months until they moved, retrained, and got one of these new jobs. Structural unemployment is painful, especially for older workers for whom the best available option might be to retire early but with a lower income than they had expected.

Sometimes, the amount of structural unemployment is small. At other times, it is large, and at such times, structural unemployment can become a serious long-term problem. It was especially large during the late 1970s and early 1980s.

**Structural unemployment**
The unemployment that arises when changes in technology or international competition change the skills needed to perform jobs or change the locations of jobs.

*Jobs lost to computer technology.*

## ■ Cyclical Unemployment

**Cyclical unemployment**
The fluctuating unemployment over the business cycle that increases during a recession and decreases during an expansion.

The fluctuating unemployment over the business cycle—higher than normal unemployment at a business cycle trough and the lower than normal unemployment at a business cycle peak—is called **cyclical unemployment.** A worker who is laid off because the economy is in a recession and who gets rehired some months later when the expansion begins has experienced cyclical unemployment.

## ■ "Natural" Unemployment

**Natural unemployment rate**
The unemployment rate when the economy is at full employment.

**Full employment**
When there is no cyclical unemployment or, equivalently, when *all* the unemployment is frictional or structural.

Natural unemployment is the unemployment that arises from frictions and structural change when there is no cyclical unemployment—when all the unemployment is frictional and structural. Natural unemployment as a percentage of the labor force is called the **natural unemployment rate.**

**Full employment** is defined as a situation in which the unemployment rate equals the natural unemployment rate.

What determines the natural unemployment rate? Is it constant or does it change over time?

The natural unemployment rate is influenced by many factors but the most important ones are

- The age distribution of the population
- The pace of structural change
- The real wage rate
- Unemployment benefits

# EYE on the UNEMPLOYED

## How Long Does it Take to Find a Job?

The average duration of unemployment spells varies over the business cycle. In 2000, at a cycle peak when the unemployment rate was below the natural rate at 4 percent, the median time to find a job was 6 weeks. In 2013, in a slow expansion when the unemployment rate was above the natural rate at 7.5 percent, the median time to find a job was 16 weeks.

The figure provides more information: It shows the percentage of the unemployed at four unemployment durations. You can see that long-term unemployment (27 weeks and over) was much greater in 2013 than it was at the cycle peak in 2000.

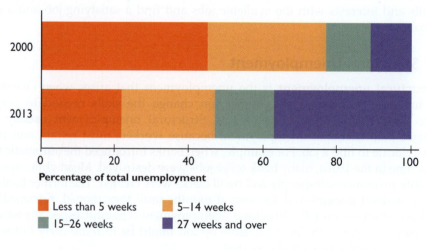

SOURCE OF DATA: Bureau of Labor Statistics.

### The Age Distribution of the Population

An economy with a young population has lots of new job seekers every year and has a high level of frictional unemployment. An economy with an aging population has fewer new job seekers and a low level of frictional unemployment.

### The Pace of Structural Change

The pace of structural change is sometimes low. The same jobs using the same machines remain in place for many years. But sometimes a technological upheaval sweeps aside the old ways, wipes out millions of jobs, and makes the skills once used to perform these jobs obsolete. The amount of structural unemployment fluctuates with the pace of technological change. The change is driven by fierce international competition, especially from fast-changing Asian economies. A high level of structural unemployment is present in many parts of the United States today.

### The Real Wage Rate

The natural unemployment rate is influenced by the level of the real wage rate. Anything that raises the real wage rate above the market equilibrium level creates a surplus of labor and increases the natural unemployment rate. The real wage rate might exceed the market equilibrium level for two reasons: a minimum wage and an efficiency wage. The federal minimum wage creates unemployment because it is set above the equilibrium wage rate of low-skilled young workers. An efficiency wage is a wage set above the going market wage to enable firms to attract the most productive workers, get them to work hard, and discourage them from quitting. When firms set their wage above the going market wage, some workers would like to work for these firms but can't get jobs.

### Unemployment Benefits

Unemployment benefits increase the natural unemployment rate by lowering the opportunity cost of job search. European countries have more generous unemployment benefits and higher natural unemployment rates than the United States. Extending unemployment benefits raises the natural unemployment rate.

There is no controversy about the existence of a natural unemployment rate. Nor is there disagreement that the natural unemployment rate changes. But economists don't know its exact size or the extent to which it fluctuates. The Congressional Budget Office estimates the natural unemployment rate and its estimate for 2013 was 6 percent—about 80 percent of the actual unemployment rate in that year.

## ■ Unemployment and Real GDP

Cyclical unemployment is the fluctuating unemployment over the business cycle—unemployment that increases during a recession and decreases during an expansion. At full employment, there is *no* cyclical unemployment. At a business cycle trough, cyclical unemployment is *positive* and at a business cycle peak, cyclical unemployment is *negative*.

Figure 15.6(a) shows the unemployment rate in the United States between 1980 and 2013. It also shows the natural unemployment rate and cyclical unemployment. The natural unemployment rate in this figure was estimated by the Congressional Budget Office (CBO).

In Figure 15.6(a), you can see that during most of the 1980s, the early 1990s, early 2000s, and during 2008–2009, unemployment was above the natural unemployment rate, so cyclical unemployment was positive (the red sections of the line). You can also see that during the late 1980s, from 1997 to 2001, and during 2005–2008 unemployment was below the natural unemployment rate, so cyclical unemployment was negative (the blue sections of the line).

As the unemployment rate fluctuates around the natural unemployment rate, real GDP fluctuates around potential GDP. **Potential GDP** is the value of real GDP when the economy is at full employment—all the economy's factors of production (labor, capital, land, and entrepreneurial ability) are employed. Real GDP equals potential GDP when the economy is at full employment. Real GDP minus potential GDP expressed as a percentage of potential GDP is called the **output gap.**

Figure 15.6(b) shows the U.S. *output gap* from 1980 to 2013. You can see that as the unemployment rate fluctuates around the natural unemployment rate, the output gap also fluctuates. When the unemployment rate is above the natural unemployment rate, in part (a), the output gap is negative (real GDP is below potential GDP), in part (b); when the unemployment rate is below the natural unemployment rate, the output gap is positive (real GDP is above potential GDP); and when the unemployment rate equals the natural unemployment rate, the output gap is zero (real GDP equals potential GDP).

You can also see in Figure 15.6 that the unemployment rate is a lagging indicator of the business cycle. Long after a recession is over, the unemployment rate is still rising.

**Potential GDP**
The value of real GDP when the economy is at full employment— all the economy's factors of production (labor, capital, land, and entrepreneurial ability) are employed.

**Output gap**
Real GDP minus potential GDP expressed as a percentage of potential GDP.

# EYE on YOUR LIFE
## Your Labor Market Status and Activity

You are going to spend a lot of your life in the labor market. Most of the time, you'll be supplying labor services. But first, you must find a job. Most likely, one job will not last your entire working life. You will want to find a new job when you decide to quit or when changing economic conditions destroy your current job.

As you look for a job, get a job, quit a job, or get laid off and look for a new job, you will pass through many and possibly all of the population categories used in the Current Population Survey that you've learned about in this chapter.

Think about your current labor market status while you are studying economics.

- Are you in the labor force or not?
- If you are in the labor force, are you employed or unemployed?
- If you are employed, are you a part-time or a full-time worker?

Now think about someone you know who is unemployed or has been unemployed. Classify the unemployment experienced by this person as

- frictional,
- structural, or
- cyclical.

How can you tell the type of unemployment experienced by this person?

The labor market conditions that you face today or when you graduate and look for a job depend partly on general national economic conditions—on whether the economy is in recession or booming.

Labor market conditions also depend on where you live. Visit the Bureau of Labor Statistics' Web site at www.bls.gov/sae/sm_mrs.htm. There you can find information on employment and unemployment for your state and metropolitan area or county. By comparing the labor market conditions in your own region with those in other areas, you can figure out where it might be easier to find work.

**FIGURE 15.6**

## The Relationship Between Unemployment and the Output Gap

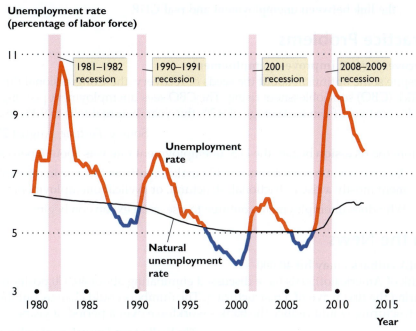

**(a) Cyclical and natural unemployment**

As the unemployment rate fluctuates around the natural unemployment rate in part (a), the output gap—real GDP minus potential GDP expressed as a percentage of potential GDP—fluctuates around a zero output gap in part (b).

When the unemployment rate *exceeds* the natural unemployment rate, real GDP is below potential GDP and the output gap is negative (red sections in both parts).

When the unemployment rate is *below* the natural unemployment rate, real GDP is above potential GDP and the output gap is positive (blue sections in both parts).

The natural unemployment rate shown in the graph is the Congressional Budget Office's estimate. It might turn out to be a substantial underestimate for the years since 2008.

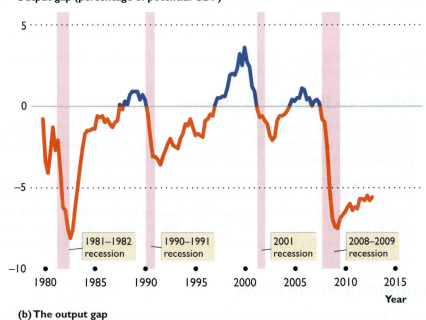

**(b) The output gap**

SOURCES OF DATA: Bureau of Economic Analysis, Bureau of Labor Statistics, and Congressional Budget Office.

## CHECKPOINT 15.3

**Describe the types of unemployment, define full employment, and explain the link between unemployment and real GDP.**

## Practice Problems

**Recovery won't improve unemployment**

Despite some optimism about the seeds of recovery, the Congressional Budget Office (CBO) sees joblessness rising. The CBO sees unemployment peaking at 10.4% next year from an average of 9.3% this year, before it falls to 9.1% in 2011.

Source: *Fortune*, August 25, 2009

Before the recession began, the U.S. unemployment rate was about 6 percent.

1.  As a recession begins, firms quickly make layoffs. Is this rise in unemployment mostly a rise in frictional, structural, or cyclical unemployment?

2.  Why does unemployment continue to rise as an expansion begins?

## In the News

**BofA cutbacks may hit 40,000**

Bank of America officials have discussed eliminating about 40,000 positions during the first wave of a restructuring. The numbers could change, but the restructuring would reduce the bank's workforce over a period of years.

Source: *The Wall Street Journal*, September 9, 2011

**Postal Service targets 220,000 job cuts**

The U.S. Postal Service plans to reduce its workforce by 220,000 jobs to remedy its dire financial situation. The Postal Service, financed mostly by postage, has been struggling as a result of the economic slowdown.

Source: *The Wall Street Journal*, August 12, 2011

What type of unemployment will arise from the cut in employment in each of these cases? Explain your answer.

## Solutions to Practice Problems

1.  When a recession starts, firms are quick to lay off workers. Most of the rise in unemployment is cyclical—related to the state of the economy. The unemployment rate rises quickly as the number of layoffs increases.

2.  The unemployment rate is a lagging indicator of the business cycle. When an expansion begins, firms start hiring. Unemployed workers get jobs, but the labor force increases as marginally attached workers start to look for jobs. In the early stages of an expansion, the number of marginally attached workers looking for jobs exceeds the number of people hired and unemployment increases.

## Solution to In the News

Bank of America is reducing its workforce as it restructures its organization in response to changing technology. Because online banking has grown, the bank will close many branches. Cuts in its workforce will create structural unemployment. The U.S. Postal Service is cutting its workforce in response to a downturn in economic activity. Cuts in its workforce will create cyclical unemployment.

## CHAPTER SUMMARY

## Key Points

1. **Define the unemployment rate and other labor market indicators.**

   - The unemployment rate is the number of people unemployed as a percentage of the labor force, and the labor force is the sum of the number of people employed and the number unemployed.
   - The labor force participation rate is the labor force as a percentage of the working-age population.

2. **Describe the trends and fluctuations in the indicators of labor market performance in the United States.**

   - The unemployment rate fluctuates with the business cycle, increasing in recessions and decreasing in expansions.
   - The labor force participation rate of women has increased, and the labor force participation rate of men has decreased.

3. **Describe the types of unemployment, define full employment, and explain the link between unemployment and real GDP.**

   - Unemployment can be frictional, structural, or cyclical.
   - Full employment occurs when there is no cyclical unemployment and at full employment, the unemployment rate equals the natural unemployment rate.
   - Potential GDP is the real GDP produced when the economy is at full employment.
   - As the unemployment rate fluctuates around the natural unemployment rate, real GDP fluctuates around potential GDP and the output gap fluctuates between negative and positive values.

## Key Terms

# CHAPTER CHECKPOINT

## Study Plan Problems and Applications

Use the following information gathered by a BLS labor market survey of four households to work Problems **1** and **2**.

- Household 1: Candy worked 20 hours last week setting up her Internet shopping business. The rest of the week, she completed application forms and attended two job interviews. Husband Jerry worked 40 hours at his job at GM. Daughter Meg, a student, worked 10 hours at her weekend job at Starbucks.
- Household 2: Joey, a full-time bank clerk, was on vacation. Wife, Serena, who wants a full-time job, worked 10 hours as a part-time checkout clerk.
- Household 3: Ari had no work last week but was going to be recalled to his regular job in two weeks. Partner Kosta, after months of searching for a job and not being able to find one, has stopped looking and will go back to school.
- Household 4: Mimi and Henry are retired. Son Hank is a professional artist, who painted for 12 hours last week and sold one picture.

1. Classify each of the 10 people into the labor market category used by the BLS. Who are part-time workers and who are full-time workers? Of the part-time workers, who works part time for economic reasons?

2. Calculate the unemployment rate and the labor force participation rate, and compare these rates with those in the United States in 2013.

3. Describe two examples of people who work part time for economic reasons and two examples of people who work part time for noneconomic reasons.

4. Explain the relationship between the percentage of employed workers who have part-time jobs and the business cycle.

5. Distinguish among the three types of unemployment: frictional, structural, and cyclical. Provide an example of each type of unemployment in the United States today.

6. Describe the relationship between the unemployment rate and the natural unemployment rate as the output gap fluctuates between being positive and being negative.

Use the following information to work Problems **7** and **8**.

### U.S. unemployment rate lowest since 2008
The Labor Department said that the economy added 146,000 jobs in November, and the unemployment rate fell to 7.7% from 7.9% in October. But it fell mainly because workers dropped out of the labor force.

Source: CNN Money, December 7, 2012

7. Explain how the new jobs change the labor force and the unemployment rate.

8. Explain why workers dropping out of the labor force lowers the unemployment rate and why by more than new jobs do.

9. Read *Eye on the Unemployed* on p. 450. In which year, 2000 or 2013, was real GDP below potential GDP? How can you tell from the graph on p. 450?

## Instructor Assignable Problems and Applications

1. In the United States,
   - Compare the duration of unemployment in 2013 with that in 2000 and explain whether the difference was most likely the result of frictions, structural change, or the business cycle.
   - How does the unemployment of marginally attached workers influence the duration of unemployment in 2013 compared with that in 2000?

2. The Bureau of Labor Statistics reported that in the second quarter of 2008 the working-age population was 233,410,000, the labor force was 154,294,000, and employment was 146,089,000. Calculate for that quarter the labor force participation rate and the unemployment rate.

3. In July 2011, in the economy of Sandy Island, 10,000 people were employed and 1,000 were unemployed. During August 2011, 80 people lost their jobs and didn't look for new ones, 20 people quit their jobs and retired, 150 people who had looked for work were hired, 50 people became discouraged workers, and 40 new graduates looked for work. Calculate the change in the unemployment rate from July 2011 to August 2011.

4. The BLS survey reported the following data in a community of 320 people: 200 worked at least 1 hour as paid employees; 20 did not work but were temporarily absent from their jobs; 40 did not have jobs and didn't want to work; 10 were available for work and last week they had looked for work; and 6 were available for work and were waiting to be recalled to their previous job. Calculate the unemployment rate and the labor force participation rate.

5. Describe the trends and fluctuations in the unemployment rate in the United States from 1949 through 2013. In which periods was the unemployment rate above average and in which periods was it below average?

6. Describe how the labor force participation rate in the United States changed between 1960 and 2013. Contrast and explain the different trends in the labor force participation rates of women and men.

7. Explain why the natural unemployment rate is not zero and why the unemployment rate fluctuates around the natural unemployment rate.

Use the following information to work Problems **8** and **9**.

**Michigan unemployment tops 15%**
The U.S. Department of Labor reported that Michigan's unemployment rate in June 2009 rose to 15.2%, becoming the first state in 25 years to suffer an unemployment rate exceeding 15%. Michigan has been battered by the collapse of the auto industry and the housing crisis and has had the highest unemployment rate in the nation for the past 12 months.

Source: CNN Money, July 17, 2009

8. Why is the reality of the unemployment problem in Michigan actually worse than the unemployment rate statistic of 15.2 percent?

9. Is this increased unemployment frictional, structural, or cyclical? Explain.

## Critical Thinking Discussion Questions

1. **Older Australians suffer from unemployment**

   With life expectancies rising, many retired Australians would like to re-enter the labor force. Several of these job seekers are experiencing difficulties in finding employment because many employers are not interested in hiring older people.

   Source: ABC, 3 November 2013

   Think about the effects of retired Australians re-entering the labor force:

   Are retired Australians who are searching for a job counted as unemployed?

   How do job-searching retirees change the labor force participation rate?

   What effect does new technology have on the senior unemployment rate?

   Should retired people who decide to re-enter the labor force be included in the country's official unemployment rate? Why or why not?

2. **Spanish unemployment falls as economy emerges from recession**

   As Spain's economy emerges from recession, its unemployment rate is beginning to fall. Spain still has one of the highest unemployment rates among European countries. With an unemployment rate of 26 %, the government believes that some people who claim to be unemployed are actually working illegally.

   Source: Bloomberg, 24 October 2013

   Think about unemployment in Spain:

   What type of unemployment is most prevalent in Spain?

   What would be the effect on Spain's labor force participation rate if some of the unemployed who are working illegally are categorized as employed?

   What would be the effect on Spain's employment-to-population ratio if some of the unemployed who are working illegally are categorized as employed?

   Does moving out of recession change Spain's natural unemployment rate?

3. **Greece jobless rate hits new record of 28 %**

   The unemployment rate in Greece increased from 27.7 % in December to 28 % in January. For those under the age of 25, unemployment hit 61.4 %.

   Source: BBC, 13 February 2014

   Think about the youth unemployment rate in Greece:

   Why is the youth unemployment rate in Greece higher than the unemployment rate for the entire labor force?

   What type of unemployment is most common among young people?

   Should an unemployment rate of zero percent for young people be the goal of the Greek government?

## Which movie *really* was the biggest box office hit?

# The CPI and the Cost of Living

**16**

**When you have completed your study of this chapter, you will be able to**

**1** Explain what the Consumer Price Index (CPI) is and how it is calculated.

**2** Explain the limitations of the CPI and describe other measures of the price level.

**3** Adjust money values for inflation and calculate real wage rates and real interest rates.

## 16.1 THE CONSUMER PRICE INDEX

**Consumer Price Index**
A measure of the average of the prices paid by urban consumers for a fixed market basket of consumption goods and services.

The **Consumer Price Index** (CPI) is a measure of the average of the prices paid by urban consumers for a fixed market basket of consumption goods and services. The Bureau of Labor Statistics (BLS) calculates the CPI every month, and we can use these numbers to compare what the fixed market basket costs this month with what it cost in some previous month or other period.

### Reading the CPI Numbers

**Reference base period**
A period for which the CPI is defined to equal 100. Currently, the reference base period is 1982–1984.

The CPI is defined to equal 100 for a period called the **reference base period.** Currently, the reference base period is 1982–1984. That is, the CPI equals 100 on the average over the 36 months from January 1982 through December 1984.

In May 2013, the CPI was 232.9. This number tells us that the average of the prices paid by urban consumers for a fixed market basket of consumption goods and services was 132.9 percent higher in May 2013 than it was on the average during 1982–1984.

In April 2013, the CPI was 232.5. Comparing the CPI in May 2013 with the CPI in April 2013 tells us that the average of the prices paid by urban consumers for a fixed market basket of consumption goods and services *increased* by 0.4 percentage points in May 2013.

### Constructing the CPI

Constructing the CPI is a huge operation that costs millions of dollars and involves three stages:

- Selecting the CPI market basket
- Conducting the monthly price survey
- Calculating the CPI

### The CPI Market Basket

The first stage in constructing the CPI is to determine the *CPI market basket.* This "basket" contains the goods and services represented in the index and the relative importance, or weight, attached to each of them. The idea is to make the weight of the items in the CPI basket the same as in the budget of an average urban household. For example, if the average household spends 2 percent of its income on public transportation, then the CPI places a weight of 2 percent on the prices of bus, subway, and other transit system rides.

Although the CPI is calculated every month, the CPI market basket isn't updated every month. The information used to determine the CPI market basket comes from a survey, called the *Consumer Expenditure Survey,* that discovers what people actually buy. This survey is an ongoing activity, and the CPI market basket in 2013 was based on a survey conducted during 2011. An astonishing 88,000 individuals and families contributed information. Some of them were interviewed every three months, and others kept detailed diaries for two weeks in which they listed absolutely everything they bought. (Before 1999, the Consumer Expenditure Survey was conducted less frequently.)

The reference base period for the CPI has been fixed at 1982–1984 for more than 20 years and doesn't change when a new Consumer Expenditure Survey is used to update the market basket.

Figure 16.1 shows the CPI market basket in May 2013. The basket contains around 80,000 goods and services arranged in the eight large groups shown in the figure. The most important item in a household's budget is housing, which accounts for 40.9 percent of total expenditure. Transportation comes next at 17.2 percent. Third in relative importance is food and beverages at 15.2 percent. These three groups account for almost three quarters of the average household budget. Medical care takes 7.0 percent, education and communication takes 6.7 percent, recreation takes 6 percent, and apparel (clothing and footwear) takes 3.6 percent. Another 3.4 percent is spent on other goods and services.

The BLS breaks down each of these categories into smaller ones. For example, education and communication breaks down into textbooks and supplies, tuition, telephone services, and personal computer services.

As you look at these numbers, remember that they apply to the average household. Each individual household is spread around the average. Think about your own expenditure and compare it with the average.

## ■ The Monthly Price Survey

Each month, BLS employees check the prices of the 80,000 goods and services in the CPI market basket in 30 metropolitan areas. Because the CPI aims to measure price changes, it is important that the prices recorded each month refer to exactly the same items. For example, suppose the price of a box of jelly beans has increased but a box now contains more beans. Has the price of a jelly bean increased? The BLS employee must record the details of changes in quality, size, weight, or packaging so that price changes can be isolated from other changes.

Once the raw price data are in hand, the next task is to calculate the CPI.

### ■ FIGURE 16.1

### The CPI Market Basket

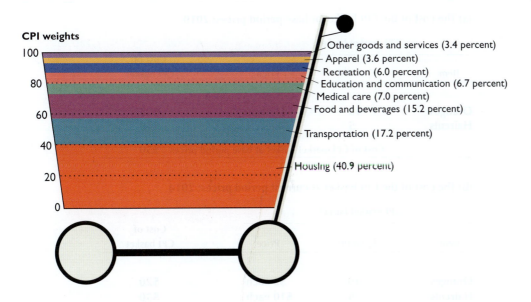

This shopping cart is filled with the items that an average urban household buys. Housing (40.9 percent), transportation (17.2 percent), and food and beverages (15.2 percent) take almost three quarters of household income.

SOURCE OF DATA: Bureau of Labor Statistics.

## ■ Calculating the CPI

The CPI calculation has three steps:

- Find the cost of the CPI market basket at base period prices.
- Find the cost of the CPI market basket at current period prices.
- Calculate the CPI for the base period and the current period.

We'll work through these three steps for a simple example. Suppose the CPI market basket contains only two goods and services: oranges and haircuts. We'll construct an annual CPI rather than a monthly CPI with the reference base period 2010 and the current period 2014.

Table 16.1 shows the quantities in the CPI market basket and the prices in the base period and the current period. Part (a) contains the data for the base period. In that period, consumers bought 10 oranges at $1 each and 5 haircuts at $8 each. To find the cost of the CPI market basket in the base period prices, multiply the quantities in the CPI market basket by the base period prices. The cost of oranges is $10 (10 at $1 each), and the cost of haircuts is $40 (5 at $8 each). So total expenditure in the base period on the CPI market basket is $50 ($10 + $40).

Part (b) contains the price data for the current period. The price of an orange increased from $1 to $2, which is a 100 percent increase ($1 ÷ $1 × 100 = 100 percent). The price of a haircut increased from $8 to $10, which is a 25 percent increase ($2 ÷ $8 × 100 = 25 percent).

The CPI provides a way of averaging these price increases by comparing the cost of the basket rather than the price of each item. To find the cost of the CPI market basket in the current period, 2014, multiply the quantities in the basket by their 2014 prices. The cost of oranges is $20 (10 at $2 each), and the cost of haircuts is $50 (5 at $10 each). So total expenditure on the fixed CPI market basket at current period prices is $70 ($20 + $50).

## ■ TABLE 16.1

### The Consumer Price Index: A Simplified CPI Calculation

**(a) The cost of the CPI basket at base period prices: 2010**

| | CPI market basket | | |
|---|---|---|---|
| Item | Quantity | Price | Cost of CPI basket |
| Oranges | 10 | $1 each | $10 |
| Haircuts | 5 | $8 each | $40 |
| | Cost of CPI market basket at base period prices | | $50 |

**(b) The cost of the CPI basket at current period prices: 2014**

| | CPI market basket | | |
|---|---|---|---|
| Item | Quantity | Price | Cost of CPI basket |
| Oranges | 10 | $2 each | $20 |
| Haircuts | 5 | $10 each | $50 |
| | Cost of CPI market basket at current period prices | | $70 |

You've now taken the first two steps toward calculating the CPI. The third step uses the numbers you've just calculated to find the CPI for 2010 and 2014. The formula for the CPI is

$$\text{CPI} = \frac{\text{Cost of CPI basket at current period prices}}{\text{Cost of CPI basket at base period prices}} \times 100.$$

In Table 16.1, you established that in 2010, the cost of the CPI market basket was $50 and in 2014, it was $70. If we use these numbers in the CPI formula, we can find the CPI for 2010 and 2014. The base period is 2010, so

$$\text{CPI in 2010} = \frac{\$50}{\$50} \times 100 = 100.$$

$$\text{CPI in 2014} = \frac{\$70}{\$50} \times 100 = 140.$$

The principles that you've applied in this simplified CPI calculation apply to the more complex calculations performed every month by the BLS.

Figure 16.2(a) shows the CPI in the United States during the 40 years between 1973 and 2013. The CPI increased every year during this period until 2009 when it fell slightly. During the late 1970s and in 1980, the CPI was increasing rapidly, but since the early 1980s, the rate of increase has slowed.

## ■ Measuring Inflation and Deflation

A major purpose of the CPI is to measure *changes* in the cost of living and in the value of money. To measure these changes, we calculate the **inflation rate**, which is the percentage change in the price level from one year to the next. To calculate the inflation rate, we use the formula

**Inflation rate**
The percentage change in the price level from one year to the next.

$$\text{Inflation rate} = \frac{(\text{CPI in current year} - \text{CPI in previous year})}{\text{CPI in previous year}} \times 100.$$

Suppose that the current year is 2014 and the CPI for 2014 is 140. And suppose that in the previous year, 2013, the CPI was 120. Then in 2014,

$$\text{Inflation rate} = \frac{(140 - 120)}{120} \times 100 = 16.7 \text{ percent}.$$

If the inflation rate is *negative*, the price level is *falling* and we have **deflation.** The United States has rarely experienced deflation, but 2009 was one of those rare years. You can check the latest data by visiting the BLS Web site. In July 2009, the CPI was 215.4, and in July 2008, it was 220.0. So during the year to July 2009,

**Deflation**
A situation in which the price level is *falling and the inflation rate is negative.*

$$\text{Inflation rate} = \frac{(215.4 - 220.0)}{220.0} \times 100 = -2.1 \text{ percent}.$$

Figure 16.2(b) shows the inflation rate in the United States between 1973 and 2013. The change in the price level in part (a) and the inflation rate in part (b) are related. When the price *level* rises rapidly, the inflation rate is high; when the price *level* rises slowly, the inflation rate is low; and when the price level is falling, the inflation rate is negative.

# EYE on the PAST

## 700 Years of Inflation and Deflation

These extraordinary data show that inflation became a persistent problem only after 1900. During the preceding 600 years, inflation was almost unknown. Inflation increased slightly during the sixteenth century after Europeans discovered gold in America. But this inflation barely reached 2 percent a year—less than we have today—and eventually subsided. The Industrial Revolution saw a temporary burst of inflation followed by a period of deflation.

SOURCES OF DATA: E.H. Phelps Brown and Sheila V. Hopkins, *Economica*, 1955, and Robert Sahr, http://oregonstate.edu/dept/pol_sci/fac/sahr/sahr.htm.

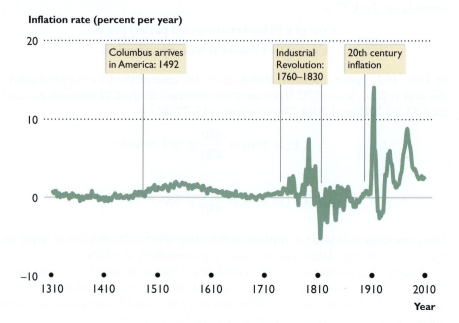

---

■ **FIGURE 16.2**

The CPI and the Inflation Rate: 1973–2013

(a) CPI: 1973–2013

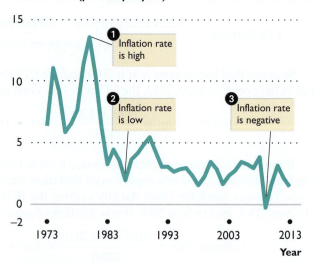

(b) CPI inflation rate: 1973–2013

SOURCE OF DATA: Bureau of Labor Statistics.

❶ The price level in part (a) was rising rapidly during the 1970s and 1980s and the inflation rate in part (b) was high.

❷ The price level was rising slowly during the 1990s and 2000s and the inflation rate was low.

❸ In 2009, the price level fell and the inflation rate was negative.

# CHECKPOINT 16.1

**Explain what the Consumer Price Index (CPI) is and how it is calculated.**

## Practice Problems

A Consumer Expenditure Survey in Sparta shows that people buy only juice and cloth. In 2012, the year of the Consumer Expenditure Survey and also the reference base year, the average household spent $40 on juice and $25 on cloth. Table 1 sets out the prices of juice and cloth in 2012 and 2014.

1.  Calculate the CPI market basket and the percentage of the average household budget spent on juice in the reference base year.

2.  Calculate the CPI in 2014 and the inflation rate between 2012 and 2014.

3.  Table 2 shows the CPI in Sparta. Calculate the inflation rates in 2010 and 2011. Did the price level rise in 2011? Did the inflation rate increase in 2011?

**TABLE 1 PRICES**

|       | 2012        | 2014        |
|-------|-------------|-------------|
| Juice | $4 a bottle | $4 a bottle |
| Cloth | $5 a yard   | $6 a yard   |

**TABLE 2**

| Year | CPI |
|------|-----|
| 2009 | 200 |
| 2010 | 219 |
| 2011 | 237 |

## In the News

**Consumer price index falls 0.4% in April**
The CPI in April 2013 was 233 and 0.4% lower than in March. In April, food prices rose 0.2% while energy prices fell 4.3%.

Source: BLS, April, 2013

Distinguish between the price level and the inflation rate and explain why the CPI fell by only 0.4 percent when energy fell by 4.3 percent.

## Solutions to Practice Problems

1.  The CPI market basket is the quantities bought during the Consumer Expenditure Survey year, 2012. The average household spent $40 on juice at $4 a bottle, so it bought 10 bottles of juice. The average household spent $25 on cloth at $5 a yard, so it bought 5 yards of cloth. The CPI market basket is made up of 10 bottles of juice and 5 yards of cloth.
    In the reference base year, the average household spent $40 on juice and $25 on cloth, so the household budget was $65. Expenditure on juice was 61.5 percent of the household budget: ($40 ÷ $65) × 100 = 61.5 percent.

2.  To calculate the CPI in 2014, find the cost of the CPI market basket in 2012 and 2014. In 2012, the CPI basket costs $65 ($40 for juice + $25 for cloth). In 2014, the CPI market basket costs $70 (10 bottles of juice at $4 a bottle + 5 yards of cloth at $6 a yard). The CPI in 2014 is ($70 ÷ $65) × 100 = 107.7. The inflation rate is [(107.7 − 100) ÷ 100] × 100 = 7.7 percent.

3.  The inflation rate in 2010 is [(219 − 200) ÷ 200] × 100 = 9.5 percent. The inflation rate in 2011 is [(237 − 219) ÷ 219] × 100 = 8.2 percent. In 2011, the price level increased, but the inflation rate decreased.

## Solution to In the News

The CPI is the price level. The percentage change in the CPI is the inflation rate. Food and beverage is 15.2 percent of the CPI basket. Energy is included in transportation and housing. For the CPI to have fallen by 0.4 percent when energy prices fell 4.3 percent, other prices must have risen by more than 0.4 percent.

## 16.2 THE CPI AND OTHER PRICE LEVEL MEASURES

**Cost of living index**
A measure of the change in the amount of money that people need to spend to achieve a given standard of living.

The purpose of the CPI is to measure the cost of living or what amounts to the same thing, the *value of money*. The CPI is sometimes called a **cost of living index** —a measure of the change in the amount of money that people need to spend to achieve a given standard of living. The CPI is not a perfect measure of the cost of living (value of money) for two broad reasons.

First, the CPI does not try to measure all the changes in the cost of living. For example, the cost of living rises in a severe winter as people buy more natural gas and electricity to heat their homes. A rise in the prices of these items increases the CPI. But the increased quantities of natural gas and electricity bought don't change the CPI because the CPI market basket is fixed. So part of this increase in spending—the increase in the cost of maintaining a given standard of living—doesn't show up as an increase in the CPI.

Second, even those components of the cost of living that are measured by the CPI are not always measured accurately. The result is that the CPI is possibly a biased measure of changes in the cost of living.

Let's look at some of the sources of bias in the CPI and the ways the BLS tries to overcome them.

### ■ Sources of Bias in the CPI

The potential sources of bias in the CPI are

- New goods bias
- Quality change bias
- Commodity substitution bias
- Outlet substitution bias

### New Goods Bias

Every year, some new goods become available and some old goods disappear. Make a short list of items that you take for granted today that were not available 10 or 20 years ago. This list includes cell phones, tablet computers, and flat-panel, large-screen television sets. A list of items no longer available or rarely bought includes audiocassette players, vinyl records, photographic film, and typewriters.

When we want to compare the price level in 2014 with that in 2004, 1994, or 1984, we must do so by comparing the prices of different baskets of goods. We can't compare the same baskets because today's basket wasn't available 10 years ago and the basket of 10 years ago isn't available today.

To make comparisons, the BLS tries to measure the price of the service performed by yesterday's goods and today's goods. It tries to compare, for example, the price of listening to recorded music, regardless of the technology that delivers that service. But the comparison is hard to make. Today's smart phone delivers an improved quality of sound and level of convenience compared to yesterday's Walkman and Discman.

How much of a new product represents an increase in quantity and quality and how much represents a higher price? The BLS does its best to answer this question, but there is no sure way of making the necessary adjustment. It is believed that the arrival of new goods puts an upward bias into the CPI and its measure of the inflation rate.

To measure the CPI, the BLS must compare the price of today's smart phone with that of the 1970s Walkman and 1980s Discman.

## Quality Change Bias

Cars, cell phones, laptops, and many other items get better every year. For example, central locking, airbags, and antilock braking systems all add to the quality of a car. But they also add to the cost. Is the improvement in quality greater than the increase in cost? Or do car prices rise by more than can be accounted for by quality improvements? To the extent that a price rise is a payment for improved quality, it is not inflation. Again, the BLS does the best job it can to estimate the effects of quality improvements on price changes. But the CPI probably counts too much of any price rise as inflation and so overstates inflation.

To compare the price of today's cars with those of earlier years, the BLS must value the improvements in features and quality.

## Commodity Substitution Bias

Changes in relative prices lead consumers to change the items they buy. People cut back on items that become relatively more costly and increase their consumption of items that become relatively less costly. For example, suppose the price of carrots rises while the price of broccoli remains constant. Now that carrots are more costly relative to broccoli, you might decide to buy more broccoli and fewer carrots. Suppose that you switch from carrots to broccoli, spend the same amount on vegetables as before, and get the same enjoyment as before. Your cost of vegetables has not changed. The CPI says that the price of vegetables has increased because it ignores your substitution between goods in the CPI market basket.

When consumers substitute lower priced broccoli for higher priced carrots, the CPI overstates the rise in the price of vegetables.

## Outlet Substitution Bias

When confronted with higher prices, people use discount stores more frequently and convenience stores less frequently. This phenomenon is called *outlet substitution*. Suppose, for example, that gas prices rise by 10¢ a gallon. Instead of buying from your nearby gas station for $4.599 a gallon, you now drive farther to a gas station that charges $4.499 a gallon. Your cost of gas has increased because you must factor in the cost of your time and the gas that you use driving several blocks down the road. But your cost has not increased by as much as the 10¢ a gallon increase in the pump price. However, the CPI says that the price of gas has increased by 10¢ a gallon because the CPI does not measure outlet substitution.

The growth of online shopping in recent years has provided an alternative to discount stores that makes outlet substitution even easier and potentially makes this source of bias more serious.

As consumers shop around for the lowest prices, outlet substitution occurs and the CPI overstates the rise in prices actually paid.

## ■ The Magnitude of the Bias

You have reviewed the sources of bias in the CPI. But how big is the bias? When this question was tackled in 1996 by a Congressional Advisory Commission chaired by Michael Boskin, an economics professor at Stanford University, the answer was that the CPI overstated inflation by 1.1 percentage points a year. That is, if the CPI reports that inflation is 3.1 percent a year, most likely inflation is actually 2 percent a year.

In the period since the Boskin Commission reported, the BLS has taken steps to reduce the CPI bias. The more frequent Consumer Expenditure Survey that we described earlier in this chapter is one of these steps. Beyond that, the BLS uses ever more sophisticated models and methods to try to eliminate the sources of bias and make the CPI as accurate as possible.

## ■ Two Consequences of the CPI Bias

Avoiding bias in the CPI is important for two main reasons. Bias leads to

- Distortion of private contracts
- Increases in government outlays and decreases in taxes

### Distortion of Private Contracts

Many wage contracts contain a cost of living adjustment. For example, the United Auto Workers Union (UAW) and Ford Motor Company might agree on a wage rate of $30 an hour initially that increases over three years at the same rate as the cost of living increases. The idea is that both the union and the employer want a contract in "real" terms. As the cost of living rises, the firm wants to pay the workers the number of dollars per hour that buys a given market basket of goods and services. And the firm is happy to pay the higher wage because it can sell its output for a higher price.

Suppose that over the three years of a UAW and Ford contract, the CPI increases by 5 percent each year. The wage rate paid by Ford will increase to $31.50 in the second year and $33.08 in the third year.

But suppose that the CPI is biased and the true price increase is 3 percent a year. The workers' cost of living increases by this amount, so in the second year, $30.90 rather than $31.50 is the intended wage. In the third year, a wage rate of $31.83 and not $33.08 compensates for the higher cost of living. So in the second year, the workers gain 60¢ an hour, or $21 for a 35-hour workweek. And in the third year, they gain $1.25 an hour, or $43.75 for a 35-hour workweek.

The workers' gain is Ford's loss. With a work force of a few thousand, the loss amounts to several thousand dollars a week and a few million dollars over the life of a 3-year wage contract.

If the CPI bias was common knowledge and large, the CPI would not be used without some adjustment in contracts. Unions and employers would seek agreement on the extent of the bias and make an appropriate adjustment to their contract. But for a small bias, the cost of negotiating a more complicated agreement might be too large.

### Increases in Government Outlays and Decreases in Taxes

Because rising prices decrease the buying power of the dollar, the CPI is used to adjust the incomes of the 55 million Social Security beneficiaries, 45 million food stamp recipients, and 4 million retired former military personnel and federal civil servants (and their surviving spouses). The CPI is also used to adjust the budget for 3 million school lunches.

Close to a third of federal government outlays are linked directly to the CPI. If the CPI has a 1.1 percentage point bias, all of these expenditures increase by more than required to compensate for the fall in the buying power of the dollar and, although a bias of 1.1 percent a year seems small, accumulated over a decade, it adds up to almost a trillion dollars of additional government outlays.

The CPI is also used to adjust the income levels at which higher tax rates apply. The tax rates on large incomes are higher than those on small incomes so, as incomes rise, if these adjustments were not made, the burden of taxes would rise relentlessly. To the extent that the CPI is biased upward, the tax adjustments over-compensate for rising prices and decrease the amount paid in taxes.

# ■ Alternative Measures of the Price Level and Inflation Rate

Several alternative measures of the price level and inflation rate are available. One based on wholesale prices and another based on producers' prices are similar to the CPI, both in the way they are constructed and their potential for bias. But three other price indexes that we'll briefly describe here are less biased. These indexes are the

- GDP price index
- Personal consumption expenditures (PCE) price index
- PCE price index excluding food and energy

## GDP Price Index

The **GDP price index** (also called the *GDP deflator*) is an average of the current prices of all the goods and services included in GDP expressed as a percentage of base year prices. Two key differences between the GDP price index and the CPI result in different estimates of the price level and inflation rate.

First, the GDP price index uses the prices of all the goods and services in GDP—consumption goods and services, capital goods, government goods and services, and export goods and services—while the CPI uses prices of consumption goods and services only. For example, the GDP price index includes the prices of paper mills bought by 3M to make Post-it® Notes, nuclear submarines bought by the Defense Department, and Boeing 747s bought by British Airways.

Second, the GDP price index weights each item using information about current quantities. In contrast, the CPI weights each item using information from a *past* Consumer Expenditure Survey. But because of the breadth of the items that the GDP price index includes, it is not an alternative to the CPI as a measure of the cost of living.

**GDP price index**
An average of the current prices of all the goods and services included in GDP expressed as a percentage of base year prices.

## Personal Consumption Expenditures (PCE) Price Index

The **Personal Consumption Expenditures price index** (or **PCE price index**) is an average of the current prices of the goods and services included in the consumption expenditure component of GDP expressed as a percentage of base year prices. The PCE price index has the same advantages as the GDP price index—it uses current information on quantities and to some degree overcomes the sources of bias in the CPI. It also has an advantage shared by the CPI of focusing on consumption expenditure and therefore being a possible measure of the cost of living.

A weakness of the PCE price index is that it is based on data that become known after the lapse of several months. So the CPI provides more current information about the inflation rate than what the PCE price index provides.

**PCE price index**
An average of the current prices of the goods and services included in the consumption expenditure component of GDP expressed as a percentage of base year prices.

## PCE Price Index Excluding Food and Energy

Food and energy prices fluctuate much more than other prices and their changes can obscure the underlying trends in prices. By excluding these highly variable items, the underlying price level and inflation trends can be seen more clearly. The percentage change in the PCE price index excluding food and energy is called the **core inflation rate**.

Figure 16.3(a) shows the three *price levels* measured by the CPI, the PCE price index, and PCE price index excluding food and energy. The two measures based on the PCE price index are very similar but the CPI measure rises above the other two and the gap widens to 100 percentage points over the 40 years shown here.

**Core inflation rate**
The annual percentage change in the PCE price index excluding the prices of food and energy.

Figure 16.3(b) shows the three consumer price *inflation rates*. These measures move up and down in similar ways, but the CPI measure exceeds the PCE price index measures. The average difference between the CPI and PCE measures is about a half a percentage point. The core inflation rate has almost the same average as the PCE inflation rate, but it fluctuates less. You can see why this measure provides a better indication of the inflation trend than the index that includes food and energy prices.

This higher CPI is a reflection of its bias and a confirmation that the PCE price index, which is based on current period actual expenditures, avoids most of the sources of bias in the CPI.

■ **FIGURE 16.3**

## Three Measures of Consumer Prices

The three measures of the *price level* in part (a) rise together, but the CPI rises above the two PCE measures reflecting the bias in the CPI.

The three measures of the *inflation rate* in part (b) fluctuate together, but the CPI inflation rate is higher than the PCE price index inflation rate or the core inflation rate. The core inflation rate fluctuates less than the other two measures.

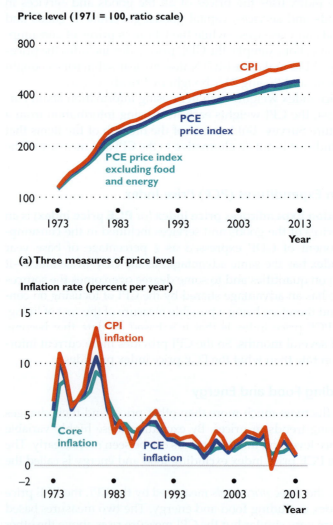

**(a)** Three measures of price level

**(b)** Three measures of inflation

SOURCES OF DATA: Bureau of Labor Statistics and Bureau of Economic Analysis.

# CHECKPOINT 16.2

Explain the limitations of the CPI and describe other measures of the price level.

## Practice Problems

Economists in the Statistics Bureau decide to check the CPI substitution bias. To do so, they conduct a Consumer Expenditure Survey in both 2012 and 2013. Table 1 shows the results of the survey. It shows the items that consumers buy and their prices. The Statistics Bureau fixes the reference base year as 2012.

1. Calculate the CPI in 2013 if the CPI basket contains the 2012 quantities.
2. Calculate the CPI in 2013 if the CPI basket contains the 2013 quantities.
3. Is there any substitution bias in the CPI that uses the 2012 basket? Explain.

**TABLE 1**

| Item | 2012 Quantity | 2012 Price | 2013 Quantity | 2013 Price |
|------|------|------|------|------|
| Broccoli | 10 | $3.00 | 15 | $3.00 |
| Carrots | 15 | $2.00 | 10 | $4.00 |

## In the News

**News release**
In 2011, the CPI increased by 1.4 percent, the GDP price index increased by 1.2 percent, and the PCE price index increased by 1.8 percent.

Source: Bureau of Economic Analysis, August 29, 2011

Why do these three measures of the price level give different inflation rates?

## Solutions to Practice Problems

1. Table 2 shows the calculation of the CPI in 2013 when the CPI basket is made of the 2012 quantities. The cost of the 2012 basket at 2012 prices is $60 and the cost of the 2012 basket at 2013 prices is $90. So the CPI in 2013 using the 2012 basket is ($90 ÷ $60) × 100 = 150.

2. Table 3 shows the calculation of the CPI in 2013 when the CPI basket is made of the 2013 quantities. The cost of the 2013 basket at 2012 prices is $65, and the cost of the 2013 basket at 2013 prices is $85. So the CPI in 2013 using the 2013 basket is ($85 ÷ $65 ) × 100 = 131.

3. The CPI that uses the 2012 basket displays some bias. With the price of broccoli constant and the price of carrots rising, consumers buy fewer carrots and more broccoli and they spend $85 on vegetables. But they would have spent $90 if they had not substituted broccoli for some carrots. The price of vegetables does not rise by 50 percent as shown by the CPI. Because of substitution, the price of vegetables rises by only 42 percent ($85 is 42 percent greater than $60). Using the 2013 basket, the price of vegetables rises by only 31 percent ($85 compared with $65). A CPI substitution bias exists.

**TABLE 2**

| Item | 2012 basket at 2012 prices | 2012 basket at 2013 prices |
|------|------|------|
| Broccoli | $30 | $30 |
| Carrots | $30 | $60 |
| Total | $60 | $90 |

**TABLE 3**

| Item | 2013 basket at 2012 prices | 2013 basket at 2013 prices |
|------|------|------|
| Broccoli | $45 | $45 |
| Carrots | $20 | $40 |
| Total | $65 | $85 |

## Solution to In the News

These three measures of the price level are based on the prices of different baskets of goods and services. The GDP price index is the broadest measure and its basket contains all the goods and services that are counted in GDP—U.S.-produced goods and services that households, firms, governments, and foreigners buy in the current year. The basket of the PCE price index contains the goods and services in GDP that households buy in the current year. The CPI basket contains the items that urban consumers buy in the most recent survey year.

## 16.3   NOMINAL AND REAL VALUES

In 2013, it cost 46 cents to mail a first-class letter. One hundred years earlier, in 1913, that same letter would have cost 2 cents to mail. Does it *really* cost you 23 times the amount that it cost your great-great-grandmother to mail a letter?

You know that it does not. You know that a dollar today buys less than what a dollar bought in 1913, so the cost of a stamp has not really increased to 23 times its 1913 level. But has it increased at all? Did it really cost you any more to mail a letter in 2013 than it cost your great-great-grandmother in 1913?

The CPI can be used to answer questions like these. In fact, that is one of the main reasons for constructing a price index. Let's see how we can compare the price of a stamp in 1913 and the price of a stamp in 2013.

### ■ Dollars and Cents at Different Dates

To compare dollar amounts at different dates, we need to know the CPI at those dates. Currently, the CPI has a base of 100 for 1982–1984. That is, the average of the CPI in 1982, 1983, and 1984 is 100. (The numbers for the three years are 96.4, 99.6, and 103.9, respectively. Calculate the average of these numbers and check that it is indeed 100.)

In 2013, the CPI was 232.1, and in 1913, it was 9.9. By using these two numbers, we can calculate the relative value of the dollar in 1913 and 2013. To do so, we divide the 2013 CPI by the 1913 CPI. That ratio is $232.1 \div 9.9 = 23.4$. That is, prices on average were 23.4 times higher in 2013 than in 1913.

We can use this ratio to convert the price of a 2-cent stamp in 1913 into its 2013 equivalent. The formula for this calculation is

$$\text{Price of stamp in 2013 dollars} = \text{Price of stamp in 1913 dollars} \times \frac{\text{CPI in 2013}}{\text{CPI in 1913}}$$

$$= 2 \text{ cents} \times \frac{232.1}{9.9} = 46.9 \text{ cents}.$$

So your great-great-grandmother paid a bit more than you pay! It really cost her almost 1 cent more to mail that first-class letter than it cost you in 2013. She paid the equivalent of 46.9 cents in 2013 money, and you paid 46 cents.

We've just converted the 1913 price of a stamp to its 2013 equivalent. We can do a similar calculation the other way around—converting the 2013 price to its 1913 equivalent. The formula for this alternative calculation is

$$\text{Price of stamp in 1913 dollars} = \text{Price of stamp in 2013 dollars} \times \frac{\text{CPI in 1913}}{\text{CPI in 2013}}$$

$$= 46 \text{ cents} \times \frac{9.9}{232.1} = 1.96 \text{ cents}.$$

The interpretation of this number is that you pay the *equivalent* of 1.96 cents in 1913 dollars. Your *real* price of a stamp is 1.96 cents expressed in 1913 dollars.

The calculations that we've just done are examples of converting a *nominal* value into a *real* value. A nominal value is one that is expressed in current dollars. A real value is one that is expressed in the dollars of a given year. We're now going to see how we convert other nominal macroeconomic variables into real variables using a similar method.

*Which postage stamp has the higher real price: the 2¢ stamp of 1913 or today's 46¢ stamp?*

## Nominal and Real Values in Macroeconomics

Macroeconomics makes a big issue of the distinction between the nominal value and the real value of a variable. Three nominal and real variables occupy a central position in macroeconomics. They are

- Nominal GDP and real GDP
- The nominal wage rate and the real wage rate
- The nominal interest rate and the real interest rate

We begin our examination of real and nominal variables in macroeconomics by reviewing what you've already learned about the distinction between nominal GDP and real GDP and interpreting that distinction in a new way.

## Nominal GDP and Real GDP

When we calculated the 1913 value of a 46-cent 2013 postage stamp, we multiplied the 2013 price by the ratio of the CPI in 1913 to the CPI in 2013. By this calculation, we found the "real" value of a 2013 stamp in 1913 dollars.

But when we calculated the real GDP of 2013 in 2009 dollars in Chapter 14 (pp. 418–419), we didn't multiply nominal GDP in 2013 by the ratio of a price index in the two years. Instead, we expressed the values of the goods and services produced in 2013 in terms of the prices that prevailed in 2009. We calculated real GDP directly.

But we can *interpret* real GDP in 2013 as nominal GDP in 2013 multiplied by the ratio of the GDP price index in 2009 to the GDP price index in 2013. The GDP price

# EYE on the U.S. ECONOMY
## Deflating the GDP Balloon

Nominal GDP increased every year between 1980 and 2013 except for 2009. Part of the increase reflects increased production, and part of it reflects rising prices.

You can think of GDP as a balloon that is blown up by growing production and rising prices. In the figure, the GDP price index or *GDP deflator* lets the inflation air—the contribution of rising prices—out of the nominal GDP balloon so that we can see what has happened to real GDP.

The small red balloon for 1980 shows real GDP in that year. The green balloon shows nominal GDP in 2013. The red balloon for 2013 shows real GDP for that year.

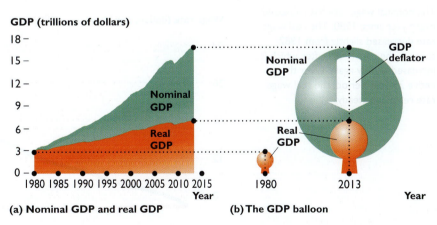

(a) Nominal GDP and real GDP

(b) The GDP balloon

SOURCE OF DATA: Bureau of Economic Analysis.

To see real GDP in 2013, we use the GDP price index to deflate nominal GDP. With the inflation air removed, we can see by how much real GDP grew from 1980 to 2013.

index in 2009 (the base year) is defined to be 100, so we can interpret real GDP in any year as nominal GDP divided by the GDP price index in that year multiplied by 100. We don't calculate real GDP this way, but we can interpret it this way.

The GDP price index, or the CPI, or some other price index might be used to convert a nominal variable to a real variable.

### ■ Nominal Wage Rate and Real Wage Rate

The price of labor services is the wage rate—the income that an hour of labor earns. In macroeconomics, we are interested in economy-wide performance, so we focus on the *average* hourly wage rate. The **nominal wage rate** is the average hourly wage rate measured in *current* dollars. The **real wage rate** is the average hourly wage rate measured in the dollars of a given reference base year.

To calculate the real wage rate relevant to a consumer, we divide the nominal wage rate by the CPI and multiply by 100. That is,

$$\text{Real wage rate in 2013} = \frac{\text{Nominal wage rate in 2013}}{\text{CPI in 2013}} \times 100.$$

In 2013, the nominal wage rate (average hourly wage rate) of production workers was \$20.10 and the CPI was 232.1, so

$$\text{Real wage rate in 2013} = \frac{\$20.10}{232.1} \times 100 = \$8.66.$$

Because we measure the real wage rate in constant base period dollars, a change in the real wage rate measures the change in the quantity of goods and

**Nominal wage rate**
The average hourly wage rate measured in current dollars.

**Real wage rate**
The average hourly wage rate measured in the dollars of a given reference base year.

---

### ■ FIGURE 16.4

Nominal and Real Wage Rates: 1980–2013

The nominal wage rate has increased every year since 1980. The real wage rate decreased slightly from 1982 through the mid-1990s, after which it increased slightly again. Over the entire 33-year period, the real wage rate remained steady.

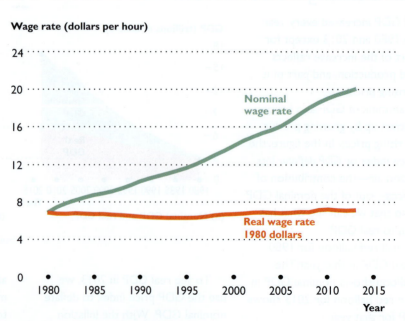

SOURCE OF DATA: Bureau of Labor Statistics.

services that an hour's work can buy. In contrast, a change in the nominal wage rate measures a combination of a change in the quantity of goods and services that an hour's work can buy and a change in the price level. So the real wage rate removes the effects of inflation from the changes in the nominal wage rate.

The real wage rate is a significant economic variable because it measures the real reward for labor, which is a major determinant of the standard of living. The real wage rate is also significant because it measures the real cost of labor services, which influences the quantity of labor that firms are willing to hire.

Figure 16.4 shows what has happened to the nominal wage rate and the real wage rate in the United States between 1980 and 2013. The nominal wage rate is the average hourly earnings of production workers. This measure is just one of several different measures of average hourly earnings that we might have used.

The nominal wage rate increased from $6.85 an hour in 1980 to $20.10 an hour in 2013, but the real wage rate barely changed. In 1980 dollars, the real wage rate in 2013 was only $7.13 an hour.

The real wage rate barely changed as the nominal wage rate increased because the nominal wage rate grew at a rate almost equal to the inflation rate. When the effects of inflation are removed from the nominal wage rate, we can see what is happening to the buying power of the average wage rate.

You can also see that the real wage rate has fluctuated a little. It decreased slightly until the mid-1990s, after which it increased slightly.

# EYE on the PAST
## The Nominal and Real Wage Rates of Presidents of the United States

Who earned more, Barack Obama in 2013, or George Washington in 1788? George Washington's pay was $25,000 (on the green line) but in 2013 dollars it was $619,000 (on the red line). Barack Obama was paid $400,000 in 2013.

But presidential accommodations are more comfortable today, and presidential travel arrangements are a breeze compared to earlier times. So adding in the perks of the job, Barack Obama doesn't get such a raw deal.

SOURCE OF DATA:
Robert Sahr, Oregon State University, http://oregonstate.edu/cla/polisci/sahr/sahr

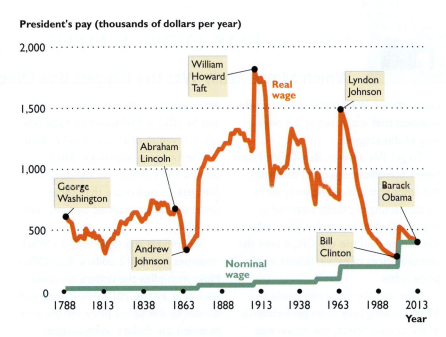

## ■ Nominal Interest Rate and Real Interest Rate

**Nominal interest rate**

The dollar amount of interest expressed as a percentage of the amount loaned.

**Real interest rate**

The goods and services forgone in interest expressed as a percentage of the amount loaned and calculated as the nominal interest rate minus the inflation rate.

You've just seen that we can calculate real values from nominal values by deflating them using the CPI. And you've seen that to make this calculation, we *divide* the nominal value by a price index. Converting a nominal interest rate to a real interest rate is a bit different. To see why, we'll start with their definitions.

A **nominal interest rate** is the dollar amount of interest expressed as a percentage of the amount loaned. For example, suppose that you have $1,000 in a bank deposit—a loan by you to a bank—on which you receive interest of $50 a year. The nominal interest rate is $50 as a percentage of $1,000, which is 5 percent a year.

A **real interest rate** is the goods and services forgone in interest expressed as a percentage of the amount loaned. Continuing with the above example, at the end of one year your bank deposit has increased to $1,050—the original $1,000 plus the $50 interest. Suppose that prices have increased by 3 percent, so now you need $1,030 to buy what $1,000 would have bought a year earlier. How much interest have you *really* received? The answer is $20, or a real interest rate of 2 percent a year.

To convert a nominal interest rate to a real interest rate, we *subtract* the *inflation rate*. That is,

$$\text{Real interest rate} = \text{Nominal interest rate} - \text{Inflation rate}.$$

Plug your numbers into this formula. Your nominal interest rate is 5 percent a year, and the inflation rate is 3 percent a year. Your real interest rate is 5 percent minus 3 percent, which equals 2 percent a year.

Figure 16.5 shows the nominal and the real interest rates in the United States between 1972 and 2012. When the inflation rate is high, the gap between the real interest rate and nominal interest rate is large. Sometimes, the real interest rate is negative (as it was in the mid-1970s) and the lender pays the borrower!

# EYE on BOX OFFICE HITS

## Which Movie *Really* Was the Biggest Box Office Hit?

*Gone with the Wind* is the answer to the question that we posed at the beginning of this chapter.

To get this answer, Box-Office Mojo (www.boxofficemojo.com) calculates the amount that a movie *really* earns by converting the dollars earned to their equivalent in current year dollars. But rather than use the CPI, it uses the average prices of movie tickets as its price index.

*Gone with the Wind* was made in 1939. Looking only at its performance in the United States, the movie was rereleased in nine subsequent years and by 2012 it had earned a total box office revenue of almost $200 million.

*The Avengers*, released in 2012, earned $623 million. So the 2012 *The Avengers* earned more than three times the dollars earned by *Gone with the Wind*.

To convert the *Gone with the Wind* revenues into 2012 dollars, Box-Office Mojo multiplies the dollars received each year by the 2012 ticket price and divides by the ticket price for the year in which the dollars were earned.

Valuing the tickets for *Gone with the Wind* at 2012 movie-ticket prices, it has earned $1,604 million, about 2.6 times *The Avengers* revenue.

Because Box-Office Mojo uses average ticket prices, the real variable that it compares is the number of tickets sold. The average ticket price in 2012 was $7.96, which means 202 million have seen *Gone with the Wind* and 78 million have seen *The Avengers*. *Gone with the Wind* was the biggest hit because it was seen by the greatest number of people.

**■ FIGURE 16.5**

Nominal and Real Interest Rates: 1973–2013

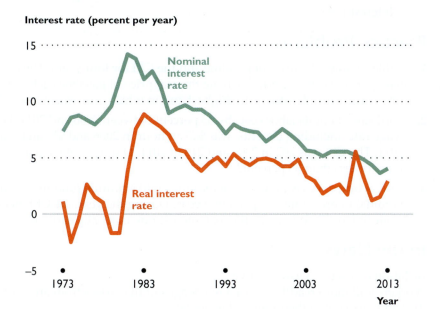

Interest rate (percent per year)

Nominal interest rate

Real interest rate

The interest rate shown here is that paid by the safest large corporations on long-term bonds (known as Moody's AAA). The real interest rate equals the nominal interest rate minus the inflation rate. The vertical gap between the nominal interest rate and the real interest rate is the inflation rate. The real interest rate is usually positive, but during the 1970s, it became negative.

Sources of data: Federal Reserve and Bureau of Labor Statistics

# EYE on YOUR LIFE
## A Student's CPI

The CPI measures the percentage change in the average prices paid for the basket of goods and services bought by a typical urban household.

A student is not a typical household. How have the prices of a student's basket of goods and services changed? The answer is by a lot more than those of an average household.

Suppose that a student spends 25 percent of her income on rent, 25 percent on tuition, 25 percent on books and study supplies, 10 percent on food, 10 percent on transportation, and 5 percent on clothing.

We can use these weights and the data collected by the BLS on individual

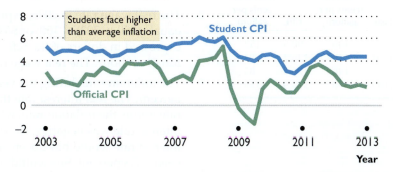

Inflation rate (percent per year)

Students face higher than average inflation

Student CPI

Official CPI

Source of data: Bureau of Labor Statistics.

price categories to find the student's CPI and the inflation rate that it implies.

The graph shows this student's inflation rate compared to that of the

official CPI. Between 2003 and 2013, a student's CPI rose 32 percent above the official CPI. Rent, textbooks, and tuition are the main items whose prices rose faster than average.

# CHECKPOINT 16.3

**Adjust money values for inflation and calculate real wage rates and real interest rates.**

## Practice Problems

1. Table 1 shows the price of gasoline and the CPI for four years. The reference base period is 1982–1984. Calculate the real price of gasoline each year. In which year was this real price highest and in which year was it lowest?

2. Ford says it cut its labor costs by 35 percent between 2006 and 2011. Ford's wage rate, including benefits, was $80 an hour in 2006 and $58 an hour in 2011. The CPI was 202 in 2006 and 218 in 2011. Did the real wage rate fall by more or less than 35 percent?

3. Sally worked all year and put her savings into a mutual fund that paid a nominal interest rate of 7 percent a year. During the year, the CPI increased from 165 to 177. What was the real interest rate that Sally earned?

**TABLE 1**

| Year | Price of gasoline (cents per gallon) | CPI |
|------|--------------------------------------|-------|
| 1981 | 138 | 90.9 |
| 1991 | 114 | 136.2 |
| 2001 | 146 | 176.6 |
| 2011 | 358 | 224.9 |

## In the News

**Inflation can act as a safety valve**

Workers will more readily accept a real wage cut that arises from an increase in the CPI than a cut in their nominal wage rate.

Source: FT.com, May 28, 2009

Explain why inflation influences a worker's real wage rate. Why might this observation be true?

## Solutions to Practice Problems

1. To calculate the real price, divide the nominal price by the CPI and multiply by 100. Table 2 shows the calculations. The real price was highest in 2011, when it was 159 cents (1982–1984 cents) per gallon. The real price was lowest in 2001, when it was 83 cents (1982–1984 cents) per gallon.

2. The real wage rate in 2006, expressed in dollars of the reference base year, equals ($80 ÷ 202) × 100, or $39.60 an hour. The real wage rate in 2011, expressed in dollars of the reference base year, equals ($58 ÷ 218) × 100, or $26.61 an hour. The real wage rate of these workers fell by 32.8 percent.

3. The inflation rate during the year equals (177 − 165) ÷ 165 × 100 = 7.3 percent. The real interest rate that Sally earned equals the nominal interest rate minus the inflation rate, which is 7.0 − 7.3 = −0.3 percent. Sally's real interest rate was negative. (If Sally had kept her savings in cash, her nominal interest rate would have been zero, and her real interest rate would have been −7.3 percent. She would have been worse off.)

**TABLE 2**

| Year | Price of gasoline (cents per gallon) | CPI | Price of gasoline (1982–1984 cents per gallon) |
|------|--------------------------------------|-------|------------------------------------------------|
| 1981 | 136 | 90.9 | 152 |
| 1991 | 114 | 136.2 | 84 |
| 2001 | 146 | 176.6 | 83 |
| 2011 | 358 | 224.9 | 159 |

## Solution to In the News

The real wage rate equals the (Nominal wage rate ÷ CPI) × 100. Two reasons why a real wage cut from inflation is more acceptable are: A rising CPI *gradually* lowers the real wage rate, while a cut in the nominal wage rate *suddenly* lowers the real wage rate. Inflation lowers everyone's real wage rate but a cut in one worker's nominal wage rate lowers only that worker's real wage rate.

# CHAPTER SUMMARY

## Key Points

**1. Explain what the Consumer Price Index (CPI) is and how it is calculated.**

- The Consumer Price Index (CPI) is a measure of the average of the prices of the goods and services that an average urban household buys.
- The CPI is calculated by dividing the cost of the CPI market basket in the current period by its cost in the base period and then multiplying by 100.

**2. Explain the limitations of the CPI and describe other measures of the price level.**

- The CPI does not include all the items that contribute to the cost of living.
- The CPI cannot provide an accurate measure of price changes because of new goods, quality improvements, and substitutions that consumers make when relative prices change.
- Other measures of the price level include the GDP price index, the PCE price index, and the PCE price index excluding food and energy.
- Both the GDP price index and the PCE price index use current information on quantities and to some degree overcome the sources of bias in the CPI.
- The PCE price index excluding food and energy is used to calculate the core inflation rate, which shows the inflation trend.

**3. Adjust money values for inflation and calculate real wage rates and real interest rates.**

- To adjust a money value (also called a nominal value) for inflation, we express the value in terms of the dollars of a given year.
- To convert a dollar value of year $B$ to the dollars of year $A$, multiply the value in year $B$ by the price level in year $A$ and divide by the price level in year $B$.
- The real wage rate equals the nominal wage rate divided by the CPI and multiplied by 100.
- The real interest rate equals the nominal interest rate minus the inflation rate.

## Key Terms

## CHAPTER CHECKPOINT

### Study Plan Problems and Applications

**TABLE 1 DATA FOR WEEK 1**

| Item | Quantity | Price (per unit) |
|------|----------|------------------|
| Coffee | 11 cups | $3.25 |
| DVDs | 1 | $25.00 |
| Gasoline | 15 gallons | $2.50 |

**TABLE 2 DATA FOR WEEK 2**

| Item | Quantity | Price (per unit) |
|------|----------|------------------|
| Coffee | 11 cups | $3.25 |
| DVDs | 3 | $12.50 |
| Gasoline | 5 gallons | $3.00 |
| Concert | 1 ticket | $95.00 |

**TABLE 3**

| Item | Price in June | Price in July |
|------|------|------|
| | (dollars per unit) | |
| Steak | 4.11 | 4.01 |
| Bread | 3.25 | 3.12 |
| Bacon | 3.62 | 3.64 |
| Milk | 2.62 | 2.62 |
| Tomatoes | 1.60 | 1.62 |
| Apples | 1.18 | 1.19 |
| Bananas | 0.62 | 0.66 |
| Chicken | 1.28 | 1.26 |
| Lettuce | 1.64 | 1.68 |

1. In Canada, the reference base period for the CPI is 2002. By 2012, prices had risen by 21.6 percent since the base period. The inflation rate in Canada in 2013 was 1.1 percent. Calculate the CPI in Canada in 2013.

2. In Brazil, the reference base period for the CPI is 2000. By 2005, prices had risen by 51 percent since the base period. The inflation rate in Brazil in 2006 was 10 percent, and in 2007, the inflation rate was 9 percent. Calculate the CPI in Brazil in 2006 and 2007. Brazil's CPI in 2008 was 173. Did Brazil's inflation rate increase or decrease in 2008?

3. Tables 1 and 2 show the quantities of the goods that Suzie bought and the prices she paid during two consecutive weeks. Suzie's CPI market basket contains the goods she bought in Week 1. Calculate the cost of Suzie's CPI market basket in Week 1 and in Week 2. What percentage of the CPI market basket is gasoline? Calculate the value of Suzie's CPI in Week 2 and her inflation rate in Week 2.

Use the following information to work Problems **4** and **5**.

The GDP price index in the United States in 2000 was about 90, and real GDP in 2000 was $11 trillion (2005 dollars). The GDP price index in 2010 was about 111, and real GDP in 2010 was $13.1 trillion (2005 dollars).

4. Calculate nominal GDP in 2000 and in 2010 and the percentage increase in nominal GDP between 2000 and 2010.

5. What was the percentage increase in production between 2000 and 2010, and by what percentage did the cost of living rise between 2000 and 2010?

6. Table 3 shows the prices that Terry paid for some of his expenditures in June and July 2013. Explain and discuss why these prices might have led to commodity substitution or outlet substitution.

7. In 2013, Annie, an 80-year-old, is telling her granddaughter Mary about the good old days. Annie says that in 1933, you could buy a nice house for $15,000 and a jacket for $5. Mary says that in 2013 such a house costs $220,000 and such a jacket costs $70. The CPI in 1933 was 16.7 and in 2013 it was 218.1. Which house and which jacket have the lower prices?

Use the following information to work Problems **8** and **9**.

**CPI: Inflation rate picks up in August**
The CPI rose 3.8% in August compared to a year earlier. Food prices rose 4.6% and clothing prices were up 4.2%, while new car prices rose 3.8% and medical care was up 3.2%.

Source: CNN Money, September 15, 2011

8. What percentage change in the CPI during the year to August 2011 is accounted for by the changes in the prices of food, clothing, and medical care?

9. Given the changes in the prices of food, clothing, and medical care, by what percentage did the prices of the other items in the CPI basket change?

 10. Read *Eye on Box Office Hits* on p. 476 and using BLS data for the CPI in 1982 and 1997, determine which movie had the greater *real* box office revenues, *E.T.: The Extra-Terrestrial*, which earned $435 million in 1982 or *Titanic*, which earned $601 million in 1997.

## Instructor Assignable Problems and Applications

**1.** Compare the method used by Box-Office Mojo to calculate real box-office receipts with the method used on p. 472 to calculate the real price of a postage stamp. Compare and contrast the real variables that each method calculates.

**2.** Pete is a student who spends 10 percent of his expenditure on books and supplies, 30 percent on tuition, 30 percent on rent, 10 percent on food and drink, 10 percent on transportation, and the rest on clothing. The price index for each item was 100 in 2000. Table 1 shows the prices in 2011. What is Pete's CPI in 2011? (Hint: The contribution of each item to the CPI is its price weighted by its share of total expenditure.) Did Pete experience a higher or lower inflation rate between 2000 and 2011 than the student whose CPI is shown on p. 467?

**TABLE 1**

| Item | Price in 2011 |
| --- | --- |
| Books and supplies | 172.6 |
| Tuition | 169.0 |
| Rent | 159.0 |
| Food and drink | 129.8 |
| Transportation | 115.4 |
| Clothing | 92.9 |

**3.** The people on Coral Island buy only juice and cloth. The CPI market basket contains the quantities bought in 2010. The average household spent $60 on juice and $30 on cloth in 2010 when the price of juice was $2 a bottle and the price of cloth was $5 a yard. In the current year, 2011, juice is $4 a bottle and cloth is $6 a yard. Calculate the CPI and the inflation rate in 2011.

**TABLE 2 DATA FOR WEEK 1**

| Item | Quantity | Price (per unit) |
| --- | --- | --- |
| Coffee | 5 cups | $3.00 |
| iTunes songs | 5 | $1.00 |
| Gasoline | 10 gallons | $2.00 |

**4.** Tables 2 and 3 show the quantities of the goods that Harry bought and the prices he paid during two consecutive weeks. Harry's CPI market basket contains the goods he bought in Week 1. Calculate Harry's CPI in Week 2. What was his inflation rate in Week 2?

Use the following information to work Problems **5** and **6**.

The base year is 2009. Real GDP in 2009 was $10 trillion (2009 dollars). The GDP price index in 2009 was 112, and real GDP in 2013 was $11 trillion (2009 dollars).

**TABLE 3 DATA FOR WEEK 2**

| Item | Quantity | Price (per unit) |
| --- | --- | --- |
| Coffee | 4 cups | $3.25 |
| iTunes songs | 10 | $1.00 |
| Gasoline | 10 gallons | $3.00 |

**5.** Calculate nominal GDP in 2009 and in 2013 and the percentage increase in nominal GDP from 2009 to 2013.

**6.** What was the percentage increase in production from 2009 to 2013, and by what percentage did the cost of living rise from 2009 to 2013?

**7.** In 1988, the average wage rate was $9.45 an hour and in 2008 the average wage rate was $18.00 an hour. The CPI in 1988 was 118.3 and in 2008 it was 215.3. Which real wage rate is higher?

**8.** Imagine that you are given $1,000 to spend and told that you must spend it all buying items from a Sears catalog. But you do have a choice of catalog. You may select from the 1903 catalog or from Sears.com today. You will pay the prices quoted in the catalog that you choose.

Which catalog will you choose and why? Refer to any biases in the CPI that might be relevant to your choice.

Use the following information to work Problems **9** and **10**.

**Money market funds are yielding almost nothing**
Last month, the interest rate on a money market fund averaged 0.08% a year and on 5-year CDs it was 2.6% a year. The inflation rate was 0.1% a year.

Source: *USA Today*, August 12, 2009

**9.** Calculate the real interest rate on each of these financial assets.

**10.** To maintain these real interest rates in the coming months, how will these nominal rates change if the inflation rate increases to 0.2 percent a year?

# Critical Thinking Discussion Questions

1. **China's CPI grew slower than expected**

   China's CPI inflation in December fell to an annual rate of 2.5 percent, down from 3 percent in November. This can be partially explained by lower food price inflation, which fell from an annual rate of 5.9 in November to 4.1 percent in December.

   Source: *Shanghai Daily*, January 9, 2014

   Think about inflation in China:

   What happened to the prices of non-food items between November and December?

   How does China's core inflation rate compare to its CPI inflation rate?

   Given the fall in food prices, do you anticipate any bias in China's CPI?

   Did China's CPI increase or decrease between November and December?

2. **Negative bank's deposit rate**

   European banks are currently receiving an interest rate of zero percent on their deposits at the European Central Bank (ECB). The ECB is considering changing this to a negative deposit rate, given Europe's weak economic growth and low inflation.

   Source: *The Wall Street Journal*, 22 November 2013

   Think about the deposit rate paid by the European Central Bank:

   With a nominal interest rate of zero percent, describe the real interest rate received on bank deposits at the ECB.

   Is it possible for banks to earn a positive real interest rate if the nominal interest rate is negative?

3. **Inflation basket drops DVD recorders in latest revision**

   Changes in households' use of digital technology have resulted in several changes to the basket of goods and services used to measure inflation. Video streaming services like Netflix are in, while DVD recorders are out. The Office for National Statistics (ONS), reports that this year 14 new items are in, while nine are out.

   Source: BBC, 13 March 2014

   Think about the CPI basket:

   Why are goods in the CPI basket being updated?

   Give examples of some goods that may have been added to and some goods that may have been deleted from the CPI basket in the last decade.

   What type of bias results if the CPI is not updated?

   If the CPI basket is not updated, would the inflation rate be higher or lower?

   Would the GDP deflator be a better measure of the inflation rate?

## Why are some nations rich and others poor?

# Potential GDP and Economic Growth

**17**

CHAPTER CHECKLIST

**When you have completed your study of this chapter, you will be able to**

**1** Explain what determines potential GDP.

**2** Define and calculate the economic growth rate, and explain the implications of sustained growth.

**3** Explain the sources of labor productivity growth.

**4** Describe policies that speed economic growth.

# MACROECONOMIC APPROACHES AND PATHWAYS

In the three previous chapters, you learned how economists define and measure real GDP, employment and unemployment, the price level, and the inflation rate—the key variables that *describe* macroeconomic performance. Your task in this chapter and those that follow is to learn the *macroeconomic theory* that *explains* macroeconomic performance and provides the basis for *policies* that might improve it.

The macroeconomic theory that we present is today's consensus view on how the economy works. But it isn't the view of all macroeconomists. Today's consensus is a merger of three earlier schools of thought that have sharply contrasting views about the causes of recessions and the best policies for dealing with them. Some economists continue to identify with these schools of thought, and the severity of the 2008–2009 recession and slow recovery intensified debate and gave economists of all shades of opinion a platform from which to present their views.

We begin with an overview of the three schools of thought from which today's consensus has emerged.

## ■ The Three Main Schools of Thought

The three main schools of macroeconomic thought are

- Classical macroeconomics
- Keynesian macroeconomics
- Monetarist macroeconomics

### Classical Macroeconomics

**Classical macroeconomics**
The view that the market economy works well, that aggregate fluctuations are a natural consequence of an expanding economy, and that government intervention cannot improve the efficiency of the market economy.

According to **classical macroeconomics**, markets work well and deliver the best available macroeconomic performance. Aggregate fluctuations are a natural consequence of an expanding economy with rising living standards, and government intervention can only hinder the ability of the market to allocate resources efficiently. The first classical macroeconomists included Adam Smith, David Ricardo, and John Stuart Mill, all of whom worked in the 18th and 19th centuries. Modern day classical economists include the 2004 Nobel Laureates Edward C. Prescott of the University of Arizona and Finn E. Kydland of Carnegie-Mellon University and the University of California at Santa Barbara.

Classical macroeconomics fell into disrepute during the Great Depression of the 1930s, a time when many people believed that *capitalism*, the political system of private ownership, free markets, and democratic political institutions, could not survive and began to advocate *socialism*, a political system based on state ownership of capital and central economic planning.

Classical macroeconomics predicted that the Great Depression would eventually end but offered no method for ending it more quickly.

### Keynesian Macroeconomics

**Keynesian macroeconomics**
The view that the market economy is inherently unstable and needs active government intervention to achieve full employment and sustained economic growth.

According to **Keynesian macroeconomics**, the market economy is inherently unstable and requires active government intervention to achieve full employment and sustained economic growth. One person, John Maynard Keynes, and his book *The General Theory of Employment, Interest, and Money*, published in 1936, began this school of thought. Keynes' theory was that depression and high unemployment occur when households don't spend enough on consumption goods and services and businesses don't spend enough investing in new capital. That is, too little *private* spending is the cause of depression (and recession). To counter the problem of too little private spending, *government* spending must rise.

This Keynesian view picked up many followers and by the 1950s it was the mainstream, but it lost popularity during the inflationary 1970s when it seemed ever more remote from the problems of that decade. The global recession of 2008–2009 and the fear of another great depression revived interest in Keynesian ideas and brought a new wave of attacks on classical macroeconomics with Nobel Laureate Paul Krugman leading the charge in the columns of the *New York Times*.

## Monetarist Macroeconomics

According to **monetarist macroeconomics**, the *classical* view of the world is broadly correct but in addition to fluctuations that arise from the normal functioning of an expanding economy, fluctuations in the quantity of money generate the business cycle. A slowdown in the growth rate of money brings recession and a large decrease in the quantity of money brought the Great Depression.

Milton Friedman, intellectual leader of the Chicago School of economists during the 1960s and 1970s, was the most prominent monetarist. The view that monetary contractions are the sole source of recessions and depressions is held by few economists today. But the view that the quantity of money plays a role in economic fluctuations is accepted by all economists and is part of today's consensus.

**Monetarist macroeconomics**
The view that the market economy works well, that aggregate fluctuations are a natural consequence of an expanding economy, but that fluctuations in the quantity of money generate the business cycle.

## ■ Today's Consensus

Each of the earlier schools provides insights and ingredients that survive in today's consensus. *Classical* macroeconomics provides the story of the economy at or close to full employment. But the classical approach doesn't explain how the economy performs in the face of a major slump in spending.

*Keynesian* macroeconomics takes up the story in a recession or depression. When spending is cut and the demand for most goods and services and the demand for labor all decrease, prices and wage rates don't fall but the quantity of goods and services sold and the quantity of labor employed do fall and the economy goes into recession. In a recession, an increase in spending by governments, or a tax cut that leaves people with more of their earnings to spend, can help to restore full employment.

*Monetarist* macroeconomics elaborates the Keynesian story by emphasizing that a contraction in the quantity of money brings higher interest rates and borrowing costs, which are a major source of cuts in spending that bring recession. Increasing the quantity of money and lowering the interest rate in a recession can help to restore full employment. And keeping the quantity of money growing steadily in line with the expansion of the economy's production possibilities can help to keep inflation in check and can also help to moderate the severity of a recession.

Another component of today's consensus is the view that the *long-term* problem of economic growth is more important than the *short-term* problem of recessions. Take a look at *Eye on the U.S. Economy,* on p. 486, and you will see why. Even a small slowdown in economic growth brings a huge cost in terms of a permanently lower level of income per person. This cost is much larger than that arising from the income lost during recessions. But the costs of recessions are serious because they are concentrated on those who are unemployed.

### ■ The Road Ahead

This book bases your tour of macroeconomics on the new consensus. We begin in this chapter by explaining what determines potential GDP and the pace at which it grows. We then study money and explain what brings inflation. Finally, we explain how real and monetary forces interact to bring about the business cycle. We also explain the policy tools available to governments and central banks to improve macroeconomic performance.

# EYE on the U.S. ECONOMY
## The Lucas Wedge and the Okun Gap

During the 1960s, U.S. real GDP per person grew at a rate of 2.8 percent a year. The black line in part (a) shows the path that would have been followed if this growth rate had been maintained. After 1970, growth slowed to 1.9 percent per year and the blue line shows the path that real GDP per person followed. University of Chicago economist Robert E. Lucas, Jr. pointed out the large output loss that resulted from this growth slowdown. Part (a) shows this loss as the *Lucas wedge*, which is equivalent to a staggering $406,000 per person or 8.2 years' income.

Real GDP fluctuates around potential GDP and when the output gap is negative, output is lost. Brookings Institution economist Arthur B. Okun drew attention to this loss. Part (b) shows this loss as the *Okun gap*, which is equivalent to $27,000 per person or about 7 months' income.

Smoothing the business cycle and eliminating the Okun gap has a big payoff. But finding ways of restoring real GDP growth to its 1960s rate has a vastly bigger payoff.

SOURCES OF DATA: Bureau of Economic Analysis and the Congressional Budget Office.

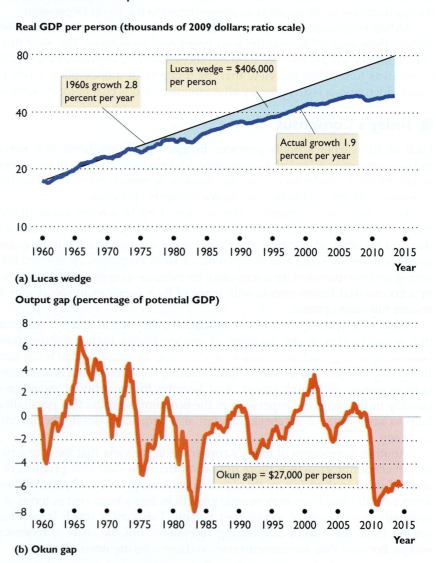

(a) Lucas wedge

(b) Okun gap

## 17.1 POTENTIAL GDP

**Potential GDP** is the value of real GDP when all the economy's factors of production—labor, capital, land, and entrepreneurial ability—are fully employed. It is vital to understand the forces that determine potential GDP for three reasons. First, when the economy is *at* full employment, real GDP equals potential GDP; so actual real GDP is determined by the same factors that determine potential GDP. Second, real GDP can exceed potential GDP only temporarily as it approaches and then recedes from a business cycle peak. So potential GDP is the *sustainable* upper limit of production. Third, real GDP fluctuates around potential GDP, which means that on the average over the business cycle, real GDP equals potential GDP.

We produce the goods and services that make up real GDP by using the *factors of production:* labor and human capital, physical capital, land (and natural resources), and entrepreneurship. At any given time, the quantities of capital, land, and entrepreneurship and the state of technology are fixed. But the quantity of labor is not fixed. It depends on the choices that people make about the allocation of time between work and leisure. So with fixed quantities of capital, land, and entrepreneurship and fixed technology, real GDP depends on the quantity of labor employed. To describe this relationship between real GDP and the quantity of labor employed, we use a relationship that is similar to the production possibilities frontier, which is called the production function.

**Potential GDP**

The value of real GDP when all the economy's factors of production—labor, capital, land, and entrepreneurial ability—are fully employed.

# EYE on the GLOBAL ECONOMY
## Potential GDP in the United States and European Union

In 2011, real GDP in the United States was $60 per hour worked. In 14 major European economies, real GDP averaged only $48 per hour worked—a gap of 25 percent. (Both numbers are measured in 2011 U.S. dollars.) Part (a) of the figure shows this difference.

Not only do Americans produce more per hour than Europeans, they work longer hours too. In 2011, Americans worked an average of 33 hours per week while Europeans worked only an average of 31 hours per week—a difference of more than 5 percent. Part (b) of the figure shows this difference.

Europeans achieve their shorter work hours by taking longer vacations

and having more sick days than Americans.

The combination of greater production per hour and longer work hours translates into a substantially larger real GDP per worker in the United States than in Europe.

In 2011, real GDP per worker in the United States was $103,000 while in Europe it was only $74,000—a gap of almost 40 percent.

This chapter enables you to understand the sources of these differences in wage rates, work hours, and production.

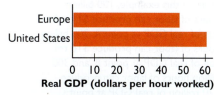

**(a) Real GDP per hour worked**

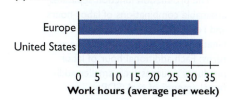

**(b) Average weekly hours**

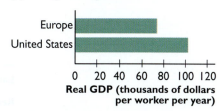

**(c) Real GDP per worker**

SOURCE OF DATA: Organization for Economic Cooperation and Development

## The Production Function

**Production function**
A relationship that shows the maximum quantity of real GDP that can be produced as the quantity of labor employed changes and all other influences on production remain the same.

The **production function** is a relationship that shows the maximum quantity of real GDP that can be produced as the quantity of labor employed changes and all other influences on production remain the same. Figure 17.1 shows a production function, which is the curve labeled *PF*.

In Figure 17.1, 100 billion labor hours can produce a real GDP of $11 trillion (at point *A*); 200 billion hours can produce a real GDP of $16 trillion (at point *B*); and 300 billion hours can produce a real GDP of $20 trillion (at point *C*).

The production function shares a feature of the *production possibilities frontier* that you studied in Chapter 3 (p. 96). Like the *PPF*, the production function is a boundary between the attainable and the unattainable. It is possible to produce at any point along the production function and beneath it in the shaded area. But it is not possible to produce at points above the production function. Those points are unattainable.

**Diminishing returns**
The tendency for each additional hour of labor employed to produce a successively smaller additional amount of real GDP.

The production function displays **diminishing returns**—each additional hour of labor employed produces a successively smaller additional amount of real GDP. The first 100 billion hours of labor produces $11 trillion of real GDP. The second 100 billion hours of labor increases real GDP from $11 trillion to $16 trillion, so the

## ■ FIGURE 17.1

### The Production Function

The production function shows the maximum quantity of real GDP that can be produced as the quantity of labor employed changes and all other influences on production remain the same. In this example, 100 billion hours of labor can produce $11 trillion of real GDP at point *A*, 200 billion hours of labor can produce $16 trillion of real GDP at point *B*, and 300 billion hours of labor can produce $20 trillion of real GDP at point *C*.

The production function separates attainable combinations of labor hours and real GDP from unattainable combinations and displays diminishing returns: Each additional hour of labor produces a successively smaller additional amount of real GDP.

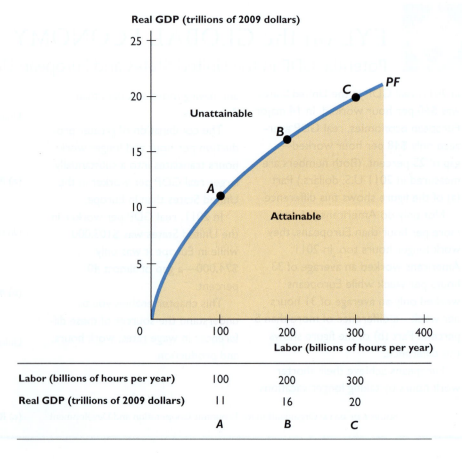

| Labor (billions of hours per year) | 100 | 200 | 300 |
|---|---|---|---|
| Real GDP (trillions of 2009 dollars) | 11 | 16 | 20 |
| | *A* | *B* | *C* |

second 100 billion hours produces only an additional $5 trillion of real GDP. The third 100 billion hours of labor increases real GDP from $16 trillion to $20 trillion, so the third 100 billion hours produces only an additional $4 trillion of real GDP.

Diminishing returns arise because the quantity of capital (and other factors of production) is fixed. As more labor is hired, the additional output produced decreases because the extra workers have less capital with which to work. For example, a forest service has three chain saws and an axe and hires three workers to clear roads and trails of fallen trees and debris during the spring thaw. Hiring a fourth worker will contribute less to the amount cleared than the amount that the third worker added, and hiring a fifth worker will add even less.

Because real GDP depends on the quantity of labor employed, potential GDP depends on the production function and the quantity of labor employed. To find potential GDP, we must understand what determines the quantity of labor employed.

## ■ The Labor Market

You've already studied the tool that we use to determine the quantity of labor employed: demand and supply. In macroeconomics, we apply the concepts of demand, supply, and market equilibrium to the economy-wide labor market.

The quantity of labor employed depends on firms' decisions about how much labor to hire (the demand for labor). It also depends on households' decisions about how to allocate time between employment and other activities (the supply of labor). And it depends on how the labor market coordinates the decisions of firms and households (labor market equilibrium). So we will study

- The demand for labor
- The supply of labor
- Labor market equilibrium

### The Demand for Labor

The **quantity of labor demanded** is the total labor hours that all the firms in the economy plan to hire during a given time period at a given real wage rate. The **demand for labor** is the relationship between the quantity of labor demanded and the real wage rate when all other influences on firms' hiring plans remain the same. The lower the real wage rate, the greater is the quantity of labor demanded.

*The Demand for Labor in a Soda Factory* You might understand the aggregate demand for labor better by thinking about a single firm rather than the economy as a whole. Suppose that the money wage rate is $15 an hour and that the price of a bottle of soda is $1.50. For the soda factory, the real wage rate is a number of bottles of soda. To find the soda factory's real wage rate, divide the money wage rate by the price of its output—$15 an hour ÷ $1.50 a bottle. The real wage rate is 10 bottles of soda an hour. It costs the soda factory 10 bottles of soda to hire an hour of labor. As long as the soda factory can hire labor that produces more than 10 additional bottles of soda an hour, it is profitable to hire more labor. Only when the extra output produced by an extra hour of labor falls to 10 bottles an hour has the factory reached the profit-maximizing quantity of labor.

### The Supply of Labor

The **quantity of labor supplied** is the number of labor hours that all the households in the economy plan to work during a given time period at a given real wage rate.

**Quantity of labor demanded**
The total labor hours that all the firms in the economy plan to hire during a given time period at a given real wage rate.

**Demand for labor**
The relationship between the quantity of labor demanded and the real wage rate when all other influences on firms' hiring plans remain the same.

**Quantity of labor supplied**
The number of labor hours that all the households in the economy plan to work during a given time period at a given real wage rate.

**Supply of labor**
The relationship between the quantity of labor supplied and the real wage rate when all other influences on work plans remain the same.

The **supply of labor** is the relationship between the quantity of labor supplied and the real wage rate when all other influences on work plans remain the same.

The real wage rate influences the quantity of labor supplied because what matters to people is not the number of dollars they earn but what those dollars will buy. The quantity of labor supplied increases as the real wage rate increases for two reasons:

• Hours per person increase.
• Labor force participation increases.

*Hours per Person* The real wage rate is the opportunity cost of taking leisure and not working. As the opportunity cost of taking leisure rises, other things remaining the same, households choose to work more. But other things don't remain the same. A higher real wage rate brings a higher income, which increases the demand for leisure and encourages less work.

So a rise in the real wage rate has two opposing effects. But for most households, the opportunity cost effect is stronger than the income effect, so a rise in the real wage rate brings an increase in the quantity of labor supplied.

*Labor Force Participation* Most people have productive opportunities outside the labor force and choose to work only if the real wage rate exceeds the value of other productive activities. For example, a parent might spend time caring for her or his child. The alternative is day care. The parent will choose to work only if he or she can earn enough per hour to pay the cost of day care and have enough left to make the work effort worthwhile. The higher the real wage rate, the more likely it is that a parent will choose to work and so the greater is the labor force participation rate.

Let's now see how the labor market determines employment, the real wage rate, and potential GDP.

## Labor Market Equilibrium

The forces of supply and demand operate in labor markets just as they do in the markets for goods and services. The price of labor services is the real wage rate. A rise in the real wage rate eliminates a shortage of labor by decreasing the quantity demanded and increasing the quantity supplied. A fall in the real wage rate eliminates a surplus of labor by increasing the quantity demanded and decreasing the quantity supplied. If there is neither a shortage nor a surplus, the labor market is in equilibrium.

Figure 17.2(a) shows the labor market equilibrium. The demand curve, *LD*, shows that the quantity of labor demanded is greater, the lower is the real wage rate. And the supply of labor curve, *LS*, shows that the quantity of labor supplied is greater, the higher is the real wage rate.

Looking at the demand and supply curves for labor in Figure 17.2(a), you can see that if the real wage rate is less than $50 an hour, the quantity of labor demanded exceeds the quantity supplied and there is a shortage of labor. In this situation, the real wage rate rises.

You can also see that if the real wage rate exceeds $50 an hour, the quantity of labor supplied exceeds the quantity demanded and there is a surplus of labor. In this situation, the real wage rate falls.

But when the real wage rate equals $50 an hour, the quantity of labor demanded equals the quantity of labor supplied and there is neither a shortage nor a surplus of labor. In this situation, the labor market is in equilibrium and the

**FIGURE 17.2**

Labor Market Equilibrium and Potential GDP

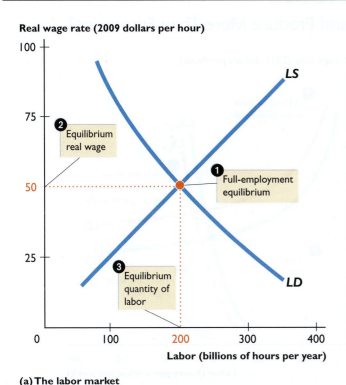

**Real wage rate (2009 dollars per hour)**

**(a) The labor market**

**Real GDP (trillions of 2009 dollars)**

**(b) Potential GDP**

**1** Full employment occurs when the quantity of labor demanded equals the quantity of labor supplied. **2** The equilibrium real wage rate is $50 an hour, and **3** the equilibrium quantity of labor employed is 200 billion hours a year.

Potential GDP is the real GDP produced on the production function by the full-employment quantity of labor. **1** The full-employment quantity of labor, 200 billion hours a year, produces a **2** potential GDP of $16 trillion.

real wage rate remains constant. The equilibrium quantity of labor is 200 billion hours a year. When the equilibrium quantity of labor is employed, the economy is at full employment. So the full-employment quantity of labor is 200 billion hours a year.

## Full Employment and Potential GDP

When the labor market is in equilibrium, the economy is at full employment and real GDP equals potential GDP.

You've seen that the quantity of real GDP depends on the quantity of labor employed. The production function tells us how much real GDP a given amount of employment can produce. Now that we've determined the full-employment quantity of labor, we can find potential GDP.

Figure 17.2(b) shows the relationship between the labor market equilibrium and potential GDP. The equilibrium quantity of labor employed in Figure 17.2(a) is 200 billion hours. The production function in Figure 17.2(b) tells us that 200 billion hours of labor produces $16 trillion of real GDP. This quantity of real GDP is potential GDP.

# EYE on the U.S. ECONOMY
## Why Do Americans Earn More and Produce More Than Europeans?

The quantity of capital per worker is greater in the United States than in Europe, and U.S. technology, on the average, is more productive than European technology.

These differences between the United States and Europe mean that U.S. labor is more productive than European labor.

Because U.S. labor is more productive than European labor, U.S. employers are willing to pay more for a given quantity of labor than European employers are. So the demand for labor curve in the United States, $LD_{US}$, lies to the right of the European demand for labor curve, $LD_{EU}$, in part (a) of the figure.

This difference in the productivity of labor also means that the U.S. production function, $PF_{US}$, lies above the European production function, $PF_{EU}$, in part (b) of the figure.

Higher income taxes and unemployment benefits in Europe mean that to induce a person to take a job, a firm in Europe must offer a higher wage rate than a firm in the United States has to offer. So the European labor supply curve, $LS_{EU}$, lies to the left of the U.S. labor supply curve, $LS_{US}$.

Equilibrium employment is higher in the United States than in Europe— Americans work longer hours—and the equilibrium real wage rate is higher in the United States than in Europe.

Potential GDP is higher in the United States than in Europe for two reasons: U.S. workers are more productive per hour of work and they work longer hours than Europeans.

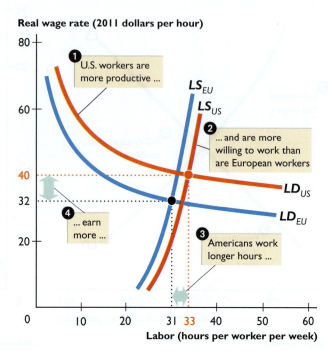

**Real wage rate (2011 dollars per hour)**

① U.S. workers are more productive ...
② ... and are more willing to work than are European workers
④ ... earn more ...
③ Americans work longer hours ...

$LS_{EU}$  $LS_{US}$  $LD_{US}$  $LD_{EU}$

**Labor (hours per worker per week)**

**(a) Labor market in Europe and the United States**

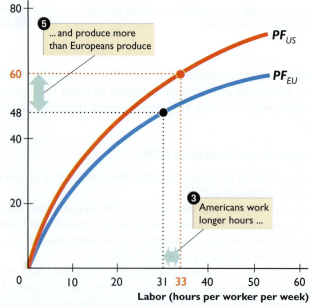

**Real GDP (2011 dollars per hour of work)**

⑤ ... and produce more than Europeans produce
③ Americans work longer hours ...

$PF_{US}$  $PF_{EU}$

**Labor (hours per worker per week)**

**(b) Production function in Europe and the United States**

CHECKPOINT 17.1

**Explain what determines potential GDP.**

## Practice Problem

1. Table 1 describes an economy's production function and demand for labor.

TABLE 1

| Quantity of labor demanded (billions of hours per year) | 0 | 1 | 2 | 3 | 4 |
|---|---|---|---|---|---|
| Real GDP (billions of 2009 dollars) | 0 | 40 | 70 | 90 | 100 |
| Real wage rate (2009 dollars per hour) | 50 | 40 | 30 | 20 | 10 |

Table 2 describes the supply of labor in this economy.

TABLE 2

| Quantity of labor supplied (billions of hours per year) | 0 | 1 | 2 | 3 | 4 |
|---|---|---|---|---|---|
| Real wage rate (2009 dollars per hour) | 10 | 20 | 30 | 40 | 50 |

Use the data in Tables 1 and 2 to make graphs of the labor market and production function. What are the equilibrium real wage rate and employment? What is potential GDP?

## In the News

### NITC bridge project

Canada is the United States' largest trading partner and 25 percent of the goods trade crosses the Detroit River. The NITC bridge, costing $1 billion, will increase capacity, reduce traffic bottlenecks and improve opportunities for businesses in both countries by providing a state-of-the-art, publicly operated border crossing.

Source: CNN, June 18, 2013

Explain how this huge project will influence potential GDP in Canada and the United States.

## Solution to Practice Problem

1. The demand for labor is a graph of the first and last row of Table 1 and the supply of labor is a graph of the data in Table 2 (Figure 1). The production function is a graph of the first two rows of Table 1 (Figure 2).

   Labor market equilibrium occurs when the real wage rate is $30 an hour and 2 billion hours of labor are employed (Figure 1). Potential GDP is the real GDP produced by the equilibrium quantity of labor (2 billion hours in Figure 1). Potential GDP is $70 billion (Figure 2).

## Solution to In the News

Potential GDP will increase, in both Canada and the United States. With increased border efficiency, the production function in both countries will shift upward. With no change in employment, real GDP would increase. But the construction project will increase the demand for U.S. and Canadian labor, increase the full-employment quantity of labor, and increase potential GDP. This project is likely to bring a boost to trade between Canada and the United States.

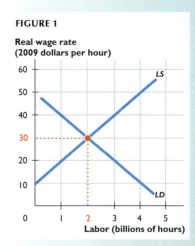

FIGURE 1

FIGURE 2

**17.2   THE BASICS OF ECONOMIC GROWTH**

**Economic growth**
A sustained expansion of production possibilities.

**Economic growth** is a sustained expansion of production possibilities. Maintained over decades, rapid economic growth can transform a poor nation into a rich one. Such has been the experience of Hong Kong, South Korea, Taiwan, and some other Asian economies. Slow economic growth or the absence of growth can condemn a nation to devastating poverty. Such has been the fate of Sierra Leone, Somalia, Zambia, and much of the rest of Africa.

Economic growth is different from the rise in incomes that occurs during the recovery from a recession. Economic growth is a sustained trend, not a temporary cyclical expansion.

## ■ Calculating Growth Rates

**Economic growth rate**
The annual percentage change of real GDP.

We express the **economic growth rate** as the annual percentage change of real GDP. To calculate this growth rate, we use the formula:

$$\text{Growth rate of real GDP} = \frac{\text{Real GDP in current year} - \text{Real GDP in previous year}}{\text{Real GDP in previous year}} \times 100.$$

For example, if real GDP in the current year is $8.4 trillion and if real GDP in the previous year was $8.0 trillion, then

$$\text{Growth rate of real GDP} = \frac{\$8.4 \text{ trillion} - \$8.0 \text{ trillion}}{\$8.0 \text{ trillion}} \times 100 = 5 \text{ percent.}$$

The growth rate of real GDP tells us how rapidly the total economy is expanding. This measure is useful for telling us about potential changes in the balance of economic power among nations, but it does not tell us about changes in the standard of living.

The standard of living depends on *real GDP per person* (also called *per capita real GDP*), which is real GDP divided by the population. So the contribution of real GDP growth to the change in the *standard of living* depends on the growth rate of real GDP per person. We use the above formula to calculate this growth rate, replacing real GDP with real GDP per person.

Suppose, for example, that in the current year, when real GDP is $8.4 trillion, the population is 202 million. Then real GDP per person in the current year is $8.4 trillion divided by 202 million, which equals $41,584. And suppose that in the previous year, when real GDP was $8.0 trillion, the population was 200 million. Then real GDP per person in that year was $8.0 trillion divided by 200 million, which equals $40,000.

Use these two values of real GDP per person with the growth formula to calculate the growth rate of real GDP per person. That is,

$$\text{Growth rate of real GDP per person} = \frac{\$41,584 - \$40,000}{\$40,000} \times 100 = 4 \text{ percent.}$$

We can also calculate the growth rate of real GDP per person by using the formula:

$$\text{Growth rate of real GDP per person} = \text{Growth rate of real GDP} - \text{Growth rate of population.}$$

In the example you've just worked through, the growth rate of real GDP is 5 percent. The population changes from 200 million to 202 million, so

$$\text{Growth rate of population} = \frac{202 \text{ million} - 200 \text{ million}}{200 \text{ million}} \times 100 = 1 \text{ percent}$$

and

Growth rate of real GDP per person = 5 percent − 1 percent = 4 percent.

This formula makes it clear that real GDP per person grows only if real GDP grows faster than the population grows. If the growth rate of the population exceeds the growth of real GDP, then real GDP per person falls.

## ■ The Magic of Sustained Growth

Sustained growth of real GDP per person can transform a poor society into a wealthy one. The reason is that economic growth is like compound interest. Suppose that you put $100 in the bank and earn 5 percent a year interest on it. After one year, you have $105. If you leave that money in the bank for another year, you earn 5 percent interest on the original $100 and on the $5 interest that you earned last year. You are now earning interest on interest! The next year, things get even better. Then you earn 5 percent on the original $100 and on the interest earned in the first year and the second year. Your money in the bank is *growing* at a rate of 5 percent a year. Before too many years have passed, you'll have $200 in the bank. But after *how many* years?

The answer is provided by a formula known as the **Rule of 70**, which states that the number of years it takes for the level of any variable to double is approximately 70 divided by the annual percentage growth rate of the variable. Using the Rule of 70, you can now calculate how many years it takes your $100 to become $200. It is 70 divided by 5, which is 14 years.

The Rule of 70 applies to any variable, so it applies to real GDP per person. Table 17.1 shows the doubling time for a selection of other growth rates. You can see that real GDP per person doubles in 70 years (70 divided by 1)—an average human life span—if the growth rate is 1 percent a year. It doubles in 35 years if the growth rate is 2 percent a year and in just 10 years if the growth rate is 7 percent a year.

We can use the Rule of 70 to answer other questions about economic growth. For example, in 2010, U.S. real GDP per person was approximately 4 times that of China. China's recent growth rate of real GDP per person was 7 percent a year. If this growth rate were to be maintained, how long would it take China's real GDP per person to reach that of the United States in 2010?

The answer, provided by the Rule of 70, is 20 years. China's real GDP per person doubles in 10 (70 divided by 7) years. It doubles again to 4 times its current level in another 10 years. So after 20 years of growth at 7 percent a year—that is by 2030—China's real GDP per person would be 4 times its current level and equal to that of the United States in 2010.

**Rule of 70**
The number of years it takes for the level of any variable to double is approximately 70 divided by the annual percentage growth rate of the variable.

**TABLE 17.1 GROWTH RATES**

| Growth rate (percent per year) | Years for level to double |
|---|---|
| 1 | 70 |
| 2 | 35 |
| 3 | 23 |
| 4 | 18 |
| 5 | 14 |
| 6 | 12 |
| 7 | 10 |
| 8 | 9 |
| 9 | 8 |
| 10 | 7 |

# EYE on the PAST

## How Fast Has Real GDP per Person Grown?

Professor Michael Kremer of Harvard University and Professor J. Bradford DeLong of the University of California, Berkeley, have constructed an extraordinary picture of real GDP in the global economy going back one million years. According to their numbers, human societies lived for a million years with no economic growth.

The top figure shows the numbers using the value of the dollar in 2009 as the measuring rod. Real GDP per person averaged $150 a year from 1,000,000 BC until 1620! It rose to $190 when Aristotle and Plato were teaching in Athens, around 500 BC, but slipped back over the next thousand years to $140 as the Roman Empire collapsed around 400 AD. When the Black Death gripped Europe in the 1340s, incomes fell to a 1-million-year low and even when the Pilgrim Fathers began to arrive in America in the 1620s, incomes were still the same as those of Ancient Greece!

Then, beginning around 1750, first in England and then in Europe and the United States, an astonishing change known as the Industrial Revolution occurred. Real GDP per person began to increase, apparently without limit. By 1850, real GDP per person was twice its 1650 level. By 1950, it was more than five times its 1850 level, and by 2000, it was four times its 1950 level.

The lower figure gives you a close-up view of U.S. real GDP per person over the past 110 years. Part (a) shows that in 2013, real GDP per person was almost eight times its level in 1903. It has grown by 2 percent a year, but the growth rate has been uneven: Almost no growth in the 1930s and the fastest growth in the 1940s.

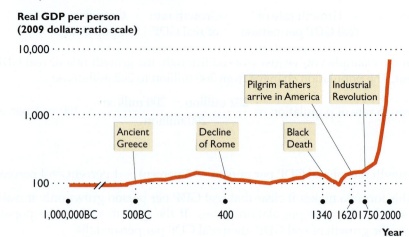

SOURCE OF DATA: J. Bradford DeLong, *"Estimating World GDP, One Million B.C.—Present."*

Part (b) shows that growth, measured decade by decade, has slowed since the 1960s and the growth rate between 2000 and 2010 was lower than that in any decade except the 1930s. But the reason is not that potential GDP growth slowed. Rather, it is because there was a deep recession in 2008 and 2009.

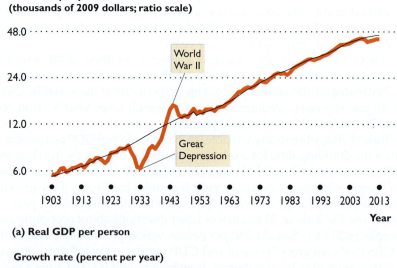

**(a) Real GDP per person**

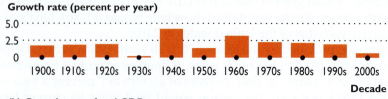

**(b) Growth rate of real GDP per person**

SOURCES OF DATA: Bureau of Economic Analysis and the Bureau of Labor Statistics.

# CHECKPOINT 17.2

**Define and calculate the economic growth rate, and explain the implications of sustained growth.**

## Practice Problems

1. Mexico's real GDP was 8,762 billion pesos in 2010 and 9,105 billion pesos in 2011. Mexico's population growth rate in 2011 was 1 percent. Calculate Mexico's economic growth rate in 2011 and the growth rate of real GDP per person in Mexico in 2011.

2. Calculate the approximate number of years it will take for real GDP per person to double if an economy maintains an economic growth rate of 12 percent a year and a population growth rate of 2 percent a year.

3. Calculate the change in the number of years it will take for real GDP per person in India to double if the growth rate of real GDP per person increases from 8 percent a year to 10 percent a year.

## In the News

**ADB reduces China growth estimate**
Since 1980 China's real GDP per person has grown at 10 percent a year. The Asian Development Bank (ADB) cut its estimate for China's growth to 9.3 percent this year.

Source: Bloomberg, September 13, 2011

If China's growth rate remains at 9.3 percent a year, how many additional years will it take for China to double its real GDP per person?

## Solutions to Practice Problems

1. Mexico's economic growth rate in 2011 was 3.9 percent. The economic growth rate equals the percentage change in real GDP:
   [(Real GDP in 2011 − Real GDP in 2010) ÷ Real GDP in 2010] × 100, which is [(9,105 billion − 8,762 billion) ÷ 8,762 billion] × 100, or 3.9 percent.
   The growth rate of real GDP per person equals 2.9 percent.
   Growth rate of real GDP per person equals (Growth rate of real GDP − Population growth rate), which is (3.9 percent − 1 percent), or 2.9 percent.

2. It will take 7 years for real GDP per person to double. The growth rate of real GDP per person equals the economic growth rate minus the population growth rate. Real GDP per person grows at 12 percent minus 2 percent, which is 10 percent a year. The Rule of 70 tells us that the level of a variable that grows at 10 percent a year will double in 70 ÷ 10 years, or 7 years.

3. Two years. The Rule of 70 tells us that a variable that grows at 8 percent a year will double in 70 ÷ 8 years, which is approximately 9 years. By increasing its growth rate to 10 percent a year, the variable will double in 7 years.

## Solution to In the News

With a growth rate of 10 percent a year, real GDP per person will double in 7 years (70 ÷ 10). If the growth rate is maintained at 9.3 percent a year, real GDP per person will double in 7.5 years (70 ÷ 9.3)—taking an additional 0.5 year.

## 17.3  LABOR PRODUCTIVITY GROWTH

Real GDP grows when the quantities of the factors of production grow or when persistent advances in technology make them increasingly productive. To understand what determines the growth rate of real GDP, we must understand what determines the growth rates of the factors of production and the rate of increase in their productivity. You're going to see how saving and investment determine the growth rate of physical capital and how the growth of physical capital and human capital and advances in technology interact to determine the economic growth rate.

We are interested in real GDP growth because it contributes to improvements in our standard of living. But our standard of living improves only if we produce more goods and services with each hour of labor. So our main concern is to understand the forces that make our labor more productive. Let's start by defining labor productivity.

### ■ Labor Productivity

**Labor productivity**
The quantity of real GDP produced by one hour of labor.

**Labor productivity** is the quantity of real GDP produced by one hour of labor. It is calculated by using the formula:

$$\text{Labor productivity} = \frac{\text{Real GDP}}{\text{Aggregate hours}}.$$

For example, if real GDP is $8,000 billion and if aggregate hours are 200 billion, then we can calculate labor productivity as

$$\text{Labor productivity} = \frac{\$8,000 \text{ billion}}{200 \text{ billion hours}} = \$40 \text{ per hour.}$$

When labor productivity grows, real GDP per person grows. So the growth in labor productivity is the basis of the rising standard of living. What makes labor productivity grow? We'll answer this question by considering the influences on labor productivity growth under two broad headings:

- Saving and investment in physical capital
- Expansion of human capital and discovery of new technologies

These two broad influences on labor productivity growth interact and are the sources of the extraordinary growth in productivity during the past 200 years. Although they interact, we'll begin by looking at each on its own.

### ■ Saving and Investment in Physical Capital

Saving and investment in physical capital increase the amount of capital per worker and increase labor productivity. Labor productivity took a dramatic upturn when the amount of capital per worker increased during the Industrial Revolution. Production processes that use hand tools can create beautiful objects, but production methods that use large amounts of capital per worker, such as auto plant assembly lines, enable workers to be much more productive. The accumulation of capital on farms and building sites; in textile factories, iron foundries and steel mills, coal mines, chemical plants, and auto plants; and at banks and insurance companies added incredibly to the productivity of our labor.

A strong and experienced farm worker of 1830, using a scythe, could harvest 3 acres of wheat a day. A farm worker of 1831, using a mechanical reaper, could harvest 15 acres a day. And a farm worker of today, using a combine harvester, can harvest and thresh hundreds of acres a day.

The next time you see a movie set in the old West, look carefully at how little capital there is. Try to imagine how productive you would be in such circumstances compared with your productivity today.

## Capital Accumulation and Diminishing Marginal Returns

Although saving and investment in additional capital is a source of labor productivity growth, without the expansion of human capital and technological change, it would not bring sustained economic growth. Eventually growth would slow and most likely stop. The reason is a fundamental fact about capital known as the **law of diminishing marginal returns**, which states that

> **If the quantity of capital is small, an increase in capital brings a large increase in production; and if the quantity of capital is large, an increase in capital brings a small increase in production.**

This law applies to all factors of production, not only to capital, and is the reason why the demand for labor curve slopes downward (see p. 491).

You can see why the law of diminishing marginal returns applies to capital by thinking about how your own productivity is influenced by the capital you own. When you got your first computer, your small quantity of capital increased and your productivity increased enormously. You most likely don't have two computers, but if you do, the productivity boost from your second computer was much smaller than that from the first. If you don't have two computers, one of the reasons is that you doubt it would be worth the expense because it would contribute such a small amount to your labor productivity

*Farm labor productivity increased from harvesting 3 acres per day in 1830 …*

*to harvesting hundreds of acres per day in the twenty-first century.*

**Productivity curve**
The relationship that shows how real GDP per hour of labor changes as the quantity of capital per hour of labor changes.

### Illustrating the Law of Diminishing Marginal Returns

Figure 17.3 illustrates the relationship between capital and productivity. The curve *PC* is a **productivity curve**, which shows how real GDP per hour of labor changes as the quantity of capital per hour of labor changes.

In Figure 17.3, when the quantity of capital (measured in real dollars) increases from $40 to $80 per hour of labor, real GDP per hour of labor increases from $30 to $50, a $20 or 67 percent increase. But when the quantity of capital increases from $180 to $220 per hour of labor, the same $40 increase as before, real GDP per hour of labor increases from $80 to $84, only a $4 or 5 percent increase. If capital per hour of labor keeps increasing, labor productivity increases by ever smaller amounts and eventually stops rising.

## ■ Expansion of Human Capital and Discovery of New Technologies

The expansion of human capital and the discovery of new technologies have a profoundly different effect on labor productivity than capital accumulation has. They don't display diminishing marginal returns.

***Expansion of Human Capital*** Human capital—the accumulated skill and knowledge of people—comes from three sources:

1. Education and training
2. Job experience
3. Health and diet

---

■ **FIGURE 17.3**

The Effects of an Increase in Capital

---

When workers are equipped with more capital, they become more productive. The productivity curve *PC* shows how an increase in capital per hour of labor increases real GDP per hour of labor.

❶ When the quantity of capital per hour of labor increases from a low $40 to $80, real GDP per hour of labor increases by $20.

❷ When the quantity of capital per hour of labor increases from a high $180 to $220, real GDP per hour of labor increases by $4.

An equal-size increase in capital per hour of labor brings a diminishing increase in output, the greater is the quantity of capital.

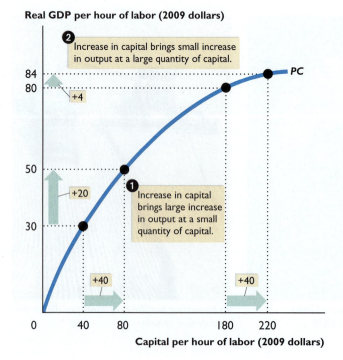

Real GDP per hour of labor (2009 dollars)

❷ Increase in capital brings small increase in output at a large quantity of capital.

❶ Increase in capital brings large increase in output at a small quantity of capital.

Capital per hour of labor (2009 dollars)

A hundred years ago, most people attended school for around eight years. A hundred years before that, most people had no formal education at all. Today, 90 percent of Americans complete high school and more than 60 percent go to college or university. Our ability to read, write, and communicate effectively contributes enormously to our productivity.

The education of thousands of scientists, engineers, mathematicians, biologists, computer programmers, and people equipped with a host of other specialist skills has made huge contributions to labor productivity and to the advance in technology.

While formal education is productive, school is not the only place where people acquire human capital. We also learn from on-the-job experience—from *learning by doing*. One carefully studied example illustrates the importance of learning by doing. Between 1941 and 1944 (during World War II), U.S. shipyards produced 2,500 Liberty Ships—cargo ships built to a standardized design. In 1941, it took 1.2 million person-hours to build a ship. By 1942, it took 600,000, and by 1943, it took only 500,000. Not much change occurred in the physical capital employed during these years, but an enormous amount of human capital was accumulated. Thousands of workers and managers learned from experience and their productivity more than doubled in two years.

Strong, healthy, well-nourished workers are much more productive than those who lack good nutrition, health care, and opportunties to exercise. This fact creates a virtuous circle. Improved health care, diet, and exercise increase labor productivity; and increased labor productivity brings the increased incomes that make these health improvements possible.

The expansion of human capital is the most fundamental source of economic growth because it directly increases labor productivity and is the source of the discovery of new technologies.

*Discovery of New Technologies* The growth of physical capital and the expansion of human capital have made large contributions to economic growth, but the discovery of new technologies has made an even greater contribution.

*Production using 1950s technology.*

The development of writing, one of the most basic human skills, was the source of some of the earliest productivity gains. The ability to keep written records made it possible to reap ever-larger gains from specialization and trade. Imagine how hard it would be to do any kind of business if all the accounts, invoices, and agreements existed only in people's memories.

Later, the development of mathematics laid the foundation for the eventual extension of knowledge in physics, chemistry, and biology. This base of scientific knowledge was the foundation for the technological advances of the Industrial Revolution 200 years ago and of today's Information Revolution.

Since the Industrial Revolution, technological change has become a part of everyday life. Firms routinely conduct research to develop technologies that are more productive, and partnerships between business and the universities are commonplace in fields such as biotechnology and electronics.

## Illustrating the Effects of Human Capital and Technological Change

Figure 17.4 illustrates the effects of the expansion of human capital and the discovery of new technologies and labor productivity: They shift the *productivity curve* upward. In the figure, these influences shift the productivity curve from $PC_0$ to $PC_1$. Imagine that $PC_0$ is the productivity curve in 1960 and $PC_1$ is the productivity curve for 2010. With capital of $180 per hour of labor, workers could

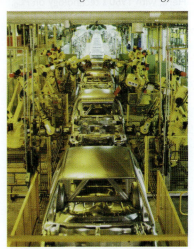

*Production using 2000s technology.*

produce $80 of real GDP per hour of labor in 2010. If workers had been equipped with the same amount of capital but with the technology of 1960, they would have produced only $40 of real GDP per hour of labor. The upward shift of the productivity curve illustrates the fact that labor and capital become more productive at each quantity of capital per hour of labor. Capital is still subject to diminishing marginal returns but the overall level of productivity is higher with expanded human capital and more productive technologies.

## ■ Combined Influences Bring Labor Productivity Growth

To reap the benefits of technological change—to use new technologies to make labor productivity grow—capital must increase. Some of the most powerful and far-reaching technologies are embodied in human capital—for example, language, writing, mathematics, physics, biology, and engineering. But most technologies are embodied in physical capital. For example, to increase the productivity of transportation workers by using the discovery of the internal combustion engine, millions of horse-drawn carriages had to be replaced by automobiles and trucks; more recently, to increase the labor productivity of office workers by using the discovery of computerized word processing, millions of typewriters had to be replaced by computers and printers.

Figure 17.5 shows how the combined effects of capital accumulation, the expansion of human capital, and the discovery of new technologies bring labor productivity growth. In 1960, the productivity curve is $PC_0$, workers have $80 of capital per hour and produce $25 of real GDP per hour. By 2010, capital has increased to $180 per hour. With no expansion of human capital or technological advance,

---

■ **FIGURE 17.4**

The Effects of Human Capital and Technological Change

When human capital expands or technology advances, labor becomes more productive—a given amount of capital per hour of labor can produce more real GDP per hour of labor.

Here, with 1960's technology on $PC_0$, $180 of capital per hour of labor can produce $40 of goods and services—real GDP per hour of labor.

With 2010's technology on $PC_1$, the same $180 of capital per hour of labor can produce $80 of goods and services—real GDP per hour of labor.

The expansion of human capital and the discovery of new technologies shift the productivity curve upward and are not subject to diminishing marginal returns.

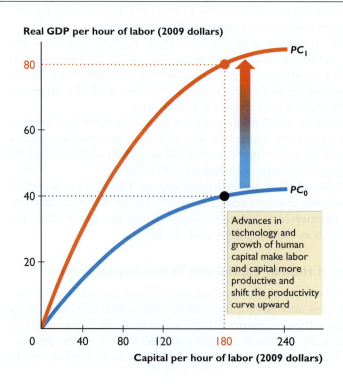

■ **FIGURE 17.5**

How Labor Productivity Grows

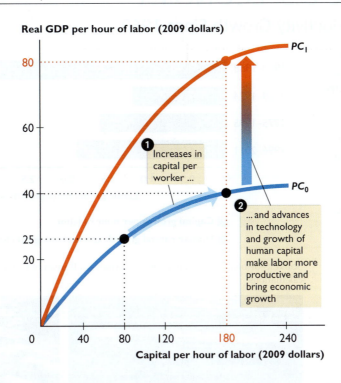

In 1960, workers had $80 of capital per hour of labor and produced real GDP per hour of $25 on $PC_0$.

❶ When the quantity of capital increased from $80 per hour of labor in 1960 to $180 per hour of labor in 2010, real GDP per hour of labor increased from $25 to $40 along $PC_0$.

❷ The expansion of human capital and discovery of new technologies shifted the productivity curve upward to $PC_1$ and increased real GDP per hour of labor from $40 to $80.

real GDP per hour of labor would have increased to $40. But with the human capital and technology of 2010, output per hour increases to $80.

You've now seen what makes labor productivity grow. *Eye on the U.S. Economy* on p. 504 looks at the quantitative importance of the sources of growth since 1960. Real GDP grows because labor becomes more productive and also because the *quantity of labor* increases. Figure 17.6 summarizes the sources of economic growth and shows how the growth in labor productivity together with the growth in the quantity of labor bring real GDP growth.

■ **FIGURE 17.6**

The Sources of Economic Growth

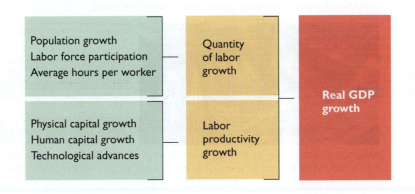

Real GDP depends on the quantity of labor and labor productivity.

The quantity of labor depends on the population, the labor force participation rate, and the average hours per worker.

Labor productivity depends on the amounts of physical capital and human capital and the state of technology.

Growth in quantity of labor and growth in labor productivity bring real GDP growth.

# EYE on the U.S. ECONOMY
## U.S. Labor Productivity Growth Since 1960

The figure shows how labor productivity growth has fluctuated over the past 50 years. It also shows the contributions to productivity growth of increases in capital per worker (the green bars) and advances in technology and the growth of human capital (the blue bars).

You can see that most of the fluctuations in productivity growth arise from changes in the pace of technological change and human capital accumulation.

## The Booming Sixties

Plastics, the laser, the computer, the transistor, the space race, the interstate highway system, the shopping mall, and the passenger jet were among the technological advances that brought extraordinary labor productivity growth during the 1960s.

## The Stagnant Seventies

An oil price hike and oil embargo as well as higher taxes and expanded regulation slowed productivity growth during the 1970s and the higher cost of energy diverted the focus of technological change toward saving energy rather than increasing labor productivity.

## The Information Age

The Internet has transformed our lives and unlocking the human genome has opened the possibility of dramatic advances in health care. But the information age increase in labor productivity is lower than that of the 1960s.

**Capital growth per hour of labor**

**Human capital growth and technological change**

SOURCES OF DATA: Bureau of Economic Analysis, Bureau of Labor Statistics, and authors' calculations.

*Passenger jets and the construction of thousands of miles of interstate highways were among the technological advances that increased labor productivity during the 1960s.*

*An embargo on oil exports to the United States and a higher cost of energy as well as tax hikes contributed to the productivity growth slowdown of the 1970s.*

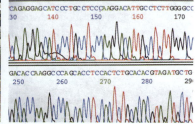

*Advances in information technologies and biotechnologies increased productivity during the 1990s and 2000s but not by as much as the technological advances of the 1960s did.*

# ■ What Keeps Labor Productivity Growing?

Labor productivity keeps growing because of the choices people make in the pursuit of profit. Paul Romer of Stanford University developed this growth theory during the 1980s, building on ideas developed by Joseph Schumpeter during the 1930s and 1940s. Romer's theory emphasizes three facts about market economies: Human capital expands because of choices; discoveries result from choices; and discoveries bring profit and competition destroys profit, bringing the incentive to keep discovering new technologies.

*Human Capital Expansion and Choices* People decide how long to remain in school, what to study, and how hard to study. And when they graduate from school, people make more choices about job training and on-the-job learning. All these choices govern the speed at which human capital expands.

*Discoveries and Choices* When people discover a new product or technique, they consider themselves lucky. They are right, but chance does not determine the pace at which new discoveries are made—and at which technology advances. It depends on how many people are looking for a new technology and how intensively they are looking.

*Discoveries and Profits* Profit is the spur to technological change. The forces of competition squeeze profits, so to increase profit, people constantly seek either lower-cost methods of production or new and better products for which people are willing to pay a higher price. Inventors can maintain a profit for several years by taking out a patent or copyright, but eventually a new discovery is copied and profits disappear.

Two other facts play a key role in the new growth theory: Many people can use discoveries at the same time, and physical activities can be replicated.

*Discoveries Used by All* Once a profitable new discovery has been made, everyone can use it. For example, when Marc Andreeson created Mosaic, the Web browser that led to the creation of Netscape Navigator and Microsoft's Internet Explorer, everyone who was interested in navigating the Internet had access to a new and more efficient tool. One person's use of a Web browser does not prevent others from using it. This fact means that as the benefits of a new discovery spread, free resources become available. These resources are free because nothing is given up when an additional person uses them.

*Replicating Activities* Production activities can be replicated. For example, there might be 2, 3, or 53 identical firms making fiber-optic cable by using an identical assembly line and production technique. If one firm increases its capital and output, that *firm* experiences diminishing returns. But the economy can increase its capital and output by adding another identical fiber cable factory, and the *economy* does not experience diminishing returns.

Because the combination of capital accumulation and technological change avoid diminishing returns, labor productivity grows indefinitely as long as people devote resources to expanding human capital and introducing new technologies.

Economic growth is like the perpetual motion machine in Figure 17.7. Growth is driven by insatiable wants that lead us to pursue profit and innovate. The economic growth rate depends on the ability and the incentive to innovate.

## ■ FIGURE 17.7

### A Perpetual Motion Machine

❶ People want a higher standard of living and are spurred by ❷ profit incentives to make the ❸ innovations that lead to ❹ new and better techniques and new and better products, which in turn lead to ❺ the birth of new firms and the death of some old firms, ❻ new and better jobs, and ❼ more leisure and more consumption goods and services. The result is ❽ a higher standard of living. But people want a yet higher standard of living, and the growth process continues.

Based on a similar figure in *These Are the Good Old Days: A Report on U.S. Living Standards*, Federal Reserve Bank of Dallas 1993 Annual Report.

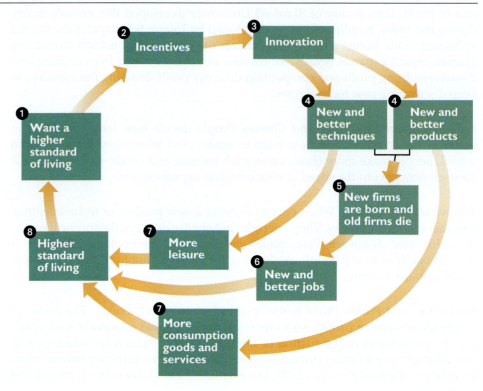

# EYE on YOUR LIFE
## How You Influence and Are Influenced by Economic Growth

Many of the choices that you make affect your personal economic growth rate—the pace of expansion of your own standard of living. And these same choices, in combination with similar choices made by millions of other people, have a profound effect on the economic growth of the nation and the world.

The most important of these choices right now is your choice to increase your human capital. By being in school, you have decided to expand your human capital.

You will continue to expand your human capital long after you finish school as your earning power rises with on-the-job experience. You might even decide to return to school at a later stage in your life.

A choice that will become increasingly important later in your life is to accumulate a retirement fund. This choice provides not only a source of income for you when you eventually retire but also financial resources that firms can use to finance the expansion of physical capital.

Not only do your choices influence economic growth; economic growth also has a big influence on you—on how you earn your income and on the standard of living that your income makes possible.

Because of economic growth, the jobs available today are more interesting and less dangerous and strenuous than those of 100 years ago; and jobs are hugely better paid. But for many of us, economic growth means that we must accept change and be ready to learn new skills and get new jobs.

# CHECKPOINT 17.3

**Explain the sources of labor productivity growth.**

## Practice Problems

Use the data in Table 1 to work Problems 1 and 2.

**TABLE 1**

| Item | 2012 | 2013 |
|------|------|------|
| Aggregate labor hours (billions) | 25.0 | 25.6 |
| Real GDP (billions of 2009 dollars) | 1,000 | 1,050 |

1. Calculate the growth rate of real GDP in 2013.
2. Calculate labor productivity in 2012 and 2013, and the growth rate of labor productivity in 2013.

## In the News

**Labor productivity on the rise**

The BLS reported the following data for the year to March 2013: In the nonfarm sector, output increased 2.4 percent as aggregate hours increased 1.5 percent; in the manufacturing sector, output increased 2.5 percent as aggregate hours increased by 0.9 percent.

Source: bls.gov/news.release

As aggregate hours increased, output increased but did labor productivity in each sector increase? In which sector was growth in labor productivity greater?

## Solutions to Practice Problems

1. The growth rate of real GDP in 2013 was 5 percent. Growth rate equals [($1,050 billion − $1,000 billion) ÷ $1,000 billion] × 100 or 5 percent.
2. Labor productivity is $40.00 an hour in 2012 and $41.02 an hour in 2013.

   Labor productivity equals real GDP divided by aggregate labor hours.

   In 2012, labor productivity was ($1,000 billion ÷ 25 billion) or $40.00 per hour of labor.

   In 2013, labor productivity was ($1,050 billion ÷ 25.6 billion) or $41.02 per hour of labor.

   The growth rate of labor productivity in 2013 was 2.55 percent.

   Labor productivity growth rate was [($41.02 − $40.00) ÷ $40.00] × 100 or 2.55 percent.

## Solution to In the News

Output = Aggregate hours × Labor productivity. In each sector, output increased by more than the increase in aggregate hours, so labor productivity must have increased. Output growth in manufacturing was almost the same as that in the nonfarm sector while growth in aggregate hours was much slower in manufacturing, so labor productivity must have increased by a larger percentage in the manufacturing sector than in the nonfarm sector.

## 17.4 ACHIEVING FASTER GROWTH

Why did it take more than a million years of human life before economic growth began? Why are some countries even today still barely growing? Why don't all societies save and invest in new capital, expand human capital, and discover and apply new technologies on a scale that brings rapid economic growth? What actions can governments take to encourage growth?

### ■ Preconditions for Economic Growth

The main reason economic growth is either absent or slow is that some societies lack the incentive system that encourages growth-producing activities. One of the fundamental preconditions for creating the incentives that lead to economic growth is economic freedom.

### Economic Freedom

**Economic freedom** is present when people are able to make personal choices, their private property is protected by the rule of law, and they are free to buy and sell in markets. The rule of law, an efficient legal system, and the ability to enforce contracts are essential foundations for creating economic freedom. Impediments to economic freedom are corruption in the courts and government bureaucracy; barriers to trade, such as import bans; high tax rates; stringent regulations on business, such as health, safety, and environmental regulation; restrictions on banks; labor market regulations that limit a firm's ability to hire and lay off workers; and illegal markets, such as those that violate intellectual property rights.

No unique political system is necessary to deliver economic freedom. Democratic systems do a good job, but the rule of law, not democracy, is the key requirement for creating economic freedom. Nondemocratic political systems that respect the rule of law can also work well. Hong Kong is the best example of a place with little democracy but a lot of economic freedom—and a lot of economic growth. No country with a high level of economic freedom is economically poor, but many countries with low levels of economic freedom stagnate.

### Property Rights

Economic freedom requires the protection of private property—the factors of production and goods that people own. The social arrangements that govern the protection of private property are called **property rights**. They include the rights to physical property (land, buildings, and capital equipment), to financial property (claims by one person against another), and to intellectual property (such as inventions). Clearly established and enforced property rights provide people with the incentive to work and save. If someone attempts to steal their property, a legal system will protect them. Such property rights also assure people that government itself will not confiscate their income or savings.

### Markets

Economic freedom also requires free markets. Buyers and sellers get information and do business with each other in *markets.* Market prices send signals to buyers and sellers that create incentives to increase or decrease the quantities demanded and supplied. Markets enable people to trade and to save and invest. But markets cannot operate without property rights.

---

**Economic freedom**
A condition in which people are able to make personal choices, their private property is protected by the rule of law, and they are free to buy and sell in markets.

**Property rights**
The social arrangements that govern the protection of private property.

Property rights and markets create incentives for people to specialize and trade, to save and invest, to expand their human capital, and to discover and apply new technologies. Early human societies based on hunting and gathering did not experience economic growth because they lacked property rights and markets. Economic growth began when societies evolved the institutions that create incentives. But the presence of an incentive system and the institutions that create it do not guarantee that economic growth will occur. They permit economic growth but do not make it inevitable.

Growth begins when the appropriate incentive system exists because people can specialize in the activities at which they have a comparative advantage and trade with each other. You saw in Chapter 3 how everyone gains from such activity. By specializing and trading, everyone can acquire goods and services at the lowest possible cost. Consequently, people can obtain a greater volume of goods and services from their labor.

As an economy moves from one with little specialization to one that reaps the gains from specialization and trade, its production and consumption grow. Real GDP per person increases, and the standard of living rises.

But for growth to be persistent, people must face incentives that encourage them to pursue the three activities that generate *ongoing* economic growth: saving and investment, expansion of human capital, and the discovery and application of new technologies.

## ■ Policies to Achieve Faster Growth

To achieve faster economic growth, we must increase the growth rate of capital per hour of labor, increase the growth rate of human capital, or increase the pace of technological advance. The main actions that governments can take to achieve these objectives are

- Create incentive mechanisms.
- Encourage saving.
- Encourage research and development.
- Encourage international trade.
- Improve the quality of education.

### Create Incentive Mechanisms

Economic growth occurs when the incentives to save, invest, and innovate are strong enough. These incentives require property rights enforced by a well-functioning legal system. Property rights and a legal system are the key ingredients that are missing in many societies. For example, they are absent throughout much of Africa. The first priority for growth policy is to establish these institutions so that incentives to save, invest, and innovate exist. Russia is a leading example of a country that is striving to take this step toward establishing the conditions in which economic growth can occur.

### Encourage Saving

Saving finances investment, which brings capital accumulation. So encouraging saving can increase the growth of capital and stimulate economic growth. The East Asian economies have the highest saving rates and the highest growth rates. Some African economies have the lowest saving rates and the lowest growth rates.

Tax incentives can increase saving. Individual Retirement Accounts (IRAs) are an example of a tax incentive to save. Economists claim that a tax on consumption rather than on income provides the best incentive to save.

### Encourage Research and Development

Everyone can use the fruits of basic research and development efforts. For example, all biotechnology firms can use advances in gene-splicing technology. Because basic inventions can be copied, the inventor's profit is limited and so the market allocates too few resources to this activity.

Governments can direct public funds toward financing basic research, but this solution is not foolproof. It requires a mechanism for allocating public funds to their highest-valued use. The National Science Foundation is one possibly efficient channel for allocating public funds to universities and public research facilities to finance and encourage basic research. Government programs such as national defense and space exploration also lead to innovations that have wide use. Laptop computers and nonstick coatings are two prominent examples of innovations that came from the U.S. space program.

### Encourage International Trade

Free international trade stimulates economic growth by extracting all the available gains from specialization and trade. The fastest-growing nations today are those with the fastest-growing exports and imports. The creation of the North American Free Trade Agreement and the integration of the economies of Europe through the formation of the European Union are examples of successful actions that governments have taken to stimulate economic growth through trade.

### Improve the Quality of Education

The free market would produce too little education because it brings social benefits beyond the benefits to the people who receive the education. By funding basic education and by ensuring high standards in skills such as language, mathematics, and science, governments can contribute enormously to a nation's growth potential. Education can also be expanded and improved by using tax incentives to encourage improved private provision. Singapore's Information Technology in Education program is one of the best examples of a successful attempt to stimulate growth through education.

## ◼ How Much Difference Can Policy Make?

It is easy to make a list of policy actions that could increase a nation's economic growth rate. It is hard to convert that list into acceptable actions that make a big difference.

Political equilibrium arises from the balance of the interests of one group against the interests of another group. Change brings gains for some and losses for others, so change is slow. And even when change occurs, if the economic growth rate can be increased by even as much as half a percentage point, it takes many years for the full benefits to accrue.

A well-intentioned government cannot dial up a big increase in the economic growth rate, but it can pursue policies that will nudge the economic growth rate upward. Over time, the benefits from these policies will be large.

# EYE on RICH AND POOR NATIONS

## Why Are Some Nations Rich and Others Poor?

Political stability, property rights protected by the rule of law, and limited government intervention in markets: These are key features of the economies that enjoy high or rapidly rising incomes and they are the features missing in economies that remain poor. All the rich nations have possessed these growth-inducing characteristics for the many decades during which their labor productivity and standard of living have been rising.

The United States started to grow rapidly 150 years ago and overtook Europe in the early 20th century. In the past 50 years, the gaps between these countries haven't changed much. (See part (a) of the figure.)

In a transition from Communism to a market economy, Eastern Europe is now growing faster.

Tribal conflict in Africa and bureaucratic overload in Central and South America have kept growth slow and the gap between the United States and these regions has widened.

Real GDP per person in East Asian economies, in part (b), has converged toward that in the United States. These economies are like fast trains running on the same track at similar speeds with roughly constant gaps between them. Hong Kong and Singapore are the lead trains and run about 15 years in front of Taiwan, 20 years in front of South Korea, and almost 40 years in front of China.

Between 1960 and 2010, Hong Kong and Singapore transformed themselves from poor developing economies to take their places among the world's richest economies.

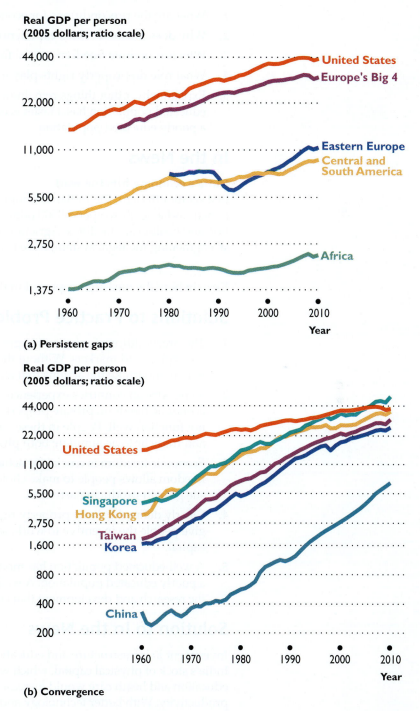

(a) Persistent gaps

(b) Convergence

Source of data: International Monetary Fund, *World Economic Outlook Database*.

# CHECKPOINT 17.4

**Describe policies that speed economic growth.**

## Practice Problems

1.  What are the preconditions for economic growth?
2.  Why does much of Africa experience slow economic growth?
3.  Why is economic freedom crucial for achieving economic growth?
4.  What role do property rights play in encouraging economic growth?
5.  Explain why, other things remaining the same, a country with a well-educated population has a faster economic growth rate than a country that has a poorly educated population.

## In the News

### India's economy hits the wall

Just six months ago, the Indian economy was growing rapidly; now growth has halted. India needs to spend $500 billion upgrading its infrastructure and education and health-care facilities. Agriculture remains unproductive; and reforms, like strengthening the legal system, have been ignored.

Source: *BusinessWeek*, July 1, 2008

Explain how the measures reported in the news clip could lead to faster growth.

## Solutions to Practice Problems

1.  The preconditions for economic growth are economic freedom, private property rights, and markets. Without these preconditions, people have little incentive to undertake the actions that lead to economic growth.
2.  Some African countries experience slow economic growth because they lack economic freedom, private property rights are not enforced, and markets do not function well. People in these countries have little incentive to specialize and trade or to accumulate both physical and human capital.
3.  Economic freedom is crucial for achieving economic growth because economic freedom allows people to make choices and gives them the incentives to pursue growth-producing activities.
4.  Clearly defined private property rights and a legal system to enforce them give people the incentive to work, save, invest, and accumulate human capital.
5.  A well-educated population has more skills and greater labor productivity than a poorly educated population. A well-educated population can contribute to the research and development that create new technology.

## Solution to In the News

Investment in infrastructure and education and heath-care facilities would increase India's stock of physical capital, which would increase labor productivity. Better education and heath care would increase human capital and again increase labor productivity. With better technology and more capital used on farms, productivity of farm workers would increase. Strengthening the legal system could better enforce property rights. Each of these measures could lead to faster growth in labor productivity and faster growth in real GDP per person in India.

## CHAPTER SUMMARY

## Key Points

1. **Explain what determines potential GDP.**

   - Potential GDP is the quantity of real GDP that the full-employment quantity of labor produces.
   - At full-employment equilibrium, the real wage rate makes the quantity of labor demanded equal the quantity of labor supplied.

2. **Define and calculate the economic growth rate, and explain the implications of sustained growth.**

   - Economic growth is the sustained expansion of production possibilities. The annual percentage change in real GDP measures the economic growth rate.
   - Real GDP per person must grow if the standard of living is to rise.
   - Sustained economic growth transforms poor nations into rich ones.
   - The Rule of 70 tells us the number of years in which real GDP doubles— 70 divided by the percentage growth rate of real GDP.

3. **Explain the sources of labor productivity growth.**

   - Real GDP grows when aggregate hours and labor productivity grow.
   - Real GDP per person grows when labor productivity grows.
   - The interaction of saving and investment in physical capital, expansion of human capital, and technological advances bring labor productivity growth.
   - Saving and investment in physical capital alone cannot bring sustained steady growth because of diminishing marginal returns to capital.

4. **Describe the policies that speed economic growth.**

   - Economic growth requires an incentive system created by economic freedom, property rights, and markets.
   - It might be possible to achieve faster growth by encouraging saving, subsidizing research and education, and encouraging international trade.

## Key Terms

Classical macroeconomics, 484
Demand for labor, 489
Diminishing returns, 488
Economic freedom, 508
Economic growth, 494
Economic growth rate, 494
Keynesian macroeconomics, 484
Labor productivity, 498
Law of diminishing marginal returns, 499

Monetarist macroeconomics, 485
Potential GDP, 487
Production function, 488
Productivity curve, 500
Property rights, 508
Quantity of labor demanded, 489
Quantity of labor supplied, 489
Rule of 70, 495
Supply of labor, 495

# CHAPTER CHECKPOINT

## Study Plan Problems and Applications

Use the events in List 1, which occur in the United States one at a time, to work Problems **1** to **4**.

**1.** Sort the items into four groups: those that change the production function, those that change the demand for labor, those that change the supply of labor, and those that do not change the production function, the demand for labor, or the supply of labor. Say in which direction any changes occur.

**2.** Which of the events increase the equilibrium quantity of labor and which decrease it?

**3.** Which of the events raise the real wage rate and which lower it?

**4.** Which of the events increase potential GDP and which decrease it?

Use the information set out in Table 1 and Table 2 about the economy of Athabasca to work Problems **5** and **6**.

**5.** Calculate the quantity of labor employed, the real wage rate, and potential GDP.

**6.** If the labor force participation increases, explain how employment, the real wage rate, and potential GDP change.

**7.** In 2005 and 2006, India's real GDP grew by 9.2 percent a year and its population grew by 1.6 percent a year. If these growth rates are sustained, in what years would
  • Real GDP be twice what it was in 2006?
  • Real GDP per person be twice what it was in 2006?

**8.** Explain how saving and investment in capital change labor productivity. Why do diminishing returns arise? Provide an example of diminishing returns. Use a graph of the productivity curve to illustrate your answer.

**9.** Explain how advances in technology change labor productivity. Do diminishing returns arise? Provide an example of an advance in technology. Use a graph of the productivity curve to illustrate your answer.

**10.** What can governments in Africa do to encourage economic growth and raise the standard of living in their countries?

**11. Slowing down growth**
China's GDP growth target for the 12th Five-Year-Plan period 2011–2015 is 7 percent a year. This largely symbolic goal (China's average growth rate for the past five years was a whopping 11 percent a year) shows that the central government wants to fundamentally restructure the economy.
Source: *The Daily Telegraph*, September 25, 2011

If China reduces its economic growth rate from 11 percent a year to 7 percent a year, how many additional years will it take for GDP to double? In what year will China's GDP quadruple?

**12.** Read *Eye on Rich and Poor Nations* on p. 511. Which nations are the richest and which are growing the fastest? What are the conditions that lead to higher incomes and faster-growing incomes?

---

### LIST 1

• Dell introduces a new supercomputer that everyone can afford.
• A major hurricane hits Florida.
• More high school graduates go to college.
• The CPI rises.
• An economic slump in the rest of the world decreases U.S. exports.

---

### TABLE 1 PRODUCTION FUNCTION

| Labor hours (millions) | Real GDP (millions of 2009 dollars) |
|---|---|
| 0 | 0 |
| 1 | 10 |
| 2 | 19 |
| 3 | 27 |
| 4 | 34 |
| 5 | 40 |

---

### TABLE 2 LABOR MARKET

| Real wage rate (2009 dollars per hour) | Quantity of labor demanded | Quantity of labor supplied |
|---|---|---|
| | (millions of hours per year) | |
| 10 | 1 | 5 |
| 9 | 2 | 4 |
| 8 | 3 | 3 |
| 7 | 4 | 2 |
| 6 | 5 | 1 |

# Instructor Assignable Problems and Applications

1. Distinguish between a low and high income and a low and high economic growth rate. What are the key features of an economy that are present when incomes are high or fast growing and absent when incomes are low and stagnating or growing slowly? Provide an example of an economy with a low income and slow growth rate, a low income and rapid growth rate, and a high income with sustained growth over many decades.

Use the following information to work Problems **2** and **3**.

In Korea, real GDP per hour of labor is $22, the real wage rate is $15 per hour, and people work an average of 46 hours per week.

2. Draw a graph of the demand for and supply of labor in Korea and the United States. Mark a point at the equilibrium quantity of labor per person per week and the real wage rate in each economy. Explain the difference in the two labor markets.

3. Draw a graph of the production functions in Korea and the United States. Mark a point on each production function that shows potential GDP per hour of work in each economy. Explain the difference in the two production functions.

Use the following events that occur one at a time to work Problems **4** and **5**.
- The Middle East cuts supplies of oil to the United States.
- The New York Yankees win the World Series.
- U.S. labor unions negotiate wage hikes that affect all workers.
- A huge scientific breakthrough doubles the output that an additional hour of U.S. labor can produce.
- Migration to the United States increases the working-age population.

4. Sort the items into four groups: those that change the production function, those that change the demand for labor, those that change the supply of labor, and those that do not change the production function, the demand for labor, or the supply of labor. Say in which direction each change occurs.

5. Which of the events increase the equilibrium quantity of labor and increase potential GDP?

6. China's growth rate of real GDP in 2005 and 2006 was 10.5 percent a year and its population growth rate was 0.5 percent a year. If these growth rates continue, in what year would real GDP be twice what it was in 2006? In what year would real GDP per person be twice what it was in 2006?

7. Explain how an increase in physical capital and an increase in human capital change labor productivity. Use a graph to illustrate your answer.

8. Table 1 describes labor productivity in an economy. What must have occured in this economy during year 1?

9. Describe and illustrate in a graph what happened in the economy in Table 1 if in year 1, capital per hour of labor was 30 and in year 2 it was 40.

10. China invests almost 50 percent of its annual production in new capital compared to 15 percent in the United States. Capital per hour of labor in China is about 25 percent of that in the United States. Explain which economy has the higher real GDP per hour of labor, the faster growth rate of labor productivity, and which experiences the more severe diminishing returns.

**TABLE 1 LABOR PRODUCTIVITY**

| Capital per hour of labor | Real GDP per hour of labor | |
|---|---|---|
| | in year 1 | in year 2 |
| 10 | 7 | 9 |
| 20 | 13 | 17 |
| 30 | 18 | 24 |
| 40 | 22 | 30 |
| 50 | 25 | 35 |
| 60 | 27 | 39 |
| 70 | 28 | 42 |

# Critical Thinking Discussion Questions

1. **Minimum wage up to £6.50 an hour**

   A million workers in the U.K. will receive their first real wage rate rise in six years. The national minimum wage will increase by 19p an hour to £6.50, the government has announced.

   Source: BBC, 12 March 2014

   Think about the U.K. minimum wage:

   How can this rise in the minimum wage lead to job rationing?

   What kind of unemployment is created by job rationing?

   What effect does a rise in the minimum wage have on the natural unemployment rate?

   Does a rise in the minimum wage have any effect on potential GDP?

2. **China's economic growth gains pace**

   China's economy grew 7.8 % in the third quarter of 2013 from a year earlier, the National Bureau of Statistics said in Beijing today.

   Source: *Sydney Morning Herald*, 18 October 2013

   Think about economic growth in China:

   What contribution does a change in China's economic growth rate make to changes in China's standard of living?

   Why is China's economic growth rate higher than the growth rate in advanced economies?

   If China's economy continues to grow at this rate, when will real GDP double?

3. **Malaysia-Singapore high-speed rail on fast track**

   The Malaysia-Singapore high-speed rail will shorten the rail journey between Kuala Lumpur and Singapore to two-and-a-half hours. The mass-rapid transit project has implemented innovative methods such as utilizing high-tech equipment, diversifying resources, and training the workforce involved in the project.

   Source: *The Rakyat Post*, 13 May 2014

   Think about the Malaysia-Singapore high-speed rail:

   What is the effect of the increase in capital provided by the Malaysia-Singapore high-speed rail on the productivity curves of Malaysia and Singapore?

   Can high-speed rail have spillover effects into other areas of the economy?

   What growth theory best describes the effects of this high-speed rail project on Malaysia and Singapore?

4. **Indian IT companies tap Africa's new-fangled fad for technology**

   India's software services companies are investing in Africa, eager to win customers and market share in a continent that is home to fast-growing enterprises and under-developed technology infrastructure.

   Source: *The Economic Times*, 13 May 2014

   Think about India's investment in Africa:

   What preconditions for economic growth are missing in Africa?

   How can India's software services companies encourage African economic growth?

   Is foreign investment necessary for African growth?

   Is Africa an example of the classical growth theory in action?

How does the Fed create money and regulate its quantity?

# Money and the Monetary System

## 18

**When you have completed your study of this chapter, you will be able to**

1  Define money and describe its functions.

2  Describe the functions of banks.

3  Describe the functions of the Federal Reserve System (the Fed).

4  Explain how the banking system creates money and how the Fed controls the quantity of money.

## 18.1 WHAT IS MONEY?

Money, like fire and the wheel, has been around for a very long time. An incredible array of items has served as money. North American Indians used wampum (beads made from shells), Fijians used whales' teeth, and early American colonists used tobacco. Cakes of salt served as money in Ethiopia and Tibet. What do wampum, whales' teeth, tobacco, and salt have in common? Why are they examples of money? Today, when we want to buy something, we use coins or notes (dollar bills), write a check, send an e-check, present a credit or debit card, or use a "smart card." Are all these things that we use today money? To answer these questions, we need a definition of money.

### ■ Definition of Money

**Money** **Money** is any commodity or token that is generally accepted as a *means of payment*.
Any commodity or token that is This definition has three parts that we'll examine in turn.
generally accepted as a *means of payment*.

#### A Commodity or Token

Money is always something that can be recognized and that can be divided up into small parts. So money might be an actual commodity, such as a bar of silver or gold. But it might also be a token, such as a quarter or a $10 bill. Money might also be a virtual token, such as an electronic record in a bank's database (more about this type of money later).

#### Generally Accepted

Money is *generally* accepted, which means that it can be used to buy *anything and everything*. Some tokens can be used to buy some things but not others. For example, a bus pass is accepted as payment for a bus ride, but you can't use your bus pass to buy toothpaste. So a bus pass is not money. In contrast, you can use a $5 bill to buy either a bus ride or toothpaste—or anything else that costs $5 or less. So a $5 bill is money.

#### Means of Payment

**Means of payment** A **means of payment** is a method of settling a debt. When a payment has been
A method of settling a debt. made, the deal is complete. Suppose that Gus buys a car from his friend Ann. Gus doesn't have enough money to pay for the car right now, but he will have enough three months from now, when he gets paid. Ann agrees that Gus may pay for the car in three months' time. Gus buys the car with a loan from Ann and then pays off the loan. The loan isn't money. Money is what Gus uses to pay off the loan.

So what wampum, whales' teeth, tobacco, and salt have in common is that they have served as a generally accepted means of payment, and that is why they are examples of money.

### ■ The Functions of Money

Money performs three vital functions. It serves as a

- Medium of exchange
- Unit of account
- Store of value

## Medium of Exchange

A **medium of exchange** is an object that is generally accepted in return for goods and services. Money is a medium of exchange. Without money, you would have to exchange goods and services directly for other goods and services—an exchange called **barter.** Barter requires a *double coincidence of wants.* For example, if you want a soda and have only a paperback novel to offer in exchange for it, you must find someone who is selling soda and who also wants your paperback novel. Money guarantees that there is a double coincidence of wants because people with something to sell will always accept money in exchange for it. Money acts as a lubricant that smoothes the mechanism of exchange. Money enables you to specialize in the activity in which you have a comparative advantage (see Chapter 3, pp. 110–112) instead of searching for a double coincidence of wants.

## Unit of Account

An agreed-upon measure for stating the prices of goods and services is called a *unit of account.* To get the most out of your budget, you have to figure out whether going to a rock concert is worth its opportunity cost. But that cost is not dollars and cents. It is the number of movies, cappuccinos, ice-cream cones, or sticks of gum that you must give up to attend the concert. It's easy to do such calculations when all these goods have prices in terms of dollars and cents (see Table 18.1). If a rock concert costs $64 and a movie costs $8, you know right away that going to the concert costs you 8 movies. If a cappuccino costs $4, going to the concert costs 16 cappuccinos. You need only one calculation to figure out the opportunity cost of any pair of goods and services. For example, the opportunity cost of the rock concert is 128 sticks of gum ($64 ÷ 50¢ = 128 sticks of gum).

Now imagine how troublesome it would be if the rock concert ticket agent posted its price as 8 movies, and if the movie theater posted its price as 2 cappuccinos, and if the coffee shop posted the price of a cappuccino as 2 ice-cream cones, and if the ice-cream shop posted its price as 4 sticks of gum! Now how much running around and calculating do you have to do to figure out how much that rock concert is going to cost you in terms of the movies, cappuccino, ice cream, or sticks of gum that you must give up to attend it? You get the answer for movies right away from the sign posted by the ticket agent. For all the other goods, you're going to have to visit many different places to establish the price of each commodity in terms of another and then calculate prices in units that are relevant for your own decision. Cover up the column labeled "price in money units" in Table 18.1 and see how hard it is to figure out the number of sticks of gum it costs to attend a rock concert. It's enough to make a person swear off rock! How much simpler it is using dollars and cents.

## Store of Value

Any commodity or token that can be held and exchanged later for goods and services is called a *store of value.* Money acts as a store of value. If it did not, it would not be accepted in exchange for goods and services. The more stable the value of a commodity or token, the better it can act as a store of value and the more useful it is as money. No store of value is completely stable. The value of a physical object, such as a house, a car, or a work of art, fluctuates over time. The value of the commodities and tokens that we use as money also fluctuates, and when there is inflation, money persistently falls in value.

**Medium of exchange**
An object that is generally accepted in return for goods and services.

**Barter**
The direct exchange of goods and services for other goods and services, which requires a double coincidence of wants.

**TABLE 18.1 A UNIT OF ACCOUNT SIMPLIFIES PRICE COMPARISONS**

| Good | Price in money units | Price in units of another good |
|---|---|---|
| Rock concert | $64.00 | 8 movies |
| Movie | $8.00 | 2 cappuccinos |
| Cappuccino | $4.00 | 2 ice-cream cones |
| Ice-cream cone | $2.00 | 4 sticks of gum |
| Stick of gum | $0.50 | |

**Fiat money**
Objects that are money because the law decrees or orders them to be money.

**Currency**
Notes (dollar bills) and coins.

**M1**
Currency held by individuals and businesses, traveler's checks, and checkable deposits owned by individuals and businesses.

**M2**
M1 plus savings deposits and small time deposits, money market funds, and other deposits.

## ■ Money Today

Money in the world today is called **fiat money.** *Fiat* is a Latin word that means decree or order. Fiat money is money because the law decrees it to be so. The objects used as money have value only because of their legal status as money.

Today's fiat money consists of

- Currency
- Deposits at banks and other financial institutions

### Currency

The notes (dollar bills) and coins that we use in the United States today are known as **currency.** The government declares notes to be money with the words printed on every dollar bill, "This note is legal tender for all debts, public and private."

### Deposits

Deposits at banks, credit unions, savings banks, and savings and loan associations are also money. Deposits are money because they can be used to make payments. You don't need to go to the bank to get currency to make a payment. You can write a check or use your debit card to tell your bank to move some money from your account to someone else's.

### Currency Inside the Banks Is Not Money

Although currency and bank deposits are money, currency *inside the banks* is *not money*. The reason is while currency is inside a bank, it isn't available as a means of payment. When you get some cash from the ATM, you convert your bank deposit into currency. You change the form of your money, but there is no change in the quantity of money that you own. Your bank deposit decreases, and your currency holding increases.

If we counted bank deposits and currency inside the banks as money, think about what would happen to the quantity of money when you get cash from the ATM. The quantity of money would appear to decrease. Your currency would increase, but both bank deposits and currency inside the banks would decrease.

You can see that counting both bank deposits and currency inside the banks as money would be double counting.

## ■ Official Measures of Money: M1 and M2

Figure 18.1 shows the items that make up two official measures of money. **M1** consists of currency held by individuals and businesses, traveler's checks, and checkable deposits owned by individuals and businesses. **M2** consists of M1 plus savings deposits and time deposits (less than $100,000), money market funds, and other deposits. Time deposits are deposits that can be withdrawn only after a fixed term. Money market funds are deposits that are invested in short-term securities.

### Are M1 and M2 Means of Payment?

The test of whether something is money is whether it is a generally accepted means of payment. Currency passes the test. Checkable deposits also pass the test because they can be transferred from one person to another by using a debit card or writing a check. So all the components of M1 serve as means of payment.

■ **FIGURE 18.1**

Two Measures of Money: June 2013

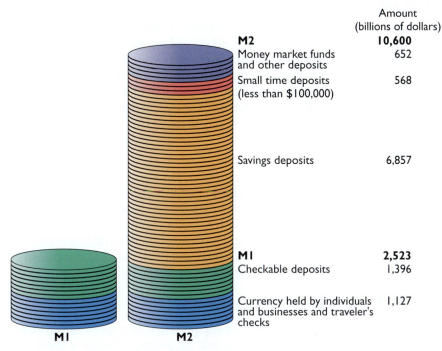

| | Amount (billions of dollars) |
|---|---|
| **M2** | **10,600** |
| Money market funds and other deposits | 652 |
| Small time deposits (less than $100,000) | 568 |
| Savings deposits | 6,857 |
| **M1** | **2,523** |
| Checkable deposits | 1,396 |
| Currency held by individuals and businesses and traveler's checks | 1,127 |

**M1** Currency held by individuals and businesses and traveler's checks plus checkable deposits owned by individuals and businesses.

**M2** M1 plus savings deposits plus small time deposits plus money market funds and other deposits.

SOURCE OF DATA: Federal Reserve.

Some of the savings deposits in M2 are also instantly convertible into a means of payment. You can use the ATM to get currency to pay for your groceries or gas. But other savings deposits, time deposits, and money market funds are not instantly convertible and are *not* a means of payment.

## ■ Checks, Credit Cards, Debit Cards, and E-Checks

In defining money and describing the things that serve as money today, we have not included checks, credit cards and debit cards, or e-checks. Aren't these things that we use when we buy something also money?

### Checks

A check is not money. It is an instruction to a bank to make a payment. The easiest way to see why a check is not money is to think about how the quantity of money you own changes if you write a check. You don't suddenly have more money because you've written a check to pay a bill. Your money is your bank deposit, not the value of the checks you've written.

### Credit Cards

A credit card is not money. It is a special type of ID card that gets you an instant loan. Suppose that you use your credit card to buy a textbook. You sign or enter your PIN and leave the store with your book. The book may be in your possession, but you've not yet paid for it. You've taken a loan from the bank that issued your credit card. Your credit card issuer pays the bookstore and you eventually get your credit card bill, which you pay using money.

### Debit Cards

A debit card works like a paper check, only faster. And just as a check isn't money, neither is a debit card. To see why a debit card works like a check, think about what happens if you use your debit card to buy your textbook. When the sales clerk swipes your card in the bookstore, the computer in the bookstore's bank gets a message: Take $100 from your account and put it in the account of the bookstore. The transaction is done in a flash. But again, the bank deposits are the money and the debit card is the tool that causes money to move from you to the bookstore.

### E-Checks

An *electronic check* (or *e-check*) is an electronic equivalent of a paper check. A group of more than 90 banks and other financial institutions have formed the Financial Services Technology Consortium to collaborate on developing the electronic check. Bank of Internet USA offers an Internet e-check system via e-mail. Like a paper check, an e-check is not money. The deposit transferred is money.

You now know that checks, credit cards and debit cards, and e-checks are not money, but one new information-age money is gradually emerging—e-cash.

## ■ An Embryonic New Money: E-Cash

*Electronic cash* (or *e-cash*) is an electronic equivalent of paper notes (dollar bills) and coins. It is an electronic currency, and for people who are willing to use it, e-cash works like other forms of money. But for e-cash to become a widely used form of money, it must evolve some of the characteristics of physical currency.

People use physical currency because it is portable, recognizable, transferable, untraceable, and anonymous and can be used to make change. The designers of e-cash aim to reproduce all of these features of notes and coins. Today's e-cash is portable, untraceable, and anonymous, but it has not yet reached the level of recognition that makes it *universally* accepted as a means of payment. E-cash doesn't yet meet the definition of money.

Like notes and coins, e-cash can be used in shops. It can also be used over the Internet. To use e-cash in a shop, the buyer uses a smart card that stores some e-cash and the shop uses a smart card reader. When a transaction is made, e-cash is transferred from the smart card directly to the shop's bank account. Users of smart cards receive their e-cash by withdrawing it from a bank account by using a special ATM or a special cell phone.

Several versions of e-cash in U.S. dollars, euros, and other currencies are available on the Internet. The most popular and widely used e-cash system is PayPal, which is owned by eBay. The most sophisticated and secure e-cash is a currency called Bitcoin, which can be used to settle debts and be traded for dollars and other currencies on the Internet.

A handy advantage of e-cash over paper notes arises when you lose your wallet. If it is stuffed with dollar bills, you're out of luck. If it contains e-cash recorded on your smart card, your bank can cancel the e-cash stored on the card and issue you replacement e-cash.

Although e-cash is not yet universally accepted, it is likely that its use will grow and that it will gradually replace physical forms of currency.

# CHECKPOINT 18.1

**Define money and describe its functions.**

## Practice Problems

1. In the United States today, which of the items in List 1 are money?

2. In January 2013, currency and traveler's checks held by individuals and businesses was $1,101 billion; checkable deposits owned by individuals and businesses were $1,365 billion; savings deposits were $6,710 billion; small time deposits were $621 billion; and money market funds and other deposits were $652 billion. Calculate M1 and M2 in January 2013.

3. In July 2013, M1 was $2,549 billion; M2 was $10,710 billion; checkable deposits owned by individuals and businesses were $1,414 billion; small time deposits were $556 billion; and money market funds and other deposits were $665 billion. Calculate currency and traveler's checks held by individuals and businesses. Calculate savings deposits.

> **LIST 1**
>
> - Your Visa card
> - The quarters inside vending machines
> - U.S. dollar bills in your wallet
> - The check that you have just written to pay for your rent
> - The loan you took out last August to pay for your tuition

## In the News

**The cell phone as wallet: Will the trend catch on?**
With the simple swipe of a phone—even when the battery's dead—consumers can now pay for their coffee, gas, or groceries. But as this technology becomes increasingly available, experts ask will it catch on?

Source: CTVNews.ca, September 24, 2011

As people use their cell phones to make payments, will currency disappear? How will the components of M1 change? Will debit cards disappear?

## Solutions to Practice Problems

1. Money is defined as a means of payment. Only the quarters inside vending machines and U.S. dollar bills in your wallet are money.

2. M1 is $2,466 billion. M1 is the sum of currency and traveler's checks held by individuals and businesses ($1,101 billion) and checkable deposits owned by individuals and businesses ($1,365 billion).

    M2 is $10,449 billion. M2 is the sum of M1 ($2,466 billion), savings deposits ($6,710 billion), small time deposits ($621 billion), and money market funds and other deposits ($652 billion).

3. Currency and traveler's checks held by individuals and businesses is $1,135 billion. Currency and traveler's checks equals M1 ($2,549 billion) minus checkable deposits owned by individuals and businesses ($1,414 billion).

    Savings deposits are $6,940 billion. Savings deposits equals M2 ($10,710 billion) minus M1 ($2,549 billion) minus small time deposits ($556 billion) minus money market funds and other deposits ($665 billion)

## Solution to In the News

Most people will probably carry less currency, but it won't disappear because currency is used in the underground economy. Most of M1 will be checkable deposits. Cell phones and debit cards will be perfect substitutes, so debit cards will probably disappear.

## 18.2 THE BANKING SYSTEM

The banking system consists of the Federal Reserve and the banks and other institutions that accept deposits and that provide the services that enable people and businesses to make and receive payments. Sitting at the top of the system (see Figure 18.2), the Federal Reserve (or Fed) sets the rules and regulates and influences the activities of the banks and other institutions. Three types of financial institutions accept the deposits that are part of the nation's money:

- Commercial banks
- Thrift institutions
- Money market funds

Here, we describe the functions of these institutions, and in the next section, we describe the structure and functions of the Fed.

### ■ Commercial Banks

A *commercial bank* is a firm that is chartered by the Comptroller of the Currency in the U.S. Treasury (or by a state agency) to accept deposits and make loans. In 2013, about 5,850 commercial banks operated in the United States, down from 13,000 a few years ago. The number of banks has shrunk because in 1997 the rules under which banks operate were changed, permitting them to open branches in every state. A wave of mergers followed this change of rules. Also, more than 130 banks failed during the financial crisis of 2008–2009.

### Bank Deposits

A commercial bank accepts three broad types of deposits: checkable deposits, savings deposits, and time deposits. A bank pays a low interest rate (sometimes zero) on checkable deposits, and it pays the highest interest rate on time deposits.

---

### ■ FIGURE 18.2

The Institutions of the Banking System

The Federal Reserve regulates and influences the activities of the commercial banks, thrift institutions, and money market funds, whose deposits make up the nation's money.

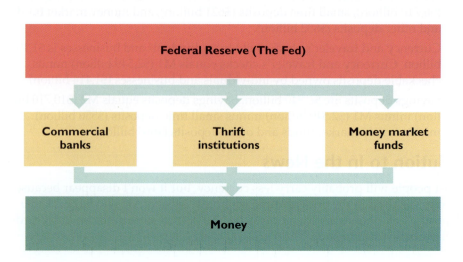

# EYE on the PAST
## The "Invention" of Banking

It is the sixteenth century somewhere in Europe: Because gold is valuable and easy to steal, goldsmiths have well-guarded safes in which people "deposit" their gold. The goldsmiths issue gold receipts entitling owners to reclaim their "deposits" on demand.

Isabella, who has a receipt for 100 ounces of gold deposited with Samuel Goldsmith, buys some land from Henry. She can pay for the land in one of two ways: She can visit Samuel, collect her gold, and hand the gold to Henry. Or she can give Henry her gold receipt, which enables Henry to claim the 100 ounces of gold.

It is a simpler and safer transaction to use the receipt. When Henry wants to buy something, he too can pass the receipt on to someone else.

So Samuel Goldsmith's gold receipt is circulating as a means of payment. It is money!

Because the receipts circulate while the gold remains in his safe, Samuel realizes that he can lend gold receipts and charge interest for doing so. Samuel writes receipts for gold that he doesn't own, but has on deposit, and lends these receipts. Samuel is one of the first bankers.

## Profit and Risk: A Balancing Act

Commercial banks try to maximize their stockholders' wealth by lending for long terms at high interest rates and borrowing from depositors and others. But lending is risky. Risky loans sometimes don't get repaid and the prices of risky securities sometimes fall. In either of these events, a bank incurs a loss that could even wipe out the stockholders' wealth. Also, when depositors see their bank incurring losses, mass withdrawals—called a run on the bank—might create a crisis. So a bank must perform a balancing act. It must be careful in the way it uses the depositors' funds and balance security for depositors and stockholders against high but risky returns. To trade off between risk and profit a bank divides its assets into four parts: reserves, liquid assets, securities, and loans.

## Reserves

A bank's **reserves** consist of currency in its vaults plus the balance on its reserve account at a Federal Reserve Bank.

The currency in a bank's vaults is a reserve to meet its depositors' withdrawals. Your bank must replenish currency in its ATM every time you and your friends have raided it for cash for a midnight pizza.

A commercial bank's deposit at a Federal Reserve Bank is similar to your own bank deposit. The bank uses its reserve account at the Fed to receive and make payments to other banks and to obtain currency. The Fed requires banks to hold a minimum percentage of deposits as reserves, called the *required reserve ratio*. Banks *desired* reserves might exceed the required reserves, especially when the cost of borrowing reserves is high.

**Reserves**
The currency in the bank's vaults plus the balance on its reserve account at a Federal Reserve Bank.

## Liquid Assets

Banks' *liquid assets* are short-term Treasury bills and overnight loans to other banks. The interest rates on liquid assets are low but these are low-risk assets. The interest rate on interbank loans, called the **federal funds rate,** is the central target of the Fed's monetary policy actions.

## Securities and Loans

*Securities* are bonds issued by the U.S. government and by other organizations. Some bonds have low interest rates and are safe. Some bonds have high interest rates and are risky. Mortgage-backed securities are examples of risky securities.

    *Loans* are the provision of funds to businesses and individuals. Loans earn the bank a high interest rate, but they are risky and, even when not very risky, cannot be called in before the agreed date. Banks earn the highest interest rate on unpaid credit card balances, which are loans to credit card holders.

## Bank Assets and Liabilities: The Relative Magnitudes

Figure 18.3 shows the relative magnitudes of the banks' assets and liabilities—deposits and other borrowing—in 2013. After performing their profit-versus-risk balancing acts, the banks kept 18 percent of total assets in reserves (and liquid assets), 22 percent in securities, and 60 percent in loans. Checkable deposits (part of M1) were 9 percent of total funds—liabilities and net worth. Another 46 percent of total funds were savings deposits and small time deposits (part of M2).

    The commercial banks' asset allocation in 2013 is not normal and is a consequence of a financial crisis in 2008 and 2009. *Eye on the U.S. Economy* on the next page contrasts normal times with the depth of the crisis.

**Federal funds rate**
The interest rate on interbank loans (loans made in the federal funds market).

---

■ **FIGURE 18.3**

### Commercial Banks' Assets, Liabilities, and Net Worth

In 2013, commercial bank loans were 60 percent of total assets, securities were 22 percent, and reserves were 18 percent. Reserves were unusually large in 2013.

The banks obtained the funds allocated to these assets from checkable deposits in M1, which were 9 percent of total funds; savings deposits and small time deposits in M2 were 46 percent; other deposits were 15 percent; other borrowing was 20 percent; and bank stockholders' net worth was 11 percent.

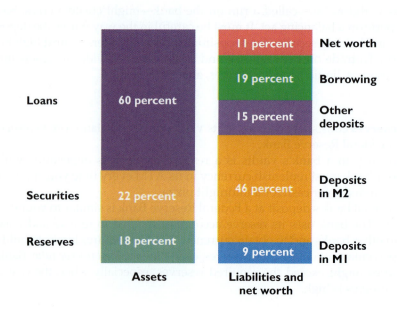

# EYE on the U.S. ECONOMY
## Commercial Banks Under Stress in the Financial Crisis

In normal times, bank reserves are less than 1 percent of total assets and liquid assets are less than 4 percent. Loans are 68 percent and securities 28 percent. July 2007 was such a normal time (the orange bars).

During the financial crisis that started in 2007 and intensified in September 2008, the banks took big hits as the value of their securities and loans fell.

Faced with a riskier world, the banks increased their liquid assets and reserves. In September 2009 (the blue bars), liquid assets were almost 10 percent of total assets and reserves were 8 percent.

The balancing act tipped away from risk-taking and toward security.

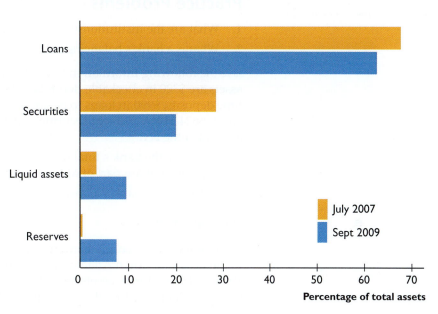

SOURCE OF DATA: Federal Reserve.

## ■ Thrift Institutions

The three types of thrift institutions are savings and loan associations, savings banks, and credit unions. A *savings and loan association (S&L)* is a financial institution that accepts checkable deposits and savings deposits and that makes personal, commercial, and home-purchase loans. A *savings bank* is a financial institution that accepts savings deposits and makes mostly consumer and home-purchase loans. The depositors own some savings banks (called mutual savings banks). A *credit union* is a financial institution owned by a social or economic group, such as a firm's employees, that accepts savings deposits and makes mostly consumer loans.

Like commercial banks, the thrift institutions hold reserves and must meet minimum reserve ratios set by the Fed.

## ■ Money Market Funds

A *money market fund* is a financial institution that obtains funds by selling shares and uses these funds to buy assets such as U.S. Treasury bills. Money market fund shares act like bank deposits. Shareholders can write checks on their money market fund accounts, but there are restrictions on most of these accounts. For example, the minimum deposit accepted might be $2,500 and the smallest check a depositor is permitted to write might be $500.

**CHECKPOINT 18.2**

**Describe the functions of banks.**

## Practice Problems

1. What are the institutions that make up the banking system?
2. What is a bank's balancing act?

Use the following information to work Problems **3** and **4**. A bank's deposits and assets are $320 in checkable deposits, $896 in savings deposits, $840 in small time deposits, $990 in loans to businesses, $400 in outstanding credit card balances, $634 in government securities, $2 in currency, and $30 in its reserve account at the Fed.

3. Calculate the bank's total deposits, deposits that are part of M1, and deposits that are part of M2.
4. Calculate the bank's loans, securities, and reserves.

## In the News

**Regulators close Georgia bank in 95th failure for the year**
Regulators shut down Atlanta-based Georgian Bank. On July 24, 2009, Georgian Bank had $2 billion in assets and $2 billion in deposits. By September 29, 2009, Georgian Bank had lost about $2 billion in home loans and other assets.

Source: *USA Today*, September 30, 2009

Explain how Georgian Bank's balancing act failed.

## Solutions to Practice Problems

1. The institutions that make up the banking system are the Fed, commercial banks, thrift institutions, and money market funds.
2. A bank makes a profit by borrowing from depositors at a low interest rate and lending at a higher interest rate. The bank must hold enough reserves to meet depositors' withdrawals. The bank's balancing act is to balance the risk of loans (profits for stockholders) against the security for depositors.
3. Total deposits are $320 + $896 + $840 = $2,056.
   Deposits that are part of M1 are checkable deposits, $320.
   Deposits that are part of M2 include all deposits, $2,056.
4. Loans are $990 + $400 = $1,390. Securities are $634.
   Reserves are $30 + $2 = $32.

## Solution to In the News

In July, Georgian Bank's $2 billion of assets (home loans and securities) balanced its deposits of $2 billion. The bank expected to make a profit on its assets that exceeded the interest it paid to depositors. The financial crisis increased the risk on all financial assets. The bank was now holding assets that were more risky than it had planned. As people defaulted on their home loans and the value of securities fell, the value of Georgian Bank's assets crashed to zero. With fewer assets than deposits, regulators had no choice other than to close the bank and sell its assets and deposits. The bank failed to balance risk against profit.

## 18.3   THE FEDERAL RESERVE SYSTEM

The **Federal Reserve System (the Fed)** is the central bank of the United States. A central bank is a public authority that provides banking services to banks and governments and regulates financial institutions and markets. A central bank does not provide banking services to businesses and individual citizens. Its only customers are banks such as Bank of America and Citibank and the U.S. government. The Fed is organized into 12 Federal Reserve districts shown in Figure 18.4.

The Fed's main task is to regulate the interest rate and quantity of money to achieve low and predictable inflation and sustained economic expansion.

**Federal Reserve System (the Fed)**
The central bank of the United States.

### ■ The Structure of the Federal Reserve

The key elements in the structure of the Federal Reserve are

- The Chairman of the Board of Governors
- The Board of Governors
- The regional Federal Reserve Banks
- The Federal Open Market Committee

### The Chairman of the Board of Governors

The Chairman of the Board of Governors is the Fed's chief executive, public face, and center of power and responsibility. When things go right, the Chairman gets the credit; when they go wrong, he gets the blame. Janet Yellen, a former University of California, Berkeley, economics professor, is the Fed's current Chair.

*Fed Chair Janet Yellen*

■ **FIGURE 18.4**

### The Federal Reserve Districts

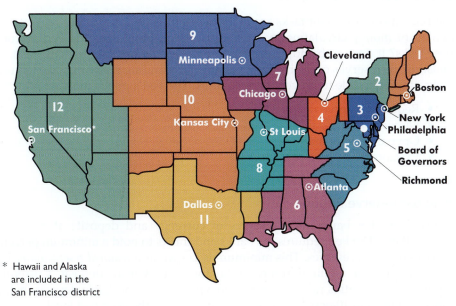

The nation is divided into 12 Federal Reserve districts, each having a Federal Reserve Bank. (Some of the larger districts also have branch banks.) The Board of Governors of the Federal Reserve System is located in Washington, D.C.

\* Hawaii and Alaska are included in the San Francisco district

SOURCE: *Federal Reserve Bulletin.*

### The Board of Governors

The Board of Governors has seven members (including the Chairman), who are appointed by the President of the United States and confirmed by the Senate, each for a 14-year term. The terms are staggered so that one seat on the board becomes vacant every two years. The President appoints one of the board members as Chairman for a term of four years, which is renewable.

### The Regional Federal Reserve Banks

There are 12 regional Federal Reserve Banks, one for each of the 12 Federal Reserve districts shown in Figure 18.4. Each regional Federal Reserve Bank has nine directors, three of whom are appointed by the Board of Governors and six of whom are elected by the commercial banks in the Federal Reserve district. The directors of each regional Federal Reserve Bank appoint that Bank's president, and the Board of Governors approves this appointment.

The Federal Reserve Bank of New York (known as the New York Fed) occupies a special place because it implements some of the Fed's most important policy decisions.

### The Federal Open Market Committee

**Federal Open Market Committee**
The Fed's main policy-making committee.

The **Federal Open Market Committee** (FOMC) is the Fed's main policy-making committee. The FOMC consists of the following twelve members:

- The Chairman and the other six members of the Board of Governors
- The president of the Federal Reserve Bank of New York
- Four presidents of the other regional Federal Reserve Banks (on a yearly rotating basis)

The FOMC meets approximately every six weeks to review the state of the economy and to decide the actions to be carried out by the New York Fed.

## ■ The Fed's Policy Tools

The Fed's most important tasks are to influence the interest rate and regulate the amount of money circulating in the United States. How does the Fed perform these tasks? It does so by adjusting the reserves of the banking system. Also, by adjusting the reserves of the banking system and standing ready to make loans to banks, the Fed is able to prevent bank failures. The Fed's policy tools are:

- Required reserve ratios
- Discount rate
- Open market operations
- Extraordinary crisis measures

### Required Reserve Ratios

You've seen that banks hold reserves of currency and deposits at a Federal Reserve Bank. The Fed requires the banks and thrifts to hold a minimum percentage of deposits as reserves. This minimum is known as a *required reserve ratio*. The Fed determines a required reserve ratio for each type of deposit. Currently, required reserve ratios range from zero to 3 percent on checkable deposits below a specified level to 10 percent on deposits in excess of the specified level.

## Discount Rate

The discount rate is the interest rate at which the Fed stands ready to lend reserves to commercial banks. A change in the discount rate begins with a proposal to the FOMC by at least one of the 12 Federal Reserve Banks. If the FOMC agrees that a change is required, it proposes the change to the Board of Governors for its approval.

## Open Market Operations

An **open market operation** is the purchase or sale of government securities—U.S. Treasury bills and bonds—by the Federal Reserve in the open market. When the Fed conducts an open market operation, it makes a transaction with a bank or some other business but it does not transact with the federal government. The New York Fed conducts the Fed's open market operations.

**Open market operation**
The purchase or sale of government securities—U.S. Treasury bills and bonds—by the New York Fed in the open market.

## Extraordinary Crisis Measures

The financial crisis of 2008, the slow recovery, and ongoing financial stress have brought three more tools into play. They are

- Quantitative easing (or QE)
- Credit easing
- Operation Twist

***Quantitative Easing (QE)*** When the Fed creates bank reserves by conducting a large-scale open market purchase at a low or possibly zero federal funds rate, the action is called *quantitative easing*. There have been three episodes of quantitative easing, QE1, QE2, and QE3—see *Eye on Creating Money* on pp. 540–541.

***Credit Easing*** When the Fed buys private securities or makes loans to financial institutions to stimulate their lending, the action is called *credit easing*.

***Operation Twist*** When the Fed buys long-term government securities and sells short-term government securities, the action is called *Operation Twist*. The idea is to lower long-term interest rates and stimulate long-term borrowing and investment expenditure. An Operation Twist was conducted in September 2011.

## ■ How the Fed's Policy Tools Work

The Fed's normal policy tools work by changing either the demand for or the supply of the monetary base, which in turn changes the interest rate. The **monetary base** is the sum of coins, Federal Reserve notes, and banks' reserves at the Fed.

**Monetary base**
The sum of coins, Federal Reserve notes, and banks' reserves at the Fed.

By increasing the required reserve ratio, the Fed can force the banks to hold a larger quantity of monetary base. By raising the discount rate, the Fed can make it more costly for the banks to borrow reserves—borrow monetary base. And by selling securities in the open market, the Fed can decrease the monetary base. All of these actions lead to a rise in the interest rate.

Similarly, by decreasing the required reserve ratio, the Fed can permit the banks to hold a smaller quantity of monetary base. By lowering the discount rate, the Fed can make it less costly for the banks to borrow monetary base. And by buying securities in the open market, the Fed can increase the monetary base. All of these actions lead to a decrease in the interest rate.

Open market operations are the Fed's main tool and in the next section you will learn in more detail how they work.

# CHECKPOINT 18.3

**Describe the functions of the Federal Reserve System (the Fed).**

## Practice Problems

1. What is the Fed and what is the FOMC?
2. Who is the Fed's chief executive, and what are the Fed's main policy tools?
3. What is the monetary base?
4. Suppose that at the end of December 2009, the monetary base in the United States was $700 billion, Federal Reserve notes were $650 billion, and banks' reserves at the Fed were $20 billion. Calculate the quantity of coins.

## In the News

**Risky assets: Counting to a trillion**
Prior to September 15, 2008, the start of the credit crisis, the Fed had less than $1 trillion in assets and most were safe U.S. government securities. By mid-December, 2008, the Fed's balance sheet had increased to more than $2.3 trillion. Much of the increase was in mortgage-backed securities. The massive expansion began when the Fed starting sending banks cash in exchange for risky assets.

Source: CNN Money, September 29, 2009

What are the Fed's policy tools and which policy tool did the Fed use to increase its assets to $2.3 trillion in 2008?

## Solutions to Practice Problems

1. The Federal Reserve (Fed) is the U.S. central bank—a public authority that provides banking services to banks and the U.S. government and that regulates the quantity of money and the banking system. The FOMC is the Federal Open Market Committee—the Fed's main policy-making committee.
2. The Fed's chief executive is the Chair of the Board of Governors, currently Janet Yellen. The Fed's main policy tools are required reserve ratios, the discount rate, and open market operations. In unusual times, extraordinary crisis measures are an additional tool.
3. The monetary base is the sum of coins, Federal Reserve notes (dollar bills), and banks' reserves at the Fed.
4. To calculate the quantity of coins, we use the definition of the monetary base: coins plus Federal Reserve notes plus banks' reserves at the Fed.

   Quantity of coins = Monetary base − Federal Reserve notes − Banks' reserves at the Fed.

   So at the end of December 2009,

   Quantity of coins = $700 billion − $650 billion − $20 billion
   = $30 billion.

## Solution to In the News

The Fed's policy tools are the required reserve ratio, discount rate, open market operations, and extraordinary crisis measures. The Fed used extraordinary crisis measures called *quantitative easing* and *credit easing.* The Fed's lending program bought risky assets of banks and increased their reserve deposits at the Fed.

## 18.4  REGULATING THE QUANTITY OF MONEY

Banks create money, but this doesn't mean that they have smoke-filled back rooms in which counterfeiters are busily working. Remember, most money is deposits, not currency. What banks create is deposits, and they do so by making loans.

### ■ Creating Deposits by Making Loans

The easiest way to see that banks create deposits is to think about what happens when Andy, who has a Visa card issued by Citibank, uses his card to buy a tank of gas from Chevron. When Andy signs the card sales slip, he takes a loan from Citibank and obligates himself to repay the loan at a later date. At the end of the business day, a Chevron clerk takes a pile of signed credit card sales slips, including Andy's, to Chevron's bank. For now, let's assume that Chevron also banks at Citibank. The bank immediately credits Chevron's account with the value of the slips (minus the bank's commission).

You can see that these transactions have created a bank deposit and a loan. Andy has increased the size of his loan (his credit card balance), and Chevron has increased the size of its bank deposit. And because deposits are money, Citibank has created money.

If, as we've just assumed, Andy and Chevron use the same bank, no further transactions take place. But the outcome is essentially the same when two banks are involved. If Chevron's bank is the Bank of America, then Citibank uses its reserves to pay the Bank of America. Citibank has an increase in loans and a decrease in reserves; the Bank of America has an increase in reserves and an increase in deposits. The banking system as a whole has an increase in loans, an increase in deposits, and no change in reserves.

# EYE on YOUR LIFE
## Money and Your Role in Its Creation

Imagine a world without money in which you must barter for everything you buy. What kinds of items would you have available for these trades? Would you keep some stocks of items that you know lots of people are willing to accept? Would you really be bartering, or would you be using a commodity as money? How much longer would it take you to conduct all the transactions of a normal day?

Now think about your own holdings of money today. How much money do you have in your pocket or wallet? How much do you have in the bank? How does the money you hold change over the course of a month?

Of the money you're holding, which items are part of M1 and which are part of M2? Are all the items in M2 means of payment?

Now think about the role that *you* play in creating money. Every time you charge something to your credit card, you help the bank that issued it to create money. The increase in your credit card balance is a loan from the bank to you. The bank pays the seller right away. So the seller's bank deposit and your outstanding balance increase together. Money is created.

You contribute to the currency drain that limits the ability of your bank to create money when you visit the ATM and get some cash to pay for your late-night pizza.

Of course, your transactions are a tiny part of the total. But together, you and a few million other students like you play a big role in the money creation process.

If Andy had swiped his card at an automatic payment pump, all these transactions would have occurred at the time he filled his tank, and the quantity of money would have increased by the amount of his purchase (minus the bank's commission for conducting the transactions).

Three factors limit the quantity of deposits that the banking system can create:

- The monetary base
- Desired reserves
- Desired currency holding

## The Monetary Base

You've seen that the monetary base is the sum of coins, Federal Reserve notes, and banks' deposits at the Fed. The size of the monetary base limits the total quantity of money that the banking system can create because banks have a desired level of reserves and households and firms have a desired level of currency holding and both of these desired holdings of the monetary base depend on the quantity of money.

## Desired Reserves

A bank's *desired* reserves are the reserves that the bank chooses to hold. The *desired reserve ratio* is the ratio of reserves to deposits that a bank wants to hold. This ratio exceeds the *required reserve ratio* by an amount that the banks determine to be prudent on the basis of their daily business requirements.

A bank's *actual reserve ratio* changes when its customers make a deposit or a withdrawal. If a bank's customer makes a deposit, reserves and deposits increase by the same amount, so the bank's reserve ratio increases. Similarly, if a bank's customer makes a withdrawal, reserves and deposits decrease by the same amount, so the bank's reserve ratio decreases.

**Excess reserves**
A bank's actual reserves minus its desired reserves.

A bank's **excess reserves** are its actual reserves minus its desired reserves. When the banking system as a whole has excess reserves, banks can create money by making new loans. When the banking system as a whole is short of reserves, banks must destroy money by decreasing the quantity of loans.

## Desired Currency Holding

We hold our money in the form of currency and bank deposits. The proportion of money held as currency isn't constant but at any given time, people have a definite view as to how much they want to hold in each form of money.

Because households and firms want to hold some proportion of their money in the form of currency, when the total quantity of bank deposits increases, so does the quantity of currency that they want to hold.

Because desired currency holding increases when deposits increase, currency leaves the banks when loans are made and deposits increase. We call the leakage of currency from the banking system the *currency drain*. And we call the ratio of currency to deposits the *currency drain ratio*.

The greater the currency drain ratio, the smaller is the quantity of deposits and money that the banking system can create from a given amount of monetary base. The reason is that as currency drains from the banks, they are left with a smaller level of reserves (and smaller excess reserves) so they make fewer loans.

## ■ How Open Market Operations Change the Monetary Base

When the Fed buys securities in an open market operation, it pays for them with newly created bank reserves and money. With more reserves in the banking system, the supply of interbank loans increases, the demand for interbank loans decreases, and the federal funds rate—the interest rate in the interbank loans market—falls.

Similarly, when the Fed sells securities in an open market operation, buyers pay for the securities with bank reserves and money. With smaller reserves in the banking system, the supply of interbank loans decreases, the demand for interbank loans increases, and the federal funds rate rises. The Fed sets a target for the federal funds rate and conducts open market operations on the scale needed to hit its target.

A change in the federal funds rate is only the first stage in an adjustment process that follows an open market operation. If banks' reserves increase, the banks can increase their lending and create even more money. If banks' reserves decrease, the banks must decrease their lending, which decreases the quantity of money. We'll study the effects of open market operations in some detail, beginning with an open market purchase.

### The Fed Buys Securities

Suppose the Fed buys $100 million of U.S. government securities in the open market. There are two cases to consider, depending on who sells the securities. A bank might sell some of its securities, or a person or business that is not a commercial bank—the general public—might sell. The outcome is essentially the same in the two cases. To convince you of this fact, we'll study the two cases, starting with the simpler case in which a commercial bank sells securities. (The seller will be someone who thinks the Fed is offering a good price for securities and it is profitable to make the sale.)

*FOMC meeting.*

*A Commercial Bank Sells* When the Fed buys $100 million of securities from the Manhattan Commercial Bank, two things happen:

1. The Manhattan Commercial Bank has $100 million less in securities, and the Fed has $100 million more in securities.

2. To pay for the securities, the Fed increases the Manhattan Commercial Bank's reserve account at the New York Fed by $100 million.

Figure 18.5 shows the effects of these actions on the balance sheets of the Fed and the Manhattan Commercial Bank. Ownership of the securities passes from the commercial bank to the Fed, so the bank's securities decrease by $100 million and the Fed's securities increase by $100 million, as shown by the red-to-blue arrow running from the Manhattan Commercial Bank to the Fed.

The Fed increases the Manhattan Commercial Bank's reserves by $100 million, as shown by the green arrow running from the Fed to the Manhattan Commercial Bank. This action increases the reserves of the banking system.

The commercial bank's total assets remain constant, but their composition changes. Its holdings of government securities decrease by $100 million, and its reserves increase by $100 million. The bank can use these additional reserves to make loans. When the bank makes loans, it creates deposits and the quantity of money increases.

We've just seen that when the Fed buys government securities from a bank, the bank's reserves increase. What happens if the Fed buys government securities from the public—say, from AIG, an insurance company?

**FIGURE 18.5**

The Fed Buys Securities from a Commercial Bank

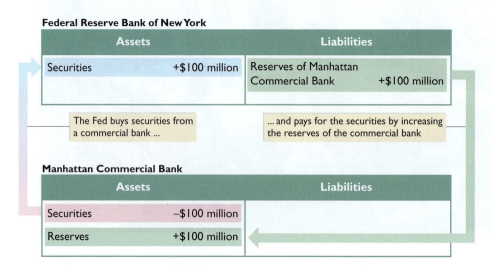

***The Nonbank Public Sells***  When the Fed buys $100 million of securities from AIG, three things happen:

1. AIG has $100 million less in securities, and the Fed has $100 million more in securities.
2. The Fed pays for the securities with a check for $100 million drawn on itself, which AIG deposits in its account at the Manhattan Commercial Bank.
3. The Manhattan Commercial Bank collects payment of this check from the Fed, and the Manhattan Commercial Bank's reserves increase by $100 million.

Figure 18.6 shows the effects of these actions on the balance sheets of the Fed, AIG, and the Manhattan Commercial Bank. Ownership of the securities passes from AIG to the Fed, so AIG's securities decrease by $100 million and the Fed's securities increase by $100 million (red-to-blue arrow). The Fed pays for the securities with a check payable to AIG, which AIG deposits in the Manhattan Commercial Bank. This payment increases Manhattan's reserves by $100 million (green arrow). It also increases AIG's deposit at the Manhattan Commercial Bank by $100 million (blue arrow). This action increases the reserves of the banking system.

## FIGURE 18.6

### The Fed Buys Securities from the Public

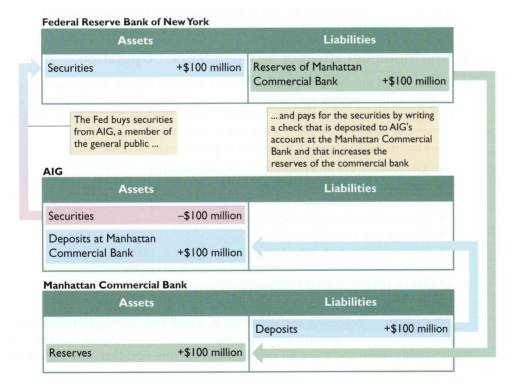

AIG has the same total assets as before, but their composition has changed. It now has more money and fewer securities. The Manhattan Commercial Bank's reserves increase, and so do its deposits—both by $100 million. Because bank reserves and deposits have increased by the same amount, the bank has excess reserves, which it can use to make loans. When it makes loans, the quantity of money increases.

We've worked through what happens when the Fed buys government securities from either a bank or the public. When the Fed sells securities, the transactions that we've just traced operate in reverse.

### The Fed Sells Securities

If the Fed sells $100 million of U.S. government securities in the open market, most likely a person or business other than a bank buys them. (A bank would buy them only if it had excess reserves and couldn't find a better use for its funds.)

When the Fed sells $100 million of securities to AIG, three things happen:

1. AIG has $100 million more in securities, and the Fed has $100 million less in securities.
2. AIG pays for the securities with a check for $100 million drawn on its deposit account at the Manhattan Commercial Bank.
3. The Fed collects payment of this check from the Manhattan Commercial Bank by decreasing its reserves by $100 million.

These actions decrease the reserves of the banking system. The Manhattan Commercial Bank is now short of reserves and must borrow in the federal funds market to meet its desired reserve ratio.

The changes in the balance sheets of the Fed and the banks that we've just described are not the end of the story about the effects of an open market operation; they are just the beginning.

### ■ The Multiplier Effect of an Open Market Operation

An open market purchase that increases bank reserves also increases the *monetary base* by the amount of the open market purchase. Regardless of whether the Fed buys securities from the banks or from the public, the quantity of bank reserves increases and gives the banks excess reserves that they then lend.

The following sequence of events takes place:

- An open market purchase creates excess reserves.
- Banks lend excess reserves.
- Bank deposits increase.
- The quantity of money increases.
- New money is used to make payments.
- Some of the new money is held as currency—a currency drain.
- Some of the new money remains in deposits in banks.
- Banks' desired reserves increase.
- Excess reserves decrease but remain positive.

The sequence described above repeats in a series of rounds, but each round begins with a smaller quantity of excess reserves than did the previous one. The process ends when there are no excess reserves. This situation arises when the increase in the monetary base resulting from the open market operation is willingly held—when the increase in desired reserves plus the increase in desired currency holding equals the increase in the monetary base. Figure 18.7 illustrates and summarizes the sequence of events in one round of the multiplier process.

An open market *sale* works similarly to an open market *purchase*, but the sale *decreases* the monetary base and sets off a multiplier process similar to that described in Figure 18.7. At the end of the process the quantity of money has decreased by an amount that lowers desired reserves and desired currency holding by an amount equal to the decrease in the monetary base resulting from the open market sale. (Make your own version of Figure 18.7 to trace the multiplier process when the Fed *sells* and the banks or public *buys* securities.)

The magnitude of the change in the quantity of money brought about by an open market operation is determined by the money multiplier that we now explain.

## ■ The Money Multiplier

The **money multiplier** is the number by which a change in the monetary base is multiplied to find the resulting change in the quantity of money. It is also the ratio of the change in the quantity of money to the change in the monetary base.

The magnitude of the money multiplier depends on the desired reserve ratio and the currency drain ratio. The smaller are these two ratios, the larger is the money multiplier. Let's explore the money multiplier in more detail.

**Money multiplier**
The number by which a change in the monetary base is multiplied to find the resulting change in the quantity of money.

■ **FIGURE 18.7**

A Round in the Multiplier Process Following an Open Market Operation

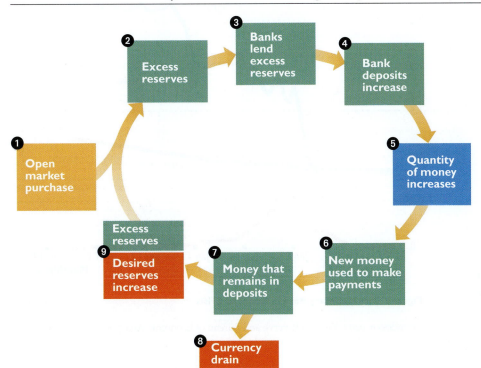

❶ An open market purchase increases bank reserves and ❷ creates excess reserves.

❸ Banks lend the excess reserves, ❹ new deposits are created, and ❺ the quantity of money increases.

❻ New money is used to make payments.

❼ Households and firms receiving payments keep some on deposit in banks and ❽ some in the form of currency—a currency drain.

❾ The increase in bank deposits increases banks' reserves but also increases banks' desired reserves.

Desired reserves increase by less than actual reserves, so the banks still have some excess reserves, but less than before. The process repeats until excess reserves have been eliminated.

To see how the desired reserve ratio and the currency drain ratio determine the size of the money multiplier, begin with two facts:

The quantity of money, $M$, is the sum of deposits, $D$, and currency, $C$, or $M = D + C$, and

The monetary base, $MB$, is the sum of reserves, $R$, and currency, $C$, or $MB = R + C$.

The money multiplier is equal to the quantity of money, $M$, divided by the monetary base, $MB$, that is:

$$\text{Money multiplier} = M/MB.$$

Because $M = D + C$ and $MB = R + C$ then:

$$\text{Money multiplier} = (D + C)/(R + C).$$

# EYE on CREATING MONEY

## How Does the Fed Create Money and Regulate Its Quantity?

During the Great Depression, many banks failed, bank deposits were destroyed, and the quantity of money crashed by 25 percent. Most economists believe that it was these events that turned an ordinary recession in 1929 into a deep and decade-long depression.

Former Fed Chairman Ben Bernanke is one of the economists who has studied this tragic episode in U.S. economic history, and he had no intention of witnessing a similar event on his watch.

Figure 1 shows what the Fed did to pump reserves into the banking system. In the fall of 2008 in an episode called QE1 (see p. 531), the Fed doubled the monetary base. In 2010 and 2011, a more gradual but sustained QE2 took the monetary base to more than three times its pre-crisis level. And in 2012 and 2013, a further gradual QE3 raised the monetary base to four times its normal level.

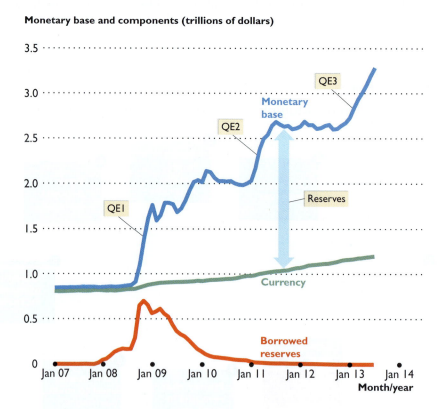

**Figure 1  The Monetary Base in Financial Crisis**

SOURCES OF DATA: Federal Reserve and Bureau of Economic Analysis

Now divide each item on the right-hand side of the previous equation by deposits, $D$, to get:

$$\text{Money multiplier} = (1 + C/D)/(R/D + C/D)$$

Notice the $D/D = 1$; $C/D$ is the currency drain ratio, and $R/D$ is the desired reserves ratio.

If the currency drain ratio is 50 percent, $C/D = 0.5$; and if the desired reserve ratio is 10 percent, $R/D = 0.1$ so the money multiplier is $1.5/0.6 = 2.5$.

The larger the reserve ratio and the larger the currency drain ratio, the smaller is the money multiplier.

The reserve ratio and the currency drain ratio that determine the magnitude of the money multiplier are not constant, so neither is the money multiplier constant. You can see in *Eye on Creating Money* below that the desired reserve ratio and money multiplier changed dramatically in 2008.

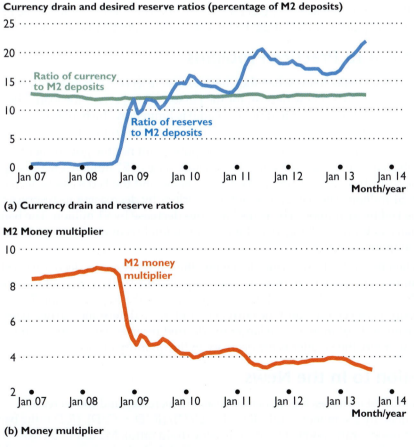

**(a) Currency drain and reserve ratios**

**(b) Money multiplier**

**Figure 2 The Changing Money Multiplier**

This extraordinary increase in the monetary base did not bring a similar increase in the quantity of money. Figure 2 shows the reason.

In 2008, the banks' desired reserve ratio, in part (a), increased tenfold from its normal level of 1.2 percent to 12 percent. This increase brought a crash in the money multiplier, in part (b), from a normal value of 9 to an unusually low value of 5.

The surge in the desired reserve ratio is the sole reason for the collapse in the money multiplier. You can see, in part (a), that the other influence on the multiplier, the currency drain ratio, barely changed.

The banks face an unusually high level of risk and this is the main source of the increase in the desired reserve ratio. As the risk faced by banks returns to normal, the desired reserve ratio will fall, and when this happens the Fed will decrease the monetary base or create an explosion in the quantity of money.

CHECKPOINT 18.4

**Explain how the banking system creates money and how the Fed controls the quantity of money.**

## Practice Problems

1. How do banks create new deposits by making loans, and what factors limit the amount of deposits and loans that they can create?

2. If the Fed makes an open market sale of $1 million of securities, who can buy the securities? What initial changes occur if the Fed sells to a bank?

3. If the Fed makes an open market sale of $1 million of securities, what is the process by which the quantity of money changes? What factors determine the change in the quantity of money?

## In the News

**Fed doubles monetary base**
During the fourth quarter of 2008, the Fed doubled the monetary base but the quantity of money (M2) increased by only 5 percent.

Source: Federal Reserve

Why did M2 not increase by much more than 5 percent? What would have happened to the quantity of M2 if the Fed had kept the monetary base constant?

## Solutions to Practice Problems

1. Banks can make loans when they have excess reserves. When a bank makes a loan, it creates a new deposit for the person who receives the loan. The amount of deposits created (loans made) is limited by the banks' excess reserves, its desired reserve ratio, and the currency drain ratio.

2. The Fed sells securities to banks or the public, but not the government. The initial change is a decrease in the monetary base of $1 million. Ownership of the securities passes from the Fed to the bank, and the Fed's assets decrease by $1 million. The bank pays for the securities by decreasing its reserves at the Fed by $1 million. The Fed's liabilities decrease by $1 million. The bank's total assets are unchanged, but it has $1 million less in reserves and $1 million more in securities.

3. When the Fed sells securities to a bank, the bank's reserves decrease by $1 million. The bank's deposits do not change, so the bank is short of reserves. The bank calls in loans and deposits decrease by the same amount. The desired reserve ratio and the currency drain ratio determine the decrease in the quantity of money. The larger the desired reserve ratio or the currency drain ratio, the smaller is the decrease in the quantity of money.

## Solution to In the News

When the Fed increases the monetary base, M2 increases and the increase is determined by the money multiplier, $(1 + C/D)/(R/D + C/D)$, ($R/D$ is the banks' desired reserve ratio and $C/D$ is the currency drain ratio). M2 didn't increase by more than 5 percent because the banks increased their desired reserve ratio, $R/D$, which decreased the money multiplier. If the Fed had kept the monetary base unchanged, M2 would have decreased because the money multiplier decreased.

## CHAPTER SUMMARY

## Key Points

**1. Define money and describe its functions.**

- Money is anything that serves as a generally accepted means of payment.
- Money functions as a medium of exchange, unit of account, and store of value.
- M1 consists of currency held by individuals and businesses, travelers' checks, and checkable deposits owned by individuals and businesses.
- M2 consists of M1 plus savings deposits, small time deposits, and money market funds.

**2. Describe the functions of banks.**

- The deposits of commercial banks and thrift institutions are money.
- Banks borrow short term and lend long term and make a profit on the spread between the interest rates that they pay and receive.

**3. Describe the functions of the Federal Reserve System (the Fed).**

- The Federal Reserve is the central bank of the United States.
- The Fed influences the economy by setting the required reserve ratio for banks, by setting the discount rate, by open market operations, and by taking extraordinary measures in a financial crisis.

**4. Explain how the banking system creates money and how the Fed controls the quantity of money.**

- Banks create money by making loans.
- The maximum quantity of deposits the banks can create is limited by the monetary base, the banks' desired reserves, and desired currency holding.
- When the Fed buys securities in an open market operation, it creates bank reserves. When the Fed sells securities in an open market operation, it destroys bank reserves.
- An open market operation has a multiplier effect on the quantity of money.

## Key Terms

Barter, 519
Currency, 520
Excess reserves, 534
Federal funds rate, 526
Federal Open Market
  Committee, 530
Federal Reserve System
  (the Fed), 529
Fiat money, 520

M1, 520
M2, 520
Means of payment, 518
Medium of exchange, 519
Monetary base, 531
Money, 518
Money multiplier, 539
Open market operation, 531
Reserves, 525

# CHAPTER CHECKPOINT

## Study Plan Problems and Applications

1. What is money? Would you classify any of the items in List 1 as money?

2. What are the three functions that money performs? Which of the following items perform some but not all of these functions, and which perform all of these functions? Which of the items are money?
   - A checking account at the Bank of America
   - A dime
   - A debit card

3. Monica transfers $10,000 from her savings account at the Bank of Alaska to her money market fund. What is the immediate change in M1 and M2?

4. Terry takes $100 from his checking account and deposits the $100 in his savings account. What is the immediate change in M1 and M2?

5. Suppose that banks had deposits of $500 billion, a desired reserve ratio of 4 percent and no excess reserves. The banks had $15 billion in notes and coins. Calculate the banks' reserves at the central bank.

6. Explain the Fed's policy tools and briefly describe how each works.

7. Table 1 shows a bank's balance sheet. The bank has no excess reserves and there is no currency drain. Calculate the bank's desired reserve ratio.

8. The Fed buys $2 million of securities from AIG. If AIG's bank has a desired reserve ratio of 0.1 and there is no currency drain, calculate the bank's excess reserves as soon as the open market purchase is made, the maximum amount of loans that the banking system can make, and the maximum amount of new money that the banking system can create.

Use the following information to work Problems **9** and **10**.

If the desired reserve ratio is 5 percent, the currency drain ratio is 20 percent of deposits, and the central bank makes an open market purchase of $1 million of securities, calculate the change in

9. The monetary base and the change in its components.

10. The quantity of money, and how much of the new money is currency and how much is bank deposits.

Use the following information to work Problems **11** and **12**.

**South Korea: Bank reserves raised**
To rein in spending, the Bank of Korea raised the required reserve ratio to 7 percent from 5 percent—the first raise in almost 17 years. With higher required reserves, banks will have to cut the amount of loans they make.

Source: The New York Times, November 24, 2006

11. Explain why the higher required reserve ratio means that banks will have to cut the amount of loans they can make.

12. Assuming that the currency drain is zero and that the desired reserve ratio equals the required reserve ratio, calculate the change in the money multiplier that results from the increase in Korea's required reserve ratio.

 13. Read *Eye on Creating Money* on pp. 540–541. By how much did the monetary base increase and why didn't M2 increase by the same percentage?

---

### LIST 1

- Store coupons for noodles
- A $100 Amazon.com gift certificate
- Frequent flier miles
- Credit available on your Visa card
- The dollar coins that a coin collector owns

---

### TABLE 1

| Assets | Liabilities | |
|---|---|---|
| (millions of dollars) | | |
| Reserves at | Checkable deposits | 80 |
| the Fed      20 | Savings deposits | 120 |
| Cash in vault    5 | | |
| Securities    75 | | |
| Loans    100 | | |

## Instructor Assignable Problems and Applications

1. When the Fed increased the monetary base between 2008 and 2011, which component of the monetary base increased most: banks' reserves or currency? What happened to the reserves that banks borrowed from the Fed?

2. What happened to the money multiplier between 2008 and 2011? What would the money multiplier have been if the currency drain ratio had increased? What would the money multiplier have been if the banks' desired reserve ratio had not changed?

3. What are the three functions that money performs? Which of the items in List 1 perform some but not all of these functions and which of the items are money?

4. Naomi buys $1,000 worth of American Express travelers' checks and charges the purchase to her American Express card. What is the immediate change in M1 and M2?

5. A bank has $500 million in checkable deposits, $600 million in savings deposits, $400 million in small time deposits, $950 million in loans to businesses, $500 million in government securities, $20 million in currency, and $30 million in its reserve account at the Fed. Calculate the bank's deposits that are part of M1, deposits that are part of M2, and the bank's loans, securities, and reserves.

6. What can the Fed do to increase the quantity of money and keep the monetary base constant? Explain why the Fed would or would not
   - Change the currency drain ratio.
   - Change the required reserve ratio.
   - Change the discount rate.
   - Conduct an open market operation.

Use Table 1, which shows a bank's balance sheet, to work Problems **7** and **8**. The desired reserve ratio on all deposits is 5 percent and there is no currency drain.

7. Calculate the bank's excess reserves. If the bank uses all of these excess reserves to make a loan, what is the quantity of the loan and the quantity of total deposits after the bank has made the loan?

8. If there is no currency drain, what is the quantity of loans and the quantity of total deposits when the bank has no excess reserves?

Use the following information to work Problems **9** and **10**.

**Inflation triggers more bank tightening**
To control inflation by limiting bank loans, the People's Bank announced that it would raise the required reserve ratio for commercial banks from 21 percent to 21.5 percent.

Source: *South China Morning Post*, June 15, 2011

9. Compare the required reserve ratio in China on June 15, 2011 and the required reserve ratio on checkable deposits in the United States today.

10. If the currency drain ratio in China and the United States is 10 percent of deposits, compare the money multipliers in the two countries.

---

**LIST 1**

- An antique clock
- An S&L savings deposit
- Your credit card
- The coins in the Fed's museum
- Government securities

---

**TABLE 1**

| Assets | Liabilities | |
| --- | --- | --- |
| (millions of dollars) | | |
| Reserves at | Checkable deposits | 90 |
| the Fed | 25 | Savings deposits | 110 |
| Cash in vault | 15 | | |
| Securities | 60 | | |
| Loans | 100 | | |

# Critical Thinking Discussion Questions

1. **The BOJ's target of increasing the purchase of government bonds**

   The Bank of Japan (BOJ), the Central Bank of Japan, revised its target of purchasing the Japanese government bonds to approximately 7 trillion yen per month.

   *Source: Bloomberg, 30 May 2013*

   Think about open market operations by the Bank of Japan:

   Suppose the BOJ buys 7 trillion yen of Japanese government bonds from the Bank of Tokyo-Mitsubishi UFJ.

   What are the immediate changes in the BOJ's total assets and total liabilities?

   What are the immediate changes in the Bank of Tokyo-Mitsubishi UFJ's total assets and total liabilities?

   What is the change in Japan's monetary base?

   Why is the Bank of Japan undertaking this open market purchase?

2. **The BOJ's target of increasing the monetary base**

   The BOJ has decided to increase the monetary base by 60 trillion yen to 70 trillion yen to meet the target of doubling the monetary base within two years.

   *Source: The Japan Times, 5 November 2013*

   Think about Japan's monetary base:

   Why does the Bank of Japan want to double the monetary base?

   Will doubling the monetary base result in a doubling of the quantity of money?

   What effect do the currency drain ratio and the desired reserve ratio have on the quantity of money created when the monetary base doubles?

3. **Glasgow store to become first in Britain to replace the pound with virtual currency Bitcoin**

   CeX, the high street chain that buys, sells, and exchanges technological and electronic products, is switching from the pound to the digital currency Bitcoin. Bitcoin is an entirely virtual currency that works without the need for a central bank, and can be sent over the internet.

   *Source: Mail Online, 12 May 2014*

   Think about the virtual currency Bitcoin:

   Does virtual currency serve all the functions of money?

   Will virtual currency eventually eliminate the need for consumers to carry cash?

   If virtual currency works without a central bank, will central banks eventually become obsolete?

# Aggregate Supply and Aggregate Demand

**19**

**When you have completed your study of this chapter, you will be able to**

**1** Define and explain the influences on aggregate supply.

**2** Define and explain the influences on aggregate demand.

**3** Explain how trends and fluctuations in aggregate demand and aggregate supply bring economic growth, inflation, and the business cycle.

## 19.1   AGGREGATE SUPPLY

The purpose of the aggregate supply–aggregate demand model is to explain how real GDP and the price level are determined. The model uses similar ideas to those that you encountered in Chapter 4 where you learned how the quantity and price are determined in a competitive market. But the *aggregate* supply–*aggregate* demand model (*AS-AD* model) isn't just an application of the competitive market model. Some differences arise because the *AS-AD* model is a model of an imaginary market for the total of all the final goods and services that make up real GDP. The quantity in this "market" is real GDP and the price is the price level measured by the GDP price index.

The *quantity of real GDP supplied* is the total amount of final goods and services that firms in the United States plan to produce and it depends on the quantities of

- Labor employed
- Capital, human capital, and the state of technology
- Land and natural resources
- Entrepreneurial talent

You saw in Chapter 17 that at full employment, real GDP equals *potential GDP*. The quantities of land, capital and human capital, the state of technology, and the amount of entrepreneurial talent are fixed. Labor market equilibrium determines the quantity of labor employed, which is equal to the quantity of labor demanded and the quantity of labor supplied at the equilibrium real wage rate.

Over the business cycle, real GDP fluctuates around potential GDP because the quantity of labor employed fluctuates around its full employment level. The aggregate supply–aggregate demand model explains these fluctuations.

We begin on the supply side with the basics of aggregate supply.

### ■ Aggregate Supply Basics

**Aggregate supply**
The relationship between the quantity of real GDP supplied and the price level when all other influences on production plans remain the same.

**Aggregate supply** is the relationship between the quantity of real GDP supplied and the price level when all other influences on production plans remain the same. This relationship can be described as follows:

**Other things remaining the same, the higher the price level, the greater is the quantity of real GDP supplied, and the lower the price level, the smaller is the quantity of real GDP supplied.**

Figure 19.1 illustrates aggregate supply as an aggregate supply schedule and aggregate supply curve. The aggregate supply schedule lists the quantities of real GDP supplied at each price level, and the upward-sloping *AS* curve graphs these points.

The figure also shows potential GDP: $16 trillion in the figure. When the price level is 105, the quantity of real GDP supplied is $16 trillion, which equals potential GDP (at point *C* on the *AS* curve).

Along the aggregate supply curve, the price level is the only influence on production plans that changes. A rise in the price level brings an increase in the quantity of real GDP supplied and a movement up along the aggregate supply curve; a fall in the price level brings a decrease in the quantity of real GDP supplied and a movement down along the aggregate supply curve.

**FIGURE 19.1**

## Aggregate Supply Schedule and Aggregate Supply Curve

| | Price level (GDP price index, 2009 = 100) | Quantity of real GDP supplied (trillions of 2009 dollars) |
|---|---|---|
| E | 115 | 17.0 |
| D | 110 | 16.5 |
| C | 105 | 16.0 |
| B | 100 | 15.5 |
| A | 95 | 15.0 |

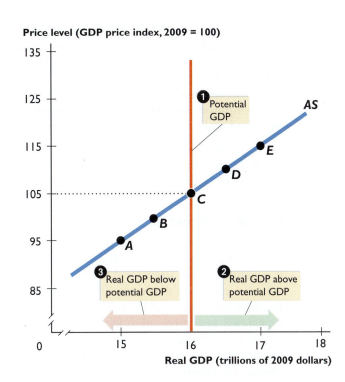

The aggregate supply schedule and aggregate supply curve, *AS*, show the relationship between the quantity of real GDP supplied and the price level when all other influences on production plans remain the same. Each point *A* through *E* on the *AS* curve corresponds to the row identified by the same letter in the schedule.

**❶** Potential GDP is $16 trillion, and when the price level is 105, real GDP equals potential GDP.

**❷** If the price level is above 105, real GDP exceeds potential GDP.

**❸** If the price level is below 105, real GDP is less than potential GDP.

Among the other influences on production plans that remain constant along the *AS* curve are

- The money wage rate
- The money prices of other resources

In contrast, along the potential GDP line, when the price level changes, the money wage rate and the money prices of other resources change by the same percentage as the change in the price level to keep the real wage rate (and other real prices) at the full-employment equilibrium level.

### Why the *AS* Curve Slopes Upward

Why does the quantity of real GDP supplied increase when the price level rises and decrease when the price level falls? The answer is that a movement along the *AS* curve brings a change in the real wage rate (and changes in the real cost of other resources whose money prices are fixed). If the price level rises, the real wage rate falls, and if the price level falls, the real wage rate rises. When the real wage rate changes, firms change the quantity of labor employed and the level of production.

Think about a concrete example. A ketchup producer has a contract with its workers to pay them $20 an hour. The firm sells ketchup for $1 a bottle. The real wage rate of a ketchup bottling worker is 20 bottles of ketchup. That is, the firm must sell 20 bottles of ketchup to buy one hour of labor. Now suppose the price of ketchup falls to 50 cents a bottle. The real wage rate of a bottling worker has increased to 40 bottles—the firm must now sell 40 bottles of ketchup to buy one hour of labor.

If the price of a bottle of ketchup increased, the real wage rate of a bottling worker would fall. For example, if the price increased to $2 a bottle, the real wage rate would be 10 bottles per worker—the firm needs to sell only 10 bottles of ketchup to buy one hour of labor.

Firms respond to a change in the real wage rate by changing the quantity of labor employed and the quantity produced. For the economy as a whole, employment and real GDP change. There are three ways in which these changes occur:

- Firms change their output rate.
- Firms shut down temporarily or restart production.
- Firms go out of business or start up in business.

### Change in Output Rate

To change its output rate, a firm must change the quantity of labor that it employs. It is profitable to hire more labor if the additional labor costs less than the revenue it generates. If the price level rises and the money wage rate doesn't change, an extra hour of labor that was previously unprofitable becomes profitable. So when the price level rises and the money wage rate doesn't change, the quantity of labor demanded and production increase. If the price level falls and the money wage rate doesn't change, an hour of labor that was previously profitable becomes unprofitable. So when the price level falls and the money wage rate doesn't change, the quantity of labor demanded and production decrease.

### Temporary Shutdowns and Restarts

A firm that is incurring a loss might foresee a profit in the future. Such a firm might decide to shut down temporarily and lay off its workers.

The price level relative to the money wage rate influences temporary shutdown decisions. If the price level rises relative to wages, fewer firms decide to shut down temporarily; so more firms operate and the quantity of real GDP supplied increases. If the price level falls relative to wages, a larger number of firms find that they cannot earn enough revenue to pay the wage bill and so temporarily shut down. The quantity of real GDP supplied decreases.

### Business Failure and Startup

People create businesses in the hope of earning a profit. When profits are squeezed or when losses arise, more firms fail, fewer new firms start up, and the number of firms decreases. When profits are generally high, fewer firms fail, more firms start up, and the number of firms increases.

The price level relative to the money wage rate influences the number of firms in business. If the price level rises relative to wages, profits increase, the number of firms in business increases, and the quantity of real GDP supplied increases. If the price level falls relative to wages, profits fall, the number of firms in business decreases, and the quantity of real GDP supplied decreases.

In a severe recession, business failure can be contagious. The failure of one firm puts pressure on both its suppliers and its customers and can bring a flood of failures and a large decrease in the quantity of real GDP supplied.

# ■ Changes in Aggregate Supply

Aggregate supply changes when any influence on production plans other than the price level changes. In particular, aggregate supply changes when

- Potential GDP changes.
- The money wage rate changes.
- The money prices of other resources change.

## Change in Potential GDP

Anything that changes potential GDP changes aggregate supply and shifts the aggregate supply curve. Figure 19.2 illustrates such a shift. You can think of point $C$ as an anchor point. The $AS$ curve and potential GDP line are anchored at this point, and when potential GDP changes, aggregate supply changes along with it. When potential GDP increases from $16 trillion to $17 trillion, point $C$ shifts to point $C'$, and the $AS$ curve and potential GDP line shift rightward together. The $AS$ curve shifts from $AS_0$ to $AS_1$.

## Change in Money Wage Rate

A change in the money wage rate changes aggregate supply because it changes firms' costs. The higher the money wage rate, the higher are firms' costs and the smaller is the quantity that firms are willing to supply at each price level. So an increase in the money wage rate decreases aggregate supply.

## ■ FIGURE 19.2

### An Increase in Potential GDP

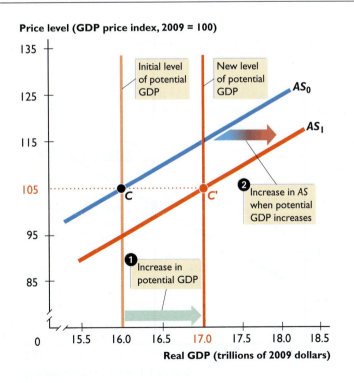

❶ An increase in potential GDP increases aggregate supply.

❷ When potential GDP increases from $16 trillion to $17 trillion, the aggregate supply curve shifts rightward from $AS_0$ to $AS_1$.

Suppose that the money wage rate is $52.50 an hour and the price level is 105. Then the real wage rate is $50 an hour ($52.50 × 100 ÷ 105 = $50)—see Chapter 16, p. 474. If the full-employment equilibrium real wage rate is $50 an hour, the economy is at full employment and real GDP equals potential GDP. In Figure 19.3, the economy is at point $C$ on the aggregate supply curve $AS_0$. The money wage rate is $52.50 an hour at all points on $AS_0$.

Now suppose the money wage rate rises to $57.50 an hour but the full-employment equilibrium real wage rate remains at $50 an hour. Real GDP now equals potential GDP when the price level is 115, at point $D$ on the aggregate supply curve $AS_2$. (If the money wage rate is $57.50 an hour and the price level is 115, the real wage rate is $57.50 × 100 ÷ 115 = $50 an hour.) The money wage rate is $57.50 an hour at all points on $AS_2$. The rise in the money wage rate *decreases* aggregate supply and shifts the aggregate supply curve leftward from $AS_0$ to $AS_2$.

A change in the money wage rate does not change potential GDP. The reason is that potential GDP depends only on the economy's real ability to produce and on the full-employment quantity of labor, which occurs at the equilibrium *real* wage rate. The equilibrium real wage rate can occur at any money wage rate.

## Change in Money Prices of Other Resources

A change in the money prices of other resources has a similar effect on firms' production plans to a change in the money wage rate. It changes firms' costs. At each price level, firms' real costs change and the quantity that firms are willing to supply changes so aggregate supply changes.

---

**■ FIGURE 19.3**

### A Change in the Money Wage Rate

A rise in the money wage rate decreases aggregate supply. The aggregate supply curve shifts leftward from $AS_0$ to $AS_2$. A rise in the money wage rate does not change potential GDP.

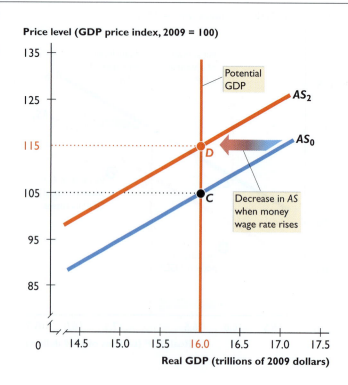

**CHECKPOINT 19.1**

**Define and explain the influences on aggregate supply.**

## Practice Problem

1. Explain the influence of each of the events in List 1 on the quantity of real GDP supplied and aggregate supply in India and use a graph to illustrate.

## In the News

### Eight states to hike minimum wage

The state minimum wage will rise by up to 37 cents an hour or $770 a year for a full-time worker in Colorado, Montana, Ohio, Oregon, and Washington. Three other states, Arizona, Florida, and Vermont, are believed to be planning similar increases.

Source: CNN Money, October 3, 2011

Explain how the rise in the minimum wage will influence aggregate supply.

## Solution to Practice Problem

1. As fuel prices rise, the quantity of real GDP supplied at the current price level decreases. The *AS* curve shifts leftward (Figure 1).

   As U.S. firms move their IT and data functions to India, real GDP supplied at the current price level increases. The *AS* curve shifts rightward (Figure 2).

   As Wal-Mart and Starbucks open, the quantity of real GDP supplied at the current price level increases. The *AS* curve shifts rightward (Figure 2).

   With more graduates, the number of skilled workers increases, and production increases at the current price level. The *AS* curve shifts rightward (Figure 2).

   As the money wage rate rises, firms' costs increase and the quantity of real GDP supplied at the current price level decreases. The *AS* curve shifts leftward (Figure 1).

   As the price level increases, other things remaining the same, businesses become more profitable and increase the quantity of real GDP supplied along the *AS* curve (Figure 3). The *AS* curve does not shift.

## Solution to In the News

The rise in the money wage rate at the current price level increases the real wage rate and decreases aggregate supply. If the rise in the minimum wage increases the natural unemployment rate, potential GDP decreases and aggregate supply decreases further.

**LIST 1**

- Fuel prices rise.
- U.S. firms move their IT and data functions to India.
- Wal-Mart and Starbucks open in India.
- Universities in India increase the number of engineering graduates.
- The money wage rate in India rises.
- The price level in India rises.

**FIGURE 1**

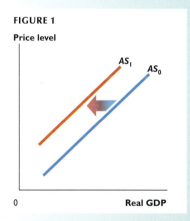

**FIGURE 2**

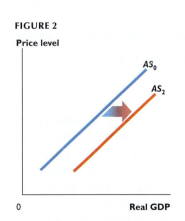

**FIGURE 3**

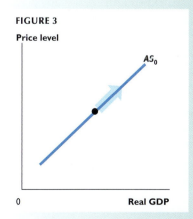

## 19.2  AGGREGATE DEMAND

The *quantity of real GDP demanded* (*Y*) is the total amount of final goods and services produced in the United States that people, businesses, governments, and foreigners plan to buy. This quantity is the sum of the real consumption expenditure (*C*), investment (*I*), government expenditure on goods and services (*G*), and exports (*X*) minus imports (*M*). That is,

$$Y = C + I + G + X - M.$$

Many factors influence expenditure plans. To study aggregate demand, we divide those factors into two parts: the price level and everything else. We'll first consider the influence of the price level on expenditure plans and then consider the other influences.

### ■ Aggregate Demand Basics

**Aggregate demand**

The relationship between the quantity of real GDP demanded and the price level when all other influences on expenditure plans remain the same.

**Aggregate demand** is the relationship between the quantity of real GDP demanded and the price level when all other influences on expenditure plans remain the same. This relationship can be described as follows:

> **Other things remaining the same, the higher the price level, the smaller is the quantity of real GDP demanded; and the lower the price level, the greater is the quantity of real GDP demanded.**

Figure 19.4 illustrates aggregate demand by using an aggregate demand schedule and aggregate demand curve. The aggregate demand schedule lists the quantities of real GDP demanded at each price level, and the downward-sloping *AD* curve graphs these points.

Along the aggregate demand curve, the only influence on expenditure plans that changes is the price level. A rise in the price level decreases the quantity of real GDP demanded and brings a movement up along the aggregate demand curve; a fall in the price level increases the quantity of real GDP demanded and brings a movement down along the aggregate demand curve.

The price level influences the quantity of real GDP demanded because a change in the price level brings a change in

- The buying power of money
- The real interest rate
- The real prices of exports and imports

### The Buying Power of Money

A rise in the price level lowers the buying power of money and decreases the quantity of real GDP demanded. To see why, think about the buying plans in two economies—Russia and Japan—where the price level has changed a lot in recent years.

Anna lives in Moscow, Russia. She has worked hard all summer and has saved 20,000 rubles (the ruble is the currency of Russia), which she plans to spend attending graduate school after she has earned her economics degree. So Anna's money holding is 20,000 rubles. Anna has a part-time job, and her income from this job pays her expenses. The price level in Russia rises by 100 percent. Anna needs 40,000 rubles to buy what 20,000 rubles once bought. To make up some of the fall in the buying power of her money, Anna slashes her spending.

■ **FIGURE 19.4**

## Aggregate Demand Schedule and Aggregate Demand Curve

| | Price level (GDP price index, 2009 = 100) | Quantity of real GDP demanded (trillions of 2009 dollars) |
|---|---|---|
| A | 125 | 15.0 |
| B | 115 | 15.5 |
| C | 105 | 16.0 |
| D | 95 | 16.5 |
| E | 85 | 17.0 |

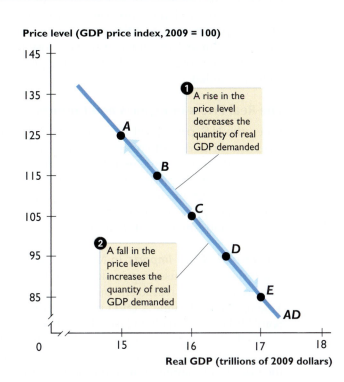

The aggregate demand schedule and aggregate demand curve, AD, show the relationship between the quantity of real GDP demanded and the price level when all other influences on expenditure plans remain the same. Each point A through E on the AD curve corresponds to the row identified by the same letter in the schedule.

The quantity of real GDP demanded

❶ decreases when the price level rises and

❷ increases when the price level falls.

Similarly, a fall in the price level, other things remaining the same, brings an increase in the quantity of real GDP demanded. To see why, think about the buying plans of Mika, who lives in Tokyo, Japan. She too has worked hard all summer and has saved 200,000 yen (the yen is the currency of Japan), which she plans to spend attending school next year. The price level in Japan falls by 10 percent; now Mika needs only 180,000 yen to buy what 200,000 yen once bought. With a rise in what her money buys, Mika decides to buy a DVD player.

### The Real Interest Rate

When the price level rises, the real interest rate rises. An increase in the price level increases the amount of money that people want to hold—increases the demand for money. When the demand for money increases, the nominal interest rate rises. In the short run, the inflation rate does not change, so a rise in the nominal interest rate brings a rise in the real interest rate. Faced with a higher real interest rate, businesses and people delay plans to buy new capital and consumer durable goods and they cut back on spending. As the price level rises, the quantity of real GDP demanded decreases.

***Anna and Mika Again*** Think about Anna and Mika again. Both of them want to buy a computer. In Moscow, a rise in the price level increases the demand for money and raises the real interest rate. At a real interest rate of 5 percent a year,

Anna was willing to borrow to buy the new computer. But at a real interest rate of 10 percent a year, she decides that the payments would be too high, so she delays buying it. The rise in the price level decreases the quantity of real GDP demanded.

In Tokyo, a fall in the price level lowers the real interest rate. At a real interest rate of 5 percent a year, Mika was willing to borrow to buy a low-performance computer. But at a real interest rate of close to zero, she decides to buy a fancier computer that costs more: The fall in the price level increases the quantity of real GDP demanded.

### The Real Prices of Exports and Imports

When the U.S. price level rises and other things remain the same, the prices in other countries do not change. So a rise in the U.S. price level makes U.S.-made goods and services more expensive relative to foreign-made goods and services. This change in real prices encourages people to spend less on U.S.-made items and more on foreign-made items. For example, if the U.S. price level rises relative to the foreign price level, foreigners buy fewer U.S.-made cars (U.S. exports decrease) and Americans buy more foreign-made cars (U.S. imports increase).

***Anna's and Mika's Imports*** In Moscow, Anna is buying some new shoes. With a sharp rise in the Russian price level, the Russian-made shoes that she planned to buy are too expensive, so she buys a less expensive pair imported from Brazil. In Tokyo, Mika is buying a DVD player. With the fall in the Japanese price level, a Sony DVD player made in Japan looks like a better buy than one made in Taiwan.

In the long run, when the price level changes by more in one country than in other countries, the exchange rate changes. The exchange rate change neutralizes the price level change, so this international price effect on buying plans is a short-run effect only. But in the short run, it is a powerful effect.

## ■ Changes in Aggregate Demand

A change in any factor that influences expenditure plans other than the price level brings a change in aggregate demand. When aggregate demand increases, the aggregate demand curve shifts rightward, which Figure 19.5 illustrates as the rightward shift of the $AD$ curve from $AD_0$ to $AD_1$. When aggregate demand decreases, the aggregate demand curve shifts leftward, which Figure 19.5 illustrates as the leftward shift of the $AD$ curve from $AD_0$ to $AD_2$. The factors that change aggregate demand are

- Expectations about the future
- Fiscal policy and monetary policy
- The state of the world economy

### Expectations

An increase in expected future income increases the amount of consumption goods (especially big-ticket items such as cars) that people plan to buy now. Aggregate demand increases. An increase in expected future inflation increases aggregate demand because people decide to buy more goods and services now before their prices rise. An increase in expected future profit increases the investment that firms plan to undertake now. Aggregate demand increases.

A decrease in expected future income, future inflation, or future profit has the opposite effect and decreases aggregate demand.

■ **FIGURE 19.5**

## Change in Aggregate Demand

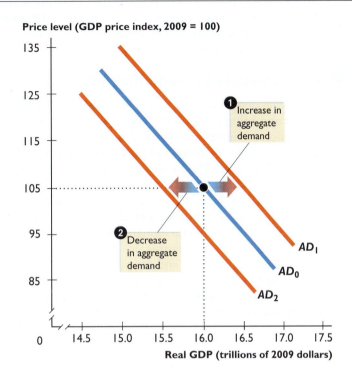

① Aggregate demand *increases if*

• Expected future income, inflation, or profits increase.
• The government or the Federal Reserve takes steps that increase planned expenditure.
• The exchange rate falls or the global economy expands.

② Aggregate demand *decreases if*

• Expected future income, inflation, or profits decrease.
• The government or the Federal Reserve takes steps that decrease planned expenditure.
• The exchange rate rises or the global economy contracts.

## Fiscal Policy and Monetary Policy

We study the effects of policy actions on aggregate demand in Chapter 20. Here, we'll just briefly note that the government can use **fiscal policy**—changing taxes, transfer payments, and government expenditure on goods and services—to influence aggregate demand. The Federal Reserve can use **monetary policy**—changing the quantity of money and the interest rate—to influence aggregate demand. A tax cut or an increase in either transfer payments or government expenditure on goods and services increases aggregate demand. A cut in the interest rate or an increase in the quantity of money increases aggregate demand.

**Fiscal policy**
Changing taxes, transfer payments, and government expenditure on goods and services.

**Monetary policy**
Changing the quantity of money and the interest rate.

## The World Economy

Two main influences that the world economy has on aggregate demand are the foreign exchange rate and foreign income. The foreign exchange rate is the amount of a foreign currency that you can buy with a U.S. dollar. Other things remaining the same, a rise in the foreign exchange rate decreases aggregate demand.

To see how the foreign exchange rate influences aggregate demand, suppose that $1 exchanges for 100 Japanese yen. A Fujitsu phone made in Japan costs 12,500 yen, and an equivalent Motorola phone made in the United States costs $110. In U.S. dollars, the Fujitsu phone costs $125, so people around the world buy the cheaper U.S. phone. Now suppose the exchange rate rises to 125 yen per dollar. At 125 yen per dollar, the Fujitsu phone costs $100 and is now cheaper than the Motorola phone. People will switch from the U.S. phone to the Japanese phone.

U.S. exports will decrease and U.S. imports will increase, so U.S. aggregate demand will decrease.

An increase in foreign income increases U.S. exports and increases U.S. aggregate demand. For example, an increase in income in Japan and Germany increases Japanese and German consumers' and producers' planned expenditures on U.S.-made goods and services.

## ■ The Aggregate Demand Multiplier

The aggregate demand multiplier is an effect that magnifies changes in expenditure plans and brings potentially large fluctuations in aggregate demand. When any influence on aggregate demand changes expenditure plans, the change in expenditure changes income; and the change in income induces a change in consumption expenditure. The increase in aggregate demand is the initial increase in expenditure plus the induced increase in consumption expenditure.

Suppose that an increase in expenditure induces an increase in consumption expenditure that is 1.5 times the initial increase in expenditure. Figure 19.6 illustrates the change in aggregate demand that occurs when investment increases by $0.4 trillion. Initially, the aggregate demand curve is $AD_0$. Investment then increases by $0.4 trillion ($\Delta I$) and the purple curve $AD_0 + \Delta I$ now describes aggregate spending plans at each price level. An increase in income induces an increase in consumption expenditure of $0.6 trillion, and the aggregate demand curve shifts rightward to $AD_1$.

■ **FIGURE 19.6**

The Aggregate Demand Multiplier

❶ An increase in investment increases aggregate demand and increases income.

❷ The increase in income induces an increase in consumption expenditure, so ❸ aggregate demand increases by more than the initial increase in investment.

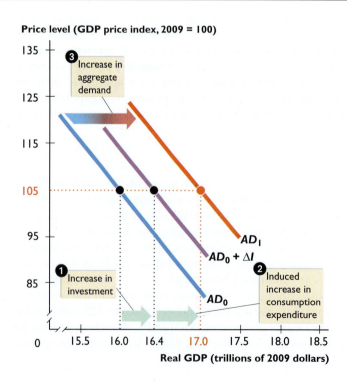

# CHECKPOINT 19.2

**Define and explain the influences on aggregate demand.**

## Practice Problems

1. Mexico trades with the United States. Explain the effect of each of the following events on Mexico's aggregate demand.
   - The government of Mexico cuts income taxes.
   - The United States experiences strong economic growth.
   - Mexico sets new environmental standards that require factories to upgrade their production facilities.
2. Explain the effect of each of the following events on the quantity of real GDP demanded and aggregate demand in Mexico.
   - Europe trades with Mexico and goes into a recession.
   - The price level in Mexico rises.
   - Mexico increases the quantity of money.

## In the News

**Durable goods orders, new-homes sales, and imports pick up**
The BEA announced that demand for durable goods rose 3.4% while new-home sales rose 13.4% in the second quarter of 2013. U.S. exports increased 5.4% while U.S. imports increased 9.5%.

Source: Bureau of Economic Analysis, July 31, 2013

Explain how the items in the news clip influence U.S. aggregate demand.

## Solutions to Practice Problems

1. A tax cut increases disposable income, which increases consumption expenditure, which increases aggregate demand. Strong U.S. growth increases the demand for Mexican-produced goods, which increases Mexico's aggregate demand. As factories upgrade their facilities, investment increases. Aggregate demand increases. In each case, the *AD* curve shifts rightward (Figure 1).
2. A recession in Europe decreases the demand for Mexico's exports, so aggregate demand decreases. The *AD* curve shifts leftward (Figure 2). A rise in the price level decreases the quantity of real GDP demanded along the *AD* curve, but the *AD* curve does not shift (Figure 3). An increase in the quantity of money increases aggregate demand, and the *AD* curve shifts rightward (Figure 1)

## Solution to In the News

The purchase of durable goods and new homes is investment, which increased aggregate demand. The rise in U.S. imports exceeded the rise in U.S. exports, which decreased the demand for U.S.-produced goods and services and decreased U.S. aggregate demand.

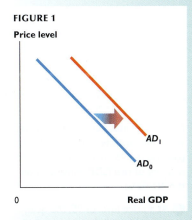

**FIGURE 1**

**FIGURE 2**

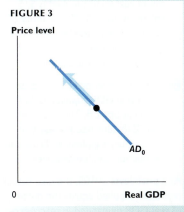

**FIGURE 3**

**19.3 EXPLAINING ECONOMIC TRENDS AND FLUCTUATIONS**

The main purpose of the *AS-AD* model is to explain business cycle fluctuations in real GDP and the price level. But the model also helps our understanding of economic growth and inflation trends that we've studied in earlier chapters. The first step toward explaining economic trends and fluctuations is to combine aggregate supply and aggregate demand and determine macroeconomic equilibrium.

### ■ Macroeconomic Equilibrium

**Macroeconomic equilibrium**
When the quantity of real GDP demanded equals the quantity of real GDP supplied at the point of intersection of the *AD* curve and the *AS* curve.

Aggregate supply and aggregate demand determine real GDP and the price level. **Macroeconomic equilibrium** occurs when the quantity of real GDP demanded equals the quantity of real GDP supplied at the point of intersection of the *AD* curve and the *AS* curve. Figure 19.7 shows such an equilibrium at a price level of 105 and real GDP of $16 trillion.

To see why this position is the equilibrium, think about what happens if the price level is something other than 105. Suppose the price level is 95 and real GDP is $15 trillion (point *A* on the *AS* curve). The quantity of real GDP demanded exceeds $15 trillion, so firms are unable to meet the demand for their output. Inventories decrease, and customers clamor for goods and services. In this situation, firms increase production and raise prices. Eventually they can meet demand when real GDP is $16 trillion and the price level is 105.

Now suppose that the price level is 115 and that real GDP is $17 trillion (point *B* on the *AS* curve). The quantity of real GDP demanded is less than $17 trillion, so firms are unable to sell all their output. Unwanted inventories pile up. Firms cut production and lower prices until they can sell all their output, which occurs when real GDP is $16 trillion and the price level is 105.

### ■ FIGURE 19.7

Macroeconomic Equilibrium

---

Macroeconomic equilibrium occurs when the quantity of real GDP supplied on the *AS* curve equals the quantity of real GDP demanded on the *AD* curve.

❶ At a price level of 95, the quantity of real GDP supplied is $15 trillion at point *A*. The quantity of real GDP demanded exceeds the quantity supplied, so firms increase production and raise prices.

❷ At a price level of 115, the quantity of real GDP supplied is $17 trillion at point *B*. The quantity of real GDP demanded is less than the quantity supplied, so firms cut production and lower prices.

At a price level of 105, the quantity of real GDP supplied equals the quantity of real GDP demanded in macroeconomic equilibrium.

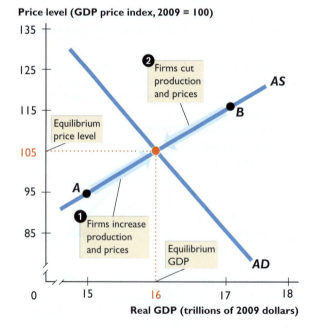

## Three Types of Macroeconomic Equilibrium

In macroeconomic equilibrium, the economy might be at full employment or above or below full employment. Figure 19.8(a) shows these three possibilities. **Full-employment equilibrium**—when equilibrium real GDP equals potential GDP—occurs where the *AD* curve intersects the aggregate supply curve *AS\**.

At a higher money wage rate, aggregate supply is $AS_1$. Real GDP is $15.5 trillion and is less than potential GDP. The economy is *below full employment* and there is a **recessionary gap**. At a lower money wage rate, aggregate supply is $AS_2$. In this situation, real GDP is $16.5 trillion and is greater than potential GDP. The economy is *above full employment* and there is an **inflationary gap**.

### Adjustment toward Full Employment

When real GDP is below or above potential GDP, the money wage rate gradually changes to restore full employment. Figure 19.8(b) illustrates this adjustment.

In a *recessionary gap*, there is a surplus of labor and firms can hire new workers at a lower wage rate. As the money wage rate falls, the *AS* curve shifts from $AS_1$ toward *AS\** and the price level falls and real GDP rises. The money wage continues to fall until real GDP equals potential GDP—full-employment equilibrium.

In an *inflationary gap*, there is a shortage of labor and firms must offer a higher wage rate to hire the labor they demand. As the money wage rate rises, the *AS* curve shifts from $AS_2$ toward *AS\** and the price level rises and real GDP falls. The money wage rate continues to rise until real GDP equals potential GDP.

**Full-employment equilibrium**
When equilibrium real GDP equals potential GDP.

**Recessionary gap**
A gap that exists when potential GDP exceeds real GDP and that brings a falling price level.

**Inflationary gap**
A gap that exists when real GDP exceeds potential GDP and that brings a rising price level.

**FIGURE 19.8**

Output Gaps and Full-Employment Equilibrium

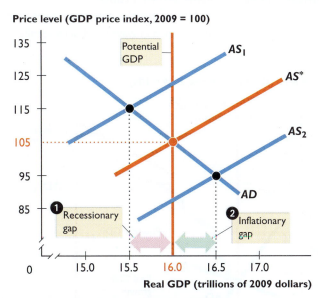

(a) Three types of macroeconomic equilibrium

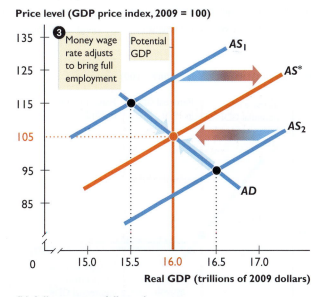

(b) Adjustment to full employment

In part (a), when equilibrium real GDP is less than potential GDP, ❶ there is a recessionary gap; when equilibrium real GDP is greater than potential GDP, ❷ there is an inflationary gap; and when equilibrium real GDP equals potential GDP, the economy is at full employment.

In part (b), when an output gap exists ❸ the money wage rate adjusts to move the economy toward full employment. With a recessionary gap, the money wage rate falls and the *AS* curve shifts rightward from $AS_1$ to *AS\**. With an inflationary gap, the money wage rate rises and the *AS* curve shifts leftward from $AS_2$ to *AS\**.

## ■ Economic Growth and Inflation Trends

Economic growth results from a growing labor force and increasing labor productivity, which together make potential GDP grow. Inflation results from a growing quantity of money that outpaces the growth of potential GDP.

The *AS-AD* model can be used to understand economic growth and inflation trends. In the *AS-AD* model, economic growth is increasing potential GDP—a persistent rightward shift in the potential GDP line. Inflation arises from a persistent increase in aggregate demand at a faster pace than that of the increase in potential GDP—a persistent rightward shift of the *AD* curve at a faster pace than the growth of potential GDP. *Eye on the U.S. Economy* below shows how the *AS-AD* model explains U.S. economic growth and inflation trends.

# EYE on the U.S. ECONOMY
## U.S. Economic Growth, Inflation, and the Business Cycle

U.S. economic growth, inflation, and the business cycle result from changes in aggregate supply and aggregate demand.

A rightward movement in the U.S. potential GDP line brings economic growth and a greater rightward movement of the U.S. *AD* curve brings inflation. Part (a) shows the shifting curves that generate growth and inflation.

Part (b) shows the history of U.S. real GDP growth and inflation from 1970 to 2013. Each dot represents the the real GDP and price level in a year—the black dot 1970 and the red dot 2013. The rightward movement of the dots is economic growth and the upward movement is a rising price level—inflation.

When the dots follow a path that is gently rising, as during the 1990s, the inflation rate is low and real GDP growth is quite rapid. When the dots follow a path that is steep, as during the 1970s, inflation is rapid and economic growth is slow.

Notice that the dots move rightward and upward in waves and occasionally

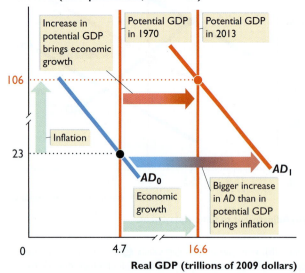

**(a) Economic growth and inflation**

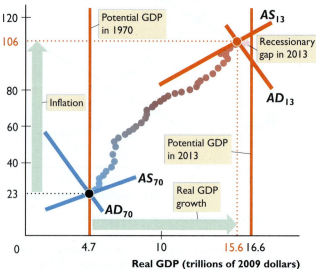

**(b) U.S. economic growth and inflation**

## ■ The Business Cycle

The business cycle results from fluctuations in aggregate supply and aggregate demand. Aggregate supply fluctuates because labor productivity grows at a variable pace, which brings fluctuations in the growth rate of potential GDP. The resulting cycle is called a **real business cycle**. But aggregate demand fluctuations are the main source of the business cycle. The key reason is that the swings in aggregate demand occur more quickly than changes in the money wage rate that change aggregate supply. The result is that the economy swings from inflationary gap to full employment to recessionary gap and back again.

*Eye on the U.S. Economy* below shows the most recent cycle interpreted as driven by aggregate demand fluctuations. But in the 2008–2009 recession, both aggregate demand and aggregate supply were at work as you can see on p. 567.

**Real business cycle**
A cycle that results from fluctuations in the pace of growth of labor productivity and potential GDP.

---

leftward. The pattern shows the business cycle expansions and recessions.

By comparing the dots with potential GDP, we can see that the economy was at full employment in 1970 and that the recessionary gap in 2013 was large.

Part (c) shows how changes in aggregate demand create the business cycle, and part (d) shows the most recent cycle from 2000 to 2013.

When the *AD* curve is $AD_0$ in part (c), the economy is at point *A* and there is an inflationary gap. Part (d) identifies the actual gap in 2000 as *A*.

A decrease in aggregate demand to $AD_1$ lowers real GDP to potential GDP and the economy moves to point *B* in parts (c) and (d).

A further decrease in aggregate demand to $AD_2$ lowers real GDP to

below potential GDP and opens up a recessionary gap at point *C* in both parts (c) and (d).

In reality, *AD* rarely decreases. It increases at a slower pace than the increase in potential GDP. Also, in reality, *AS* fluctuates. But the relative positions of the *AS* and *AD* curves and the potential GDP line are like those shown in part (c).

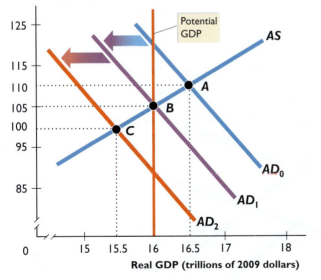

**(c) Aggregate demand fluctuations**

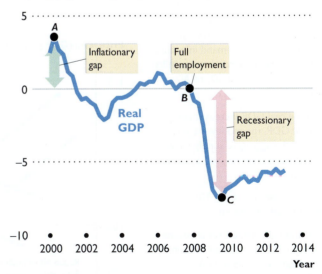

**(d) The U.S. output gap**

SOURCES OF DATA: Bureau of Labor Statistics, Bureau of Economic Analysis, and Congressional Budget Office.

## ■ Inflation Cycles

You've seen that inflation occurs if aggregate demand grows faster than potential GDP. But just as there are cycles in real GDP, there are also cycles in the inflation rate. And the two cycles are related. To study the interaction of real GDP and inflation cycles, we distinguish between two sources of inflation:

- Demand-pull inflation
- Cost-push inflation

### Demand-Pull Inflation

**Demand-pull inflation**

Inflation that starts because aggregate demand increases.

Inflation that starts because aggregate demand increases is called **demand-pull inflation**. Demand-pull inflation can be kicked off by any of the factors that change aggregate demand but the only thing that can sustain it is growth in the quantity of money.

Figure 19.9 illustrates the process of demand-pull inflation. Potential GDP is $16 trillion. Initially, the aggregate demand curve is $AD_0$, the aggregate supply curve is $AS_0$, and real GDP equals potential GDP. Aggregate demand increases, shifting the aggregate demand curve to $AD_1$. Real GDP increases and the price level rises. There is now an *inflationary gap*. A shortage of labor brings a rise in the money wage rate, which shifts the aggregate supply curve to $AS_1$. The price level rises further and real GDP returns to potential GDP.

The quantity of money increases again, and the aggregate demand curve shifts rightward to $AD_2$. The price level rises further, and real GDP again exceeds potential GDP. Yet again, the money wage rate rises and decreases aggregate supply. The $AS$ curve shifts to $AS_2$, and the price level rises further. As the quantity of money continues to grow, aggregate demand increases and the price level rises in an ongoing demand-pull inflation spiral.

■ **FIGURE 19.9**

A Demand-Pull Inflation

Each time the quantity of money increases, aggregate demand increases and the aggregate demand curve shifts rightward from $AD_0$ to $AD_1$ to $AD_2$, and so on.

Each time real GDP increases above potential GDP, the money wage rate rises and the aggregate supply curve shifts leftward from $AS_0$ to $AS_1$ to $AS_2$, and so on.

The price level rises from 105 to 108, 116, 120, 128, and so on.

A demand-pull inflation spiral results with real GDP fluctuating between $16 trillion and $16.5 trillion.

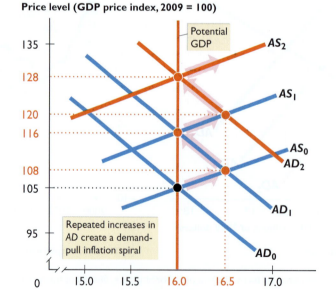

## Cost-Push Inflation

Inflation that begins with an increase in cost is called **cost-push inflation**. The two main sources of cost increases are increases in the money wage rate and increases in the money prices of raw materials such as oil.

Cost-push inflation can be kicked off by an increase in costs but the only thing that can sustain it is growth in the quantity of money.

Figure 19.10 illustrates cost-push inflation. The aggregate demand curve is $AD_0$, the aggregate supply curve is $AS_0$, and real GDP equals potential GDP. The world price of oil rises, which decreases aggregate supply. The aggregate supply curve shifts leftward to $AS_1$, the price level rises, and real GDP decreases so there is a *recessionary gap*.

When real GDP decreases, unemployment rises above its natural rate and the Fed increases the quantity of money to restore full employment. Aggregate demand increases and the $AD$ curve shifts rightward to $AD_1$. Real GDP returns to potential GDP but the price level rises further.

Oil producers now see the prices of everything they buy rising so they raise the price of oil again to restore its new higher relative price. The $AS$ curve now shifts to $AS_2$, the price level rises again and real GDP decreases again.

If the Fed responds yet again with an increase in the quantity of money, aggregate demand increases and the $AD$ curve shifts to $AD_2$. The price level rises even higher and full employment is again restored. A cost-push inflation spiral results.

The combination of a decreasing real GDP and a rising price level is called **stagflation**. You can see that stagflation poses a dilemma for the Fed. If the Fed does not respond when producers raise the oil price, the economy remains below full employment. If the Fed increases the quantity of money to restore full employment, it invites another oil price hike that will call forth yet a further increase in the quantity of money.

**Cost-push inflation**
An inflation that begins with an increase in cost.

**Stagflation**
The combination of recession (decreasing real GDP) and inflation (rising price level).

### FIGURE 19.10

A Cost-Push Inflation

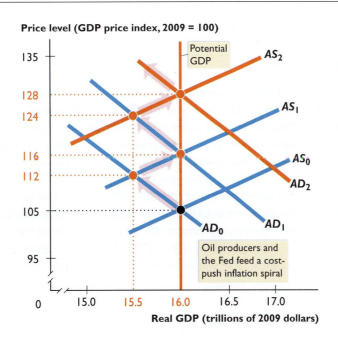

Each time a cost increase occurs, the aggregate supply curve shifts leftward from $AS_0$ to $AS_1$ to $AS_2$, and so on.

Each time real GDP decreases below potential GDP, the Fed increases the quantity of money and the aggregate demand curve shifts rightward from $AD_0$ to $AD_1$ to $AD_2$, and so on.

The price level rises from 105 to 112, 116, 124, 128, and so on.

A cost-push inflation spiral results with real GDP fluctuating between $16 trillion and $15.5 trillion.

## ◼ Deflation and the Great Depression

When a financial crisis hit the United States in October 2008, many people feared a repeat of the dreadful events of the 1930s. From 1929 through 1933, the United States and most of the world experienced deflation and depression—the *Great Depression*. The price level fell by 22 percent and real GDP fell by 31 percent.

The recession of 2008–2009 turned out to be much less severe than the Great Depression. Real GDP fell by less than 4 percent and the price level continued to rise, although at a slower pace. Why was the Great Depression so bad and why was 2008–2009 so mild in comparison? You can answer these questions with what you've learned in this chapter.

During the Great Depression, banks failed and the quantity of money contracted by 25 percent. The Fed stood by and took no action to counteract the collapse of buying power, so aggregate demand also collapsed. Because the money wage rate didn't fall immediately, the decrease in aggregate demand brought a large fall in real GDP. The money wage rate and price level fell eventually, but not until employment and real GDP had shrunk to 75 percent of their 1929 levels.

In contrast, during the 2008 financial crisis, the Fed bailed out troubled financial institutions and doubled the monetary base. The quantity of money kept growing. Also, the government increased its own expenditures, which added to aggregate demand. The combined effects of continued growth in the quantity of money and increased government expenditure limited the fall in aggregate demand and prevented a large decrease in real GDP.

The challenge that now lies ahead is to unwind the monetary and fiscal stimulus as the components of private expenditure—consumption expenditure, investment, and exports—begin to increase and return to more normal levels and so bring an increase in aggregate demand. Too much stimulus will bring an inflationary gap and faster inflation. Too little stimulus will leave a recessionary gap.

You will explore these monetary and fiscal policy actions and their effects in Chapter 20.

## EYE on YOUR LIFE
### Using the *AS-AD* Model

Using all the knowledge that you have accumulated over the term, and by watching or reading the current news, try to figure out where the U.S. economy is in its business cycle right now.

First, can you determine if real GDP is currently above, below, or at potential GDP? Second, can you determine if real GDP is expanding or contracting in a recession?

Next, try to form a view about where the U.S. economy is heading. What do you see as the main pressures on aggregate supply and aggregate demand, and in which directions are they pushing or pulling the economy?

Do you think that real GDP will expand more quickly or more slowly over the coming months? Do you think the gap between real GDP and potential GDP will widen or narrow?

How do you expect the labor market to be affected by the changes in aggregate supply and aggregate demand that you are expecting? Do you expect the unemployment rate to rise, fall, or remain constant?

Talk to your friends in class about where they see the U.S. economy right now and where it is heading. Is there a consensus or is there a wide range of opinion?

# EYE on the BUSINESS CYCLE
## Why Did the U.S. Economy Go into Recession in 2008?

What causes the business cycle and what caused the 2008–2009 recession?

### Business Cycle Theory

The mainstream business cycle theory is that potential GDP grows at a steady rate while aggregate demand grows at a fluctuating rate.

Because the money wage rate is slow to change, if aggregate demand grows more quickly than potential GDP, real GDP moves above potential GDP and an inflationary gap emerges. The inflation rate rises and real GDP is pulled back toward potential GDP.

If aggregate demand grows more slowly than potential GDP, real GDP moves below potential GDP and a recessionary gap emerges. The inflation rate slows. Because the money wage rate responds very slowly to the recessionary gap, real GDP does not return to potential GDP until another increase in aggregate demand occurs.

Fluctuations in investment are the main source of fluctuations in aggregate demand. Consumption expenditure responds to changes in income.

A recession can also occur if aggregate supply decreases to bring stagflation. And a recession might occur because both aggregate demand and aggregate supply decrease.

### The 2008–2009 Recession

The 2008–2009 recession is an example of a recession caused by a decrease in both aggregate demand and aggregate supply. The figure illustrates these two contributing forces.

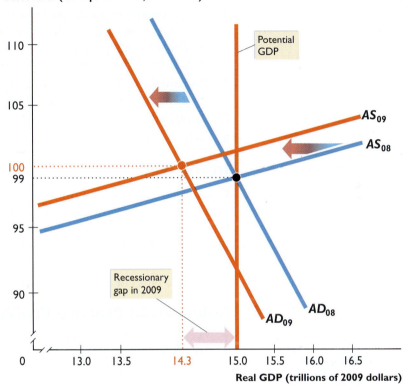

SOURCES OF DATA: Bureau of Economic Analysis and Congressional Budget Office.

At the peak in 2008, real GDP was $15 trillion and the price level was 99. In the second quarter of 2009, real GDP had fallen to $14.3 trillion and the price level had risen to 100.

The financial crisis that began in 2007 and intensified in 2008 decreased the supply of loanable funds and investment fell. In particular, construction investment collapsed.

Recession in the global economy decreased the demand for U.S. exports, so this component of aggregate demand also decreased.

The decrease in aggregate demand was moderated by a large injection of spending by the U.S. government, but this move was not enough to stop aggregate demand from decreasing.

We cannot account for the combination of a rise in the price level and a decrease in real GDP with a decrease in aggregate demand alone. Aggregate supply must also have decreased. The rise in oil prices in 2007 and a rise in the money wage rate were the two factors that brought about the decrease in aggregate supply.

CHECKPOINT 19.3

**Explain how trends and fluctuations in aggregate demand and aggregate supply bring economic growth, inflation, and the business cycle.**

## Practice Problems

The U.S. economy is at full employment when the following events occur:
- A deep recession hits the world economy.
- The world oil price rises by a large amount.
- U.S. businesses expect future profits to fall.

1. Explain the effect of each event separately on aggregate demand and aggregate supply. How will real GDP and the price level change in the short run?

2. Explain the combined effect of these events on real GDP and the price level.

3. Which event, if any, brings stagflation?

## In the News

**U.S. incomes fall for first time in 2 years**
Consumer spending rose 0.2 percent in August, down from 0.7 percent in July. Incomes fell 0.1 percent—the first decline since October 2009. Consumer spending accounts for 70 percent of economic activity.

Source: Associated Press, September 30, 2011

Explain the effect of these events in terms of the *AS-AD* model.

## Solutions to Practice Problems

1. A deep recession in the world economy decreases U.S. aggregate demand. The *AD* curve shifts leftward. In the short run, U.S. real GDP decreases and the price level falls (Figure 1). A rise in the world oil price decreases U.S. aggregate supply. The *AS* curve shifts leftward. In the short run, U.S. real GDP decreases and the price level rises (Figure 2). A fall in expected future profits decreases U.S. aggregate demand. The *AD* curve shifts leftward. In the short run, U.S. real GDP decreases and the price level falls (Figure 1).

2. All three events decrease U.S. real GDP (Figures 1 and 2). The deep world recession and the fall in expected future profits decrease the price level (Figure 1). The rise in the world oil price increases the price level (Figure 2). So the combined effect on the price level is ambiguous.

3. Stagflation is a rising price level and a decreasing real GDP together. The rise in the world oil price brings stagflation because it decreases aggregate supply, decreases real GDP, and raises the price level (Figure 2).

## Solution to In the News

The news clip gives no information about aggregate supply. Consumption expenditure is 70 percent of aggregate demand, so an increase in consumption expenditure would increase aggregate demand, real GDP, and aggregate incomes. But incomes fell, so the other components of aggregate demand (investment, government expenditure, net exports) must have decreased, moving the economy down along the *AS* curve. Or aggregate supply must have decreased, moving the economy up along the *AD* curve.

**FIGURE 1**

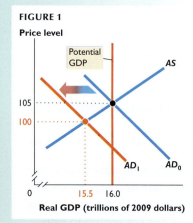

Real GDP (trillions of 2009 dollars)

**FIGURE 2**

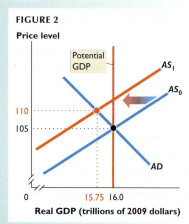

Real GDP (trillions of 2009 dollars)

**CHAPTER SUMMARY**

## Key Points

**1. Define and explain the influences on aggregate supply.**

- Aggregate supply is the relationship between the quantity of real GDP supplied and the price level when all other influences on production plans remain the same.

- The *AS* curve slopes upward because with a given money wage rate, a rise in the price level lowers the real wage rate, increases the quantity of labor demanded, and increases the quantity of real GDP supplied.

- A change in potential GDP, a change in the money wage rate, or a change in the money price of other resources changes aggregate supply.

**2. Define and explain the influences on aggregate demand.**

- Aggregate demand is the relationship between the quantity of real GDP demanded and the price level when all other influences on expenditure plans remain the same.

- The *AD* curve slopes downward because a rise in the price level decreases the buying power of money, raises the real interest rate, raises the real price of domestic goods compared with foreign goods, and decreases the quantity of real GDP demanded.

- A change in expected future income, inflation, and profits; a change in fiscal policy and monetary policy; and a change in the foreign exchange rate and foreign real GDP all change aggregate demand—the aggregate demand curve shifts.

**3. Explain how trends and fluctuations in aggregate demand and aggregate supply bring economic growth, inflation, and the business cycle.**

- Aggregate demand and aggregate supply determine real GDP and the price level in macroeconomic equilibrium, which can occur at full employment or above or below full employment.

- Away from full employment, gradual changes in the money wage rate move real GDP toward potential GDP.

- Economic growth is a persistent increase in potential GDP, and inflation occurs when aggregate demand grows at a faster rate than potential GDP.

- Business cycles occur because aggregate demand and aggregate supply fluctuate.

- Demand-pull and cost-push forces bring inflation and real GDP cycles.

## Key Terms

Aggregate demand, 554
Aggregate supply, 548
Cost-push inflation, 565
Demand-pull inflation, 564

Fiscal policy, 557
Full-employment equilibrium, 561
Inflationary gap, 561
Macroeconomic equilibrium, 560

Monetary policy, 557
Real business cycle, 563
Recessionary gap, 561
Stagflation, 565

# CHAPTER CHECKPOINT

## Study Plan Problems and Applications

1.  As more people in India have access to higher education, explain how potential GDP and aggregate supply will change in the long run.

2.  Explain the effect of each of the following events on the quantity of U.S. real GDP demanded and the demand for U.S. real GDP:
    *   The world economy goes into a strong expansion.
    *   The U.S. price level rises.
    *   Congress raises income taxes.

3.  The United States is at full employment when the Fed cuts the quantity of money, other things remaining the same. Explain the effect of the cut in the quantity of money on aggregate demand in the short run.

4.  Table 1 sets out an economy's aggregate demand and aggregate supply schedules. What is the macroeconomic equilibrium? If potential GDP is $600 billion, what is the type of macroeconomic equilibrium? Explain how real GDP and the price level will adjust in the long run.

5.  Suppose that the U.S. economy has a recessionary gap and the world economy goes into an expansion. Explain the effect of the expansion on U.S. real GDP and unemployment in the short run.

6.  Explain the effect of the Fed's action that increases the quantity of money on the macroeconomic equilibrium in the short run. Explain the adjustment process that returns the economy to full employment.

Use Figure 1 to work Problems **7** to **9**. Initially, the economy is at point *B*.

7.  Some events change aggregate demand from $AD_0$ to $AD_1$. Describe two possible events. What is the new equilibrium point? If potential GDP is $1 trillion, describe the type of macroeconomic equilibrium.

8.  Some events change aggregate supply from $AS_0$ to $AS_1$. Describe two possible events. What is the new equilibrium point? If potential GDP is $1 trillion, does the economy have an inflationary gap, a recessionary gap, or no gap?

9.  Some events change aggregate demand from $AD_0$ to $AD_1$ and aggregate supply from $AS_0$ to $AS_1$. What is the new macroeconomic equilibrium?

10. **Japan economic recovery under way as deflation eases**
    Consumer prices excluding fresh food declined 0.4 percent from a year earlier—the smallest drop since 2009. The unemployment rate unexpectedly fell to 4.9 percent from 5.1 percent—the first decrease since September. The economy will emerge from its slump "soon."

    Source: Bloomberg, January 27, 2011

    On an *AS-AD* graph show the macroeconomic equilibrium in Japan in 2010. Show why economic recovery is under way and deflation is easing.

 11. Read *Eye on the Business Cycle* on p. 567. What caused the 2008–2009 recession and how do we know that a decrease in aggregate supply played a role?

**TABLE 1**

| Price level (GDP price index) | Real GDP demanded | Real GDP supplied |
|---|---|---|
| | (billions of 2009 dollars) | |
| 90 | 900 | 600 |
| 100 | 850 | 700 |
| 110 | 800 | 800 |
| 120 | 750 | 900 |
| 130 | 700 | 1,000 |

**FIGURE 1**

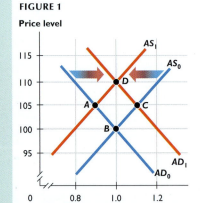

# Instructor Assignable Problems and Applications

1. What, according to the mainstream theory of the business cycle, is the most common source of recession: a decrease in aggregate demand, a decrease in aggregate supply, or both? Which is the most likely component of aggregate demand to start a recession? How does the aggregate demand multiplier influence a recession?

2. Suppose that the United States is at full employment. Explain the effect of each of the following events on aggregate supply:
   - Union wage settlements push the money wage rate up by 10 percent.
   - The price level increases.
   - Potential GDP increases.

3. Suppose that the United States is at full employment. Then the federal government cuts taxes, and all other influences on aggregate demand remain the same. Explain the effect of the tax cut on aggregate demand in the short run.

Use the following information to work Problems **4** and **5**.

Because fluctuations in the world oil price make the U.S. short-run macroeconomic equilibrium fluctuate, someone suggests that the government should vary the tax rate on oil, lowering the tax when the world oil price rises and increasing the tax when the world oil price falls, to stabilize the oil price in the U.S. market.

4. How would such an action influence aggregate demand?

5. How would such an action influence aggregate supply?

6. Table 1 sets out the aggregate demand and aggregate supply schedules in Japan. Potential GDP is 600 trillion yen. What is the short-run macroeconomic equilibrium? Does Japan have an inflationary gap or a recessionary gap and what is its magnitude?

7. Suppose that the world price of oil rises. On an *AS-AD* graph, show the effect of the world oil price rise on U.S. macroeconomic equilibrium in the short run. Explain the adjustment process that restores the economy to full employment.

8. Explain the effects of a global recession on the U.S. macroeconomic equilibrium in the short run. Explain the adjustment process that restores the economy to full employment.

### TABLE 1

| Price level (GDP price index) | Real GDP demanded | Real GDP supplied |
|---|---|---|
| | (trillions of 2005 yen) | |
| 75 | 600 | 400 |
| 85 | 550 | 450 |
| 95 | 500 | 500 |
| 105 | 450 | 550 |
| 115 | 400 | 600 |
| 125 | 350 | 650 |
| 135 | 300 | 700 |

Use the following information to work Problems **9** and **10**.

**House GOP changes course on infrastructure**

House Republicans abandoned plans to slash U.S. infrastructure spending and now say they are trying to find ways to pay for a multiyear highway-construction program, which will exceed $300 billion.

Source: *The Wall Street Journal*, September 30, 2011

9. Explain the effect of the government's increased expenditure on infrastructure on U.S. aggregate demand and aggregate supply.

10. The United States in 2011 has a recessionary gap. Use the *AS-AD* model to show the effect on U.S. real GDP as the new infrastructure is completed.

# Critical Thinking Discussion Questions

1. **Singapore tightens foreign-worker restrictions**

   To reduce reliance on overseas labor in the manufacturing sector, Singapore's government is tightening its foreign-worker restrictions. With this policy, Singapore is losing its manufacturing capacity. Even though there have been more sales orders resulting from the economic recovery of other Southeast Asian countries, firms do not have enough manpower to produce.

   Source: Bloomberg, 13 January 2014

   Think about Singapore's foreign-worker restrictions:

   What is the effect of Singapore's foreign-worker restrictions on aggregate supply and potential GDP?

   What is the effect of the economic recovery of other Southeast Asian countries on Singapore's economy?

   How do Singapore's real GDP and price level change as a result of these two events?

2. **NZ immigration at 10-year high**

   New Zealand immigration has risen to a 10-year high. The Reserve Bank said net migration is boosting demand for housing and consumer spending, and is seen as an inflationary pressure.

   Source: *Sydney Morning Herald*, 21 March 2014

   Think about immigration to New Zealand:

   How does immigration influence New Zealand's aggregate supply and potential GDP?

   How does immigration influence New Zealand's aggregate demand?

   How does immigration lead to inflationary pressure?

   What type of inflation is created?

3. **Russian economy minister says country heading for recession**

   The Russian economy may slide into recession in the second quarter as fear of sanctions harms investment activity. Russia's economy contracted 0.5% in the first quarter from the fourth quarter. The central bank's policy also harmed economic growth by increasing interest rates twice since early March, citing rising inflationary risks.

   Source: *The Wall Street Journal*, 13 May 2014

   Think about the Russian economy:

   Describe the Russian macroeconomic equilibrium prior to the actions of the central bank.

   What is the effect on Russia's aggregate supply, potential GDP and aggregate demand of a rise in interest rates and a decrease in investment activity?

   What policies can the government take to increase economic growth?

Can fiscal stimulus end a recession?
Did the Fed save us from another
Great Depression?

# Fiscal Policy and Monetary Policy

**20**

**When you have completed your study of this chapter,
you will be able to**

**1** Describe the federal budget process and explain the effects of fiscal policy.

**2** Describe the Federal Reserve's monetary policy process and explain the effects of monetary policy.

## 20.1 THE FEDERAL BUDGET AND FISCAL POLICY

**Fiscal policy**
The use of the federal budget to achieve the macroeconomic objectives of high and sustained economic growth and full employment.

**Fiscal policy** is the use of the federal budget to achieve the macroeconomic objectives of high and sustained economic growth and full employment. What is the federal budget and how is it made?

### ■ The Federal Budget

The *federal budget* is an annual statement of the tax revenues, outlays, and surplus or deficit of the government of the United States.

#### Budget Time Line

The President and Congress make the federal budget on the time line shown in Figure 20.1. The President proposes and approves the budget, but Congress makes the tough decisions on spending and taxes. The House of Representatives and the Senate develop their ideas in their respective budget committees, and conferences between the two houses resolve differences and draft the bills that become the Budget Act.

### ■ Budget Balance and Debt

**Budget balance**
Tax revenues minus outlays.

The government's **budget balance** is equal to tax revenues minus outlays. That is,

$$\text{Budget balance} = \text{Tax revenues} - \text{Outlays}.$$

If tax revenues equal outlays, the government has a *balanced budget*. The government has a *budget surplus* if tax revenues exceed outlays. The government has a *budget deficit* if outlays exceed tax revenues. Table 20.1 shows the tax revenues, outlays, and budget balance for the fiscal 2014 year.

■ **FIGURE 20.1**

The Federal Budget Time Line for Fiscal 2015

The federal budget process begins with the President's proposals in February.

Congress debates and amends the President's proposals and enacts a budget before the start of the fiscal year on October 1.

The President signs the budget act into law.

Throughout the fiscal year, Congress might pass supplementary budget laws. The budget outcome is calculated after the end of the fiscal year.

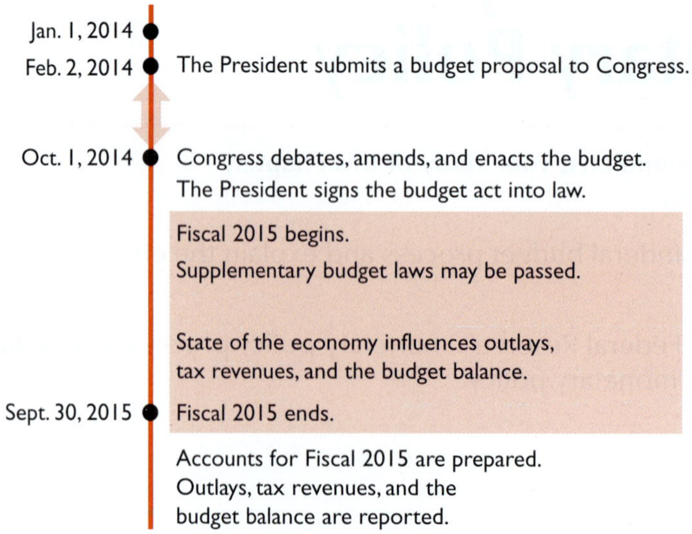

Jan. 1, 2014 ●
Feb. 2, 2014 ● The President submits a budget proposal to Congress.

Oct. 1, 2014 ● Congress debates, amends, and enacts the budget.
The President signs the budget act into law.

Fiscal 2015 begins.
Supplementary budget laws may be passed.

State of the economy influences outlays, tax revenues, and the budget balance.

Sept. 30, 2015 ● Fiscal 2015 ends.

Accounts for Fiscal 2015 are prepared.
Outlays, tax revenues, and the budget balance are reported.

■ **TABLE 20.1**

The Federal Budget in Fiscal 2014

| Item | Projections (billions of dollars) | |
|---|---|---|
| **Tax Revenues** | **3,000** | |
| Personal income taxes | | 1,358 |
| Social Security taxes | | 1,031 |
| Corporate income taxes | | 335 |
| Indirect taxes | | 276 |
| **Outlays** | **3,627** | |
| Transfer payments | | 2,253 |
| Expenditure on goods and services | | 1,152 |
| Debt interest | | 222 |
| **Balance** | **−627** | |

The federal budget for 2014 was expected to be in a large deficit. Tax revenues of $3,000 billion were expected to be $627 billion less than outlays of $3,627 billion.

Personal income taxes are the largest revenue source and transfer payments are the largest outlay.

SOURCE OF DATA: *Budget of the United States Government, Fiscal Year 2014.*

## Surplus, Deficit, and Debt

To finance a budget deficit, the government borrows, and it repays debt when it has a surplus. The amount of debt outstanding that has arisen from past budget deficits is called **national debt**. The national debt at the end of a fiscal year equals the national debt at the end of the previous fiscal year plus the budget deficit or minus the budget surplus. For example,

Debt at the end of 2015 = Debt at the end of 2014 + Budget deficit in 2014

*Eye on the Past* on p. 576 shows the history of the U.S. budget deficit and debt.

**National debt**
The amount of government debt outstanding—debt that has arisen from past budget deficits.

## A Personal Analogy

The government's budget and debt are like your budget and debt, only bigger. If you take a student loan each year to go to school, you have a budget deficit and a growing debt. After graduating, if you have a job and repay some of your loan each year, you have a budget surplus each year and a shrinking debt.

## Types of Fiscal Policy

Fiscal policy actions can be

- Discretionary fiscal policy
- Automatic fiscal policy

**Discretionary Fiscal Policy** A fiscal action that is initiated by an act of Congress is called **discretionary fiscal policy**. It requires a change in a spending program or in a tax law. For example, an increase in defense spending or a cut in the income tax rate is a discretionary fiscal policy.

**Discretionary fiscal policy**
A fiscal policy action that is initiated by an act of Congress.

**Automatic Fiscal Policy** A fiscal action that is triggered by the state of the economy is called **automatic fiscal policy**. For example, an increase in unemployment induces an increase in payments to the unemployed. A fall in incomes induces a decrease in tax revenues.

**Automatic fiscal policy**
A fiscal policy action that is triggered by the state of the economy.

# EYE on the PAST
## Federal Tax Revenues, Outlays, Deficits, and Debt

In 1940, in the first year of World War II, for every dollar earned, the federal government collected 6.5 cents in taxes and spent 9.3 cents. By 1943, at the depth of the most terrible war in history, the government was spending 40 cents of every dollar earned and collecting 12 cents in taxes. The government deficit in 1943 was almost 30 percent of GDP and more than 30 percent in 1944.

The result of these enormous deficits was a mushrooming government debt. By 1946, when the debt-to-GDP ratio (debt as a percentage of GDP) peaked, the government owed more than a year's GDP.

During the 1950s and 1960s, the government's debt-to-GDP ratio tumbled as balanced budgets combined with rapid real GDP growth. By 1974, the debt-to-GDP ratio had fallen to a low of 23 percent.

Budget deficits returned during the 1980s as the defense budget swelled and some tax rates were cut. The result was a growing debt-to-GDP ratio that climbed to almost 50 percent by 1995.

Expenditure restraint combined with sustained real GDP growth lowered the debt-to-GDP ratio during the 1990s, but a surge in expenditures on defense and homeland security, further tax cuts, and a spending surge in 2009 and 2010 to fight the global financial crisis and recession, all combined to swell the debt-to-GDP ratio again. During the 2010s, the government will struggle to balance its budget.

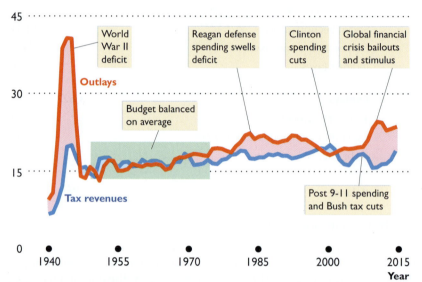

**Tax revenues and outlays (percentage of GDP)**

**(a) Tax revenues, outlays, and deficits**

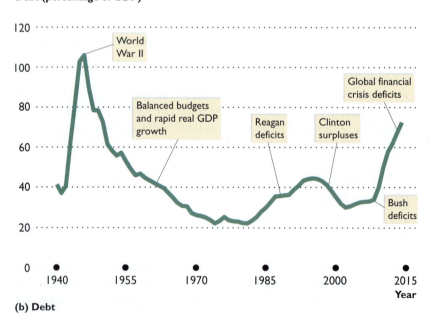

**Debt (percentage of GDP)**

**(b) Debt**

SOURCE OF DATA: *Budget of the U.S. Government, Fiscal Year 2014*, Historical Tables, Tables 7.1 and 14.1.

# ■ Discretionary Fiscal Policy: Demand-Side Effects

Discretionary fiscal policy influences both aggregate demand and aggregate supply. We'll look first at the demand-side effects. Changes in government expenditure and changes in taxes have multiplier effects on aggregate demand similar to the multiplier effect that you met in Chapter 19.

## The Government Expenditure Multiplier

The **government expenditure multiplier** is the effect of a change in government expenditure on goods and services on aggregate demand. Government expenditure is a component of aggregate expenditure, so when government expenditure increases, aggregate demand increases. Real GDP increases and induces an increase in consumption expenditure, which brings a further increase in aggregate expenditure. A multiplier process like the one described in Chapter 19 (p. 558) ensues.

**Government expenditure multiplier**
The effect of a change in government expenditure on goods and services on aggregate demand.

## The Tax Multiplier

The **tax multiplier** is the magnification effect of a change in taxes on aggregate demand. A *decrease* in taxes *increases* disposable income, which increases consumption expenditure. A decrease in taxes works like an increase in government expenditure. But the magnitude of the tax multiplier is smaller than the government expenditure multiplier because a $1 tax cut generates *less than* $1 of additional expenditure. The marginal propensity to consume determines the initial increase in expenditure induced by a tax cut and the magnitude of the tax multiplier. For example, if the marginal propensity to consume is 0.75, then the initial increase in consumption expenditure induced by a $1 tax cut is only 75 cents. In this case, the tax multiplier is 0.75 times the magnitude of the government expenditure multiplier.

**Tax multiplier**
The effect of a change in taxes on aggregate demand.

## The Transfer Payments Multiplier

The **transfer payments multiplier** is the effect of a change in transfer payments on aggregate demand. This multiplier works like the tax multiplier but in the opposite direction. An *increase* in transfer payments *increases* disposable income, which *increases* consumption expenditure. The magnitude of the transfer payments multiplier is similar to that of the tax multiplier. Just as a $1 tax cut generates *less than* $1 of additional expenditure, so also does a $1 increase in transfer payments. Again, it is the marginal propensity to consume that determines the increase in expenditure induced by an increase in transfer payments.

**Transfer payments multiplier**
The effect of a change in transfer payments on aggregate demand.

## The Balanced Budget Multiplier

The **balanced budget multiplier** is the magnification effect on aggregate demand of a *simultaneous* change in government expenditure and taxes that leaves the budget balance unchanged. The balanced budget multiplier is not zero. It is greater than zero because a $1 increase in government expenditure injects a dollar more into aggregate demand while a $1 tax rise (or decrease in transfer payments) takes less than $1 from aggregate demand. So when both government expenditure and taxes increase by $1, aggregate demand increases.

**Balanced budget multiplier**
The effect on aggregate demand of a *simultaneous* change in government expenditure and taxes that leaves the budget balance unchanged.

The magnitudes of the multiplier effects that we've just described are the subject of debate and disagreement among economists and we look at the range of views in *Eye on Fiscal Stimulus* on p. 584. For now, we will sidestep that debate and see how a successful discretionary fiscal policy works.

## ■ A Successful Fiscal Stimulus

**Fiscal stimulus**
An increase in government outlays or a decrease in tax revenues designed to boost real GDP and create or save jobs.

Cash for Clunkers stimulated aggregate demand.

**Fiscal stimulus** is achieved by increasing government outlays or decreasing tax revenues when real GDP is below potential GDP and the government wants to boost real GDP and create or save jobs. Figure 20.2 shows us how a successful stimulus package increases aggregate demand.

In Figure 20.2(a), potential GDP is $16 trillion but real GDP is only $15 trillion. The economy is at point *A* and there is a *recessionary gap* (see Chapter 19, p. 561).

To eliminate the recessionary gap and restore full employment, the government introduces a fiscal stimulus. An increase in government expenditure or a tax cut increases aggregate expenditure by $\Delta E$. If this were the only change in spending plans, the *AD* curve would become $AD_0 + \Delta E$ in Figure 20.2(b). But the initial increase in government expenditure sets off a multiplier process, which increases consumption expenditure. As the multiplier process plays out, aggregate demand increases and the *AD* curve shifts rightward to $AD_1$.

With no change in the price level, the economy would move from the initial point *A* to point *B* on $AD_1$. But the increase in aggregate demand combined with the upward-sloping aggregate supply curve brings a rise in the price level, and the economy moves to a new equilibrium at point *C*. The price level rises to 105, real GDP increases to $16 trillion, and the economy returns to full employment.

■ **FIGURE 20.2**

Fiscal Stimulus

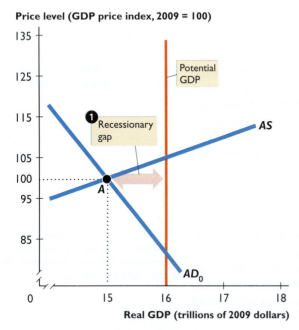

**(a) Below full-employment equilibrium**

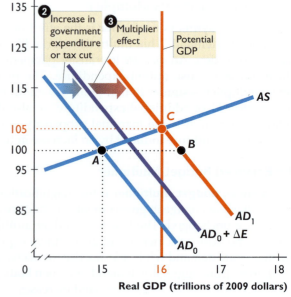

**(b) Full employment restored**

Potential GDP is $16 trillion. At point *A*, real GDP is $15 trillion, and ❶ there is a $1 trillion recessionary gap. ❷ An increase in government expenditure or a tax cut increases expenditure by $\Delta E$.

❸ The multiplier increases induced expenditure. The *AD* curve shifts rightward to $AD_1$, the price level rises to 105, real GDP increases to $16 trillion, and the recessionary gap is eliminated.

# ■ Discretionary Fiscal Policy: Supply-Side Effects

Both government expenditure and taxes influence potential GDP and aggregate supply, and we now look at the supply-side effects of fiscal policy.

## Supply-Side Effects of Government Expenditure

Government provides services such as law and order, public education, and public health that increase production possibilities. For example, one of the reasons why we are more productive than are the citizens of the poor developing countries is that we are better educated and healthier than they are. Government also provides social infrastructure capital such as highways, bridges, tunnels, and dams that increase our production possibilities.

Government services and capital could be overprovided to the point at which they no longer increase production possibilities. But it is unlikely that we have reached such a point.

An *increase* in government expenditure that increases the quantities of productive services and capital increases potential GDP and increases aggregate supply.

The construction of the Hoover Dam during the 1930s and the interstate highway system that was begun during the 1950s are two of the most spectacular examples of an increase in productive government expenditures. The Hoover Dam increased the production of electricity, improved water management, and brought expanded recreation facilities. The interstate highway system improved transportation services, increased the productivity of truck drivers and other road users, and provided the foundation for the development of suburban shopping malls and entertainment centers.

## Supply-Side Effects of Taxes

To pay for the productive services and capital that the government provides, it collects taxes. All taxes create disincentives to work, save, and provide entrepreneurial services.

Taxes on labor income decrease the supply of labor. A smaller supply of labor means a higher equilibrium real wage rate and a smaller equilibrium quantity of labor employed. With a smaller quantity of labor employed, potential GDP and aggregate supply are smaller than they would otherwise be.

Taxes on the income from capital decrease saving and decrease the supply of capital. A smaller supply of capital means a higher equilibrium real interest rate and a smaller equilibrium quantity of investment and capital employed. With a smaller quantity of capital, potential GDP and aggregate supply are smaller than they would otherwise be.

Taxes on the incomes of entrepreneurs weaken the incentive to take risks and create new businesses. With a smaller number of firms, the quantities of labor and capital employed are lower and potential GDP and aggregate supply are smaller than they would otherwise be.

An *increase* in taxes strengthens the disincentive effects that we've just described. It decreases the supply of labor, capital, and entrepreneurial services; decreases potential GDP; and decreases aggregate supply. And a tax cut has the opposite effects. It strengthens the incentives to work, save, and provide entrepreneurial services. So a tax cut increases potential GDP and increases aggregate supply.

### Scale of Government Supply-Side Effects

If both government expenditure and taxes increase, the scale of government grows. More productive government expenditure increases potential GDP, but higher taxes to pay for the expenditure decrease potential GDP. So an increase in the scale of government might increase or decrease potential GDP and aggregate supply depending on which effect is stronger. Some economists (and politicians) believe that a larger scale of government increases potential GDP and aggregate supply despite the weakened incentives from higher tax rates. Others believe that the incentive effects are so powerful that smaller government is more productive and brings a greater potential GDP and aggregate supply.

### Supply-Side Effects on Potential GDP

Figure 20.3 illustrates the effects of fiscal policy on potential GDP. Initially, the production function is $PF_0$, the full employment quantity of labor is 200 billion hours, and potential GDP is $16 trillion (see Chapter 17, pp. 490–491).

A tax cut strengthens the incentive to work, which increases the supply of labor and increases the equilibrium level of employment at full employment. In Figure 20.3, employment increases to 210 billion hours a year. The tax cut also strengthens the incentive to save and invest, which increases the quantity of capital. With more capital per worker, labor productivity increases and the production function shifts upward to $PF_1$.

At the increased level of employment and on the new higher production function, potential GDP is $17 trillion. An increase in potential GDP increases aggregate supply, which also increases actual real GDP.

■ **FIGURE 20.3**

The Supply-Side Effects of Fiscal Policy

❶ A tax cut strengthens the incentive to work, increases the supply of labor, and increases employment.

❷ A tax cut strengthens the incentive to save and invest, which increases the quantity of capital and increases labor productivity.

❸ The combined effect of a tax cut on employment and labor productivity increases potential GDP.

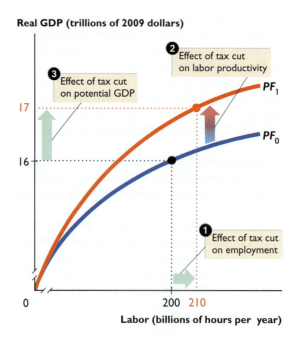

## ■ Limitations of Discretionary Fiscal Policy

Discretionary fiscal stabilization policy is hampered by four problems:

- Law-making time lag
- Shrinking area of discretion
- Estimating potential GDP
- Economic forecasting

### Law-Making Time Lag

The law-making time lag is the amount of time it takes Congress to pass the laws needed to change taxes or spending. The economy might benefit from fiscal stimulation today, but by the time Congress acts, a different fiscal medicine might be needed.

### Shrinking Area of Discretion

During the 2000s, federal spending increased faster than in any other peacetime period. An increased security threat brought increased expenditure on the military and homeland security, and an aging population brought a increased expenditure on entitlement programs such as Social Security and Medicare.

The growth of entitlement programs has not only shrunk the area of discretionary spending. It has also created a time bomb that has a potentially devastating effect on economic growth and future fiscal policy. (See *Eye on the U.S. Economy* below.)

Today, 80 percent of the federal budget is effectively off limits for discretionary policy action, and the remaining 20 percent of items are very hard to cut.

# EYE on the U.S. ECONOMY
## A Social Security and Medicare Time Bomb

The age distribution of the U.S. population today is dominated by the surge in the birth rate after World War II that created what is called the "baby boom generation." There are 77 million "baby boomers" and the first of them started collecting Social Security pensions in 2008 and became eligible for Medicare benefits in 2011. By 2030, all the baby boomers will be supported by Social Security and Medicare and benefit payments will have doubled.

The government's Social Security and Medicare obligations are a debt and are just as real as the bonds that the government issues to finance its current budget deficit.

How big is this debt? Economists Jagadeesh Gokhale and Kent Smetters estimate that it was $80 trillion in 2010 and that it grows by $2 trillion a year. To put $80 trillion in perspective, U.S. GDP in 2012 was $14 trillion. So the fiscal imbalance was 5.7 times the value of one year's production.

The time bomb points to a catastrophic future. How can the federal government meet its Social Security and Medicare obligations? There are four alternatives:

- Raise income taxes
- Raise Social Security taxes
- Cut Social Security benefits
- Cut other government spending

Gokhale and Smetters estimate that income taxes would need to be raised by 69 percent, or Social Security taxes raised by 95 percent, or Social Security benefits cut by 56 percent. Even if the government stopped all other spending, including that on national defense, it would not be able to pay its bills. By combining the four measures, the pain from each could be lessened, but the pain would still be severe.

Congress has appointed a "Super Committee" to find ways of trimming the federal budget by $1.5 trillion. Even this spending cut looks almost impossible to achieve. Some tough fiscal policy choices lie ahead.

582 Part 5 • UNDERSTANDING THE MACROECONOMY

### Estimating Potential GDP

Potential GDP is hard to estimate and sometimes we don't even get the sign of the output gap right. Because it is not always possible to tell whether real GDP is below, above, or at potential GDP, a discretionary fiscal action might move real GDP *away* from potential GDP instead of toward it.

### Economic Forecasting

Fiscal policy changes take a long time to become effective. So fiscal policy must target forecasts of where the economy will be in the future. Economic forecasting is inexact and subject to error and might mislead Congress.

These four limitations of discretionary fiscal policy do not affect automatic fiscal policy, which we now describe.

## ■ Automatic Fiscal Policy

**Automatic stabilizers**
Features of fiscal policy that stabilize real GDP without explicit action by the government.

**Induced taxes**
Taxes that vary with real GDP.

Automatic fiscal policy is a consequence of tax revenues and outlays that fluctuate with real GDP. These features of fiscal policy are called **automatic stabilizers** because they stabilize real GDP without explicit action by the government.

On the revenue side of the budget, tax laws define tax *rates,* not tax *dollars.* Tax dollars paid depend on tax rates and incomes. But incomes vary with real GDP, so tax revenues depend on real GDP. Taxes that vary with real GDP are called **induced taxes**. When real GDP increases in an expansion, wages and profits rise, so the taxes on these incomes—induced taxes—rise. When real GDP decreases in a recession, wages and profits fall, so the induced taxes on these incomes fall.

On the expenditure side of the budget, the government creates programs that entitle suitably qualified people and businesses to receive benefits. The spending on such programs is called *needs-tested spending,* and it results in transfer payments that depend on the economic state of individual citizens and businesses. When the economy is in a recession, the number of people experiencing unemployment and economic hardship increases, and needs-tested spending on unemployment benefits and food stamps increases. When the economy expands, the number of people experiencing unemployment and economic hardship decreases, and needs-tested spending decreases.

Automatic stabilizers give rise to cyclical fluctuations in the budget balance that we distinguish from structural changes in the budget.

## ■ Cyclical and Structural Budget Balances

**Structural surplus or deficit**
The budget balance that would occur if the economy were at full employment.

**Cyclical surplus or deficit**
The budget balance that arises because revenues and outlays are not at their full-employment levels.

To identify the government budget deficit that arises from the business cycle, we distinguish between the structural and cyclical budget balances. The **structural surplus or deficit** is the budget balance that would occur if the economy were at full employment. That is, the structural balance is the balance that the full-employment level of real GDP would generate given the spending programs and tax laws that Congress has created. The **cyclical surplus or deficit** is the budget balance that arises purely because tax revenues and outlays are *not* at their full-employment levels. That is, the cyclical balance is the balance that arises because tax revenues rise and outlays fall in an inflationary gap or tax revenues fall and outlays rise in a recessionary gap. The *actual* budget balance equals the sum of the structural balance and cyclical balance. A cyclical deficit corrects itself when full employment returns. A structural deficit requires action by Congress. *Eye on the U.S. Economy* on p. 583 looks at the recent history of the U.S. structural and cyclical budget balances.

# EYE on the U.S. ECONOMY
## The U.S. Structural and Cyclical Budget Balances

The U.S. federal budget balance in 2013 was a deficit of $1 trillion and the recessionary gap was close to $1 trillion. With such a large recessionary gap, you would expect some of the deficit to be cyclical. But how much of the 2013 deficit was cyclical? How much was structural?

According to the Congressional Budget Office (CBO), a half of the 2013 deficit was cyclical and a half was structural. The figure shows the actual and cyclical balances as percentages of GDP from 1990 through 2013.

The structural balance equals the actual balance minus the cyclical balance. You can see that the structural deficit was small in 2007, increased in 2008, and exploded in 2009. The 2009 fiscal stimulus package created most of this structural deficit.

When full employment returns, which the CBO says will be in 2018, the cyclical deficit will vanish, but the structural deficit must be addressed by further acts of Congress. No one knows the discretionary measures that will be taken to reduce the structural deficit and this awkward fact creates uncertainty.

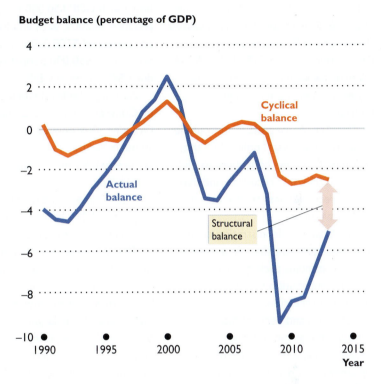

SOURCE OF DATA: Congressional Budget Office.

## Schools of Thought and Cracks in Today's Consensus

The macroeconomic events of 2008 and 2009 have created cracks in the consensus among economists about the effects of fiscal policy.

Keynesians such as the 2008 Nobel Prize Winner Paul Krugman (Princeton University) and Christina Romer (University of California, Berkeley and President Obama's former chief economic adviser) say that fiscal stimulus boosts real GDP and employment with a large multiplier effect.

Mainstream economists such as Robert J. Barro (Harvard University), the 1995 Nobel Prize Winner Robert E. Lucas Jr. (University of Chicago), and John B. Taylor (Stanford University) say that Keynesians overestimate the multiplier effects of fiscal stimulus, which "crowds out" private consumption expenditure and investment. The durable results of a fiscal stimulus, these economists say, are bigger government, lower potential GDP, a slower real GDP growth rate, and a greater burden of government debt on future generations.

# EYE on FISCAL STIMULUS
## Can Fiscal Stimulus End a Recession?

In February 2009, in the depths of the 2008–2009 recession, Congress passed the American Recovery and Reinvestment Act, a $787 billion fiscal stimulus package that the President signed at an economic forum in Denver.

This Act of Congress is an example of discretionary fiscal policy. Did this action by Congress contribute to ending the 2008–2009 recession and making the recession less severe than it might have been?

The Obama Administration economists are confident that the answer is yes: The stimulus package made a significant contribution to easing and ending the recession.

But many, and perhaps most, economists think that the stimulus package played a small role and that the truly big story is not discretionary fiscal policy but the role played by automatic stabilizers.

Let's take a closer look at the fiscal policy actions and their likely effects.

### Discretionary Fiscal Policy

In a number of speeches, President Obama promised that fiscal stimulus would save or create 650,000 jobs by the end of the 2009 summer. In October 2009, the Administration economists declared the promise fulfilled. Fiscal stimulus had saved or created the promised 650,000 jobs.

This claim of success might be correct but it isn't startling and it isn't a huge claim. To see why, start by asking

how much GDP 650,000 people would produce. In 2009, each employed person produced $100,000 of real GDP on average. So 650,000 people would produce $65 billion of GDP.

Although the fiscal stimulus passed by Congress totalled $787 billion, by October 2009 only 20 percent of the stimulus had been spent (or taken in tax breaks). So the stimulus was about $160 billion.

If government outlays of $160 billion created $65 billion of GDP, the multiplier was 0.4($65/160 = 0.4$).

This multiplier is much smaller than the 1.6 that the Obama economists say will eventually occur. They believe, like Keynes, that the multiplier starts out small and gets larger over time as spending plans respond to rising incomes. An initial increase in expenditure increases aggregate expenditure. But the increase in aggregate expenditure generates higher incomes, which in turn induces greater consumption expenditure.

### Automatic Fiscal Policy

Government revenue is sensitive to the state of the economy. When personal incomes and corporate profits fall, income tax revenues fall too. When unemployment increases, outlays on unemployment benefits and other social welfare benefits increase. These fiscal policy changes are automatic. They occur with speed and without help from Congress.

The scale of automatic fiscal policy changes depends on the depth of recession. In 2009, real GDP sank to 6 percent below potential GDP—a recessionary gap of $800 billion.

Responding to this deep recession, tax revenues crashed and transfer payments skyrocketed. The figure below shows the magnitudes as percentages of GDP. You can see that the automatic stabilizers were much bigger than the discretionary actions—six times as large. This automatic action, not the stimulus package, played the major role in limiting job losses.

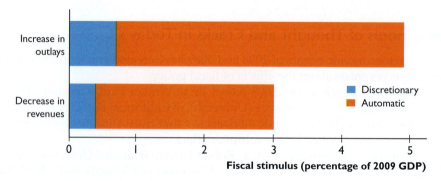

SOURCES OF DATA: Budget of the United States, 2010, Bureau of Economic Analysis, and White House press releases.

## CHECKPOINT 20.1

**Describe the federal budget process and explain the effects of fiscal policy.**

## Practice Problems

1.  Classify the following items as automatic fiscal policy, discretionary fiscal policy, or not part of fiscal policy.
    - A decrease in tax revenues in a recession
    - Additional government expenditure to upgrade highways
    - An increase in the public education budget
    - A cut in infrastructure expenditure during a boom

2.  Explain how aggregate demand changes when government expenditure on national defense increases by $100 billion.

3.  Explain how aggregate demand changes when the government increases taxes by $100 billion.

4.  Explain how aggregate demand changes when the government increases both expenditure on goods and services and taxes by $100 billion.

## In the News

**How to curb the deficit**
Senator Evan Bayh, Democrat of Indiana, noted that Democrats want to spend more than we can afford; Republicans tend to want to cut taxes more than we can afford. So we are stuck with large deficits.

Source: *The New York Times*, October 31, 2009

What policy will change aggregate demand the most: Democrats agreeing to cut the budget outlays or Republicans agreeing to raise taxes?

## Solutions to Practice Problems

1.  A decrease in tax revenues in a recession is an automatic fiscal policy. Expenditure to upgrade highways is a discretionary fiscal policy. An increase in the public education budget is a discretionary fiscal policy. A cut in infrastructure expenditure is a discretionary fiscal policy.

2.  Aggregate demand increases by more than $100 billion because government expenditure increases induced expenditure.

3.  Aggregate demand decreases by more than $100 billion because the tax increase has a multiplier effect that decreases induced expenditure.

4.  An increase in government expenditure of $100 billion increases aggregate demand by more than $100 billion. An increase in taxes of $100 billion decreases aggregate demand by more than $100 billion. The increase is greater than the decrease, so together aggregate demand increases.

## In the News

The effect of a cut in budget outlays on aggregate demand depends on whether the items cut are expenditures on goods and services (government expenditure multiplier) or transfer payments (transfer payments multiplier). An increase in taxes will decrease aggregate demand (tax multiplier). The magnitude of the government expenditure multiplier exceeds the other two multipliers, so a cut in government expenditure on goods and services will decrease aggregate demand the most.

**Monetary policy**
The adjustment of interest rates and the quantity of money to achieve the dual objectives of price stability and full employment.

**Monetary policy** is the adjustment of interest rates and the quantity of money to achieve the dual objective of price stability and full employment. The Board of Governors of the Federal Reserve System (the Fed) conducts monetary policy independently of the government but under the terms of the Federal Reserve Act of 1913 and its subsequent amendments, the most recent of which was passed in 2000. The Act defines the Fed's goals as the attainment of "maximum employment" and "stable prices," goals known as the *Fed's dual mandate*.

### ■ The Monetary Policy Process

The Fed makes monetary policy in a process that has three elements:

- Monitoring economic conditions
- Decisions of the Federal Open Market Committee (FOMC)
- Monetary Policy Report to Congress

### Monitoring Economic Conditions

Each Federal Reserve Bank monitors its district by talking with business leaders, economists, market experts, and others. The Fed summarizes the state of the economy in the *Beige Book*, which the Federal Open Market Committee uses in its deliberations.

The Beige Book is available on the Fed's Web site and is a good source of up-to-date information on the current state of the economy.

### Decisions of the Federal Open Market Committee (FOMC)

The FOMC, which meets eight times a year, makes the monetary policy decisions. The FOMC's first and fourth meetings of the year run for two days (the other six meetings run for one day) and are opportunities for the committee to assess the longer-term outlook as well as the current period's open market operations.

After each meeting, the FOMC announces its decisions and describes its view of the likelihood that its goals of price stability and full employment will be achieved. The FOMC publishes the minutes of its meetings after they have been confirmed as a correct record of the meeting at the next scheduled meeting. For example, the minutes of the first meeting of the year are published after the second meeting of the year.

Full transcripts of FOMC meetings are published with a five-year time lag. This delay enables the members of the FOMC to have a frank exchange of views without worrying about how their discussions might be interpreted by the traders in financial markets. The eventual publication of the transcripts permits a detailed public scrutiny of the FOMC's decision-making process.

### Monetary Policy Report to Congress

Twice a year, in February and July, the Fed prepares a Monetary Policy Report to Congress, and the Fed chairman testifies before the House of Representatives Committee on Financial Services. The report and the chairman's testimony review the monetary policy and economic developments of the past year and the economic outlook for the coming year.

# The Federal Funds Rate Target

Following each FOMC meeting, the Fed announces its monetary policy decision as a target for the federal funds rate. Figure 20.4 shows the federal funds rate since 2000.

You can see that the federal funds rate was 5.5 percent a year at the beginning of 2000 and during 2000 and 2001, the Fed increased the rate to 6.5 percent a year. The Fed raised the interest rate to this high level to lower the inflation rate.

Between 2002 and 2004, the federal funds rate was set at historically low levels. The reason is that with inflation well anchored at close to 2 percent a year, the Fed was less concerned about inflation than it was about recession so it wanted to lean in the direction of avoiding recession.

From mid-2004 through early 2006, the Fed was increasingly concerned about the build-up of inflation pressures and it raised the federal funds rate target on 17 occasions to take it to 5.25 percent a year, a level it held until September 2007.

When the global financial crisis began, the Fed acted cautiously in cutting the federal funds rate target. But as the crisis intensified, rate cuts became more frequent and larger, ending in December 2008 with an interest rate close to zero. The normal changes of a quarter of a percentage point (also called 25 *basis points*) were abandoned as the Fed slashed the rate, first by an unusual 50 basis points and finally, in December 2008, by an unprecedented 100 basis points. Since the end of 2008, the federal funds rate has been close to zero.

To hit its target for the federal funds rate, the FOMC instructs the New York Fed to conduct open market operations to adjust the banking system's reserves to the level that makes banks want to make loans to each other at the target rate.

## FIGURE 20.4

### The Fed's Key Monetary Policy Instrument: The Federal Funds Rate

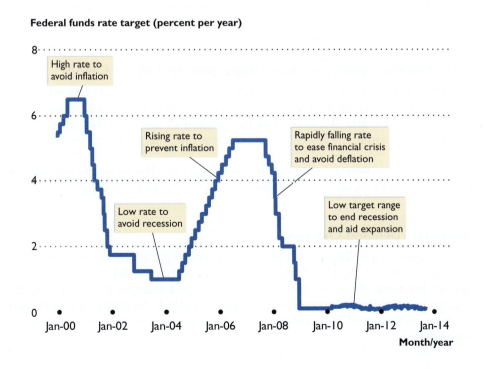

The Fed sets a target for the federal funds rate and then takes actions to keep the rate close to the target.

When the Fed wants to slow inflation, it raises the federal funds rate target.

When the inflation rate is below target and the Fed wants to avoid recession, it lowers the federal funds rate target.

When the Fed focused on restoring financial stability, it cut the federal funds rate target aggressively to almost zero.

SOURCE OF DATA: Board of Governors of the Federal Reserve System.

## ■ The Ripple Effects of the Fed's Actions

When the Fed changes the federal funds rate, it sets up a ripple effect that runs all the way to a change in real GDP and the price level. Figure 20.5 provides a schematic summary of these effects, which stretch out over a period of between one and two years. Let's look at each stage in the transmission process.

### Other Interest Rates Change

The first effect of a change in the federal funds rate is a change in other short-term interest rates. This effect occurs quickly and predictably. The reason is that an overnight loan to another bank is a close substitute for short-term securities such as Treasury bills so the interest rates on these very similar assets keep close to each other.

### The Exchange Rate Changes

A rise in the U.S. interest rate relative to the interest rate in other countries brings funds into the United States from other countries to take advantage of the higher interest rate. When people move funds into the United States, they buy dollars, the demand for dollars rises and the exchange rate rises.

### The Quantity of Money and Bank Loans Change

When the federal funds rate changes, it is because the Fed has changed the quantity of bank reserves in the opposite direction. With a change in reserves, banks change their volume of loans, which changes deposits and the quantity of money. When the Fed cuts the federal funds rate, the quantity of money and bank loans increases.

### The Long-Term Real Interest Rate Changes

A fall in the federal funds rate that increases the supply of bank loans increases the supply of funds and lowers the equilibrium real interest rate. A rise in the federal funds rate that decreases the supply of bank loans decreases the supply of funds and raises the equilibrium real interest rate.

### Consumption Expenditure, Investment, and Net Exports Change

The interest rate influences people's spending decisions. Other things remaining the same, the lower the real interest rate, the greater is the amount of consumption expenditure and the smaller is the amount of saving. Also, other things remaining the same, the lower the real interest rate, the greater is the amount of investment.

A fall in the interest rate lowers the exchange rate. The lower price of the dollar means that foreigners now pay less for U.S.-made goods and services, so U.S. exports increase.

### Aggregate Demand Changes

Consumption expenditure, investment, and net exports are all components of aggregate demand. So when these items change, aggregate demand also changes, and in the same direction. But aggregate demand changes by more than the change in these items because of the multiplier effect. A change in expenditure changes income, and the change in income induces a change in consumption expenditure.

**FIGURE 20.5**

## Ripple Effects of the Fed's Actions

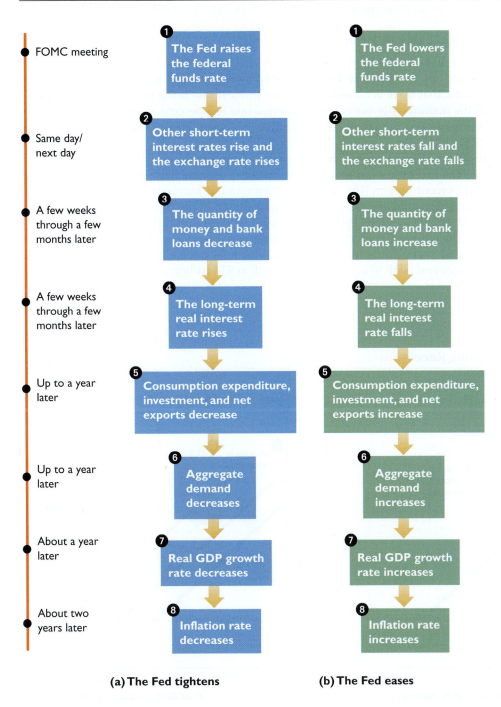

(a) The Fed tightens          (b) The Fed eases

The Fed changes its interest rate target and conducts open market operations to **1** change the federal funds rate. The same day **2** other short-term interest rates change and so does the exchange rate. A few weeks through a few months after the FOMC meeting, **3** the quantity of money and bank loans change, which **4** changes the long-term real interest rate.

Up to a year after the FOMC meeting, **5** consumption, investment, and net exports change, so **6** aggregate demand changes. Eventually, the change in the federal funds rate has ripple effects that **7** change real GDP and about two years after the FOMC meeting, **8** the inflation rate changes.

## ■ Monetary Stabilization in the *AS-AD* Model

We've described the broad outline of how the Fed's actions influence the economy. Let's now see how monetary policy might be used to stabilize real GDP.

### The Fed Eases to Fight Recession

Figure 20.6(a) shows investment demand. Think of investment demand as representing all the interest-sensitive components of aggregate expenditure. Also, assume that there is no inflation, so the interest rate is the real interest rate as well as the nominal interest rate. The interest rate is 5 percent a year, and the quantity of investment demanded is $2 trillion. In Figure 20.6(b), aggregate demand is $AD_0$, aggregate supply is $AS$, and equilibrium real GDP is $15 trillion, which is less than potential GDP. There is a recessionary gap.

The Fed now conducts an open market purchase that lowers the interest rate to 4 percent a year. The quantity of investment increases to $2.5 trillion. Other interest-sensitive expenditure items (not shown in the figure) also increase. If this were the only change, aggregate demand would increase to $AD_0 + \Delta I$.

The multiplier increases aggregate expenditure further and the aggregate demand curve shifts to $AD_1$. The Fed's actions have eliminated a recession and brought real GDP to equal potential GDP at $16 trillion and the price level to 105.

---

■ **FIGURE 20.6**

Monetary Stabilization: Avoiding Recession

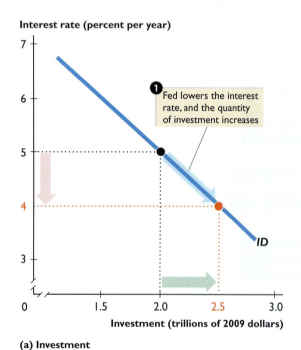

**(a) Investment**

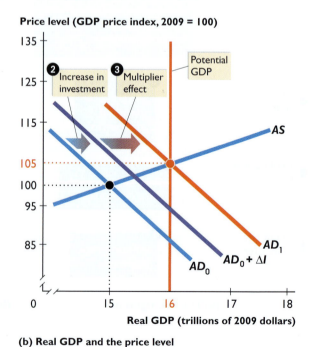

**(b) Real GDP and the price level**

Real GDP is less than potential GDP (part b). To avoid recession, ❶ the Fed lowers the interest rate (part a). ❷ Expenditure increases by Δ*I*, and ❸ the multiplier induces additional expenditure. The ag-

gregate demand curve shifts rightward to $AD_1$. Real GDP increases to potential GDP, and recession is avoided.

## The Fed Tightens to Fight Inflation

In Figure 20.7(a) the interest rate is 5 percent a year and the quantity of investment is $2 trillion. At this level of investment, aggregate demand is $AD_0$ in Figure 20.7(b). The aggregate supply curve is $AS$, so equilibrium real GDP is $17 trillion, which exceeds potential GDP. There is an inflationary gap.

The Fed now conducts an open market sale that increases the interest rate to 6 percent a year. The quantity of investment demand decreases to $1.5 trillion. If this were the only change in aggregate expenditure, aggregate demand would be $AD_0 - \Delta I$. But the multiplier decreases aggregate expenditure further, and the aggregate demand curve shifts leftward to $AD_1$.

The Fed's actions have eliminated an inflation threat and brought real GDP to equal potential GDP.

## The Size of the Multiplier Effect

The size of the multiplier effect of monetary policy depends on the sensitivity of expenditure plans to the interest rate. The larger the effect of a change in the interest rate on aggregate expenditure, the greater is the multiplier effect and the smaller is the change in the interest rate that achieves the Fed's objective.

■ **FIGURE 20.7**

Monetary Stabilization: Avoiding Inflation

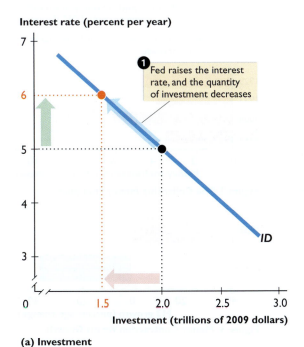

**(a) Investment**

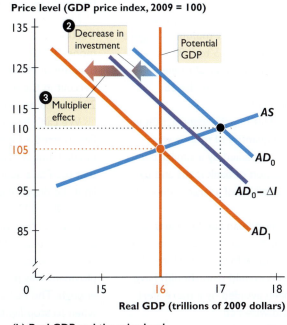

**(b) Real GDP and the price level**

Real GDP exceeds potential GDP in part (b). To avoid inflation, ❶ the Fed raises the interest rate in part (a). ❷ Expenditure decreases by $\Delta I$, and ❸ the multiplier induces additional expenditure

cuts. The aggregate demand curve shifts leftward to $AD_1$. Real GDP decreases to potential GDP, and inflation is avoided.

# EYE on the FED IN A CRISIS

## Did the Fed Save Us From Another Great Depression?

The story of the Great Depression is complex and even today, after almost 80 years of research, economists are not in full agreement on its causes. But one part of the story is clear and it is told by Milton Friedman and Anna J. Schwartz: The Fed got it wrong.

An increase in financial risk drove the banks to increase their holdings of reserves and everyone else to lower their bank deposits and hold more currency.

Between 1929 and 1933, (Figure 1) the banks' desired reserve ratio increased from 8 percent to 12 percent and the currency drain ratio increased from 9 percent to 19 percent.

The money multiplier (Figure 2) fell from 6.5 to 3.8.

The quantity of money (Figure 3) crashed by 35 percent.

This massive contraction in the quantity of money was accompanied by a similar contraction of bank loans and by the failure of a large number of banks.

Friedman and Schwartz say that this contraction of money and bank loans and failure of banks could (and should) have been avoided by a more alert and wise Fed.

The Fed could have injected reserves into the banks to accommodate their desire for greater security by holding more reserves and to offset the rise in currency holdings as people switched out of bank deposits.

Ben Bernanke's Fed did almost exactly what Friedman and Schwartz said the Fed needed to do in the Great Depression.

At the end of 2008, when the banks faced increased financial risk, the Fed flooded them with the reserves that they wanted to hold (Figure 1).

The money multiplier fell from 9.1 in 2008 to 2.5 in 2013 (Figure 2)—much more than it had fallen between 1929 and 1933—but there was no contraction of the quantity of money (Figure 3). Rather, the quantity of M2 increased by 37.5 percent in the 5 years to August 2013, a 6.6 percent annual rate.

We can't be sure that the Fed averted a Great Depression in 2009, but we can be confident that the Fed's actions helped to limit the depth and duration of the 2008–2009 recession.

In 2013, the "dual mandate" put the Fed in a dilemma. The recovery was slow and unemployment was not falling quickly enough. The Fed's dilemma was when to stop fighting the slow recovery and start worrying about unleashing inflation.

*Milton Friedman and Anna J. Schwartz, authors of* A Monetary History of the United States, *who say the Fed turned an ordinary recession into the Great Depression.*

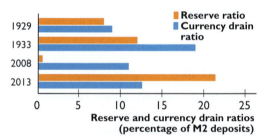

**Figure 1  The Flight to Safety: Reserve and Currency Ratios Increase**

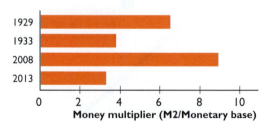

**Figure 2  The Collapsing Money Multiplier**

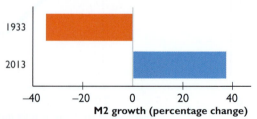

**Figure 3  Money Contraction Versus Growth**

SOURCE OF DATA: Federal Reserve Board.

## ■ Limitations of Monetary Stabilization Policy

Monetary policy has an advantage over fiscal policy because it cuts out the law-making time lags. The FOMC meets eight times a year and can conduct telephone meetings between its scheduled meetings if the need arises. And the actual actions that change the quantity of money are daily actions taken by the New York Fed operating under the guidelines decided by the FOMC. So monetary policy is a continuous policy process and is not subject to the long decision lag and the need to create a broad political consensus that confronts fiscal policy.

But monetary policy shares the other two limitations of fiscal policy: Estimating potential GDP is hard, and economic forecasting is error-prone. Monetary policy suffers an additional limitation: Its effects are indirect and depend on how private decisions respond to a change in the interest rate. These responses are themselves hard to forecast and vary from one situation to another in unpredictable ways. A related problem is that the time lags in the operation of monetary policy are longer than those for fiscal policy, so the forecasting horizon must be longer.

## EYE on YOUR LIFE
### Fiscal and Monetary Policy and How They Affect You

Consider the U.S. economy right now. Using all the knowledge that you have accumulated during your course and by reading or watching the current news, try to determine the macroeconomic policy issues that face the U.S. economy today.

Do we have a cyclical problem? Is the economy at full employment or do we have a recessionary gap or an inflationary gap?

In light of your assessment of the current state of the U.S. economy, what type of fiscal policy would you recommend and vote for? What type of monetary policy would you recommend?

Are you concerned about the size of the federal deficit? If so, how would you propose lowering it?

Consider recent changes in fiscal policy that you have seen reported in the media. What do you think these changes say about the federal government's views of the state of the economy? Do these views agree with yours?

Thinking further about recent changes in fiscal policy, how do you expect these changes to affect you? How might your spending, saving, and labor supply decisions change?

Using your own responses to fiscal policy changes as an example, are these policy changes influencing aggregate supply, aggregate demand, or both? How do you think they will change real GDP?

By reading or watching the current news, try to determine the monetary policy issues that face the U.S. economy today.

What is the greater monetary policy risk: inflation or recession? If the risk is inflation, what action do you expect the Fed to take? If the risk is recession, what do you expect the Fed to do? Which of these problems, inflation or recession, do you care most about? Do you want the Fed to be more cautious about inflation and keep the interest rate high, or more cautious about recession and keep the interest rate low?

When Ben Bernanke (the former Fed Chairman) was an economics professor at Princeton, he studied inflation targeting and found that it works well.

Do you think the United States should join the ranks of inflation targeters? Should the Fed announce an inflation target? Watch the media for commentary on the Fed's interest rate decisions and evolving monetary policy strategy.

**CHECKPOINT 20.2**

Describe the Federal Reserve's monetary policy process and explain the effects of monetary policy.

## Practice Problems

1. List the sequence of events in the transmission process from a rise in the federal funds rate to a change in the inflation rate.

The economy has slipped into recession and the Fed takes actions to lessen its severity. Use this information to work Problems **2** and **3**.

2. What action does the Fed take? Explain the effects of the Fed's actions in the money market and the market for loans.

3. Explain how the Fed's actions change aggregate demand and real GDP. Use a graph to illustrate your answer.

## In the News

**The Fed is open to changing its policy**
Fed policymakers signaled for the first time that they could increase or decrease stimulation of the economy in the future, but not now.

Source: *Los Angeles Times,* May 1, 2013

What are the ripple effects and time lags that the Fed must consider in deciding when to increase or decrease stimulation of the economy?

## Solutions to Practice Problems

1. When the Fed raises the federal funds rate, other short-term interest rates rise and the exchange rate rises; the quantity of money and bank loans decrease and the long-term real interest rate rises; consumption, investment, and net exports decrease; aggregate demand decreases; and eventually the real GDP growth rate and the inflation rate decrease.

2. The Fed lowers the federal funds rate, which lowers other short-term interest rates, and increases the supply of money. The increase in the supply of money increases the supply of bank loans and the real interest rate falls.

3. A lower real interest rate (and lower exchange rate) and greater quantity of money and loans increases investment (and other expenditures), which increases aggregate expenditure. Aggregate demand increases and the $AD$ curve shifts to $AD_0 + \Delta E$. A multiplier effect increases aggregate demand and the $AD$ curve shifts rightward to $AD_1$. Real GDP increases and recession is avoided (Figure 1).

## Solution to In the News

Figure 20.5 (p. 589) describes the ripple effects and the time lags. The Fed can influence interest rates quickly but several months pass before the quantity of money and bank loans respond, up to a year before expenditure plans respond, and up to two years before the inflation rate responds to the Fed's interest rate actions.

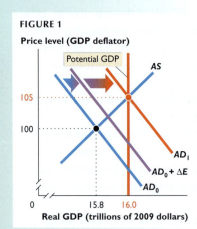

**FIGURE 1**

Price level (GDP deflator)

Potential GDP

AS

105

100

$AD_1$

$AD_0 + \Delta E$

$AD_0$

0    15.8    16.0

**Real GDP (trillions of 2009 dollars)**

## CHAPTER SUMMARY

## Key Points

1. **Describe the federal budget process and explain the effects of fiscal policy.**

   - The federal budget is an annual statement of the tax revenues, outlays, and surplus or deficit of the government of the United States.
   - Fiscal policy is the use of the federal budget to finance the federal government and to stabilize the economy.
   - Fiscal policy can be either discretionary or automatic.
   - Changes in government expenditure and changes in taxes have multiplier effects on aggregate demand and can be used to try to keep real GDP at potential GDP.
   - In practice, law-making time lags, the difficulty of estimating potential GDP, and the limitations of economic forecasting seriously hamper discretionary fiscal policy.
   - Automatic stabilizers arise because tax revenues and outlays fluctuate with real GDP.

2. **Describe the Federal Reserve's monetary policy process and explain the effects of monetary policy.**

   - The Fed makes monetary policy in an open and transparent process that involves three main elements: the Beige Book, meetings of the Federal Open Market Committee, and the Monetary Policy Report to Congress.
   - When the FOMC announces a policy change, it is in terms of a target for the federal funds rate.
   - When the Fed changes the federal funds rate, other interest rates change and the effects ripple through the economy by changing aggregate demand.
   - The size of the multiplier effect of monetary policy depends on the sensitivity of expenditure plans to the interest rate.
   - Monetary policy has no law-making time lag, but its effects are indirect and depend on how the interest rate influences private decisions.

## Key Terms

| | | |
|---|---|---|
| Automatic fiscal policy, 575 | Discretionary fiscal policy, 575 | Monetary policy, 586 |
| Automatic stabilizers, 582 | Fiscal policy, 574 | National debt, 575 |
| Balanced budget multiplier, 577 | Fiscal stimulus, 578 | Structural surplus or deficit, 582 |
| Budget balance, 574 | Government expenditure multiplier, 577 | Tax multiplier, 577 |
| Cyclical surplus or deficit, 582 | Induced taxes, 582 | Transfer payments multiplier, 577 |

# CHAPTER CHECKPOINT

## Study Plan Problems and Applications

1. Suppose that in an economy, investment is $400 billion, saving is $400 billion, tax revenues are $500 billion, exports are $300 billion, and imports are $200 billion. Calculate government expenditure and the government's budget balance.

2. Classify the following items as automatic fiscal policy actions, discretionary fiscal policy actions, or neither.
   - An increase in expenditure on homeland security
   - An increase in unemployment benefits paid during a recession
   - Decreased expenditures on national defense during peace time
   - An increase in Medicaid expenditure brought about by a flu epidemic
   - A cut in farm subsidies

3. The U.S. economy is in recession and has a large recessionary gap. Describe what automatic fiscal policy might occur. Describe a fiscal stimulus that could be used that would not increase the budget deficit.

4. **IMF reduces forecast for U.S. growth**
   The IMF expects U.S. economic growth to slow to 2% in 2012 and 2.25% in 2013. That's down from its earlier estimates of 2.15% in 2012 and 2.4% in 2013. Christine Lagarde, the IMF's managing director, said that Congress should "promptly" raise the debt ceiling and adopt strong fiscal policies.

   Source: *The New York Times*, July 3, 2012

   Explain the effects of strong fiscal stimulus if it is implemented well.

5. The Canadian Prime Minister Stephen Harper warned on November 6, 2008, that if policy makers adopt too strong a fiscal stimulus then long-term growth might be jeopardized. Explain what he meant.

Use the following information to work Problems **6** to **8**.

Figure 1 shows the aggregate demand curve, *AD*, and the short-run aggregate supply curve, *AS*, in the economy of Artica. Potential GDP is $300 billion.

6. What are the price level and real GDP? Does Artica have an unemployment problem or an inflation problem? Why?

7. What do you predict will happen if the central bank takes no monetary policy actions? What monetary policy action would you advise the central bank to take and what do you predict will be the effect of that action?

8. Suppose that a drought decreases potential GDP in Artica to $250 billion. Explain what happens if the central bank lowers the federal funds rate. Do you recommend that the central bank lower the interest rate? Why?

9. Read *Eye on Fiscal Stimulus* on p. 584. How big was the fiscal stimulus package of 2008–2009, how many jobs was it expected to create, and how large was the multiplier implied by that expectation? Did the stimulus work?

10. Read *Eye on the Fed in a Crisis* on p. 592. What are the key differences in monetary policy between the Great Depression and the slow recovery from the 2008–2009 recession?

**FIGURE 1**

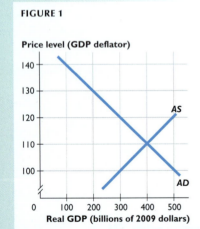

## Instructor Assignable Problems and Applications

1. From the peak in 1929 to the Great Depression trough in 1933, government tax revenues fell by 1.9 percent of GDP and government expenditure increased by 0.3 percent. Real GDP fell by 25 percent. Compare and contrast this experience with the fiscal policy that accompanied the 2008–2009 recession. What did fiscal policy do to moderate the last recession that was largely absent during the Great Depression?

2. In which episode, the Great Depression or the 2008–2009 recession, did the banks' desired reserve ratio and the currency drain ratio increase by the larger amount and the money multiplier fall by the larger amount?

3. Suppose that the U.S. government increases its expenditure on highways and bridges by $100 billion. Explain the effect that this expenditure would have on aggregate demand and real GDP.

4. Suppose that the U.S. government increases its expenditure on highways and bridges by $100 billion. Explain the effect that this expenditure would have on needs-tested spending and the government's budget surplus.

5. Describe the supply-side effects of a fiscal stimulus and explain how a tax cut will influence potential GDP.

6. Use an aggregate supply–aggregate demand graph to illustrate the effects on real GDP and the price level of a fiscal stimulus when the economy is in recession.

Use the following information to work Problems **7** and **8**.

**CBO estimates $1.3 trillion deficit for 2011**

The Congressional Budget Office (CBO) predicts that the federal budget deficit hit a near-record $1.3 trillion in the just-completed fiscal year. The 2011 deficit equaled 8.6% of GDP, a slight drop from the 8.9% of GDP in 2010. It'll take some combination of new revenues and major spending cuts to get the deficit down to about 3% of GDP, the level that many analysts say is sustainable.

Source: *USA Today*, October 8, 2011

7. If the plan to reduce the deficit includes a cut in transfer payments and a rise in taxes of the same amount, how will this policy influence the budget deficit and real GDP?

8. If the plan to reduce the deficit includes an increase in taxes on the wealthy, explain how this policy might have serious supply-side consequences for both potential GDP and the growth rate of real GDP.

9. Suppose that inflation is rising toward 5 percent a year, and the Fed, Congress, and the White House are discussing ways of containing inflation without damaging employment and output. The President wants to cut aggregate demand but to do so in a way that will give the best chance of keeping investment high to encourage long-term economic growth. Explain the Fed's best action for meeting the President's objectives.

10. Compare and contrast the Fed's monetary policy response to the surge in desired reserves and currency holdings in the Great Depression and the 2008–2009 recession.

# Critical Thinking Discussion Questions

**1. Japan's Prime Minister is breaking his budget-balancing promise**

Shinzo Abe, Japan's Prime Minister, promised to balance Japan's budget deficit within five years. Japan is running a deficit of 23.2 trillion yen ($227 billion) in the current fiscal year. Forecasters believe that it will be difficult for Abe to keep his promise, and he will have to raise taxes or cut government expenditure in the near future.

Source: Reuters, 24 January 2014

Think about Japan's budget deficit:

What is more important—eliminating a cyclical budget deficit or a structural budget deficit?

Why does Prime Minister Abe want to eliminate the budget deficit?

How can eliminating the government budget deficit result in a crowding-out effect?

**2. Coming: 35% income tax slab for super-rich**

The Cabinet is likely to bring in sweeping changes in India's income tax regime, including a higher 35% tax for the super-rich and a wealth tax on a host of new assets, such as expensive watches and paintings.

Source: *Hindustan Times*, 22 August 2013

Think about income taxes in India:

What effect do these new taxes have on India's tax wedge?

Will these new taxes have any effect on India's labor market and potential GDP?

What is stronger—the supply-side effect or the demand-side effect of a rise in income taxes?

**3. Iran president vows to tackle inflation and unemployment**

With the combination of inflation and recession, Iran's president, Hassan Rouhani, considers job creation to be the most significant issue.

Source: *Financial Times*, 8 December 2013

Think about Iran's inflation and recession policies:

What monetary policy can Iran implement to combat recession and create jobs?

What monetary policy can Iran implement to combat inflation?

Are these policies compatible?

Why does Iran's president consider job creation to be more significant than fighting inflation?

**4. Pressure on the European Central Bank to cut interest rates**

The inflation in the 18-country Eurozone fell to 0.7% in January. To avoid suffering from deflation, the ECB is expected to cut the interest rate at which the ECB lends money to commercial banks, from 0.25% to 0.1%.

Source: CTV News, 31 January 2014

Think about the Eurozone's monetary policy:

Is the ECB following an instrument rule or a targeting rule?

Why is the ECB concerned about deflation?

What are the ripple effects of the ECB's actions?

What is the lag time associated with the implementation of this policy?

# Glossary

**Abatement technology** A technology that reduces or prevents pollution. (p. 267)

**Absolute advantage** When one person (or nation) is more productive than another—needs fewer inputs or takes less time to produce a good or perform a production task. (p. 109)

**Adverse selection** When a seller is better informed than a buyer or a buyer is better informed than a seller, and the deal that gets made benefits the one who is better informed. (p. 280)

**Aggregate demand** The relationship between the quantity of real GDP demanded and the price level when all other influences on expenditure plans remain the same. (p. 554)

**Aggregate supply** The relationship between the quantity of real GDP supplied and the price level when all other influences on production plans remain the same. (p. 548)

**Allocative efficiency** A situation in which the quantities of goods and services produced are those that people *value most highly*—it is not possible to produce more of a good or service without giving up some of another good that people *value more highly*. (p. 179)

**Automatic fiscal policy** A fiscal policy action that is triggered by the state of the economy. (p. 575)

**Automatic stabilizers** Features of fiscal policy that stabilize real GDP without explicit action by the government. (p. 582)

**Average cost pricing rule** A rule that sets price equal to average total cost to enable a regulated firm to avoid economic loss. (p. 368)

**Average fixed cost** Total fixed cost per unit of output. (p. 303)

**Average product** Total product divided by the quantity of a factor of production. The average product of labor is total product divided by the quantity of labor employed. (p. 298)

**Average total cost** Total cost per unit of output, which equals average fixed cost plus average variable cost. (p. 303)

**Average variable cost** Total variable cost per unit of output. (p. 303)

**Balanced budget multiplier** The magnification effect on aggregate demand of a *simultaneous* change in government expenditure and taxes that leaves the budget balance unchanged. (p. 577)

**Barrier to entry** Any constraint that protects a firm from competitors. (p. 346)

**Barter** The direct exchange of goods and services for other goods and services, which requires a double coincidence of wants. (p. 519)

**Benefit** The benefit of something is the gain or pleasure that it brings, measured by what you are willing to give up to get it. (p. 47)

**Big tradeoff** A tradeoff between efficiency and fairness that recognizes the cost of making income transfers. (p. 197)

**Black market** An illegal market that operates alongside a government-regulated market. (p. 213)

**Budget balance** Tax revenues minus outlays. (p. 574)

**Business cycle** A periodic but irregular up-and-down movement of total production and other measures of economic activity. (p. 422)

**Capital** Tools, instruments, machines, buildings, and other items that have been produced in the past and that businesses now use to produce goods and services. (p. 73)

**Capital goods** Goods bought by businesses and governments to increase productive resources to use over future periods to produce other goods. (p. 70)

**Capture theory** The theory that regulation serves the self-interest of the producer and results in maximum profit, underproduction, and deadweight loss. (p. 366)

**Cartel** A group of firms acting together to limit output, raise price, and increase economic profit. (p. 390)

**Chained-dollar real GDP** The measure of real GDP calculated by the Bureau of Economic Analysis. (p. 433)

**Change in demand** A change in the quantity that people plan to buy when any influence on buying plans other than the price of the good changes. (p. 124)

**Change in the quantity demanded** A change in the quantity of a good that people plan to buy that results from a change in the price of the good with all other influences on buying plans remaining the same. (p. 126)

**Change in the quantity supplied** A change in the quantity of a good that suppliers plan to sell that results from a change in the price of the good with all other influences on selling plans remaining the same. (p. 133)

**Change in supply** A change in the quantity that suppliers plan to sell when any influence on selling plans other than the price of the good changes. (p. 131)

**Circular flow model** A model of the economy that shows the circular flow of expenditures and incomes that result from decision makers' choices and the way those choices interact to determine what, how, and for whom goods and services are produced. (p. 84)

**Classical macroeconomics** The view that the market economy works well, that aggregate fluctuations are a natural consequence of an expanding economy, and that government intervention cannot improve the efficiency of the market economy. (p. 484)

**Coase theorem** The proposition that if property rights exist and transactions costs are low, then priate are involved, and transactions costs are low, then private transactions are efficient and the outcome is not affected by who is assigned the property right. (p. 267)

**Command system** A system that allocates resources by the order of someone in authority. (p. 177)

**Comparative advantage** The ability of a person to perform an activity or produce a good or service at a lower opportunity cost than anyone else. (p. 109)

**Complement** A good that is consumed with another good. (p. 124)

**Complement in production** A good that is produced along with another good. (p. 131)

**Constant returns to scale** Features of a firm's technology that keep average total cost constant as output increases. (p. 310)

**Consumer Price Index** A measure of the average of the prices paid by urban consumers for a fixed market basket of consumption goods and services. (p. 460)

**Consumer surplus** The marginal benefit from a good or service in excess of the price paid for it, summed over the quantity consumed. (p. 185)

**Consumption expenditure** The expenditure by households on consumption goods and services. (p. 409)

**Consumption goods and services** Goods and services that individuals and governments buy and use in the current period. (p. 70)

**Core inflation rate** The annual percentage change in the PCE price index excluding the prices of food and energy. (p. 469)

**Cost of living index** A measure of the change in the amount of money that people need to spend to achieve a given standard of living. (p. 466)

**Cost-push inflation** An inflation that begins with an increase in costs. (p. 565)

**Cross elasticity of demand** A measure of the responsiveness of the demand for a good to a change in the price of a substitute or complement when other things remain the same. (p. 167)

**Cross-section graph** A graph that shows the values of an economic variable for different groups in a population at a point in time. (p. 60)

**Currency** Notes (dollar bills) and coins. (p. 520)

**Cyclical surplus or deficit** The budget balance that arises because revenues and outlays are not at their full-employment levels. (p. 582)

**Cyclical unemployment** The fluctuating unemployment over the business cycle that increases during a recession and decreases during an expansion. (p. 450)

**Deadweight loss** The decrease in total surplus that results from an inefficient underproduction or overproduction. (p. 193)

**Decreasing marginal returns** When the marginal product of an additional worker is less than the marginal product of the previous worker. (p. 296)

**Deflation** A situation in which the price level is *falling* and the inflation rate is *negative*. (p. 463)

**Demand** The relationship between the quantity demanded and the price of a good when all other influences on buying plans remain the same. (p. 121)

**Demand curve** A graph of the relationship between the quantity demanded of a good and its price when all the other influences on buying plans remain the same. (p. 122)

**Demand for labor** The relationship between the quantity of labor demanded and the real wage rate when all other influences on firms' hiring plans remain the same. (p. 489)

**Demand-pull inflation** An inflation that starts because aggregate demand increases. (p. 564)

**Demand schedule** A list of the quantities demanded at each different price when all the other influences on buying plans remain the same. (p. 122)

**Depreciation** The decrease in the value of capital that results from its use and from obsolescence. (p. 416)

**Deregulation** The process of removing regulation of prices, quantities, entry, and other aspects of economic activity in a firm or an industry. (p. 366)

**Diminishing returns** The tendency for each additional hour of labor employed to produce a successively smaller additional amount of real GDP. (p. 488)

**Direct relationship** A relationship between two variables that move in the same direction. (p. 62)

**Discouraged worker** A marginally attached worker who has not made specific efforts to find a job within the past four weeks because previous unsuccessful attempts to find a job were discouraging. (p. 440)

**Discretionary fiscal policy** A fiscal policy action that is initiated by an act of Congress. (p. 575)

**Diseconomies of scale** Features of a firm's technology that make average total cost rise as output increases. (p. 310)

**Dumping** When a foreign firm sells its exports at a lower price than its cost of production. (p. 252)

**Duopoly** A market with only two firms. (p. 390)

**Economic depreciation** An opportunity cost of a firm using capital that it owns—measured as the change in the *market value* of capital over a given period. (p. 291)

**Economic freedom** A condition in which people are able to make personal choices, their private property is protected by the rule of law, and they are free to buy and sell in markets. (p. 508)

**Economic growth** The sustained expansion of production possibilities. (pp. 106, 494)

**Economic growth rate** The annual percentage change of real GDP. (p. 494)

**Economic model** A description of the economy or part of the economy that includes only those features assumed necessary to explain the observed facts. (p. 50)

**Economic profit** A firm's total revenue minus total cost. (p. 291)

**Economics** The social science that studies the choices that individuals, businesses, government, and entire societies make as they cope with *scarcity*, the influences on those choices, and the arrangements that coordinate them. (p. 40)

**Economies of scale** Features of a firm's technology that make average total cost fall as output increases. (p. 309)

**Efficient scale** The quantity at which average total cost is a minimum. (p. 383)

**Elastic demand** When the percentage change in the quantity demanded exceeds the percentage change in price. (p. 152)

**Elastic supply** When the percentage change in the quantity supplied exceeds the percentage change in price. (p. 162)

**Entrepreneurship** The human resource that organizes labor, land, and capital to produce goods and services. (p. 74)

**Equilibrium price** The price at which the quantity demanded equals the quantity supplied. (p. 136)

**Equilibrium quantity** The quantity bought and sold at the equilibrium price. (p. 136)

**Excess burden** The amount by which the burden of a tax exceeds the tax revenue received by the government—the deadweight loss from a tax. (p. 208)

**Excess capacity** The amount by which the efficient scale exceeds the quantity that the firm produces. (p. 383)

**Excess reserves** A bank's actual reserves minus its desired reserves. (p. 534)

**Explicit cost** A cost paid in money. (p. 291)

**Export subsidy** A payment by the government to a producer to cover part of the cost of production that is exported. (p. 249)

**Exports** The goods and services that firms in one country sell to people and firms in other countries. (p. 234)

**Exports of goods and services** Items that firms in the United States produce and sell to the rest of the world. (p. 410)

**Externality** A cost or a benefit that arises from production and that falls on someone other than the producer; or a cost or benefit that arises from consumption and that falls on someone other than the consumer. (p. 262)

**Factor markets** Markets in which the services of factors of production are bought and sold. (p. 84)

**Factors of production** The productive resources that are used to produce goods and services—land, labor, capital, and entrepreneurship. (p. 72)

**Federal funds rate** The interest rate at which banks can borrow and lend reserves (interbank loans) in the federal funds market. (p. 526)

**Federal Open Market Committee** The Fed's main policy-making committee. (p. 530)

**Federal Reserve System (the Fed)** The central bank of the United States. (p. 529)

**Fiat money** Objects that are money because the law decrees or orders them to be money. (p. 520)

**Final good or service** A good or service that is produced for its final user and not as a component of another good or service. (p. 408)

**Firms** The institutions that organize the production of goods and services. (p. 84)

**Fiscal policy** Changing taxes, transfer payments, and government expenditure on goods and services. (p. 557) The use of the federal budget to achieve the macroeconomic objectives of high and sustained economic growth and full employment. (p. 574)

**Fiscal stimulus** An increase in government outlays or a decrease in tax revenues designed to boost real GDP and create or save jobs. (p. 578)

**Four-firm concentration ratio** The percentage of the total revenue in an industry accounted for by the four largest firms in the industry. (p. 380)

**Frictional unemployment** The unemployment that arises from normal labor turnover—from people entering and leaving the labor force, from quitting jobs to find better ones, and from the ongoing creation and destruction of jobs. (p. 449)

**Full employment** When there is no cyclical unemployment or, equivalently, when all the unemployment is frictional or structural. (p. 450)

**Full-employment equilibrium** When equilibrium real GDP equals potential GDP. (p. 561)

**Full-time workers** People who usually work 35 hours or more a week. (p. 441)

**Game theory** The tool that economists use to analyze *strategic behavior*—behavior that recognizes mutual interdependence and takes account of the expected behavior of others. (p. 395)

**GDP price index** An average of the current prices of all the goods and services included in GDP expressed as a percentage of base-year prices. (p. 469)

**Goods and services** The objects (goods) and the actions (services) that people value and produce to satisfy human wants. (p. 41)

**Goods markets** Markets in which goods and services are bought and sold. (p. 84)

**Government expenditure multiplier** The effect of a change in government expenditure on goods and services on aggregate demand. (p. 577)

**Government expenditure on goods and services** The expenditure by all levels of government on goods and services. (p. 410)

**Great Depression** A period of high unemployment, low incomes, and extreme economic hardship that lasted from 1929 to 1939. (p. 443)

**Gross domestic product (GDP)** The market value of all the final goods and services produced within a coountry in a given time period. (p. 408)

**Herfindahl-Hirschman Index** The square of the percentage market share of each firm summed over the 50 largest firms (or summed over all the firms if there are fewer than 50) in a market. (p. 380)

**Households** Individuals or groups of people living together. (p. 84)

**Human capital** The knowledge and skill that people obtain from education, on-the-job training, and work experience. (p. 73)

**Implicit cost** An opportunity cost incurred by a firm when it uses a factor of production for which it does not make a direct money payment. (p. 291)

**Import quota** A quantitative restriction on the import of a good that limits the maximum quantity of a good that may be imported in a given period. (p. 247)

**Imports** The goods and services that people and firms in one country buy from firms in other countries. (p. 234)

**Imports of goods and services** Items that households, firms, and governments in the United States buy from the rest of the world. (p. 410)

**Incentive** A reward or a penalty—a "carrot" or a "stick"—that encourages or discourages an action. (p. 49)

**Income elasticity of demand** A measure of the responsiveness of the demand for a good to a change in income when other things remain the same. (p. 168)

**Increasing marginal returns** When the marginal product of an additional worker exceeds the marginal product of the previous worker. (p. 296)

**Induced taxes** Taxes that vary with real GDP. (p. 582)

**Inelastic demand** When the percentage change in the quantity demanded is less than the percentage change in price. (p. 152)

**Inelastic supply** When the percentage change in the quantity supplied is less than the percentage change in price. (p. 162)

**Infant-industry argument** The argument that it is necessary to protect a new industry to enable it to grow into a mature industry that can compete in world markets. (p. 251)

**Inferior good** A good for which demand decreases when income increases and demand increases when income decreases. (p. 125)

**Inflation rate** The percentage change in the price level from one year to the next. (p. 463)

**Inflationary gap** A gap that exists when real GDP exceeds potential GDP and that brings a rising price level. (p. 561)

**Interest** Income paid for the use of capital. (p. 75)

**Intermediate good or service** A good or service that is used as a component of a final good or service. (p. 408)

**Inverse relationship** A relationship between two variables that move in opposite directions. (p. 63)

**Investment** The purchase of new *capital goods*—tools, instruments, machines, buildings, and additions to inventories. (p. 409)

**Keynesian macroeconomics** The view that the market economy is inherently unstable and needs active government intervention to achieve full employment and sustained economic growth. (p. 484)

**Labor** The work time and work effort that people devote to producing goods and services. (p. 73)

**Labor force** The number of people employed plus the number unemployed. (p. 438)

**Labor force participation rate** The percentage of the working-age population who are members of the labor force. (p. 440)

**Labor productivity** The quantity of real GDP produced by one hour of labor. (p. 498)

**Land** The "gifts of nature," or *natural resources*, that we use to produce goods and services. (p. 72)

**Law of decreasing returns** As a firm uses more of a variable input, with a given quantity of fixed inputs, the marginal product of the variable input eventually decreases. (p. 298)

**Law of demand** Other things remaining the same, if the price of a good rises, the quantity demanded of that good decreases; and if the price of a good falls, the quantity demanded of that good increases. (p. 121)

**Law of diminishing marginal returns** If the quantity of capital is small, an increase in capital brings a large increase in production; and if the quantity of capital is large, an increase in capital brings a small increase in production. (p. 499)

**Law of market forces** When there is a surplus, the price falls; when there is a shortage, the price rises. (p. 136)

**Law of supply** Other things remaining the same, if the price of a good rises, the quantity supplied of that good increases; and if the price of a good falls, the quantity supplied of that good decreases. (p. 128)

**Legal monopoly** A market in which competition and entry are restricted by the granting of a public franchise, government license, patent, or copyright. (p. 347)

**Linear relationship** A relationship that graphs as a straight line. (p. 62)

**Long run** The time frame in which the quantities of *all* resources can be varied. (p. 294)

**Long-run average cost curve** A curve that shows the lowest average total cost at which it is possible to produce each output when the firm has had sufficient time to change both its plant size and labor employed. (p. 310)

**Loss** Income earned by an entrepreneur for running a business when that income is negative. (p. 75)

**M1** Currency held by individuals and firms, traveler's checks, and checkable deposits owned by individuals and businesses. (p. 520)

**M2** M1 plus savings deposits and small time deposits, money market funds, and other deposits. (p. 520)

**Macroeconomic equilibrium** When the quantity of real GDP demanded equals the quantity of real GDP supplied at the point of intersection of the *AD* curve and the *AS* curve. (p. 560)

**Macroeconomics** The study of the aggregate (or total) effects on the national economy and the global economy of the choices that individuals, businesses, and governments make. (p. 41)

**Margin** A choice on the margin is a choice that is made by comparing *all* the relevant alternatives systematically and incrementally. (p. 48)

**Marginal benefit**  The benefit that arises from a one-unit increase in an activity. The marginal benefit of something is measured by what you *are willing to* give up to get *one additional* unit of it. (p. 48)

**Marginal cost**  The opportunity cost that arises from a one-unit increase in an activity. The marginal cost of something is what you *must* give up to get one additional unit of it. (p. 48) The marginal cost of producing a good is the change in total cost that results from a one-unit increase in output. (p. 302)

**Marginal cost pricing rule**  A rule that sets price equal to marginal cost to achieve an efficient output. (p. 366)

**Marginal external benefit**  The benefit from an additional unit of a good or service that people other than the consumer of the good or service enjoy. (p. 274)

**Marginal external cost**  The cost of producing an additional unit of a good or service that falls on people other than the producer. (p. 264)

**Marginal private benefit**  The benefit from an additional unit of a good or service that the consumer of that good or service receives. (p. 274)

**Marginal private cost**  The cost of producing an additional unit of a good or service that is borne by the producer of that good or service. (p. 264)

**Marginal product**  The change in total product that results from a one-unit increase in the quantity of labor employed. (p. 296)

**Marginal revenue**  The change in total revenue that results from a one-unit increase in the quantity sold. (p. 319)

**Marginal social benefit**  The marginal benefit enjoyed by society—by the consumer of a good or service and by everyone else who benefits from it. It is the sum of marginal private benefit and marginal external benefit. (p. 274)

**Marginal social cost**  The marginal cost incurred by the entire society—by the producer and by everyone else on whom the cost falls. It is the sum of marginal private cost and marginal external cost. (p. 264)

**Marginally attached worker**  A person who does not have a job, is available and willing to work, has not made specific efforts to find a job within the previous four weeks, but has looked for work sometime in the recent past. (p. 440)

**Market**  Any arrangement that brings buyers and sellers together and enables them to get information and do business with each other. (p. 84)

**Market equilibrium**  When the quantity demanded equals the quantity supplied—buyers' and sellers' plans are in balance. (p. 136)

**Market failure**  A situation in which the market delivers an inefficient outcome. (p. 193)

**Means of payment**  A method of settling a debt. (p. 518)

**Medium of exchange**  An object that is generally accepted in return for goods and services. (p. 519)

**Microeconomics**  The study of the choices that individuals and businesses make and the way these choices interact and are influenced by governments. (p. 40)

**Minimum wage law**  A government regulation that makes hiring labor services for less than a specified wage illegal. (p. 219)

**Monetarist macroeconomics**  The view that the market economy works well, that aggregate fluctuations are the natural consequence of an expanding economy, but that fluctuations in the quantity of money generate the business cycle. (p. 485)

**Monetary base**  The sum of coins, Federal Reserve notes, and banks' reserves at the Fed. (p. 531)

**Monetary policy**  Changing the quantity of money and the interest rate. (p. 557) The adjustment of interest rates and the quantity of money to achieve the dual objective of price atability and full employment. (p. 586)

**Money**  Any commodity or token that is generally accepted as a means of payment. (p. 518)

**Money multiplier**  The number by which a change in the monetary base is multiplied to find the resulting change in the quantity of money. (p. 539)

**Monopolistic competition**  A market in which a large number of firms compete by making similar but slightly different products. (p. 318)

**Monopoly**  A market in which one firm sells a good or service that has no close substitutes and a barrier blocks the entry of new firms. (pp. 318, 346)

**Moral hazard**  A situation that arises after a deal is done when the actions of the person with private information impose costs on the uninformed party. (p. 280)

**Nash equilibrium** An equilibrium in which each player takes the best possible action given the action of the other player. (p. 396)

**National debt** The amount of government debt outstanding—the debt that has arisen from past budget deficits. (p. 575)

**Natural monopoly** A monopoly that arises because one firm can meet the entire market demand at a lower average total cost than two or more firms could. (p. 346)

**Natural unemployment rate** The unemployment rate when the economy is at full employment. (p. 450)

**Negative externality** A production or consumption activity that creates an external cost. (p. 262)

**Negative relationship** A relationship between two variables that move in opposite directions. (p. 63)

**Net exports of goods and services** The value of exports of goods and services minus the value of imports of goods and services. (p. 410)

**Net taxes** Taxes paid minus cash benefits received from governments. (p. 410)

**Nominal GDP** The value of the final goods and services produced in a given year expressed in terms of the prices of that same year. (p. 418)

**Nominal interest rate** The dollar amount of interest expressed as a percentage of the amount loaned. (p. 476)

**Nominal wage rate** The average hourly wage rate measured in *current* dollars. (p. 474)

**Normal good** A good for which demand increases when income increases and demand decreases when income decreases. (p. 125)

**Normal profit** The return to entrepreneurship. Normal profit is part of a firm's opportunity cost because it is the cost of not running another firm. (p. 291)

**Oligopoly** A market in which a small number of independent firms compete. (p. 318)

**Open market operation** The purchase or sale of government securities—U.S. Treasury bills and bonds—by the New York Fed in the open market. (p. 531)

**Opportunity cost** The opportunity cost of something is the best thing you *must* give up to get it. (p. 46)

**Output gap** Real GDP minus potential GDP expressed as a percentage of potential GDP. (p. 452)

**Part time for economic reasons** People who work 1 to 34 hours per week but are looking for full-time work and cannot find it because of unfavorable business conditions. (p. 441)

**Part-time workers** People who usually work less than 35 hours a week. (p. 441)

**Payoff matrix** A table that shows the payoffs for each player for every possible combination of actions by the players. (p. 396)

**PCE price index** An average of the current prices of the goods and services included in the consumption expenditure component of GDP expressed as a percentage of base year prices. (p. 469)

**Perfect competition** A market in which there are many firms, each selling an identical product; many buyers; no barriers to the entry of new firms into the industry; no advantage to established firms; and buyers and sellers are well informed about prices. (p. 318)

**Perfect price discrimination** Price discrimination that extracts the entire consumer surplus by charging the highest price that consumers are willing to pay for each unit. (p. 362)

**Perfectly elastic demand** When the quantity demanded changes by a very large percentage in response to an almost zero percentage change in price. (p. 152)

**Perfectly elastic supply** When the quantity supplied changes by a very large percentage in response to an almost zero percentage change in price. (p. 162)

**Perfectly inelastic demand** When the percentage change in the quantity demanded is zero for any percentage change in the price. (p. 152)

**Perfectly inelastic supply** When the percentage change in the quantity supplied is zero for any percentage change in the price. (p. 162)

**Positive externality** A production or consumption activity that creates an external benefit. (p. 262)

**Positive relationship** A relationship between two variables that move in the same direction. (p. 62)

**Potential GDP** The value of real GDP when all the economy's factors of production—labor, capital, land, and entrepreneurial ability—are fully employed. (pp. 421, 452, 487)

**Price cap** A government regulation that places an upper limit on the price at which a particular good, service, or factor of production may be traded. (p. 212)

**Price cap regulation** A rule that specifies the highest price that a firm is permitted to set—a price ceiling. (p. 371)

**Price ceiling** A government regulation that places an *upper* limit on the price at which a particular good, service, or factor of production may be traded. (p. 212)

**Price-discriminating monopoly** A monopoly that sells different units of a good or service for different prices not related to cost differences. (p. 348)

**Price elasticity of demand** A measure of the responsiveness of the quantity demanded of a good to a change in its price when all other influences on buyers' plans remain the same. (p. 150)

**Price elasticity of supply** A measure of the responsiveness of the quantity supplied of a good to a change in its price when all other influences on sellers' plans remain the same. (p. 162)

**Price floor** A government regulation that places a *lower* limit on the price at which a particular good, service, or factor of production may be traded. (p. 218)

**Price support** A price floor in an agricultural market maintained by a government guarantee to buy any surplus output at that price. (p. 225)

**Price taker** A firm that cannot influence the price of the good or service that it produces. (p. 319)

**Prisoners' dilemma** A game between two prisoners that shows why it is hard to cooperate, even when it would be beneficial to both players to do so. (p. 395)

**Producer surplus** The price of a good in excess of the marginal cost of producing it, summed over the quantity produced. (p. 188)

**Product differentiation** Making a product that is slightly different from the products of competing firms. (p. 378)

**Production efficiency** A situation in which the economy is getting all that it can from its resources and cannot produce more of one good or service without producing less of something else. (p. 98)

**Production function** A relationship that shows the maximum quantity of real GDP that can be produced as the quantity of labor employed changes and all other influences on production remain the same. (p. 488)

**Production possibilities frontier** The boundary between the combinations of goods and services that can be produced and the combinations that cannot be produced, given the available factors of production and the state of technology. (pp. 96, 179)

**Productivity curve** The relationship that shows how real GDP per hour of labor changes as the quantity of capital per hour of labor changes. (p. 500)

**Profit** Income earned by an entrepreneur for running a business. (p. 75)

**Property rights** Social arrangements that govern the protection of private property—legally established titles to the ownership, use, and disposal of factors of production and goods and services that are enforceable in the courts. (pp. 267, 508)

**Public provision** The production of a good or service by a public authority that receives most of its revenue from the government. (p. 276)

**Quantity demanded** The amount of any good, service, or resource that people are willing and able to buy during a specified period at a specified price. (p. 121)

**Quantity of labor demanded** The total labor hours that all the firms in the economy plan to hire during a given time period at a given real wage rate. (p. 489)

**Quantity of labor supplied** The number of labor hours that all the households in the economy plan to work during a given time period at a given real wage rate. (p. 489)

**Quantity supplied** The amount of any good, service, or resource that people are willing and able to sell during a specified period at a specified price. (p. 128)

**Rate of return regulation** A regulation that sets the price at a level that enables a firm to earn a specified target rate of return on its capital. (p. 370)

**Rational choice** A choice that uses the available resources to best achieve the objective of the person making the choice. (p. 47)

**Real business cycle** A cycle that results from fluctuations in the pace of growth of labor productivity and potential GDP. (p. 563)

**Real GDP** The value of the final goods and services produced in a given year expressed in terms of the prices in a *base year*. (p. 418)

**Real interest rate** The goods and services forgone in interest expressed as a percentage of the amount loaned and calculated as the nominal interest rate minus the inflation rate. (p. 476)

**Real wage rate** The average hourly wage rate measured in the dollars of a given reference base year. (p. 474)

**Recession** A period during which real GDP decreases for at least two successive quarters; or defined by the NBER as "a period of significant decline in total output, income, employment, and trade, usually lasting from six months to a year, and marked by contractions in many sectors of the economy." (p. 422)

**Recessionary gap** A gap that exists when potential GDP exceeds real GDP and that brings a falling price level. (p. 561)

**Reference base period** A period for which the CPI is defined to equal 100. Currently, the reference base period is 1982–1984. (p. 460)

**Regulation** Rules administered by a government agency to influence prices, quantities, entry, and other aspects of economic activity in a firm or an industry. (p. 366)

**Rent** Income paid for the use of land (p. 75)

**Rent ceiling** A regulation that makes it illegal to charge more than a specified rent for housing. (p. 212)

**Rent seeking** Lobbying and other political activity that aims to capture the gains from trade. The act of obtaining special treatment by the government to create economic profit or divert consumer surplus or producer surplus away from others. (pp. 255, 357)

**Reserves** The currency in the bank's vaults plus the balance on its reserve account at a Federal Reserve Bank. (p. 525)

**Rule of 70** The number of years it takes for the level of any variable to double is approximately 70 divided by the annual percentage growth rate of the variable. (p. 495)

**Saving** The amount of income that is not paid in net taxes or spent on consumption goods and services. (p. 410)

**Scarcity** The condition that arises because wants exceed the ability of resources to satisfy them. (p. 40)

**Scatter diagram** A graph of the value of one variable against the value of another variable. (p. 60)

**Search activity** The time spent looking for someone with whom to do business. (p. 214)

**Self-interest** The choices that are best for the individual who makes them. (p. 42)

**Short run** The time frame in which the quantities of some resources are fixed. In the short run, a firm can usually change the quantity of labor it uses but not its technology and quantity of capital. (p. 294)

**Shutdown point** The point at which price equals minimum average variable cost and the quantity produced is that at which average variable cost is at a minimum. (p. 423)

**Single-price monopoly** A monopoly that must sell each unit of its output for the same price to all its customers. (p. 348)

**Slope** The change in the value of the variable measured on the $y$-axis divided by the change in the value of the variable measured on the $x$-axis. (p. 65)

**Social interest** The choices that are best for society as a whole. (p. 42)

**Social interest theory** The theory that regulation achieves an efficient allocation of resources. (p. 366)

**Stagflation** A combination of recession (falling real GDP)

and inflation (rising price level). (p. 565)

**Strategies** All the possible actions of each player in a game. (p. 396)

**Structural surplus or deficit** The budget balance that would occur if the economy were at full employment. (p. 582)

**Structural unemployment** The unemployment that arises when changes in technology or international competition change the skills needed to perform jobs or change the locations of jobs. (p. 449)

**Subsidy** A payment by the government to a producer to cover part of the cost of production. (pp. 225, 277)

**Substitute** A good that can be consumed in place of another good. (p. 124)

**Substitute in production** A good that can be produced in place of another good. (p. 131)

**Supply** The relationship between the quantity supplied and the price of a good when all other influences on selling plans remain the same. (p. 128)

**Supply curve** A graph of the relationship between the quantity supplied of a good and its price when all the other influences on selling plans remain the same. (p. 129)

**Supply of labor** The relationship between the quantity of labor supplied and the real wage rate when all other influences on work plans remain the same. (p. 490)

**Supply schedule** A list of the quantities supplied at each different price when all the other influences on selling plans remain the same. (p. 129)

**Tariff** A tax imposed on a good when it is imported. (p. 243)

**Tax incidence** The division of the burden of a tax between the buyer and the seller. (p. 206)

**Tax multiplier** The effect of a change in taxes on aggregate demand. (p. 577)

**Time-series graph** A graph that measures time on the $x$-axis and the variable or variables in which we are interested on the $y$-axis. (p. 60)

**Total cost** The cost of all the factors of production used by a firm. (p. 301)

**Total fixed cost** The cost of the firm's fixed factors of production—the cost of land, capital, and entrepreneurship. (p. 301)

**Total product** The total quantity of a good produced in a given period. (p. 295)

**Total revenue** The amount spent on a good and received by the seller and equals the price of the good multiplied by the quantity of the good sold. (p. 158)

**Total revenue test** A method of estimating the price elasticity of demand by observing the change in total revenue that results from a price change (with all other influences on the quantity sold remaining unchanged). (p. 159)

**Total surplus** The sum of consumer surplus and producer surplus. (p. 191)

**Total variable cost** The cost of the firm's variable factor of production—the cost of labor. (p. 301)

**Tradeoff** An exchange—giving up one thing to get something else. (pp. 46, 99)

**Transactions costs** The opportunity costs of making trades in a market or conducting a transaction. (p. 195)

**Transfer payments multiplier** The effect of a change in transfer payments on aggregate demand. (p. 577)

**Trend** A general tendency for the value of a variable to rise or fall over time. (p. 60)

**Unemployment rate** The percentage of the people in the labor force who are unemployed. (p. 439)

**Unit elastic demand** When the percentage change in the quantity demanded equals the percentage change in price. (p. 152)

**Unit elastic supply** When the percentage change in the quantity supplied equals the percentage change in price. (p. 162)

**Voucher** A token that the government provides to households, which they can use to buy specified goods or services. (p. 278)

**Wages** Income paid for the services of labor. (p. 75)

**Working-age population** The total number of people aged 16 years and over who are not in jail, hospital, or some other form of institutional care or in the U.S. Armed Forces. (p. 438)

# Index

# Photo Credits

# The Pearson Series in Economics

**Abel/Bernanke/Croushore**
*Macroeconomics**

**Bade/Parkin**
*Foundations of Economics**

**Berck/Helfand**
*The Economics of the Environment*

**Bierman/Fernandez**
*Game Theory with Economic Applications*

**Blanchard**
*Macroeconomics**

**Blau/Ferber/Winkler**
*The Economics of Women, Men, and Work*

**Boardman/Greenberg/ Vining/Weimer**
*Cost-Benefit Analysis*

**Boyer**
*Principles of Transportation Economics*

**Branson**
*Macroeconomic Theory and Policy*

**Bruce**
*Public Finance and the American Economy*

**Carlton/Perloff**
*Modern Industrial Organization*

**Case/Fair/Oster**
*Principles of Economics**

**Chapman**
*Environmental Economics: Theory, Application, and Policy*

**Cooter/Ulen**
*Law & Economics*

**Daniels/VanHoose**
*International Monetary & Financial Economics*

**Downs**
*An Economic Theory of Democracy*

**Ehrenberg/Smith**
*Modern Labor Economics*

**Farnham**
*Economics for Managers*

**Folland/Goodman/Stano**
*The Economics of Health and Health Care*

**Fort**
*Sports Economics*

**Froyen**
*Macroeconomics*

**Fusfeld**
*The Age of the Economist*

**Gerber**
*International Economics**

**González-Rivera**
*Forecasting for Economics and Business*

**Gordon**
*Macroeconomics**

**Greene**
*Econometric Analysis*

**Gregory**
*Essentials of Economics*

**Gregory/Stuart**
*Russian and Soviet Economic Performance and Structure*

**Hartwick/Olewiler**
*The Economics of Natural Resource Use*

**Heilbroner/Milberg**
*The Making of the Economic Society*

**Heyne/Boettke/Prychitko**
*The Economic Way of Thinking*

**Holt**
*Markets, Games, and Strategic Behavior*

**Hubbard/O'Brien**
*Economics**

*Money, Banking, and the Financial System**

**Hubbard/O'Brien/Rafferty**
*Macroeconomics**

**Hughes/Cain**
*American Economic History*

**Husted/Melvin**
*International Economics*

**Jehle/Reny**
*Advanced Microeconomic Theory*

**Johnson-Lans**
*A Health Economics Primer*

**Keat/Young/Erfle**
*Managerial Economics*

**Klein**
*Mathematical Methods for Economics*

**Krugman/Obstfeld/Melitz**
*International Economics: Theory & Policy**

**Laidler**
*The Demand for Money*

**Leeds/von Allmen**
*The Economics of Sports*

**Leeds/von Allmen/Schiming**
*Economics**

**Lynn**
*Economic Development: Theory and Practice for a Divided World*

**Miller**
*Economics Today**

*Understanding Modern Economics*

**Miller/Benjamin**
*The Economics of Macro Issues*

**Miller/Benjamin/North**
*The Economics of Public Issues*

**Mills/Hamilton**
*Urban Economics*

**Mishkin**
*The Economics of Money, Banking, and Financial Markets**

*The Economics of Money, Banking, and Financial Markets, Business School Edition**

*Macroeconomics: Policy and Practice**

**Murray**
*Econometrics: A Modern Introduction*

**O'Sullivan/Sheffrin/Perez**
*Economics: Principles, Applications and Tools**

**Parkin**
*Economics**

**Perloff**
*Microeconomics**

*Microeconomics: Theory and Applications with Calculus**

**Perloff/Brander**
*Managerial Economics and Strategy**

**Phelps**
*Health Economics*

**Pindyck/Rubinfeld**
*Microeconomics**

**Riddell/Shackelford/ Stamos/Schneider**
*Economics: A Tool for Critically Understanding Society*

**Roberts**
*The Choice: A Fable of Free Trade and Protection*

**Rohlf**
*Introduction to Economic Reasoning*

**Roland**
*Development Economics*

**Scherer**
*Industry Structure, Strategy, and Public Policy*

**Schiller**
*The Economics of Poverty and Discrimination*

**Sherman**
*Market Regulation*

**Stock/Watson**
*Introduction to Econometrics*

**Studenmund**
*Using Econometrics: A Practical Guide*

**Tietenberg/Lewis**
*Environmental and Natural Resource Economics*

*Environmental Economics and Policy*

**Todaro/Smith**
*Economic Development*

**Waldman/Jensen**
*Industrial Organization: Theory and Practice*

**Walters/Walters/Appel/ Callahan/Centanni/ Maex/O'Neill**
*Econversations: Today's Students Discuss Today's Issues*

**Weil**
*Economic Growth*

**Williamson**
*Macroeconomics*

---

*denotes MyEconLab titles

Visit www.myeconlab.com to learn more.

# Macroeconomic Data

These macroeconomic data series show some of the trends in GDP and its components, the price level, and other variables that provide information about changes in the standard of living and the cost of living—the central questions of macroeconomics. You will find these data in a spreadsheet that you can download from your MyEconLab Web site.

| | | NATIONAL INCOME AND PRODUCT ACCOUNTS | 1967 | 1968 | 1969 | 1970 | 1971 | 1972 | 1973 | 1974 | 1975 | 1976 |
|---|---|---|---|---|---|---|---|---|---|---|---|---|
| | | **EXPENDITURE APPROACH** | | | | | | | | | | |
| the sum of | 1 | Personal consumption expenditure | 507 | 557 | 605 | 648 | 701 | 769 | 851 | 932 | 1,033 | 1,150 |
| | 2 | Gross private domestic investment | 143 | 157 | 174 | 170 | 197 | 228 | 267 | 275 | 257 | 323 |
| | 3 | Government expenditure | 208 | 227 | 240 | 254 | 269 | 288 | 306 | 343 | 383 | 406 |
| | 4 | Exports | 44 | 48 | 52 | 60 | 63 | 71 | 95 | 127 | 139 | 150 |
| less | 5 | Imports | 40 | 47 | 51 | 56 | 62 | 74 | 91 | 128 | 123 | 151 |
| equals | 6 | Gross domestic product | 862 | 943 | 1,020 | 1,076 | 1,168 | 1,282 | 1,429 | 1,549 | 1,689 | 1,878 |
| | | **INCOME APPROACH** | | | | | | | | | | |
| | 7 | Compensation of employees | 483 | 532 | 586 | 625 | 667 | 734 | 815 | 890 | 950 | 1,051 |
| plus | 8 | Net operating surplus | 208 | 222 | 228 | 222 | 247 | 280 | 317 | 323 | 357 | 405 |
| equals | 9 | Net domestic product at factor cost | 691 | 754 | 814 | 847 | 914 | 1,013 | 1,132 | 1,214 | 1,307 | 1,457 |
| | 10 | Indirect taxes less subsidies | 64 | 72 | 79 | 87 | 96 | 101 | 112 | 122 | 131 | 141 |
| plus | 11 | Depreciation (capital consumption) | 104 | 113 | 125 | 137 | 149 | 161 | 178 | 206 | 238 | 259 |
| equals | 12 | GDP (income approach) | 858 | 939 | 1,018 | 1,071 | 1,158 | 1,275 | 1,423 | 1,541 | 1,676 | 1,857 |
| plus | 13 | Statistical discrepancy | 3 | 3 | 2 | 5 | 10 | 7 | 6 | 7 | 13 | 21 |
| equals | 14 | GDP (expenditure approach) | 862 | 943 | 1,020 | 1,076 | 1,168 | 1,282 | 1,429 | 1,549 | 1,689 | 1,878 |
| | 15 | Real GDP (billions of 2009 dollars) | 4,351 | 4,565 | 4,708 | 4,718 | 4,873 | 5,129 | 5,418 | 5,390 | 5,380 | 5,669 |
| | 16 | Real GDP growth rate (percent per year) | 2.7 | 4.9 | 3.1 | 0.2 | 3.3 | 5.2 | 5.6 | –0.5 | –0.2 | 5.4 |
| | | **OTHER DATA** | | | | | | | | | | |
| | 17 | Population (millions) | 199 | 201 | 203 | 205 | 208 | 210 | 212 | 214 | 216 | 218 |
| | 18 | Labor force (millions) | 77 | 79 | 81 | 83 | 84 | 87 | 89 | 92 | 94 | 96 |
| | 19 | Employment (millions) | 74 | 76 | 78 | 79 | 79 | 82 | 85 | 87 | 86 | 89 |
| | 20 | Unemployment (millions) | 3 | 3 | 3 | 4 | 5 | 5 | 4 | 5 | 8 | 7 |
| | 21 | Labor force participation rate (percent of working–age population) | 59.6 | 59.6 | 60.1 | 60.4 | 60.2 | 60.4 | 60.8 | 61.3 | 61.2 | 61.6 |
| | 22 | Unemployment rate (percent of labor force) | 3.8 | 3.6 | 3.5 | 5.0 | 6.0 | 5.6 | 4.9 | 5.6 | 8.5 | 7.7 |
| | 23 | Real GDP per person (2009 dollars per year) | 21,893 | 22,739 | 23,222 | 23,003 | 23,463 | 24,432 | 25,565 | 25,200 | 24,907 | 25,996 |
| | 24 | Growth rate of real GDP per person (percent per year) | 1.6 | 3.9 | 2.1 | –0.9 | 2.0 | 4.1 | 4.6 | –1.4 | –1.2 | 4.4 |
| | 25 | Quantity of money (M2, billions of dollars) | 504 | 545 | 579 | 602 | 674 | 758 | 832 | 881 | 964 | 1,087 |
| | 26 | GDP deflator (2009 = 100) | 19.8 | 20.6 | 21.7 | 22.8 | 24.0 | 25.0 | 26.4 | 28.7 | 31.4 | 33.1 |
| | 27 | GDP deflator inflation rate (percent per year) | 2.9 | 4.3 | 4.9 | 5.3 | 5.1 | 4.3 | 5.5 | 9.0 | 9.3 | 5.5 |
| | 28 | Consumer price index (1982–1984 = 100) | 33.4 | 34.8 | 36.7 | 38.8 | 40.5 | 41.8 | 44.4 | 49.3 | 53.8 | 56.9 |
| | 29 | CPI inflation rate (percent per year) | 2.8 | 4.2 | 5.4 | 5.9 | 4.2 | 3.3 | 6.3 | 11.0 | 9.1 | 5.8 |
| | 30 | Current account balance (billions of dollars) | 3 | 1 | 0 | 2 | –1 | –6 | 7 | 2 | 18 | 4 |

| 1977 | 1978 | 1979 | 1980 | 1981 | 1982 | 1983 | 1984 | 1985 | 1986 | 1987 | 1988 | 1989 |
|---|---|---|---|---|---|---|---|---|---|---|---|---|
| 1,277 | 1,426 | 1,590 | 1,755 | 1,938 | 2,074 | 2,287 | 2,498 | 2,723 | 2,898 | 3,092 | 3,347 | 3,593 |
| 397 | 478 | 540 | 530 | 631 | 581 | 638 | 820 | 830 | 849 | 892 | 937 | 1,000 |
| 436 | 477 | 526 | 591 | 655 | 710 | 766 | 825 | 908 | 975 | 1,031 | 1,078 | 1,152 |
| 159 | 187 | 230 | 281 | 305 | 283 | 277 | 302 | 303 | 321 | 364 | 445 | 504 |
| 182 | 212 | 253 | 294 | 318 | 303 | 329 | 405 | 417 | 453 | 509 | 554 | 591 |
| 2,086 | 2,357 | 2,632 | 2,863 | 3,211 | 3,345 | 3,638 | 4,041 | 4,347 | 4,590 | 4,870 | 5,253 | 5,658 |
| 1,169 | 1,320 | 1,481 | 1,626 | 1,795 | 1,895 | 2,014 | 2,218 | 2,389 | 2,546 | 2,726 | 2,951 | 3,144 |
| 457 | 526 | 564 | 576 | 670 | 684 | 767 | 921 | 983 | 987 | 1,059 | 1,175 | 1,242 |
| 1,626 | 1,846 | 2,045 | 2,202 | 2,465 | 2,578 | 2,782 | 3,139 | 3,372 | 3,533 | 3,785 | 4,126 | 4,386 |
| 153 | 162 | 172 | 191 | 224 | 226 | 242 | 269 | 287 | 299 | 317 | 345 | 372 |
| 288 | 325 | 371 | 426 | 485 | 534 | 561 | 594 | 637 | 682 | 728 | 782 | 836 |
| 2,067 | 2,334 | 2,587 | 2,819 | 3,174 | 3,338 | 3,584 | 4,002 | 4,296 | 4,513 | 4,830 | 5,253 | 5,594 |
| 19 | 23 | 45 | 44 | 37 | 7 | 54 | 39 | 51 | 77 | 41 | −1 | 64 |
| 2,086 | 2,357 | 2,632 | 2,862 | 3,211 | 3,345 | 3,638 | 4,041 | 4,347 | 4,590 | 4,870 | 5,253 | 5,658 |
| 5,931 | 6,260 | 6,459 | 6,443 | 6,611 | 6,484 | 6,785 | 7,277 | 7,586 | 7,852 | 8,124 | 8,465 | 8,777 |
| 4.6 | 5.6 | 3.2 | −0.2 | 2.6 | −1.9 | 4.6 | 7.3 | 4.2 | 3.5 | 3.5 | 4.2 | 3.7 |
| 220 | 223 | 225 | 228 | 230 | 232 | 234 | 236 | 239 | 241 | 243 | 245 | 247 |
| 99 | 102 | 105 | 107 | 109 | 110 | 112 | 114 | 115 | 118 | 120 | 122 | 124 |
| 92 | 96 | 99 | 99 | 100 | 100 | 101 | 105 | 107 | 110 | 112 | 115 | 117 |
| 7 | 6 | 6 | 8 | 8 | 11 | 11 | 9 | 8 | 8 | 7 | 7 | 7 |
| 62.2 | 63.2 | 63.7 | 63.8 | 63.9 | 64.0 | 64.0 | 64.4 | 64.8 | 65.2 | 65.6 | 65.9 | 66.4 |
| 7.1 | 6.1 | 5.9 | 7.2 | 7.6 | 9.7 | 9.6 | 7.5 | 7.2 | 7.0 | 6.2 | 5.5 | 5.3 |
| 26,922 | 28,120 | 28,694 | 28,295 | 28,741 | 27,923 | 28,953 | 30,784 | 31,805 | 32,624 | 33,453 | 34,544 | 35,479 |
| 3.6 | 4.5 | 2.0 | −1.4 | 1.6 | −2.8 | 3.7 | 6.3 | 3.3 | 2.6 | 2.5 | 3.3 | 2.7 |
| 1,221 | 1,322 | 1,426 | 1,540 | 1,679 | 1,831 | 2,055 | 2,219 | 2,417 | 2,614 | 2,784 | 2,934 | 3,056 |
| 35.2 | 37.6 | 40.8 | 44.4 | 48.6 | 51.6 | 53.6 | 55.5 | 57.3 | 58.5 | 59.9 | 62.0 | 64.5 |
| 6.2 | 7.0 | 8.3 | 9.0 | 9.3 | 6.2 | 3.9 | 3.5 | 3.2 | 2.0 | 2.6 | 3.5 | 3.9 |
| 60.6 | 65.2 | 72.6 | 82.4 | 90.9 | 96.5 | 99.6 | 103.9 | 107.6 | 109.7 | 113.6 | 118.3 | 123.9 |
| 6.5 | 7.6 | 11.3 | 13.5 | 10.4 | 6.2 | 3.2 | 4.4 | 3.5 | 1.9 | 3.6 | 4.1 | 4.8 |
| −14 | −15 | −0 | 2 | 5 | −6 | −39 | −94 | −118 | −147 | −161 | −121 | −99 |

# Macroeconomic Data

These macroeconomic data series show some of the trends in GDP and its components, the price level, and other variables that provide information about changes in the standard of living and the cost of living—the central questions of macroeconomics. You will find these data in a spreadsheet that you can download from your MyEconLab Web site.

| | | NATIONAL INCOME AND PRODUCT ACCOUNTS | 1990 | 1991 | 1992 | 1993 | 1994 | 1995 | 1996 | 1997 | 1998 | 1999 |
|---|---|---|---|---|---|---|---|---|---|---|---|---|
| | | **EXPENDITURE APPROACH** | | | | | | | | | | |
| the sum of | 1 | Personal consumption expenditure | 3,826 | 3,960 | 4,216 | 4,471 | 4,741 | 4,984 | 5,268 | 5,561 | 5,903 | 6,317 |
| | 2 | Gross private domestic investment | 994 | 944 | 1,013 | 1,107 | 1,257 | 1,318 | 1,432 | 1,596 | 1,735 | 1,884 |
| | 3 | Government expenditure | 1,238 | 1,298 | 1,345 | 1,366 | 1,404 | 1,452 | 1,496 | 1,554 | 1,614 | 1,726 |
| | 4 | Exports | 552 | 595 | 633 | 655 | 721 | 813 | 868 | 954 | 953 | 989 |
| less | 5 | Imports | 630 | 624 | 668 | 720 | 813 | 903 | 964 | 1,056 | 1,116 | 1,251 |
| equals | 6 | Gross domestic product | 5,980 | 6,174 | 6,539 | 6,879 | 7,309 | 7,664 | 8,100 | 8,609 | 9,089 | 9,666 |
| | | **INCOME APPROACH** | | | | | | | | | | |
| | 7 | Compensation of employees | 3,345 | 3,455 | 3,674 | 3,824 | 4,014 | 4,207 | 4,426 | 4,719 | 5,082 | 5,418 |
| plus | 8 | Net operating surplus | 1,258 | 1,270 | 1,341 | 1,432 | 1,590 | 1,721 | 1,896 | 2,059 | 2,154 | 2,251 |
| equals | 9 | Net domestic product at factor cost | 4,603 | 4,725 | 5,015 | 5,256 | 5,604 | 5,928 | 6,322 | 6,779 | 7,236 | 7,669 |
| plus | 10 | Indirect taxes less subsidies | 398 | 430 | 453 | 466 | 513 | 523 | 546 | 578 | 603 | 628 |
| | 11 | Depreciation (capital consumption) | 887 | 931 | 960 | 1,004 | 1,056 | 1,123 | 1,176 | 1,240 | 1,310 | 1,401 |
| equals | 12 | GDP (income approach) | 5,888 | 6,086 | 6,428 | 6,726 | 7,172 | 7,574 | 8,044 | 8,596 | 9,149 | 9,698 |
| plus | 13 | Statistical discrepancy | 91 | 88 | 111 | 152 | 137 | 91 | 57 | 12 | –60 | –32 |
| equals | 14 | GDP (expenditure approach) | 5,980 | 6,174 | 6,539 | 6,879 | 7,309 | 7,664 | 8,100 | 8,609 | 9,089 | 9,666 |
| | 15 | Real GDP (billions of 2009 dollars) | 8,945 | 8,939 | 9,257 | 9,511 | 9,895 | 10,164 | 10,550 | 11,023 | 11,513 | 12,071 |
| | 16 | Real GDP growth rate (percent per year) | 1.9 | –0.1 | 3.6 | 2.7 | 4.0 | 2.7 | 3.8 | 4.5 | 4.4 | 4.8 |
| | | **OTHER DATA** | | | | | | | | | | |
| | 17 | Population (millions) | 250 | 254 | 257 | 260 | 263 | 267 | 270 | 273 | 276 | 279 |
| | 18 | Labor force (millions) | 126 | 126 | 128 | 129 | 131 | 132 | 134 | 136 | 138 | 139 |
| | 19 | Employment (millions) | 119 | 118 | 118 | 120 | 123 | 125 | 127 | 130 | 131 | 134 |
| | 20 | Unemployment (millions) | 7 | 9 | 10 | 9 | 8 | 7 | 7 | 7 | 6 | 6 |
| | 21 | Labor force participation rate (percent of working–age population) | 66.5 | 66.2 | 66.4 | 66.3 | 66.6 | 66.6 | 66.8 | 67.1 | 67.1 | 67.1 |
| | 22 | Unemployment rate (percent of labor force) | 5.6 | 6.9 | 7.5 | 6.9 | 6.1 | 5.6 | 5.4 | 4.9 | 4.5 | 4.2 |
| | 23 | Real GDP per person (2009 dollars per year) | 35,756 | 35,258 | 36,029 | 36,540 | 37,557 | 38,125 | 39,114 | 40,383 | 41,692 | 43,216 |
| | 24 | Growth rate of real GDP per person (percent per year) | 0.8 | –1.4 | 2.2 | 1.4 | 2.8 | 1.5 | 2.6 | 3.2 | 3.2 | 3.7 |
| | 25 | Quantity of money (M2, billions of dollars) | 3,224 | 3,342 | 3,403 | 3,438 | 3,482 | 3,553 | 3,724 | 3,910 | 4,190 | 4,497 |
| | 26 | GDP deflator (2009 = 100) | 66.8 | 69.1 | 70.6 | 72.3 | 73.9 | 75.4 | 76.8 | 78.1 | 78.9 | 80.1 |
| | 27 | GDP deflator inflation rate (percent per year) | 3.7 | 3.3 | 2.3 | 2.4 | 2.1 | 2.1 | 1.8 | 1.7 | 1.1 | 1.4 |
| | 28 | Consumer price index (1982–1984 = 100) | 130.7 | 136.2 | 140.3 | 144.5 | 148.2 | 152.4 | 156.9 | 160.5 | 163.0 | 166.6 |
| | 29 | CPI inflation rate (percent per year) | 5.4 | 4.2 | 3.0 | 3.0 | 2.6 | 2.8 | 2.9 | 2.3 | 1.5 | 2.2 |
| | 30 | Current account balance (billions of dollars) | –79 | 3 | –52 | –85 | –122 | –114 | –125 | –141 | –215 | –301 |

| 2000 | 2001 | 2002 | 2003 | 2004 | 2005 | 2006 | 2007 | 2008 | 2009 | 2010 | 2011 | 2012 |
|---|---|---|---|---|---|---|---|---|---|---|---|---|
| 6,802 | 7,107 | 7,385 | 7,764 | 8,258 | 8,790 | 9,298 | 9,744 | 10,006 | 9,843 | 10,202 | 10,712 | 11,150 |
| 2,034 | 1,929 | 1,925 | 2,028 | 2,277 | 2,527 | 2,681 | 2,644 | 2,425 | 1,878 | 2,101 | 2,232 | 2,475 |
| 1,834 | 1,959 | 2,095 | 2,221 | 2,357 | 2,494 | 2,642 | 2,802 | 3,003 | 3,089 | 3,174 | 3,159 | 3,167 |
| 1,094 | 1,029 | 1,005 | 1,043 | 1,183 | 1,310 | 1,479 | 1,666 | 1,843 | 1,584 | 1,844 | 2,101 | 2,196 |
| 1,474 | 1,398 | 1,430 | 1,544 | 1,798 | 2,026 | 2,241 | 2,376 | 2,556 | 1,976 | 2,362 | 2,670 | 2,743 |
| 10,290 | 10,625 | 10,980 | 11,512 | 12,277 | 13,095 | 13,858 | 14,480 | 14,720 | 14,418 | 14,958 | 15,534 | 16,245 |
| 5,863 | 6,054 | 6,150 | 6,373 | 6,749 | 7,098 | 7,514 | 7,909 | 8,090 | 7,796 | 7,975 | 8,287 | 8,620 |
| 2,344 | 2,410 | 2,517 | 2,665 | 2,886 | 3,176 | 3,483 | 3,307 | 3,179 | 3,214 | 3,557 | 3,811 | 4,033 |
| 8,207 | 8,464 | 8,667 | 9,038 | 9,634 | 10,274 | 10,997 | 11,216 | 11,269 | 11,010 | 11,532 | 12,098 | 12,653 |
| 663 | 669 | 721 | 759 | 818 | 874 | 940 | 980 | 989 | 968 | 1,001 | 1,037 | 1,066 |
| 1,514 | 1,604 | 1,662 | 1,727 | 1,832 | 1,982 | 2,136 | 2,264 | 2,363 | 2,368 | 2,382 | 2,453 | 2,543 |
| 10,384 | 10,737 | 11,050 | 11,524 | 12,284 | 13,129 | 14,073 | 14,460 | 14,621 | 14,346 | 14,915 | 15,588 | 16,262 |
| -95 | -112 | -70 | -12 | -7 | -34 | -215 | 20 | 99 | 72 | 43 | -54 | -17 |
| 10,290 | 10,625 | 10,980 | 11,512 | 12,277 | 13,095 | 13,858 | 14,480 | 14,720 | 14,418 | 14,958 | 15,534 | 16,245 |
| 12,565 | 12,684 | 12,910 | 13,270 | 13,774 | 14,236 | 14,615 | 14,877 | 14,834 | 14,418 | 14,779 | 15,052 | 15,471 |
| 4.1 | 0.9 | 1.8 | 2.8 | 3.8 | 3.4 | 2.7 | 1.8 | -0.3 | -2.8 | 2.5 | 1.8 | 2.8 |
| 282 | 285 | 288 | 291 | 293 | 296 | 299 | 302 | 305 | 307 | 310 | 312 | 314 |
| 143 | 144 | 145 | 147 | 147 | 149 | 151 | 153 | 154 | 154 | 154 | 154 | 155 |
| 137 | 137 | 136 | 138 | 139 | 142 | 144 | 146 | 145 | 140 | 139 | 140 | 142 |
| 6 | 7 | 8 | 9 | 8 | 8 | 7 | 7 | 9 | 14 | 15 | 14 | 12 |
| 67.1 | 66.8 | 66.6 | 66.2 | 66.0 | 66.0 | 66.2 | 66.0 | 66.0 | 65.4 | 64.7 | 64.1 | 63.7 |
| 4.0 | 4.7 | 5.8 | 6.0 | 5.5 | 5.1 | 4.6 | 4.6 | 5.8 | 9.3 | 9.6 | 8.9 | 8.1 |
| 44,495 | 44,472 | 44,832 | 45,660 | 46,968 | 48,094 | 48,910 | 49,311 | 48,708 | 46,927 | 47,710 | 48,239 | 49,226 |
| 3.0 | -0.1 | 0.8 | 1.8 | 2.9 | 2.4 | 1.7 | 0.8 | -1.2 | -3.7 | 1.7 | 1.1 | 2.0 |
| 4,769 | 5,179 | 5,562 | 5,950 | 6,237 | 6,506 | 6,847 | 7,269 | 7,765 | 8,386 | 8,594 | 9,222 | 10,011 |
| 81.9 | 83.8 | 85.1 | 86.8 | 89.1 | 92.0 | 94.8 | 97.3 | 99.2 | 100.0 | 101.2 | 103.2 | 105.0 |
| 2.3 | 2.3 | 1.5 | 2.0 | 2.7 | 3.2 | 3.1 | 2.7 | 2.0 | 0.8 | 1.2 | 2.0 | 1.7 |
| 172.2 | 177.0 | 179.9 | 184.0 | 188.9 | 195.3 | 201.6 | 207.3 | 215.3 | 214.6 | 218.1 | 224.9 | 229.6 |
| 3.4 | 2.8 | 1.6 | 2.3 | 2.7 | 3.4 | 3.2 | 2.9 | 3.8 | -0.3 | 1.6 | 3.1 | 2.1 |
| -416 | -397 | -458 | -519 | -629 | -740 | -798 | -713 | -681 | -382 | -449 | -458 | -440 |